Muslim Spain
Its History and Culture

تاريخ وثقافة الأندلس

Muslim Spain
Its History and Culture

أنور شحنة

Anwar G. Chejne

THE UNIVERSITY OF MINNESOTA PRESS • MINNEAPOLIS

Printed in the United States of America
at North Central Publishing Co.
St. Paul, Minnesota.
Published in the United Kingdom
and India by the Oxford University Press,
London and Bombay, and in Canada
by the Copp Clark Publishing Co.
Limited, Toronto

Library of Congress Catalog Card Number: 73-87254
ISBN 0-8166-0688-9

Preface

THE FIELD OF Hispano-Arabic studies is vast, and it cannot be compressed into a single volume. In consequence, this book is not intended to be a definitive work on the subject, but rather a general study of the history, culture, and intellectual life of Muslim Spain. It is an attempt to give a panoramic view of the whole field of Hispano-Arabic culture; to indicate its nature, scope, and importance; and to show its dependence on and relation to the mainstream of Islamic culture. In fact, Muslim Spain was always an integral part of the literary and intellectual mainstream of the East and, as such, was as Islamic as Syria or Egypt. The great affinity and interdependence were facilitated by the unhampered travel of students and scholars and the circulation of publications throughout the Islamic Empire despite the political division that separated Muslim Spain from the heartland of Islam.

The present work is the outgrowth of several years of research and teaching of graduate courses and seminars at the University of Minnesota. The task of teaching was made quite difficult and students were often frustrated by the absence of works on al-Andalus in English. It was necessary to refer to materials in Arabic and other languages which were either not ordinarily accessible or beyond the students' linguistic competence.

This emphasized the pressing need for a volume that would fill the gap in the available writings on al-Andalus. I am fully aware that such a task is not only difficult, but perhaps beyond the competence of a single individual.

Flaws and shortcomings will certainly appear. An enormous amount of literature in Arabic and Western languages has been surveyed. Some Arabic manuscripts have been used, though not to the extent that I would have liked. In all this, my hope is to present a succinct account of the main features and manifestations of a great culture and literature with reference to major periods, main themes, authors, and some of the most important writings. The task of selecting the most relevant material in order to bring to the fore the scope and nature of Hispano-Arabic culture was not easy. Many important questions could only be discussed briefly. To remedy this deficiency a lengthy bibliography is included, and it forms an essential part of the book. The reader is also referred to footnotes and studies in the various languages, with the hope that these will enable him to pursue further reading and research. For the benefit of non-Arabists, whenever possible reference is made to translations of Arabic texts and studies in Western languages. I can only express my great indebtedness to their authors, as noted in footnotes and bibliography. Thus, by treating the subject in more detail than has been done previously, I hope that this volume will fill a gap and bring full awareness of the importance of Hispano-Arabic studies to cultured persons, students, Islamists, and Romance scholars.

The Arabs were present in Spain for almost eight centuries, from 711 to 1492, to be exact. During most of this long period, and despite recurrent internal wars and convulsions, Spain was by far the most advanced country of Europe. It was culturally a bridge between Asia, Africa, and Europe. It was a melting pot of many people: Romans, Visigoths, Berbers, Arabs, Jews, and others. In its heyday, al-Andalus (the name applied to the Iberian Peninsula by the Arabs) was one of the major Islamic intellectual centers; it had many educational institutions, libraries, gorgeous palaces and mosques, public baths, and beautiful gardens. It achieved a great culture in the Arabic language, expressed in an immense literature containing abundant poetry, grammar and lexicography, belles lettres, history and geography, and religious, speculative, and natural sciences. It manifested itself as well in art and architecture; in highly advanced urban centers in cities like Cordova, Seville, Toledo, and Granada; in music, agriculture, commerce, and industry. Hence, the field of Hispano-Arabic culture should be important for the student of Islam as well as for those committed to Spanish studies and comparative literature. Its importance lies in the fact that it was inspired by and based on an Islamic background besides being a composite of many cultures.

The origin of Hispano-Arabic civilization may be traced to the Near East,

Greece, Rome, and other countries. The Arabs were able to forge a synthesis from diverse elements, and to give an Arabic or an Islamic stamp to their culture. Spain served as a bridge between the Orient and the West in this connection. As early as the twelfth century, scholars from France, England, Italy, and Germany came to Spain in pursuit of knowledge and became conversant with Arabic culture. It was to their credit that the task of translating Arabic works into Latin began in earnest. This contributed not only to an exchange of ideas and borrowings, but to the appearance of a new intellectual perspective in Europe which manifested itself in the European Renaissance. In this connection, Hispano-Arabic culture left its mark on Spain and Europe even in unsuspected areas. When the late Spanish Arabist, Asín Palacios, pointed to the possibility that the topic of Dante's *Divine Comedy* was inspired by an Islamic theme, his suggestion was received with dismay and caused a heated controversy among European scholars. But later investigations by other scholars produced enough data to prove that Asín's contentions were not without foundation. Arabic influences can be seen in other areas of European literature and thought. The Andalusian philosopher Averroës had a great impact on European thought. Although quite misunderstood by both Christians and Muslims, his philosophical system, known as Averroism, was the subject of animated discussions in Europe. It came to influence Thomism, which advocated the harmony between faith and reason — a problem that had been discussed frequently among Muslims. Moreover, Arabic influences are found in the works of Alfonso el Sabio, Raymond Lull, Raymond Martin, Juan Manuel, Juan Ruíz, and other European writers. Arabic words abound in Spanish and other Western languages. "Moorish" architecture is still much alive in Spain itself as well as outside it in such places as Latin America, Florida, and California.

The field of Hispano-Arabic culture has been neglected even by the general Islamist or Arabist, whose main concern has been the study of Eastern Islam. It may be argued that since Muslim Spain constituted part of the Islamic community, its culture should be confined within the cultural sphere of Islam. Although this may be true, al-Andalus is unique by virtue of its position on the periphery of the Islamic Empire, and by its independent posture from Islamic polity almost immediately after its conquest. Its unique position on European soil and its role as the spiritual and intellectual leader of Christians from the north and Berbers from North Africa to the south gives the country added significance. As an Islamic enclave in Europe, al-Andalus played the greatest role in the transmission of ideas from Arabic into Latin and other

European languages. In the light of all this, al-Andalus deserves more attention in Middle Eastern as well as in medieval European studies. At present, the field of Hispano-Arabic culture has been appallingly neglected even in the better Romance departments throughout this country. This neglect may possibly be due to the fact that the study of humanities in general is a thankless task and in this particular instance requires broad training in Arabic, Romance, modern Spanish, and other languages. A further difficulty is presented by the lack of trained personnel in the field. Nonetheless, one cannot pretend that the field does not exist. This repudiates the true spirit of scholarship.

Despite this state of affairs, occasional lonely voices have called attention to the importance of the field. In the eighteenth century, in his work *Dell'origine progressi e stato attuale d'ogni letteratura* (Parma, 1782–1799), Juan Andrés, a Jesuit renegade, suggested many Arabic elements found in Western culture. The response to the call of Andrés was rather slow. In the eighteenth century the cleric Ghazīrī (Casiri), a Lebanese, was called from the Vatican to Spain to take charge of the Arabic manuscripts at the Escorial. During his stay he catalogued the existing Arabic manuscripts under the title *Bibliotheca arabico-hispana escurialensis*, which was published in two volumes (Madrid, 1760–1770). The work contains a description of more than 1,700 manuscripts which were preserved from some 10,000 or more manuscripts burned in the fire of 1671. Casiri's work was put to good use during the nineteenth and twentieth centuries when a number of European scholars became interested in Arabic lore. Their number included such names as Dozy of Holland; von Schack of Germany; Simonet, Codera, Ribera, Lafuente, Pons Boïgues, Amador de las Ríos, Altamira, Nieto, Asín Palacios, Menéndez Pidal, González Palencia, García Gómez, Millás-Vallicrosa, Sánchez-Albornóz, Américo Castro, and others of Spain; G. LeBon, E. Renan, Lévi-Provençal, and Pérès of France; Washington Irving of the United States; Thomas Bourke and George Power of England; and Imamuddin of Pakistan. All these scholars made distinct contributions to the field of Hispano-Arabic studies, and their numerous and still valuable works aroused great interest. It is quite understandable that the majority of these individuals were Spaniards. In recent decades, Spanish scholars have taken a keen interest in Hispano-Arabic culture. Interest in these studies resulted in the establishment in 1933 of the quarterly journal, *al-Andalus*, which publishes numerous and valuable articles on the history, literature, and culture of al-Andalus. An increasing interest in the study of Arabic lore has been shown at a number of Spanish universities. In 1950 the Egyptian Institute of Islamic Studies was established in Madrid. Likewise, the Arabs who emulated Western scholarship have displayed a keen interest in the field of Hispano-Arabic culture. A number of valuable works and editions by Arab authors have appeared. Among these scholars are ʻAbbās, Ahwānī, al-Dāyah, al-Ḥajjī, ʻInān, al-Makkī, Mu'nis, Muṭlaq, and Sālim.

Unfortunately, many of the works of these scholars are known only to a small audience and are often not available. However pioneering and valuable, they have barely scratched the surface of the fund of knowledge. A great mine of material still remains to be exploited, if we are to judge from the bibliographical works that have reached us, and by the presence of numerous manuscripts that may be found in Madrid, the Vatican, Berlin, Cairo, Istanbul, Rabat, Fez, Tunis, and other cities. The remains of the great Andalusian legacy constitute a small fraction of a large and rich literature that vanished in the passing of time, or because of wanton destruction at the hands of such fanatics as Cardinal Jiménez of Toledo, who made a bonfire of Arabic books. Nonetheless, the data available still remain sizable and challenging.

A. G. C.

Minneapolis
January 1973

Acknowledgments

I WISH TO EXPRESS my gratitude to the Graduate School, the McMillan Committee, and the Office of International Programs at the University of Minnesota for their financial assistance which permitted me to travel to Spain, Morocco, and Tunisia for research and publication help. A special word of thanks goes to Mrs. Mary Lundsten; to Bruce Craig, Middle Eastern bibliographer at the University of Minnesota; and to Professor James Monroe of the University of California, who read the manuscript and offered valuable suggestions on editorial and factual matters. I am equally indebted to Wendy Becker for the maps, as well as to Professor Hosni Iskander for his generosity in preparing the calligraphy for the title page. Don Ramón Paz, Chief of the Manuscript Section of the National Library of Madrid; Reverend Gregorio de Andrés, Chief of the Biblioteca del Escorial; Ana María Vicent Taragoza, Directora del Museo Anquelógico of Cordova; Don Jesús Bermudez, Director of the Alhambra; Professor Juan Vernet of the University of Barcelona, and the officers of the Central Library of Barcelona, Archivo de Aragón, Archivo Nacional de Madrid were generous beyond the call of duty in assisting and supplying me with the necessary material and help while I was working in Spain. I wish to express my warmest appreciation to them. A special word of thanks goes to the staff of the University of Minnesota Press for their patience and vigilance during the preparation of the manuscript for publication. It is of course understood that these people are in no way responsible for whatever defects or inadequacies may be found in this work. Last, but not least, I wish to express my appreciation to my students Linda Johnson and Susan Iskander and secretary, Linda Foster, who enthusiastically and expeditiously dispatched the tedious task of typing the manuscript. I am also thankful to Professor A. Donchenko for her help on some editorial matters.

And, finally, I wish to thank my wife and my daughter Cecilia for their help in the preparation of the index.

Transliteration

TERMINAL	MEDIAL	INITIAL	ALONE	TRANSLITERATION
ـا	ـا	ا	ا	’
ـب	ـبـ	بـ	ب	b
ـت	ـتـ	تـ	ت	t
ـث	ـثـ	ثـ	ث	th
ـج	ـجـ	جـ	ج	j
ـح	ـحـ	حـ	ح	ḥ
ـخ	ـخـ	خـ	خ	kh
ـد	ـد	د	د	d
ـذ	ـذ	ذ	ذ	dh
ـر	ـر	ر	ر	r
ـز	ـز	ز	ز	z
ـس	ـسـ	سـ	س	s
ـش	ـشـ	شـ	ش	sh
ـص	ـصـ	صـ	ص	ṣ
ـض	ـضـ	ضـ	ض	ḍ
ـط	ـطـ	طـ	ط	ṭ
ـظ	ـظـ	ظـ	ظ	ẓ
ـع	ـعـ	عـ	ع	‘
ـغ	ـغـ	غـ	غ	gh
ـف	ـفـ	فـ	ف	f
ـق	ـقـ	قـ	ق	q
ـك	ـكـ	كـ	ك	k
ـل	ـلـ	لـ	ل	l
ـم	ـمـ	مـ	م	m
ـن	ـنـ	نـ	ن	n
ـه	ـهـ	هـ	ه	h
ـو	ـو	و	و	w
ـي	ـيـ	يـ	ي	y

VOWELS: short a ـَ u ـُ i ـِ long a ـَا u ـُو i ـِي

DIPHTHONGS: aw ـَوْ ay ـَيْ

Table of Contents

Muslim Spain
Its History and Culture

1

The Conquest of Spain and the Emirate

AROUND A.D. 570, a child was born in the city of Mecca in northwestern Arabia. He became the founder of a religious movement, Islam, which has had a tremendous impact on peoples inhabiting a large area of the world. The man was Muḥammad. His immediate successors, generally known as Orthodox Caliphs (*al-Rāshidūn*; 632–661), spread Islam into and established a state in Arabia proper, Syria-Palestine, Iraq and Iran, and Egypt. Their newly founded empire was for the most part established at the expense of the two big contemporary empires, Byzantine and Sāsānid. Soon afterward, the politico-religious center of the state shifted from Mecca-Medina to the provinces, mainly Syria and Iraq. In 661, an Umayyad dynasty (611–750) was established in Damascus and pushed Arab expansion into a vast territory stretching from the Atlantic Ocean in the west to Central Asia in the east. It was under the Umayyads that North Africa and Spain were conquered and that repeated forays were made into Southern France. When in 750 the dynasty was displaced by the 'Abbāsids (750–1258), the Umayyad legacy was retained and strengthened, thereby deeply affecting the religious life, intellectual perspective, and mores of most people around the Mediterranean basin. As a result, the Arabic-Islamic legacy may be discerned in Crete, Sicily, southern Italy, North Africa, and particularly in Spain.[1]

Spain was known to the Arabs as al-Andalus. Like the other countries of the Mediterranean, it was a melting pot of many peoples and cultures.

Europeans and Berbers had been settled there since ancient times. The Phoenicians had established colonies as early as the tenth century B.C. Next came the Greeks, who named the Peninsula Iberia and built colonies. Spain became a Roman province in the first century B.C. and adopted the Latin language, Roman customs and law, and Christianity, proclaimed the official religion of the Empire in the fourth century. As the Roman Empire weakened, the Peninsula fell victim to the successive invasions of German hordes such as the Suevi, the Vandals, and the Visigoths.[2] In the early part of the fifth century, the Visigoths occupied the northeastern part of the Peninsula. At first they espoused Arianism, a Christian heresy, but soon shifted to the Catholicism practiced by the majority of the population. This gave unity to the country that was ruled from Toledo, often referred to as the Royal City (*Ciudad regia*). The Visigoths fused into the population, forming a ruling aristocracy which shared some of its power with the ecclesiastical hierarchy and the native nobility. They had enormous power over the masses, which were exploited and restricted to serfdom. This situation led to socioeconomic instability and was aggravated by contention within the ruling class.

Some of the Visigothic kings, who were elected by the nobility and clergy, proved themselves able to rule without the tutelage of Rome or Byzantium. However, at the end of the seventh century, a crisis erupted and reached alarming proportions by the first decade of the eighth century. This no doubt facilitated the swift conquest of the peninsula by the Arabs. The nobility and clergy enjoyed all privileges and wealth, while serfs and slaves suffered numerous deprivations. The Jews, who played an important role in the economic life of the country, were subjected to such harsh measures as forced baptism, confiscation of property, and persecution. The intrigues and intolerance of the nobility, the problem of succession, economic difficulties, and other factors all contributed to the final dissolution of the Visigothic kingdom. The situation deteriorated in 700 when Witiza succeeded his father Egica to the throne. At the beginning of his reign he tried to redress many ills, but he nonetheless committed serious blunders in exiling his son Pelayo and suppressing the partisans of his general Roderick. Witiza arbitrarily appointed his infant son Achila to succeed him; Achila assumed the governorship of two provinces and was placed under the guardianship of Witiza's own brother. This act may have antagonized the electors and encouraged usurpation attempts by eligible candidates. Thus, upon Witiza's death in 710 opinions were divided, some supporting Achila and others Roderick.

In the midst of tension, Roderick assumed the royal title and Achila fled, either to the north or to Ceuta, where he is alleged to have sought the help of the Arabs to regain his throne.

The Arab conquest of Spain is ultimately connected to that of North Africa, which was dominated by the Byzantines. The Arabs considered the whole of North Africa enemy territory, and they could not feel safe so long as the Byzantines remained there and were able to strike from land or sea. Consequently, the Arabs felt that the conquest of North Africa west of Egypt was a major objective, to be attained as soon as the opportunity offered itself.[3]

The Arabs at first gave the name *Ifrīqiyah* to North Africa from Libya to the Atlantic. Afterward, *Ifrīqiyah* was applied to the area from Egypt to Bougie in Tunis. The land stretching from Tripoli in the East to the Atlantic in the West was called al-Maghrib (the West; i.e., North Africa). It was divided by the Arabs into the Near Maghrib (*al-Maghrib al-adnā*) from Tripoli to Bougie, the Middle Maghrib (*al-Maghrib al-awsaṭ*) from Bougie to the Tāzah Mountains, and the Far Maghrib (*al-Maghrib al-aqṣā*) from the mountains to the Atlantic.

After the conquest of Egypt in 639–641, it took the Arab army almost sixty years to gain control of the area from Libya to the Atlantic Ocean. 'Amr ibn al-'Āṣ, the conqueror of Egypt, made attempts to march westward but did not go beyond Tripoli. His aim was obviously to check the Byzantine navy on the shore of the Mediterranean. The caliphs seemed reluctant to commit large numbers of troops for the conquest; their hesitation was due probably to the difficult terrain, made up of mountains and wide desert tracts, to the unruly tribes, and to the absence of sufficient booty to make the conquest attractive. Although attempts were constantly made to push the conquest westward, political crises in Medina and the removal of the government from that city to Damascus in A.D. 661 slowed progress. It was not until the appointment of 'Uqbah Ibn Nāfi' as governor of Ifrīqiyah in about 667[4] that the conquest began to make headway. 'Uqbah, who had assisted 'Amr ibn al-'Āṣ in the movement westward, is generally considered the actual conqueror of most of North Africa. In 670, he established south of Carthage a military settlement, Qayrawān, which first became an important fortress against the enemy and later was one of the major cities of Muslim North Africa. The military settlement was soon provided with facilities — a great mosque, markets, and streets — which attracted many Berbers. 'Uqbah's initial success was interrupted by the appointment of Maslamah as governor of Egypt and Ifrīqiyah. Maslamah replaced ʻUqbah with his own client, Abū al-Muhājir Dīnār, who destroyed the settlement built by ʻUqbah at Qayrawān and reached as far west as Tilimsān.[5] However, ʻUqbah returned to his former post in 682, and proceeded to consolidate his domain and to push the conquest farther west. Up to this time, Islamization had taken place concurrently with the conquest of North Africa, but ʻUqbah faced the problem of apostasy when Berbers, under the tutelage and encouragement of Christian Byzantium, resisted Arab domination. Nevertheless, he took Carthage and reached the Atlas Mountains, then pushing forward until he reached Tangier and the Atlantic Ocean. At this point, revolt in Qayrawān forced him to return to fight Berber tribes. ʻUqbah died in 683 near Biskra in present-day Algeria. He left behind him a large territory that was temporarily conquered but never subjugated.

After ʻUqbah's death, Qayrawān and the rest of the territory to the west remained to be reconquered. This task fell to Zuhayr Ibn Qays, an associate of ʻUqbah's. He took Qayrawān in 688 but soon afterward headed east to face the Byzantines. He perished on the battlefield, leaving the area west of Qayrawān in utter confusion. At that time, the central government in Damascus was faced with a serious internal revolt. The conquest was not renewed until 692 when the caliph ʻAbd al-Malik, now free from strife at home, sent a 40,000-man army under Ḥassān Ibn al-Nuʻmān al-Ghassānī.[6] This able general reached Qayrawān, from which he marched against Carthage and retook it. His initial success was soon upset by a priestess, the queen of Jirārāh, whose Berber army defeated the Muslim forces. Ḥassān was compelled to retreat to Barqah and await reinforcements from Damascus. When help came, in 694, he renewed the fighting against the priestess, who took refuge in the mountains. It was not until 701 that Ḥassān defeated her, thus becoming the master of the entire Maghrib from his headquarters in Qayrawān. Among his accomplishments was the building of the city of Tunis on the site of a small village. He made it a naval base and provided it with the Zaytunah mosque, a palace, and quarters for soldiers. He gave impetus to Islamization and Arabization by sending missionaries among the tribes. However, he was recalled to Damascus about 705, leaving one of his soldiers in his place.[7]

Ḥassān Ibn al-Nuʻmān was succeeded by Mūsā Ibn Nuṣayr in about 707. When the new governor reached Qayrawān, he found the country in need of stability and he set out to provide it with firmness and determination. He sent missionaries to various regions to pacify the Berbers, and he delegated his two sons to lead forces into restive areas. In 708, he took Tangier and appointed his lieutenant, Ṭāriq, the future conqueror of Spain, to govern it. He ruled the conquered territories with an iron hand from Qayrawān. For the first time a measure of tranquility prevailed.

Now the Arabs held sway all over North Africa from Egypt to the Atlantic. This posture enabled them to gain control of the eastern and southern Mediterranean basin and gave them the potential of defeating the Byzantine navy, hitherto the mistress of the seas. Perhaps it was to encircle the Byzantine navy completely that the conquest of Spain received serious consideration. Aside from this, Spain offered the attraction of great wealth and hence booty for an army that could not easily be kept loyal for long periods of inactivity. These are some of the considerations that may have induced Mūsā Ibn Nuṣayr to undertake the conquest of Spain.

The history of the conquest of Spain is distorted by legendary accounts. It is reported that Julian,[8] who may have been a merchant or a former governor of Ceuta under the Byzantines or Visigoths, encouraged the conquest as revenge upon Roderick, then the ruler of Spain, who had dishonored Julian's daughter Florinda. But a look at the Peninsula in the first part of the eighth century may suggest a better reason for the conquest. In the first place, the Peninsula was close to Africa, and the Arab conquerors or their Berber subjects must have known about the fertility and beauty of the country and the possibility of securing handsome booty. Furthermore, the Peninsula was undergoing serious sociopolitical crises, and that, too, must have been known to the Arabs through their effective espionage system. Still, the Arabs may have been encouraged by the partisans of Achila, who was dethroned by Roderick, and by the disgruntled Jews, whose persecution has been noted.

The Arab conquest of Spain was swift and successful. This fact may justify the assumption that there was a good deal of planning before the undertaking and that Julian of Ceuta and others from the Peninsula may have contributed enormously to that success. In 710, Mūsā b. Nuṣayr permitted an officer, Ṭarīf, to head a reconnaissance group of 100 cavalry and 400 men on an exploratory mission.[9] Ṭarīf met with great success in the occupation of the southern tip of the Peninsula, where the city of Tarifa bears his name. He returned with an impressive amount of booty. Reports of this initial enterprise may have encouraged Mūsā Ibn Nuṣayr to allow his client and lieutenant, Ṭāriq, to pursue the conquest further. Thus, in 711 Ṭāriq left Tangier at the head of an army of about 9,000 Berbers, crossed the strait, and landed with ease at a fortress that became known after him

(Jabal Ṭāriq, hence, Gibraltar). At the moment of his landing, Ṭāriq was determined to triumph or perish, according to his oration, which became famous in Arabic literature. He is said to have burned the ships which had been supplied to him by Julian and to have addressed his followers, stating that there was no escape except in triumph: "Whither can you fly? — The enemy is before you and the sea behind you."

Ṭāriq made Gibraltar the base of operation from which he marched to the north. When informed of the invasion, Roderick marched against the intruder at the head of an army which is reported to have numbered forty to a hundred thousand men.[10] The two armies met at the Barbate River (*wādī lakkah*) and engaged in a battle that lasted seven days. Roderick's army suffered heavy casualties, probably because of defections among his soldiers. What happened to Roderick after this crushing defeat is uncertain; he either drowned or escaped. At any rate, Ṭāriq lost no time in continuing his march to the north. He conquered several cities on his way to the capital city of Toledo, and simultaneously sent contingents against Málaga, Elvira, Murcia (Tudmir), and Cordova. Through Jaén he reached Toledo without much opposition. He found the city deserted except for the Jews. It was here that he secured an enormous amount of booty consisting of gold, silver, precious stones, vestments, crowns, horses, and many other prizes, such as the Table of Solomon, reportedly made of solid gold and silver and profusely decorated with precious stones.[11] True or not, these things must have captivated the imagination of the conqueror and induced him to advance into Castile, León, and the Asturias.

With an army of modest size, Ṭāriq spread too thinly in the Peninsula. However, as he moved northward, he delegated the administration of the conquered territories to the natives, especially to the Jews, who were supervised by the conqueror. Ṭāriq's success was such that it must have prompted his master, Mūsā Ibn Nuṣayr, to come to assist him and, at the same time, to share in the glory of the conquest. Mūsā, who is said to have been angered by and jealous of his lieutenant's remarkable successes, gathered around him some 18,000 men, mostly Arabs, and landed in the Peninsula in 712. He followed a different route from that of his lieutenant, proceeding to Algeciras with guides supplied him by Julian. He headed for and took Seville after he had conquered Sidonia, Carmona,[12] Huelva, and Beja. Following the Guadiana River he took Mérida and other towns with relative ease. He joined forces with Ṭāriq near or in Toledo.

Mūsā's reported whipping of his lieutenant cannot be taken seriously.

The two men appear to have combined their forces and marched northward to Salamanca, Alba de Tormas, and other points. After the winter of 713, they went on to Saragossa and Lérida, Barcelona and Narbonne, reaching beyond the Pyrenees into Avignon and to Lyons on the Rhône River.[13] Meeting stiff opposition, the Muslim army retreated and turned to the northwestern part of the Peninsula, where it conquered León and Galicia and pushed the last opponents, under the leadership of Pelayo, into the Asturias. Mūsā had hoped to reach Damascus by way of Europe through Constantinople and Asia Minor. This intent caused consternation in Damascus and led the caliph al-Walīd to recall him.[14] The caliph may have felt that the invasion had gone too far, and beyond caliphal authorization. Mūsā procrastinated for a while and pushed the conquest forward until he felt that the conquered territory was safe. In 714, he and Ṭāriq headed for Damascus while Mūsā's son, 'Abd al-'Azīz, remained in Seville in charge of the affairs of the Peninsula. Mūsā took with him a huge retinue of Arabs and captive Visigoths and precious gifts of gold, silver, and pearls, slaves, and other booty. Reaching Africa he appointed one son to govern Tangier and another Ifrīqiyah. He marched leisurely and with great pomp at the head of his caravan through North Africa, Egypt, and Palestine while the caliph al-Walīd (705–715) was ailing. Soon after he reached Damascus al-Walīd died. The newly inaugurated caliph, Sulaymān, treated him coolly and finally disgraced Mūsā and his lieutenant.

Thus ended the careers of two competent military leaders who added a new and significant dimension to the Islamic state. The new land, hereafter known as al-Andalus, became a province of an enormous empire ruled by the Umayyad family, a branch of the Quraysh tribe to which Muḥammad belonged. A new chapter in the history of Spain had begun. The conquest marked a new departure in the life and thought of the country. Two societies with different ethnic, linguistic, religious, and cultural backgrounds came together and succeeded in forging a new civilization.

It would seem that the conquered population accepted the new intruders with little or no resistance, and that their lot was an improvement over that under the Visigoths. While they reconciled themselves to the new conditions, the conqueror had as yet to make considerable adjustments in his new environment. The first crisis began with the departure of Ṭāriq and Mūsā, who had not had time to consolidate their conquest. Mūsā had delegated the power to his son 'Abd al-'Azīz b. Mūsā (714–716), a capable ruler who made Seville his capital.[15] He extended the conquest in the east, west, and south of the Peninsula and consolidated his power in areas such as Portugal, Málaga, Granada, Orihuela, Gerona, and Barcelona.[16] Simultaneously, he organized the country, formulated administrative and financial policies, settled the difference among the contending groups of Arab and Berber tribes, and bridged the cleavage separating them. He encouraged marriage between the conquerors and native Christian women. Although 'Abd al-'Azīz seems to have been successful in his policies toward the conquered population, he encountered enormous difficulties among his fellow Muslims, who accused him of undue partiality to his Christian subjects. His marriage to Egilona, the widow or daughter of Roderick, appears to be at the root of his troubles. Egilona is said to have insisted that he wear a crown and act in the manner of Christian kings. This created tensions in his relations with leading members of his army and coincided with the reported ill treatment of his father by the caliph. He was killed on the pretext that he was seceding from the caliphate.[17]

The Successors of 'Abd al-'Azīz b. Mūsā (716–756)

At the time 'Abd al-'Azīz Ibn Mūsā died, the central government in Damascus was witnessing a critical period. The Umayyad dynasty was faced with serious sociopolitical problems and was rapidly declining. Under the circumstances, Spain was too far from the center of the Empire to warrant much attention and was left to the invaders contending for supremacy among themselves. This situation lasted from 716 to 756 and led to confusion, mixed loyalties, and recurrent bloody wars. During this period, the country saw some twenty-one governors, about nine of whom were appointed by the soldiers; the remaining governors were named by the caliph in Damascus or the governor of North Africa in Qayrawān. From 725 to 730 alone, six governors were put on the throne by soldiers. In addition to the internal problems, the Muslims were far from secure in the north. Already in 718 Pelayo had won a victory over the Muslims at Covadonga in northwest Spain, and the Muslims suffered further reverses at Toulouse in 721 and near Tours in 732.

After the assassination of 'Abd al-'Azīz b. Mūsā in 716, al-Andalus had no governor, and the army nominated Ayyūb b. Ḥabīb, a nephew of Mūsā.[18] Ayyūb had ruled only for a few months when he was replaced by an appointee of the governor of North Africa. Ayyūb's most significant act was to move the capital from Seville to Cordova, which, located in the center of the

Peninsula, had more strategic value. To the north of Toledo he established a fortress that bore his name (Calatayud). Ayyūb's successor, al-Ḥurr, found the country torn asunder by tribal wars between Arabs and Berbers. He failed to achieve a complete pacification and was replaced by al-Samḥ b. Mālik (d. 721), who was appointed by the caliph 'Umar (717–720). Al-Samḥ proved to be a good administrator. He built the canal of Cordova and made raids to the north as far as Narbonne and Toulouse in France. The army appointed a successor who lasted until 'Anbasah, an appointee of the governor of Ifrīqiyah, arrived. 'Anbasah (722–725) was an able general and good administrator who faced successfully the problems of organization, pacification, and continuation of raids into southern France. His sudden death in 725 left a vacuum in al-Andalus for the next five years, during which six men assumed the governorship, but with little tangible results.

Among the succession of emirs, one of the more important was 'Abd al-Raḥmān b. Abdallah al-Ghāfiqī (730–732). He had to pacify quarreling tribes before he could undertake any raid to the North. Afterward he gathered an army of eighty thousand men and marched into France, where he was met by the army of Charles Martel between Tours and Poitiers. An initial and undecisive skirmish took place, lasting almost a week. Al-Ghāfiqī perished on the battlefield. Facing the serious loss of its leader, the Arab army fled by night. This was in 732 at the famous battle variously known as the Battle of Tours or the Battle of Poitiers. This rather uneventful confrontation is often considered one of the greatest battles in the world.[19] Muslim historians, usually inclined toward details, hardly mention its significance. The Arab withdrawal from Tours was not the first withdrawal of its kind. The Arabs may have learned that intrusion into France was not profitable enough owing to the terrain, climate, the great distance from supplies, and, most important, the unsettled situation in the Peninsula that required the constant presence of the ruler. Moreover, the Arabs were neither prepared nor able to undertake a prolonged war. In fact, a war of individual raids (*ghazw*) persisted throughout Muslim occupation of Spain from 711 to 1492. From beginning to end, the country was never consolidated; it was the scene of offensives and counteroffensives without a conclusion or a lasting peace.

No doubt the Arabs had the initial advantage and the means to impose a permanent peace, but their internal difficulties — Arabs against Arabs, Berbers against Arabs, and the revolts that constantly broke out — were the major deterrent to firm consolidation and tranquility in the country. This, of course, contributed to the eventual success of the Reconquista, which began with Alfonso I, King of Asturias (739–756), and continued under his successors who established various states in northern Spain. The defeat at Tours together with the internal problems in al-Andalus marked the limit of Islamic expansion into Europe.

With the death of al-Ghāfiqī, al-Andalus lost a great general and administrator at a most critical stage of its history. His successor could not cope with general unrest and was soon replaced by 'Uqbah Ibn al-Ḥajjāj (734–739), an able soldier and administrator, who brought some measure of stability to the country and kept the Carolingians at bay in southern France. However, his career came to an abrupt end when 'Abd al-Malik Ibn Qaṭan instigated a revolt against him. Ibn Qaṭan encountered numerous problems, the gravest of which was the Berber revolt, which started in North Africa and had significant repercussions in al-Andalus.[20] The Berbers had always felt that they were discriminated against by the Arabs. They rose in open revolt and were inspired by the puritan and democratic ideology of the Islamic sect, the Khawārij, who advocated that any "true" Muslim — be he black or Berber — was not only deserving of equality but eligible to hold the highest office in the Islamic community.

The Berbers took Tangier in 740; in response, the governor of North Africa ordered his lieutenant in al-Andalus to meet the crisis. Ibn Qaṭan's attempts to subdue the rebels failed, and the situation was further aggravated by another Berber revolt in northern al-Andalus. This alarmed the government at Damascus. From there some thirty thousand soldiers were sent to the scene, but they were badly defeated in Morocco in 741. Another expeditionary force headed by the governor of Ifrīqiyah finally quenched the revolt.

No doubt these events contributed to a new problem in al-Andalus. The defeated soldiers sent from Damascus were besieged in Ceuta under their proud general Balj Ibn Bishr. These soldiers, numbering some seven thousand, were originally from different parts of Syria (Damascus, Emesa, Qinnasrīn), Palestine, Jordan, and some from Egypt. As their plight became untenable in Ceuta, Balj sought and was granted entry into al-Andalus along with his soldiers. Ibn Qaṭan had hoped that the newcomers would help him to put down the Berber revolt which was threatening Cordova itself, and that they would then leave al-Andalus to go back home. The Balj's army dealt a swift blow to the Berbers, but soon became entangled in the governor's machinations. After promising Balj's army a safe return to North Africa, Ibn Qaṭan wanted to send them back to Ceuta. In despair, perhaps, Balj's soldiers besieged Cordova in 741, overthrew the governor, and installed Balj in his stead.

Balj was overtly partial to his soldiers, who were for the most part Qaysites or northern Arabs. This situation aroused the indignation of the deposed governor's partisans, who were mostly Yemenites or southern Arabs. This situation set the stage for bitterness between the two contending groups and led to untold bloodshed and suffering.

In 743, Abū al-Khaṭṭār was sent as governor of al-Andalus. His main task was to establish peace in the country. In order to curb the danger of Balj's army, he distributed it into various regions: Elvira, Seville, Sidonia, Algeciras, Jaén, Beja, and Murcia. He also put down various revolts, but failed to secure a lasting peace. The polarization between northern and southern Arabs became more pronounced, and Abū al-Khaṭṭār could not avoid an alignment with the southern Arabs. His entanglement with al-Ṣumayl, a proud northern Arab and able soldier, sparked new hostilities. To avoid further bloodshed, the two contending groups decided to alternate the governorship on a yearly basis. In 747, they agreed on Yūsuf al-Fihrī, a northerner, to rule for one year, after which he would be succeeded by a southerner. This arrangement might have worked well had Yūsuf honored it. Instead, he began to purge the government of southern elements, an act that precipitated a bitter and bloody war followed by secession everywhere. This situation lasted for almost a decade during which the followers of Pelayo in the Asturias and Carolingians in France regained a large portion of territory. Al-Andalus was now divided against itself and threatened from the north.

Thus, the 740's presaged ominous events for Arab rule in al-Andalus. All might have ended soon had it not been for the advent of 'Abd al-Raḥmān I, a refugee who succeeded in establishing a dynasty under which al-Andalus saw moments of glory and great splendor.

The Independent Umayyad Emirate (756–929)

'Abd al-Raḥmān I (756–788)
- Hishām I (788–796)
- al-Ḥakam I (796–822)
- 'Abd al-Raḥmān II (822–852)
- Muḥammad I (852–886)
- al-Mundhir (886–888)
- 'Abdallah (888–912)
  - Muḥammad
  - 'Abd al-Raḥmān III (912–929)

The situation in Spain was deteriorating at a time when the central government in Damascus was experiencing a grave crisis. Already in the 720's all signs indicated that the Umayyads of Damascus were heading for serious and compounded troubles: social tension, economic difficulties, the problem of succession to the rule, and indecisive wars against Byzantium. Although all this was apparent, secret cells were also organizing to overthrow the regime. They gathered around the Hāshimite descendants of the Prophet's family, and in 749 launched a revolt which ended in their victory. A new caliph, of the 'Abbāsid family, was installed in 750 in Kūfah, and the last Umayyad caliph, Marwān II, was captured and put to death.

The new 'Abbāsid regime was determined to eliminate any danger from the fallen Umayyad house and treacherously put all its members to death at a carefully staged banquet. Only 'Abd al-Raḥmān,[21] who was almost twenty years old, escaped with his faithful servant Badr. He wandered incognito through Palestine, Egypt, and North Africa. He had no means of support except his sagacity and a great natural instinct for survival.

The governor of North Africa was then 'Abd al-Raḥmān Ibn Ḥabīb al-Fihrī, who denied hospitality to the wandering prince and even made attempts upon his life. Failing to secure any promise of support in North Africa, the prince 'Abd al-Raḥmān turned his eyes hopefully to al-Andalus, then torn with civil war. In 754 he sent Badr on a reconnaissance mission to the Peninsula. Badr returned with encouraging reports. The recently defeated Yemenites, now extremely resentful of the opposing Qaysites, pledged their support and sent a boat with twenty men to bring 'Abd al-Raḥmān. The party landed on Spanish soil in 755 at a village near Elvira. 'Abd al-Raḥmān proceeded to establish rapport with various leaders. He was given supplies and men, and the number of his supporters increased steadily. The Yemenites in particular saw in 'Abd al-Raḥmān an opportunity for avenging their humiliating defeat at the hands of the Qaysites. Other supporters saw in his leadership the best chance for establishing peace and security. Yūsuf al-Fihrī, the governor of al-Andalus, was at that time with his general, al-Ṣumayl, pursuing their opponents in the north. Yūsuf received the news of the arrival of the Umayyad prince with great apprehension. He rushed to Cordova, but since a good number of his army was deserting him, Yūsuf felt that a military encounter would be risky; he decided to neutralize the newcomer by offering him his daughter in marriage, an estate, money, and safe conduct to live in peace. Yūsuf's delegation arrived before 'Abd al-Raḥmān at a place near Loja. After heated deliberation amont his partisans, 'Abd al-Raḥmān emphatically rejected the offer and began to augment his army. To a nucleus of about three hundred cavalrymen from the Umayyads, many others from neighboring districts were soon joined. The army, now consisting of about three thousand horsemen, marched northward to the capital city of Cordova. 'Abd al-Raḥmān gathered more and more adherents on his march to the north and was rendered the oath of allegiance as emir, a title which he was still to earn in the battlefield. He went through Archidona, Sidonia, and reached Seville in 756. From here he marched against Cordova without a flag of his own. An enthusiastic follower hoisted a green turban on a spear, which served for a time as his emblem. He occupied Cordova in 756. At the age of twenty-six he became emir and founder of the Umayyad dynasty that was to rule al-Andalus until 1031.

The conquest of Cordova was by no means the end of the struggle. 'Abd al-Raḥmān was faced with a number of grave problems. His Yemenite partisans entered the city in vengeance and began looting and pillaging. His task was to control them and thereby demonstrate his magnanimity and moderation, two qualities not generally appreciated at the time and for which he risked his throne. The soldiers were embittered to the point of revolt, believing that they had been deprived of their due reward.

Moreover, Yūsuf al-Fihrī and his shrewd general, al-Ṣumayl, continued the struggle. Yūsuf fled to Toledo, and al-Ṣumayl headed for Jaén to gather an army and continue the war. Al-Ṣumayl remained in Elvira afterward, encouraging 'Abd al-Raḥmān to pursue him so Yūsuf's son could enter Cordova and occupy the government palace — a stratagem that probably would have succeeded had Yūsuf's son been able to hold the city. Yūsuf offered to recognize 'Abd al-Raḥmān as emir provided that he, Yūsuf, be granted a safe conduct and be allowed to retain his property and money. 'Abd al-Raḥmān accepted the proposal in 757 on the condition that Yūsuf leave his two sons as hostages; he invited the two to reside in Cordova, where they remained under surveillance. It was in A.H. 139/A.D. 757 that 'Abd al-Raḥmān cursed the black flag of the 'Abbāsids, and forbade the mentioning of the 'Abbāsid caliph al-Manṣūr in the Friday prayer.[22]

A policy of moderation and magnanimity earned for 'Abd al-Raḥmān the respect and admiration of friends and foes alike. But there were those who resented him and called upon Yūsuf al-Fihrī to take arms against him. Yūsuf fled first to Mérida and then to Alicante and surrounded himself with Berber and Yemenite supporters. He then headed for Seville to gather more partisans. After he failed to capture Cordova, he was compelled to flee

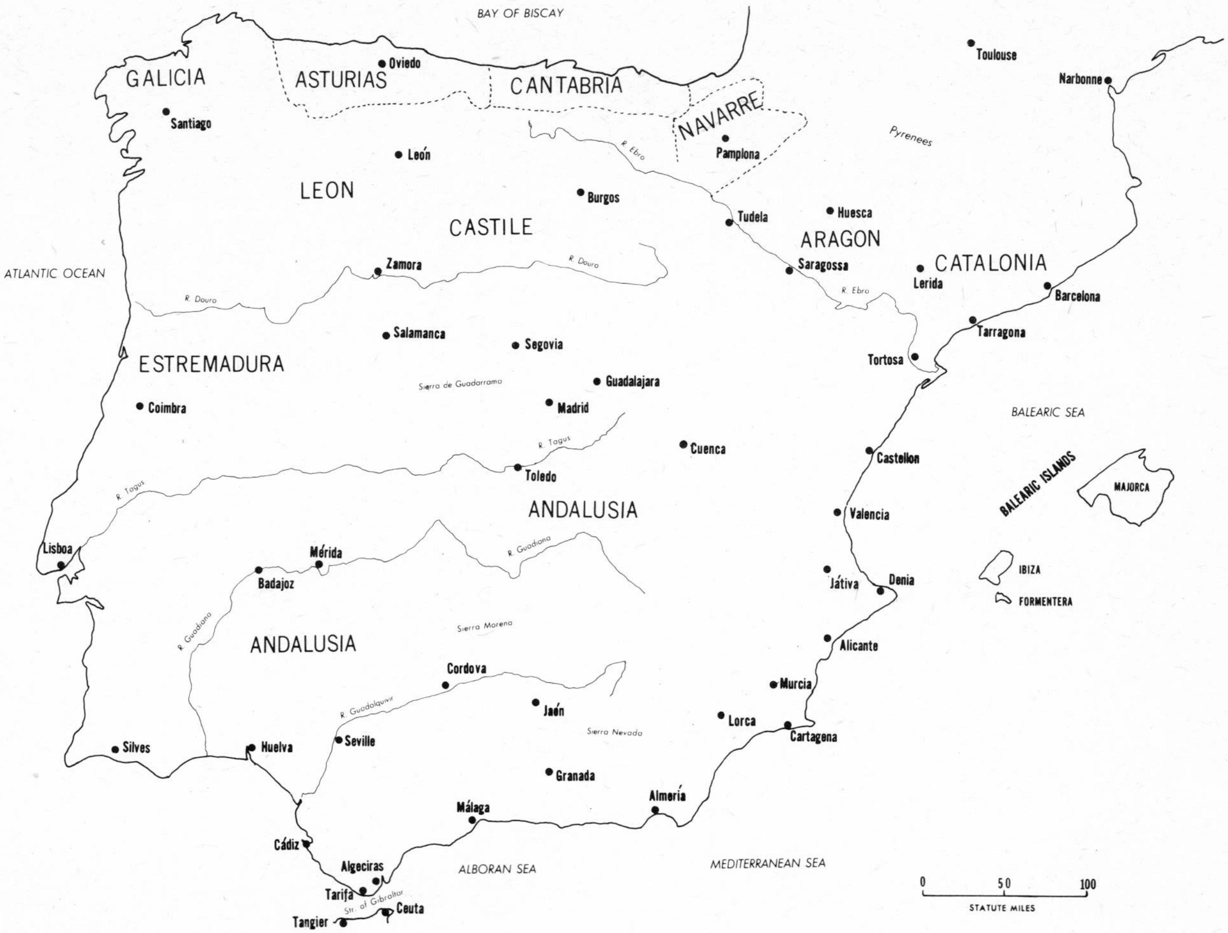

The Iberian Peninsula in the Ninth Century

to Toledo where he hoped to find refuge. In A.H. 142/A.D. 760, before he could reach the city, a loyal subject of ʻAbd al-Raḥmān intercepted and killed him. His head was sent to ʻAbd al-Raḥmān, who displayed it for all to see. In the meantime, ʻAbd al-Raḥmān disposed of al-Ṣumayl and Yūsuf's sons.

Now ʻAbd al-Raḥmān turned his attention to the task of pacifying the country and repelling the Christian enemy to the north. At Toledo in 761 he had to squelch a revolt instigated by a Qaysite. At Beja in 763 he put down another revolt, this time instigated by al-ʻAlā' Ibn Mughīth, an ʻAbbāsid agent, who hoisted the ʻAbbāsid flag. ʻAbd al-Raḥmān viewed this act with great consternation and marched against the intruder, who had moved on to Carmona. After stubborn resistance he defeated ʻAlā', cut off his head, wrapped it in the black ʻAbbāsid banner, and shipped it off in a trunk to Mecca where the caliph al-Manṣūr was on a pilgrimage. Upon seeing the head, the caliph is supposed to have said, "Thanks to God for placing the sea between us and this devil." [23]

In 766, ʻAbd al-Raḥmān also put down a revolt headed by a Yemenite in Niebla, and another in Seville instigated by its former governor who had been dismissed. In 769, a Shiʻite-inspired revolt erupted in Lusitania. Subsequently, other revolts took place in Tudmir, Barcelona, Saragossa, and Algeciras.

During these numerous revolts, ʻAbd al-Raḥmān was also feeling pressure from the north. Beyond the Pyrenees a powerful empire had been forged by the Carolingian king, Charlemagne, who is said to have had diplomatic relations with the ʻAbbāsid court in Baghdād. In 774 Sulaymān al-Aʻrābī and other rebels sought the help of Charlemagne and pledged their assistance to help conquer Cordova and become his loyal subjects. Charlemagne answered the call and marched against al-Andalus in 778. He occupied Pamplona and headed for Saragossa. Although he besieged the city, he had to withdraw and return to attend to pressing problems at home. On his way back, Charlemagne's army was surprised in the narrow passes of Roncesvalles, to the northeast of Pamplona. His army was decimated and lost many of its leaders, including Roland, who became celebrated in the *Chanson de Roland*.[24]

ʻAbd al-Raḥmān displayed great ability and statesmanship. He may be said to have saved Muslim Spain from disintegration, pacifying the country and, to some degree, consolidating it. He appointed able and trustworthy governors to the provinces. Faithful perhaps to the Muslim tradition, or to avoid political complications, he did not assume the title of caliph but rather remained satisfied with emir or king or "son of the caliph."

He embellished the old city of Cordova with buildings and gardens, for which he imported fruit trees and vegetables from the Orient. His garden, al-Ruṣāfah, was a wonder of his day. In it he built a palace known both as the Damascus Palace and the Ruṣāfah Palace. He initiated the construction of the Mosque of Cordova, which became the model for future mosques. He is justly regarded as one of the great Muslim rulers. In addition, he was an able poet, composing nostalgic and suggestive verses reminiscing about his Syrian homeland.

'Abd al-Raḥmān was shortsighted in the selection of his successor. Some sources[25] tell us that he instructed his son 'Abdallah to pass the rule to whichever of his other two sons, Hishām or the older Sulaymān, arrived in Cordova first. Hishām was then in Mérida and Sulaymān was in Toledo. Upon hearing of the death of their father, the two sons rushed to the capital. Hishām I (789–796), who appears to have been the more capable, arrived first; he was given the "ring of the emirate" as instructed and was rendered the oath of allegiance by the notables and common people. It is likely that he was the first choice. Sulaymān did not accept his father's dictum and forced the people of Toledo to render him the oath of allegiance. Then he gathered an army and headed toward the capital. Hishām met him at Jaén and forced his brother to flee to Toledo, where he assumed an independent posture. In the meantime, Hishām's relations with his brother 'Abdallah deteriorated to the extent that the latter left Cordova and joined Sulaymān in Toledo. In view of this development, Hishām, who had so far shown great tolerance, intended at first to march against Toledo at the head of a large army. When Sulaymān marched against Cordova, however, leaving 'Abdallah behind, Hishām decided to stay in Cordova and to send his son to fight Sulaymān; the latter soon fled to Mérida. Hishām besieged Toledo for two months and forced 'Abdallah to come with him to Cordova. Afterward, he impelled Sulaymān to surrender and to leave al-Andalus together with 'Abdallah and their immediate families.[26]

The struggle for succession took almost one year of Hishām's reign, and, at the same time, a rebel in Saragossa had to be subdued in 791. In addition, Hishām launched raids against Bermudo I in Alava, Castilla la Vieja, and Galicia, which were followed by an attack against Narbonne, Oviedo, and others.

It is plausible that under Hishām Mālikism was made the official legal doctrine in al-Andalus, thus displacing the school of the Damascene jurist al- Awzā'ī (d. 774). The Mālikite school was introduced by native Spaniards who had studied under Mālik Ibn Anas himself in the East.

Hishām is reported to have had wide knowledge of Prophetic Traditions and Qur'ānic studies. Inclined toward asceticism and piety, he fell under the influence of the jurists. He continued the construction of the Mosque of Cordova initiated by his father. He also built the great canal of Cordova, but was accused of using it mainly for his pleasure and hunting.[27]

Hishām nominated his son al-Ḥakam (796–822) to succeed him, bypassing an older son. Al-Ḥakam ascended to the throne at the age of twenty-six and had to earn his title to the throne against pretenders and seceders in various regions of al-Andalus, including his two uncles, 'Abdallah and Sulaymān, who had been exiled to Africa. This strife lasted for almost four years until Sulaymān was killed and 'Abdallah was granted amnesty and was given Valencia to rule. Al-Ḥakam's experience with his kinsmen may have influenced him to prefer the advice of his governors to that of relatives and courtiers.[28]

Al-Ḥakam was stern, determined, and just. He was an accomplished poet, and several love poems have been attributed to him (he used a poem, we are told, to put down a revolt launched by five of his concubines). Aware of the tendency for revolts in the provinces, he introduced an effective espionage system; he had at the palace gate a thousand horses and spies who were constantly ready to move against attempted rebellion. In his army he made use of some five thousand slaves who could not speak Arabic and were referred to as mute.[29] In 798, suspecting a revolt in Toledo, he forestalled it by massacring about five thousand men.[30] Except for his two uncles, the situation remained calm in the Peninsula until 817, when the revolt of the suburb (*rabaḍ*), presumably instigated by hostile jurists, broke out in Cordova. Al-Ḥakam further antagonized the jurists by limiting their hitherto influential role at court. When they tried to undermine his authority, he crucified seventy-two men, some of whom were quite prominent. This created great resentment and tension between the religious scholars and the throne. Then a civil war broke out when a boy was killed by one of the emir's guards in 202/820. Cries for unseating the emir spread in the city, and an armed mob surrounded the palace.[31] Hopelessly besieged, al-Ḥakam sent word to his horsemen to go to the suburbs and set fire to the houses. This stratagem succeeded. The mob withdrew when they saw their homes aflame; relieved from the siege, al-Ḥakam's guards pursued the rebels and killed more than ten thousand.[32] Some three hundred survivors were crucified one by one. The following day, al-Ḥakam ordered the destruction of the whole suburb and expulsion of its inhabitants to North Africa. Some of them went to Morocco. Others, some fifteen thousand,[33] occupied Alexandria, but were soon driven out by 'Abdallah Ibn Ṭāhir. They settled in Crete, where they ruled for more than a century.

Al-Ḥakam's relations with the Christians to the north followed a pattern of raids and counterraids. He had several reverses: the Franks took Barcelona in 801, and the Arab army was badly defeated during its attack of Alava and Castilla la Vieja. However, al-Ḥakam struck back successfully in 808 in Galicia and Asturias against Alfonso II (791–842). One of the factors perhaps most damaging to his rule was a famine rampant throughout al-Andalus in 199/813, which played havoc on the hard-pressed economy of the country.

Al-Ḥakam was more feared than loved. Thus, when he died, the suppressed tension would probably have exploded throughout al-Andalus had it not been for the foresight and ability of his successor. Al-Ḥakam's older and able son 'Abd al-Raḥmān II (822–852) succeeded him, ascending the throne at the age of thirty. He had extensive military experience and was a good administrator. In addition, he had a broad education and a taste for poetry and the amenities of life. This wide exposure definitely affected his character and outlook, contributing to his moderation and consequently to peace and prosperity.

He was a great builder and statesman. He enlarged the mosque of Cordova and built many others in Jaén, Seville, and Cordova. He reorganized the government in the 'Abbāsid manner by delegating some of his duties to viziers, but always exercising absolute power. He struck coins in his name and imported goods and talents from the Orient. In the words of Ibn 'Idhārī, 'Abd al-Raḥmān II was "The first one to follow the customs [*sunan*] of the caliphs with respect to feast, form and arrangement of the civil service [*khidmah*]. He dressed the caliphate [sic] with great majesty; erected palaces to which he brought water; constructed a dam to which he devoted great skill. He also built mosques; devoted himself to irrigation; introduced embroideries and determined their use; and struck coinage in Cordova."[34]

His court had an impressive entourage of poets, religious scholars, litterateurs, musicians, and boon-companions. He is said to have fallen under the influence of the following: Yaḥyā b. Yaḥyā (d. 849), a jurist who was a strong advocate of Mālikism; Ziryāb, an accomplished singer and poet who had emigrated from Baghdād and who came to exert a great influence on Cordovan fashion;[35] Ṭarūb, a concubine whom he showered with great wealth and for whom he composed beautiful songs[36] (he even forgave her when he discovered her plotting against him); Naṣr, the eunuch who cared for his harem and was a confidant of Ṭarūb.

At first, 'Abd al-Raḥmān faced problems identical to those of his predecessors. 'Abdallah, unsuccessful pretender for the third time, rebelled but died in 823. And there was a revolt between Yemenite and Qaysite Arabs and other revolts in Mérida (833), Toledo (829), and Algeciras (850).

One unusual event during the reign was the appearance of a rough people from the North. They were called Majūs, but were most probably from the Scandinavian countries. In 844, they were found off the eastern and western coast of al-Andalus with a fleet of sixty of more ships. They landed in Lisbon and then headed for Seville, Cadiz, and Sidonia.[37] They looted and killed wherever they went and were soon confronted by 'Abd al-Raḥmān's army. Most of their fleet was destroyed and some sixteen thousand were killed. This menace influenced 'Abd al-Raḥmān to enlarge his fleet, which proved useful in the following century when al-Andalus was threatened by the rising power of the Fāṭimids. Moreover, 'Abd al-Raḥmān was involved in several raids on Alava, Castilla la Vieja, Galicia, Barcelona, Asturias, and elsewhere. He had to fight not only the Christians there, but the *Muwallad* Mūsā Ibn Mūsā Ibn Qasī of Tudela who rebelled several times (*Muwalladūn* were Muslims born of Spanish ancestry). It was perhaps the Banū Qasī, who had confessed Islam overtly, who inspired and encouraged other *Muwallad* revolts following the death of 'Abd al-Raḥmān II. Although they disappeared from the scene in 884, their place was taken by the Arab Tujībids who became the masters of Saragossa.

In 851 another unusual movement came from some of the extremist Mozarabs of Cordova who were aroused by the Christian cleric Eulogio and Alvaro to insult the prophet Muḥammad in public, knowing that such conduct would carry the death penalty. They hoped to gain martyrdom by acts amounting to suicide. Many of them would not desist. Flora, the daughter of a Muslim father and Christian mother, committed the insult of Muḥammad and attracted much attention for her defiance of the authorities. The latter displayed unusual leniency on her behalf, but Flora stubbornly persisted in her insults and left the judge little choice but to decree her death in 851, along with her zealous friend María. Both earned not only coveted martyrdom but sainthood as well.[38] A further display of religiosity was made in 852 by a man who proclaimed himself a prophet and advocated living according to nature. He thus forbade the cutting of hair and nails. He was crucified upon his refusal to desist from his claims.[39]

Although this kind of aberration was for the most part under control, it must have had serious repercussions later with regard to Muslim-Christian relations in general. Moreover, two major famines in 823 and 846 were followed by a devastating flood in 850; these combined events surely crippled the economy and contributed to the general unrest which became quite perceptible after the death of 'Abd al-Raḥmān II.

On the whole, 'Abd al-Raḥmān presided over a state which gained the respect and admiration of even distant Byzantium and the states of North Africa. In 840, he received a diplomatic mission from Byzantium bearing gifts and seeking mutual cooperation against their common foe, the 'Abbāsids. 'Abd al-Raḥmān returned the courtesy by sending an embassy headed by the able and handsome poet Yaḥyā al-Ghazāl.[40]

Thus, 'Abd al-Raḥmān II had the country under control during his lifetime, but his failure to consolidate this control became more evident under his immediate successors, who faced numerous revolts instigated by ambitious governors and accelerated by social tensions, especially from among *Muwalladūn*. Thus, from almost 852 to 920, al-Andalus was on the path toward political disintegration and would have disintegrated had it not been for the determination and statesmanship of 'Abd al-Raḥmān III (912–961).

In 852 'Abd al-Raḥmān was succeeded by his son Muḥammad. He was about thirty years old, had served as governor of the High March, and had participated in various expeditions. The able chamberlain 'Īsā b. Shuhayd exacted the oath of allegiance from the nobility and the common people. Muḥammad inherited what appeared to be a stable and prosperous kingdom, but though he followed his father's policies, weaknesses soon appeared following 'Īsā's death. Court unrest set in when the emir appointed Hishām b. 'Abd al-'Azīz as chamberlain. Ambitious and cunning, Ibn 'Abd al-'Azīz influenced policies and recruited inexperienced favorites to sensitive posts. This led to abuses and no doubt to restiveness among the populace. The situation was aggravated by socio-religious tension. Toledo, the nest of revolts, dismissed and imprisoned the emir's governor and openly sought alliance with Ordoño I, King of Asturias, who sent an army in 854. Muḥammad met the enemy, defeated him, and killed eight thousand or more soldiers, whose heads he made into a mountain.[41] He later succeeded in reaching Alava to the north. These skirmishes lasted until 858. The revolt had great repercussions, since it had been inspired by Christian clerics and supported by *Muwalladūn* who called for emancipation from Muslims and Arab rule. In spite of Muḥammad's initial successes, the socio-religious tension continued unabated, and rose following the execution in 859 of the cleric Eulogio, who became a martyr to his followers. Similar revolts inspired by Christians and supported by *Muwalladūn* took place in Mérida in 868, Badajoz, Huesca, the High and Middle Marches, and the southern part of al-Andalus.[42]

The emir Muḥammad was overwhelmed. The Norsemen reappeared on the scene in 240/855 and succeeded for a while in occupying Algeciras, Tudmir, and other posts (859). Next came Christian harassment in the north and the tacit secession of Mūsā Ibn Mūsā Ibn Qasī from the central government; Mūsā now allied himself with neighboring Christians. When Mūsā died (862), his successors continued to espouse the *Muwallad* cause. This situation was further aggravated by the occurrence of two famines in 867 and 874, respectively.[43] All this seems to have contributed to the rise of two individuals who became the principal figures in al-Andalus. They were Ibn Marwān al-Jillīqī and Ibn Ḥafṣūn.

Time of Trouble

Ibn Marwān al-Jillīqī belonged to a *Muwallad* family. His father was the governor of Mérida, and seemed to have enjoyed the favor of the central government. Taking advantage of unrest in the north in 868, Ibn al-Jillīqī declared himself independent and had the full support of fellow *Muwallads* and Mozarabs. The central government besieged Mérida and was successful in recapturing the city and bringing Ibn al-Jillīqī to Cordova. He stayed in the capital city until 875, when he left it in anger following his humiliation by the chamberlain Ibn 'Abd al-'Azīz. He renewed his rebellion in and around Mérida, and the central government sent against him an army headed by the chamberlain himself. It was a memorable victory when Ibn al-Jillīqī defeated the emir's army and captured the hated chamberlain. With gusto, Ibn al-Jillīqī sent the captive chamberlain to Alfonso III of Asturias (he was released two years later upon the payment of a hundred thousand dinars in ransom). This audacious act had a great psychological effect among other rebels and was humiliating to the central government, which soon forced Ibn al-Jillīqī to seek refuge at the court of Alfonso III. In 884, Ibn al-Jillīqī returned and was able to hold sway over Badajoz and a large area in the south. He died in 889 and was succeeded by his descendants, who ruled that territory until 929.

Ibn Ḥafṣūn was likewise a *Muwallad*, from Ronda. In his youth, he killed a man and became a highway robber in the mountainous areas. Being sought by the authorities, he decided to go to North Africa, where he became an apprentice in a tailor shop. In 850, he returned to al-Andalus and continued his early pursuits with headquarters in the almost impregnable fortress of Bobastro. In 883, he surrendered to an invading army which he joined but deserted after a fight with a fellow officer. He returned to Bobastro and extended his power over many villages, holding his own under four emirs and becoming for a time the major figure of al-Andalus. He would enter into a truce or an agreement with the emir only to break it when the pressure was lifted. The repeated failures of the central government to subdue him contributed to his gaining prestige and more partisans. Certainly, the emir Muḥammad lacked determination in subduing the rebel, who continued to be a major threat to the government for several decades. Even the powerful 'Abd al-Raḥmān III had to negotiate with him.

Ibn Ḥafṣūn possessed all the gifts of revolutionary ability, cunning, shrewdness, perceptiveness, and courage. Ibn 'Idhārī tells us: "When he rebelled, he found support and acceptance from among the people due to the similarity and harmony of views. The people rallied about him. He mingled with and befriended the people saying: 'The sultan has for a long time treated you harshly, taken away your property, and imposed demands beyond your ability. The Arabs have humiliated and enslaved you. But I wish to avenge you and emancipate you from your enslavement.' "[44]

Many followed Ibn Ḥafṣūn out of interest in adventure and booty; some sympathized because of justified grievances against Muḥammad. Ibn Ḥafṣūn commanded the respect of his followers by his fair but stern decisions. He imposed justice even on his own son; he was devoted to his men and honored the brave among them. He was respectful to women to the point that one was able to travel from one town to another without being molested.[45]

Like other *Muwalladūn* Ibn Ḥafṣūn exploited the discontent of his fellow Muslims. In addition, he flirted with 'Abbāsid agents through the Aghlabids and other North African dynasties.[46]

Ibn Ḥafṣūn was under attack in 886 by Muḥammad's son, al-Mundhir, the heir apparent; when Muḥammad died, al-Mundhir had to rush to Cordova to assume the throne. This respite allowed Ibn Ḥafṣūn to consolidate his forces and extend his power in Beja, Cabra, Jaén, and other towns. Al-

Mundhir (886–888), an able military man, was determined to dispose of the rebel once and for all. With a large army he succeeded in taking some fortresses. A number of leaders were captured and put to the cross — one of them, ʻAyshūn, was crucified with a pig at his right and a dog at his left. Hard pressed, Ibn Ḥafṣūn asked for amnesty, and al-Mundhir accepted. However, after he had received mules and provisions from al-Mundhir as part of the terms, Ibn Ḥafṣūn fled by night to Bobastro, where he was besieged for some forty-three days. He was relieved only when al-Mundhir became ill and returned to Cordova. Though it had seemed that the central government had finally secured the upper hand, al-Mundhir died and the rebel was granted a new lease of life.

At this juncture, the deteriorating situation in al-Andalus called for a decisive and determined man. But ʻAbdallah (888–912), who succeeded his brother al-Mundhir, is said to have been a pious and humble man, knowledgeable in the Qur'ān, Arabic, history, and poetry. (In spite of his avowed piety, he killed two brothers and his own son who intrigued against the heir apparent, another son, and caused his death.) He was not able to cope with the situation, which gradually deteriorated to the point that central authority was limited to the capital city. Ibn Ḥafṣūn extended his power over most of southern al-Andalus and threatened Cordova itself. Revolts were instigated by *Muwalladūn* in Murcia, Jaén, Mérida, Écija, Seville, Granada, Badajoz, Saragossa, and other centers.[47] Most of the rebels were in touch with Ibn Ḥafṣūn. Similarly, the Arabs and Berbers undertook revolts, some of which — like those of the *Muwalladūn* — resulted in the establishment of autonomous states. At first, ʻAbdallah used diplomacy with Ibn Ḥafṣūn. He called on him to render the oath of allegiance, in return for which Ibn Ḥafṣūn was made governor of the district of Rayyah, to be aided by an appointee of the court. This gave the rebel an opportunity to build up his position in harmony with his future plans. He soon dismissed his co-governor and pursued his ambitions. ʻAbdallah sent an army but was defeated, thereby enhancing Ibn Ḥafṣūn's power and prestige. Now many flocked to him from all sectors of al-Andalus. In fact, he felt confident that he could become the sole ruler of al-Andalus if he took Cordova itself.

In 891, Ibn Ḥafṣūn established himself in the fortress of Poley southeast of Cordova but was repelled and pursued by the emir's army up to Bobastro after Elvira, Jaén, and other cities were taken from him. When hard pressed he sued for peace, which was granted. However, it did not take him long to break his truce, and the emir was forced in 893 again to send an army against him. Ibn Ḥafṣūn was checked but not defeated. The emir's army withdrew to counter a revolt elsewhere, and in the meantime Ibn Ḥafṣūn recaptured cities such as Écija. Raid after raid proved inconclusive until 901 when Ibn Ḥafṣūn negotiated a truce, which he broke the following year, leading to further indecisive encounters. In 899, Ibn Ḥafṣūn embraced Christianity. By doing so he lost many Muslim followers, but gained Christian sympathies.

In the meantime the position of the central government remained tenuous. Conflicts between *Muwalladūn* and Arabs appeared in Elvira, Seville, and elsewhere, starting as feuds and ending in massacres. The rise of the Banū Ḥajjāj[48] of Seville exemplifies the deteriorating situation in al-Andalus. Ibrāhīm Ibn Ḥajjāj (d. 910) emerged as a leader after a bitter conflict between Arabs and *Muwalladūn*. In 899 he broke his alliance with the Khaldūn, another prominent family of the city, and declared himself independent. He built an army, collected taxes, and had his court in the manner of kings. He rendered lip service to the central government, but kept on good terms with Ibn Ḥafṣūn. He was succeeded by his son 'Abd al-Raḥmān (d. 301/914) in Seville and another son ruled Carmona. It was not until the coming of 'Abd al-Raḥmān III that those areas were reunited with the central government.

The politicosocial situation in al-Andalus was chaotic under the emir 'Abdallah.[49] He was indecisive and overextended his army in meeting threats to the central government. There were occasions when he could have disposed of Ibn Ḥafṣūn but other pressing problems diverted his attention. Ibn Ḥafṣūn may have symbolized the widespread discontent that led to the virtual political disintegration of the country in 912. 'Abdallah inherited numerous problems, some of which had remained unresolved from the time of the conquest. To the chronic rivalry among the conquerors may be added their failure to consolidate the northern area of the country and to make it attractive for settlement. Instead, they left it exposed to the ambitions of Muslim and Christian rebels who received early encouragement and support from the Carolingians in southern France. This situation eventually led to the establishment of independent Christian kingdoms, the earliest of which was Asturias. Pelayo was the first paragon of the Reconquista. He took refuge in the almost impregnable region of the Asturias and is said to have defeated a Muslim army at Covadonga in 718. In the course of time, he gained more followers, establishing a kingdom that grew while the Muslims were preoccupied with internal unrest. After Pelayo died in 737, his son ruled for a short time. In the absence of any successor, Pelayo's daughter married Alfonso, the duke of Cantabria, who incorporated a number of fortresses and towns, becoming the ruler of a kingdom that was never to disappear. The successors of Alfonso I (739–756) were able to take important towns, and establish a religio-nationalist ideology that was kept alive for centuries. This religio-nationalist fervor took strength under the reign of Alfonso II (791–842) from the discovery of the tomb of St. Jacob in what came to be known as the city of Santiago of Compostela. The city was provided with an impressive cathedral and with a shrine that became the source of spiritual inspiration and national aspiration for Christian Spain.

In brief, the conquest of Spain was achieved with relative smoothness, but the conqueror failed to pacify and consolidate his domains. A number of reasons can be suggested for both success and failure. The descendants of the Visigothic king Witiza and their partisans rendered an immeasurable help during the conquest. They had hoped that they would regain the throne, but they were soon disappointed and had to resign themselves to holding their titles and large estates. Also the role of Julian of Ceuta and that of Oppas, Bishop of Seville, could not be overestimated. They continued their cooperation with the conqueror and were handsomely rewarded. Some of Julian's descendants enjoyed the favors of the court of Cordova, and were accomplished scholars and administrators. The prince Ardabastro, the minor son of Witiza, preserved many privileges, resided in Cordova, and became very influential in relations between Muslims and Christians. He was known as the leader of Christians (*za'īm 'ajam al-dhimmah*); his power grew considerably at the death of his brother Olemundo. His niece Sara opposed him when he tried to incorporate her property into his already large estates, and went to Damascus to complain to the caliph, who foiled her uncle's plan. Upon her return, she married an Arab leader in Seville, whose clan came to play a significant role in the affairs of the city.

Moreover, the administration of towns and provinces was, by and large, relegated to natives, depending on the terms of surrender. If a city surrendered peacefully (*ṣulḥan*), a favorable treaty was usually drawn allowing the local leadership to continue administering it in return for a specified amount of taxes. For instance, such a treaty was made with Tudmīr (Theodomir), who ruled the southeast of the Peninsula (Malága-Murcia) with great autonomy until 'Abd al-Raḥmān II revoked the treaty and limited those privileges. 'Abd al-Raḥmān also reduced the size of the enormous estate of Ardabastro's family, allowing one of them to assume the post of *qūmis al-Andalus*, "the count of al-Andalus."

However, if a city was taken forcibly (*'anwatan*), it became subject to the whims of the conqueror, who could dispose of it at will or govern it by an appointee of his own choice. But in either case, the conquered population was governed by its own religious leaders, who were responsible to the central government. This arrangement seems to have worked well, but only in areas south of Toledo. In areas north of this restless city, the situation remained tenuous from beginning to end. Forays into France had little or no tangible results, and the same may be said about the numerous offensive and counteroffensives in areas north of Toledo. Those areas constituting the High, Middle, and Low Marches were never colonized and were sparsely inhabited by Berbers, who remained disaffected.

Moreover, the conquerors failed to resolve the chronic differences among themselves, mainly the cleavage between Arabs and Berbers. Repeated internal revolts among Arab tribes made of the country a bloodbath resulting in grave consequences for the Arabs themselves and the rest of the population. This situation became thornier when many Christians adopted Islam. In the course of time, these converts constituted the majority of the Muslim population, becoming increasingly disgruntled that they were not receiving their just share in the life and wealth of the country. Their status may be equated to that of the *mawālī* (clients) in the East who accepted Islam in good faith but felt the discrimination of the ruling class. The rank and file of the neo-Muslims was increased by the import of mercenaries drawn from slaves or brought from Africa and Europe.

Finally, the remainder of the Christian population could not escape the consequences of the unsettled situation and were not free from abuses and exploitations. Some decided to join the resistance movement in the north, while others resigned themselves to second-class citizenry. But as their number was reduced substantially by conversion to Islam or by sweeping arabization, staunch Christians were alarmed and felt a genuine concern for the grave threat to their beliefs, their old way of life, and their law. Their reaction against this state of affairs was violent and uncompromising and found eloquent expression in the movement of martyrdom wherein Christian zealots encouraged by clergymen would vilify Islam and its founder in order to receive capital punishment and, thus, earn the coveted designation of martyrs and saints. The movement lasted for almost a decade (850–859) while the government failed to find a viable solution. The harsh punishment imposed by the government — crucifixion, display of corpses in public for days, and denial of burial — aggravated rather than minimized the religious fervor of many who cherished such an end. More often than not their corpses were eaten by vultures, thrown into the river, or cremated to avoid their resting places' becoming shrines. But this did not deter their partisans from getting the remains and taking them to churches or monasteries, thereby keeping the spirit of martyrdom alive. The situation became so serious that the authorities summoned the bishops to a council in 852 to have them put an end to such suicidal acts. The Council failed in its effort and could not stop Eulogio, the ringleader of the would-be martyrs, whose desire for martyrdom never ceased until the government had him put to death. Many Christians objected to the methods of the would-be martyrs, creating thereby a cleavage among Christians themselves. This cleavage was aggravated by certain Christian heresies; one advocated, among other things, that Christ was not the natural but the adopted son of God; others denied the actual distinction of the Trinity, refused fasting on Saturdays, believed in predestination, and permitted mixed marriages of Muslims and Christians and concubinage among the clergy.

This religious convulsion within Christianity, besides its confrontation with Islam, gave impetus to the Reconquista, which carried with it the idea of purifying the land from infidelity. In consequence, the Muslims found themselves involved in constant wars with the Christians to the north, who had a stronghold in the Marches as well as in Galicia, Luisitania, Cantabria, Cataluña, and Gaul. But the most serious danger to the government came from Muslims of non-Arabic ancestry (*Muwalladūn*) who rose in rebellions in the north, center, and south of the Peninsula. Their revolts supported by Christians lasted for decades and did not subside until the reign of 'Abd al-Raḥmān III, who succeeded in pacifying the country only after he allowed his coreligionists to have a share in the wealth and management of the country.

In short, Muslim Spain went through the painful stages of revolts and convulsion that were to mark the rest of its history. A clear pattern of conquest and reconquest was set and fluctuated according to circumstances. Moreover, Arab defeat at the battle of Tours-Poitiers in 732 not only put an end to further Muslim forays into southern France, but reversed the coin in favor of the Carolingians, who often attacked Muslim territory.

Although al-Andalus became an independent political entity as early as 756, preserving much of the primitive features brought to it by the conquerors, it continued to receive its inspiration and guidance from the East in the cultural and intellectual fields, notwithstanding the political obstacles separating it from the heartland of Islam. Al-Andalus thus transcended its provincialism, and its presence was strongly felt throughout the Peninsula, southern France, and the Mediterranean. Its navy patrolled its shores on the Atlantic and the Mediterranean. The presence of Andalusians in the Mediterranean — Balearic Islands, Malta, Sicily, Crete, and elsewhere — was quite apparent. Their role in this area cannot be separated from that of their coreligionists. It must be recalled that the Arabs attacked and plundered the various islands in the Mediterranean following the conquest of North Africa and Spain. Andalusian refugees numbering some 15,000 occupied the island of Crete in 827 and held it until 961. In the meantime, the conquest of Sicily from Tunisia was undertaken in 827 and was completed in 902, making the island Muslim territory until 1091.[50] Also, Malta was conquered in 869 and was held until 1090. Besides, Italian cities such as Salerno, Naples, Amalfi, Capua, and Rome were constantly harassed and plundered by Muslims, thereby giving ample evidence of the enormous power of the Arabs throughout the Mediterranean basin.[51]

2

The Caliphate, 929–1031

The Rise of ʻAbd al-Raḥmān III (912–967)

ʻABDALLAH had nominated his son Muḥammad as his successor, but Muḥammad perished at the hand of his jealous brother, al-Muṭarrif, who in turn was put to death by ʻAbdallah.[1] Filled with remorse, ʻAbdallah nominated Muḥammad's son, ʻAbd al-Raḥmān III, who was born in 277/891, the same year in which Muḥammad was killed. ʻAbdallah had great affection for his grandson. He brought him up, gave him a good education, and entrusted him at an early age with various responsibilities. Thus, in 912, ʻAbd al-Raḥmān was rendered the oath of allegiance by his uncles and other elders of the Umayyad family. He ascended the throne at the age of about twenty-one with considerable experience behind him, but there remained the great task of unifying a state hopelessly divided from within and threatened by powerful foes from without. "Al-Nāṣir li-Dīn Allāh [ʻAbd al-Raḥmān] assumed power," Ibn al-Khaṭīb relates, "while al-Andalus was ablaze and the fire was kindled with increasing contention and hyprocrisy, and the provinces were in a state of convulsion. By virtue of his [ʻAbd al-Raḥmān's] good fortune and indomitable spirit, God pacified it. He is usually compared to ʻAbd al-Raḥmān al-Dākhil. He subdued rebels, built palaces, gave impetus to agriculture, immortalized ancient deeds and monuments (*āthār*), inflicted great damage on infidels to a point

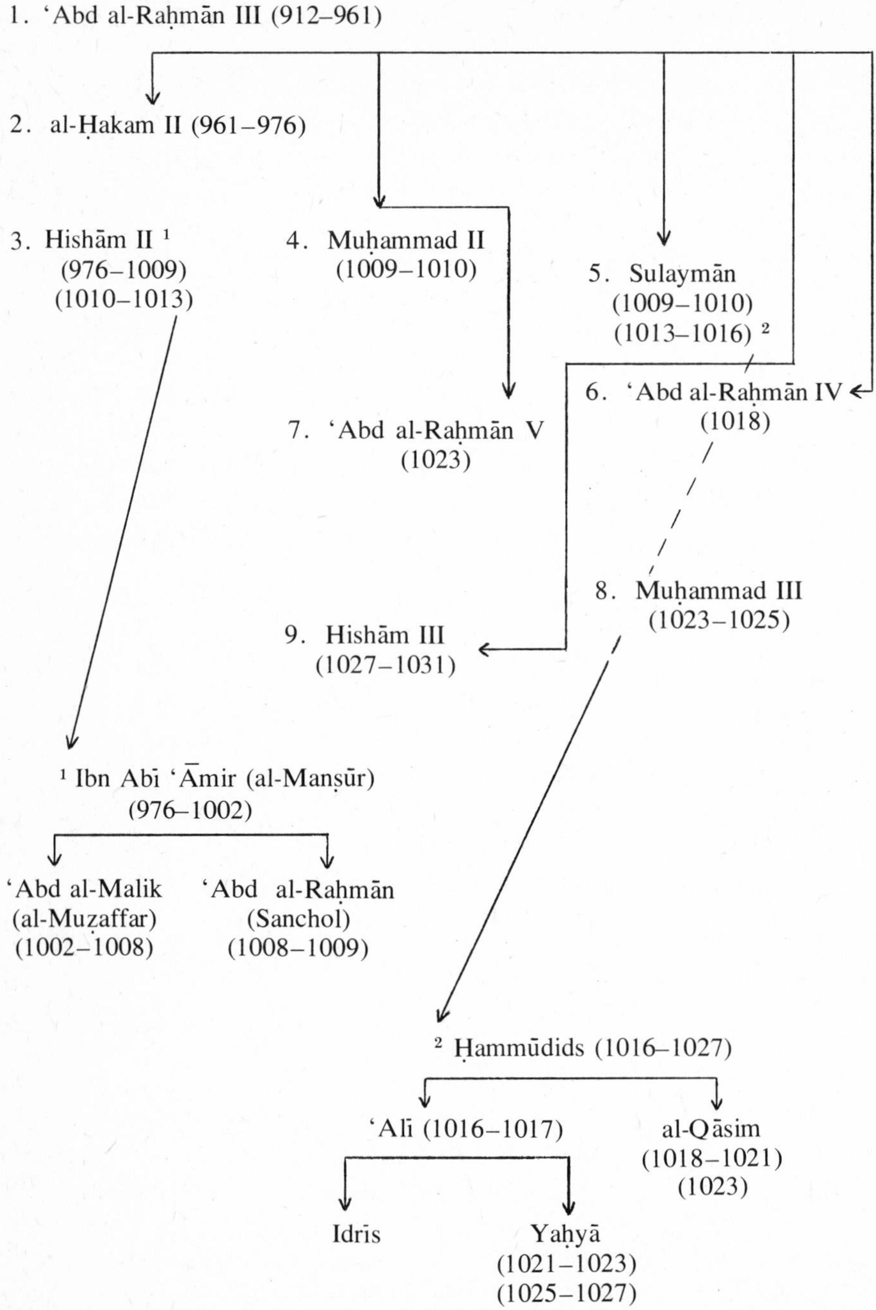
1. ‘Abd al-Raḥmān III (912–961)
2. al-Ḥakam II (961–976)
3. Hishām II [1] (976–1009) (1010–1013)
4. Muḥammad II (1009–1010)
5. Sulaymān (1009–1010) (1013–1016) [2]
6. ‘Abd al-Raḥmān IV (1018)
7. ‘Abd al-Raḥmān V (1023)
8. Muḥammad III (1023–1025)
9. Hishām III (1027–1031)
[1] Ibn Abī ‘Āmir (al-Manṣūr) (976–1002)
‘Abd al-Malik (al-Muẓaffar) (1002–1008)
‘Abd al-Raḥmān (Sanchol) (1008–1009)
[2] Ḥammūdids (1016–1027)
‘Alī (1016–1017)
al-Qāsim (1018–1021) (1023)
Idrīs
Yaḥyā (1021–1023) (1025–1027)

that no opponent or contender remained in al-Andalus. People obeyed in mass and wished to live with him in peace.''[2]

This statement is not without foundation. 'Abd al-Raḥmān III inherited a post which no one seemed to want, ascending the throne without visible opposition within the Umayyad family. Undisturbed by the chaotic situation, he proceeded slowly and surely in the difficult task of pacifying and uniting al-Andalus.

Upon his inauguration 'Abd al-Raḥmān sent emissaries to the governors of the Peninsula and asked them to render him the oath of allegiance. His appeal got some response, but was ignored by many. He lost no time in confronting his opponents with military force or with persuasive diplomacy. He first marched at the head of his army toward the south and captured many fortresses. In 913, Seville, which had become independent under Banū Ḥajjāj, was brought under the control of Cordova without much bloodshed.[3] He then directed his attention in 914 against Ibn Ḥafṣūn, who at one time dominated an area from Algeciras to the proximity of Cordova itself. Ibn Ḥafsūn was surrounded and deprived of access to the sea by the capture of Algeciras and other towns.[4] However, he continued his stubborn opposition until his death in 917. He was succeeded by his sons, who followed the tactics of their father, making peace one day and breaking it the next. Ja'far was killed in 920 and was succeeded by his brother Sulaymān, who made peace with 'Abd al-Raḥmān, later rebelled, and died in 927. He was succeeded by his brother Ḥafṣ, who was impelled in 928 to relinquish Bobastro, the last stronghold of the Ḥafṣūnids. 'Abd al-Raḥmān III took Ḥafṣ into his employ[5] and thereby was able to visit the fortress of Bobastro. He destroyed the churches there and unearthed the corpses of the Ḥafṣūnids and put them on crosses in Cordova for all to see.[6]

Having secured the important city of Seville and having terminated the menace of the Ḥafṣūnids, 'Abd al-Raḥmān won Badajoz (929), Beja, Toledo, Saragossa, and other strongholds. Thus, by 932, he had pacified, if not consolidated, al-Andalus.

In addition to the difficult task of pacification, 'Abd al-Raḥmān from the outset faced grave external danger to the south of the Peninsula as well as to the north. In North Africa there appeared a Shī'ah movement, the Fāṭimids, who claimed to be the sole legitimate rulers of the entire Islamic community. They soon established the most powerful Islamic state in the tenth century. They began to harass al-Andalus and constituted the greatest danger during the first years of 'Abd al-Raḥmān's rule. Through diplomacy and show of force, 'Abd al-Raḥmān III checked once and for all the Fāṭimid ambitions. His navy, built by 'Abd al-Raḥmān II, greatly deterred their advances. By 931 the naval force took and occupied Ceuta and other coastal areas, which served as a cordon between al-Andalus and North Africa. Also, the navy was used to halt the Norsemen who reappeared in 964 in Almería and other cities.

No doubt, the Fāṭimids had hoped to rule the whole of North Africa and al-Andalus, for they had an able body of missionaries and propagandists in those areas. 'Abd al-Raḥmān counteracted their moves with agents and money, and allied himself with such powerful Berber tribes in North Africa as the Zanātah and leaders of the Shī'ite Idrīsids and the Khārijite 'Ibāḍiyyah.[7]

It is significant to note that the Umayyads up to 929 had abstained from assuming the title of the caliphate, owing perhaps to religious sensitivity. At that time, the caliphal institution in Baghdād was in decline while the Fāṭimids, through their ever-increasing power and prestige, were beginning to give the institution the desired respectability. Perhaps in order to counteract Fāṭimid ambition to rule the Islamic world, 'Abd al-Raḥmān III decided to adopt the title of the caliphate in the name of orthodoxy.

On Thursday, the second of Dhu-l-Ḥijjah, 316 (A.D. 929), 'Abd al-Raḥmān ordered his governors to address him as "Commander of the Faithful" in all correspondence. He thus served notice that he was the legitimate caliph and that anyone else recognized as such was a pretender, intruder, and usurper of the title.

The salient points of the text follow: "We are, indeed, more entitled than those who have received their right and more deserving than those who have received their share in full. . . . Consequently, we feel that we should be henceforth addressed as Commander of the Faithful and that all correspondence emanating from or addressed to us should bear such title. For, any person other than us who arrogates it to himself, assumes it unduly and falsely and without being entitled to it. We are convinced that to delay any longer what is due to us would be tantamount to the loss of our right and to an outright renunciation. Therefore, instruct the preacher of your locality to mention it in the prayers, and include it yourself in your correspondence to us."[8]

This audacious move was followed in 931 by the occupation of Ceuta on the African mainland, thereby protecting the southern frontiers from Fāṭimids, who often gave encouragement and support to Andalusian rebels.

Moreover, ʻAbd al-Raḥmān secured the allegiance of leading Berber tribes. As a result, the Fāṭimids, who had hoped to entrench themselves in the Far Maghrib and al-Andalus, moved east and established their headquarters in Egypt, where they founded their capital city of Cairo.

While ʻAbd al-Raḥmān was busy quenching internal revolts and Fāṭimid threats, he also found it imperative to attend to the fluid situation in the north, where dissidents never ceased to ally themselves with Christian rulers, particularly those of León and Navarre.[9] Taking advantage of the deteriorating conditions in Muslim territories, those Christian rulers were able to make successful forays. In 914, Ordoño II (914–924) attacked Mérida and took neighboring fortresses with ease. This attack prompted ʻAbd al-Raḥmān to retaliate and attack San Esteban. This kind of offensive and counteroffensive prevailed for a number of years and proved inconclusive. ʻAbd al-Raḥmān himself headed several expeditions, but was badly defeated at Simancas in 939. After barely escaping death, he decided to delegate military action to his generals, who were not able to bring peace until the 950's. Then ʻAbd al-Raḥmān was able to exact peace on his own terms.

ʻAbd al-Raḥmān III gave ample proof of his statesmanship in other areas. He was outstanding in both war and peace. He not only unified al-Andalus, but he brought it great prosperity. Cordova was the most prosperous city of Europe; it was the intellectual and political center, outshining by far both Constantinople and Baghdād. The best talents of al-Andalus and the East gathered in his court and were amply rewarded. Many diplomatic delegations converged at Cordova from inside and outside the Peninsula. There were delegations from the powerful North African tribes of Zanātah, Adārisah (Idrīsid), and others; from the Christian kings to the north, from France and Germany, and from Constantinople.[10] These delegates were dazzled by the luxury and prosperity of Cordova and by the splendor of ʻAbd al-Raḥmān's court.

An enthusiastic builder,[11] ʻAbd al-Raḥmān assigned one-third of the state budget, more than six million dinars, to canals, irrigation systems, and other projects. He enlarged the mosque of Cordova and provided it with an imposing minaret topped with three spheres in the shape of pomegranates — two of gold and one of silver, each weighing one ton. In 325/937 he began the construction of the famous al-Zahrā', a government city which housed the caliphal family, 3,500 youths, and 6,750 women, among others. For this project he recruited the best talents of the day. The material for its construction was brought in from distant places: marble from Carthage, golden cisterns from Constantinople and Damascus, and so forth.

He is said to have had fourteen days of leisure throughout his reign of about fifty years.[12] He put his own son to death for having proclaimed himself caliph.[13] As the builder of a state and as a statesman he was determined to attain his objectives, but he also possessed the ability to compromise with his enemies — he would enter into a truce with some factions, accept hostages from others, bring some into his employ, and put others to the sword.[14] Perhaps to neutralize the various factions within his realm, Arab Qaysites versus Arab Kalbites or Arabs versus Berbers, he introduced Slavs (*Ṣaqālibah*)[15] of European origin into his court for protection; this group, docile at the beginning, came to play an important role at the court and in the affairs of al-Andalus. He also introduced reforms into the army and improved the navy; agriculture, commerce, and industry flourished and contributed to the increase of state revenue. More significant still, he introduced a program of social integration in which the hitherto disgruntled neo-Muslims (*al-Muwalladūn*) were able to participate in government and to have a share in the wealth and life of the country. But at no time did 'Abd al-Raḥmān lose control of the situation, or relegate his responsibilities to a special group of bureaucrats.

'Abd al-Raḥmān III may justifiably be compared with 'Abd al-Raḥmān I in that he established from chaos a stable and prosperous kingdom which earned the respect of Christians, rebels, North Africans, and Byzantines. He forced the Fāṭimids who emerged as a power in Qayrawān to move east to Egypt, for they had failed to dominate the Maghrib, let alone al-Andalus. Moreover, he was praised by poets such as Ibn 'Abd Rabbihi[16] and has been regarded in Muslim traditions as one of the great rulers in Islamic history.

'Abd al-Raḥmān III left the throne to his son al-Ḥakam II (961–976),[17] who was nominated when he was eight years old. Al-Ḥakam had received the best education of the day and had accompanied his father on various expeditions. He ascended the throne at the mature age of forty-seven and inherited a relatively stable and prosperous state. It was common practice for a new ruler to lead or order raids into Christian territories, and al-Ḥakam was no exception. However, he preferred to settle questions through peaceful rather than military means. In fact, he instructed his governors neither to impose oppressive taxes nor to indulge in bloodshed. Except for the appearance of the Norsemen (*Majūs*) in 967[18] and 971[19] and the defiance of the Idrīsid Ḥasan Ibn Qannūn[20] in Tunis, the reign of al-Ḥakam was on the whole a peaceful one. Both threats were resolved satisfactorily.

Al-Ḥakam seems to have been more interested in books than in state affairs. It is said that his library contained more than four hundred thousand volumes, most of which he had read.[21] He established a scriptorium (*ṣināʿat al-naskh*) and a bindery.[22] He secured the *Book of Songs* by Abū-l-Faraj al-Iṣfahānī for one thousand dinars.[23] Moreover, he took a particular interest in the poor and in public instruction. He built a charity hall (*dār al-ṣadaqah*) near the mosque where money was distributed to the poor. He built some twenty-seven public schools and set the learned to teaching the poor and the orphans[24] in return for handsome salaries.

By and large al-Ḥakam II continued his father's policies. In the north he had a number of confrontations with Christian rulers, and in North Africa he had to subdue several leaders who had rebelled.[25] Moreover, delegates from both regions often visited Cordova and were received with splendor.[26] He also enlarged and embellished the mosque of Cordova[27] and undertook other public works. Al-Ḥakam was able to preserve the state of stability and prosperity in al-Andalus. However, unlike his father, ʿAbd al-Raḥmān, al-Ḥakam relied more and more on his officials, mainly the chamberlain al-Muṣḥafī,[28] the vizier Ibn Abī ʿĀmir,[29] and the general Ghālib.[30] These men were eminently able and served al-Ḥakam well. However, they contributed to the end of the dynasty because of al-Ḥakam's failure to nominate a suitable and qualified person to succeed himself. In his old age, his concubine, Ṣubḥ from Navarre, bore him a son, Hishām, whom he named successor. He made his nomination public and ordered that an oath of allegiance be rendered to Hishām by the notables and the common people throughout the provinces and in that part of North Africa under his suzereignty. He also instructed that Hishām be mentioned in the Friday prayers and other holidays.[31] As al-Ḥakam approached death, he confirmed Hishām's nomination in 976, thus leaving wide room for contention among powerful and ambitious leaders who occupied the limelight after his death. Ominous signs were noted which foretold the end of the Umayyad dynasty. For one, the great thinker and statesman, Ibn al-Khaṭīb[32] expressed his astonishment at the nomination and made an extensive list of eligible and well-qualified candidates who tolerated and even witnessed the inauguration of Hishām. His remarks are revealing:

> And when al-Ḥakam al-Mustanṣir bi-llāh was rendered the oath of allegiance, surely the caliphate had achieved the utmost degree and attained its prime. Its cycle was reached and its turn has ended. It was a calyx, then became a smiling flower, then a beautiful and an appetizing fruit. . . .[33]

It was agreed to nominate Hishām as caliph in spite of the presence of mature paternal uncles and their virile sons — the lions of battle and productive rain for barren soil.[34]

At the time the oath of allegiance was rendered to Hishām Ibn al-Ḥakam, there were among the outstanding men unshakable mountains, great men of learning, and others whose saying is respected, whose probity is prescribed and whose action is followed.[35]

The Captive Hishām (976–1009/1010–1013) and the ʻĀmirids (976–1009)

When al-Ḥakam died, the question of succession posed a serious problem because the heir apparent was only about eleven years old. The *Ṣaqālibah*, the Slav bodyguards of the palace, attempted to put al-Mughīrah, a brother of the deceased caliph, on the throne.[36] But the vizier Ibn Abī ʻĀmir and the powerful chamberlain al-Muṣḥafī connived the death of al-Mughīrah and hastened to install the young Hishām on the throne with the apparent acquiescence of the religious scholars and other leading men. This act proved fatal to the caliphal institution, which was deprived of all power.

Hishām remained under the guardianship of Ibn Abī ʻĀmir, presumably until he came of age. However, Ibn Abī ʻĀmir had different plans; he arrogated all powers and maintained Hishām only as a figurehead who, throughout his whole reign, acquiesced to the will and ambitions of his guardian. In this connection, Ibn al-Khaṭīb says: "At the time Hishām was secluded by his protector, the chamberlain al-Manṣūr, may God have mercy upon him, neither administration could be related to him, nor big nor small matters. For he was a weakling, contemptible, and preoccupied with pastime and amusement with boys and girls."[37]

Moreover, Ibn Abī ʻĀmir began the purge of all potential enemies and soon succeeded in ruling al-Andalus with an iron hand. "He would not leave a hand which he suspected to strike without paralyzing it, nor an eye with a stern look without plucking it."[38] Under these circumstances the reign of Hishām marked the beginning of the downfall of the Umayyad dynasty and the gradual decline of Arab political power in al-Andalus.

The career of Ibn Abī ʻĀmir has attracted the attention of Arab historians.[39] Ibn al-Khaṭīb's *Aʻlām* devotes ample space to Ibn Abī ʻĀmir's fantastic rise to power. He belonged to an Arab family which came to al-Andalus at the time of the conquest in 711. Members of the family served the Umayyads in various capacities. His father was a religious man and gave him a good education. With that background Ibn Abī ʻĀmir took advantage of every opportunity given to him. He was alert and industrious in addition to being handsome and intelligent. He had hoped to become a judge, but instead he opened a shop in the vicinity of the caliphal palace. It was from his shop that he became acquainted with the palace personnel and served as copier. His handwriting and style were quite impressive and enabled him to establish contact with Ṣubḥ, Hishām's mother. Ṣubḥ interceded on his behalf and secured a position for him in the palace. She was assisted by al-Muṣḥafī, the powerful chamberlain and the "sword of the dynasty."[40] From that time, Ibn Abī 'Āmir climbed the ladder of success without any apparent hitch, to the point that "there was not a day in which he was not promoted or gained influence."[41] Al-Ḥakam appointed him judge (*qāḍī*) in some village in the south, then entrusted him with the important post of administrator of almsgiving and inheritance (*zakā wa-l-mawārith*) in Seville, chief of police over the mint, chief judge in the Gharb (northwest Africa), and other posts.[42] More important still, he was made guardian (*wakīl*) at the time of Hishām's nomination as heir apparent in 356/967 and, previously, during the nomination of another son who had died.[43] Moreover, his relationship with the Queen Mother, Ṣubḥ, was very cordial and was interpreted as amorous. He was generous and quite extravagant in spending. He showered Ṣubḥ with expensive and curious gifts, among which was a "palace of silver."[44] While he was in charge of the mint, he was accused of misuse of state funds. However, a friend bailed him out, enabling Ibn Abī 'Āmir to continue his rise to power without stigma.

Ibn Abī 'Āmir was well established during al-Ḥakam's reign. He enjoyed great prestige and wealth, which he always put to maximum use. Thus, upon the death of al-Ḥakam, he was able to manipulate the leading men, including the powerful chamberlain al-Muṣḥafī, who served al-Ḥakam well and had his full confidence. No doubt, he was the key figure at the time of Hishām's accession. As guardian of the minor caliph, he ruled in the name of the latter. One of the new caliph's first decrees was the abrogation of taxes on olives,[45] an act which delighted the people and, at the same time, increased their esteem of Ibn Abī 'Āmir.

Ibn Abī 'Āmir had the distinct advantage of being aided by the beautiful and youthful Ṣubḥ, a woman of Basque origin, who climbed from a mere concubine of al-Ḥakam to a full-fledged and favorite wife. She seems to have exerted an enormous influence at the court. Even al-Muṣḥafī looked up to her and acquiesced to her will; thus, he helped her bring Ibn Abī 'Āmir into the limelight. Ṣubḥ's influential role continued after the death of al-

Ḥakam. It would appear that she ruled with the help of Ibn Abī ʻĀmir on behalf of the young Hishām, and that she played an important role in upsetting the balance of power in favor of Ibn Abī ʻĀmir.

At first, Ibn Abī ʻĀmir was careful not to introduce radical changes which might antagonize the leading men of the court. He prevailed upon the boy-caliph Hishām to confirm him as vizier and al-Muṣḥafī as chamberlain, the most important post. His plans soon became clear. He used al-Muṣḥafī, who had power over both money and appointments, to dispose of the increasing influence of the *Ṣaqālibah*. Now, Ibn Abī ʻĀmir turned his attention to the army, which he soon headed. Especially after his successful expedition into Galicia in 366/977, which brought a great amount of booty, he was the unquestioned military leader. He was given a hero's welcome upon his return to Cordova, and he earned the affection of the army by handsomely rewarding the soldiers, a practice which he continued in the successful raids which followed.[46]

Having eliminated the danger of the *Ṣaqālibah*, and having earned the esteem and admiration of the people and the army, Ibn Abī ʻĀmir felt secure to confront and eventually dispose of the chamberlain al-Muṣḥafī and other potential contenders.[47] He went about it with his usual cunning, using a second party. He chose the general Ghālib, the "knight of al-Andalus" and the hero of many battles, who was at odds with al-Muṣḥafī. Ibn Abī ʻĀmir married Ghālib's daughter, and the two men conspired against the chamberlain, who was dismissed in 977 on charges of treason, placed in prison and eventually killed in 982. Now Ibn Abī ʻĀmir was on his way to assume absolute power.

Ibn Abī ʻĀmir took care at first that his relationship with his father-in-law remained cordial. In fact, they undertook joint campaigns to the north which enhanced their power and prestige. Moreover, Ibn Abī ʻĀmir consented to share the office of chamberlain with Ghālib. However, it soon appeared that Ibn Abī ʻĀmir was determined to be the sole power behind the throne.

He drew closer and closer to Berber elements in preference to either *Ṣaqālibah* or Arabs on whom he could not rely. In order to ensure necessary security, he decided as early as 978 to move the seat of government outside Cordova. For that purpose he began the construction of al-Zāhirah, which came to equal if not surpass the famous al-Zahrāʼ of ʻAbd al-Raḥmān III in elegance and splendor.[48] Once completed, al-Zāhirah consisted of a palace, gardens, and several office buildings. In 980 he moved his guards and state employees to the new palace, leaving Hishām in the caliphal palace under constant surveillance and in virtual imprisonment. He ordered the governors of the provinces to send taxes and address all government business to the new city, and he claimed that the caliph had invested him with full power to look after the affairs of the government.

Ibn Abī ʻĀmir's intentions became quite evident. It was then that the Queen Mother, Ṣubḥ, was alienated and even attempted to unseat him, but without success. He was able to silence her without much difficulty. Now the only potential contender that remained was his father-in-law, who may have disapproved of his radical and seemingly reckless action. The relation between the two men was strained, degenerated into war, and ended with the death of Ghālib in 981. Ibn Abī ʻĀmir disposed of Ghālib by lining up a prominent Berber general, Jaʻfar Ibn ʻAlī Ibn Ḥamdūn, against him — succeeding in this plan just as he later succeeded in eliminating the Berber general.[49]

By now, there was no doubt who was the actual ruler. As the Umayyad house became increasingly disgruntled, he encouraged the immigration of North African Berbers, who became the mainstay of his power.

It was in 981 that Ibn Abī ʻĀmir assumed the surname (*laqab*) of al-Manṣūr, the Victorious. He ordered that his name be mentioned in the Friday prayer after that of the caliph, and he had his name appear on coins, embroidery, and correspondence emanating from or addressed to him. Moreover, he instructed his viziers and other courtiers to kiss his hand in the same manner they greeted the caliph.[50]

To be sure, Ibn Abī ʻĀmir filled a political vacuum and he may be justly considered among the greatest rulers of al-Andalus. He ruled al-Andalus with an iron hand. In this respect he preserved the unity of the kingdom as ably as the great ʻAbd al-Raḥmān III, and he continued to exert considerable influence in North African affairs. He not only kept the Christian kingdoms to the north at bay, but he inflicted on them many crushing defeats. He initiated various public works, built a canal at a cost of 140,000 dinars, and enlarged the Mosque of Cordova.[51] He may have been ambitious and cunning, but he was a great statesman who brought al-Andalus stability and prosperity. He may have been cruel, but at the same time, he behaved justly toward many of those who worked with him.

Ibn Abī ʻĀmir was a religious man who kept a copy of the Qur'ān written in his own hand. Perhaps to cater to the religious scholars, he was averse to philosophy, religious disputations, and astrology. He is said to have burned the books on these subjects in the famous library of al-Ḥakam II.[52] He cut out the tongue of an astrologer who predicted the fall of his dynasty, and he exiled the poet ʻAbd al-ʻAzīz Ibn al-Khaṭīb, who criticized him for arrogating too much power to himself and who warned him that fate, and not al-Manṣūr, determines all things.

Ibn Abī ʻĀmir was full of confidence. In 991, he nominated his eighteen-year-old son ʻAbd al-Malik to the important post of chamberlain.[53] At his death in 1002 he advised his son to be neither extravagant in spending nor oppressive to the governors and to be considerate to the caliph, from whom no unpleasant things could come. However, he urged him to deal sternly with the Umayyads in the event that they should try to create difficulties for him.[54]

Ibn Abī ʻĀmir was right in both instances. ʻAbd al-Malik,[55] who assumed the title of al-Muẓaffar (1002–1008), received all necessary cooperation from Hishām II, who was twenty-six. The caliph entrusted him with the important office of chamberlain and bestowed upon him the title of al-Muzaffar (Victorious). On the other hand, attempts to unseat him came from the *Ṣaqālibah*, who were still faithful to the Umayyads. With no vacillation, al-Muẓaffar eliminated the opposition and soon directed his attention to the Christians, who attempted to take advantage of the change of rule. Again, al-Muẓaffar faced this danger with the same ability that characterized his father. He led most of the raids himself, having left the situation in Cordova under the control of the increasingly numerous Berbers whom he added to his army and guards. Among these newcomers was Zāwī b. Zīrī, who came to play an important role in the affairs of al-Andalus.

Al-Muẓaffar may not have had the magnetic personality of his father, but he proved himself able to manage the State for some six years without losing ground. His ability, determination, and decisiveness may have accounted for the continued general stability and prosperity of the State. Like his father, he maintained a friendly and proper relationship with the caliph.

Up to now, friends and foes were reconciled to the rule of the ʻĀmirids in the presence of a caliph who refused to take any initiative or assume any responsibility. He was satisfied with mere frivolities within the palace walls. He was now of age and nothing could be done on his behalf under the circumstances so long as the person of the caliph and the dignity of his office were respected. Ibn Abī ʻĀmir as well as his son had the wisdom to respect the sensitivity of the members of the ruling dynasty in particular and the religious susceptibility of the Muslims in general.

However, when al-Muẓaffar died in 1008, respect for the caliphate was disregarded by his brother and successor 'Abd al-Raḥmān,[56] who displayed from the outset erratic behavior and illusions of grandeur. This led to the tragic end of the 'Āmirids. 'Abd al-Raḥmān was known as Sanchol, a diminutive of Sancho. He soon secured from the caliph the post of chamberlain with the triple titles of al-Ma'mūn (the Trustworthy), al-Nāṣir (the Victorious), and al-ḥājib al-a'lā (the Supreme Chamberlain). He was not satisfied with those titles but instead aimed at securing the caliphate himself by making the weakling Hishām appoint him as his successor.

He had the caliph write a document of nomination in triplicate,[57] and had it signed by nineteen viziers and one hundred eighty persons from the police and palace administration. He soon sent letters to all governors, even in the Mahgrib, informing them of the nomination and instructing them to mention his name along with the caliph in the Friday sermons. Moreover, he called upon the people to congratulate him and pay their respects!

This recklessness was accompanied by indulgence in wine and women in company of the caliph and people who commanded little respect. This ignited a dormant resentment throughout the Peninsula, especially among the Umayyad family and their partisans. Moreover, he appointed his own son chamberlain and bestowed on him the title of Sword of the Dynasty (*sayf al-dawlah*).

With all this done, he ventured to leave the capital and lead a raid against the Christians. This was tantamount to an invitation for trouble, which he got and which led to his ruin and the downfall of the 'Āmirids.

The Great Revolt and Political Disintegration

The end of the 'Āmirids marked the beginning of the most critical period in the history of al-Andalus. It was a time of bloody revolts, lawlessness, and coups d'état.[58] To begin with, the Cordovan people's disgust with the last 'Āmirid ruler could be measured by their almost unqualified support of a rebel who had neither the capacity to govern nor the kind of ability required by the situation. His only asset was that he belonged to the Umayyad family. He was Muḥammad b. Hishām b. 'Abd al-Jabbār b. 'Abd al-Raḥmān III. This Muḥammad declared a revolt at the beginning of 1009. He successfully occupied the caliphal palace in Cordova and compelled Hishām II to transfer the caliphate to him. He assumed the title of al-Mahdī.[59] In the course of the revolt he allowed his partisans, drawn for the most part from the populace and including criminals from jails, to indulge in looting, pillaging, destruction, and wanton killing.[60] They marched against al-Zāhirah, the palace built at great expense by Ibn Abī 'Āmir, and reduced it to rubble. They took everything portable, such as money, jewels, and other objects and they destroyed furniture, gates, and doors.[61]

Upon hearing this ominous news, the 'Āmirid 'Abd al-Raḥmān, who was on his way in an expedition against the Christians, returned along with his ally García Gómez. They attempted to regain Cordova but were killed before they arrived there.

The new caliph Muḥammad showed the same recklessness that characterized the 'Āmirid 'Abd al-Raḥmān. He became identified with the mob, from whose ranks he picked his viziers. He hid the caliph, but soon declared him dead by producing the corpse of a Jew or a Christian, which he buried with great pomp.[62] He dismissed and forced from power all who were connected with the 'Āmirids; he unleashed his anger against Berbers such as the powerful Zīrids, and ordered their extermination. He offered a prize for each Berber head.[63] This behavior intensified the social tension and accentuated the ethnic division, leading thereby to extensive suffering and bloodshed.

The Berbers retaliated in kind. They attempted to enthrone a person of their choice. First they proclaimed a Umayyad, Hishām, but he was killed. Then they selected Sulaymān, an accomplished poet and a descendant of 'Abd al-Raḥmān III, and proclaimed him caliph.[64] They sought and received the help of Sancho García of Castile, and together they overran Toledo and then marched against Cordova. Muḥammad could not prevent them from entering the city and, in despair, he produced the deposed Hishām, who was supposed to be dead. His stratagem did not work. He was forced to flee to Toledo after nine months' rule without relinquishing his claims and in spite of his assertion that Hishām was still the legitimate caliph.

Sulaymān entered the city and was soon confirmed as caliph with the title of al-Musta'īn bi-l-lāh. He managed to rule for about seven months as captive of his Berber supporters. The Berbers, full of revenge, indulged in looting, burning, and killing. For his part, Sulaymān lacked insight into the explosive situation and underestimated the feeling of the inhabitants of Cordova against his Berber supporters. To make things worse, he nominated his son to succeed him. As a result his days were short. With the help of the Christians of Barcelona, the ousted Muḥammad organized an army in Toledo and marched against Cordova, which was taken with ease. Sulaymān soon fled, and Muḥammad regained the throne. The victorious army repeated the sad performance of indiscriminately killing Berbers and looting their homes. But again Muḥammad's victory was a short one, lasting only forty-nine days.[65] He had pursued the Berbers, but they struck back furiously, killing some three thousand of his Christian followers and compelling Muḥammad to flee and return to Cordova.[66] Inasmuch as he did not offer any promise of peace and stability, he was finally put to death in 1010 by his chamberlain and former supporter Wāḍiḥ, who had decided to reinstate Hishām as the rightful caliph.

Hishām II resumed the throne for the next three years, although most of his power resided in the hands of his new chamberlain, Wāḍiḥ. The latter sent Muḥammad's head to Sulaymān and his Berber followers and called upon them to give up the revolt and render the oath of allegiance to the legitimate caliph.[67] However, Sulaymān's partisans were not willing to accept Hishām and persisted in their own cause even though it meant all-out revolution and bloodshed. They spread into Málaga, Elvira, Almería, and other areas and gave vent to their disaffection.[68] Tensions ran high, and Cordova was feeling economic pressure in the midst of lawlessness and uncertainty. The Cordovans disposed of Wāḍiḥ, leaving a free hand for Hishām to act. But Hishām proved his inability once more. He was not capable of filling a vacuum or governing the divided community in an impartial manner. Moreover, he was vulnerable to anyone who happened to have political ambitions. In the meantime, Sulaymān was threatening armed intervention, which was averted when he was admitted again to Cordova to assume the coveted title of the caliphate.

This was accomplished in 1013. Sulaymān brought the helpless Hishām before him and obligated him once more to transfer the title of the caliphate. He is said to have reprimanded Hishām, but there is no agreement whether or not he killed him. At any rate, Sulaymān appealed to the provinces for calm and distributed some of the provinces — Elvira, Saragossa, Jaén, Sidonia, Morón, Ceuta, and Tangier — among his Berber supporters.[69] Henceforth the Berbers ruled as they saw fit, to the bitter discontent of both the 'Āmirid and Arab elements. This was a prelude to the "party-kings" (*mulūk al-ṭawā'if*). Thus, under the circumstances, there is no evidence that Sulaymān was actually acknowledged outside of Cordova, except for the lip service of his supporters who had received the fairest provinces of al-Andalus.

Sulaymān won a victory but failed to achieve peace. His three years' reign accentuated rather than ameliorated the social tensions. His complete dependence on the Berbers and the favoritism shown them aroused the anger not only of many leaders but also of several former supporters as well. Both groups clamored for the return of the caliph Hishām. Oddly enough, it was 'Alī Ibn Ḥammūd of Ceuta, a recipient of Sulaymān's favor, who waved the flag of indignation. He was encouraged by some 'Āmirid and Hāshimite leaders, mainly Khayrān of Almería, who claimed that Hishām was still alive and that he had nominated 'Alī to succeed him.[70] 'Alī left Ceuta, passed through Málaga, and headed for Cordova. Sulaymān's army offered little resistance and fled, but Sulaymān was apprehended along with his father and a brother, and put to death for having killed the legitimate caliph Hishām.[71] This inaugurated the rule of a new dynasty, the Ḥammūdid dynasty.

The Ḥammūdid (1016–1023)

The Ḥammūdids[72] were an 'Alīd group that traced its origin to 'Alī, the son-in-law of the prophet Muḥammad. It was under Sulaymān that they came to prominence in the affairs of al-Andalus, especially in Ceuta, Tangier, Málaga, and Seville. When 'Alī, the founder of the dynasty, entered Cordova, it became clear that his motive was not so much to espouse the cause of a legitimate caliph as to further his own aggrandizement. In fact, he soon exacted the oath of allegiance to himself and adopted the sonorous surname of al-Nāṣir li-dīn-Allāh (the Defender of the Religion of God). The inhabitants of Cordova, hitherto conservative but now tired of the civil war and its deprivations, did not indicate aversion to an 'Alīd dynasty in their midst nor did they show much regret for the summary liquidation of the Umayyad dynasty. Moreover, they were reassured at first when 'Alī displayed great impartiality and determination to bring to justice any extremist — whether Berber, Arab, or 'Āmirid.

However, an increasingly dangerous situation soon affected 'Alī's impartial policy. An Umayyad pretender, 'Abd al-Raḥmān, who assumed the surname of al-Murtaḍā,[73] was making headway in the east of al-Andalus with the support of the 'Amirid Khayrān, the same man who induced 'Alī Ibn Ḥammūd to march against Cordova.[74] Agents working on 'Abd al-Raḥmān's behalf secured many supporters. This development alarmed 'Alī, who drew closer to the Berber elements for support, thus antagonizing the rest of the population. Under the circumstances, the situation became as tense as when he entered Cordova. He was soon apprehended in his bathroom by some of his guards and was put to death. All of this occurred after scarcely one year of rule.

The Berbers viewed the deteriorating situation with deep concern. They hastened to inform al-Qāsim, 'Alī's brother, and urged him to come to Cordova. Al-Qāsim (1018–1021) rushed into the city and assumed the title of al-Ma'mūn. He punished the culprits for the death of his brother but soon ran into difficulties because of his dependence on the Berbers, some 'Āmirid leaders, and Negroes. In the meantime, the Umayyad pretender, 'Abd al-Raḥmān, was gaining more adherents and was able to muster a respectable force made up of 'Āmirids, Umayyad sympathizers, and Christian mercenaries. The force was sufficient to overwhelm Cordova, but the pretender blundered perhaps in marching against the Zīrids of Granada, who were tough Berber warriors. 'Abd al-Raḥmān appears to have had the upper hand at first, but his ambivalent supporters abandoned him and contributed to his death in 1018.[75]

This Umayyad threat was eliminated only temporarily. The social tension in Cordova remained as high as ever before. It was aggravated by the rebellion of al-Qāsim's two nephews, Yaḥyā and Idrīs, who set out to unseat him. Yaḥyā, who was the governor of Ceuta and Tangier, felt he was the one most entitled to the throne of Cordova; he marched against the city and forced his uncle out. Yaḥyā entered Cordova in 1021 and was proclaimed caliph while his uncle ended up in Seville. He made a display of generosity and distributed important posts among men of humble origin. This did not solve the social tension and the situation remained untenable. As a result, after one and a half years of rule, he was removed by his former partisans and the Cordovan aristocracy. He fled to Málaga and his uncle was recalled from Seville, only to be removed in the same year (1023) following bloody clashes between Berbers and the people of Cordova. Now both uncle and nephew were claiming the title "Commander of the Faithful" but neither actually possessed the throne. The uncle was put to death at the hand of the nephew, who soon made another attempt to regain the throne of Cordova.

The Re-establishment of the Umayyad Caliphate and its Abolition (1023–1031)

Disillusioned with the rule of the Ḥammūdids, the people of Cordova decided to elect a caliph from the Umayyad family. They chose three eligible candidates from whom emerged 'Abd al-Raḥmān V, surnamed al-Mustaẓhir,[76] a brother of the twice deposed Muḥammad II. This 'Abd al-Raḥmān forced himself on the people without the due process of election.

After only forty-six days he was replaced by Muḥammad III, surnamed al-Mustakfī.[77] The new caliph showed an unrestrained revenge against opponents, but when he was urged to confront the Ḥammūdid Yaḥyā, who was besieging Cordova, he disguised himself as a woman and disappeared. Thus, Yaḥyā assumed the throne for the second time (1025–1027). Yaḥyā's tenure lasted for about a year, after which he was forced away to Carmona where he was harassed by the rising power of the 'Abbādids of Seville.

Once again, Cordova was without a ruler. They chose the Umayyad, Hishām III (1027–1031), surnamed al-Mu'tadd,[78] who was then somewhere in the eastern part of al-Andalus. The new caliph showed little enthusiasm for coming to the capital and assuming his caliphal powers. In fact, it took almost two and a half years before he entered Cordova in 1029 at the head of a small, unimpressive retinue. Before long he antagonized leaders and people alike when he nominated as his vizier a common, crude individual who was a weaver by profession. The new vizier, who was entrusted with the important task of government, assumed an arrogant attitude and indulged in abuses. This was aggravated further by lack of revenue and by the depletion of the treasury. The people asked Hishām to restrain him but received no satisfaction. Then they took matters into their own hand and put the vizier to death.

A revolt ensued, and the Cordovans found themselves in a predicament. A bloody civil strife had continued from 1009, and had played havoc on all walks of life. Perhaps people became convinced, although belatedly, that neither the Umayyads nor the Berbers and other adventurers could give them the much needed peace and stability. Under the circumstances, the elders of the city met under the leadership of Abū Ḥazm Ibn Jahwar and agreed to abolish the caliphate once and for all and to replace it with a governing council. Hishām III was put in a cell along with members of his family, but they were soon released to live in an abject condition.

In conclusion, the end of the caliphate marked the loss of central authority, or semblance thereof. It had grave repercussions on the future history of al-Andalus. The aftermath left the country in chaotic conditions that were never redressed. Al-Andalus reached the apogee of its power under 'Abd al-Raḥmān III, his son al-Ḥakam II, and the chamberlain al-Manṣūr, and witnessed a period of stability and prosperity that was conducive to the cultivation of the arts and rich literature. In fact, their reign represents the golden age of al-Andalus and marks Andalusian ascendancy throughout the Peninsula and in a portion of North Africa. Al-Andalus was a great power that inspired admiration for its high culture and awe for its military prowess and affluence. This coincided with Muslim ascendance in the Mediterranean. The Andalusians were still holding Crete while other Muslims were deeply entrenched in Sicily, from which they attacked and plundered Italian cities as far north as Pisa and Genoa. Broadly, the Mediterranean became a Muslim lake during most of the tenth and a good part of the eleventh century.

On the other hand, while 'Abd al-Raḥmān III achieved a great degree of cohesiveness among heterogeneous elements of the population, he relied more and more on mercenary soldiers for defense and for his own protection. Al-Ḥakam II continued the same policy, but disengaged himself from decisive participation in state affairs by relegating much of his power to his chamberlain and military commander. This precedent proved fatal to the caliphal institution when the chamberlain al-Manṣūr arrogated to himself all the powers of the office. In order to keep a firm grip on the state, al-Manṣūr isolated and manipulated the incumbent caliph at will and imported Berber soldiers in numbers that upset the social balance and led to tension. The urbane and sophisticated Andalusians, who had acquired a strong sense of identity, resented the privileges and arrogance of the newcomers. The able and determined al-Manṣūr had control over this situation as long as he lived, but the seeds of unrest and violence had been planted and were to erupt in the absence of an able and decisive man. In such a vacuum, al-Andalus reverted to a state of division and chaos, the effect of which lasted for centuries. It was at this juncture in the eleventh century that the Christian states to the North, hitherto dependent and kept in check, began to reassert themselves and pursued the Reconquest with a great measure of success.

3

The Party-Kings, 1031–1090

WITH the fall of the Umayyad dynasty, al-Andalus became an agglomeration of feudal city states. This situation actually began as early as 1009 when al-Andalus had already lost any semblance of unity. Consequently, the year 1031, which marks the final abolition of the Umayyad dynasty, is in reality an arbitrary date for the beginning of the rule of the Mulūk al-Ṭawā'if, "party-kings."[1]

The abolition of the caliphate did not resolve any problem, but rather expressed the political reality that in 1031 there was already a multiplicity of states. At the fall of the 'Āmirids in 1009, Berber chieftains became entrenched in certain areas of al-Andalus and assumed an independent posture. This was true of 'Āmirid, Arab, and Slav leaders as well. These leaders belonged to a family or tribe (hence, their designation as Ṭawā'if (sing.: *Ṭā'ifah*), or Spanish *Taifas*) which included their clients and mercenary soldiery. Although some of them were at first governors, others were given certain areas in fief for services rendered. For example, in 1013 the caliph Sulaymān distributed the fairest provinces among his Berber supporters.[2] Concurrently, the 'Āmirids, their clients, and other groups settled in various sectors of al-Andalus.

There were no fixed boundaries, and many a city often changed hands. One could easily discern twenty or more states.[3] Ibn al-Khaṭīb mentions other states which came into being as a result of inheritance. For instance, one of the Hūd rulers of Saragossa divided his realm among his five sons, who attempted to rule autonomously. This was also true of other rulers.

At any rate, the party-kings gave eloquent expression to the tribal mentality — in place of a national consciousness resting on language, culture, or religion, individualism based on tribal loyalties prevailed. There were leaders everywhere who aspired to rule a kingdom. They battled among themselves and sought alliances with fellow Muslims and Christians. In their mutual conflict, they often allied themselves with Christians to the point of becoming mere tributaries. By and large, there prevailed a general sociopolitical dislocation which led to the decline of religious sentiments and to ambivalence in popular loyalty. The common man — whether Muslim, Christian, or Jew — was called upon to finance and sustain a state at a great sacrifice without visible return in the protection of his life and property. Under the circumstances, he lacked confidence in the government. The hitherto harmonious modus vivendi between Muslims and Christians was affected adversely. Mercenary soldiers from both religious camps were always available to serve anyone willing to pay them well. They may not have taken their respective religions seriously at first, but soon the religious element became the most distinctive dividing line between them. With the onslaught of the Christians from the north, the Arabized Christians (Mozarabs) were torn between their fellow Andalusians of the Muslim faith and their northern coreligionists. This was also true of the Mudejars — those Muslims who were allowed to remain in territories conquered by Christians. These two groups not only suspected each other but were the object of suspicion from their own religious communities. This precarious position contributed enormously to social tension and eventually to mutual religious intolerance.

By mere coincidence, a great number of scholars flourished during this chaotic period. That they did so is not to the credit of the party-kings but rather owing to the great literary traditions that had been established under the Umayyads. Scholars who had ornamented the caliphal court now became wandering solicitors of the munificence of a tyrant, whether or not he had any taste for scholarship. Even religious scholars sought accommodations with ambitious rulers and lost their self-respect in the process. Ibn Ḥazm (d. 1064), the most prolific scholar of the century, launched a sweeping criticism in which he spared no one of the period, including religious scholars, poets, and rulers. He lamented the fact that beliefs were destroyed; that rulers were the enemies of God and disseminators of corruption, their soldiers were bandits, they made Jews overlords for collecting taxes, and they would worship the cross if this helped attain their objectives.[4]

Significantly, each party-king still considered himself the true and majestic ruler. He adopted sonorous and honorific titles in the manner of a caliph, and he nominated his son or relative to succeed him. His court, almost a replica of former caliphal courts, was the meeting place for the best talents of the day: poets, litterateurs, historians, religious scholars, physicians, boon-companions, buffoons, jesters, and musicians. In fact, many of the rulers competed with one another in this and other respects. They had their own armies which, more often than not, consisted of mercenary soldiers. They built canals, luxurious palaces, mosques, and public baths. They minted their own coins, appointed their own diplomats, and retained a large body of civil servants. Ibn al-Khaṭīb makes the following incisive observations:

The people of al-Andalus went from disruption, disunion and separation in a manner never done by any nation in spite of the peculiarity of the country with respect to its proximity to the land of the worshippers of the Cross. None of them possessed [the right] of inheritance to the caliphate, a reasonable claim for the emirate, a lineage for bravery, or any quality of the conditions of the Imamate.

[In spite of all this] they took regions in fief; divided the great cities among themselves; exacted taxes on districts and cities; built armies; appointed judges; and adopted surnames. Distinguished authors wrote about them, and poets praised them. They registered their poetical collections. Testaments giving them the right to rule were made. Scholars stood at their doors; and the learned sought their favor.

[They were of different brands:] lowmen, imported Berbers, hated recruits; negligent and unimportant people. Some were satisfied with being called rebels and would not take the side of right. Those who were accomplished among them would say, "I hold on to what I have until someone who is entitled to it is appointed." However, if 'Umar Ibn 'Abd al-'Azīz[5] were to come to him, he would not accept him, or find any good in him.

With this, they received full respite and endured. They left legacies. However, they beguiled themselves with titles such as: "Reliant," "Supporter," "Pleasing," "Successful," "Sufficient," "Conqueror," "Helper," "Victorious," "Victor," and "Trusty." As the poet would say:

> That which I reject in al-Andalus are names such as
> "Supporter" and "Reliant";
> Surnames of kingdoms without a place
> Like a cat making too much noise as if it were a lion.[6]

The party-kings lived in a perpetual strife among themselves and were the objects of harassment from the Christian powers to the north. They committed a slow but certain suicide. While the hitherto disorganized Christians had been held at bay, often as tributaries to the Umayyad government of Cordova, they now emerged into ascendance and reversed the coin in their favor. Although they were still disorganized themselves, their disunity was far less than that prevailing among Muslim rulers. A number of important Christian kingdoms emerged following the fall of the central government of Cordova in 1009: Navarre, León, Castile, Asturia, Galicia, Aragón, and Barcelona. To be sure, they warred among themselves and faced problems identical to those plaguing their Muslim counterparts. On the other hand, they had a common goal: to regain what they strongly felt to be the land of their ancestors. Moreover, they were spared the grave problem of ethnic grouping that played havoc among their Muslim enemies. At any rate, the Christians were able, after decades of internal wars, to forge coalitions in their confrontations with the Muslims. They succeeded in gaining the upper hand under Fernando I (1037–1065), king of Castile and León, who began the Reconquista in earnest; it continued, interrupted only by periodic internal strife, for four centuries. Fernando himself had to fight his brothers, who aspired to the throne. When he emerged victorious, he launched an attack against the kingdom of Badajoz in 1057 and forced its ruler to pay a tribute of six thousand dinars. Subsequently, he attacked the kingdom of Toledo in 1062 and that of Seville in the following year, and imposed heavy tributes on them. At the time of his death, he was the most powerful ruler of the Peninsula.

Fernando divided his realm among his sons, who quarrelled among themselves. One of them, Alfonso VI, was given León but lost it to a brother. He sought refuge at the Muslim court of Toledo, returning in 1072 after the assassination of his brother to become the leading Christian ruler. After consolidating his position, he directed his attention against Muslim rulers and was able to exact heavy tributes from the most powerful of them. Moreover, in 1085 he took the strategic city of Toledo, thereby upsetting the balance of power in the Peninsula. Valencia was also within his reach, but it fell to the Cid in 1094. Muslim rulers were alarmed, but unable to present a unified front. All this coincided with the rise in North Africa of the Almoravids, who were invited by the quarreling Muslim rulers to rescue them in the name of Islam. The rescuers decided to stay, bringing to an end the rule of the party-kings.

It is almost impossible to determine accurately the number of petty states in al-Andalus following the breakdown of the central government of Cordova

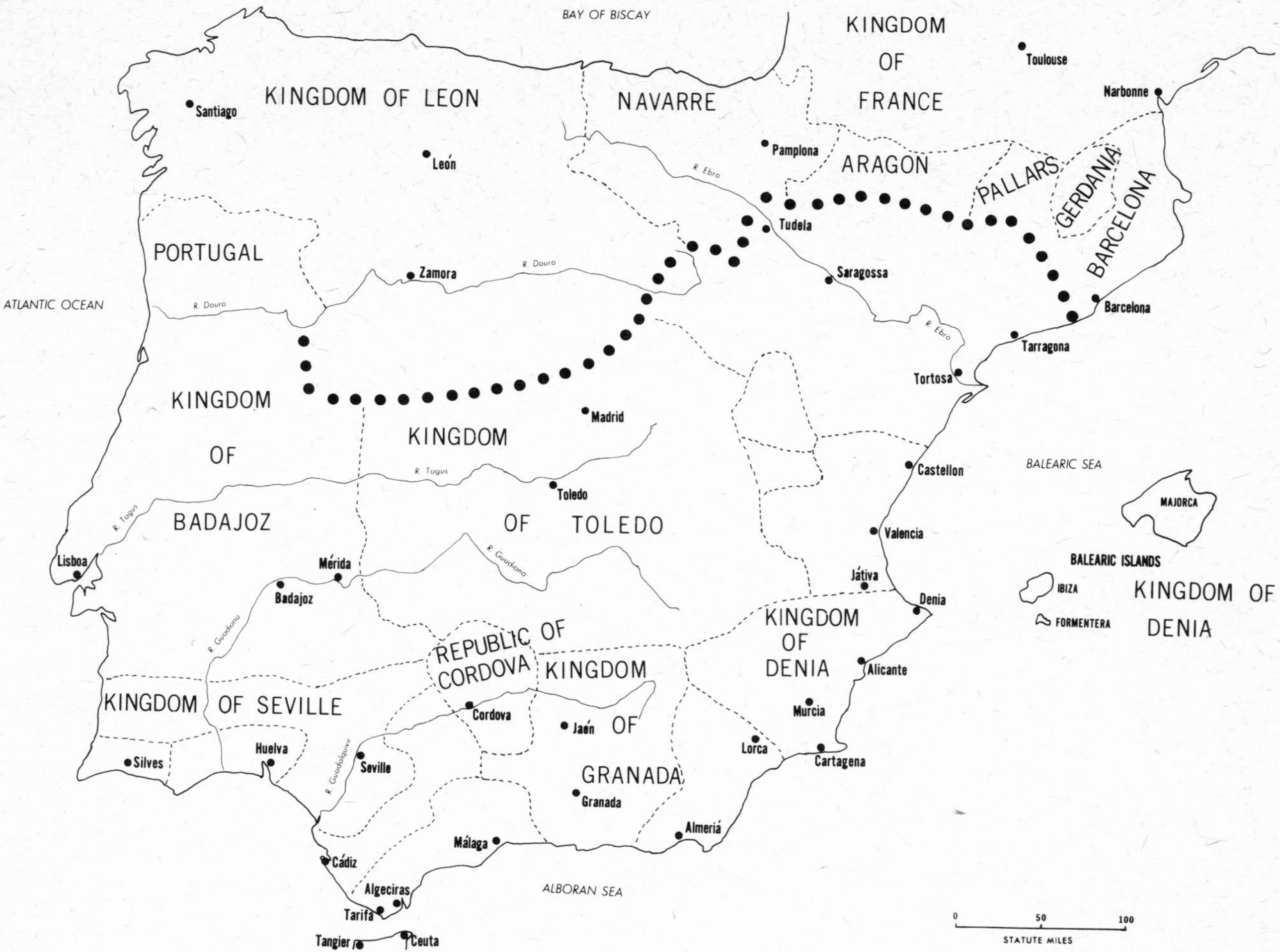

Spain after the Fall of the Umayyad Caliphate in the Eleventh Century

in 1009. The following survey of the most important petty states is meant to give a general idea about their geographical distribution among three major groups: ʻĀmirids and their clients, Arabs, and Berbers.

ʻĀmirids and Their Clients

The ʻĀmirids, their "Slav" clients, and sympathizers with the Umayyads found themselves in a great predicament during the overthrow of the unpopular and reckless ʻĀmirid ʻAbd al-Raḥmān (d. 1009). The indignation over the latter's abuses and the dormant resentment against the ʻĀmirids in general came to the fore with fury; these feelings were also given expression in overthrowing the legitimate caliph Hishām II. Although the universal sentiment was for the continuance of the Umayyad caliphate, the subsequent tragic events gave food for thought to many leaders who now entertained mixed feelings in the midst of uncertainty and anarchy. No doubt, some of the ʻĀmirid leaders attempted to recapture their political power and sought better horizons outside the confines of Cordova. At the same time they avowedly favored the restoration of the Umayyad caliphate, but did not seem to be willing to give up their holdings or to produce a suitable candidate. This ambivalence was characteristic of the major social groups contending for power.

During the great revolt in Cordova in 1009, the ʻĀmirid leaders and their followers were certainly in danger of being decimated. Many of them perished in mob violence, whereas others escaped the onslaught and established principalities on the eastern shores of al-Andalus and in the Balearic Islands. Like other dynasties, their very existence was precarious and they were often at war among themselves and with their neighbors.

One of the ablest ʻĀmirid clients was Khayrān (d. 1029),[7] a competent military man who had discharged an important function at the court of Hishām II. Forced to leave Cordova during the revolt, he joined his partisans in eastern Andalus. He took Orihuela, then Murcia[8] and Almería. He first espoused the cause of the deposed caliph Hishām II by joining ʻAlī Ibn Ḥammūd, but soon fought with the latter[9] and supported the candidacy of al-Murtaḍā — only to abandon him on the battlefield.[10] Khayrān also had to contend with the ʻĀmirid Muḥammad, a descendant of the last ʻĀmirid ruler, ʻAbd al-Raḥmān. Muḥammad[11] appeared in Jaén at the head of a well-financed army and was probably invited by Khayrān to share in the administration of his kingdom. But differences between the two men eventually led to the displacement of Muḥammad. At any rate, Khayrān was able to hold sway over Orihuela, Murcia, and Almería. He made Almería his capital, fortified and beautified it, and added new buildings and running water.

Khayrān nominated his brother Zuhayr (d. 1038), the governor of Murcia, to succeed him. Zuhayr continued Khayrān's policies and proved himself an able administrator. He extended his realm from Almería to a point not far from Cordova and Toledo and over Játiva and Baeza.[12] However, he had serious reverses during his struggle with Bādīs of Granada, and perished on the battlefield in 1038. The news of his death was received with great consternation in Almería; the inhabitants of the city nominated one of their leaders to rule them pending the arrival of the ʻĀmirid ʻAbd al-ʻAzīz of Valencia, who was recognized as the leader of the ʻĀmirids.[13]

Another prominent ʻĀmirid client was Mujāhid (d. 436/1045).[14] He was the master of Denia and the Balearic Islands.[15] He was the son of a Christian woman who continued to practice that faith, but he himself was a devout Muslim and a man of wide erudition. His court attracted the best talents of the day. As a statesman, he brought tranquility and prosperity to his realm and extended his power for a while over a portion of Sardinia, which he raided with a fleet of one hundred twenty ships carrying one thousand cavalrymen.[16] He was repulsed later on and suffered great losses, including the capture of his wives and daughters. Another adventurous undertaking was the appointment of a caliph on whom he bestowed the surname of al-Muntaṣir bi-l-lāh.

Mujāhid was succeeded by his son ʻAlī, who spoke the Romance language and who had been brought up a Christian.[17] This notwithstanding, Mujāhid called on the son to embrace Islam before going ahead with the nomination, and ʻAlī acquiesced, becoming for all intents and purposes a good Mulsim. ʻAlī had at first to contend with his brother who aspired to the throne; and in 468/1076 he was compelled by his brother-in-law, the ruler of Saragossa, to give up Denia and accept instead an estate in Saragossa.

Of course there were other ʻĀmirid leaders who exerted their influence on some cities and even ruled others. Mubārak and Muẓaffar had great influence in the affairs of Valencia,[18] which changed hands many times. Khayrah al-Ṣaqlabī and Labīb al-Ṣaqlabī ruled over Játiva and Tortosa, respectively.[19]

Other rulers who appeared in the eastern part of al-Andalus were the Banū Ṣumādiḥ,[20] who were of Yemenite origin and related to the Tujībid of Saragossa; their ancestor had ruled Huesca during the reign of the caliph

Hishām II. Ma'n, founder of the dynasty, was the vizier and brother-in-law of the 'Āmirid 'Abd al-'Azīz. When 'Abd al-'Azīz had to march against Mujāhid of Denia, he entrusted Ma'n with Almería. In 1041, Ma'n declared himself independent, thereby displacing his brother-in-law. After a rule of about ten years, he was succeeded by his son Muḥammad, who assumed the sonorous title of al-Mu'taṣim bi-l-lāh.[21] He enlarged his kingdom at the expense of his neighbors of Granada and ruled for over forty years until 1091, when the Almoravids took his territory.

The Arabs or ''Andalusians''

The Arabs and their descendants began to lose their influential role in the affairs of al-Andalus as early as the reign of 'Abd al-Raḥmān III in the tenth century. This caliph imported Slavs (*Ṣaqālibah*) to serve as his Praetorian guard. The Slavs soon emerged as a separate power at the court though their influence was reduced enormously by the 'Āmirids, who replaced them with loyal Berber subjects from North Africa. Under the circumstances, the influence of the Arab elements who identified themselves as Andalusians reached its lowest ebb at the beginning of the eleventh century. They eventually lost the office of the caliphate, which had been the major symbol of their pre-eminent position, notwithstanding the ineffectiveness of the caliphal institution. Their individualism and contentious behavior in the past had contributed greatly to their declining influence. In spite of this, some families were able to achieve and hold power in important regions of al-Andalus: the Jahwars in Cordova, the 'Abbādids in Seville, the Hūds in Saragossa; the Qāsims in the small principality of Alpuente until its fall at the hand of the Cid in 1087;[22] and the Ṣumādiḥ of Almería.

The Jahwars of Cordova (1031–1069)

Abū Ḥazm (1031–1043)
Muḥammad (1043–1058)
'Abd al-Malik (1058–1069)

The founder of the ''dynasty''[23] was Abū Ḥazm b. Jahwar, who was instrumental in enthroning the last Umayyad caliph, Hishām III (1027–1031) and in removing him. Abū Ḥazm was a member of an old family, one of whose ancestors, a client of the Umayyads, had entered al-Andalus in the eighth century. Members of the family had served rulers in various capacities and possessed wealth and prestige. Abū Ḥazm was the most respected leader of his time. His influence must have been great in order to abolish the caliphate once and for all and to replace it by a council of elders to administer the province of Cordova and all of al-Andalus. He became the chief of the council (*shaykh al-jamā'ah*) at the insistence of the leading citizens of Cordova, and he was entrusted with the power of governing the city. He seems to have shown great reluctance to assume the awesome responsibility of ruling a city accustomed to anarchy. With his acceptance, he made the following conditions: that his power should be shared by two viziers; that the adoption of a title should be avoided; and that the site of government should be a place other than the caliphal residence.

Perhaps naïvely, Abū Ḥazm sent messages to the various leaders of al-Andalus to come and recognize the authority of his group over al-Andalus. As he might have expected, his call was completely ignored in some circles and was challenged by many others who felt that they were more entitled to rule than he. However, he was wise enough not to press the issue; instead he contented himself with governing Cordova for more than a decade. Moreover, he chose the path of peacemaker among his quarreling neighbors.[24]

Abū Ḥazm Ibn Jahwar was succeeded by his able son, Muḥammad, who followed in his father's footsteps. Muḥammad avoided entanglement with neighboring rulers and concentrated on the affairs of Cordova, which he ruled with justice and democratic spirit. His major mistake was to leave his post to his inept son, 'Abd al-Malik, a vain and incompetent man. 'Abd al-Malik soon undid what his grandfather and his father had accomplished out of devotion and a sense of civic duty. 'Abd al-Malik arrogated to himself all powers, adopted a sonorous title, and required that his name be mentioned in the Friday prayers. By so doing, he antagonized the leaders and the populace at a time when neighboring states coveted Cordova. He soon became easy prey for the Dhū-l-Nūns of Toledo, who besieged the city for a time, and the 'Abbādids of Seville, who annexed it to their domain in 1069.

The 'Abbādids of Seville (1023–1091)

Muḥammad (1023–1042)
al-Mu'taḍid (1042–1068)
al-Mu'tamid (1068–1091)

The 'Abbādids[25] were by far the most powerful among the party-kings. Starting from their base in Seville, they succeeded not only in filling the political vacuum in Cordova but also in extending their power in all directions.

The family sprang from Yemenite ancestry. Their first leader entered al-Andalus in the 740's. The 'Abbādids enjoyed pre-eminence in Seville from the time of the caliph al-Ḥakam II through the 'Āmirid period. Ibn Abī 'Āmir had appointed their ancestor Ismā'īl a judge of the city. Ismā'īl, who was known for his integrity, held the post under the Ḥammūdids, 'Alī and al-Qāsim, and endeavoured to keep Seville beyond the reach and influence of quarreling Berbers.[26] When he grew old and his eyesight failed, he handed down the office of judge to his son Muḥammad, who became the founder of the dynasty.

Muḥammad inherited great wealth from his father. He is said to have owned one-third of the land of Seville[27] and to have enjoyed the respect and esteem of the people. All these assets may have influenced the Ḥammūdids to make him the governor of the city. When the Ḥammūdid al-Qāsim was overthrown in 1023 and denied entry to the city, Muḥammad became a member of the three-man council entrusted with administering the city. Subsequently, he was asked by the people to assume full power, but he consented on the condition that he would have two viziers to assist and advise him.

Muḥammad ruled for nearly two decades, during which he was able to establish an autonomous state. He succeeded in building a volunteer army made up of Arabs, Berbers, Christians, and even criminals.[28] Perhaps to silence the pretensions of the Berbers and the many other aspiring leaders, he claimed that the deposed caliph Hishām II, who was probably dead, was alive in Seville. Muḥammad argued that he was still bound to Hishām by an oath of allegiance.[29] The pseudo-Hishām assumed the dignity of the caliphate, clothed himself with the caliphal robes, and conducted the Friday prayers. Muḥammad himself assumed the post of chamberlain and worked vigorously on behalf of the "legitimate" caliph. Furthermore, he asked all the provinces to render the oath of allegiance to Hishām II. This took place about 1035. Some 'Āmirid clients and Abū Ḥazm of Cordova cooperated with Muḥammad, but other rulers ignored the appeal. He encountered difficulties with his neighbors, mainly the Ḥammūdids and the Banū al-Afṭas of Badajoz. He marched against the ruler of Málaga, one of the Berber leaders, killed him, and occupied Carmona. Afterward, he attacked the ruler of Almería, who soon sought an alliance with the Berbers of Granada. In one encounter with this alliance in 1039, his army was badly defeated and his son Ismāʿīl was killed on the battlefield. At Muḥammad's death in 1042, the situation did not appear promising for the ʿAbbādids. The coalition of Berbers would have succeeded had it not been for his son and successor al-Muʿtaḍid, an able and determined man who extended his power over Portuguese cities such as Silves, Niebla, and Gibraleon and in the south over Carmona and Algeciras, Huelva, Ronda, and other cities and fortresses. Moreover, he had successful military engagements with his neighbor Ibn al-Afṭas of Badajoz. On the other hand, al-Muʿtaḍid was forced to negotiate with the Christians and to pay an annual tribute to Fernando I, who as early as 1056 had made great inroads into Muslim territories in the Marches and who attacked Seville in 1063.

Al-Muʿtaḍid assumed the helm of government at the age of twenty-six. At first, he was satisfied with the title of chamberlain under the pseudo-caliph Hishām II. But in 1059 al-Muʿtaḍid decided to omit Hishām's name from the Friday prayer after declaring him dead for the third time.[30]

Al-Muʿtaḍid disposed of his enemies on the slightest suspicion and treasured their skulls. Among the many persons he killed was his own son who, in fear of his father's wrath, had fled to the south and was later put to the sword on suspicion of treason. Al-Muʿtaḍid once disposed of a number of guests in baths prepared for the occasion.[31]

Al-Muʿtaḍid combined his cruelty with a great political astuteness. He was an able poet and administrator. He encouraged learning, held literary sessions once a week, and established a house of poets (*dār al-shuʿarāʾ*), which was headed by a chief poet (*raʾīs al-shuʿarāʾ*). In addition, he built palaces such as the Qaṣr al-Mubārak, acquired fine horses and luxurious vestments, and lived in the style of a great potentate.

Al-Muʿtaḍid was quite strict with his children and was feared by them. He groomed one, the future al-Muʿtamid, for the succession. He appointed this son chamberlain, commander of the army, and governor of various western cities. Thus, when Muʿtaḍid died, al-Muʿtamid was already experienced in the conduct of state affairs.

Al-Muʿtamid was a great and tragic figure. He was an excellent poet of love and a good statesman whom destiny had chosen to taste both the gaiety and bitterness of life. He ascended the throne in 1068 at the age of thirty. He had assumed the governorship of Silves in 1063, assisted by his boon-companion and fellow poet, Ibn ʿAmmār. He is famous for his love poetry to his wife, Iʿtimād, a former slave girl whom he showered with love and precious gifts. His friendship with Ibn ʿAmmār, whom he had befriended from youth, is equally moving and even tragic. The men were very close and enjoyed many frivolities. Al-Mu'tamid bestowed many gifts and honors on his companion. When Ibn 'Ammār later betrayed him, al-Mu'tamid killed him with his own hands. But al-Mu'tamid's greatest tragedy was the result of his relationship with the Almoravid Ibn Tāshfīn, who was asked to rescue him from the Christians but who instead led him into captivity and humiliation.

Al-Mu'tamid followed in his father's footsteps. His policy toward his neighbors was expansionist. He took Cordova, Murcia, Jaén, and other centers, and emerged as the most powerful Muslim ruler of al-Andalus. Nevertheless, the Christians at the same time had made great gains under Alfonso VI, who forced a number of party-kings, including al-Mu'tamid, to pay annual tributes. The most ominous sign was yet to come from North Africa.

THE HŪD OF SARAGOSSA (1040–1142)

Sulaymān (1040–1046)
Aḥmad I (1046–1082)
Muḥammad (1082–1085)
Aḥmad II (1085–1108)
'Abd al-Malik (1108–1110)
Aḥmad III (1110–1142)

The region of Saragossa was ruled by the descendants of the Tujībids, an Arab dynasty which had been established in the neighboring area since the latter part of the ninth century. They became independent during the great revolt in Cordova but lost their power to Sulaymān, a descendant of an Arab named Hūd who had entered al-Andalus during its conquest. Sulaymān was an able general and the actual founder of the Hūd dynasty.[32] He appeared on the political scene about 1039 when he wrested Lérida and Monzón from Abū al-Muṭarrif al-Tujībi. Before long he held power over Saragossa and had acquired jurisdiction over Huesca, Tudela, and Calatayud as well. He was at war with Toledo from 435/1043 to 438/1046, during which he sought alliances with the Christians. Sulaymān divided his dominion among his five sons, who quarrelled among themselves until one of them, Aḥmad, emerged victorious. Aḥmad assumed the sobriquet of al-Muqtadir bi-l-lāh. He asserted his sovereignty over the Low March and soon added Tortosa to his realm. As was the case with other party-kings, Aḥmad could not avoid entanglement with Christian neighbors, who wrested Barbastro from him after he lost a large number of his army.[33] However, he regained Barbastro and added Denia to his realm. He thus became a great power among the party-kings, renowned for his many public works and buildings, among them the Palace of Joy (*dār al-surūr*). His son and successor preserved the integrity of the realm and even challenged al-Mu'tamid of Seville by giving refuge to the poet Ibn 'Ammār, the former boon-companion of al-Mu'tamid turned deserter and his chief enemy. The next Hūd ruler, Aḥmad II, could not withstand the harassment of the Christians, who inflicted a crushing defeat on him at Huesca and at whose hand he perished in 1108. However, the Hūd were able to preserve their independence even from the Almoravids until 1110 when the Hūdid ruler 'Abd al-Malik allied himself with the Christians, which provoked the Almoravids to send an army to occupy Saragossa. However, they allowed Aḥmad III to occupy the throne up to 1118, when Alfonso I el Batallador and Ramiro II of Aragón displaced him.

The Berbers

From the time of the conquest of al-Andalus, the Berbers remained a disaffected group in the country and always felt that they did not receive their fair share of the wealth and power of the country. They often revolted against the central government and had frequent contention among themselves. From the end of the tenth century Berbers were brought in large numbers from North Africa to serve in the army and in other important posts. Thus, they constituted the most important element in the government at the beginning of the eleventh century, and were able to influence the course of war and peace. They pushed their own candidate to the caliphate and were in actual control of a huge area stretching from the Middle March in the north to the tip of the Peninsula in the south. There were also minor principalities such as the Albarracin in the south of the High March, ruled by the Razīn. But the most important were the Dhū-l-Nūn, the al-Afṭas, and the Zīrids.[34]

The Dhūl-Nūn of Toledo (ca. 1016–1085)

Ismā'īl (ca. 1016–1043)
Yaḥyā (1043–1075)
his grandson Yaḥyā (1075–1085)

Throughout Arab rule in al-Andalus, Toledo was perhaps the most active city of the country. Revolt followed revolt, and the city was always prone to secession. The opportunity for independence offered itself in the second decade of the eleventh century during the chaotic period in Cordova. For a while, the city was ruled by a local citizen, but the Toledans became dissatisfied with him and invited Ismā'īl, a member of the Dhū-l-Nūn, to rule them. The Dhū-l-Nūn[35] were Berbers who appeared during the 'Āmirid period and settled in Shantamariyyah, a district northeast of Toledo. Some of them discharged important functions as commanders of the army and governors. At first, Ismā'īl seems to have shared the administration of the city with Abū Bakr al-Ḥadīdī, a respected citizen and scholar. Al-Ḥadīdī continued in his role of close adviser under Yaḥyā, Ismā'īl's son and successor. Through alliances Yaḥyā was able to withstand the harassment of both fellow Muslims and Christians. When he faced danger from the Hūd of Saragossa, he sought an alliance with Fernando I of Castile and León. He also allied himself with the 'Abbādids of Seville and went along with them in recognizing the pseudo-Hishām as caliph.[36] However, he was soon in conflict with them over the fate of Cordova. He was also at war with the al-Afṭas of Badajoz. By and large, his reign was successful and marked with great splendor and prosperity. However, after his death in 1075 the situation began to deteriorate. His grandson and successor Yaḥyā lacked the ability for rulership and presided over the liquidation of the dynasty. He disposed of Ibn al-Ḥadīdī, who was the mainstay of the dynasty, and others who protested such policies as his expensive alliance with Alfonso VI, who imposed on him heavy tributes.

The situation became untenable owing to the pressure of the Hūd of Saragossa. The inhabitants rebelled and invited the intervention of Ibn al-Afṭas of Badajoz. The latter occupied Toledo in 472/1079, forcing its last ruler, Yaḥyā, into exile. Yaḥyā sought the help of Alfonso VI, who obligingly regained the city for him, though only for a short time. In 1085, Alfonso VI decided to give Valencia to Yaḥyā, he himself remaining in Toledo permanently. This was done with the knowledge and consent of al-Mu'tamid of Seville.[37] The fall of Toledo had grave repercussions for the Muslims: it represented the major blow against Muslim power in al-Andalus and provided the key to further Christian successes in the Reconquista.

The al-Afṭas of Badajoz (1022–1094)

'Abdallah (1022–1045)
Muḥammad (1045–1068)

'Umar (1068–1094) Yaḥyā (d. 1068)

The kingdom of Badajoz, squeezed between the kingdoms of Toledo to the east and Seville to the south, included such important cities as Mérida, Lisbon, Santarem, and Coimbra. Its rulers were the al-Afṭas,[38] who traced their origin to the Berber Tribe of Miknāsah.

During the revolt in Cordova Sābūr, a slave of al-Ḥakam II, occupied Badajoz, Santarem, and the Low March (*al-thaghr al-jawfī*). Upon his death one of his aides, the Berber 'Abdallah, took over. He succeeded in ruling the Algarve but had strained relations with his close neighbors, the 'Abbādids of Seville. His son, Muḥammad, called al-Muẓaffar, was a worthy successor who excelled as soldier, administrator, and scholar. He held on firmly against the 'Abbādids of Seville but lost ground to the advancing Christians, who wrested Coimbra, Santarem, and other fortresses from him and required the payment of a heavy tribute. In spite of recurring wars, Muḥammad's kingdom witnessed moments of prosperity and splendor. His court was visited frequently by scholars, and he himself had a taste for good poetry. He is also credited with a number of writings, one of which, entitled *al-Muẓaffarīyah,* consisted of some fifty volumes on literary and historic matters.

After Muḥammad's death in 1068, the kingdom steadily declined for both internal and external reasons. In the first place, he was succeeded by his two quarreling sons, 'Umar and Yaḥyā. Their wars led them to depend on neighboring Christians and Muslims. Yaḥyā allied himself with the Dhū-l-Nūns of Toledo, and 'Umar was allied with the powerful kingdom of Seville. In the process, the brothers weakened their position, and the Christians made exacting demands on the kingdom. The internal strife subsided when Yaḥyā died in 1068, and 'Umar emerged as the ruler. His capital, Badajoz, became "the abode of letters, poetry, grammar, and the sciences."[39] He organized the state on a sound basis and his fame was such that the people of Toledo invited him to rule over them. Quite aware of the Christian danger, he cooperated fully with the 'Abbādids of Seville and invited the Almoravids to help. However, he soon saw that the Zīrids and the 'Abbādids were forcibly absorbed by the Almoravids and that his turn would only be a matter of time. 'Umar was able to hold on until 1094. When he saw that his plight was desperate, he asked the help of Alfonso VI, but to no avail — the people clamored for the Almoravids. 'Umar was captured, his property was confiscated, and he was put to death at his own request along with members of his family. However, one stayed in a fortress and joined Alfonso VI.

The Zīrīds of Granada (ca. 1010–1090)

Zāwī (1010–1018) ⟶ Maksan
Ḥabūs (1010–1018)
(1029–1037)
Bādīs (1037–1073)
'Abdallah (1073–1090)

Primary information about the Zīrīds and their relation with other party-kings is contained in the memoirs of 'Abdallah, the last ruler of the dynasty.[40] The Zīrīds were originally a branch of the Ṣinhājah tribe and came from Tunis during the reign of Ibn Abī 'Āmir (976–1002), who recruited them to the army. Their leader, Zāwī Ibn Zīrī, played an important role in al-Andalus under the 'Āmirids. In 1010, after the fall of the 'Āmirids, Zāwī decided to return home, but on the way he was persuaded by the people of Elvira to stay and protect them.[41] It is probable, however, that Zāwī was forced to leave Cordova soon after the cause of the Umayyad Sulaymān failed; it is equally probable that he was confirmed in his post upon Sulaymān's inauguration in 1013 as caliph.

At any rate, Zāwī ruled Elvira, and his nephew Ḥabūs ruled Jaén. Soon their realm included Granada, Cabra, Málaga, Écija, and part of the province of Cordova. Here they assumed an independent role, and their prestige rose when in 1018 they inflicted a crushing defeat on the Umayyad pretender al-Murtaḍā and his partisans.[42] After this impressive victory, Zāwī decided to return to his homeland, hoping perhaps to assume the leadership in Qayrawān, then torn by internal politics. Before he left, he delegated power to the council of elders instead of to one of his sons. No sooner had he left al-Andalus than his nephew Ḥabūs assumed power, to the disappointment of the elders and Zāwī's own sons. However, in order to counteract opposition, Ḥabūs ruled with his relatives in a loose federation.[43]

A crisis of succession followed Ḥabūs's death, but it was resolved with the accession of his son, Bādīs, who was supported by a Jewish financial magnate named Ibn Naghrilah. Bādīs rewarded his supporter handsomely by making him his most trusted confidant, financier, and vizier. (Ibn Naghrilah's successor, his son Yūsuf, assumed virtual rulership, to the indignation of enemies who concocted a scheme for his demise.) The Zīrīd power reached its apogee under Bādīs. Bādīs was able to defeat and kill Zuhayr, the ruler of Almería, and also to check the ambitions of the 'Abbādids of Seville, who had been making great strides in the neighboring area. After his death, the Zīrid kingdom was divided between his inept grandsons, Tamīm and ʿAbdallah, who were at odds. Tamīm ruled over Málaga and always felt that he was the one most entitled to rule the Zīrids. On the other hand, ʿAbdallah was the titular ruler of the kingdom, but his jurisdiction was limited to Granada and its immediate surroundings. He was a minor when he came to the throne and his guardian Simāja, a shrewd and ambitious man, arrogated all powers to himself even long after ʿAbdallah had come of age. All this coincided with external harassment of the kingdom from the ʿAbbādids of Seville and the Christians, who made considerable encroachment into Zīrid territory. Moreover, the Zīrids faced internal economic and military difficulties besides considerable rivalry among the various leaders.

When Simāja was dismissed, he went to the court of Ibn Ṣumādiḥ of Almería and created trouble for ʿAbdallah. ʿAbdallah also had to fight his brother Tamīm of Málaga. In the meantime, Alfonso VI exploited the confusion; he asked and received 10,000 *mithqāls* in return for protection. It was at this juncture that the Zīrids, who like the other party-kings were in a desperate plight, decided to invite the increasingly powerful Almoravids to bail them out.

The period of the party-kings was essentially a time of confusion and anarchy. It was marked by constant fluctuation and represented a small ocean in which the large fish prey on the small. The absence of established frontiers led to perpetual wars that played havoc with the spiritual, political, and economic life of the country. There was complete awareness of the existence of a vacuum and of the need to fill it, but in spite of the shortcomings of the Umayyads, no viable substitute was found for them. Under the circumstances, the party-kings came to realize — too late — that they were committing suicide. They found themselves hopelessly squeezed between two mighty forces: one in the north from the Christians, and the other in the south from a new Muslim movement prompted by the Almoravids.

One may safely conjecture that al-Andalus would have fallen into Christian hands as early as 1009 had the Christians themselves been united. As it happened, the Christian kingdoms to the north were experiencing a situation identical with that of the party-kings: costly wars, dynastic quarrels, and chronic jealousies. However, the Christians began to make steady strides from the middle of the eleventh century and overwhelmed the Muslims almost without interruption. From about 1057, they exacted tributes from the most powerful of the party-kings: Ibn al-Afṭas of Badajoz, the Dhū-l-Nūns of Toledo, the Zīrids of Granada, and al-Mu'tamid of Seville.

But the most ominous sign came when the city of Toledo fell in 1085 to Alfonso VI (1072–1109) and Valencia to the Cid in 1094. The fall of Toledo marks the beginning of the end and was followed by other Christian victories. These developments coincided with the rising power of the Almoravids in northwest Africa.

The eleventh century signaled disaster for the Muslims in Spain as well as in the Mediterranean basin. It marks the beginning of the end of Muslim rule in the Iberian Peninsula. The decisive events in the Peninsula and elsewhere in the Mediterranean prepared the way for the First Crusade of 1098, which was called by Pope Urban II at Clermont. The astonishing success of the Crusades, which hit at the heart of the Muslim world in Syria-Palestine, is one of the yardsticks for assessing the degree of the political dislocation of Muslims and their apathy toward outside forces. The general situation in the eleventh century marked an increasing Western ascendance and constituted a complete reversal from that of the tenth century in which the Muslims ruled almost unchallenged in the Mediterranean. Although the Reconquest was kept at bay in the tenth century, it continued in full vigor in the eleventh. The party-kings of al-Andalus became tributaries of Fernando I (1037–1065) and his son Alfonso VI (1072–1109). These two rulers raided Muslim territory as far south as Seville and Granada. But the most ominous sign for the Andalusians was when Alfonso VI took the strategic and important city of Toledo in 1085. This event upset the balance of power in the Peninsula.

In spite of Alfonso's reverses at the battle of Zallāqah (Sagrajas) in 1086, the fate of al-Andalus was determined. It was only a question of time. Powerful forces from outside al-Andalus took active roles in the life of the country. As early as 1064, Catalans, French knights, Normans, and other foreigners began to appear with frequency in the Christian-Muslim wars of al-Andalus. The monastic order of Cluny — to which Hildebrand, the future Pope Gregory VII (d. 1085), belonged — often intervened in the affairs of Spain and kept the religious passion much alive. The order was aided by the Papacy, which from this time on began to have an increasing influence and to assert its authority over the monarchies by claiming that the Pope was God's viceroy on earth. Subsequently, the Papacy had an enormous impact on the secular conduct and policies of monarchs. Also, the merchants of Pisa, Genoa, and others — once the object of harassment and attacks by Muslims in the previous century — took the offensive, attacked Sardinia and other Muslim outposts, and made successful raids into Tunisia itself. They had a decisive role in the Mediterranean and, more often than not, were able to dictate their terms as their commercial interests dictated. In fact, they participated in the Crusades and influenced their course.

Concurrently, the power of the Normans was felt among the Muslims of Sicily. The island was inflicted by division and strife. Petty rulers called upon Byzantines and North Africans for help, only to find out that those powers were not willing to intervene altruistically. In 1060, the Sicilian ruler Ibn al-Ṭumnah asked the help of Roger Guiscard of Calabria to come to his rescue against local contenders. Roger acquiesced and was able to conquer a number of cities. This marks the beginning of the Norman conquest, which lasted until 1091, marking the end of Muslim rule in the island.

At this juncture, the Almoravids in North Africa rose to power and gave al-Andalus a temporary lease on life.

4

The Berber Dynasties, 1056–1269

The Almoravids (1056–1147)

(Yaḥyā b. Ibrāhīm (d. ca. 1042); 'Imrān al Fāsī (d. 1039); Ibn Yāsīn (d. ca. 1056))
Yaḥyā b. 'Umar (d. 1056)
Abū Bakr b. 'Umar (d. 1087)
Yūsuf b. Tāshfīn (1061–1106)
'Alī (1106–1143)
Tāshfīn (1143–1145)
Ibrāhīm (1145)
Isḥāq (1145–1147)

THE situation in northwest Africa during the first half of the eleventh century was in many respects similar to that in al-Andalus. Northwest Africa turned to tribalism with all the attending quarrels and uncertainty. It was perhaps a mere accident that members of the powerful Berber Ṣanhājah tribe, or a branch thereof, the Lamtūnah, made their pilgrimage to Mecca about 1038, under the leadership of Yaḥyā b. Ibrāhīm. On their return, they passed through Qayrawān, then an important intellectual center, where they became imbued with Islamic teachings and recognized their tribesmen's ignorance concerning the true religious practices of Islam. While in Qayrawān, Yaḥyā b. Ibrāhīm befriended Abū 'Imrān al-Fāsī, a distinguished jurist, and prevailed upon him to recommend a religious scholar to come with them and teach their people the principles of Islam. Abū 'Imrān referred them to one of his pupils in the Maghrib, 'Abdallah Ibn Yāsīn, who was to become the moving force behind a new religious zeal in an area extending from the Niger River (Senegal) in the south to the Mediterranean Sea in the north.

'Abdallah Ibn Yāsīn became the Lamtūnahs' spiritual leader and devoted his time to teaching and preaching. His success was limited at first, since he was able to muster only a small, though articulate and enthusiastic, group. In the face of a violent opposition from tribesmen who found the new teaching too rigorous to follow, Ibn Yāsīn decided to establish a "retreat" (*ribāṭ*) for his followers, from which *al-Murābiṭūn* is derived — hence, Spanish Almorávides or English Almoravids. They are also referred to as "veil-wearers" (*Mulaththamūn*).[1]

At first, the Almoravids led a reclusive, devout life, full of tribulations and deprivations. As his following grew, Ibn Yāsīn embarked upon missionary activities which proved quite successful. From a stage of passivity limited to preachings, Ibn Yāsīn took a more militant attitude and appointed able commanders to bring the several tribes within his movement. Of course, Yaḥyā b. Ibrāhīm was the temporal leader. When Yaḥyā died in 1042, Ibn Yāsīn chose as his successor Yaḥyā b. 'Umar, a man who was known for his devotion, asceticism, and zeal in war. The two men worked in harmony and were able to unite all the surrounding tribes in the new faith. For Yaḥyā Ibn 'Umar's participation in a battle, Ibn Yāsīn is said to have given him a few lashes, alleging that a prince should not enter hostilities in person, for "his life is the life of his army and his perdition is its perdition."[2] Yaḥyā b. 'Umar, who was known as the Prince of Truth (*amīr al-ḥaqq*), followed the orders of Ibn Yāsīn, who was in reality the "emir who sanctioned and denied."[3] (In addition to his religious and administrative activities, Ibn Yāsīn had a great passion for beautiful women, and married and divorced a number of them every month.[4]) Dara'ah and Sijilmāsah to the south fell to the Almoravids. They pushed their conquest to the north causing grave consternation in the entire Maghrib, which was now beset by wars and dissension. In their successful march, they acquired a great amount of booty to distribute among their followers.

When Yaḥyā b. 'Umar died in 1056, he was succeeded by his brother Abū Bakr with the consent and approval of Ibn Yāsīn, who exacted the oath of allegiance from their followers. Abū Bakr left Sijilmāsah in 450/1057 at the head of an army of about two thousand men[5] and took the city of Āghamāt, which he then made his headquarters. He married Zaynab, a beautiful and shrewd woman, the widow of the former ruler of Āghamāt.[6] From this capital Abū Bakr sent his generals for further conquest, and his cousin Yūsuf Ibn Tāshfīn went to the northern Maghrib, where he eventually succeeded in establishing a state that stretched from the central part of present-day Algeria in the east to the Atlantic Ocean in the west.

In 1061, Abū Bakr[7] was impelled to leave Āghamāt in order to quell a revolt in the south. He recalled Yūsuf Ibn Tāshfīn, put him in charge of the Maghrib, divorced his wife Zaynab, and gave her in marriage to him.[8] Worthy of leadership, Yūsuf Ibn Tāshfīn assumed command and became his own master. He founded the city of Marrākush in 1062, which he made his capital and provided with a mosque, government buildings, and fortifications. He bought a large number of Negro and Spanish slaves for his army of more than forty thousand men. He minted coins and established various ministries. He soon conquered whatever was left of the Maghrib, including Fez, and by 1075 a new and vigorous empire based on religious zeal was born. This empire came to play a significant role in the destiny of al-Andalus, especially after the conquest of Tangier, Ceuta, Tlemcen, and the coastal areas of the Maghrib.

When Abū Bakr returned in 1073 to take his throne, he found Yūsuf so entrenched that he did not venture a showdown. Instead, he accepted numerous gifts from his cousin.[9] In the following year, 1074, Yūsuf refused to assume the title of the caliphate, alleging that he was the subject of the 'Abbāsid caliph. But he did not refuse the title Commander of the Muslims, which actually was the same as Commander of the Faithful, reserved for the caliph only.[10]

Precisely at this juncture, the party-kings were facing the greatest dangers from the north. However, they were willing to compromise with the Christian kings by paying tributes and even making concessions of fortresses and towns. It would thus seem that they feared the Almoravids more than the Christians, with whom they had much in common. Moreover, they must have felt secure as long as the Christians were preoccupied with serious internal problems. But when the situation drastically changed, especially after the fall of Toledo in 1085, the party-kings were forced to choose between two dangerous alternatives. They opted for their fellow Muslims, the Almoravids, to come and rescue them.

The precise date of the party-kings' initial communication with Ibn Tāshfīn is uncertain. The year 1079, in which Alfonso VI declared war against Seville and after which he made further demands, may be considered the starting point of negotiations. It was in 1083 that Alfonso's Jewish agent came to Seville at the head of a large retinue in order to collect the tribute. However, when the agent made indiscreet remarks and questioned the genuineness of the money, al-Mu'tamid lost his temper and put him to death. Al-Mu'tamid foresaw the consequences and appealed to some of his fellow party-kings to analyze the deteriorating situation. In response, delegates from Badajoz, Granada, and other cities met in Seville. When al-Mu'tamid was questioned about the danger of the Almoravid intervention, he is said to have retorted, "I'd rather be a camelherd [in the Maghrib] than a swineherd [in a Christian land]."[11]

Inasmuch as they could not agree among themselves concerning the formation of a united front, the party-kings decided to ask help from the Almoravids; they sent a delegation of *qāḍīs* (judges) from the various cities, thus giving the mission a religious overtone. The delegation arrived in Fez in 474/1082 and began deliberations with Ibn Tāshfīn, who showed grave reservations but left the door open. In the meantime, al-Mu'tamid was receiving threatening letters from Alfonso VI, who referred to himself therein as the Emperor of the Two Religions.[12]

In 1085, al-Mu'tamid made a direct appeal to Ibn Tāshfīn, imploring him in the name of Islam to come and save the situation. He says in part: "He [Alfonso VI] has come to us demanding pulpits, minarets, *miḥrābs*, and mosques, so that crosses may be erected in them, and so that monks may run them . . . God has given you a kingdom because of your Holy War and the defense of His right, because of your endeavor . . . And you have now many soldiers of God who through their fighting may win paradise in their own lifetime."[13]

Ibn Tāshfīn still showed reluctance to intervene militarily in the affairs of al-Andalus. Pressured by his advisers and religious scholars from the Peninsula, he consented to come on the condition that Algeciras be placed at his disposal.[14] Al-Mu'tamid lost no time in complying — he made his fleet available and even went in person to meet Ibn Tāshfīn somewhere in the Maghrib, probably in Marrākush.[15]

In 1086, the Almoravid army crossed the Straits, and with great expectations landed in Algeciras. Ibn Tāshfīn was given a sumptuous reception by the emirs, military commanders, noblemen, and religious scholars who had been campaigning for him.[16] After preliminary preparations were made, they proceeded to Seville, where another extravagant reception was given to the would-be liberating army. The armies of Granada, Málaga, Badajoz, Seville, and others joined in. A strategy was agreed upon. Al-Mu'tamid was made commander in chief of the party-kings' forces on order of Ibn Tāshfīn, who himself commanded the elite of the Almoravid army. Hoping the enemy would penetrate into the south and then be surrounded, they entrenched themselves at Zallāqah (Sagrajas) two or three miles north of Badajoz. But Alfonso VI, at the head of an army about fifty thousand strong, made a surprise attack on Friday, October 23, 1086.[17] The Andalusian army in the front line was thrown into panic. Al-Mu'tamid fought bravely and was badly wounded. However, he received relief from the Almoravid army stationed in the rear, which inflicted a crushing defeat on the enemy. Alfonso VI had to flee, leaving the bulk of his army dead on the battlefield.

The Battle of Zallāqah lasted only a few days. Although it resulted in a great victory for the Muslims, it solved little except to give the party-kings a temporary boost in morale and a great deal of excitement. The credit for the victory goes, no doubt, to the army of Ibn Tāshfīn, who was convinced by now of the Andalusians' chronic weakness. He soon left for North Africa, leaving the Andalusians to their squabbles and problems.

Alfonso VI lost no time in recruiting a new army and strengthening his position. He proceeded to avenge the defeat at Zallāqah and to harass the Muslims once more with astonishing success. He ran deep into Muslim territory and reached the gates of Seville as early as 1087, impelling al-Mu'tamid again to seek Ibn Tāshfīn's help. Moreover, Alfonso built the strong fortress of Aledo between Lorca and Murcia and garrisoned it with some fifteen thousand men. Strategically located, the fortress threatened eastern al-Andalus, mainly the cities of Valencia, Lorca, and Murcia. Al-Mu'tamid, suzereign of Murcia, was alarmed, and Ibn Rashīq, ruler of the city, felt the Christian pressure. Ibn Rashīq's attempts to liquidate the fortress were abortive because of lack of cooperation from fellow Muslim rulers. Once again al-Mu'tamid appealed to Ibn Tāshfīn for help. The latter obliged and landed in 1088 at Algeciras, where al-Mu'tamid met him. This led to a general conference which was attended by several delegates and which was marked by acrimonious debate over whether or not the siege of the fortress of Liyyīṭ (Aledo) should continue.[18] After four months of siege a decision was made to abandon it for Alfonso VI to raze owing to its vulnerability. Ibn Tāshfīn went out of his way to warn the petty rulers of the consequences that would surely result from their lack of cooperation.

His advice went unheeded even at the conference, where some of them made spectacles of their conflicts — for example, the king of Granada was accused by his own brother of being a usurper.

Following the conference, Ibn Tāshfīn left for North Africa. In one sense he was filled with misgivings, but on the other hand, he felt reassured of support from the religious scholars and the people. Soon afterward, he received alarming reports of new and ominous developments which might threaten his own North African dominion. Many party-kings looked upon the Almoravids with grave mistrust and were more inclined to compromise with the Christians than to risk losing their kingdoms to the Almoravids. Many of them had already acquiesced to Christian demands for retroactive tributes and even for acquisitions of new territories.[19] Quite alarmed, the religious scholars made an urgent appeal in the name of Islam and presented Ibn Tāshfīn with a *fatwa* (legal decision) from the theologians al-Ghazālī and al-Turṭūshī; this *fatwa* authorized Ibn Tāshfīn to occupy and administer al-Andalus and to assume the title of *Amīr al-Muslimīn* (Commander of the Muslims).[20]

Such an enterprise offered enormous strategic, political, religious, and economic possibilities. And in the light of the prevalent confusion in al-Andalus, it offered relatively little risk. Thus, Ibn Tāshfīn decided in 1090 to land in al-Andalus and assume the role of liberator. According to the Emir ʻAbdallah, he headed for Cordova and summoned the various rulers, who complied by attending. An exception among the rulers was ʻAbdallah of Granada, now a tributary of Alfonso VI. Ibn Tāshfīn retaliated against ʻAbdallah by enchaining his emissaries and by sending an army against Granada. ʻAbdallah attempted to muster a force for defense, but his subjects from all walks of life chose to welcome the invader, leaving ʻAbdallah no choice but unconditional surrender.[21] He received humiliating treatment at the hand of Ibn Tāshfīn's emissary. All of his properties, including personal belongings, were placed at the disposal of the invader. ʻAbdallah and his mother were undressed to make sure they possessed no jewels or money. After this indignity they were allowed to have three hundred dinars, three servants, and five mules for the transport of their essential belongings. They were taken to Algeciras, then to Ceuta, and finally to Āghamāt, to the north-east of Marrākush. ʻAbdallah was soon joined by his brother Tamīm of Málaga, who had been plotting against him.

It may be possible that al-Muʻtamid encouraged Ibn Tāshfīn to dispose of Granada, hoping thereby to rule this territory himself.[22] Other rulers were watchful and continued to intrigue against one another. This situation made them easy prey for Ibn Tāshfīn, who proceeded systematically to liquidate the Andalusian rulers under one pretext or another. Almería, then held by Ibn Ṣumādiḥ, offered little resistance; al-Mu'tamid of Seville and Ibn al-Afṭas of Badajoz remained.

To his great disappointment, al-Mu'tamid soon found himself in serious conflict with Ibn Tāshfīn, who began to exert undue pressure on him. Sīr Ibn Abū Bakr (d. 507/1114), Ibn Tāshfīn's general, took Tarifa and headed for Seville, while other military contingents headed for Jaén, Ronda, and Cordova. Sīr asked al-Mu'tamid to surrender peacefully, with a guarantee for his life and property. The proud al-Mu'tamid offered stubborn resistance; to the astonishment of the religious scholars and Ibn Tāshfīn, he sought and received help from Alfonso VI. Al-Mu'tamid could no longer rely on the support of the populace of Seville, but he fought on and is said to have told one of his sons, "Do not fear, for death is easier than humiliation and the road of kings is from the palace to the grave."[23] However, the city surrendered in 1091 after six days of fierce fighting, and al-Mu'tamid was put in chains along with some one hundred members of his family. He was taken to Āghamāt where he spent his last days in abject poverty and humiliation. The fall of Seville was followed by the capture of Badajoz in 1094, Valencia in 1102, and Saragossa, Lisbon, and Santarem in 1110. The Almoravids failed to regain Toledo or to acquire new territory from the Christians.

From about 1090 to 1145, al-Andalus became an Almoravid province and was governed from Marrākush. Military commanders, usually relatives of Ibn Tāshfīn, were appointed over the major cities. They kept the Christians at bay and worked with the religious scholars toward religious rejuvenation. By and large, al-Andalus regained its posture under Ibn Tāshfīn and his son and successor 'Alī (1106–1143), who relied on able and trustworthy governors. However, the Almoravids failed to consolidate al-Andalus and to bring it lasting stability. Powerful factors from within and without worked against them. Christian Spain — although divided — had become inspired by religious zeal and a strong crusading spirit. This was to clash with the political ambition and the religious overtones of the Almoravid movement in a confrontation which coincided with an international *jihād* and crusade transcending the boundaries of al-Andalus and the Maghrib. The confrontation played havoc with the hitherto harmonious relationship between Christians and Muslims, who now looked upon each other with mistrust and

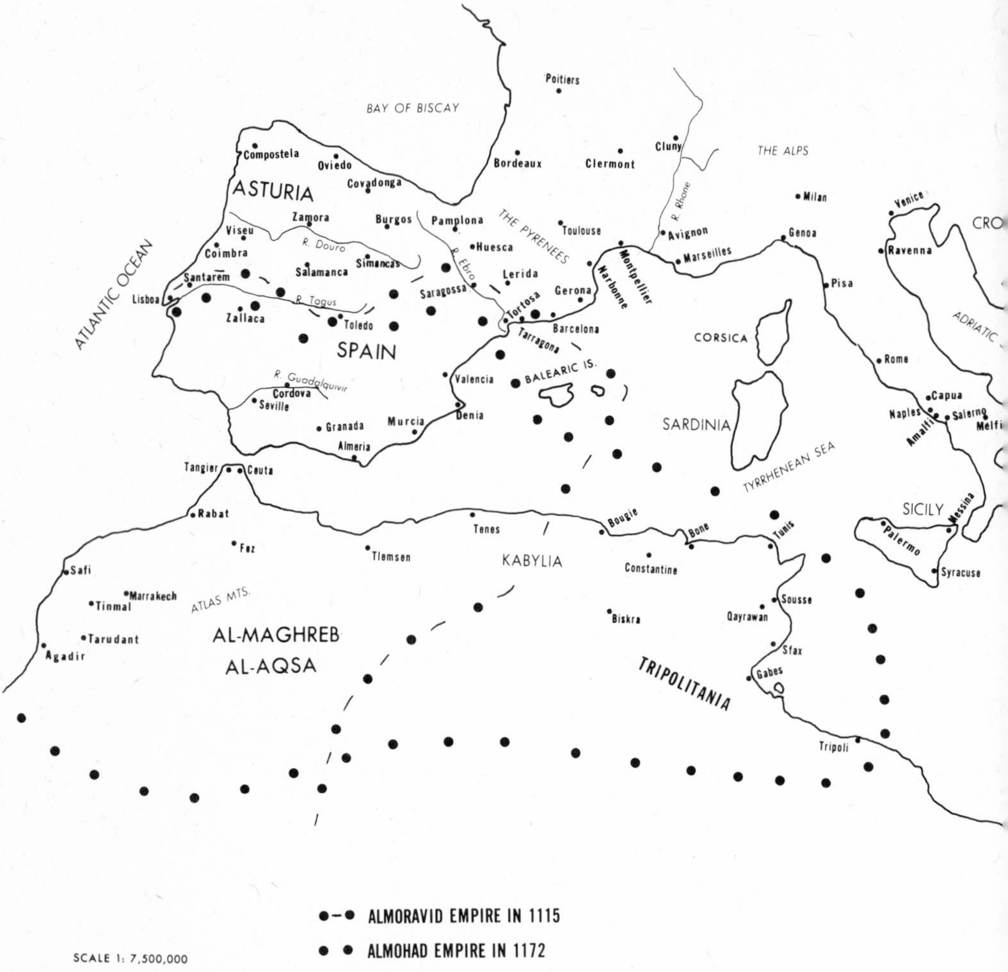

The Muslim West in the Twelfth Century

disdain. In 1118, Alfonso I of Aragón conquered the important city of Saragossa after having acquired several towns and fortresses in the High March. He made Saragossa his capital, converted its main mosque into a church, and impelled many Muslims to leave the city. With the conquest of Saragossa, Alfonso I upset the balance of power in favor of the Christians in the same way Alfonso VI had with the capture of Toledo in 1085. Encouraged by the call of Christians under Muslim rule, Alfonso I made an auda-

cious march against Granada in 1125. At the head of an army of some eight thousand men, he passed through Lérida, Valencia, Denia, Játiva, Murcia, and other towns, reaching Granada itself. Although he was impelled to turn back, his deep inroads into Muslim territory showed the vulnerability of Muslim defenses at a time when the Almoravids were threatened by the nascent Almohad movement in the heart of their North African domain.

Under the circumstances, 'Alī was more concerned with the affairs of the Maghrib. In 1128, he appointed his son Tāshfīn governor of Granada, recalling him ten years later to make him his successor and to confront the growing menace of the Almohads. Tāshfīn proved himself an able general, but the divisive factors within the Almoravid empire were overwhelming. These conditions prevailed under his rule of about four years and were aggravated by internal unrest expressed in revolts, further Christian encroachment, and the growing power of the Almohads in the Maghrib.

The Almoravids gave a new lease on life to the Muslim state in al-Andalus. Their rule filled a political vacuum and contributed in its initial stage to considerable stability and prosperity. Moreover, they satisfied the emotional and spiritual needs of both the religious scholars and the masses. For one thing, the Almoravids made a great display of religiosity at the expense of free thought. The religious scholars, who had had great influence in state affairs under the Umayyads, regained their privileged position and even had the power now to blacklist any book which they thought contained subversive statements. The books of al-Ghazālī (d. 1111), the greatest theologian of Islam, were burned and their author was declared a heretic.[24] Moreover, they subjected Christians and Jews to dire measures. All this conformed to the ideology of the Almoravids.

However, no sooner had the Almoravids established themselves when trouble arose. Their dynasty, once puritan, succumbed to luxury and eventually deteriorated. Disaffection became rampant in all sectors of society and gained momentum with the renewed attacks of the Christians. Under the circumstances, it became clear that the rule of the Almoravids was no more secure than that of the party-kings. In fact, revolts and sedition appeared in 1145 in the Algarve, Niebla, Santarem, Jeréz de la Frontera, the Eastern Coast, Cádiz, Badajoz, and other centers.[25] Some of the revolts resulted in the establishment of various city states similar to those of the party-kings.

The revolts seem to have been instigated by religious men or by the *qāḍīs*. They were backed by the people, who rendered them an oath of allegiance as rulers. Only a few can be mentioned here: A ṣūfī by the name of Abū-l-Qāsim Ibn Qasī,[26] calling himself Mahdī, gathered a number of followers and launched a revolt in Silves and Niebla. When one of his leaders was killed, he took refuge in Sidonia but one of his followers continued the fight. In Cordova, Aḥmad Ibn Ḥamdīn (d. 1152) was made the judge of the city in 536/1142, but three years later he was rendered the oath of allegiance as the supreme ruler with a sonorous title, the Commander of the Muslims and Defender of the Religion. Ibn Ḥamdīn formed his own cabinet, built an army, and ruled Cordova for about eleven months, after which he was displaced by another rebel. He went to Castile, and subsequently to Málaga, where he died.[27] Two other judges did likewise in Málaga and Valencia, respectively.[28] But the most important of the new rulers were Ibn 'Iyāḍ (d. 1146)[29] and Ibn Mardanīsh (d. 1172). Both appeared in eastern al-Andalus and spread their power over Valencia, Murcia, Jaén, Ubeda, and Baeza. Ibn Mardanīsh later besieged Cordova and Seville and penetrated deep into the south as far as Granada.

This situation coincided with the rise of a new religious movement in northwest Africa. The Almohads made their influence felt in al-Andalus first and eventually occupied it under circumstances similar to those which prevailed during the last days of the party-kings. Al-Marrākushī sums up the deteriorating situation as follows:

> The state of affairs under the commander of the Muslims — may God have mercy upon him — deteriorated enormously in the fifth century [twelfth century]. Many abominable things appeared in his realm due to its appropriation by Almoravid leaders and to their sweeping despotism in which they indulged openly.
> Each leader became an imposing figure claiming that he was better than the Commander of the Muslims 'Alī and more deserving to rule than he. Women took control of things; and the affairs of state rested on them. Each woman of the Lamtūnah and Masūfah tribes became associated with evil and corrupt people: bandits, drunkards, and libertines. In spite of all this, the negligence of the Commander of the Muslims and his weakness increased. He was satisfied with the name of the office of governing [*imrah*] of the Muslims and with collecting taxes. He devoted himself to prayer and chastity! He used to stay up at night and fast during the day! He was famous for this! He neglected the affairs of the community to the extreme. For this reason, many things deteriorated in al-Andalus, which almost returned to its former state, especially since the time of Ibn Tūmart's call in Sūs.[30]

Almohads (ca. 1121–1269)

Ibn Tūmart (1121–1130)
'Abd al-Mu'min (1130–1163)
Yūsuf I (1163–1184)
Ya'qūb (1184–1199)
Muḥammad (1199–1213)
Yūsuf II (1213–1223)

Once again a religious movement[31] from the Maghrib came to rescue al-Andalus from internal trouble and the Christians. The Almohads had a number of things in common with the Almoravids: a Berber origin, a strong religious base, and similar development. Moreover, the Almohads filled a role in al-Andalus not unlike that of the Almoravids, and they came to a similar abrupt end, leaving al-Andalus to itself with old and grave problems that contributed to further decline and the ultimate disappearance of Muslim rule in Spain.

The Almohad movement had an interesting beginning. Its founder was Muḥammad Ibn Tūmart,[32] born about 1084 to the Harghah tribe in a village in the region of Sūs in the anti-Atlas Mountains of southern Morocco. His father was lamplighter (*sarrāj*) in a mosque. The young Muḥammad received his elementary education in his native town and subsequently lived and studied in Cordova. He became disenchanted with many things in al-Andalus, among them the burning of al-Ghazālī's works and the prevalence of rigid orthodoxy. He decided to emigrate to the East about 500/1107 to further his education. He went through North Africa to Alexandria, Baghdād, and other cities. In the East he became acquainted with the teachings of jurists and theologians, mainly those who followed the teachings of al-Ash'arī and al-Ghazālī — the two men most responsible for the formulation of an orthodox theology. He was exposed to such leaders as al-Turṭūshī and others, and to the ideas of the Shī'ah and Mu'tazilah.

He stayed in the East about ten years. Upon his return home he began to preach everywhere and to attack the religious practices and mores of the day, whether in Alexandria, Tripoli, al-Mahdiyah, Tlemcen, Fez, or Marrākush.[33] His passionate preaching gained for him both followers and foes. The governors of Alexandria and Bougie ordered him to leave,[34] but this did not deter him. It was in that journey that he acquired one of his staunchest supporters, 'Abd al-Mu'min, who became his right-hand man.

After he was banished from Marrākush, he headed home to Sūs, where he built a mosque in a place called Tīnmall, about a day's journey from the city of Fez. Here he taught and preached his doctrine, calling upon his followers to fill the earth with justice and righteousness and to repress reprehensible actions. His eloquence and devotion earned his adherents' respect and loyalty. He sent leaders to spread the new faith among other tribes. With the undivided loyalty of his followers he ventured in 1121 to proclaim himself the infallible Mahdi (*al-mahdī al-ma'ṣūm*) and to trace his genealogy back to the Prophet.[35] He expounded his doctrine in two major works. His teaching was eclectic, containing orthodox, Mu'tazilite, and Shī'ite elements.[36] He advocated the concept of *tawḥīd* (unity) of God, who is indivisible, limitless, undefinable. It is from this basic doctrine of unity that the term *Muwaḥḥidūn* comes, from which the Spanish *Almohades* and English *Almohads* are derived. He thus assumed a role of both spiritual and secular leadership.

In the manner of Ibn Ḥazm (d. 1064), who may have influenced his teaching,[37] he condemned the doctrine of *taqlīd* (blind acceptance of authority) and insisted on going back and studying the revealed texts. He accepted with enthusiasm allegorical interpretation (*ta'wīl*), which gave him flexibility to disseminate his new version of Islam. And in the manner of the Mu'tazilah he advocated the denial of divine attributes. He made a distinction between those who believed in God, the Prophet, and himself, and those who did not: his followers were considered the people of Paradise, while his opponents constituted "the people of Hell."[38] Once he crucified a jurist for questioning his judgment when he put a follower to death.[39] Moreover, his followers were so submissive and obedient that they would kill fathers, brothers, or sons if ordered to do so,[40] despite the fact that they were taught not to shed blood.

Ibn Tūmart's early career was marred by strong opposition, and his movement made little headway through mere sermons. His small group of articulate followers, designated the faithful ones, *al-mu'minūn*, included a council of ten who worked in closely with him. As his adherents increased, Ibn Tūmart organized them into a governmental hierarchy. To the council of ten disciples, he added a council of fifty representatives from the various Berber tribes.[41] Henceforth, he began to press his claims to righteousness by violent means. He challenged the Almoravids as early as 1122 and engaged them in several encounters. In 1127, Ibn Tūmart attracted discontented Moroccan mountaineers and subsequently marched against Āghamāt and the capital city of Marrākush.[42] He retreated to the mountains without engaging the enemy, but in 1130 sent his lieutenant, 'Abd al-Mu'min, at the head of an army numbering some forty-four thousand men. 'Abd al-Mu'min attacked Marrākush, but was repulsed swiftly by the Almoravid ruler, 'Alī b. Yūsuf.[43] Though his army suffered crushing defeat, Ibn Tūmart persisted in his struggle until he died in 1130. Shortly before his death, he summoned his two councils and exhorted them to adhere faithfully to his doctrine and to pursue the struggle.

Ibn Tūmart may have chosen 'Abd al-Mu'min (1130–1163)[44] as his successor at that meeting. The new leader was confirmed by the two governing councils. But Ibn Tūmart's ambitious claims to infallibility made it difficult for his friend to assume the spiritual and temporal leadership of the nascent community. In view of this, the appointment of 'Abd al-Mu'min was not revealed to the public until three years later, when he proved himself able to assume undisputed leadership and to carry on the struggle.

'Abd al-Mu'min, the son of a potter, was born in 1095 at a village in the district of Tlemcen. He was one of the early followers and became the closest associate of Ibn Tūmart; he served as a member of the council of ten (*jamā'ah*) and as a military commander. 'Abd al-Mu'min, like his predecessor, had a great interest in the various sciences. He gathered around him a number of scholars who aided him in the formulation of the new religious doctrine. Moreover, he proved himself an able commander, leading his followers from victory to victory over the waning but still powerful Almoravids.

After his defeat during the siege of Marrākush, 'Abd al-Mu'min became fully aware of the fact that he could not confront, let alone defeat, the Almoravid calvary on the plains. Instead, he proceeded cautiously and took enough time to organize and consolidate his forces. He remained entrenched in the mountainous areas, resorting to guerrilla tactics and limiting his activities to the region of Sūs. It was not until 1140 that he headed to the northeast and took several towns and fortresses. His followers increased considerably and he became the general of a large army after the death in 1143 of the Almoravid ruler 'Alī.

Tāshfin (1143–1145), 'Alī's son and successor, was not capable of coping with the Almohads' increasing power. In 1145, he perished and his army was badly defeated near Tlemcen, which fell to 'Abd al-Mu'min. Soon afterward, Fez (1146), Āghamāt, Ceuta, Tangier, and finally Marrākush (1147) itself were captured.

'Abd al-Mu'min's success lay in the fact that the Almoravids had lost mass support and were plagued by dissensions and revolts in the Maghrib as well as in al-Andalus. This restiveness coincided with the inroads of Christians into Muslim territories. It is probable that Almohad propagandists were stirring more trouble at this juncture.[45]

After the fall of Marrākush, Almoravid power disappeared and gave way to the Almohad dynasty. After the city was purged and purified from infidelity, the Almohads made it their capital. Soon afterward, 'Abd al-Mu'min turned his attention to the south, where rebellious tribes seceded from his movement. He acted swiftly, defeated them, and put many of them to death. He laid the foundations of Rabat as a military settlement to prevent any future uprising in the south. Once the area was pacified, 'Abd al-Mu'min concentrated wholly upon the affairs of northwest Africa, suppressing all opposition in Ceuta and elsewhere. At this time, the Normans of Sicily had become entrenched in a wide territory of North Africa stretching from Tripoli to Tunis. 'Abd al-Mu'min marched east and took Bougie (1153). He had to return to Marrākush to put down revolts and conspiracy, but he returned in 1159 and took al-Mahdiyah the following year. On his way home, he encountered unruly Arab tribes; instead of fighting, he persuaded them to come to Morocco and enter his military service. He hoped to use them for the conquest of al-Andalus.

'Abd al-Mu'min could not have remained indifferent to al-Andalus, particularly in view of its involvement with outside forces on a zealous crusade against Muslims. Tortosa (1148) and Lérida (1149), two major cities in the north, were lost to the Christians along with the rest of the towns and fortresses in the High March. Even Almería to the south fell in 1147 before the joint forces of Castile, Genoa, Pisa, and other Christian powers. The Papacy was urging Christian rulers to purge the land of the infidel. Moreover, the internal situation in al-Andalus was deteriorating rapidly. Cordova, Valencia, Murcia, Málaga, and other cities had assumed independent postures under local leaders, and were unwilling to relinquish their sovereignty to an outsider. Ibn 'Iyāḍ (d. 1147) had proclaimed himself master of Valencia and other cities, and his domain stretched from that city in the north to Cartagena in the south. He was succeeded by Ibn Mardanīsh, who allied himself with the Christian ruler of Barcelona and Castile, and contracted treaties with the merchants of Genoa and Pisa which entitled them to the use of the ports of Valencia and Denia.

For their part, the Almohads held sway over Seville (1147), Cordova (1149), Granada, and other cities that came to accept their rule. In 1157, Almería fell and was followed by Baeza, Jaén, Ubeda, and more. This notwithstanding, Almohad rule in al-Andalus was loose and precarious. The country remained restless and beset by divisive forces, especially after 1158 when Ibn Mardanīsh and his father-in-law Ibn Hamshuk, supported by Christians, took Jaén with ease and attacked Cordova and Seville; in 1160, they took Carmona and threatened other towns. 'Abd al-Mu'min received the news with consternation and ordered his two sons, Abū Ya'qūb, ruler of Seville, and Abū Sa'īd, ruler of Granada, to launch an offensive. He sent military contingents and ordered the building of a city on Gibraltar so that he could visit it. The city was completed within the year and was provided with a mosque, a royal palace, villas, gardens, fortifications, and running water. ʻAbd al-Mu'min landed in Gibraltar in 1161 at the head of an army made up of Berbers and Arab contingents. Given a hero's welcome by his two sons and large retinues of Andalusian notables, he was showered with the praise of poets.[46] He stayed two months planning the attack, after which he returned to the Maghrib.

The Almohad offensive proceeded without delay. While Carmona was being attacked in 1161, Ibn Hamshuk entered Granada with the help of the Jews.[47] The Almohad contingent offered stubborn resistance and were relieved only by two Almohad reinforcements. This kind of threat reinforced ʻAbd al-Mu'min's belief that a large-scale army was needed. In 1163, he mustered some two hundred thousand men to march against al-Andalus, but he fell ill and died soon afterward. His dream of conquering Spain was not fulfilled, and it was left to his successors to push on.[48]

ʻAbd al-Mu'min was a highly successful leader and great statesman who earned the respect of religious followers. With all his apparent religiosity, however, in 1155 he nominated his oldest son Muḥammad to succeed him, despite the latter's frivolities such as the partaking of wine, which was reprehensible to the Almohads. In consequence, opinions were divided concerning Muḥammad, and he was ousted after forty-five days' rule.[49] It was to the good fortune of the Almohads that he was succeeded by competent rulers who brought Almohad power to its apogee. Their territory comprised all of North Africa from the border of Egypt in the east to the Atlantic in the west, as well as al-Andalus.

Yūsuf I (1163–1184),[50] who had been the governor of Seville, was recalled to Marrākush by his father ʻAbd al-Mu'min with the apparent intention of making Yūsuf his successor instead of Muḥammad. This last-minute decision was pregnant with danger since Yūsuf had to contend with relatives who appear to have rendered him the oath of allegiance with some misgiving. In fact, he was not able to assume the coveted title of Commander of the Faithful until five years after his accession to the throne. Although he followed in his father's footsteps with respect to military and religio-intellectual fields, he was far less decisive in managing state affairs and in attending quickly to urgent problems. On the other hand, he was an erudite scholar in Arabic, Arabic literature, religious sciences, medicine, and philosophy. He was a great bibliophile and had a library almost equal to that of the

Umayyad caliph al-Ḥakam II.[51] He surrounded himself with scholars, including philosophers, who had hitherto been discredited. Among these were the two great philosophers of al-Andalus, Ibn Ṭufayl and Averroes.[52] Moreover, he had the ablest men of his day serving as chamberlains, viziers, judges, and secretaries.[53]

At first, Yūsuf paid special attention to the consolidation of his empire and showed a great preoccupation with the affairs of North Africa. Although Almohad influence in al-Andalus was quite strong, the country was by no means under their control. Various Muslim principalities existed there, and the situation was similar in some respects to that existing at the coming of the Almoravids in 1090. While some of the Andalusian rulers were willing to accept Almohad rule, others were determined to preserve their independence at all costs. Among the latter was Muḥammad b. Sa'd b. Mardanīsh (d. 1172), who still held sway over a large area of the eastern part of al-Andalus, including Murcia. In 1165, Yūsuf sent a military contingent against Ibn Mardanīsh, who offered stubborn resistance. It was not until 1171 that Yūsuf decided to come to al-Andalus at the head of a large army, hoping to bring the whole Peninsula under his rule. He crossed the Strait to Seville, which he made his permanent headquarters against Ibn Mardanīsh and his Christian allies. The military encounter dragged on until Ibn Mardanīsh's death in 1172. Ibn Mardanīsh's relatives found it expedient to acknowledge Yūsuf, who in turn allowed them to continue discharging important functions in areas they once occupied. Free from any serious Muslim opposition, Yūsuf directed his attention to the Christian kingdoms which threatened Almohad power. The kingdom of León under Fernando II proved an effective ally after 1168, whereas those of Castile and Portugal were engaged in expansionist policies which threatened Muslim cities nearly everywhere. Giraldo Sn Pavor, an adventurer in the service of Alfonso Enriquez of Portugal, created havoc in Extremadura and took several towns and fortresses — Trujillo, Evora, Montanchez, and Serpa. He besieged Badajoz in 1169 and took Beja in 1172. These ominous events prompted Yūsuf to send a large army which was able to regain those outposts. He was assisted by Fernando II of León. Yūsuf was then able to besiege Toledo for a while but was forced to abandon the siege and to face the enemy in places where there was less risk. He met with relative success, and the Andalusian question was resolved temporarily through the signing of a truce with his enemies.

During his almost five years' stay in al-Andalus, Yūsuf undertook the construction of several public works in Seville and gave vent to his intellectual pursuits. He was able to attain a modicum of pacification in the country, but by no means its consolidation or permanent peace with its neighbors. He lived to regret this failure. In 1176, Yūsuf left al-Andalus for Marrākush and then Sūs in order to quench a revolt. While he was thus engaged, alarming news about conditions in al-Andalus were reaching him constantly: Portugal attacked Beja in 1178 and threatened the coast, including Ceuta on the African mainland. Alfonso VIII of Castile attacked al-Andalus in 1182, encamped near Cordova, then headed for Seville and Algeciras. Fernando II of León allied himself with Castile in 1183 and pledged to break his good relations with the Almohads. All this led Yūsuf to frantic preparation of a large army for a campaign against the Christian rulers. In 1184, he crossed the Strait and headed for Seville. He then marched against Santarem in the Algarve, which was defended by the forces of Portugal and León. The Almohad army besieged it but found it impossible to take because of its excellent fortifications and good defenses. The army retreated in near panic after Yūsuf died of a wound received in his tent. While the Almohads were mourning their dead leader and were preoccupied with the succession, the Christian rulers were preparing more ambitious plans for al-Andalus. Once more, Muslim Spain was left in a precarious position.

Yūsuf's death was kept secret for a time to avoid contention. It appears that he had nominated his son Ya'qūb to succeed him. Ya'qūb was first rendered the oath of allegiance in the Alcázar of Seville by the notables and public. He departed for Rabat, where he was proclaimed Commander of the Faithful;[54] then he proceeded to Marrākush, where he was again rendered the oath of allegiance. After this oath, the governors of North Africa were notified of Ya'qūb's succession. Some of his relatives objected to his appointment because of dissipations in his early youth, but they came to accept it after Ya'qūb had "filled their hands with money and given them extensive lands in fief."[55]

Ya'qūb (1184–1199)[56] began his administration with emphasis on the implementation of justice, enhancing morale, and construction of public works. He forbade the use of alcoholic beverages and attacked high living by restricting the use of embroideries and silken vestments.[57] He provided Rabat with the biggest mosque in North Africa, and he enlarged the caliphal residence in Marrākush through the addition of several palaces and a large mosque. In 1185, he had to attend to the threat of the Banū Ghāniyah of Majorca,[58] who had ruled the Balearic Islands in the name of the Almoravids from the time of Yūsuf b. Tāshfīn. Although they acknowledged the 'Abbāsid caliph, they were at first on tolerable terms with the Almohads. They indulged in piracy and now challenged the Almohads not only by refusing to acknowledge them but by taking the North African city of Bougie and other conquests to the east. Their leader, 'Alī b. Ghāniyah, entered Bougie with the help of some inhabitants, captured two Almohad princes, and held them for ransom. He proceeded to Algiers, took it along with another town, and returned to Bougie where he hoisted the black flag of the 'Abbāsids. Ya'qūb received this news with consternation and ordered a squadron of galleys and strong army to regain the lost territory. 'Alī was badly defeated, but fled and continued to stir trouble in North Africa with the help of Arab tribesmen and Almoravid supporters. Ya'qūb was compelled to send another contingent, but the rebellion continued for some time by 'Alī and his brother and successor Yaḥyā.

No sooner had Ya'qūb emerged victorious over 'Alī in 1188 than he had to rush back to subdue and dispose of some defecting relatives, who questioned his title to the throne. In the meantime, the situation in al-Andalus was deteriorating rapidly. Ya'qūb began to prepare for a *jihād* against the Christians of Portugal, who had besieged and taken Silves in 1189, assisted by French, German, and English Crusaders. Simultaneously, Alfonso VIII of Castile was besieging a number of towns and fortresses and exacting heavy booty from the Muslims. Ya'qūb was slow in coming, but in 1191, at the head of a large army, he left for al-Andalus, disembarked in Tarifa, and continued on his way to Cordova. Alarmed and fearful Christian delegates from León rushed to Cordova and Seville and pleaded with Ya'qūb for a truce. This gave Ya'qūb a free hand to march against Portugal and recapture Silves. Unable to conquer it at first because of illness, he succeeded in doing so late in the year. He went back to Marrākush but returned to al-Andalus in 1195 when Alfonso VIII of Castile attacked the region of Seville. He met Alfonso's army at Alarcos, north of Cordova, and imposed a crushing defeat. The magnitude and repercussions of the Christian defeat at Alarcos are compared with those of the Battle of Zallāqah.[59] Ya'qūb pushed his conquest to the north and was able to take the towns of Guadalajara, Salamanca, and others. In 1196, he laid siege to Toledo but withdrew to Seville. The Almohads appeared to be in a position to regain all of al-Andalus. However, Ya'qūb was unable to exploit his success and had to hurry back to Marrākush to put down a revolt. Tired and ill, he reached his capital in 1198. His task of stabilization remained unfinished when he died the following year.

Among the pending and crucial problems that faced Ya'qūb late in life was the question of religious thinking and practice. He fell under the influence of religious scholars who were concerned about the danger facing Islam from within among the "free thinkers." To appease the conservative scholars, he ordered the burning of what seemed to them to be subversive materials.[60] He also exiled the great philosopher Averroës and banished his books.[61]

Ya'qūb was the last of the great Almohad rulers. He was an able statesman and a great builder.[62] Many forts, bridges, palaces, and mosques were built under his reign, and the hospital he built in Marrākush was considered superior to any other hospital in the world.[63]

The Almohads, like the Almoravids, had failed to retain their empire for an appreciable time. The raison d'être of both dynasties was a religious zeal that brought together a basically heterogeneous society. But as the religious zeal waned and was lost in mundane pursuits, that society reverted to its fragmented state. This was true in al-Andalus, as in the Maghrib. Many independent principalities appeared at a time when the Christians, particularly in Spain, were making considerable gains and ultimately were able to strike the final blow. This was becoming apparent after the death of Ya'qūb in 1199, who was succeeded by incompetent and feeble rulers. Muḥammad (1199–1213), the son and successor of Ya'qūb, faced various revolts in Africa and even witnessed the emergence of independent states there. Although the situation remained stable in al-Andalus during the first years of Muḥammad's rule, it deteriorated enormously at the end of his reign. Alfonso VIII of Castile made considerable penetrations into Muslim territory and inflicted great damage there. Muḥammad headed for Spain at the head of a large army and hoped to contain or even eliminate Christian inroads. But by this time he could not count on the loyalty of his own army, let alone that of the Andalusians. In 1212 he met the combined forces of León, Castile, Navarre, and Aragón and suffered a crushing defeat at Las Navas de Tolosa. His army, estimated at some three hundred thousand, was decimated, leaving him with a few thousand. Muḥammad barely escaped with his life; he was forced to return to Fez and leave al-Andalus to his fourteen-year-old son, Yūsuf, who soon succeeded him.

Yūsuf II (1213–1223), who ruled in name only, witnessed the breakdown of Almohad power in al-Maghrib as well as in al-Andalus. After his death in 1223, quarrels within the ruling family diverted attention from more pressing business and hastened the disappearance of a central administration. In both al-Maghrib and al-Andalus several pretenders arose, each claiming to be most entitled to the throne. Al-Andalus itself had at least two pretenders, one in Murcia and a second in Baeza. The pretenders were at war, in which Christians helped one against the other in return for territorial concessions. This situation led to instability and confusion, encouraging native groups to assume independent postures in a pattern like that which characterized the last days of the Almoravids. Thus, one may say with some qualifications that a fourth cycle of party-kings came into being in al-Andalus.

After about 1228, new states began to appear in al-Andalus. These kingdoms existed precariously, with constant warfare among themselves. In their struggles they received help from the Christians, who exploited the situation and penetrated deep into al-Andalus under the leadership of Fernando III, king of Castile and León.

During the breakdown of Almohad power in al-Andalus, Zayyān, a descendant of the Banū Mardanīsh, entrenched himself in Valencia, Denia, and other neighboring cities as early as 1229. He did not fare well and had to relinquish Valencia in 1238.[64] When the religious man Ibn Khaṭṭāb (d. 1239) forged a principality in Murcia, the inhabitants revolted and called upon Zayyān Ibn Mardanīsh to take over.[65] In Minorca, Ibn Ḥakam (d. 1288) ruled with an iron hand for about fifty years, but after his death the island fell to the ruler of Barcelona.[66]

Perhaps the most important of the new group of independent rulers was Muḥammad b. Yūsuf b. Hūd (d. 1237), a descendant of the rulers of Saragossa. When the Banū Hūd lost the kingdom in 1118, members of the family lived under the protection of Christian rulers, and appear to have lost their influence in subsequent decades. At the beginning of the thirteenth century Muḥammad Ibn Hūd made his debut in the midst of a political vacuum. He was stationed in the army at Murcia, but deserted along with an officer and engaged in highway robbery. In time, he acquired a great amount of booty and a large number of followers. He championed the cause of Islam against Christianity. In 1228 he took Murcia, and subsequently extended his power over Cordova, Seville, Granada, Almería, Ceuta, and Algeciras.[67] Ibn Hūd acknowledged the ʿAbbāsid caliph, al-Mustanṣir, who sent him a verbose letter of confirmation.[68] Ibn Hūd had adopted the sonorous titles of Commander of the Muslims and al-Mutawakkil bi-l-lāh, and emerged the strongest Muslim ruler in al-Andalus. He soon found himself in direct confrontation with fellow Muslims, mainly Zayyān Ibn Mardanīsh of Valencia and Muḥammad Ibn Yūsuf Ibn Naṣr. In 1231, Ibn Naṣr declared himself the ruler of his native town, Arjona, and began to build a kingdom for himself. The following year, Ibn Naṣr took Jaén, Guadix, Baeza, and other districts and eventually clashed with Ibn Hūd. In the meantime, Fernando III of Castile (1217–1252) took advantage of the unsettled situation, marched to the south, and compelled Ibn Hūd to give up some fortresses and to pay a tribute of one thousand dinars a day. This arrangement freed the hand of Ibn Hūd and allowed him to compel Ibn Naṣr to acknowledge his authority in 1234.

Ibn Hūd's leadership was short-lived and marked by constant harassment from the kingdoms of Castile and Aragón. In 1236, Cordova fell to Fernando III of Castile. After Ibn Hūd's death in 1238, the whole of al-Andalus fell prey to the Christian kingdoms and was actually divided into three spheres to be incorporated whenever the opportunity would permit. The powerful kingdom of Castile would conquer the central and southeastern portion, the Aragonese the northeastern, and the Portuguese the western. Their conquests proceeded almost simultaneously. In addition to Cordova, the Castilians took Málaga in 1241, Jaén and Arjona in 1246, Seville in 1248, and other important cities.[69] They made Ibn Naṣr, ruler of Granada and other southern cities, their tributary. The Aragonese under Jaime (1227–1274) were able to conquer the Balearic Islands in 1229–1287, Valencia in 1238, Denia in 1244, Játiva in 1246, and other cities. As for the Portuguese, they took Silves in 1242, Santarem in 1249, and the rest of the Algarve by 1250. Only the tributary kingdom of Granada remained under Ibn Naṣr. All this marks the beginning of the end of Muslim rule in Spain.

In conclusion, the Berber dynasties held sway over al-Andalus for one and a quarter centuries. To be sure, they filled a temporary vacuum in areas inhabited by Muslims, but they did little to alter the balance of power in the Peninsula or to resolve some of its sociopolitical problems. Christian rulers were barely kept at bay. The Berbers' vows to reconquer the whole Peninsula were not pursued seriously, and the few attempts made were frustrated by strong Christian opposition and by the unsettled state of affairs in North Africa, which often required the ruler's presence there. Significantly, the Berbers, except for the Almohad leadership, were on the whole unsophisticated and lacked the education and refinement of the Andalusians. This made their presence in al-Andalus quite tenuous and even resented by the rank and file of the Andalusians, who were conscious and proud of their material culture and refinement. Moreover, the Berbers remained a minority. There is no evidence that they brought along with them a large number of people for settlement. In consequence, they were never integrated into the mainstream of the population and thus remained foreigners. This becomes more apparent when compared with the extensive settlement and resettlement of people made by Christian rulers.

The Berber dynasties lacked a strong central government. They distributed the administration of the provinces among relatives and army commanders, who often asserted their independence and even rebelled against the central government. This was true of al-Andalus as well as North Africa. The mere fact that al-Andalus was governed from Marrākush made the task of stabilizing the country more difficult, especially at a time when there existed a number of relatively strong Christian states to the North who were imbued with the spirit of the Reconquista and the Crusades.[70]

One could venture to say that the Andalusians would have preferred coexistence with their Christian neighbors had it not been for the harshness and religious intolerance of the Christian conquerors. Under the circumstances, the Andalusians had not much choice except to ask the help of their fellow Muslims of North Africa. It was a marriage of convenience which was based on religious zeal. This religious feeling in fact served as a rallying cry and motto for the Berber dynasties. It coincided with an equally intense religious consciousness among the Christians. A call for a crusade was matched by a call to *jihād*. Christianity and Islam were embarked on a collision course. The Andalusians, who were known for their tolerance and conviviality, found themselves in an unavoidable predicament. They had hoped that the Berber dynasties would protect them and bring them unity and peace, but they found themselves hoping in vain when the end came.

All considered, the Berber dynasties had a religious base in common, but failed to achieve a socio-religious cohesiveness within or without their tribal conglomerate. In fact, their tribalism came to the fore whenever there was a crisis or weakness in the central authority. At first their religious fanaticism was backed ruthlessly by tough and courageous tribesmen. More often than not, they depended on religious scholars, who influenced policies. In their eagerness to recreate a puritan Islam, they attempted to formulate a new theology. Concomitant with this, the Almoravids forbade the use of the writings of the great Eastern theologian al-Ghazālī (d. 1111). The

Almohads advocated, contrary to established doctrine, reliance on allegorical interpretation and the literalism of the revealed texts. Encouragement of the study of philosophy by Almohad leadership was one way, perhaps, to arrive at a new theology. Be this as it may, the Berber dynasties succeeded in disseminating Islam among lukewarm Berbers and among the black people of Ghana, Mali, Mauritania, and elsewhere. Moreover, they kept the spirit of *jihād* (Holy War) much alive in its confrontation with Christian Spain, and elsewhere in the Mediterranean basin.

On the other hand, the Berber dynasties were confronted with numerous and difficult problems. The internal situation in the empire never seemed stable. A gain in al-Andalus was more often than not nullified in North Africa and vice versa. From the eleventh century on, friction between Berbers and Andalusian Muslims was the rule rather than the exception. Numerous and bloody revolts marked this relationship until the end of the two Berber dynasties. It appears that the Almoravids were welcomed to intervene and take over al-Andalus, but the same cannot be said about the Almohads. It would seem that the Andalusians were convinced that the newcomers from North Africa would not fare any better than the Almoravids and opposed them bitterly. Revolts in Valencia, Murcia, and elsewhere led to the rise in 1147 of an uncompromising leader who defied and fought both dynasties until his death in 1172. He was Ibn Mardanīsh, who allied himself with Christian neighbors at the price of paying tribute to halt the intrusion of the Almohads. Moreover, he signed a commercial treaty with the merchants of Pisa and Genoa, allowing them the use of his ports in eastern al-Andalus.

This antagonism to the Almohads is also reflected in the opposition of the Ghāniyah, masters of the Baleares. Their impressive fleet raided southern France and other cities in the Mediterranean. They assumed an independent role, and felt safe as long as Ibn Mardanīsh had control over the Eastern part of al-Andalus. In 1177, they contracted a peaceful agreement with Genoa and Pisa, but in 1182 they were given an ultimatum by the Almohads to accept their sovereignty or else. They refused and proceeded to attack and occupy several coastal cities in North Africa. Although the Almohads succeeded in conquering Majorca in 1203, they were impelled to fight the Banū Ghāniyah for almost three decades on African soil.

Moreover, the emergence of the Berber dynasties coincided with the ongoing Crusades and the presence of the strong kingdoms of Portugal, Castile, and Aragón in the Iberian Peninsula. These kingdoms met with great success in their encounters with the Muslims. The fall of Saragossa to Aragón in 1118 had a repercussion on the balance of power in the Peninsula as grave as the fall of Toledo in 1085. It was followed in 1125 by deep inroads into Muslim territory as far as Seville and Granada. Local Christians felt secure in supporting their coreligionists, resulting in further tension between Christians and Muslims. In this connection, the Berber dynasties may have given a new lease on life to al-Andalus, but they contributed enormously to an intense socio-religious tension. Of course, the tension had been there from the time of the First Crusade, which precipitated religious fervor and brought Christians from outside Spain to fight the Muslims. This is one of the reasons why Christians were subjected to harsh measures and often expelled to Morocco, where they served as soldiers under the Almoravids and succeeding dynasties. In time, they were allowed to practice their religion in public. The building of a church in Marrākush must have been what encouraged the Pope in 1146 to write to the Almohad ruler inviting him to embrace Christianity.

In fact, the Crusades not only had a great impact on Spain, but were strongly felt at various levels. The merchants of Pisa, Genoa, and Venice and Crusaders from France, Germany, England, and elsewhere played a decisive role in the affairs of the Peninsula. A few instances will suffice. In 1115, the merchants of Genoa and Pisa raided the Baleares, took Majorca, and held it for almost one year. In 1147, the king of Portugal, supported by Crusaders from England, Germany, and Holland, took Lisbon, Santarem, and Beja. In the same year, joint forces of Castile, Catalan, Navarre, Genoa, and Pisa held Almería. In 1211, the king of Castile urged the Pope to sanction a Crusade against the Muslims of Spain. Subsequently, French volunteers, clerics, and monks from the various religious orders and knights met the joint armies of Castile, Aragón, and Navarre in Toledo and crushed the Muslims at Las Navas de Tolosa in 1212. Finally, Jiménez de Rada, Bishop of Toledo, organized a Crusade in 1217 and took several fortresses in eastern al-Andalus.

One can hardly overestimate the gravity of this international involvement. The Berber dynasties were quite aware of its implications, but were busy at home settling their internal problems. It would seem that both dynasties gave low priority to the conquest and internal problems of al-Andalus. Ibn Tāshfīn entered al-Andalus with great vacillation, never took advantage of his victory at Zallāqah (Sagrajas), and did little to reconquer Toledo and consolidate his power in al-Andalus. Like his successors, he engaged the enemy in a sporadic manner and whenever the opportunity presented itself. The Almohads, who had similar problems in the African mainland, did likewise. 'Abd al-Mu'min, the actual founder of the dynasty, seemed to be more concerned about the threat of the Normans in Tunisia than the precarious situation of al-Andalus during the 1140's and following. In 1158, he responded to the call of the Zīrīd ruler of Tunisia after the Normans had extended their power from Tripoli in the east to Tunis in the west. He marched at the head of a large army and ordered his navy to reinforce it by sea; this action succeeded in displacing the Normans. Returning triumphantly 'Abd al-Mu'min made preparations to take al-Andalus. No sooner had his plans materialized than he returned to Morocco to attend to pressing problems. His subsequent death created further crises and delayed any major interventions in al-Andalus. As a result, the country remained in a tenuous situation, and the Almohads' victories remained indecisive. Their major victory at Alarcos in 1195 can be compared with that of Zallāqah in having little effect on the course of events. It was nullified by the Christian victory at the battle of Las Navas de Tolosa. The disaster of Las Navas de Tolosa marks the turning point of the Reconquest and the steady decline of Almohad power in al-Andalus as elsewhere in the empire. In fact, the Almohads, in spite of their numerical strength, fell short of expectations and held less territory in al-Andalus than did their Almoravid predecessors.

No doubt the unsettled situation in North Africa prevented both dynasties from pursuing a more successful *jihād* in al-Andalus. Besides, their administrative machinery left much to be desired. Their army was heterogeneous and made up of mercenary soldiers, captive Christians, and tribesmen. Provinces of the empire were given to relatives and military commanders who ruled them as private estates. Ordinary legal taxes were not sufficient to maintain an army always on the move, and were supplemented by extra taxes on sales and manufactured goods. Frequently, Christians were tax collectors and viewed with contempt by the populace.

In balance, the Berber dynasties lacked the sophistication and refined culture of the Andalusians. Like other invaders before and after them, the Berbers succumbed to the amenities of Andalusian life. More often than not, they depended on Andalusian skills and knowledge. Andalusian civil servants at all levels assisted them within and outside al-Andalus. Secretaries, viziers, religious scholars, philosophers, poets, and so forth adorned their courts.

In fact, the Berbers did little to alter the intellectual current, but followed the long-established cultural tradition of al-Andalus. From the twelfth century to the seventeenth, the influx of Andalusian Muslims into North Africa was considerable and had an enormous impact on North African life in the arts, architecture, administration, agriculture, and literature.[71]

While al-Andalus was disintegrating and being absorbed by Christian kingdoms in the early part of the thirteenth century, the Almohad domain in the African continent was undergoing a similar fate. Although the dynasty lingered on until 1269, they lost their empire to three dynasties which appeared almost simultaneously: the Ḥafṣids in Tunisia, the Zayyānids in Tlemcen, and the Marīnids in Morocco. These dynasties displayed features similar to their predecessors: tribal structure, internal wars, and conflicts among themselves. Many Christians and Andalusian Muslims could be found among their subjects. Aragón vied for influence among the Ḥafṣids and Zayyānids, and Castile sought a sphere of influence in the Marīnid domain.

The Ḥafṣids, who served the Almohads in various important capacities, took advantage of the unsettled situation in Tunis and shook off Almohad rule in 1229. They claimed to be the legitimate heirs of the Almohads and continued to mention Ibn Tūmart's name in the Friday prayer up to 1311. In 1236, Ḥafṣid rulers began to assume the caliphal title of Commander of the Faithful. They extended their power into Algeria, and homage was paid them in Morocco and al-Andalus. However, they hardly got involved in Andalusian affairs. On the contrary, they established commercial relations with Venice (1231), Pisa (1234), and Aragón which from 1240 on began to have a decisive role in the internal and external affairs of the Ḥafṣids.

The Zayyānids, a branch of the Zañatah tribe, ruled in the central Maghrib from the important city of Tlemcen. Yaghmurāsan, the founder of the dynasty, fought his neighbors the Ḥafṣids to the east and the Marīnids to the west. He survived their harassment. In the 1290's, the Zayyānid state extended over the Algerian coast from the Mulawiyah River to Shammun (wādi-l-kabīr) in the west. Like the Ḥafṣids, they had commercial relations with Aragón.

The Marīnids, probably of Berber origin, claimed Arab ancestry. They were essentially nomads, clashed with the Almohads in 1145, and were impelled to live in the Sahara. In 1216, they revolted in Fez, and emerged successful in subsequent encounters with the Almohads. In spite of their internal division, they took Tāzah in 1248, Fez in 1250, Sijilmāsah in 1257,

Salé in 1260, the Almohad capital of Marrākush in 1269, Tangiers in 1273 and Ceuta in 1275. Unlike the Ḥafṣids and the Zayyānids, they played an important role in the affairs of al-Andalus from the outset. In the fourteenth century, they had hoped to establish a large empire, thereby counteracting the influence of Aragón and Castile, but their attempts failed in this respect as well as in protecting the last outpost in the Peninsula.

5

The Naṣrid Dynasty of Granada, 1231–1492

THE Naṣrid kingdom[1] was the only state that survived the Christian Reconquest in the thirteenth century. Its founder, Muḥammad b. Yūsuf b. Aḥmad b. Naṣr, was able to forge a kingdom for himself on the southern fringes of al-Andalus. His kingdom comprised a narrow region along the coast, extending from Tarifa in the west beyond Almería in the east and from the Mediterranean in the south to a point beyond Granada in the north.

The kingdom of Granada led a precarious life from the very outset. It was squeezed between the North African states to the south and the Christian kingdoms to the north for about two and a half centuries, and was looked upon with covetous eyes from either side. More often than not, Granada sought either protection by the Christians with payment of heavy tributes or the rescue by the Marīnids of Morocco, depending on which was attacking. It was only through adroit maneuvering that the Naṣrids were able to survive.

The kingdom resulted from the breakdown of Almohad power in 1228, when al-Andalus became once more a maze of confusion and uncertainty. Muḥammad b. Yūsuf b. Hūd,[2] Zayyān Ibn Mardanīsh,[3] and other leaders cropped up to carve principalities for themselves and to claim rule over al-Andalus. One leader went so far as to secure the sanction of a powerless 'Abbāsid caliph to rule; another acknowledged the Almohad ruler of Morocco; still others sought help from the Christian states or acknowledged their neighbors for a while only to fight them shortly afterward. Ibn Hūd, who received the sanction of the 'Abbāsid caliph, held Murcia and extended his power over eastern al-Andalus, while Zayyān Ibn Mardanīsh became the master of Valencia and neighboring towns. Muḥammad b. Yūsuf b. Naṣr (1231–1273),[4] who traced his ancestry to an Arabian tribe, was recognized in 1231 as the ruler of his native town of Arjona, located to the north of Jaén. He was assisted by his in-laws, the Ashqīlūlah clan, who shared the government of the kingdom. In 1232, he extended his power over Jaén and Guadix. At first he acknowledged the Almohad ruler of Morocco, but he found it expedient to pay allegiance to Ibn Hūd after the latter received a letter of investiture from the 'Abbāsid caliph.[5] After the death of Ibn Hūd in 1238, Ibn Naṣr joined forces with the Castilians under Fernando III (d. 1252). He may have assisted his new master in the conquest of Cordova in 1236, and perhaps in return he was allowed to conquer the city of Granada in 1238 and to retain it as the capital of his newly acquired kingdom. However, he found himself in grave difficulty in 1244 when Fernando's forces took Jaén and the surrounding areas and then threatened Granada itself. This threat ended with a peace treaty requiring Ibn Naṣr to acknowledge the suzerainty of Fernando in his own territory, to assist him militarily, and to pay an annual tribute of one hundred fifty thousand pieces of gold.[6] It was under these conditions that Ibn Naṣr was able to rule a kingdom consisting of the important cities of Málaga, Almería, and neighboring towns. In 1247, he had the unpleasant task of assisting Fernando in the siege of Seville. In 1248, after eight months of siege, the conquering army entered the city and soon converted its main mosque into a church. The role of Ibn Naṣr in the conquest of the most important Muslim city did not endear him to his coreligionists. Moreover, he found himself once more in difficulty with his Christian allies, who, in 1264, attacked his kingdom. Ibn Naṣr was able to repulse the attack with the aid of Marīnids of North Africa. This respite did not last long, and he was impelled in 1267 to give up a number of fortresses in return for a peace treaty.

In spite of this precarious existence, Ibn Naṣr was able to consolidate his power and retain it during a reign of forty-two years. He assumed the title of al-Ghālib bi-l-lāh, and kept a watchful eye on his neighbors. Granada became a great metropolis under his rule and the haven of Muslims who converged upon it from the north. He provided it with numerous new mosques, buildings, and public baths. He chose for himself the hilly terrace in the southeast of the city — once a fortress called al-Ḥamrā' — and initiated the building of a magnificent complex that came to be known by that name (Alhambra).

On the whole, the Naṣrid kingdom led a tenuous existence between two powerful external forces for most of its duration. Muḥammad II (1273–1302), the son and successor of Ibn Naṣr, known as the *faqīh* (jurist) because of his religious erudition, attempted to shake off the Christian pressure from Alfonso X (1252–1284) and Sancho (1284–1295) but met with little success. He got help from the Marīnids, whose strong army defeated the Christians but soon departed, leaving Muḥammad alone after he had ceded Algeciras and Tarifa to his North African ally. This new alliance between Granada and North Africa proved as dangerous for the Naṣrids as former alliances with Christian rulers. North African involvement in the internal affairs of Spain may have contributed enormously to the deterioration of relations between Muslims and Christians, and may have provided an excuse for Christian rulers to introduce oppressive measures against Muslims living in their territories. The Christian armies often retaliated by attacking the major towns of the kingdom, including the capital city of Granada — military pressures which often ended with short-lived peace treaties. This pattern of military forays followed by truces prevailed throughout the history of the kingdom of Granada.

At the death of Muḥammad II in 1302, Granada was at peace with the Marīnids and the kingdom of Aragón. His son and successor Muḥammad III (1302–1308), known as the *Makhlū*ʻ (deposed), was a scholar, poet, and builder, who erected the Great Mosque at the Alhambra. However, he failed as a statesman with the management of state affairs, which he relegated entirely to a secretary and a vizier. His relationship with the Marīnids became strained when he decided to enter into peace negotiations with Castile. He also had the difficult task of coping with internal problems which arose from the revolts of his governors in Guadix and Almería. Finally, his brother Naṣr, backed by the leadership of the dynasty, killed the hated vizier and compelled Muḥammad to step down.

Naṣr (1308–1313), though knowledgeable in mathematics and astronomy, was not able to resolve the problems facing the kingdom. His subjects remained restless. This was aggravated when Castile decided to take Gibraltar and Algeciras in 1310. With no hope of receiving any help from the Marīnids, Naṣr became tributary of Fernando IV, king of Castile. The Naṣrids accepted the political reality of the time and managed to survive their dependence on and harassment by the ever-growing Castile and other Christian kingdoms. However, they were not able to check internal dissensions. This internal strife was quite apparent after the reign of Muḥammad III and may have been the principal factor in the Naṣrids' decline and ultimate downfall. Naṣr, a usurper, was in turn overthrown by his nephew Ismā'īl (1313–1325).[7] This pattern repeated itself again and again, adding confusion and instability to the already precarious existence of the small kingdom.

Ismā'īl was able to regain some territory from the Christians, who became divided following the death of Fernando IV (1296–1312). In fact, a Christian army reaching the plain of Granada was soundly defeated in his reign. However, Ismā'īl was assassinated by his cousin, then governor of Algeciras, and succeeded by his nine-year-old son, Muḥammad IV (1325–1333).[8] In spite of his being a minor, Muḥammad IV was rendered the oath of allegiance by jurists, scholars, devout and virtuous men.[9] He was the captive of his ambitious guardian, Ibn Aḥmad al-Maḥrūq. Muḥammad IV showed great promise. He recaptured Gibraltar and other fortresses from the Christians and held invading North African armies at bay. However, his career came to an end at the hand of a Christian assassin.

Muḥammad's brother and successor, Yūsuf I (1333–1354),[10] was raised to the throne by the capable minister Riḍwān. Ibn al-Khaṭīb, who knew him, describes Yūsuf as a reserved and cautious man.[11] It was during his reign that attempts were made from Morocco to reconquer the whole of Spain. Yūsuf encouraged such a move. In fact, he allowed the ruler of Fez to land an army in Algeciras and Gibraltar. The North African army was met by the combined forces of Aragón, Castile, and Portugal and was badly defeated at Saledo in 1340. The Battle of Saledo frustrated North African plans to regain al-Andalus in the same manner as had the Battle of Navas de Tolosa in 1212. Subsequently, Tarifa and Algeciras fell into Christian hands. Under the circumstances, Yūsuf found it expedient to conclude a peace treaty with Aragón, wich allowed him to live in peace and prosperity for almost fifteen years.

The successors of Yūsuf I lived in the shadow of court intrigues and were for the most part either incompetent or manipulated by courtiers. His son, Muḥammad V (1354–1359),[12] was overthrown by the intrigues of his mother-in-law and replaced by her son, Ismā'īl II,[13] who was overthrown by his brother-in-law, Muḥammad b. Ismā'īl (1360–1362),[14] who was overthrown in turn. Muḥammad V (1362–1391), a scholar and able administrator, was brought back and ruled the kingdom with ability. He surrounded himself with able officials, among them the great statesman-scholar, Ibn al-Khaṭīb.[15] This prolific author left us diplomatic correspondence addressed to the Marīnid ruler describing the desperate state of affairs in Granada and imploring him to come to its rescue. He also foresaw the grave danger facing Muslims and appealed to his coreligionists to launch a *jihād* against Christians in order to save their religion and homes.[16]

Muḥammad V was succeeded by his son, Yūsuf II (1391–1392), who died of poison after scarcely a year, and by a second son, Muḥammad VII (1392–1407), who witnessed the beginning of a persistent attempt by Christian rulers to dispose of the kingdom once and for all. His brother, Yūsuf III (1407–1417), was able to sign a peace treaty with Castile for two years, after which the Christians chose to renew their attacks. In addition to this serious situation, Yūsuf had to face invading African forces. Nonetheless, he was able to survive both dangers and to bring a great measure of peace and prosperity to his kingdom. Yūsuf III was succeeded by his frivolous son, Muḥammad VIII (1417–1428), who was driven out of the country, returned to his throne (1430–1432), and was ousted again only to return for a third time (1432–1444). In the interim, Muḥammad IX (1427–1429) and Yūsuf IV (1432) ruled, but ineffectively. Civil wars became more frequent and did violence to the economy.

By the end of the first half of the fifteenth century, Granada could no longer count on any help from the Marīnids of Morocco, who were then in decline. In despair, the Granadines appealed for help to Egypt,[17] and to the Ottomans after their conquest of Constantinople in 1453.[18] They felt completely isolated after the fall of Gibraltar in 1462, which was the last outpost between Granada and the African mainland. In the meantime, the Christians were becoming more insistent upon peace agreements or tribute; they invaded Granada during the reigns of Sa‘d b. ‘Alī (1445–1446) and his son ‘Alī (1462–1482) and captured a number of fortresses such as Archidona and Gibraltar. At that time, the Christian rulers were divided. However, the internal difficulties among the Naṣrids made the position of Granada especially weak at a time when the Christians were gaining unity and were becoming more intolerant of Muslim presence in the Peninsula. After his initial success in recapturing lost territory, ‘Alī had hoped to secure peace with Castile, but Fernando of Aragón insisted on terms which ‘Alī could not accept. ‘Alī was able to take some fortresses in 1481, but internal unrest prevented him from consolidating his power. In fact, he relegated most of his duties to viziers and became indulgent in pleasure and pastime.[19]

Mismanagement and abuses caused wide discontent and led to a revolt. To complicate things further, his wife and his Christian concubine were pushing the cause of their respective sons to the throne. This was resolved by the elevation to the throne of Abū 'Abdallah Muḥammad, a son of his legitimate wife. 'Alī fled to Málaga, then ruled by his brother, while his son ruled Granada until he was taken captive during an expedition against the Castilians in the north. 'Alī was recalled to the throne but turned it over to his brother, Abū 'Abdallah, in 1485. In the meantime, the captive Abū Abdallah Muḥammad was released from captivity in return for 400 Christian prisoners, payment of 12,000 pieces of gold, and recognition of Fernando's suzerainty over Granada upon his returning to the throne.[20] He finally took office in 1487, thus displacing his uncle, who ruled the southeastern part of the kingdom. Under this Muḥammad, known as Abū 'Abdallah (Sp. Boabdil), Granada fell to the enemy. He (1487–1492) began his second rule with a great handicap. He allowed himself to be the captive of Fernando with whom he cooperated in the conquest of the major towns and fortresses of the kingdom of Granada. Thus, the situation of the Granadines was becoming more and more vulnerable, especially after the union of Aragón and Castile in 1479 through the marriage of Fernando and Isabella. These two rulers, pressured by the clergy, emphasized their religiosity and were committed to conquer the whole Peninsula in the name of Christianity. In 1482, they were able to take the important fortress of al-Ḥāmah located to the southwest of Granada. Subsequently major cities and fortresses were captured. Ronda fell in 1485; Loja and nearby fortresses were taken in 1486 with the help of Abū 'Abdallah. In 1487, the important city of Málaga was besieged by land and sea; its inhabitants fought bravely until supplies of food and weapons were exhausted. In their surrender they were promised safety, but their conqueror broke his pledges and took many of the inhabitants captive.[21] In similar manner, the fortress of Baeza, Almería (1489), and others were taken peacefully from Abū 'Abdallah's uncle in return for what appeared to be full guarantees for the safety of the people and their religious and civil freedom.[22] Only Granada with its famous fortress, Alhambra, was left.[23]

While this systematic conquest was going on, the Naṣrid ruler made a desperate appeal to the Marīnid ruler. He sent a delegation of prominent men to Fez pleading for help.[24] In the meantime, Fernando mustered an army of some fifty thousand cavalrymen and one hundred thousand foot soldiers, and he marched against Granada. The inhabitants of Granada became alarmed, especially when Fernando demanded the surrender of the city from Abū 'Abdallah. The latter, though amenable to the idea, was pressured by the notables, jurists, military commanders, and the people to refuse. They were united under the leadership of Mūsā b. Abī Ghassān, who sent word to Fernando that he would have to take the city by force. Fernando lost no time in marching against Granada in 1490. He still hoped that the city would surrender without a fight; he called upon its inhabitants to surrender or have their harvest destroyed. They ignored his demand, and war ensued. Fernando was able to damage the harvest and take some fortresses, but he withdrew unexpectedly. In the interim, the Granadines recaptured the lost territory and gained ground to the east. However, their success was short-lived: Fernando's army returned in 1491 and besieged Granada for seven months, through part of the winter when the source of supplies to the city was cut. The enemy drew closer to the city gates. In the city itself the food supply was becoming scarce and inflation was rampant. There was no hope for relief. In view of this, Abū 'Abdallah summoned the leaders of the city and informed them of the desperate situation. He also revealed to them the proposed terms of surrender which would guarantee Muslims the exercise of their religion and the preservation of their language and customs. Following are some of the terms:[25]

> To guarantee safety of young and old people with respect to their persons, family, and property;
> To preserve their law as it was and judge Muslims by it;
> To allow mosques and religious foundations to function as they did in the past;
> Not to let Christians enter the home of Muslims or coerce them;
> Not to appoint Christians or Jews over the affairs of Muslims;
> To release and give amnesty to all prisoners from Granada and to all those who fled;
> To allow emigrations to North Africa for anyone wanting to go;
> Not to apprehend an innocent individual for the crime of another;
> Not to punish converts from Christianity to Islam and vice versa;
> Not to hold responsible anyone who may have killed a Christian in time of war;
> Not to oblige Muslims to render hospitality to Christian soldiers;
> Not to permit Christians to enter mosques;
> To permit Muslims freedom of travel in Christian territory with full protection of life and property;
> To give freedom to leaders of prayer and observants of fasting to practice their religious obligations without any hindrance.[26]

These terms of surrender, among others, were quite generous — too generous, indeed, to be kept by the victors. The Granadines, hard pressed and defeated, could hardly reject them. Abū 'Abdallah received the conqueror and delivered the key to the city on January 2, 1492. The enemy entered triumphantly and on the Alhambra they hoisted the cross by the side of the flag of Castile and Aragón. Abū 'Abdallah is said to have wailed, which prompted his mother to admonish "Should you cry, O my son, as women do for the loss of a city which you were not able to defend as men should have done?"

Thus fell the last Muslim outpost in Spain. If the end seems tragic, the subsequent events in the Peninsula with regard to the Muslim-Christian relationship had, indeed, all the intensity of a drama. Abū 'Abdallah seems to have been pressed to leave the country and to give up villages and estates granted to him by the terms of surrender.[27] Before his departure, he wrote a moving letter in prose and verse to the ruler of Fez informing him of what had befallen him and his fellow Muslims. His letter offers an apologia and defends him against the accusations of treason; it attributes his failure to fate as well as to his own shortcomings.[28] He soon left for North Africa and established himself in Fez, where he built palaces and gardens in emulation of those of his native land. Many others followed him to escape the harsh policies of the conqueror. They settled in Morocco, Fez, Tlemcen, Tunis, and other North African cities. They transplanted their skills and knowledge, built new homes, gardens, palaces, and public baths, and spread their great legacy in their new homeland. The monuments built by them are eloquent testimony to their potential accomplishments in the Peninsula, had they been given the chance.

The fall of Granada had grave repercussions for the Muslims of the Peninsula. Soon the conqueror made a mockery of pledges contained in the terms of surrender. In 1501, Fernando and Isabella decreed that "God chose them to purify the kingdom of Granada from unbelief."[29] They not only submitted the subjected population to extreme hardship but demanded from it complete effacement of its personality, beliefs, customs, and language under the threat of death. Some acquiesced to these measures; others rebelled only to be crushed, and many others were forced to emigrate. This relentless policy prevailed up to 1609–1614 when the last Muslims were expelled en masse.[30]

The significance of Granada to the Muslims cannot be underestimated. It had been the place of refuge for many Muslims who were dispossessed and persecuted elsewhere. More important still, it preserved and continued

Hispano-Arabic culture and built such great monuments such as the beautiful Alhambra and the Generalife, numerous gardens, gorgeous homes, and public baths. Thus, its fall not only marked the disappearance of the last Arab political unit in al-Andalus, but the discontinuance of a hitherto brilliant culture. Its fall also meant the loss of personal dignity for a people who were deeply attached to the land of their birth.

In retrospect, the kingdom of Granada and the rest of the Muslims in the Peninsula lacked unity. From its founding, Granada was beset by internal strife over the succession. Frequent revolts made the kingdom vulnerable to foreign intervention from the Christian and Muslim sides. Heavy expenditures for maintaining a sizable army drained the resources of the country and contributed to social unrest and economical crisis. Granadine rulers were, for the most part, less than average statesmen who frequently were manipulated by viziers and military commanders. These public officials often influenced policy and assumed all the functions of the ruler.

But the greatest threat to Granada came from the outside. For one thing, the kingdom served as a buffer zone between the North African powers and the Christian kingdoms of the Peninsula. It was simply a matter of time before the kingdom was absorbed by either side. But this depended, of course, on the longevity of the powers surrounding it. The North African powers, mainly the Marīnids, proved themselves ephemeral and went through a trajectory similar to that of their Almohad predecessors. The parallel is striking indeed in terms of attitude and accomplishments. The relationship of the Granadines and Marīnids was marked by mutual ambivalence and mistrust from the outset. When hard pressed, the Granadine rulers sent impressive delegations to the Marīnid court pleading for help and inviting them to come and rescue al-Andalus from the hands of the Christian "infidels." In 1275 the Marīnids complied but only after their demand to place at their disposal Ronda, Tarifa, and Algeciras had been met. No sooner had the Marīnids triumphed against the Christians as far as Cordova than the Granadine ruler began to have second thoughts about the wisdom of the invitation, alleging that the Marīnids were interfering with the internal affairs of Granada. In fact, Marīnid victory on the outskirts of Écija was almost reminiscent of the battles of Zallāqah and Alarcos. After other successful skirmishes against the Christians, they decided to return to Morocco, much as the Almoravid Ibn Tāshfīn had done almost two hundred years before.

Marīnid victories had little or no effect on the course of events except to arouse the suspicions of the Granadine ruler, who felt that the Marīnids were determined to support his relatives who were ruling Málaga. Again in 1278, the Marīnids entered al-Andalus at Málaga, from which they marched against Christian territory, reaching Seville. This confirmed the suspicions of the Granadine ruler, who, with the help of Castile, occupied Málaga, but in return had to allow the Castilians to occupy Algeciras, hitherto the headquarters of the Marīnids. But Granada found itself once more at the mercy of the Castilians, who did not honor their pledges and whose policy appeared to absorb the kingdom of Granada. In 1285, the Marīnids intervened once more, penetrated deep into Castilian territory, and imposed conditions on Castile such as noninterference with the life of Muslims under Castilian rule. Following this impressive success, relations between Granada and the Marīnids improved, but the chronic suspicion between the two powers remained. Castile continued its policy of military intervention. As a result, in 1299 Granada was forced to enter a defense agreement with Aragón, which was meant to check the ambitions of both Castilians and Marīnids. The agreement gave Granada a temporary respite, but did not prevent Castilian interference in its internal affairs. In 1310, Castile took the strategic fortress of Gibraltar, thereby enormously restricting Marīnid entry into al-Andalus. In fact, subsequent Marīnid military intervention in al-Andalus was sporadic and ineffectual, and lacked a sense of urgency.

On the whole, the Marīnids failed to achieve any permanent success in Spain. Although their early interventions resulted in victories on the battlefield, they gained next to nothing in terms of territory or permanent influence on Granada. Like their Almoravid and Almohad predecessors, they were more concerned about the internal situation in North Africa than in al-Andalus. This was the case during the fourteenth and fifteenth centuries, when the Marīnids chose to ignore the plight of Granada altogether. In despair, its rulers turned their attention to other Muslim countries for help. As early as 1440, a Granadine delegation went to Egypt and pleaded for help. It was followed by another delegation in 1487, which explained the desperate plight of Granada in particular and that of other Muslims under Christian rule in general. The Egyptian ruler limited himself to sending a delegation to Castile to remind them that he had control over the holy places in Palestine and had many Christian subjects in his empire. Mindful of possible repercussions, the Castilians sent an embassy in 1501 to Egypt which was headed by Pietro Martiri de Angleria, a man of great erudition.

Pietro made a record of his mission in his *Legatio Babylonico*. He assured the Egyptian ruler that Muslim subjects were treated with magnanimity and would continue to receive such treatment. Granada made similar appeals to the Ottoman rulers, which resulted in empty promises.

All this did not deter the Christians from vigorously pursuing the Reconquest, which was animated now by a strong crusading fervor, nor did it relax the harsh measures imposed on Muslims. The fall of Constantinople to the Ottoman Muḥammad the Conqueror in 1453 contributed, no doubt, to arousing Christian sentiments against Muslims and to precipitating the downfall of Granada. As soon as Spain settled its internal problems, it began in earnest to displace the Muslims once and for all from the Peninsula. The unity of the kingdom of Aragón and Castile made of Spain a power to be reckoned with, and the small kingdom of Granada was not a match for it. With the fall of Granada, the Reconquest was completed.

The fall of Granada had also grave consequences for the attitude and psychology of the Christian conquerors. They feared retaliation from the Ottomans who had penetrated into Europe and who made their presence felt in Syria-Palestine, Egypt, North Africa, and the Mediterranean. The Spanish fear of imminent invasion of Spain was increased by piratical activities conducted by Muslims in the Mediterranean. In 1517, the brothers Barbarossa and other pirates terrorized the Mediterranean, particularly when Algiers and a good part of North African coast fell under their sway. They attacked ships and raided several ports from which they took, among other things, captives to be sold into slavery. In addition, pirates transported Muslims or Moriscos who chose to escape the harsh measures imposed upon them by the inquisitors and who probably participated in piracy or cooperated with pirates.

In addition to the religious intolerance, this kind of activity must have hardened the attitude of Spanish Christians toward their Muslim Morisco subjects. These people were quite numerous, and lived throughout the Peninsula. After 1492, the Spanish Muslims lost all sorts of protection from within and without and became the objects of stringent measures concerning their beliefs, customs, language, freedom of movement, and individual dignity. Rightly or wrongly, they were considered a fifth column and enemy of the state and religion. In the light of an outright persecution, Muslims and Moriscos revolted in Valencia, Granada, and elsewhere, but they were so disorganized that the state did not have much difficulty in crushing them. The affluent among them emigrated, but the majority were forced to stay and accept their lot with resignation, with a hope for deliverance. In the process, they had forgotten Arabic, the language of their ancestors, and even the religious practices of Islam. The staunchest among the Moriscos wanted to perpetuate their Islamic legacy; they translated Arabic texts into their own dialect and wrote in it, using the Arabic script, thus producing a sizable amount of writing which is known as *aljamiado* literature.

As indicated elsewhere, Christian attitudes toward Muslims may be traced to an earlier period, almost from the time of the First Crusade. However, Muslims living under Christian rule (Mudéjares) were tolerated at first, because of their skill. They were allowed to serve in the army, buy and sell land, and even build mosques and practice their religion. Documents continued to be written in Arabic as late as the fifteenth century. But these privileges began to be rescinded as early as the thirteenth century according to local conditions and the policy of a particular Christian ruler. By and large, Mudéjares were tolerated as long as the kingdom of Granada lasted. They lived, like the Jews, in ghettos (Ar. *ḥayy*, Sp. *morería*). No doubt they were exploited by their Christian masters and frowned upon by coreligionists living in Muslim territory who felt that emigration from the land of unbelief to Islamic land was a religious duty (*farīḍah*). More often than not, Christian rulers ignored papal bulls which called for the exile and conversion of Muslims. However, papal policy began to have effect, particularly after the establishment of the Inquisition. Conversion to Christianity and intermarriage reduced the number of Mudéjares and Jews. The Jews who embraced Christianity were known as *conversos*. Even the *conversos*, not to mention those who remained true to their faith, became in course of time a target for fanaticism and persecution. The Jewish problem was resolved by mass exile in 1492.

As for the Muslims and Moriscos, they had no choice but emigration under the rule of the Inquisition. They took advantage of every opportunity available to them, using the ships of pirates or their own means of transportation. The exodus began in the twelfth century and continued increasing up to the seventeenth, when expulsion was forced upon them. The majority found new homes in the major North African cities: Ceuta, Tangiers, Tetuan, Fez, Salé, Tlemcen, Tunis, and others. They established new villages and contributed enormously to the material and intellectual life of their adopted land. More often than not, they preserved some of their Andalusian identity, including customs, Spanish names, music, and other skills.

In sum, this mass exodus may have satisfied the national and religious aspirations of Spain, but it created a serious socioeconomic dislocation in the country which adversely affected its future development. The considerable loss of skilled population led to the decline of agriculture, industry, and commerce. The contention that the presence of Muslims in the Peninsula was responsible for all the ills of Spain must be viewed in the context of the Reconquest and the inquisitional policies of extortion, confiscation of property, persecution, and the mass exodus of a people, who, by any account, made of Spain one of the most progressive countries of Europe in the Middle Ages.

6

Social Structure and Socio-Religious Tensions

IF WE are to contemplate the factors that led to the decline and ultimate fall of al-Andalus, we can hardly omit the structure and ethnic composition of Andalusian society. This composite society consisted of several layers, including Visigoths, old Semitic stock and Arabs, Hamitic Berbers, imported white and black slaves, and others.[1] Its ethnic distinctions remained acute and influenced the orientation and loyalty of the respective groups, especially in time of crisis. To ethnic distinctions, one may add the religious affiliations which also played a divisive role in society and eventually resulted in intolerance and persecution.

Spain was conquered by some twenty thousand Berber and Arab Muslims. They constituted a tiny minority in the large Christian population of the country, though subsequent waves of immigration increased — perhaps doubled — their number. This notwithstanding, they remained an ethnic and religious minority for many decades after the conquest. In course of time, however, they succeeded in attracting to their religion a majority of the population inhabiting territory which was firmly conquered. Many Christians and Jews, although fully arabized, remained faithful to their respective religions. By and large, Andalusians became united in language and custom but remained faithful to their ethno-religious affiliation. This chapter will clarify the position and role of each of the major social groups — Muslims; Non-Muslims; and Muslims known as Moros, Mudéjares, or Moriscos, who lived under Christian rule. Finally, religious attitudes are discussed, with special attention to the views of Alfonso X and the subsequent Inquisition.

Muslims

We do not have statistics on the actual numerical strength of Muslims. It is certain, however, that they were a minority at first and managed to outnumber both Christians and Jews by the ninth century. No doubt they were united in Islam, the Arabic language, and Arabic culture. They comprised a number of ethnic groups which were jealous of their ancestry as well as of their provenance. It is because of this clanishness that one is able to discern the following major groups: Arabs, Berbers, Musālimah, and Muwalladūn and Slavs.

As an ethnic minority, the Arabs nonetheless constituted the ruling class from the time of the conquest in 711 to the fall of the Umayyad dynasty in 1031. They occupied a predominant position in the social, economic, and political life of the country. In addition to important positions, they owned large estates, towns, and fortresses which they named after themselves.[2] Also, they imposed their language, Arabic, and their religion, Islam, on a large proportion of the population.

When the Arabs entered al-Andalus as conquerors, their number could not have exceeded ten thousand. These original settlers, who occupied the fairest portions of the land, were known as *baladiyyūn*; they were later joined by new larger waves of soldiers or immigrants. These newcomers, known as Syrians or *shāmiyyūn*, were resented by the older Arab settlers.

Subsequently, the Arabs' numerical strength increased greatly through adoption and intermarriage with the native population. The Arabs freely married natives or took many as concubines and slaves. Other natives became clients and identified themselves with their masters; these clients inflated the ranks of the Arabs and were largely responsible for the success of both Islamization and Arabization. In fact, they adopted Arabic names, customs, and genealogy — all of which became the distinctive marks of ''Arabness.'' Those who were Arabs or identified themselves as Arabs amounted to a considerable portion of the population.

In their pre-eminent position, the Arab leaders failed to integrate the various Arab tribes into an organized whole. Strong individualism, rivalry, and envy characterized inter-Arab relationships to the extent that an Arab group would ally itself with Christians or Berbers against fellow Arabs.

In this respect, old rivalries and quarrels which had divided them in their original locales were preserved. The traditional division between the northern, Qaysite Arabs and southern, Kalbite Arabs played havoc with inter-Arab relations in the newly acquired land. Settlement or colonization according to tribal allegiance not only preserved the seeds of division but also contributed enormously to social tension and bloody conflict, which led ultimately to the Arabs' loss of influence and their eventual downfall.

It seems that the hatred resulting from intermittent wars between Qaysites and Kalbites in Syria was transplanted in all its intensity to al-Andalus. The defeat of the Qaysites in 684 at Marj Rāḥiṭ, Syria, remained vivid in their memories. Emotions inflamed by old grievances in the East ran high in al-Andalus. Before the coming of 'Abd al-Raḥmān I in 756, al-Andalus was torn with strife. To avenge a defeat inflicted on them by the Qaysites, the Kalbites allied themselves with the Berbers but were badly defeated. The Qaysites showed no magnanimity in victory; they sold captive Kalbites to the lowest bidder. One Kalbite was exchanged for a dog, and another was traded for a stick.[3] After bitter fighting, peace was restored for a while. The new Kalbite governor, Abū al-Khaṭṭār, felt it expedient to distribute the Qaysite soldiers in an attempt to avoid another holocaust. He placed the Damascenes in Elvira, the Palestinians in Sidonia, men from Ḥimṣ in Seville, and those from Qinnasrīn in Jaén.[4] But this arrangement was not successful, since war erupted shortly. The Qaysites gathered around al-Ṣumayl, an able and ambitious soldier. Both parties engaged themselves in a civil war so bloody that the historian Ibn 'Idhārī compared it with the two great *fitnahs* of early Islam — the battle of the Camel in 656 and that of Ṣiffīn in 657.[5] The Qaysites won the day amid much bitterness. This unsettled situation no doubt facilitated the success of 'Abd al-Raḥmān I, who relied heavily on the defeated Kalbites.

This sort of alignment had grave repercussions for the central government, which had to contend with revolts instigated not only by Arabs but also by other discontented groups. Under the circumstances, the Arab ruling class in Cordova was often compelled to recruit non-Arab elements in order to safeguard their persons and ensure a dependable and loyal army for the defense of the country.

Berbers. The Berbers were perhaps the most important group participating in the conquest of al-Andalus. They constituted the first wave to enter al-Andalus under Ṭāriq b. Ziyād, who succeeded in conquering a good portion of the Peninsula. The Berbers were disaffected from the outset, partly because their share of the booty did not equal that of their Arab coreligionists. Initially they outnumbered the Arabs, and after the conquest their numbers increased through immigration, which reached its high point during the eleventh and twelfth centuries. Already at the end of the tenth century, Berber soldiers were the mainstay of the government under the 'Āmirids. Subsequently, in the key regions of al-Andalus they were able to forge a number of independent states such as Badajoz and Toledo in the north and Málaga, Elvira, Granada, and Algeciras in the south.

The conquering armies of Berbers and Arabs were never integrated. After the conquest, the various components of those armies settled in regions distinguished by ethnic lines, the Arabs taking the fertile plains and the Berbers the mountains. Like the Arabs, the Berbers were divided by tribal allegiance and internal war. They suffered from the same malady which plagued the Arabs: they were not able to present a united front in their struggle with either Christians or Arabs. Their organization remained essentially tribal in spirit not only under the Umayyads but also during and following the period of the party-kings.

The Berbers had common bonds with the Arabs through Islam and, to a lesser degree, through the Arabic language, but the relationship between the two groups was marked by constant friction and bloody wars. The Berbers were restless in both North Africa and al-Andalus. They were imbued with an independent spirit and frequently rose in open revolts that proved costly in human life and materials. In 741, the caliph Hishām, who was preoccupied with problems in Damascus, sent a large army to put down a Berber revolt. The defeat of the army encouraged the Andalusian Berbers to revolt and indulge in wanton killings. Many revolts followed and were accompanied by bitter resentment against the Arabs. In their discontent, they did not hesitate to espouse some extremist causes, such as those of Khārijites and Shī'ites. By the end of the eleventh century, they became the masters of al-Andalus and continued in this role during the twelfth and part of the thirteenth centuries. Rule then passed to the Almoravids and Almohads, who sent governors from Marrākush. Subsequently the influence of the Berbers in the affairs of al-Andalus remained great until the fall of Granada.

Nevertheless, the Berbers emulated the Arabs in language, religion, and outlook. Their courts were meeting places for poets and literary men. They produced many scholars, including the able poet and litterateur Al-Muẓaffar.

Muwalladūn and Musālimah. The *Muwalladūn* and *musālimah* were Muslims of Spanish stock. Muslim authors make a distinction between these two groups. The *Muwalladūn* (Sp. *Muladíes*), known to Spanish Christians as "renegados," were born Muslims of either Arab or Berber fathers who had married Spanish women, a practice that was quite prevalent, especially at the time of the conquest. On the other hand, the *musālimah* had adopted Islam out of either conviction or convenience. Although there are instances in which *Muwalladūn* preserved their maternal names and felt pride in their Spanish ancestry, they were by and large as devout Muslims as the *musālimah*. In the course of time, they became the largest portion of the Islamic community of al-Andalus. They may be compared with the *mawālis* (clients) of the East. Of different ethnic backgrounds, they emulated the Arabs in custom, dress, and language; they identified themselves with the Arabs to the extent of adopting Arabic names and even Arabic genealogies.

Like the *mawālis* in the East, the *Muwalladūn* and the *musālimah* were the backbone of al-Andalus by virtue not only of their large numbers but also their pre-eminent positions in the religious, political, and intellectual life of the country. More often than not, they showed as much zeal in the cause of Islam as did the Arabs. Many religious scholars, judges, viziers, secretaries, military commanders, and others came from their ranks — among them, the historian Ibn al-Qūṭiyah and the great theologian and thinker Ibn Ḥazm.

And like other groups, the *Muwalladūn* and *musālimah* had moments of disaffection which often led to open revolts against the central government. This discontent did not cease, being based in resentment of the Arab aristocracy, which they felt was exploiting them and depriving them of equality in Muslim polity.

Ṣaqālibah.[6] More often than not, the Umayyads felt that they could not rely on their Arab supporters, let alone the other segments of society which resented their power. In consequence, they made use of slaves imported from North Africa, the Mediterranean basin, France, Germany, and other European countries.

The *Ṣaqālibah* ("Slavs") appeared on the political scene under 'Abd al-Raḥmān III, who used them in the palace in preference to the quarreling Arabs and Berbers. Their presence at the court is reminiscent of ninth-century Baghdād, when the 'Abbāsid caliphs could depend on neither Arabs nor Persians and turned to Turkish mercenaries.

The *Ṣaqālibah* were originally captives or slaves from northern Spain, France, Germany, and Eastern European countries. As slaves, they were bought in the market places at a tender age. They were easily indoctrinated into the Arabic language and the religious practices and mores of the court. They are said to have numbered over thirteen thousand under 'Abd al-Raḥmān III. From minor and humble positions in the court, the *Ṣaqālibah* were soon elevated to such sensitive and influential positions as advisers and commanders of the army. They also acquired great wealth and large estates. As a result, they were resented by both Arabs and Berbers. However, they remained loyal to the Umayyad cause during the last days of the dynasty. Ibn Abī 'Āmir removed most of them from power and replaced them by imported Berber elements. However, they succeeded after the fall of the 'Āmirids in establishing various states in Denia, Tolosa, Valencia, and the Baleares.

Non-Muslims

To be sure, non-Muslims constituted a minority in the Islamic Empire. As such they occupied a position which, as may be expected, differed from that of Muslims. The position of non-Muslims in al-Andalus may be compared with that elsewhere in the Muslim world. Christians and Jews entered into the mainstream of Islamic society and were eventually arabized so that they were no longer distinct from Muslims. They were granted the protection of the religious law based on Qur'ānic injunction, which considered both groups the "People of the Book" (*ahl al-kitāb*) or the "People of the Contract" (*ahl al-dhimmah*) by virtue of having received divine revelation. As such they were allowed to practice their own religions; to have complete jurisdiction governing marriage, divorce, dietary laws, and other family and civil affairs; to own property; and to engage in all crafts. On the other hand, they had to pay a poll tax (*jizyah*) and land tax (*kharāj*) in return for protection; they were forbidden to propagate their own faiths, to bear arms, or to bear witness against a Muslim in a legal case involving a Muslim and a non-Muslim. By and large, these privileges and restrictions entered into the canon law and remained an integral part of it throughout the centuries. It is significant to point out that, according to the law books, non-Muslims could not build new churches and synagogues or hold official positions. In practice, however, numerous churches and synagogues were erected in newly established cities, and many important posts, including that of vizier, were held by Jews and Christians.

Non-Muslims were in some instances subjected to stiff regulations but never to persecution of the sort practiced under the Byzantines or in Spain under the Visigoths. For instance the second caliph, 'Umar (634–644), promulgated a constitution whereby non-Muslims were forbidden to remain in Arabia. In the early part of the eighth century another caliph, who is remembered for his piety, instituted an edict whereby all Muslims, regardless of origin or race, were equal and exempt from taxes; the same edict applied higher taxes to Jews and Christians and restricted their liberty and movement. A similar edict was promulgated in the following century. It is noteworthy to point out that these measures, however discriminatory, were set down during a time of national crisis and affected both Muslims and non-Muslims. They were an infringement of Muslim canon law and occurred in scattered instances, never amounting to systematic persecution.

On the whole, Islam remained faithful to a policy of scrupulous tolerance throughout the Muslim countries, including al-Andalus. Consequently, the non-Muslim population made full use of the opportunities given to them and made contributions to social life. The Jews developed a close kinship with the Arabs and cultivated their talents to the fullest extent. During the expansion of the seventh and eighth centuries, the Jews in Syria-Palestine, Egypt, and Spain welcomed the Arab conquerors as their liberators from persecution. They "ceased to be an out-cast community persecuted by the ruling church and became part of a vast class of subjects with special status."[7] Subsequently, they led a harmonious life with Muslims and together witnessed periods of ascendancy and decline. By the tenth century, the Jewish communities were totally arabized to the point that Sa'adya Gaon (d. 942), a leader of the Egyptian Jewish community, felt the need to translate the Bible into Arabic and even to explain Hebrew grammar in that language for the benefit of his co-religionists. It was at that time that many Jewish merchants, artisans, bankers, public officials, and authors made remarkable contributions.[8] In the following two centuries came a Jewish golden age in literature, which was written in both Arabic and Hebrew: "There, under Arab-Muslim influence, Jewish thought and philosophy and even Jewish law and religious practice were systematized and finally formulated. Even the Hebrew language developed its grammar and vocabulary on the model of the Arab language."[9]

The Jews of al-Andalus. When Spain was conquered by the Arabs in 711, we are told, the Jews of the Iberian Peninsula had been placed under harsh restrictions by the Visigoth rulers, and they encouraged and helped the Arabs. While the conqueror advanced to the north, the administration of many cities was left to the Jews. To be sure, they found relief under Islam. Subsequently, they played an important role in the political, economic, and intellectual life of the country. They cooperated with the conqueror until both Muslims and Jews fell victim to the Spanish Inquisition. Those who escaped the bigotry and wanton massacre of the inquisitors found homes and refuge in Muslim countries such as Morocco, Tunisia, Algeria, Egypt, and Turkey. There they lived unmolested for centuries. The great philosopher Maimonides left intolerant Spain for Cairo, and served as the court physician of Saladin, the conqueror of Jerusalem. Similarly, Joseph of Nassus sought the Ottoman court, where he occupied a prominent position as adviser and boon-companion to the Ottoman sultan.

In Spain, as elsewhere in the Arab countries, the Jews preserved their religion but assimilated the culture and the mores of the land in which they lived. Muslim Spain may serve as an example of social integration and cooperation. During the tenth century, Hasdai ben Shaprut, a Jew, served 'Abd al-Raḥmān III, one of the ablest rulers of Muslim Spain, in the capacity of close adviser, court physician, and trusted emissary to the Christian kings. Ben Shaprut also appears to have encouraged the caliph to enter into diplomatic negotiations with the Byzantine emperor, Constantine VII, who subsequently sent gifts to 'Abd al-Raḥmān.[10] Another Jewish statesman was Samuel Ibn Naghrīlah (993–1055), the financier and prime minister of the Zīrīd king of Granada. Samuel was the virtual ruler and was succeeded by his son Yūsuf. Both allowed their co-religionists to participate in the administration of the State and to enlist in the army.

The Jews, whether converts to Islam or devout adherents to their own faith, were fully arabized and made their presence felt throughout the Empire. They used the Arabic language for self-expression and adopted the Arabic lore. Thus, it is hardly possible to differentiate the mental process or intellectual outlook of a Jew and an Arab of the time. Moreover, the indebtedness of Arabic and Arabic lore to the Jews is not hard to demonstrate, nor is it difficult to show the influence of the Arabic language and literature on later Jewish writers who used Hebrew as the medium of self-expression. The list of Jewish intellectuals in Muslim Spain is, indeed, an impressive one. Only a few names of a long list can be mentioned here.

Yahūda Ibn Dāwūd wrote the first scientific Hebrew grammar in Arabic using Arabic grammar for a model. A number of Jewish poets initiated a neo-Hebraic poetry, taking Arabic poetry as a model of form and often of content. For instance, Moses Ibn Ezra (d. 1138) was a poet of wine, women, and song in the best Arab manner. Yahūda Halevi (1085–1143), poet, philosopher, and physician, composed several poems in Arabic "with a rare elegance.'' Finally, Abraham Ibn Ezra (1092–1167) was an expert in the use of Arabic prosody and an astronomer, poet, and traveller as well. Although al-Harizī (ca. 1170–ca. 1230) tried to prove that Hebrew was as great a language as Arabic, he often preferred to use Arabic and undertook the difficult task of translating the famous *Maqāmāt* of al-Ḥarīrī into Hebrew.

In philosophy and medicine, many outstanding Jews used Arabic as the medium of expression and Arabic learning as the basis of their intellectual orientation. When Arabic-speaking scholars — Jews, Christians, and Muslims — were deliberating philosophical questions and cultivating the sciences, Europe was in a period of slumber. The Jews played an important role in transmitting Arabic lore to Europe. Many Jews knew Arabic, Hebrew and Latin well. Under the sponsorship of Christian rulers in Spain and Sicily, they began to translate Arabic works from all disciplines into Latin. The transmission of ideas was a prime factor in the subsequent resurgence of Europe.

The Mozarabs. Originally, the Mozarabs[11] constituted the native population which, from all available indications, had welcomed and subsequently accepted the Muslim conquerors. In course of time many natives embraced Islam. A substantial group remained faithful to Christianity but became arabized by the influence of Arabic language and culture. Hence, their designation as Mozarabs (Ar. *al-Musta'ribūn*).[12]

Their status as ''People of the Contract'' required them to pay the poll and land taxes in return for protection. Like the Jews, they had their own courts and enjoyed freedom of worship in their churches and monasteries. Although their status was not equal to that of Muslims, they seem to have lived in harmony with their Muslim neighbors. In large cities, they lived in their own quarters, but this did not prevent them from circulating among Muslims in their daily activities. They had their own judges but litigation of cases involving a Mozarab and a Muslim required a special Muslim judge who knew both Muslim and customary law. They were headed by a governor or Count (*comes*, Ar. *qūmis*) who was an intermediary between them and the central government, and had their own laws (*Fuero Juzgo*) based on the Visigothic system.

Mozarabs were much in evidence in the major cities of Cordova, Seville, Granada, Murcia, Valencia, Toledo, and Saragossa. A large number of them lived in villages and rural areas and devoted themselves to agriculture.

The Mozarabs often adopted Arabic names and were often criticized by their clergy for overindulgence in Arabic customs. However, in times of political and economic crisis they were prone to resent and challenge the Muslim authorities. Under 'Abd al-Raḥmān II some of the Mozarabs were prompted by clerics to vilify the memory of Muḥammad in order to earn martyrdom in this life and eternal bliss in the hereafter[13] (see Ch. 1). Subsequently, they joined or assisted their close Muslim kinsmen, the *Muwalladūn*, in rebelling against the central government.[14]

On the other hand, the Mozarabs often enlisted as mercenaries in Muslim armies and fought their co-religionists from the north. They also held important posts at the courts of Muslim rulers, thus playing a significant role in the social, economic, political, and intellectual life of the country. Marriage between them and Muslims was not uncommon. Often a Muslim married a Mozarab woman who continued to practice her Christian religion. More often than not, members of the same family were divided in their religious beliefs, some professing Islam and others Christianity. They spoke both Arabic and Romance. They constituted the best intermediaries between Muslims and Christians to the north, contributing, thus, to the transmission of ideas. In fact, their influence on the customs, weapons, coins, arts, and architecture of northern Spain was enormous.[15]

The role of the Mozarabs in the process of sociocultural interaction can hardly be underestimated. They enjoyed tranquility under Muslim rule in the tenth century, especially during the reigns of 'Abd al-Raḥmān III and al-Ḥakam II. They contributed enormously to Andalusian life as artisans, builders, public officials, and writers. They had a great fascination with the Arabic language and culture. Although no detailed study has been made of their literary productions in Arabic, there are indications of their literary activities and interest in the Arabic sciences. Bishop Recemundo, known in Arabic as Rabī' b. Zayd al-Usqūf al-Qurṭubī, was knowledgeable in the Arabic sciences and wrote on astronomy.[16] About 955, he was sent on a diplomatic mission to Germany and visited Jerusalem and Constantinople. 'Arīb b. Sa'd, a renegade, was an accomplished physician and served as secretary to 'Abd al-Raḥmān III.

On the whole, a remarkable accommodation and tolerance between Muslims and Christians prevailed up to the eleventh century. However, following the great revolt in 1009 and the political disintegration in al-Andalus, the Mozarabs found themselves caught in a net of contending forces. Like the rest of the population, they became the victims of disorder and lawlessness. Subsequently, the unsettled situation in the Peninsula under the party-kings placed Muslims and Mozarabs in a tenuous position and the hitherto harmonious relationship between them was affected adversely. With the inroads of northern Christians into Muslim territory, the question affecting Mozarabs was not a problem of nationality but a seemingly endless collision of Christianity and Islam provoked by outside forces. The religious element, hitherto insignificant, increasingly became a divisive factor and the cause of intense social tension and religious intolerance. As a result, the Mozarabs were placed under stringent regulations by the Almoravids and Almohads. They were made to wear special clothing to distinguish them from Muslims. While these and similar restrictions were going on under Muslim domination, more restrictive measures were being applied to those Muslims living under Christian rule.

Moros and Mudéjares

Owing to constant warfare between Muslims and Christians living in northern al-Andalus, it is quite difficult to determine the number of Muslims living in Christian territory or under Christian rule. However, during the eleventh century, particularly after the fall of Toledo in 1085, one can assume that a large number of Muslims lived under Christian domination. These Muslims were known as Moros (Moors), a term probably derived from Mauritania in northwest Africa. By and large, the designation of Moros referred to Berbers, whereas the pure-blooded Arabs were known as Alárayes. After the Reconquest, the Muslims forced to convert to Christianity were known as Moriscos. Those Muslims who remained faithful to their religion and lived in Christian territories were known as Mudéjares, from the Arabic *mudajjan*, meaning "tamed" or "permitted to remain." Their number increased enormously in proportion to the advance of the Reconquista, which was completed in 1492 with the fall of Granada.

The Mudéjares,[17] like the Mozarabs, lived under ever-changing political and military conditions and hence were subjected to the vicissitude of time. At first, they were allowed to live in Christian territories in return for payment of taxes. Moreover, the Christian rulers employed their talents in commerce, industry, agriculture, arts, and architecture, and allowed them freedom of worship, their own customs, and local government organizations.[18] However, in time, harsh measures aiming at de-islamizing and de-arabizing the Mudéjares contributed not only to the decline and disappearance of their cultural heritage, as expressed in religious practices, customs, and language, but to their eventual extermination and expulsion. This aspect can better be understood through a review of the confrontation of Christianity and Islam in terms of religious attitude and coexistence.

Religious Attitudes and the Inquisition

The attitudes of Christians and Muslims toward each other, which eventually led to the Inquisition, have been the subjects of several works and numerous articles.[19] In the case of al-Andalus in particular, Christian-Muslim relations appear to have been congenial from the eighth century to the end of the eleventh century, when they began to deteriorate, becoming by degrees strained, intransigent, and intolerable as time went on. No serious attempts were made to improve them, and the result was the establishment in the fifteenth century of the Inquisition, which ended with the extermination and expulsion of a whole people in the name of religion.

In spite of the fact that Christianity and Islam share certain basic beliefs — the existence of one God, Creator of all things, Rewarder and Punisher on the Day of Judgment; a common tradition; and a similar moral code — they have been in conflict from the seventh century to the present. The hostility between the two religions, by virtue of its duration and consequences, makes the present-day struggle between communism and capitalism appear insignificant. The religious conflict has been perpetuated for centuries by both the pen and the sword. The underlying motivations have been not only religious but economic and political as well. As a result, it has engendered inflexible attitudes and an atmosphere of prejudice.

The Arab or Muslim has been and continues to be looked upon with disdain and ridicule. He is regarded as an inferior, incredulous, sensual, and backward human being. He is associated with the camel, the tent, and the turban, and in his best posture is seen as an obese and sensual man presiding over a crowded harem of appealing and obliging dancing girls. His religion is considered a farce allowing for much laxity, and at its best, it is thought to be a corruption of the Judeo-Christian doctrine promulgated by an ignorant and ambitious man.

This image of the Muslim or Arab and of his religion had been perpetuated by clerics, humanists, politicians, and even some modern scholars. There are historical and psychological reasons for its existence. Indeed, Islam has from the outset presented a threat to Christendom. It shook the very foundation of Christian polity at a critical moment in Christian history and wrested from it an enormous territory, thereby acquiring supremacy in the political, economic, social, and cultural fields during various centuries of the Middle Ages. It was, consequently, a natural reaction on the part of Christianity to oppose Islam by all the means at its disposal. Under the circumstances, facts were of no consequence and were often disfigured in order to show that whatever a Muslim did or thought was radically wrong. This feeling crystallized into a tradition that was perpetuated by apologists, and had its violent expression in the race for martyrdom in Spain, in the Crusades, and in the Spanish Inquisition.

In considering the attitudes of Christians toward Islam, one may make reference to Norman Daniel's invaluable work, *Islam and the West*. This scholar produces ample documentation showing Christians' negative attitudes toward Islam. He has shown that Christians could not conceive of the Qur'ān's being true or of Muḥammad as a prophet. Both the Qur'ān and Muḥammad were thought to represent forgery and falsehood at their best, the former being disorganized dicta lacking style and content,[20] and the latter having been, by generous account, a mere pseudo-prophet who could not lay claim to prophecy since he could not fulfill its requirements. Principally, Muḥammad's failings were said to include his inability to produce miracles, to bring out something new of the past, or to foretell something unknown in the present or the future. His claims to prophecy lie mainly in the fact that he was possessed by a devil, who excited people to sensual pursuits rather than to spiritual ones. Moreover, his life was far from meeting acceptable standards of behavior, let alone justifying a claim to prophecy. He was a low-born pagan with great ambition claiming revelation to suit his whims among ignorant nomads. At best, he was inspired by either a heretic Christian or a malicious Jew who claimed Muḥammad to be a man of vast learning, whereas in reality he was a mere magician. He became important only when he married a rich widow with whom he had lived in sin.[21]

This image of Islam and of its prophet is consistent enough to have been derived from a single source; it lasted up to the time of Alfonso X and continued unhampered in the following centuries. On the whole, the arguments, facts, and fictions used by Peter the Venerable, Peter Alfonso, Rodrigo Jiménez de Rada, Mark of Toledo, and St. Peter Pascual, among others, do not differ much from those used later by Alfonso X, whose views will presently be discussed.

As for Christian attitudes toward Islam in al-Andalus, one must look into the relationship between Christians and Muslims. This relationship underwent two main stages — one of peaceful coexistence and harmony and another of intolerance and persecution. As already pointed out, a remarkable accommodation between the two groups prevailed in al-Andalus from the eighth century through most of the eleventh century. This coexistence allowed for a great degree of acculturation. Christian kings, princes, and clerics emulated Muslims in their dress, customs, and institutions;[22] and Muslims did not feel inhibited to emulate Christians. The fusion of the two religious groups was so thorough that Africans were scandalized at the "hispanization" of Muslims in the same manner that Europeans were scandalized at the Islamization of Christians.[23] Even after the fall of Toledo, Muslims and Christians continued to live with a great measure of tolerance despite recurrent wars. Alfonso VI, the conqueror of Toledo, was the most powerful Christian ruler in the Peninsula and was able to exact tributes from Muslim rulers such as al-Mu'tamid, the proud and powerful king of Seville. It is significant to note that Alfonso VI himself had found refuge at the Muslim court of Toledo when he was defeated by his brother Sancho[24] in their struggle for the succession. Moreover, it was not uncommon at that time for Christians to serve in Muslim armies and vice versa. Alliances between Muslim and Christian states against a common enemy, Christian or Muslim, were often undertaken. That was the political reality in the country. Alfonso VI prided himself on the title of "king of the three religions" — Jewish, Christian and Muslim — and showed a great desire to emulate the skill and the know-how of the Muslims. He was assisted by the Mozarabs and by Jews and Muslims. The Cid, contrary to the myth surrounding him as an uncompromising national hero and emancipator, lived among and dealt with Muslims and even found refuge among them when he was exiled by his king, Alfonso VI. When he attained ascendancy with the conquest of Valencia, he showed a remarkable degree of tolerance for and understanding of the problems of his Muslim subjects. This policy of coexistence was continued by succeeding Christian rulers, in spite of pressure from the clergy, who incited their congregations to rise against Jews and Muslims in proof of their unshaken faith in Christianity.

On the other hand, the eleventh century witnessed a number of political, military, and social problems which came to have grave repercussions for both the religious attitudes and the social relations of Christians and Muslims. The roots of the trouble can be traced to a series of events following the year 1009, when a Muslim state represented by a stable central government ceased to exist in al-Andalus. Following revolts and chaos, the central government superseded by numerous petty states represented by the party-kings which rivaled one another and the emerging Christian states to the north. The situation was chaotic, and prompted the fourteenth-century thinker and statesman Ibn al-Khaṭib to look back critically at both the Muslim and the Christian leaders. To him the party-kings were cats claiming to be lions.

The Cid was the "enemy of God"[25] and did not spare the killing of children and women after the conquest of Valencia;[26] so was the "accursed tyrant" Alfonso VI.[27]

The Muslims began for the first time to lose ground to the Christian principalities to the north, and in the absence of a strong government they began to develop a strong religious consciousness. In the last quarter of the eleventh century the Muslim kingdoms not only became tributary states, but they were subjected to more exacting demands so that their existence became precarious. This situation coincided with the emergence of the Almoravids in North Africa. The religious scholars of al-Andalus, who had been relegated to oblivion under the party-kings, appealed to the religious sentiments of the people and prevailed on Muslim rulers to seek the help of the Almoravids in the name of Islam and to rescue their co-religionists from the hands of the Christian "infidels." This paved the way for the coming of the Almoravids and Almohads to al-Andalus, and for the appearance in al-Andalus of foreign Christian clerics who urged an all-out Crusade against Muslims. The African dynasties followed policies with intensely religious overtones that did great violence to the hitherto prevailing situation of tolerance and peaceful coexistence. The Christians were already responding in kind. "For the first time in Spanish history intolerance had appeared, but it is curious that it should have appeared almost simultaneously in both camps, being introduced by the Berber fanatics in the South and the Cluniac monks in the North."[28] The lives of both Jews and Christians (Mozarabs) were becoming vulnerable in Muslim territories, and their positions grew worse when the Almohad ruler 'Abd al-Mu'min decreed the expulsion of all Christians and Jews who refused to become Muslims.[29]

It was at this juncture in the twelfth century that Spain became the pawn of international pressure. Neighboring Christian rulers and the Papacy were encouraged by the astonishing success of the First Crusade, and became fully committed to fight the infidels. It became Church policy not to have any compromises with the Muslims of al-Andalus. When a town was conquered, the Church insisted that all properties be confiscated and the inhabitants be put to death or taken captive.[30] This policy found acceptance at the Third Lateran Council (1177), which also prohibited Christians from having any sort of contact with Muslims. Similarly, the Fourth Lateran Council (1215) decreed, among other things, that Jews and Muslims wear special garments to distinguish them from Christians.[31]

Although Spanish rulers did not always find it expedient and practical to implement Church policies, Christian clerics aroused popular sentiments and writers attacked Islam and Muslims at the intellectual level. Their aim was to discredit everything Muslim. Peter Alfonso, a translator and a man of great learning in the sciences of the Muslims, was a convert from Judaism to Christianity. In two of his treatises, he attacked Islam and Judaism with all the zeal of a convert.[32] Peter the Venerable visited Spain in 1142 and commissioned various individuals to translate the Qur'ān for the purpose of attacking Islam from within. In fact, he wrote a book on "Islamic heresy."[33] Rodrigo Jiménez de Rada (1176–1247), the Bishop of Toledo, gained the favor of Alfonso VIII. In his *Historia Arabum*[34] he included the life of Muḥammad and the history of Islam. He also wrote *Historia Gothica*, in which he emphasized the past greatness of the Visigoths in the same manner as Alfonso X had in his *Crónica general*.[35] These authors were followed by Mark of Toledo, who translated the Qur'ān to prove that it was not in agreement with the Old and New Testaments. Later Peter Pascual (d. 1300) stated that Muḥammad was possessed by the devil,[36] and that the Qur'ān was a hodge-podge of contradictions, lies, and fables.[37]

But the most relevant and significant views on Islam are those of Alfonso X (1252–1284), a king and scholar, who "enjoyed being in the company of Muslim scholars but never realized the aspiration of the Muslim inhabitants for justice."[38] Before assuming the throne, Alfonso X was in intimate contact with Muslims, first as governor of Murcia and later as a King who surrounded himself with Muslim savants. He knew the plight of the Mudéjares, but the pressure of the clergy must have been so great that he ignored their suffering. In fact, like his immediate predecessors and contemporaries he gave serious consideration to the expulsion of the Moors.[39] This was not feasible at the time, but Alfonso remained faithful to the policies of his father, Ferdinand III (1217–1252), who introduced, at the urging of his wife, the practice of burning those accused of heresy. Moreover, Alfonso articulated his feelings and attitudes toward Islam in a manner reflecting thirteenth-century prejudices.

Alfonso X, like some of his Spanish predecessors, arrogated to himself the title of "king of the three religions" — Christian, Islamic and Jewish. But this attitude owed its raison d'être, perhaps, more to political realities in thirteenth-century Spain than to a change of attitude toward non-Christians. Actually, he was a fervent and devout Christian who could find no merit in any religion other than Christianity. In his *Crónica general de España*, Alfonso X faithfully reflects the Christian attitude toward Islam, an unbending and negative attitude toward anything "mohametano." He discusses all conquerors of Spain — Greeks, Carthaginians, Romans, Germans, Vandals, Alans — without much praise or condemnation.[40] But when he writes of the Visigoths and the Arabs he relates in polemical language and pious laments how the devil inflicted the powerful, religious, and peaceful Visigoths with all calamities; and how their noble kingdom, "devoto en religion," "claro et limpio por ell ensenamiento de los concilios"[41] fell when King Roderick opened the charmed palace, thereby violating the secret of a sacred palace and thus serving as an omen of the Muslim invasion.[42] Alfonso X narrated the ominous situation of the Visigoths in the following manner:

The devil, who is the enemy of humanity and in whose envy there always remained the search for doing it harm, sowed the evil and black seed in the kingdom of Spain, and caused pride in the powerful; laziness and negligence in the religious men; discord among those who had enjoyed peace and love; luxury and great lust among the rich and the well-to-do; complete indifference among the wise and people of understanding; to such an extent that he made the bishops and the clerics like vile men of the people, and kings and princes like thieves. It was in this manner, as we have said, that the kingdom of the Goths of Spain was destroyed, a kingdom that was great and large, so great that its dominion lasted long and stretched from sea to sea, to the city of Tangier in Africa to the Rhône River.[43]

He went on to praise the glorious past of the Visigoths and to lament that such a noble, rich, powerful, and honorable kingdom could be overthrown, destroyed by internal vicissitudes at the hands of "moros," those vile, cruel, deceitful people, whose knights are "more cruel and dangerous than a wolf among sheep at night":

All the Moorish soldiers were dressed with silk and black wool that had been forcibly acquired; the reins of their horses were like fire; their black faces were like pitch and the most handsome of them was like a cooking pan; thus, their eyes shone like flames; their horses fast as leopards and their knights were more cruel and more harmful than a wolf in the midst of a herd of lambs at night. The vile people of Africa, who were not used to kindness and all of whose deeds were accomplished with tricks and deceits and who were not used to protect but to exploit great riches, are now exalted . . . "Poor Spain. Your death was so afflicted that none remained to lament you in your dire suffering, for you are [considered] more dead than alive."[44]

That was not all. The conquest of Spain by the Arabs presaged horror, pillage, destruction, and slavery:

Here the sanctity and the religion of bishops and priests came to an end; here the bounty of clerics who served the churches diminished and came to a standstill; here the understanding of prelates and people of order perished; here the teachings of the law and of the Holy Faith died. Fathers and lords all perished as one; the sanctuaries were destroyed, the churches crushed; the places in which God was eulogized with gaiety are now abused and ill treated; the crosses and the altars were thrown out of churches; the charism, books, and all things in honor of Christianity were put to bad use and made the object of amusement; all festivals and religious ceremonies were forgotten; all reverence for the saints and beauty of the church were turned into ugliness and vileness; the churches and the towers from which God used to be praised are now a place of confession [of Islam] and a call to Muḥammad; the ecclesiastical robes, the chalices and other vases of the sanctuaries were put to bad use and defiled by infidels.

The enemies put to waste all the land; destroyed things; killed men; destroyed cities, trees, vineyards; and cut down all that they found green. This pestilence and this menace were pushed to such a point that neither a good village, nor a city remained with a bishop. They were either burned, or demolished, or retained by the Moors. As for the cities which the Arabs could not conquer, they were taken through deceit and false pacts."[45]

With this sweeping condemnation and exaggeration, it is evident that Alfonso X had no regard for facts or historical truth in spite of his admiration for Arabic culture. He was intent on discrediting the Arabs at any cost. He completely ignored almost five centuries of Arabic contributions to the artistic and intellectual life of Spain. Instead, he took up the sensitive subject of the life of Muḥammad, intentionally weaving facts and fiction into a maze of falsehood and hatred. Although he knew a great deal about Arabic sources, he seems deliberately not to have used them, precisely so that he could present a distorted picture of Islam and its founder drawn from his Christian predecessors. It is a strange biography of Muḥammad, and must have been written not for the enlightened individuals of the day but for the credulous and uncultured pious. His account can be paraphrased as follows:

Muḥammad was born in 580[46] at a time when there was a drought and an inflation in Arabia that obliged many people to eat grass and roots, and when the Arabs as well as the people of Africa were torn between Judaism, Christianity, and Arianism. The coming of Muḥammad was foretold to his father ʻAbdallah and his mother Amīnah by a Jewish astrologer, who said that the boy was going to be a vigorous, exalted, and powerful man as a king and lawmaker.[47] His father ʻAbdallah went to Jerusalem and died after Muḥammad's birth;[48] he was buried in Yathrib (Medina).

At the age of four, according to the Jewish astrologer, the angels took

Muḥammad's heart out, divided it, and took out a black clot of blood; they cleaned it, weighed it against ten hearts, then against one thousand hearts, but the heart of Muḥammad weighed more than all of them. This prompted an angel to say that if it were put against all the hearts of Arabia, it would weigh more. Alfonso remarks that all these events were lies of the Jewish astrologer, who even said that these were the words of the Archangel Gabriel.

When Muḥammad was eight years old, he began to study the natural sciences and the laws of Christians and Jews. He borrowed a great deal from them and added to his horrible sect which he established for the perdition of those who came to believe in it.[49]

At the age of thirteen, his uncle Abū Ṭālib took him to Jerusalem. Upon his return, he entered in the midst of inflation into the service of a widow, a relative of his by the name Hadaya,[50] and at the age of twenty-five, he entered into the service of Queen Khadījah ("reina Cadiga") when he was already well versed in the art of magic ("muy sabidor en las artes a que llaman magicas"). He became a merchant and made trips to Egypt and Palestine with the Monk Juan, a heretic from whom he learned many things about the old and the new laws (testaments) so well as to be able to defend himself against Christians and Jews. All that he learned from the monk was against God and the law in the manner of heresy.[51] It is from this moment on that he began to confide in Khadījah that he was the expected Messiah of the Jews. Jews as well as Arabs believed in him and marveled at his deeds and sayings. But in his preaching he deceitfully made new laws on the basis of the old and new testaments; thus managing in this way to destroy the Law of Our Lord God ("la ley de Nuestro Señor Dios").[52]

For the Moors, Muḥammad's commandments constitute the law of God ("ley de Dios"), and he himself is the messenger of God ("mandadero de Dios"). It was when he had many adherents that Khadījah married him and he became rich and powerful, king and lord of the earth.[53]

Supposed attacks of epilepsy worried Khadījah a great deal until she was assured by Muḥammad that that was not a malady but visitations from the Archangel Gabriel.

It was in this manner that he continued his preaching by means of charms and magical tricks and helped by the devil, who guided him to make miracles and who penetrated into him and made him foretell the future.[54]

Muḥammad began to preach his evil sect ("su mala secta") in Spain,[55] but the devil warned him of the arrival of the men of St. Isodore against him, and he had to flee the Peninsula. However, he continued to preach in Africa and Arabia, confusing and deceiving many people.

Muḥammad made a journey to Jerusalem on a winged beast. There he met Abraham, Moses, and Jesus, who had gone to say their prayers. The assension of Muḥammad (*mi'rāj*) to Seventh Heaven is described in some detail, conforming in many respects to Muslim tradition. Muḥammad was directed by the Archangel Gabriel to the first heaven, where he was received by other angels. In the second heaven he met Jesus and St. John; in the third, Joseph, who appeared like a full moon; in the fourth, Arobo;[56] in the fifth, Aaron; in the sixth, Moses; and in the seventh, Abraham. In Paradise proper, there was a beautiful girl. Finally, Muḥammad is found in the presence of God, who demanded from Muḥammad that his followers should recite fifty prayers a day; but in view of the excessive number, Muḥammad sought the help of Moses, who asked that the prayer be reduced to five a day.[57]

Muḥammad began his preaching at the age of forty-eight — that is, nine years after he had been elevated to king.[58]

He preached that he who killed his enemies would go directly to heaven, a place where there is delicious food and where there are three rivers: one of wine, a second of honey, and a third of milk. In addition, there are virgins.[59] He preached many a lie and said many other false things making believe that the Archangel Gabriel had communicated them to him. The truth of the matter was that he imposed himself on the people of Mecca, who worshiped many idols. From this moment on he began to preach his doctrine openly by inciting people against the faith of Christ.[60] From all this, he gave them laws and commandments [Ar. *Sūras*, Sp. *Zoharas*], which came to constitute what they call *alcoran*. And how many a falsehood he wrote in those *Zoharas*! It is shameful to say or hear it, let alone to follow it. Those unhappy people, inebriated by the devil and sedated by the sin of lechery, accepted those *Zoharas*. Even today, they firmly adhere to them and are unwilling to embrace the true Faith, or the law of God and his teachings.[61]

When Muḥammad died, his resurrection was expected within three days; but the expectation was in vain. After eleven days, his body was found eaten by dogs. Thus ends the story of Muḥammad. That year the earth trembled, and a sign appeared in heaven in the form of a sword for thirty days, which indicated the lordship the Moors were going to have.[62]

It is evident that Alfonso X revealed a more deeply rooted attitude toward Islam and its founder rather than earnest search for historical truth. One would expect him as the "king of the three religions" to understand or to show some tolerance for a religion which was still flourishing on Spanish soil, but this is perhaps too much to expect in view of the fact that Islam and Christianity fought each other in long and bloody wars, engendering great bitterness and hatred. Moreover, as a leader of the Reconquista with which he had little success, he would feel doubly bitter against Islam. However, it would be erroneous to attribute his bitterness either to this fact alone or to his own prejudice. One has to go back to the unbroken tradition of prejudice which was tantamount to an article of faith for a good Christian. Such a man was, without a doubt, convinced of the superiority of his religion, just as the Muslim was convinced of the superiority of his. Thus the religious question remained essentially a matter of disposition and faith, with little or no concern whether one or the other should have validity or claim to the truth. Consequently, both Christianity and Islam remained vulnerable to attacks and the objects of vituperation and prejudice. This religious question has remained unresolved. Consequently, it would be quite harsh to put the blame on an Alfonso, who was a man of his age.

In sum, when the Almoravids and Almohads disappeared, they left behind a bitter religious legacy and acute political chaos. Territories once held by them fell into Christian hands. An exception was the small kingdom of Granada, which continued its vulnerable existence for more than two centuries. On the whole, Muslims and Jews were left defenseless and without any viable organization. However, their skills in various crafts and professions allowed them to play an important role in the economic life of the country and to occupy a prominent place in society. This advantageous position came under attack from the Church and avaricious fortune seekers who made it their business to exploit these non-Christians in the name of Jesus Christ. Non-Christians were deprived of the opportunity for advancement and were subjected to all sorts of harassments including forced conversion.

Relations between Christians and Muslims not only deteriorated but reached an alarming state of tension during the thirteenth century. At first, the Mozarabs and Mudéjares, the most skilled elements in society, suffered the brunt of the situation. Both groups had to live in a hostile environment, whether under Christian or Muslim rule.[63] The Mozarabs back under Christian rule were suspect by their fellow-Christians for their Arab customs and habits, although their skills and financial status may also have engendered great resentment. The Mudéjares and Jews were also resented by virtue of their status in addition to their affiliation with Islam and Judaism, respectively.

While the Mozarabs managed in time to survive the onslaught of their co-religionists, the Mudéjares and the Jews remained the object of intolerance and were subjected to stringent measures, violent outbursts, and forced conversion. Even those who adopted Christianity were not free from harassment. The clergy openly attacked Islam, pressed the courts for repressive measures against Muslims and Jews, and demanded their conversion to Christianity. In 1391, a cleric in Seville urged people to destroy the Jews as an act of their faith in Christianity. This coincided with anti-Jewish riots in Castile and Aragón, but this time the Muslims were spared because the

Christians feared reprisal. However, the Muslims were required to pay taxes on their mosques and often were forbidden to conduct prayers in public.

The fifteenth century intensified religious intolerance. John II (1406–1454) made a great display of his fanaticism. This was relaxed by his successor, Henry IV (1404–1474), who was then accused of having committed an unpardonable crime.[64] The fanaticism was unrelenting: Muslims and Jews were forced either to adopt Christianity or to emigrate — mainly to Granada, which remained the only Muslim place of refuge until it fell into Christian hands in 1492.

The reign of Fernando V (1452–1516) and Isabella (1451–1504) began a new phase of a systematic persecution, forced conversion, and expulsion. Ironically, conversion to Christianity, which was the aim of Christian rulers, often proved inadequate. To deal with the problem of converts and the eradication of heresy, the clergy insisted on the establishment of the Inquisition, authorized in 1478 and implemented two years later. Anyone baptized willingly or forcibly fell under its jurisdiction, which soon broadened to include all sorts of crimes. Converts were always suspect and considered a threat to religious unity.[65] A person could be apprehended on the slightest pretext and was considered guilty until proved innocent, a difficult task under the procedure of the Inquisition. Arrests were made without due process and were accompanied with the confiscation of the victims' property in order to defray the costs of the trial.[66] A confession of guilt or innocence was accepted only if accompanied by a list of the unfaithful acquaintances of the accused, including members of his immediate family. The victim was entirely at the mercy of the Inquisition — "the inquisitors were both judge and jury, both prosecution and defense, and the prisoner's fate depended entirely on the mood and character of the inquisitors."[67]

The Inquisition had a free hand after the fall of Granada in 1492, which presaged many ominous things to come. For one thing, Isabella issued an edict in 1492 which required that all Jews be expelled and their valuable belongings be left behind. Next came the turn of the Muslims who, henceforth, were designated Moriscos. In spite of the fact that Fernando and Isabella pledged themselves to uphold the rights of the Muslims to practice their religion, to continue the use of their language and customs, and to receive protection of life and property, such pledges were soon disregarded on the insistence of Cardinal Jiménez de Cisneros, who argued that a contract with Muslims was not binding on a Christian. In 1498 the Cardinal went to Granada and compelled many Muslims to take the sacrament of baptism and to accept Christianity as the true faith. This harsh measure was opposed by Fr. Hernando de Talavera, who hoped to achieve the same end through preaching, education, and persuasion, but Cardinal Jiménez prevailed. In one day, some three thousand persons were forced to take the sacrament of baptism. This action led to a revolt and the Crown quickly declared that the Muslims had forfeited all their rights and gave them a choice of baptism or expulsion. "The last Muslims of Spain, insofar as they failed to emigrate, were conducted by the Inquisition into the bosom of the one and only saving Church without heed to the terms of surrender."[68] Many accepted baptism and, in this way, fell under the jurisdiction of the Church, which now could try them on heresy charges carrying stiff penalties, imprisonment, confiscation of property, expulsion, or the death penalty.

This policy was implemented everywhere in the Peninsula. Mosques were closed and converted into churches. Arabic was forbidden, and Arabic manuscripts were committed to fire. Charles I (1516–1556), after pledging to respect the rights of Muslims, asked the Pope to release him from his sworn oath. In 1526, he issued an edict prohibiting Muslims from using their language, dress, and family names. His successor Philip II (1556–1596) forbade Muslims to purchase or possess slaves, enforced Charles's decree of 1526, and added an edict of his own in 1568 requiring the registration of children between the ages of three and fifteen with a view of educating them in the Christian faith. Revolts followed in Granada, but these resulted in expulsion and wholesale confiscation of property. The end was near when the clergy persuaded Philip III (1598–1621), a weak ruler, to banish all the Moors from his kingdom on religious grounds and on the allegation that they were cooperating with the Turks.[69] On September 22, 1609, an edict for expulsion of the Moors was proclaimed and was carried out in less than five years. The last Moors, some five hundred thousand, were ordered to leave their native land with no hope of return. This settled the Moorish problem once and for all, but it also deprived Spain of a great human resource that adversely affected its future history.

7

Society and Administration

THE division of Andalusian society into religious and ethnic groups adversely affected social integration. Consequently, Andalusian society remained heterogeneous and discordant and was often beset by grave troubles in which religion and/or ethnic association provided the main lines of cleavage.

In theory, Islam recognized the equality of all adherents regardless of ethnic origin or social station. In practice, however, differences were common, arising mainly from economic and political factors. *Muwalladūn*, Berbers, and other groups felt they were not getting their due as prescribed by the ideas of Islam; they often rose in open revolt against the ruling class.

It should be emphasized, however, that Andalusian society was flexible and open. A man of humble station, whether Muslim or non-Muslim, could climb the social ladder and occupy any high position except that of supreme ruler. Moreover, the various social groups were united in language and culture — the two major elements in a common national identity. But this did not prevent social inequality, tension, and recurrent revolts whenever there was a political vacuum. Economic and social factors also contributed to restiveness. In this connection, one may distinguish the following groups according to their position in the social pyramid:[1] nobility (*al-khāṣṣah*), the masses (*al-ʻāmmah*), and the slaves.

From 711 to 1031, an Arab elite whose blood had become diluted through mixture and intermarriage held the peak of the social pyramid. This group represented the dynasty from which the supreme ruler and other high officials were drawn. Known as Qurayshites, or Umayyads, they received ample pensions (*rizq*) and were given large estates (*qaṭā'i'*). Under the emirate, there were five important families which held key positions as governors of provinces, commanders of the army, judges, viziers, and so on. In the course of time, however, many of these posts were filled by non-Arabs who, through ability and wealth, succeeded in moving up the social ladder and becoming an integral part of the nobility (*ahl al-khāṣṣah*). By and large, they lived in cities and received their incomes from the court and from their estates.

With the downfall of the Umayyad dynasty, this Arab aristocracy was soon replaced by a number of lesser aristocracies consisting of Berbers, *Ṣaqālibah*, and others who forged petty states for themselves. After the eleventh century, the Berbers became the predominant element in society. However, they soon lost their influential position to the Christians, who eventually managed to gain full control of the destiny of al-Andalus.

The masses constituted the bulk of population and included the middle and lower classes. They were the mainstay of society. To them belonged the crafts, commerce, agriculture, and all the minor civil posts. They were made up of heterogeneous elements — Arabs, Berbers, Mozarabs, and Jews. The last two groups inhabited their own quarters, but they moved freely for business and social intercourse. A prosperous segment, or a middle class, lived in comfortable homes, whereas others merely subsisted. Ibn 'Abdūn[2] and Ibn al-Ra'ūf[3] give us a glimpse of the many civil service employees, tradesmen, and craftsmen during the eleventh and twelfth centuries in Seville. There were wardens, gatekeepers, caretakers of mosques and public buildings, street cleaners, garbage collectors, bakers, perfumers, wheat dealers, butchers, cooks, fishermen, and traders of figs, oil, perfume, linen, milk, cheese, meat, fruit and vegetables, leathers, furs, and other products. Moreover, both Ibn 'Abdūn and Ibn al-Ra'ūf mention a set of regulations regarding the function of each guild and the quality of each commodity.

In view of the scanty information available, one cannot be sure of the composition of the rural population.[4] One may assume, however, that it was more homogeneous than that of cities, grouped along ethnic or religious lines. Although many probably had their own land, the rest worked for absentee landlords on a share-cropping basis which may have amounted to between 25 per cent and 50 per cent. The recurrent revolts and instability in the countryside made their lives insecure — a situation that must have prompted many to settle in large towns where they could engage in menial labor. This may partly explain the frequent famines and economic troubles in al-Andalus.

In ancient and medieval times, slavery was a common and flourishing business. Islam condoned the institution, though manumission was considered an act pleasing to God. Al-Andalus had many slave markets and a large number of individuals who prospered through slave trade. Slaves were often victims of war, but they were also sought throughout the Mediterranean region by specialized merchants who knew the market demands for human chattel. The slaves included blacks from the Sudan and other parts of Africa and Christians from Spain and elsewhere in western and eastern Europe. The aristocracy and the well to do had a large number of slaves of both sexes. They used them for domestic help, menial labor, and so forth. For instance, some male *Ṣaqālibah* were castrated to become eunuchs in the caliphs' harems, and others served as guards in the palace. Female *Ṣaqālibah* with fair skin and blue eyes were eagerly sought as concubines. The price could be very high, depending upon a girl's talents as dancer or singer and upon her physique. A female had a better chance of being declared free, especially after she bore children. The freed woman was thus called "the mother of the son" (*umm al-walad*).

Social Life

Medieval literature, which was essentially aristocratic, reflects the mode of thinking, the taste, and way of life of an elite. Little is known about the manner in which the average and poor citizen lived. Andalusian nobility and the rich lived in refinement and luxury. They enjoyed an urban life, taking pleasure in sumptuous palaces, mansions, gardens, country houses, and public baths. In the tenth century, Cordova was, perhaps, the most cosmopolitan and sophisticated city in the Muslim world and Europe. It served as a model for building and fashion. There was the great mosque of Cordova and a number of splendid palaces, such as al-Zahrā' built by 'Abd al-Raḥmān III and al-Zāhirah built by Ibn Abī 'Āmir. According to al-Maqqarī[5] Cordova had under Ibn Abī 'Āmir in the tenth century some 1,600 mosques; 900 public baths; 213,077 homes for the general populace; 60,300 mansions for notables, viziers, secretaries, army commanders, and other high officials; and 80,455 shops. One is inclined to doubt these figures, since they suggest that Cordova would have had, by conservative estimate, more than one million inhabitants. However exaggerated they may be, these figures give us an idea of the high development and vigor of urban life under Muslim rule. In fact, each city came to excel in some area. Cordova was famous for its libraries and books; Málaga for its songs; and Seville for its musical instruments — lute, *qanūn*, rebec, drums, which were most common for a musical ensemble.

Ordinarily, the homes of the wealthy had two stories, gardens, and running water. It was fashionable to include an ample room for a library.[6] Men of means had also their country houses (*munyah*) which were located in the suburbs or the countryside. The government palaces resembled self-contained cities. They provided not only government offices and ample sleeping quarters but also storage for large amounts of food, clothing, and furniture. In addition, they contained recreation areas and gardens with many beautiful flowers and fruit trees.

To this may be added a great refinement in personal care. There was a wide selection of clothes and jewels for men and women. Cleanliness was a daily practice maintained in private baths for the wealthy households or in public baths which were a major feature in every city. These public baths were well managed, and each had several attendants. Ordinarily, they were accessible to women in the morning and to men at noon.[7]

The Andalusians enjoyed indoor and outdoor pastimes. In their homes the ruling class and the well-to-do had literary salons (*majlis*, pl. *majālis*), to which men of letters and boon-companions gathered for serious literary discussions and/or lighthearted pursuits such as drinking wine, listening to music and singing,[8] watching dancing girls, or playing chess and backgammon.[9] Although these pleasurable entertainments were frowned upon by the jurists and religious scholars, they were so widely pursued that the judges could hardly penalize a musician, wine drinker, or other violator.

This was equally true of popular outdoor sports, such as hunting[10] and polo. Many of the rulers were so fascinated with these sports that the religious scholars grudgingly accepted them. Horse racing, marksmanship, and animal fighting were not uncommon.[11]

Finally, some remarks should be made about the status of women in al-Andalus. In theory, a woman was subjected to the traditional restrictions imposed on her by religion and Islamic custom: inequality with men and limited freedom of movement and social intercourse. For instance, Andalusian propriety required that women should not be allowed to walk alone, to follow a funeral, or to visit cemeteries;[12] they should be kept whenever possible from the company of men at weddings and other gatherings unless accompanied.[13] They should not wash in streamlets or sit at the edge of a *wādi* (river), for they would provoke men;[14] they should not be jailed with men, and their warden should be old and married.[15] Moreover, women should not enter churches because of the corruption attributed to priests, who were said often to cohabit with more than one woman.[16]

In practice, however, Andalusian women seemed to have enjoyed a great deal of freedom, as attested to by their poetry and biographies. They seemed to have circulated freely in the streets and to have enjoyed all sorts of gatherings. It would seem that women had more freedom in al-Andalus than in the eastern part of the Muslim world. Significant too is the fact that when a Muslim in al-Andalus married a Christian woman, she often was allowed to continue practicing her religion. A great number of rulers were quite submissive to their wives or concubines, who often displayed an independent attitude and whimsical behavior. Vast numbers of poems were composed in their names exalting their beauty and good qualities. The emir al-Ḥakam I composed a poem to his five rebellious concubines and became overjoyed when he was reconciled with them. ʿAbd al-Raḥmān II showered his wife Ṭarūb with expensive and precious gifts and composed numerous verses in her name. The great poet-king al-Muʿtamid showed a great deal of submissiveness to the whims and arbitrary demands of his beloved Iʿtimād. Wallādah (d. 1091), daughter of the caliph al-Mustakfī, was an able poetess. She had a salon frequented by the leading talents of the day. She had a complete disregard for the veil and circulated freely among the high circles of eleventh-century Cordova. She frequently met her lover Ibn Zaydūn at night in the beautiful gardens of Cordova, exchanged pleasantries until dawn, and often partook wine with him.[17]

Other interesting glimpses about Andalusian women may be gained from the famous *Dove's Ring*,[18] a valuable treatise on love by the prolific Ibn Ḥazm. In Chapter 5, dealing with love at first sight, Ibn Ḥazm refers to the gathering of women at the Gate of Perfumers in Cordova. One day, the poet al-Ramādī saw a slave girl (*jāriyah*) who took possession of his heart and love. He followed her, succeeded in engaging her in a conversation, and set a rendezvous for Friday at the Gate of the Perfumers.[19] Lovers corresponded extensively,[20] making use of male or female messengers.[21] In addition, lovers frequently visited each other.[22]

In conclusion, the status and role of women varied according to the social pyramid. Women of the low class (*ʿāmmah*) were not inhibited by social stricture. They performed numerous domestic duties and helped support the family. It was among the wealthy class and aristocracy that the status of women was complicated by economic and social considerations and by the taste and proclivity of the husband. A woman may have been quite submissive to her husband, thus conforming to legislation favoring the male, or quite independent and inventive, thereby subverting the law and the social mores. In the latter case, she appeared as a towering figure exerting great influence on her husband, including a decisive role in politics. This notwithstanding, she did not attempt to encroach on the freedom of her husband to have a multiplicity of wives and concubines. In fact, she seemed to resign herself to a life of competition in the harem, and to the expectation of becoming the favorite wife. In this way, she would become the prima donna of the harem and would be served by an array of servants (*jawārī al-khidmah*). There were many gifted women who excelled in dancing, singing, and poetry. Their talents were highly appreciated for pleasurable purposes (*ladhdhah*) or for more serious pursuits. They were the object of love and a source of inspiration for an enormous quantity of tender lyrical poetry.

Administration

From 711 to 750 al-Andalus constituted an integral part of the Islamic Empire with its capital at Damascus. Administratively, al-Andalus was part of the province of the Maghrib, ruled from the city of Qayrawān in present-day Tunisia. Its governor was appointed by either the caliph in Damascus or the governor of the Maghrib, but in time of crisis he was also elected by the Andalusians themselves.

As for the internal administration of al-Andalus, the Arabs, like the Church and the Visigoths before them, adopted the existing administration, which was traceable to the Romans. The Arabs had done the same in the East by adopting Sāsānid and Byzantine institutions, which were eventually arabized.

Al-Andalus was divided into three main districts: central, eastern and western. The central district included the cities of Cordova, Granada, Málaga, Almería, Jaén and Toledo.[23] In the western district were Seville, Jeréz, Gibraltar, Tarifa, Beja, Badajoz, Mérida, Lisbon, and Silves.[24] In the eastern district were Saragossa, Valencia, Murcia, Cartagena, and Albarracín.[25] These three main divisions were subdivided into provinces, to each of which a governor (*wālī*) was appointed by the governor of al-Andalus and by the emir or caliph under the Umayyads. Although we do not possess an exact account of the number of provinces,[26] one can distinguish some twenty or more which were designated by the name of a city or region. Each province (*kūrah*) had its capital (*ḥaḍrah*) where the governor resided. In addition to the provinces there were three regions known as the Marches (*thughūr*). The High, Middle, and Low Marches extended from Saragossa to Toledo. They were zones of war, ordinarily governed by a military commander (*qā'id*) whose troops were in constant readiness against Christian intrusions from the north.

By and large, the provincial administration was patterned after the central government in Cordova and remained essentially the same under the party-kings, the Almoravids, and the Almohads. Under the Umayyads, the governor was appointed for an unspecified time. More often than not he would assume independent jurisdiction, especially at the death of one ruler and the inauguration of a new one. To regain control the ruler frequently resorted to force.

For a while the capital of al-Andalus was Seville, but soon after the conquest it was moved to Cordova, where it remained until the fall of the Umayyad dynasty in 1031. For a long time Cordova was both the political and intellectual center of al-Andalus. Al-Maqqarī[27] said that it had no equal on earth, not even the city of Baghdād; he quoted Ibn Sa'īd al-Ḥijārī as saying, "Its relation to al-Andalus is like that of the head to the body."[28] Cordova was famous for four things: the sciences, the Umayyad Mosque, al-Zahrā' palace, and al-Zāhirah palace.[29] It became the model for all the provincial capitals, which even came to surpass it in splendor under the party-kings and afterward.

From 711 to 750, the government of al-Andalus was vested in the hands of a military commander appointed by the viceroys in Qayrawān who were themselves appointed by the caliph of Damascus. These governors controlled army and civil affairs and were directly responsible to the caliph. After the fall of the Umayyad dynasty in 750, al-Andalus was ruled by local governors in the midst of contention and political upheaval. With the advent of 'Abd al-Raḥmān I in 756, al-Andalus became politically independent from the Muslim East. Nevertheless, the Andalusians looked to the East as a model. This was evident not only in the adoption of Arabic names for public offices but also in the structure of the official hierarchy. The country was ruled by the Umayyad dynasty until 1031. Until 929, the Umayyad rulers assumed the title of emir in spite of the fact that their ancestors had been overthrown by the ʻAbbāsids. During this period, they were content to refer to themselves as the "sons of caliphs" or "emirs," and not as caliphs, which would imply sovereignty over the whole Islamic community. This conformed to the political reality of the day, since the ʻAbbāsids actually remained supreme over a large area of the Muslim world. With the decline of the ʻAbbāsids in the tenth century and the emergence of the Shiʻite Fāṭimid dynasty in North Africa, the Umayyads of Spain under ʻAbd al-Raḥmān III felt justified in assuming the title of caliph — though in practice their power did not extend much beyond the Peninsula.

Like his counterpart in the East, the emir or caliph had absolute power over his subjects. He was the temporal and spiritual ruler: the *imām* or leader of prayer on Friday and commander in chief of the army on military expeditions. He delegated his power to whom he wished; he appointed and dismissed his functionaries at will. He coined money in his own name. From the tenth century onward he adopted sonorous titles (*laqāb*). His inauguration was attended by great pomposity; an oath of allegiance was rendered to him first by the nobility and high functionaries and afterward by the masses. His name was expected to be mentioned throughout al-Andalus in the Friday sermon (*khuṭbah*).

Whether under the emirate or the caliphate, the Umayyad rulers nominated their successors during their own lifetime. Their criteria for the nominee were as inconsistent as those in the East.[30] By and large, a son or relative was appointed to the throne after the incumbent's death, but the heir apparent (*walī-l-ʻahd*) more often than not had to earn his throne on the battlefield against contending members of the ruling family. The unrest and uncertainty of this situation constituted one of the major factors that led to the decline and ultimate fall of the dynasty.

The Umayyad rulers constantly strove for strong central government, but the actual degree of centralization always depended on the ability and determination of the individual ruler. ʻAbd al-Raḥmān III had full control of al-Andalus. However, after his death power was arrogated almost solely by the chamberlain (*ḥājib*), who made the major decisions on behalf of the caliph. After the great *fitnah* (civil war) of 1009, chaos prevailed in al-Andalus, and a viable central government hardly existed. Revolt followed revolt, and a number of caliphs emerged but were ineffectual and always captives of military commanders and princes.

During the breakdown of Umayyad power and the subsequent downfall of the dynasty in 1031, governors of provinces and commanders of the army forged for themselves a number of principalities. These rulers, known as party-kings, held authority from about 1009 to 1091; they emulated the Umayyads of Cordova in every respect and arrogated to themselves the role of caliphs. They adopted sonorous titles, nominated their successors, and surrounded themselves with all sorts of bureaucrats: secretaries, viziers, judges, military commanders, eunuchs, literati, and others. Soon after 1091, the Almoravids, followed by the Almohads, governed al-Andalus from Marrākush. They appointed their relatives or commanders of the army to govern the various provinces of al-Andalus. Their administration remained essentially the same as it had been under the Umayyads, but began to lose its Arabic character with the advance of the Reconquest.

Under both the Umayyads and subsequent dynasties, the ruler relied on many individuals for the administration of his domain.[31] Important among them were the following officials:

The *ḥājib* (chamberlain) was the most influential figure at the court. He was the intermediary between the ruler, on the one hand, and the rest of the courtiers and people, on the other. His functions were similar to those of the vizier in the East.[32] He executed the ruler's orders and often made decisions and formulated policies for him. Furthermore, he was in charge of the central administration, public security, and military and provincial affairs,[33] and he presided over the council of functionaries. His power was enormous since he oversaw all branches of administration: foreign relations, justice, finance, provision and equipment of troops, and so on. Al-Ḥakam II delegated most of his powers to his *ḥājib*, al-Muṣḥafī. This powerful chamberlain was succeeded by Ibn Abī 'Āmir who ruled al-Andalus under the title of *ḥājib*, and was assisted by a number of viziers.[34]

The vizier[35] was a secondary figure accountable to the chamberlain. There were a number of viziers, each of whom had under his control one branch of administration: finance, foreign relations, justice, etc. They formed a council over which the emir and/or the *ḥājib* presided. The title of vizier soon became honorary and was assumed by military commanders and other individuals.[36] However, the office of the vizirate developed in time and seems to have overshadowed the post of *ḥājib*. It took on a dual character and was conferred upon people who were both good administrators and erudite, hence their appelation of "Holder of the Two Vizirates" (*dhū-l-wizāratayn*).[37]

The secretary (*kātib*)[38] was an important official. There were several secretaries, each in charge of a specific function. The two most important were the secretary of correspondence (*kātib al-rasā'il*), who excelled in the epistolary art and drafted and wrote official documents, and the secretary of finance (*kātib al-dhimām*), who took charge of budgetary matters and accounting, with particular concern for the affairs of Christians and Jews. ". . . so long as this [latter] office subsisted in al-Andalus and in the Maghrib no Christian or Jew ever needed the protection and assistance of the great and powerful."[39]

The postmaster (*ṣāḥib al-barīd*)[40] held a very important, sensitive post concerned not only with the distribution of mail but also with gathering intelligence about the state of affairs in the provinces.

The treasurer (*khāzin al-māl*) took care of the caliph's coffers and supervised tax revenue from the provinces.

A judge (*qāḍī*)[41] was an appointee of the ruler. He was known at first as *qāḍī al-jund* (the judge of a military contingent) and later as *qāḍī al-jamā'ah* (the judge of the people) or *qāḍī al-qudāt* (the chief judge); in a small town, he was known as *ḥākim*. Judges belonged to the Mālikite school of law. They were extremely influential and highly respected owing to the great independence and power which the office gave its holders; it is even maintained that if a *qāḍī* summoned the ruler, the latter would immediately obey the summons.[42] In theory the chief *qāḍī* had the power to appoint judges to the various provinces, but it is unlikely that he actually exercised such power. They had jurisdiction over religious foundations (*waqf*, pl. *awqāf*) and the Treasury of Muslims (*bayt māl al-muslimīn*), which differed from the state treasury.[43] In addition, a *qāḍī* conducted the Friday prayer in the main mosque. He was often assisted by an advisory council (*majlis al-shūrā*) of people familiar with the law; the council deliberated legal questions. The *qāḍī* dealt with civil cases pertaining to marriage, divorce, wills, inheritance, and so on, whereas police inspectors dealt with criminal cases. He was supposed to be a man of great learning, high moral standards, and integrity.

The prefect of the city (*ṣāḥib al-madīnah* or *ṣāḥib al-layl*), known in the East as *ṣāḥib al-shurṭah* (chief of police),[44] seems to have been the principal official for administering the city. He had almost unlimited authority, even to the point of sentencing anyone he pleased.[45] He was in charge of detecting and punishing crimes against public morality. At times appointment to this office had to be sanctioned by a *qāḍī*. The prefect of the city had a number of assistants, each of whom had subordinates.[46] For instance, night guards were assigned to each gate of the city to ensure that suspicious characters were questioned or arrested.

The market inspector (*muḥtasib*, also known as *ṣāḥib al-sūq*) fell under the jurisdiction of the city prefect or the *qāḍī*, but acted independently of both. Ibn ʿAbdūn said that inspection (*iḥtisāb*) is the twin of adjudication,[47] and that the inspector is "the tongue of the judge, his chamberlain, his vizier, and his successor."[48] Ibn ʿAbdūn[49] considered *iḥtisāb* the most important branch of government, requiring much legal knowledge. The inspector was concerned with all sorts of things: making sure that weights and measures were in order; correcting irregularities, regulating sales and purchases with respect to the quality of goods and their prices; ascertaining that all foods, beverages, and clothing were clean and up to standard, and that mosques, roads, rivers, and other places were kept in good order so as not to endanger public safety or offend public morality. Along with these broad functions, the *muḥtasib* had the full power to impose a sentence at the scene of the offense. If a violation were committed, he would serve a warning or impose a fine. After repeated violations, he would flog or banish the culprit.

The judge of appeal (*ṣāḥib al-maẓālim*) was empowered to correct abuses of power by those in authority. This function was often performed by the ruler himself or by his delegate.

The collector of taxes (*ṣāḥib al-ashghāl*) was one of the most important and feared officials. He was considered "more powerful and influential than a vizier . . . all necks bowed before him, all hands were stretched out to him, and he kept the provinces in awe by means of his overseers and informers."[50]

The director of religious foundations (*ṣāḥib al-awqāf*) managed estates endowed for religious purposes. The commander of the army had responsibility for the defense of the country. The governors of the provinces had executive power in their territories but were ultimately accountable to the central government.

In addition to this array of officials, the ruler was surrounded by a large number of religious scholars who exerted great influence on both the religious and secular life of al-Andalus. At his court could also be found a galaxy of poets, litterateurs, boon-companions, and entertainers of all sorts. The people ordinarily met in *majālis* to discuss literary questions or to entertain, depending on the proclivity of the ruler.

One can hardly omit the military institution[51] on which depended the defense, peace, and security of the realm. The Arab conquerors relied on the army for conquest and pacification. Their success depended on its strength, discipline, and loyalty. Once these elements were lacking al-Andalus fell into a state of confusion — which happened frequently. The underlying reasons may be found in the organization of the military and its objectives. The army remained heterogeneous throughout, and its loyalty was identified with group consciousness rather than with national consciousness. The call for *jihād* was often made but was frequently superseded by self-interest.

The composition of the army followed ethnic lines from the outset. Its early components were Berbers and Arabs. These two groups conflicted, each further torn by serious tribal divisions. After the army's resounding success in conquering most of the Peninsula, nothing was done to bridge these differences. Army contingents for a long time identified primarily with their tribes — for example, the Syrian contingents were given grants of land (*qaṭā'i'*) in the various southern cities, according to their place of origin, and the Berbers were given certain areas in the north. The central government soon discovered that it could rely on neither Syrians nor Berbers and introduced mercenaries. Al-Ḥakam I (796–822) is said to have been the first emir to introduce Christian slaves into the army. This practice was continued by his successors, who brought Negroes, "Slavs," Berbers, and others. The *Ṣaqālibah* became the mainstay of the dynasty under the great 'Abd al-Raḥmān III and his successor, al-Ḥakam II. As the power of the *Ṣaqālibah* became decisive, Ibn Abī 'Āmir substituted loyal Berbers whom he brought from Africa.

Al-Andalus existed in a state of war throughout its history. There was hardly a decade of continuous peace. Wars and skirmishes with the Christians coupled with frequent internal revolts required the presence of a standing army of 25,000 to 50,000 men. In an emergency the ruler called for volunteers to fight in a *jihād*. Fortresses (*qalā'i'*), castles, and other fortifications were erected and constantly manned.

The army consisted of cavalrymen (*fursān*) and infantrymen (*rajjālah*). A general (*amīr*) commanded 5,000 men and had under him several officers: a *qā'id* who commanded 1,000 men, a *nakīb* (200 men), an *'arīf* (40 men), and other minor officers.

Up to the time of 'Abd al-Raḥmān II (823–852), al-Andalus had no viable navy. However, when threatened by the Norsemen (*majūs*), 'Abd al-Raḥmān II took immediate steps to strengthen the navy. This force soon proved effective in checking Norse inroads as well as the menace of the Fāṭimids in the Mediterranean. Moreover, the navy succeeded under 'Abd al-Raḥmān III in occupying and holding the strategic cities of Ceuta and Tangier in northwest Africa.

Economic policy in al-Andalus conformed to general Islamic practice. At first the conqueror introduced, at the expense of the Visigothic nobility and the Church, a land reform more tolerable to the peasants. The conqueror himself soon became the major landowner, and many of the conquered or contested lands passed on to the State. Land ownership meant wealth, and agriculture was the mainstay of the economy. The early Umayyad rulers fully realized the importance of agriculture in the economic life of the country and endeavored to improve irrigation by constructing canals. They also improved agricultural produce by introducing vegetables, spices, rice, sugar, oranges, and cotton from the East. These products were widely cultivated.

In the major cities a number of new industries appeared, including metalworks, textiles, ceramics, and paper, among others. Public works of various kinds — mosques, palaces, bridges — provided employment for many people. Although al-Andalus was torn by many wars, it traded with its neighbors to the north as far as France and in North Africa as far as Egypt.

The state had a monopoly on minting silver and gold coins.[52] 'Abd al-Raḥmān II appears to have been the first ruler to strike coins. A number of taxes were exacted, to be paid in cash or kind. Muslims were required as a part of their religious obligation to pay alms (*ṣadaqā*), which represented about 10 per cent of the mobile property. The Christians and Jews were required to pay the poll tax (*jizyah*) in return for protection. A more general tax was the *kharāj* imposed on land. In addition, there were extraordinary and oppressive taxes imposed on animals, wine, olives, and other goods.[53]

Al-Andalus had periods of prosperity and acute depressions, the latter owing to natural disasters or the ravages of war. We have only scanty information about the net revenue of a few rulers. The annual income (*jibāyah*) under al-Ḥakam I amounted to 600,000 dinars. It reached 1,000,000 under 'Abd al-Rahmān II; it seems to have declined afterward, but it reached a maximum of 5,480,000, in addition to 765,000 collected from Crown properties, under 'Abd al-Raḥmān III. This caliph allocated from land taxes 300,000 dinars each for the army, administration, and reserve.[54] He is said to have left 20,000,000 dinars in the treasury upon his death. Such prosperity continued under Ibn Abī 'Āmir but declined considerably under his immediate successors. During the political chaos and recurrent internal wars from 1009 onward, the financial situation in al-Andalus deteriorated to the extent that the central government could not maintain an army. As a result, political disorder was accompanied by an economic breakdown. The many newly established states could maintain themselves only through oppressive taxes and extortion. Internal wars forced them to maintain mercenary armies in constant readiness and to pay tributes to avoid being absorbed by the Christians. Moreover, the local rulers indulged in extravagant spending. Under the circumstances, al-Andalus gradually fragmented until it ceased to exist as a recognizable political entity.

8

Acculturation and Self-Appraisal

Some of the factors that ultimately led to the decline and fall of al-Andalus may in retrospect appear to have been insurmountable. Indeed, one might ponder how a country could survive under such adverse conditions for almost eight centuries much less reach a degree of culture far superior to that existing anywhere else in Europe during the Middle Ages.

It may be said that the Arab conquerors failed to consolidate their position in the Peninsula, especially in the north. For lack of colonization, northern al-Andalus became a nest of Christian rebels who, in the course of time, forged a number of states for themselves and ultimately dealt the final blow to the Muslim intruders. There were continual military encounters between Muslims and Christians from the beginning. Although many and composite factors plagued al-Andalus for a long time, perhaps the foremost was the prevalence of tribalism, which largely prevented social integration. Through tribal loyalties, ethnic differences were maintained and manifested themselves in times of crisis. This cleavage was quite apparent in the fragmented military institution, within which tribal leaders commanded the loyalties of different factions. Later, when it became customary to rely on mercenary soldiers, the highest bidder received the greatest following. Despite the great cost, it was imperative to maintain an army in order to repel the Christians from the north and to control revolts within al-Andalus. This expenditure, coupled with extravagant spending on luxuries, played havoc with the economy, affecting especially the peasants. In sum, political, social, and economic instability led to demoralization and general decay.

However great the diversity, al-Andalus enjoyed a unity in its midst derived from a culture, the Arabic language, and to a small degree the Islamic religion. These three elements kept Muslim polity much alive and contributed to preserving a unity that transcended social stresses, economic crises, military failures, and political vicissitudes.[1] For all intents and purposes, al-Andalus assumed an autonomous political posture vis-à-vis the East as early as 750 — barely four decades after its conquest. On the other hand, it remained dependent upon the East in the religious and cultural spheres. Muslim institutions and intellectual life in al-Andalus were patterned after those of the East. The Eastern influences are quite discernible in the political organization, treatment of minorities, agricultural and economic policies, art and architecture, customs, and, more significantly still, in the various intellectual manifestations of the Arabic language, which often transcended ethnic and religious boundaries, although they were deeply influenced by Islamic thought.

The interactions of peoples and ideas continued unhampered among the Muslim countries despite the political animosity dividing them. Freedom of movement between the East and al-Andalus remained almost unbroken. Several authors — Ibn Khayr (d. 1180),[2] al-Ḍabbī (d. 1203),[3] Ibn al-Khaṭīb (d. 1374),[4] al-Maqqarī (d. 1632),[5] among others — give an impressive list of talented men who came from the East and settled in al-Andalus and of Andalusians who went to the East in search of education and other pursuits. These men no doubt left an indelible mark upon the religious, social, political, and intellectual life of al-Andalus.

Consequently, Eastern influences on al-Andalus can hardly be underestimated. From the beginning of the conquest until the middle of the eleventh century, al-Andalus looked to the East for inspiration and guidance in practically all pursuits. In fact, Andalusian scholars were satisfied to emulate and imitate Eastern authors in grammar and lexicography, Qur'ānic studies, the study of Prophetic Tradition, poetry, belles lettres, mathematics, geography, botany, and philosophy. Favorable comparison with Eastern standards was generally considered the mark of excellence. An eleventh-century ruler of Badajoz would not listen to any poet unless his poetry equaled the great Eastern poets al-Mutanabbī and al-Ma'arrī.[6] Henceforth, the Hispano-Arabic scholar was satisfied only with exceeding the status of his Eastern counterpart.

No doubt by the eleventh century the Hispano-Arabic scholar had attained virtuosity and facility in practically all the disciplines known at the time. Religious scholars, grammarians, lexicographers, poets, historians, belletrists, and others appeared in large numbers and could be compared with the best talents of the East. For instance, Ibn ʻAbd Rabbihi and Ibn Ḥazm are only two of many men of letters. In the eleventh century Abū Walīd al-Ḥimyarī (d. 1048) complained that Oriental poetry had preoccupied and charmed Andalusians for centuries and it was high time that they pay attention to their own poetry, which possessed "an original beauty." Moreover, he considered Andalusian poetry superior to that of the East with respect to metaphors (*tashbīhāt*) and description (*waṣf*).[7] Likewise, his contemporary Ibn Ḥazm (d. 1064), one of the most brilliant minds of Islamic culture, called attention to Andalusian creativity in a famous treatise.[8] He lamented that Andalusian talent was not given the recognition it deserved; he mentioned some of the native scholars who were equal or even superior to any talent the East had ever produced. In the following verses, Ibn Ḥazm displays self-praise but also all the bitterness of not being appreciated or noticed, let alone honored in his homeland:

> I am the sun shining in the sky of knowledge,
> My only fault is that I rose in the West:
> Had I risen in the firmament of the East,
> Nothing would have been lost then of my fame!
> I have a deep love for the ʻIrāq regions, and
> No wonder that a lover finds himself lonesome here.[9]

This complaint was voiced to some degree by a number of Andalusian authors, principal among them are Ibn Khāqān (d. 1137),[10] Ibn Bassām (d. 1148),[11] al-Shaqundī (d. 1232),[12] and Ibn Saʻīd (d. 1274),[13] who called attention to the ranking Hispano-Arabic scholars as equal to or above their Eastern counterparts.[14]

These authors may be justified in describing in glowing terms the Andalusian contribution to general Islamic culture. Although there appears to be strong pride in Andalusian accomplishments in the various sciences, one need not assume that those authors intended to disassociate themselves from the mainstream of Islamic culture or to deny their indebtedness to the East. It would be erroneous to suggest that al-Andalus had broken away from the East and asserted its cultural independence. Actually, from the tenth century onward, al-Andalus had become a major cultural center, like many others following the political decline of Baghdād in the tenth century.

It was from these centers that Arabic culture radiated in all directions; from them that Muslim scholars contributed to the preservation of Arabic lore. In al-Andalus itself, the city of Cordova became, during the tenth and part of the eleventh century, one of the great cultural centers of the Muslim world. It was soon superseded by other Andalusian cities, such as Seville, Badajoz, Almería, Granada, and others.

One may gain fuller appreciation of and insight into the almost unbroken continuity of Muslim culture, especially between al-Andalus and the East, by considering, first, the migration of peoples and ideas from the East to al-Andalus, and from al-Andalus to the East, and second, self-appraisal (*faḍā'il*) and contributions of al-Andalus to Islamic culture as conceived by Hispano-Arabic authors.

For many centuries, the interaction of peoples and ideas remained unhindered throughout the Mediterranean basin, in spite of the political animosity among the Muslims themselves and between Muslims and Christians. The individual had freedom of movement even in time of war, and there is no indication that he needed a passport to go from one country to another. Travel was by land and by sea, and the traveller followed certain routes, having at his disposal travel guides known under the rubric *al-masālik wa-l-mamālik* (roads and countries). One rarely reads that ''foreigners'' were either interned or expelled during time of war. For instance, the bitter and continuous animosity between the Umayyads and the 'Abbāsids hardly stopped the flow of goods and people between the eastern and western parts of the Muslim world. Scholars, merchants, and pilgrims frequently travelled and were never denied freedom of movement even when spies and propagandists were suspected to be among them. Moreover, travellers had more often than not the option of settling in a new land and of engaging in gainful employment, including important government posts. In time of crisis and persecution, émigrés were able to settle in another Muslim country. When thousands of people were forced by the emir al-Ḥakam I to leave al-Andalus, they settled in North Africa, Alexandria, and eventually on the island of Crete. The same phenomenon occurred again and again during the Reconquista when Andalusians found new homes in North Africa and were able to build and perpetuate a culture and a way of life similar to those of their native land.

Under the circumstances, travel and emigration took different forms and had various purposes, mainly commerce, pilgrimage, and education. The mercantile class included many who were multilingual, prosperous, and highly educated. All sorts of commodities flowed between the East and al-Andalus. Andalusian products such as oil, wine, wheat, leather, woodwork, paper, textiles, and metalwork found markets throughout the Mediterranean basin and beyond. Similarly, al-Andalus imported goods such as horses, dates, ivory, slaves, books, marble, carpets, furs, musk, camphor, aloe, and other items, and had widespread commercial relations with Christian Spain and souther France, North Africa, Italy, Greece, Syria, Iraq, India, and China.

But the most important interaction was through the institution of pilgrimage and the search for knowledge. The holy cities of Mecca and Medina are the object of pilgrimage once in the lifetime of the faithful. Moreover, they were in the first century of Islam major educational centers where students sought first-hand information about Islamic practices and the conduct of leading followers of Islam. Even mundane pursuits such as acquiring virtuosity in music, singing, and dancing were sought in the holy cities. Medina in particular attracted many Andalusian students who studied at the feet of the great jurist Mālik Ibn Anas (d. 795). It was disciples such as al-Ghāzī Ibn Qays (d. 815), Ziyād Shabṭūn (d. 819), and Yaḥyā Ibn Yaḥyā (d. 849) who were responsible for introducing and making the legal rite of Mālik the sole basis of law in al-Andalus.

Of course, travel was not limited to Mecca and Medina, but was extended to the major Islamic centers of the Muslim world: Kūfah, Baṣrah, Baghdād, Damascus, Qayrawān, Alexandria, Cairo, and others.

It is not feasible to give here an exhaustive list of the many outstanding persons who emigrated either from the East to al-Andalus or from al-Andalus to the East. These people had an enormous role in the transmission and interaction of ideas. Ibn al-Khaṭīb gives in his *Iḥāṭah* a long list of distinguished men who visited Granada and either settled or moved on. Among them are kings, emirs, notables, judges, Qur'ān readers, traditionalists, jurists, secretaries, poets, ascetics, ṣūfis, and others. For each, Ibn al-Khaṭīb gives a biographical sketch of his background, place of origin, accomplishments, literary works, and the dates of his birth and death. Similarly, al-Maqqarī devotes most of volumes II, III, and IV of his *Nafḥ al-Ṭīb* to Easterners who came to al-Andalus and to those Andalusians who went to the East.

These two authors, among others, definitely recognized the cultural interdependence of Andalusians and Easterners, an interdependence which existed throughout the history of al-Andalus. The migration to al-Andalus consisted of professional soldiers, adventurers, preachers, teachers, Qur'ānic readers, poets, administrators, and so forth. Al-Maqqarī states that "those who entered al-Andalus from the East are many. The notables among them cannot be reckoned, let alone the others. There were those who settled for good until they died, and those who returned to the East when their desire was fulfilled."[15]

The newcomers — conquerors and immigrant followers alike — carried with them their families, belongings, customs, and beliefs. In their position of ascendancy, they soon imposed their religion, customs, and language on the native population. They were remarkably successful in their attempts at Islamization and Arabization. These were helped, no doubt, by the influx of people conversant in the religion of Islam and Arabic.

Al-Maqqarī[16] mentions a number of Muḥammad's companions of the second generation (*al-tābi'īn*) who entered al-Andalus and helped to spread the message of Islam. These companions were aided by Qur'ānic readers (*qurrā'*), Qur'ānic memorizers (*ḥuffāẓ*), traditionists (*muḥaddithūn*), poets, and linguists. Their task was encouraged by the emirs (governors), who were Arabic-speaking Muslims. One of the most important early immigrants was 'Abd al-Raḥmān I. He not only put an end to the chaotic conditions in al-Andalus, but he also established a regime that enjoyed a great measure of stability. He was an able statesman, poet, and orator who looked back to the East with great nostalgia. As the uncontested sovereign of al-Andalus, he gave impetus to the process of Arabization and Islamization and surrounded himself with Arabic-speaking individuals. He also gave refuge to many who emigrated from the East, especially to members of his family. His policies of Arabization and Islamization were followed by his successors, who tended more and more to look to the East for example and inspiration. 'Abd al-Raḥmān II "orientalized" the administration by introducing and encouraging many Eastern fashions. The scholar-caliph al-Ḥakam II was led by his interest in scholarship to send agents all over the Muslim world in search of Arabic manuscripts. His library was the largest possessed by any ruler in the Muslim world up to his time. Moreover, al-Ḥakam II had at his court leading intellectuals from inside and outside al-Andalus. By the tenth century, al-Andalus was for the most part Arabized and Islamized under the Umayyad rulers, and it stayed this way under their successors.

But the process of acculturation could not have been successful had it not been for the talents of many individuals. One of the most colorful figures from the East was Ziryāb (d. 857), a former client of the 'Abbāsid caliph al-Mahdī. This singer revolutionized the social modes of al-Andalus and came to exert a great influence at the court as well as in the city of Cordova.[17]

Equally important was Abū Ismā'il Ibn al-Qāsim, known as al-Qālī,[18] whose influence in al-Andalus was felt for generations. He was born somewhere in Armenia and went to Baghdād in 916. He received his education there from the great masters of the day but found little appreciation for his talent. He immigrated to al-Andalus in 941. Whether he went there on his own or at the invitation of the Umayyad princes is not clear. However, he may have come to take the place of the famous belletrist and poet Ibn 'Abd Rabbihi (d. 940), whose *The Unique Necklace* (*al-'Iqd al-farīd*) remains one of the most important works in Arabic literature. He was a man of wide erudition and was known as "the most learned man of his time in lexicography, poetry, and grammar according to the school of Baṣrah."[19] Attached to the court of 'Abd al-Raḥmān III, he became the tutor and close companion of the prince and future caliph al-Ḥakam II. Al-Qālī taught and wrote in al-Andalus for almost three decades. His fame rests on his *adab* work *Kitāb al-Amālī*[20] which was dedicated to his patron, 'Abd al-Raḥmān III. The work contains a large number of prophetic traditions and much information concerning the Arabs — their language, poetry, proverbs, stories, and anecdotes.[21] He wrote other important works and had a number of able pupils, such as the historian Ibn al-Qūṭiyah (d. 977) and the grammarian al-Zubaydī (d. 989), both of whom greatly influenced Andalusian thought. Also, dancers, songstresses,[22] musicians, poets, and other talented individuals made their way to al-Andalus in this period.

It was during the reign of al-Ḥakam II that Ẓafr al-Baghdādī,[23] the dean of bookbinders and scribes (*ra'īs al-warrāqīn*), arrived in al-Andalus and joined the court. Another immigrant was Aḥmad al-Shaybānī (d. 902), who died in Qayrawān at the age of 72. He had travelled extensively "east and west from Khurāsān to Andalus."[24] He was exposed to leading traditionists, jurists, grammarians, belletrists, and poets whose ideas he disseminated in the West. Like many other Easterners, these men made their presence felt not only by their particular skills but also through their teaching and introducing of literary works, mannerisms, fashions, and customs.

This ascendancy of Eastern Islamic modes was reinforced by the large number of Andalusians who travelled to the East. These Andalusians sought, in addition to Mecca and Medina, the cultural centers of Kūfah, Baṣrah, Baghdād, Alexandria, and others, and in doing so they became exposed to the multifarious ideas and ideologies of the East. They brought back with them major literary works dealing with religion, Qur'ānic studies, Prophetic Traditions, jurisprudence, language, belles lettres (*adab*), history, and the sciences. Hardly any important work was written in the East that the Andalusians did not know. Their libraries were replete with Eastern books of all types, and the leading Eastern authors were household names among the cultural circles of al-Andalus. Collections of pre-Islamic and Islamic poetry were readily accessible. Among these were the *Mufaḍḍaliyāt*, the *Aṣma'iyāt*, the *Ḥamāsah*, and the collections of Abū Nuwās (d. 810), Abū-l-'Atāhiyah (d. 828), al-Mutanabbī (d. 965), and Abū 'Alā' al-Ma'arrī (d. 1057). In *adab*, there were the works of al-Jāḥiẓ (d. 869) and Ibn Qutaybah (d. 885); in grammar and lexicography, the *Kitāb* of Sībawayhi (d. ca. 800), the *Kitāb al-'ayn* of al-Khalīl, the *Faṣīḥ* of Tha'lab (d. 904), and *al-Kāmil* of al-Mubarrad (d. ca. 897); in religious studies, the various versions of Prophetic Traditions, the seven Qur'ānic readings, the legal codes, especially the *Muwaṭṭa'* of Mālik Ibn Anas, and Qur'ānic commentaries. Also there were historical works and others dealing with philosophy and the natural sciences.[25]

Among the most prominent Andalusians who travelled to the East was Yaḥyā b. Yaḥyā,[26] one of the most influential religious scholars of his time. After receiving his education in Cordova, Yaḥyā went to Medina and studied law under Mālik b. Anas, returning to al-Andalus full of zeal for the legal doctrine of his master. It is probable that he was among those responsible for persuading the court to adopt Mālikite doctrine as the legal system in al-Andalus. Mālikism had far-reaching consequences on the religious life of al-Andalus. The Mālikite code of law guaranteed the unity of dogma in the country and, at the same time, exerted great influence on state affairs and on intellectual life through the religious scholars (*'ulamā'*) and jurists (*fuqahā'*). Yaḥyā's early advocacy of Mālikism was endorsed by other prominent scholars who had visited the East. Among them was Ibn Ḥabīb (d. 845),[27] known as "the scholar of al-Andalus," who distinguished himself in jurisprudence, Prophetic Traditions, linguistic studies, belles lettres, and poetry. Qāsim Ibn Thābit (d. 915)[28] and his father introduced a number of sciences (*'ilmān kathīran*) into al-Andalus; they are said to have also introduced the famous lexicon, *Kitāb al-'ayn*, of al-Khalīl Ibn Aḥmad. Qāsim Ibn Aṣbagh (d. 862)[29] went to the East and became acquainted with the leading men of the time. He was quite knowledgeable concerning the works of Ibn Qutaybah, al-Mubarrad, Tha'lab, Ibn al-Jahm, among others, and he had a number of followers. Finally, Ibn 'Abdūn[30] and Abū Bakr

Ibn Zuhr[31] received their training in hospital management and discharged their functions as directors of hospitals in both the East and al-Andalus.

If there appeared to be a lack of cultural dependence on the East from the eleventh century onward, it was because the Andalusians had by then digested the lore of the East and were possibly superior to their Eastern counterparts. In fact, Eastern scholars began to look to Andalusian lore for inspiration, just as the Andalusians had formerly looked to the East. This process continued almost unabated, reaching great heights with Ibn Mālik (d. 1274), author of the famous grammatical work in verse, the *Alfiyyah*; the poet-grammarian, Abū Ḥayyān (d. 1344); and the great thinkers Ibn al-Khaṭib and Ibn Khaldūn (d. 1406). However, the old Eastern masters were never forgotten in Andalusian soil.

This interdependence can be gauged from the *Fahrasah*, a work of the twelfth century by Ibn Khayr (d. 575/1180). The *Fahrasah*, which contains some 1,045 titles in various disciplines, reveals much about the education of a scholar. Ibn Khayr travelled throughout al-Andalus in search of knowledge and received his education at the feet of the leading scholars of Cordova, Almería, Málaga, Algeciras, and other cities. His education consisted of Qur'ānic studies, Prophetic Traditions, the *Muwaṭṭa'* of Mālik, biography, genealogy, the roots (*uṣūl*) of jurisprudence, vision, asceticism, grammar, lexicography, belles lettres, and poetry. More important, Ibn Khayr indicated how certain Eastern books had been introduced to al-Andalus and which people had studied them by the twelfth century. Whenever he mentioned a book, he adopted the method used in relating the Prophetic Traditions; he stated that he had studied it orally or textually (*udhnan aw mushāfahatan*) under so-and-so, who studied it under so-and-so, who studied it under so-and-so, etc., until he brought the chain of transmission to the author of the work.

The Merits of al-Andalus

Although at first Eastern scholars may have looked upon the Andalusians as inferior and unproductive, and though the Andalusians were consciously dependent on Eastern talents, there arose the intense feeling that al-Andalus had, after all, great merits (*faḍā'il*). In consequence, from the eleventh century on, authors began repeatedly to recount the merits and wonders of al-Andalus and to describe them in glowing terms. The marvels included its topography, mountains, rivers, valleys, resources, fruits, vegetables, brooks, and groves; its people, their character, qualities, religion, customs, and above all the men of letters; its cities with their palaces, promenades, gardens, bridges, streets, baths, mosques, estates, and so forth.

Ibn al-Khaṭīb [32] and al-Maqqarī [33] provide abundant detail about their predecessors' opinions of al-Andalus. They considered al-Andalus an earthly paradise, since the Almighty endowed it with a clear sky, a beautiful sea full of fish, ripe and delicious fruits, and lovely women; had the Almighty given it a good government it would have been Paradise itself.

Ibn al-Khaṭīb, who served as vizier to the Naṣrid rulers of Granada, speaks of fourteenth-century Granada as "the mother of the kingdom" (*umm al-miṣr*) by virtue of its impregnable position, its good air, its flowing water, and its great wealth. He points out, not without exaggeration: "It is the axis of al-Andalus, the abode of kingship, the entertainment of princes. . . . It is nowadays the capital of the world [country], the loftiest dwelling, the capital of rulership, the dome of justice and beneficence. No city can be compared to it as to its exterior or interior, and no country is like it with respect to the extent of its buildings, and the excellence of its position." [34]

Al-Maqqarī [35] devotes ample space to the main cities of al-Andalus and describes aspects which made them famous. It should suffice here to mention some salient points from his account of Cordova. His detailed descriptions, which are derived from old authorities, deal with its location, extent, suburbs, palaces, gates, resting places (*muntazihāt*), gardens, mosques, public baths, shops, houses, canals, bridges, and mansions.[36]

Cordova was famous for many things: the Umayyad Mosque, the al-Zahrā' palace built by 'Abd al-Raḥmān III, the al-Zāhirah palace built by Ibn Abī 'Āmir, and for its sciences — the greatest of the virtues.[37] "There is no city like it on earth not even the famous city of Baghdād," says al-Maqqarī, and, quoting al-Ḥijārī,[38] he adds, "Its position in al-Andalus is that of the head to the body and the chest to the lion." [39] And, on the authority of Ibn Sa'īd,[40]

> It has more books than any city of al-Andalus and its inhabitants pay most attention to libraries (*khazā'in al-kutub*). This became among them one of the yardsticks (*ālāt*) of prestige and leadership to a point that if a leader did not possess any education (*ma'rifah*) he would see to it to have a library in his house with a discriminating selection not merely for saying that so-and-so has a library, but rather that such a book is not found anywhere . . ." [41]

In connection with books and libraries, al-Maqqarī relates a story that reveals the taste and fashion of the well-to-do in al-Andalus.

Al-Ḥaḍramī said, "I stayed once in Cordova and spent some time at the book market in search of a book in which I was interested until I found it. It was in clear handwriting and had a good commentary. I became exceedingly happy about it. I began to offer higher prices for it in auction, but the auctioneer would come back with a higher price to a point that it reached the highest limit. Then I said to him: 'Show me the one who is making this high bidding for this book to such a point that the price is more than the book is worth.' Then he showed me a man who had on an attire of leadership (*riyāsah*). I came near him and said: 'May God exalt our lord and scholar, if you have a purpose in this book I would leave it to you since bidding between us has reached the extremes.' He said to me: 'I am not a scholar (*faqīh*) and I do not know what is in the book. However, I set up a library to which I have added things not found among the leaders of the town, and there remains in it a place just for this book. Thus, when I saw it in a good handwriting and beautiful binding I liked it and I do not care how much I bid for it.'

Al-Ḥaḍramī relates that he was impelled to retort: 'Praise be to God for the great wealth He bestows. Yes, indeed, wealth is abundant only among people like you. Walnuts are given to those who do not have teeth! And here am I who knows what is in the book and seek to put it to a good use, yet I have little wealth and scarcity comes between me and it!' "[42]

Whereas Cordova was famed for its books and public and private libraries, the city of Seville was known, among other things, for its musical instruments. Ibn Sa'īd relates a conversation between the scholars, Abū al-Walīd Ibn Rushd (Averroës, d. 1198) and Abū Bakr Ibn Zuhr (d. 1198), in which the former said: "I know that if a scholar dies in Seville and if his books are for sale, they would be taken to Cordova, and if a musician dies in Cordova and his estate is for sale, it would be taken to Seville."[43]

However, authors looked back to the glory of Cordova nostalgically and lamented what befell the city after the downfall of the 'Āmirids in 1009. Cordova became the victim of looting and pillage both by unruly Berbers and by its own inhabitants. From that time, it declined in importance and lived for decades in a state of anarchy which contributed to wanton destruction of many of its great monuments. The Cordovans themselves may be blamed for the chaos, for it seemed that no ruler could satisfy them. This situation may have prompted the saying: "The inhabitants of Cordova are like a camel. It will scream if you put on a light load, and it will do the same if you put on a heavy load."[44]

Be this as it may, Cordova never lost its fascination for later writers, nor did al-Andalus as a whole. If its cities were full of marvels, so were its people; they were said to possess supreme qualities. Al-Maqqarī says

"Know that the merit (*faḍl*) of the people is evident just as the beauty of their country is dazzling." He refers to Ibn Ghālib, the author of *Farḥat al-anfus*,[45] who maintains on the authority of Ptolemy that the Andalusians possess good taste in matters of clothes, food, cleanliness, probity, and singing and composition of songs by virtue of the influence of Venus. And by virtue of the influence of Mercury, they are good managers, seekers of knowledge, and lovers of wisdom, philosophy, justice, and fair play.[46] And he adds on the authority of Ibn Ghālib:

> The people of al-Andalus are Arabs in genealogy, honor (*'izzah*), pride, high-mindedness, eloquence of the tongue, cheerfulness, avoidance of inequity, impatience in enduring humiliation, generosity, freedom, and the elimination of infamy.
>
> They are Indians by their great devotions to, love for, and preservation of the sciences; they are Baghdadis by virtue of their cleanliness, gracefulness, subtle manners, nobility, intelligence, good appearance, the excellence of their natural disposition, the sophistication of their intellect, the keenness of thinking, and the effectiveness of their ideas.
>
> They are Greeks in discovery of liquids, in cultivation, selection of different kinds of fruits, management of assembling trees, beautification of gardens with all sorts of vegetables and flowers.[47]

And according to Ibn Ḥazm:

> The Andalusians are Chinese in the mastery of crafts and pictorial representation, Turks in the pursuit of wars and manipulation of its instruments. . . . Moreover, they travelled to North Africa and became pioneers in agriculture, industry, administration, buildings, and gardens.[48]

A Berber once questioned whether al-Andalus had any men of talents, and if so, why there were not recorded; the able theologian Ibn Ḥazm took it upon himself to answer the query in a famous treatise.[49] In the first place, Ibn Ḥazm said, Aḥmad Ibn Muḥammad al-Rāzī[50] wrote a voluminous history of al-Andalus showing its roads, principal cities, and military settlements. Moreover, the Prophet had already made reference to our fighting ancestors and in this alone is there a sufficient distinction. Our fair climate and geographical position are conducive to sagacity and intelligence. Experience has shown that the people of al-Andalus have been able to grasp the various sciences — Qur'ānic readings, jurisprudence, grammar, poetry, lexicography, history, medicine, mathematics, and astronomy — in a manner unequalled elsewhere, including the city of Qayrawān. The Andalusians are not unusual in not perpetuating the memory of their great men: evidence of this is the saying "People do not appreciate a scholar of their own," or in the saying of Jesus, "A prophet is not without honor, save in his own country, and in his own house." In spite of all this, we have had, says Ibn Ḥazm, a great number of excellent works that can be compared with the best works ever written anywhere. He proceeds to enumerate the major authors and their works in the major disciplines. There are many works on the Mālikite school of law, including *al-Hidāyah* of 'Īsā Ibn Dīnār;[51] Qur'ānic commentaries such as that of Abū 'Abd al-Raḥmān Baqī Ibn Makhlad,[52] which excels even the commentary of al-Ṭabarī. At its best, Ibn Ḥazm's treatise is a compact anthology that covers what he conceived to be a good selection of men of letters who could withstand comparison with the great luminaries of the East. In sum:

This country of ours! In spite of being distant from the source of knowledge and in spite of being removed from the skill of scholars, we have been able to mention some of the works of its people which would be difficult to get if one were to seek the like of them in Persia, al-Ahwāz, Muḍar, Rabī'ah, Yemen, Syria, notwithstanding their proximity to Iraq which is the abode of emigration (*hijrah*) of understanding and the home of the sciences and its leaders.

And if we mention Abū al-Ajrab Ja'ūnah Ibn al-Ṣimah al-Kilābī[53] in poetry, we think of Jarīr[54] and al-Farazdaq,[55] his contemporaries. If one were to be impartial, his poetry would serve as evidence, for he followed the school of the classicists (*awā'il*) and not that of the modernists (*al-muḥdathūn*).

And if we mention Baqī Ibn Makhlad, we match him with Muḥammad Ibn Ismā'īl al-Bukhārī,[56] Muslim Ibn al-Ḥajjāj al-Naysābūrī,[57] Sulaymān Ibn al-Ash'ath al-Sijistānī,[58] and Aḥmad Ibn Shu'ayb al-Nisā'ī.[59]

And if we mention Qāsim Ibn Muḥammad[60] we think of al-Qaffāl,[61] and Muḥammad Ibn 'Aqīl al-Faryābī.[62] He is, like them, the companion and pupil of al-Mazanī Abū Ibrāhīm.[63]

If we single out 'Abdallah Ibn Qāsim Ibn Hilāl[64] and Mundhir Ibn Sa'īd[65] we reckon them with Abū-l-Ḥasan Ibn al-Muflis,[66] al-Khalīl,[67] al-Daybājī,[68] and Ruwaym Ibn Aḥmad. . . .[69]

If we make reference to Muhammad Ibn 'Umar Lubābah[70] and his uncle, Muḥammad Ibn 'Isā,[71] and Faḍl Ibn Salāmah,[72] we have them as contenders for Muḥammad Ibn 'Abdallah Ibn 'Abd al-Ḥakam,[73] Muḥammad Ibn Saḥnūn,[74] and Muḥammad Ibn 'Abdūs.[75]

If we bring up the names of Muḥammad Ibn Yaḥyā al-Riyāḥī[76] and Abū 'Abdallah Muḥammad Ibn 'Āṣim,[77] they do not fall short of the leading followers of Muḥammad Ibn Yazīd al-Mubarrad.[78]

And even if our only leading poet were Aḥmad Ibn Muḥammad Ibn Darrāj al-Qasṭallī[79] who does not fall behind Bashshār (Ibn Burd),[80] Ḥabīb,[81] and al-Mutanabbī.[82] How then? And we have in addition to him Ja'far Ibn 'Uthmān al-Ḥājib,[83] Aḥmad Ibn 'Abd al-Malik Ibn Marwān,[84] Aghlab Ibn

Shu'ayb,[85] Muḥammad Ibn Shukhays,[86] Aḥmad Ibn Faraj,[87] and 'Abd al-Malik Ibn Sa'īd al-Murādī,[88] each of whom is a stallion (*faḥl*) and a horse with a blaze on its forehead![89]

This enthusiastic exaltation of Andalusian men of letters is corroborated by Ibn Sa'īd (d. 1287)[90] and al-Shaqundī (d. 1231),[91] who not only reiterated Ibn Ḥazm's praise but added their own extensive lists of literary men. Ibn Sa'īd tried to supplement Ibn Ḥazm's list of authors in the various disciplines, whereas al-Shaqundī concentrates on the outstanding poets of al-Andalus and quotes generously from their poems. This procedure had already been adopted by Ibn Bassām (d. 1148) in *al-Dhakhīrah* and by Ibn Khāqān (d. 1137) in *Qālā'id*; both men dealt mainly with contemporaries and immediate predecessors.

In addition to the list of prominent poets, al-Shaqundī devotes a good portion of the treatise to the major cities of al-Andalus. It is interesting to note that his treatise was the result of a controversy between him and a Berber who claimed the superiority of North Africa over al-Andalus. In an apologetic vein, al-Shaqundī exclaims that to place Berberland above al-Andalus is like giving precedence to the left hand over the right hand or like claiming that night is brighter than day![92] He then asked whether there was a man like so-and-so who excelled in this or that discipline? And he proceeded to enumerate a large number of talented individuals who, in his estimate, would do honor to any court anywhere in the Muslim world. Andalusian knights (*fursān*) are the paragons of courage and the source of pride by virtue of their great deeds of heroism.[93] Moreover, Andalusian cities are earthly paradise, and each possesses certain qualities not found anywhere outside of al-Andalus. There is Seville, clean and gay, that is superior even to Cairo or Damascus. The banks of its river are adorned with estates, gardens, and trees in a sequence not found on the banks of the Nile. It is famous for its fruit trees, musical instruments, women, and wine.[94] Cordova — once the site of government, the center of the sciences, the beacon of religion, and the seat of nobility — is remembered by its palaces al-Zāhirah and al-Zahrā' and by its main mosque. Jaén is the fortress and home of heroes and is known for its silkworm. Granada is the Damascus of al-Andalus and possesses high walls and splendid buildings. Málaga has the virtues of being favored by the sea and land, and possessing a great stretch of vineyard and beautiful mansions that resemble stars in the sky. It is famous for a rare specie of fig and delectable wine. And he relates that when a dying debauchee was told to ask forgiveness from the Lord, he retorted, "O Lord, of all the things in Paradise, I only wish the wine of Málaga and the raisin of Seville."[95]

Al-Andalus was a melting pot of peoples and ideas which went through various stages of cultural development. At first, it depended slavishly on the East for religious, linguistic, and cultural guidance and inspiration. It then acquired consciousness of itself and of its merit vis-à-vis the rest of the Muslim world. This consciousness, however, did not lead to a break with the mainstream of Islam, even when al-Andalus became more of a contributor to the general Islamic culture. It was roughly from the eleventh century on that Andalusian talents could be seen everywhere in North Africa and farther East, where they could compete easily with the best talents of the day. One of the main reasons for this close interaction is that Arabization and Islamization took deep roots in the country, particularly in areas south of Toledo. It resulted in making al-Andalus an extension of the Islamic world, part and parcel of Arabic culture.[96] This relationship can be amply documented not only in terms of extensive travels to and from al-Andalus but in terms of conscious borrowing in grammar, lexicography, religious and legal texts, poetry, and other areas. On the whole, al-Andalus developed eastern themes and forms rather than created new literary genres. This notwithstanding, Andalusian culture as manifested in its arts and literature betrays a personality of its own which is discernible in poetry in its popular form, in the simplicity and directness of its prose, and in the lucidity of all sorts of commentaries often used for teaching purposes. All in all, al-Andalus must be studied within the context of Islam, the Arab Empire, the Arabic language, and Arabic culture and not within the narrow provincialism of the Iberian Peninsula. This can be seen clearly in the enormous amount of literature produced in al-Andalus which is Arabic in form and content and which will be the subject of the following chapters.

9

The Sciences and Education

THE following chapters will show that al-Andalus indeed produced in the Arabic language a great literature, covering every subject known in medieval times: religious studies, language, history, belles lettres, geography, medicine, mathematics, astronomy, philosophy, and finally, poetry, the most expressive artistic manifestation of the Arabs in pre-Islamic and Islamic times. This intellectual efflorescence was taking place at a time when most of Europe was going through a period of transition and slumber. The highly advanced Arabic culture directly influenced later Spanish life and thought; in addition, through the translation of Arabic works into Latin or Romance, the Arabic heritage indirectly affected European culture from the eleventh century onward. The following statements give a panoramic view of the fecund Arabic culture as well as several leading conceptions of the sciences.

The year 711 marks not only the conquest of the Iberian Peninsula but also the beginning of a new chapter in its cultural history. This chapter, covering eight centuries, witnessed many changes in linguistic distribution and practices, the religion and social mannerisms of the Spaniards, and Spanish arts and crafts — most of which are discernible even to the present day.

At first, the Arab conquerors had very little in common with the conquered population; they differed in language, religion, and customs. They constituted a minority and remained so long after the conquest. They were even outnumbered by their coreligionists, the Berbers. It is doubtful that there were many literate Arabs at the time of the conquest. In the early part of the eighth century, intellectual life as manifested in the Arabic language was still in its infancy, even in the East. However, the Arabic language did have the Qur'ān, some oral traditions and legends, and poetry. On the whole, the Qur'ān and poetry could be said to have contributed the first and most important literary elements on Spanish soil, and thus served as the principal ingredients for future development. To them may be added official documents, coins, sermons, and the like, which constitute the main documentary evidence from the eighth century.

It was in the ninth century however that the process of Arabization of the Peninsula made great strides, especially among the urban populations, containing a large number of Christians and Jews. With the dissemination of the language over a broader population there emerged a literature, mainly dependent on that of the East and consisting for the most part of poetry. Literary activities were encouraged by rulers who appreciated scholarship and surrounded themselves with scholars. For one, 'Abd al-Raḥmān II was greatly inclined toward religious and secular sciences, poetry, and music, and secured books from the East. During his reign the famous singer Ziryāb[1] arrived in Cordova and enjoyed his generous patronage. Among the other interesting personages of his court were 'Abbās Ibn Firnās (d. 888) and Yaḥyā al-Ghazāl (d. 865). Ibn Firnās was a man of unusual abilities. He invented a formula for manufacturing crystals, constructed a simulated sky with lightning and thunder, and conceived the possibility of flying. Al-Ghazāl was an able poet and satirist. He was reputed for his sharp tongue and quick answers, for which he was feared even by the powerful jurist Yaḥyā Ibn Yaḥyā.[2] The encouragement and generous patronage of learning by the Umayyad emirs, principally 'Abd al-Raḥmān II, contributed enormously to the establishment of a literary tradition that continued at the Umayyad court in succeeding generations and bore fruits in the tenth and eleventh centuries.

For education, al-Andalus counted at first on a large body of scholars who had received their education in the East and who had brought back many works of outstanding Eastern scholars. The numerous mosques became educational centers for anyone who wished to learn. Private and public libraries were founded in great numbers. All of these paved the way for enormous literary activity in the tenth century. Cordova was the nerve center of politics and the major intellectual center of al-Andalus. On it converged many students from all over the country to study at the feet of scholars. This center reached the pinnacle of its glory during the reigns of 'Abd al-

Raḥmān III and his son al Ḥakam II. They sponsored the leading intellectuals of the day: Ibn 'Abd Rabbihi,[3] al-Qālī,[4] al-Zubaydī,[5] and Ibn al-Quṭiyah,[6] among many others. Moreover, al-Ḥakam II founded a number of schools, thereby making education available to anyone who sought it.

The pursuit of learning continued unhampered after al-Ḥakam II's death in 976, although Ibn Abī 'Āmir attempted to restrict freedom of thought and even to purge al-Ḥakam's library of materials that seemed offensive to the religious scholars.[7] However annoying these restrictions were, al-Andalus continued its intellectual upsurge in the eleventh century, though Cordova lost ground as the principal intellectual center. This decline took place in 1009 when the city's gorgeous palaces, libraries, and other monuments became objects of wanton destruction. The famous library of al-Ḥakam II was sacked, and many books were sold and found their way into other cities. In later years, Cordova was overshadowed by the capital cities of the party-kings, each of which tried to recapture Cordova's former glory. This kind of competition in the midst of constant quarrels and bloody wars may have saved literary activities from stagnation or even dissolution. Cities such as Seville, Almería, Badajoz, Granada, Toledo, Valencia, Málaga, and Denia became centers to which scholars converged to receive rulers' patronage. No doubt many scholars were inconvenienced and uprooted, but they always found patrons. It seems that the poet had the best chance of success, and for this reason, perhaps, the period 1031–1090 produced an enormous number of poets, who overshadowed the rest of the scholars. The 'Abbādid rulers of Seville, like other rulers, could count among them a number of able poets. The emir al-Mu'tamid, for instance, was an outstanding poet, as was his vizier and boon-companion Ibn 'Ammār (d. 1086).[8] The great poet Ibn Zaydūn (1003–1071)[9] and his beloved princess-poetess Wallādah are examples of many outstanding poets of the century.

Besides poets, many outstanding men of letters appeared in the eleventh century. The gifted scholar Ibn Ḥazm (994–1064) may be considered the first intellectual giant of Muslim Spain and one of the greatest thinkers in the intellectual history of Islam. He was a poet, theologian, jurist, historian, moralist, and one of the ablest polemicists in Islam. He always spoke what he thought at a time when discretion would have guaranteed him the highest honors at any court of his days. As a polemicist it is said of him that his "tongue was as sharp as the sword of al-Ḥajjāj."[10] When his books were ordered to be burned by the ruler of Seville, he defiantly retorted in a famous poem "Although you may burn the paper, you shall never burn what is on it, for this will remain in my breast." [11] Among other outstanding savants of the eleventh century were the blind lexicographer Ibn Sīdah (d. 1066), [12] the historian Abū Marwān Ibn Ḥayyān (d. 1075), [13] the traditionist Yūsuf Ibn 'Abd al-Barr (d. 1071).[14]

However noteworthy the literary accomplishments, the political conditions were becoming chaotic by the end of the century and had repercussions on all aspects of life. The coming of the Almoravids and later the Almohads from North Africa brought temporary stability. Both dynasties came to power with strong religious platforms, and both imposed heavy restrictions on free thought. Nonetheless, great intellectuals appeared during their rule in the twelfth and thirteenth centuries. Subjected by the less educated Berbers, the Andalusian authors displayed their national pride by emphasizing native talents[15] in anthologies such as those of Ibn Bassām (d. 1148), Ibn Khāqān (d. 1137), and Ibn Bashkuwāl (d. 1183),[16] who dealt for the most part with the men of the century in which they lived. Among other prominent names one may mention the geographers al-Idrīsī (d. 1115) [17] and Ibn Jubayr (d. 1217),[18] the physician Ibn Zuhr (d. 1162),[19] the botanist Ibn Bayṭār (d. 1248),[20] and the two great mystics Ibn 'Arabī (d. 1240)[21] and Ibn Sab'īn (d. 1269).[22] It is significant to note that philosophy now flourished for the first time on Andalusian soil, paradoxically in the midst of religious intolerance. The major philosophers[23] were Ibn Bājjah (d. 1138); Ibn Ṭufayl (d. 1185); Ibn Rushd, better known as Averroës (d. 1198); and Maimonides (d. 1204). Their influence was felt beyond al-Andalus, especially in the rise and development of Christian Scholasticism in the thirteenth century.

From about the middle of the thirteenth century, Muslim ascendancy in al-Andalus was being shattered at its very foundations. The Muslim domain comprised only a small pocket in the southern fringes of the Peninsula ruled by the Naṣrid dynasty (1232–1492) and constantly in a precarious position. In Granada Arabic culture had extended life but none of the vigor that had characterized it in former times. The single exception was Ibn al-Khaṭīb, who was an able statesman and thinker. However, the dynasty excelled in erecting great buildings and monuments, among which is the famous Alhambra, still one of the most magnificent monuments in the world.

In 1492, the Reconquista attained its ultimate objective by liquidating the last Muslim hold on the Peninsula. The loss of political power led to the decline of the culture that was expressed in the Arabic language. In fact, there was a concerted effort to erase the influence of Arabic culture and to forbid the use of Arabic as the medium of written or spoken expression.

Under the circumstances, persecuted Muslims complied with the wishes of the inquisitors and expressed themselves in a local Spanish dialect, but they used Arabic characters. This literature, known as *aljamiado*, represented the last cultural vestiges; it consisted of poems, stories, and religious and legal accounts. Such was the fate of a fascinating, if not brilliant, chapter of intellectual adventure.

The Andalusians had developed a strong tradition for learning. That they were avid students of Muslim culture is attested by their great literary legacy in all branches of knowledge. As already indicated, they sought knowledge wherever they could find it. They travelled far and wide in its pursuit, often risking their lives. Moreover, they were great and devoted teachers. They built numerous libraries, which became not only the symbol of learning but also a mark of prestige among non-scholars who found it fashionable to have libraries in their homes.

As a result the pursuit and dissemination of knowledge became one of the most precious goals of the Andalusians. Many Prophetic Traditions emphasizing the importance of knowledge were put to work. The classical tradition, "Seek knowledge even if it were in China," became a maxim among Muslim scholars. Its pursuance and dissemination were conceived to represent the highest attainment in this world and in the Hereafter, especially if the knowledge happened to bear upon religion. In this case, it was tantamount to an article of faith.

All in all, Muslim scholars pondered not only on the meaning of knowledge (*'ilm*), but on its various kinds, and its utility. The Arabic term *'ilm* denotes "knowledge," "learning," "intellect," or "science." As a rule, the connotation of science or sciences is conveyed in the plural formation (*'ulūm*). The term *'ilm* is also attached to a particular discipline, such as *'ilm al-ḥisāb*, the literal meaning being "the knowledge of accounting," mathematics; *'ilm al-nabāt*, "the knowledge of plants," botany;[24] and so forth.

In this connection, the tenth-century belletrist Ibn 'Abd Rabbihi devoted a whole book to knowledge and education in *al-'Iqd al-farīd* (*The Unique Necklace*).[25] No doubt, Ibn 'Abd Rabbihi reiterated an already established tradition among Eastern scholars concerning knowledge and education. He faithfully reproduced Muslim conceptions on the subject as they occurred in the *adab* works of his Eastern predecessors and contemporaries. He stressed the importance of knowledge, its usefulness, and its virtues; he exhorted people to pursue it; and he presented the reflections of his predecessors on its various aspects. He referred to leading scholars, their qualities and prominent positions. He defines knowledge and education as "the pillars upon which rest the axis of religion and the world. They distinguish man from the beast, and the rational from the irrational being. They are the substance of the intellect, the lantern of the body, the light of the heart, and the pole of the soul. . . . The proof is that the intellect grasps the sciences in the same manner sight receives colors; and hearing receives sounds. Indeed, the intelligent person who is not taught anything is like not having intellect (*'aql*) at all. And if a child were not educated and taught to read and write he would be the most stupid of animals and the most wandering beast." [26]

Thus, knowledge is not only useful but indispensable for every man. Although the sciences are many, Muslims should interest themselves in all of them. Some sciences are indispensable for people who occupy certain positions. For instance, kings should know about genealogy and history; warriors about biography; and merchants about mathematics.[27] There are two types of knowledge: that of the body and that of religion.[28] He who pursues one discipline is called a scholar, and the one who pursues various disciplines is an educated man. However, blemishes may be found among the three kinds of people: those who seek religion through philosophy do not escape heresy, those who seek wealth through alchemy do not escape poverty, and those who seek rare traditions are not safe from lies.[29] All in all, knowledge serves as a distinctive mark among people who are either learned or grubs. It is for this reason that knowledge should be the aim of every individual for it is the best possession, as expressed in the admonition "Let knowledge be your possession and education your ornament." [30] The famous philologist al-Khalīl Ibn Aḥmad was asked, "Which is better, knowledge or wealth?" He said, "Knowledge." Then he was asked, "Why do scholars then gather at the doors of kings and not these at the doors of scholars?" He replied, "It is because scholars know the position of kings, but kings are ignorant of the position of scholars." [31] Finally, knowledge is acquired through education, which has five stages: the first stage is silence, the second listening, the third learning by heart, the fourth action, and the fifth dissemination.[32]

These conceptions held by Eastern scholars soon became known to Andalusians, and it was for Ibn 'Abd Rabbihi in the tenth century to articulate them in *al-'Iqd al-farīd*, which became one of the major tools in the educational system of al-Andalus. Thus, the Andalusians from the tenth century on were pondering knowledge and received further impetus from their Eastern counterparts regarding its nature, nobility, and content.[33] The three great philosophers al-Kindī,[34] al-Fārābī,[35] and Ibn Sīnā,[36] the mathematician al-Khuwārizmī,[37] and other Eastern scholars not only contemplated knowledge but attempted in the manner of the Greeks before them to classify the sciences in terms of their value, utility, and nobility. They were followed by Andalusians who did likewise. Three men of the eleventh century deserve mention. They are Ibn 'Abd al-Barr (d. 1071), Ibn Ḥazm (d. 1064), and Ṣā'id (d. 1070).

Ibn 'Abd al-Barr was a religious scholar who wrote a work on knowledge and its excellence.[38] The work consists of a number of traditions attributed to the Prophet Muḥammad and his companions concerning knowledge and its virtue; its superiority over all pursuits, including piety; the need for seeking it; the relationship of teacher to pupil and that of scholar to ruler.

But the most comprehensive and articulate treatment of the subject of knowledge and sciences is contained in the works of Ibn Ḥazm, mainly in *Marātib al-'ulūm* (*Categories of the Sciences*)[39] and in *Kitāb al-akhlāq* (*Book of Conduct*),[40] consisting of his admonitions and reflections on the good and virtuous life. In the latter, Ibn Ḥazm devoted to the sciences a chapter which began: "Even if knowledge did not have any purpose other than making the ignorant respect and honor you and the scholar esteem and do honor to you, it would suffice to pursue it."[41] He went on to inquire, How is it possible not to seek knowledge in the light of its many other advantages in this world and in the Hereafter? The anathema of ignorance causes harm both in this world and in the Hereafter. Ibn Ḥazm conceived knowledge as having a great utility for practicing virtue. Knowledge enables the individual to see the ugliness of vices and the manner of avoiding them.[42] He expressed his delight with scholars when he was ignorant and was taught by them, and when he became scholar and conversed with them.[43] Moreover, in wealth, social station, and health, one should compare himself with those who have less, but in religiosity, sciences, and virtue, one should compare himself with those who have more.[44] Knowledge ought to be disseminated, but its dissemination among untalented and inept people is not only a waste of time, but prejudicial as well,[45] for a great harm is done to the sciences by these intruders and inept people who pretend that they are scholars, but who actually are ignorant.[46] Those who aim at acquiring honors, wealth, and pleasure seek the company of people who, by virtue of their qualities, resemble angry dogs and shifty wolves.[47] However, he who is greedy with his knowledge is worse than one who is greedy with his material possessions. All in all, knowledge is associated with virtue, and ignorance with vices

— though he qualifies this statement by saying that he knew untutored people whose conduct was irreproachable, whereas that of some scholars was such as to make them the vilest and most corrupt people on earth.[48] This leads him to the conclusion that virtues are, after all, gifts from the Almighty, who bestows or denies them as He pleases.

These reflections of Ibn Ḥazm are for the most part reiterated in *Marātib al-'ulūm*, in which he reflects on the sciences, their actual worth, and the manner of pursuing them. The treatise is very important since it was the first work of its kind known in al-Andalus. It shed light on the sciences as conceived by a thinker who attempted to classify them according to their value, and to distinguish the spurious from the genuine sciences. It consisted of two major parts: the first dealing with the education of the individual, and the second with the division of the sciences according to an Islamic framework.

To Ibn Ḥazm, knowledge is beneficial to its seeker in this world and in the Hereafter as well.[49] However, "he who seeks knowledge in order to be boastful about it or to be praised or to acquire wealth and fame is far away from success, for his object is to ascertain something other than knowledge."[50] Acquiring knowledge is as much of a virtue as transmitting it,[51] from which follows the importance of the teacher and of books. He considers books to be the best tools for transmission. Contrary to the view that an abundance of books is harmful, he maintains that the more books there are the better.[52]

Ibn Ḥazm attaches a great importance to the religious sciences, or *Sharī'ah*. After praising God, he describes Muḥammad as "the best of mankind and the purest of the descendants of Adam" and says that Muḥammad "was sent to guide and save his followers from the darkness of unbelief and blind ignorance [and bring them] to the light of knowledge."[53] He continues that the Almighty God preferred man to all his other creatures and distinguished him with freedom to pursue the sciences and the crafts. In consequence, it is incumbent upon the individual neither to squander nor to neglect this gift but to use and discharge it to the fullest extent. Reflecting back on history, Ibn Ḥazm sees that the sciences and conditions differ from time to time and from place to place. The ancients had sciences which they transmitted to posterity. Some of these survived and others disappeared, leaving no trace except in name. There are blameworthy sciences such as music, melody, sorcery, magic, and alchemy, whose claimants are swindlers, liars, and insolent. For instance, the alchemist, who intends to convert copper into gold, or vice versa, is like converting a man into a donkey or a donkey into a man. Such a pursuit cannot be called a science. On the other hand, there are legitimate, useful sciences which should be pursued gradually, starting with those having immediate bearing on this world and ending with those pertaining to the Hereafter. This is so because this world is a temporary abode and the sciences concerning it are utilitarian, aiming at the acquisition of wealth and the preservation of health. These limited and narrow objectives are easy to obtain, and occupation with them is both troublesome and devious. Their pursuers confront the thorniest road in acquiring them and use a supreme quality, reason, for acquiring a stone without knowing when it is going to leave them, or vice versa. They are like the person who made a beautiful sword but used it for cutting bones and grass; or they resemble the one who built a mansion and used it for depositing waste! All in all, the pursuit of the sciences for personal gains in this world is of little benefit, although it may appear that the conditions of these seekers is more respectable than scholars'. He remarks, "We ask God's help and may He protect us from desertion."[54]

On the other hand, Ibn Ḥazm conceives that the best sciences are those which lead to eternal salvation. The student of these sciences, unlike the one pursuing sciences aimed at worldly gains, is amply rewarded. He gives little but receives much in return; that is, he labors little and receives the tranquility of an eternal life.

After stating the two main objectives of the sciences, Ibn Ḥazm passes on to show the manner of attaining them, the extent to which they should be pursued, and a classification of those possessing supreme qualities and values and those not possessing them. He says that any intelligent person is fully aware that he cannot attain the sciences without searching, and that searching requires hearing, reading, and writing.

As a result, a child should be entrusted to a teacher by the time he is about five years old, or when he is able to understand and communicate. At this stage, he should be taught how to write legibly and spell correctly. Anything beyond this, such as an emphasis on the aesthetic value of writing, is superfluous and wastes time. Here Ibn Ḥazm seems to have little or no appreciation for the art of calligraphy. This art, in his opinion, would not serve any constructive purpose except as a pretext to attach oneself to the court of a ruler, thereby wasting a whole life "in the shadow of people drafting documents with false items and lies."[55] Here, as in other instances, Ibn Ḥazm shows his contempt for rulers and, most probably, for the rulers of his day. At any rate, he compares the expert in decorative and intricate writing with the person who secures a lot of musk for charming the soul but instead uses it to delight the beasts or spills it wastefully on the road.

As for reading, the student should acquire proficiency such as to enable him to read any book that should fall in his hand. Of course, he should begin with the Qur'ān, which will serve both as a drill in recitation and as a meritorious obligation.

Next come grammar and lexicography, which should be studied until one grasps the structure and morphology of the language and the meaning of most frequently used words and expressions. Anything beyond the material contained in some standard grammar or *The Book* of Sībawayhi is rather useless since the time spent in such pursuits could be put to a better use. The same is true of the study of lexicography, which could stop after acquainting oneself with the lexicons of Abū 'Ubayd[56] and of al-Zubaydī.[57]

To reinforce grammatical and lexical studies, Ibn Ḥazm suggests with great reluctance the study of poetry, but only poetry containing counsels and good examples. He was fully aware of the strong attachment the Andalusians had for poetry and suspected he would be criticized severely for his stringent limitations. He defends his position by calling attention to his knowledge in the field and his contribution to the art of versification. Though fully aware of its merits, he strongly feels that poetry is not good material for educating the young, since most of it is not edifying but instead adversely affects the individual. The poetical forms that should be avoided are: (1) love poetry (*ghazal*), which provokes fervent longings, invites temptations, incites youth, turns the soul to dissipation and pleasure, and leads to deceit, passion, corruption of religious sentiments, extravagant spending, and other objectionable pursuits; (2) poetry of separation (*tagharrub*) and description of deserts which encourages abandonment of dwellings and has other adverse effects; (3) poetry connected with destitution and wars which agitates the soul and leads to destruction and crimes, and other abominable actions; (4) satirical poetry (*hijā'*), which is the vilest of all since it leads the individual to the company of insolent people, dope addicts, and street sweepers; in addition, it aims at tearing people's honor to pieces, and at indulging in imperfections and defilements; and (5) panegyrics (*madḥ*) and eulogy (*rithā'*) which may be licit but are distasteful since they tend to exaggerate, distort, and falsify.

After studying writing, reading, grammar, lexicography, and selected poetry, the student should pass on to study the science of numbers (*'ilm al-'adad*). He should master addition, subtraction, multiplication, division, fractions, and plane geometry (*masāḥah*). Then he should take arithmetic, which is the science of the nature of number (*'ilm ṭabī'at al-'adad*). He should read and grasp Euclid's work, which will gain him knowledge about the earth and its surface, about the celestial bodies, their positions, distances, and so forth. He should also read Ptolemy's *Almagest*, which teaches him about the eclipses, the width and length of countries, the duration of day and night, the rising tide, the rise and setting of the sun, moon, and the bright stars.

At this point, Ibn Ḥazm interjects his thought on the supposed influence of the stars on people. He says that such an influence defies experimentation or proof. Thus, the belief that the stars can change the course of things is absurd since "there is no way of changing the species or eliminating the nature of things."[58] Such pursuits are unscientific, and those who occupy themselves in them are outcasts who look for something which they will never find. He further refutes the validity of astrology by saying that if kingdoms fall, it is because of wars, raids, poor conditions, corruption, and similar factors, and not because of the influence of the stars.

At this stage, the individual should take up logic and the science of the species (*'ilm al-ajnās*) and related subjects in order to get at proofs (*burhān*) and contentions (*shaghab*). It is by means of logic that the individual is able to learn the truth and distinguish it from falsehood and to understand the natural sciences, atmospheric conditions, the composition of the elements, animals, plants, minerals, and medicine. Of course, he should not neglect the history (*akhbār*) of ancient and contemporary people; he should learn about their decline, destruction, and the causes of these processes, and he should study people of virtue in order to imitate them. All these are useful and teach things leading in turn to the knowledge of their Maker.

The scholar should also seek proof whether or not the world is created, and if so, he should inquire whether it has a creator. Once this answer is obtained, he should inquire further whether the creator is one or more than one. Then, he should ponder whether or not prophecy is possible. He should find out that it is possible and within the will of God. This will lead to the confirmation of Muḥammad's prophecy as attested in the Qur'ān, which contains God's covenants.

This brings Ibn Ḥazm to the most important subject which an individual should pursue: the religious law (*sharī'ah*). He who neglects its study in preference to something else not only errs, but does great injustice to himself, for he "espouses the base and less useful pursuits for the loftiest and most useful."[59]

After a digression on the virtue of teaching, the true objective of knowledge, the evil company of the sultan, and the usefulness of books, he divides the sciences into seven groups which are, he says, universal among all peoples. The first three (law, history, and language) distinguish one nation from another, whereas the remaining four (astronomy, number, medicine, and philosophy) are common to all people.

After stating that the religious law (*sharīʻah*) is the only true law, he recognizes its main components which constitute the following discipline:

1. Religious law (*sharīʻah*)
    a. Qur'ān: reading and meaning (*maʻna*)
    b. Prophetic Traditions (*ḥadīth*): texts (*matn*) and chain of transmitters (*ruwāt*)
    c. Jurisprudence (*fiqh*): Qur'ānic ordinance, *ḥadīth* ordinance, consensus (*ijmāʻ*)
    d. Theology (*kalām*)
2. Language
    a. Grammar
    b. Lexicography
3. History
    a. Dynastic (*mamālik*)
    b. Annalistic
    c. Countries
    d. Categories (*ṭabaqāt*)
    e. Genealogy
4. Astronomy
5. Numbers: Ascertaining their rules and then their proofs
6. Logic, rational or metaphysical and sensory
7. Medicine: Spiritual medicine and corporeal medicine

Perhaps as an afterthought he adds poetry, rhetoric (*balāgha*), and idioms (*ʻilm al-ʻibārah*). He argues that anything which is known can be called knowledge (*fa kull mā ʻulima fa huwa ʻilm*) and thus commerce, construction, tailoring, weaving, shipbuilding, agriculture, horticulture, and the like can be called science (*ʻilm*). But these are limited to this world for gaining a livelihood.

Ibn Ḥazm makes other recommendations to students, and he concludes with reflections on the interrelationship of the various disciplines and with criticisms of those persons not meeting the standards of good and wholesome education. The latter would include those who have little knowledge yet make pretence of knowing it all or those who have a specialized knowledge and frown on the rest of the sciences. It is worthwhile to scrutinize his views in some detail. He cautions that a person should not attribute fault to what he does not know, for this would prove his shortcoming; nor should he be conceited in what he knows, or his virtue may become obliterated; nor should he be envious of those more knowledgeable than he or look down on those who are less knowledgeable; nor should he talk about a science without knowledge of it or use his knowledge for worldly gain alone.

Ibn Ḥazm reiterates his initial points and states that all the sciences are connected and none can dispense with the others, for "pursuing the sciences aims at learning the knowledge of what the Almighty God had wished for us"[60] — which, in the final account, is knowledge of the religious law, its promulgation, and conformity with it. Therefore, one cannot reach true knowledge without knowing God's ordinances as revealed in the Qur'ān, and knowing what Muḥammad and his companions commanded us to do. Consequently, reading the Qur'ān becomes imperative. However, such reading could not be possible without a knowledge of Arabic lexicography and grammar. Also, true knowledge requires some knowledge of poetry; the knowledge of genealogy to determine who is eligible for the caliphate; arithmetic to determine the position of the *Qiblah*; the knowledge of astronomy (*hay'ah*), theology, and medicine for determining defects, diseases, and their cure; writing, rhetoric, and even astrology so that one can distinguish between right and wrong.

However, if the individual is not able to master all of the sciences, it becomes necessary for him to have a smattering of each one, however small this may be. Ibn Ḥazm argues for a general and integrated education in all the sciences by comparing the outcome to the construction of a building which requires the participation and interdependence of many skillful hands. He also points to the interdependence of the disciplines by indicating the need of man to live and participate with his fellows, with whom he exchanges knowledge. A man will perform the noblest task when he is able to teach the religious disciplines. In consequence, Ibn Ḥazm cautions against those who have some knowledge and who are basically ignorant but who claim erudition. He also reproaches the specialist who downgrades all the sciences except his specialty; as an example he mentions the religious scholars who frown on the secular sciences when actually they should know them for the performance of their religious tasks. For instance, the knowledge of the Qur'ān is not sufficient without a knowledge of Prophetic Traditions and related disciplines and without the knowledge of language, medicine, and other disciplines. Thus, if the religious scholar intends to make a legal decision without the knowledge of the various sciences, he would be like a donkey which cannot distinguish right from wrong. Similarly, there are those who boast knowledge of the various sciences, yet they neglect the most important of these, that is, the *sharī'ah*, without which life in this world and in the Hereafter is meaningless. He concludes: "It does not follow that we wish to take away anything from these sciences. God forbid — for if we did, we would enter the company of those whom we are criticizing and we would have embarked upon despicable belief. But he who aims at a short cut for attaining a science will do violence to and belittle the rest of the sciences. If a person is unable to pursue all the sciences and to recognize their merit, he is still charitable, laudable, and virtuous, for he cannot be blamed for what the Almighty God did not make available to him. In the same manner, he who studies what he needs from all the sciences, and uses his knowledge as he should, is the most virtuous person because he has attained nobility of soul conducive to enrichment in this world and bliss in the Hereafter. He has rescued himself from the circle of the ignorant people and those who make use of the sciences for utilitarian purposes."[61]

Ibn Ḥazm could find justification for his views concerning the pursuit of knowledge and its dissemination in the Prophetic Traditions. The religious scholar Ibn Khayr in his *Fahrasah*[62] includes a number of traditions concerning knowledge, its pursuits, and its dissemination. The following traditions are revealing:

There is nothing greater in the eye of God than a man who learned a science (*ta'allama 'ilman*) and who taught it to people.[63]

A Muslim cannot bestow on his brother a better gift than a word of wisdom. If the brother hears, grasps, and then transmits it, God will guide him, and divert him from evil, since the word of wisdom leads to the uplifting of the soul.[64]

The bearers of knowledge (*ḥamlah*) are the successors of the prophets in this world and martyrs in the Hereafter.[65]

Scholars and teachers are partners in reward, and there is no better people than they.[66]

The knowledge that is not used is like a treasure from which nothing is spent. Its possessor labored in collecting it, but never benefited from it.[67]

And if God directs you to one single man [who is learned], it is better for you than the whole world and all in it.[68]

The exaltation of knowledge and its acquisition among the Muslims may account, no doubt, for the abundant literary activities in al-Andalus. These activities also contributed to the belief that knowledge, or the possession of erudition in the sciences, constituted a mark of distinction among the several peoples of the world and an index for determining the degree of their civilization. Arabic authors referred to various peoples as civilized or barbarian on the basis of what they possessed or lacked of knowledge. This tendency is conveyed quite clearly by the eleventh-century Ṣā'id in his *Ṭabaqāt al-umam* (*The Categories of Nations*).[69] Abū Qāsim Ṣā'id Ibn Aḥmad was born in 1029 in Almería, and became a judge in Toledo, where he died in 1070. In addition to his *Ṭabaqāt*, he wrote a universal history, a history of al-Andalus, and a work on astronomy, in which he had a keen interest.

It is particularly interesting to note that Ṣā'id, unlike Ibn Ḥazm and Ibn Khayr, is more inclined to the speculative and the natural sciences — mainly philosophy and astronomy — than to the linguistic and religious sciences. This tendency is evident in his *Ṭabaqāt*. Moreover, Ṣā'id does not, like Ibn Ḥazm, attempt to exalt one science over another or to imply that the acquisition of the religious sciences constitutes the culmination of knowledge. On the contrary, the *Ṭabaqāt* has a plan and a specific theme to show the extent of the sciences among the various people from antiquity to his own time. Thus, the work offers a cultural history of the various peoples with reference to their governments, geographic position, customs, religions, and more important, to the sciences and their leading representatives. The *Ṭabaqāt* is important in two main respects: first, it gives an insight into the origin and cultivation of the sciences as they were known by the Andalusians of the eleventh century, and second, it enables us to gauge the extent of their cultivation and appreciation on Andalusian soil.

Ṣā'id distinguishes seven groups of people — Persians, Chaldean-Assyrian-Babylonians, Greco-Romans, Copts, Turks, Indians, and Chinese — all of whom differ mainly in language, history, and religion.[70] He then places people into two main categories: those who have cultivated the sciences and those who neither possessed nor cultivated them.

Those who did not interest themselves in the sciences are the Chinese, Turks, Khazars, Slavs, Russians, Berbers, Sudanese, Negroes, and other related groups.[71] Although the Chinese excel in the practical crafts (*al-ṣanā'i' al-'amaliyyah*) and the Turks in the art of war, they all to some degree resemble beasts more than human beings; all are victims of geographic accident, either by extreme cold or heat. He compares Chinese craftsmanship with that of the bees and ants and Turkish military dexterity with the lion's prowess. In both instances, the characteristics are more animal than human.

Those who interest themselves in the sciences are the Indians, Persians, Chaldeans, Greeks, Romans, Egyptians, Arabs, and Jews. He devotes a section to each of these and describes them as "The quintessence (*ṣafwah*) of God's creation and the humblest of His servants because they directed their attention to attaining the virtues of the active and rational soul (*faḍā'il al-nafs al-nāṭiqah al-ṣāni'ah*) which is characteristic of the human specie." [72] He adds, "Scholars (*ahl al-'ilm*) were the lamps of darkness and the banners of guidance, the lords of people, and the choicest of nations, who understood what the Almighty expected of them and knew the objective assigned for them." [73]

He devotes ample space to those people who interested themselves in the sciences. Following are some of the salient points of his evaluation:

India is called "the pasture of Wisdom" because of its devotion to the sciences and because it is "the treasure-trove of wisdom and the fountain of justice and political management (*siyāsah*)." [74] In spite of the fact that its people were nearly black, they were devoted to mathematics, geometry, astronomy, virtuous conduct, and perfect government.[75] Moreover, they are the most knowledgeable in medicine and the most discerning in determining the effects of drugs.[76] The Arabs are indebted to them in these disciplines, and owe them the famous book of fables, *Kalīlah wa-Dimnah*.[77]

Persia,[78] "the King of Kings," is famed for its long and orderly duration of government with an excellent administration and for knowledge of medicine and astronomy.

The Chaldeans[79] excelled in mathematics, metaphysics, and astronomy. Hermes was the most renowned and venerable of their scholars in the field of astronomy.

The Greeks[80] had the richest language; their scholars are called "philosophers," who "occupy the loftiest position and are most highly regarded among scholars for their genuine interest in the various aspects of wisdom pertaining to the sciences of mathematics, logic, the natural sciences, metaphysics, and domestic and city management." [81] They had Empedocles, Pythagoras, Socrates, Plato, Aristotle, Apolinus, Euclid, and Ptolemy, who greatly influenced Muslim scholars such as al-Rāzī, al-Fārābī, and al-Kindī.

The Romans[82] appear to be the intermediary between the Greeks and the Muslims through the Syriac-speaking people who transmitted Greek lore into Arabic. Those "Romans" include the Bakhtishū' family, Ḥunayn Ibn Isḥāq, Thābit Ibn Qurrah, and others, who were translators and also physicians and authors of books on the various sciences.

The Egyptians[83] had a great culture, as attested by their monuments and temples which are unequalled anywhere.[84] Their early knowledge in medicine and astronomy is traced again to a "Hermes" who built the pyramids and temples against the forthcoming flood. Afterward, the Egyptians cultivated philosophy, mathematics, the natural sciences, talisman, and chemistry.

The Arabs[85] are treated in greater detail. In fact, he devotes more than half of the *Ṭabaqāt* to them, taking into consideration three main periods by regions: pre-Islamic times,[86] Islamic times,[87] and al-Andalus.[88]

Among the pre-Islamic Arabs, there are those who did not leave any traces of knowledge and those who did. Among the latter are the Southerners, or Qaḥṭānites, who left a great legacy and who include the Ḥimyarites, Lakhmids, and others. The Northerners, on the other hand, were sedentary people, cultivators and merchants who did not possess any scholar to speak of. Others were simply Bedouins. He observes that the Arabs did not have any gift for philosophy and to the best of his knowledge no one excelled in it in pre-Islamic or Islamic times except al-Kindī, who was generally known as the "philosopher of the Arabs."[89] However, the Arabs took pride in their language, poetry, oratory, stories, and legends.

At the time of the emergence of Muḥammad, the Arabs were disorganized, having only their customary laws and some notion of medicine. Muḥammad led them to believe in God. Muḥammad's successors established a great empire, through which they came into contact with many peoples. Ṣā'id believes that the Umayyads of Damascus (661–750) did not improve the situation much with regard to the sciences.[90] It was only with the coming of the 'Abbāsids (750–1258), particularly with the emergence of the second caliph al-Manṣūr (754–775), that interest in philosophy and astronomy was given impetus by the rulers. This interest continued unabated, reaching its apogee with the caliph al-Ma'mūn (813–833), who "sought knowledge of the various subjects and brought it from its hiding place."[91] He got from the Byzantines the works of Plato, Aristotle, Galen, Euclid, Ptolemy, and others and committed them into Arabic. The process of translation led to the cultivation of the philosophical and natural sciences; there was al-Kindī and his pupil al-Sarakhsī, who wrote numerous works on the various sciences; al-Rāzī was a physician, logician, and philosopher; and al-Fārābī was known as "the philosopher of the Muslims." In addition to these celebrities (*mashāhīr*), who had a wide range of knowledge, a large number excelled in a particular discipline. There were the Banū Shākir—Mūsā and his sons Muḥammad, Aḥmad, and Ḥusayn — who excelled in astronomy, a subject that was pursued by many others.[92]

After he mentions a large number of Iraqis, Syrians, and Egyptians who excelled in the various sciences, Ṣā'id then passes on to his homeland, al-Andalus.[93]

Except for the language and law, al-Andalus did not possess any science before the coming of the Arabs, according to Ṣā'id. It was only after the coming of the Muslims that al-Andalus began to cultivate the various sciences. He describes their dramatic development, reaching an apogee under al-Ḥakam II, whose great library contained books about all the sciences. Al-Ḥakam II was known for collecting books on philosophy, mathematics, and astronomy. Ibn Abī 'Āmir, the ambitious general and chamberlain, purged them and committed many to the fire. This notwithstanding, the intellectual life continued, and a great number of mathematicians, astronomers, physicians, and philosophers appeared.

Ṣā'id concludes his book with the Jews.[94] He says that the Jews did not have any philosophy, but their main concern was with religious law and biographies of prophets. They are "the people of prophecy and the recipients of Revelation from among the descendants of Adam";[95] they possessed an exact system of calculating legal transactions and of figuring the lunar calendar. They inhabited a portion of Syria but were exiled all over the world under the Romans. It was in the various countries of exile, mainly in the Muslim world, that some of them interested themselves in the sciences and served Muslim rulers.

Finally, one can hardly omit Ibn Khaldūn's long discussion of the sciences in his valuable *al-Muqaddimah*.[96] Here Ibn Khaldūn devotes an ample space to man's ability to think, learn, and cultivate the various sciences — Qur'ānic studies, Prophetic Traditions, jurisprudence and its subdivisions, theology, Sufism, dream interpretation, mathematics and geometry, astronomy, logic, physics, medicine, agriculture, metaphysics, sorcery and talisman, the secrets of letters, and alchemy. He surveys all these sciences and refutes some such as astrology and alchemy as being both spurious and harmful. Some of Ibn Khaldūn's reflections on the manner of and the tools for acquiring the sciences are quite incisive and interesting. For instance, he believes that severity to students is extremely harmful[97] and that travelling in quest of knowledge will enhance enormously the education of a scholar.[98] Unlike Ibn Ḥazm[99] Ibn Khaldūn contended that a superabundance of books constitutes a major obstacle to attaining sound scholarship. The student would have to familiarize himself with all of them and the various methods used therein. This would be impossible, since the student's lifetime would not suffice to know all the literature in a single discipline, let alone in the various fields.[100]

Ibn Khaldūn's statement was no doubt influenced by the existence of an abundant and overwhelming literature in the Arabic language, most of which comprised compendia, commentaries, and commentaries on commentaries. At any rate, it is evident from the previous paragraphs that the Andalusians had a high regard for knowledge and attempted to pursue and disseminate it to the fullest extent. The search for education did not know any boundaries. Ordinarily, elementary education consisting of memorizing the Qur'ān, reading, and writing began at home and was given by the parents of the child or by a tutor. It might continue there depending on the educational level of the parents or their affluence. Also, the student was able to seek his education at the mosque, which was the main educational center. There he would receive his training in the Qur'ān, Prophetic Traditions, jurisprudence, grammar, lexicography, and other related subjects. This training could be received at all levels and under seasoned teachers who often were renowned authorities in this or that discipline.

Both Ibn Ḥazm and Ibn Khayr[101] give us a good idea of the content of the curriculum and of the ways and the manner of acquiring an education. Scholars travelled far and wide in search of knowledge; they sought the great authorities wherever these may have been, in Cordova, Seville, or Saragossa, or in the East in cities such as Qayrawān, Alexandria, Kūfah, Baṣrah, or Baghdād. They came into contact with leading teachers and intellectuals and received diplomas (*ijāzah*) from them upon the completion of a certain work or works. Once in full command of their subject, they became teachers (*mudarrisūn* or *mu'addibūn*), and were respected and in great demand at the court of rulers and in the homes of notables. They were often self-employed. There are references to the effect that teachers conducted classes at home and some of them had dozens of students. Aḥmad Ibn Sa'īd al-Anṣārī (d. 403/1012), a professor (*shaykh*) of Toledo used to have as many as forty students in his home, which was comfortably furnished and heated during the winter. At mealtime, students were served olives, meat, yoghurt, and sweets.[102]

Seeking training under a particular professor offered the advantage of getting the type of education or specialty the student wanted. For instance, the teaching of philosophy and the natural sciences was not favored by the religious scholars, and it was left for the student to pursue such subjects under scholars who seem to have conducted their classes in a clandestine manner. As a result, al-Andalus produced a good number of scholars in those disciplines.

Scholars, rulers, and notables had salons or literary clubs (*majālis*, sing. *majlis*)[103] in their homes which were attended by select people. Literary debates pertaining to grammar, lexicography, poetry, religion, law, and other topics took place. Often the host presided over those debates and supplied food and entertainment afterward. Bookshops also served as a meeting place for leading scholars who conducted spirited discussions on almost every conceivable subject.

By and large, rulers were men of culture, encouraged learning, and took pride in having the best talents at their court. Moreover, they established a great number of libraries and vied for the honor of having the best collection of books.[104] Their agents brought them books from distant places, and scribes copied books which were not readily available. They sponsored the establishment of a number of schools as to make education available for all. All in all, libraries — public and private — were the hallmark of culture and a source of pride even for those who did not have much interest in books.[105]

10

Arabic and Linguistic Studies

THE intimate relationship between the Arabic language and the "clear Arabic Qur'ān" has been recognized throughout the centuries. In fact, the revealed Book, the Qur'ān, could not possibly be comprehended without the study and mastery of the Arabic language. This makes the two almost inseparable and equally sacrosanct in Muslim tradition. It is because of this phenomenon that one can hardly separate the process of Arabization from that of Islamization. The two went hand in hand and, in the course of time, assumed universal posture. It was only with the emergence of a great literary tradition that Arabic was espoused by non-Muslims, mainly Christians and Jews, who used it as the language of intellectual expression. As such, Arabic became the mark of culture among Muslims and non-Muslims during medieval times. Thus, it became the most important unifying factor in al-Andalus and the most permanent link between it and the East. To be sure, the literary language remained one and the same in both East and West. It contained a vast and universal literature, some of which from the twelfth century onward was committed to Latin or Romance. Thereby the Arabic language helped to bring about and accelerate the European Renaissance.

The evolution and development of Arabic into a language of religion, state, and culture constitute the most fascinating chapter of Arab history.[1] During the rise of Islam in the seventh century, Arabic was basically a tribal language lacking a written grammar, lexicons, and the terms of the sciences as they were known in the great urban centers of the Near East. However, soon after the expansion of Islam over a wide territory, including the area from the Indus River to the Atlantic Ocean, special care was taken to study the language in which the Qur'ān was revealed and to preserve its purity in conformity with the Holy Book, pre-Islamic poetry, and Bedouin speech as it was known in and around the city of Mecca. This interest in the language eventually led to intensive linguistic studies which comprised not only grammar (*naḥw*) and lexicography (*lughah*) but every aspect of the language.[2]

The inception of Arabic linguistic studies appears to have taken place simultaneously in the cities of Kūfah and Baṣrah, which were military settlements during the early expansion of Islam, although they became cosmopolitan centers soon afterward. These two cities competed in the political and intellectual arena, and each developed its own outlook with regard to some linguistic problems. It was a debate between analogists and anomalists. Although these differences appear to be minor, they were magnified at the courts by rival scholars. The difference in approach between the two cities pervaded philological thinking in East and West alike, including al-Andalus. Controversy aside, both cities appear to be the home of the formulation of important linguistic criteria with respect to codification of the language and development of Arabic philology. As a consequence, what was agreed upon or established in either Baṣrah or Kūfah became something close to a linguistic dogma which was scrupulously followed in the other major intellectual centers of the Muslim empire. This is true of the grammar and lexicography which are associated with the Baṣran and Kūfan schools. It is significant to note that the Andalusian Jūdī al-Naḥawī was the first to introduce in al-Andalus the work of al-Kisā'ī of Kūfah, thus making the Kūfan tradition dominant until al-Qālī from Baghdād ultimately succeeded in giving precedence to the Baṣran school. As a rule, Arab philologists were both grammarians and lexicographers. Every educated Arab was expected not only to be conversant in grammar and lexicography but also to hold his own in any linguistic discussion. In addition, status required a good knowledge of the religious disciplines, poetry, and belles lettres (*adab*) — all of which were intimately related to the language. These Eastern and traditional qualifications were common among the Hispano-Arabic scholars. In sum, linguistic studies in Muslim Spain cannot be separated from those of the East, for the simple reason that they were emulations and imitations of them. Therefore, whether in grammar, lexicography, or other linguistic studies, Andalusians did not deviate much from the East. More often than not, they contained some of the conflicting outlooks that separated the Eastern philologists into the schools of Kūfah and Baṣrah.

As far as it can be ascertained, the Arabic language was still in a state of flux at the time of the conquest of al-Andalus. To be sure, though in the process of codification and development, the language of the Qur'ān was then, perhaps, the most common expression among the Muslims. But the language was attended by numerous problems at the source, and they became more acute in distant places, where the challenges were enormous and even overwhelming. In al-Andalus in particular, large-scale Arabization seemed unlikely because of many divisive factors. First, the linguistic mix of the country included Latin, which was the language of the Church, State, and literature; Romance dialects derived from Latin, which were the spoken idioms of the majority of the population; and Hebrew, which was used by the Jewish population, particularly for religious purposes. Secondly, it is doubtful whether the Arab and Berber conquerors themselves enjoyed a linguistic uniformity, although there is no reason to doubt that they all were Muslims and spoke a form of Arabic. Even the Arabs spoke different dialects and settled in various regions according to their tribal affiliations, thereby perpetuating certain peculiarities of their speech. They occupied roughly the southern region of the Peninsula up to Toledo. The region north of Toledo was either no man's land or sparsely inhabited by Berber settlers. In addition to some Arabic, the Berbers spoke a variety of Berber dialects.

On the other hand, there were positive factors which helped to give impetus to Arabization. Although the newcomers constituted a minority, their number increased by new waves of immigrants or military contingents. These immigrants, mostly men, took numerous slaves, wives, and concubines. Their offspring became Muslims and learned the languages of both father and mother. As the number of converts to Islam increased, the Arabic language came to have wider significance and served as the medium of unity among Muslims first and among these and non-Muslims afterward. Equally important initially was the presence of the Umayyads, under whose rule in the East Arabic was made the official language of empire about the turn of the seventh century. The Umayyads were proud of their Arab ancestry and their language. In the East as well as in al-Andalus, they contributed enormously to the Arabization of the empire through Islam, the Arabic language, and Arab mores. With the ascendancy of the Umayyads in al-Andalus, it became common among the non-Muslim population to adopt and learn the

Arabic language for daily communication and to use it as the medium of literary expression. From the ninth century onward, Arabic increasingly became the language of daily communication and the instrument of literary expression. It is no wonder that the ninth-century Álvaro of Cordova expressed his concern about the sweeping Arabization and the consequent neglect of Latin among Christians. He complained in one of his epistles: "Many of my coreligionists read verses and fairy tales of the Arabs, study the works of the Muḥammadan philosophers and theologians not in order to refute them but to learn to express themselves properly in the Arabic language more correctly and more elegantly. Who among them studies the Gospels, and Prophets and Apostles? Alas! All talented young men know only the language and literature of the Arabs and read and assiduously study the Arab books. If somebody speaks of Christian books they contemptuously answer that they deserve no attention whatever. Woe! The Christians have forgotten their own language, and there is hardly one among a thousand to be found who can write to a friend a decent greeting in Latin. . . ."[3]

Many of these Mozarabs adopted Arabic names in addition to their Latin family names. They served as civil servants in the administration, often as interpreters and translators. As noted earlier, the Bishop of Cordova, Recemundo (known as Rabīʿ Ibn Zayd), knew both Arabic and Latin, and was sent by ʿAbd al-Raḥmān III on a diplomatic mission to Germany. The Jews of Spain became fully arabized and wrote their most important works in Arabic, besides actively participating in the economic, commercial, and political life of the country.

However, the supremacy of Arabic did not put an end to the Romance dialects. The political situation in al-Andalus was such that it was imperative for both Muslims and non-Muslims to learn each other's language. This led to a widespread bilingualism consisting of knowledge of the literary Arabic and/or a dialect thereof on the one hand, and a Romance dialect on the other. In his *History of the Judges of Cordova*[4] al-Khushanī gives ample indication that Romance dialects were used widely in Cordova and even in courts of law.

Judging from the enormous amount of Arabic literature, however, Arabic enjoyed supremacy in the rather polyglot society, and its study was intensely pursued to a degree that enabled it to become the language of culture par excellence. Linguistic studies inspired by the Eastern model occupied the forefront in the Andalusian curriculum. Moreover, being quite distant from the source, the Andalusians were particularly careful and conscious about the eloquence, or correctness (*faṣāḥah*), of the language. In this connection, Ibn Khaldūn compares the ability of Andalusians with North Africans: "The Arabic philologists and teachers of Arabic in Spain are closer to acquiring and teaching the [linguistic] habit than others. They use evidential Arab verses and proverbs in this connection and investigate a good deal of [Arabic] word combinations in the classroom. Thus, a good deal of [linguistic] habit comes to the beginners early in [their] instruction. [Their] souls are impressed by it and prepared to obtain and accept it."[5] Furthermore, study of the language was an integral part of the study of the religious sciences. As a result of this, teachers (*mu'addibūn*) were in great demand and enjoyed the esteem and admiration of the people.

At first, the Andalusians depended wholly on Eastern scholars for their education — some teachers coming from the East, and others being Andalusians who had been educated in the East.[6] Among the latter one may mention: Jūdī (d. 814),[7] who earned the title of grammarian (*naḥawī*); al-Ghāzī Ibn Qays (d. 815);[8] 'Abd al-Malik Ibn Ḥabīb (d. 845);[9] Qāsim Ibn Thābit (d. 915);[10] and Qāsim Ibn Aṣbagh (d. 951).[11] These men studied under the leading authorities of the East and returned to al-Andalus where they were renowned teachers. Some of their pupils became outstanding philologists.[12] Although there was little composition of grammatical and lexical works in the ninth century, from the tenth century on a number of philologists composed works which could be compared favorably with the writings of leading Eastern scholars.

Like their Eastern counterparts, Andalusian scholars were first and foremost philologists. They concerned themselves with all aspects of the language: structure, morphology, idioms, grammar, origin, purity, and so forth.[13] They wrote grammars, lexicons, and even tried their hand at works dealing with the faulty idiom of the common people and writers. They held animated linguistic sessions and called attention to the inroads of colloquialisms and foreign elements into the written language. But their most outstanding accomplishment perhaps lay in their commentaries and abridgements of the great Eastern works, making these masters household words in al-Andalus. Eastern works were not only carefully studied and memorized but were explicated for students. Among the major works were *The Book* of Sībawayhi (d. ca. 800) of Baṣrah,[14] the *Amthāl* of al-Aṣmā'ī (d. 830),[15] the *Adab al-kuttāb* of Ibn Qutaybah (d. 885),[16] *The Kāmil* of al-Mubarrad (d. 897),[17] the *Alfāẓ* of Ibn Sikkīt (d. 857),[18] the *Majālis* of Tha'lab (d. 904),[19] the *Jumal* of al-Zajjājī (d. 949),[20] the *Gharīb al-muṣannaf* of Abū 'Ubayd,[21] and the works of many other writers.[22]

No doubt, early Andalusian writers were mere imitators of Eastern works in approach and content. At first they were students and teachers who made lexical and grammatical compilations. Jūdī is said to have written a text on grammar.[23] Other works were attributed to Ibn Ḥabīb,[24] Muḥammad Ibn 'Abd al-Salām al-Khushanī (d. 899), and Qāsim Ibn Thābit. These men and such others as Qāsim Ibn Aṣbagh and al-Ghāzī Ibn Qays left a great legacy which was continued by their pupils in the ninth and tenth centuries. From the tenth century on, however, Andalusians began to compose truly original works, some of which, according to Andalusian estimate, were unequalled.[25] Be that as it may, the most outstanding figures of the tenth century are al-Qālī (d. 967), Ibn al-Qūṭīyah (d. 978), and al-Zubaydī (d. 989). These men's teaching was kept much alive by an array of pupils throughout al-Andalus.

The name of al-Qālī has been mentioned in connection with his role of disseminating Eastern lore in al-Andalus.[26] Although he was an emigré from Baghdād, the Andalusians claim him as one of their own. Among his teachers were Ibn Durayd (d. 933) and Ibn al-Anbārī (d. 940), both authors of important philological works.[27] Furthermore, he was conversant with the works of al-Aṣmā'ī, Ibn Qutaybah, Sībawayhi, and others. He was a staunch advocate of the philological school of Baṣrah as represented by its foremost leaders al-Khalīl and Sībawayhi. He is credited with several monographs explaining pre-Islamic poetry, proverbs, grammar, and lexicography. His well-known and valuable *adab* work *al-Amālī wa-l-nawādir*[28] contains many lexical and grammatical items, historical information, poems, and proverbs. It has been compared with *al-Kāmil* of al-Mubarrad, but the former contains more items on lexicography and poetry whereas *al-Kāmil* contains more grammar and historical information.[29]

Of great significance in the development of Arabic lexicography is al-Qālī's *al-Kitāb al-bārī' fī-l-lughah* (*The Excellent Book on Lexicography*). It is said that al-Qālī spent some fifteen years in its preparation. He did not live to see it published; two of his pupils published it after his death. It appears to be the most comprehensive lexicon written up to that time and is said to have consisted of some five thousand folios. Only a small fraction has survived.[30] It was highly esteemed in learned circles, who considered it to be unique. The work is arranged according to the *Kitāb al-'ayn* of al-Khalīl Ibn Aḥmad — that is, on the basis of phonetic principles. Each entry is illustrated with poems and other literature and explained according to leading Eastern authorities.

Al-Qālī's fame rests also on his enormous influence on the philologists of the tenth century, chief among them the historian Ibn al-Qūṭiyah and the grammarian al-Zubaydī. His works were studied and commented on for generations.

Ibn al-Qūṭiyah (the son of the Gothic woman)[31] was born in Seville but made his home in Cordova, where he received his education and subsequently served the Umayyad court, most notably under al-Ḥakam II. In addition to his knowledge of Prophetic Tradition, history, anecdotes, and poetry, he was considered the most knowledgeable man of his age in Arabic and lexicography. Two of his works are of great linguistic interest. One consists of an explanation of *Adab al-kātib* of Ibn Qutaybah, and the other is a monograph dealing with the verb[32] — its classification, verbal derivations and their relationships, and in the bulk of the work, the relationship between the first form (*fa'ala*) and the fourth (*af'ala*), where Ibn al-Qūṭiyah attempts to show when *fa'ala* and *af'ala* coincide in meanings and when they differ.

But the most outstanding tenth-century Andalusian philologist was perhaps al-Zubaydī,[33] whom the biographer Ibn Khallikān calls "the ablest grammarian and the most learned philologer of his age." [34] Al-Zubaydī was born in Seville in 928 and moved to Cordova, where he received his education and subsequently the generous patronage of al-Ḥakam II. He came into close contact with al-Qālī, through whose works he became familiar with the leading Eastern scholars. He was highly regarded at the court and was appointed tutor of the future caliph Hishām II, Judge of Cordova, and Chief of Police. He is reported to have gathered a large fortune. Al-Zubaydī had a great enthusiasm and fascination for the Arabic language, considering it "the most palatable of all languages to utter, the most accurate in its formation, the clearest in the meaning of expression, and the richest in the various branches of knowledge." [35] In addition to being an excellent grammarian and lexicographer, he was an able poet and jurist. He was the author of a number of works, most of which appear to have been written at the behest of his patron al-Ḥakam II. Principal among them are *An Abridgment of "Kitāb al-'Ayn" of al-Khalīl*,[36] *Laḥn al-'awwām* (*The Faulty Speech of the Common People*),[37] a grammar entitled *al-Wāḍiḥ* (*The Clear One*), and a work dealing with derivations and explanations of portions of Sībawayhi's *Kitāb*.[38] Of great historical importance is his *Categories of Grammarians and Lex-*

icographers,[39] which includes an extensive list of both Eastern and Western philologists from the eighth century up to his own time. In it al-Zubaydī gives biographical sketches of scholars, their works, the places in which they flourished, and the methods they had followed. He categorizes the scholars with regard to their association with a school or region: Baṣrah, Kūfah, Egypt, Qayrawān, or al-Andalus. He treats first the grammarians and then the lexicographers of each category. Although he does not mention the sources of his information, the work was widely used by his successors and today remains an indispensable tool for philological studies.

Al-Zubaydī valued both al-Khalīl and Sībawayhi, although he attempted to correct and elucidate some of their findings. For instance, he attributed some of al-Khalīl's mistakes to later interpolations or to negligence by copyists. In the same manner, in his *Istidrāk* he criticized authors who had neglected the work of Sībawayhi and had written their own grammars which added little or nothing to grammatical studies. This work is important, too, for its insights into al-Zubaydī's linguistic ability, especially in cases where he takes issue with Sībawayhi, as on derivations (*abniyah*).

We are equally fortunate to have his *The Faulty Speech of the Common People*, a subject that occupied the attention of many Eastern philologists before and after him. The work is extremely valuable for its insight into the spoken and written errors of tenth-century Andalusians, particularly the inhabitants of Cordova. The aim of the work is to point to these mistakes, consisting of misused words, mispronunciation, and shifting vowels and consonants. He attempted to correct those mistakes by availing himself of Qur'ānic passages, proverbs, poetry, and sayings of the Arabs.

In sum, linguistic studies reached high development in the tenth century, with al-Qālī, Ibn al-Qūṭīyah, and al-Zubaydī as the best representatives. Their work was continued by their numerous pupils.[40] These pupils, first and foremost teachers, played an important role in fostering linguistic studies in the eleventh century. For the most part, they occupied themselves with explaining and commenting on the works of their predecessors, especially those of the East.[41] However, a number of authors went beyond abridgment and commentary to try their hand at original works.

It should be emphasized that in spite of the unsettled political situation in the eleventh century — that is, during the period of the party-kings — there was much scholarly activity in Cordova, Seville, Almería, Toledo, Denia, and other major cities. While the majority of the scholars at the time were poets, many of them were at the same time able philologists.

The most prominent eleventh-century scholars who displayed more than a passing interest in the language are Ibn al-Iflīlī (d. 1049), Ibn Ḥazm, Ibn Sarrāj (d. 1097), and Ibn Sayyīd (d. 1127) in Cordova; Abū al-Ḥajjāj al-A'lam (d. 1083) and Abū 'Ubayd al-Bakrī (d. 1094) in Seville; and Ibn Sīdah in Murcia, the greatest lexicographer of al-Andalus.

Only a few observations can be made in connection with several of these scholars. Although Ibn Ḥazm was more theologian and jurist than philologist, he offered his views on the manner and extent of studying the language.[42] He also discussed its origins and excellence and other linguistic questions.[43] For example, Ibn Ḥazm posed the seemingly eternal question of whether language was originated by divine teaching or by human convention — a question that received the attention of many of his predecessors and successors. He granted, like many Arab-Muslim scholars before him, the divine origin of language as attested by the Qur'ānic verse, "God taught Adam all the names."[44] He attempted to give a rational proof to this pious statement by arguing that if language had been the result of human convention, people must have convened to invent language without having a means of communication, intelligence, and skill — all of which are required to identify things and to know their essence. Therefore, it is false to assume that language was the result of human convention, a natural act, or dictated by physical environment. He concludes that the origin of language owes its very existence to God, who is both man's Creator and Teacher. With remarkable detachment, however, Ibn Ḥazm does not venture to say, like many of his Muslim predecessors, that Arabic was the first language taught by God to Adam. Nor does he commit himself to the excellence or superiority of one language over another, saying that many people claim their language to be the best and most excellent of languages, and that such a belief is, in his opinion, utter nonsense.

The most prominent philologist of the century was Ibn Sīdah,[45] whose influence on Arabic lexicography was felt for generations. He was born blind in Murcia and received his early education from his father. He developed a fantastic memory which aided him in compiling voluminous lexicons. Very little is known about him except that he was at the court of Mujāhid al-'Āmirī, the ruler of Denia to whom he dedicated his works with glowing praise. He was able to explain the lexical work (*gharīb al-muṣannaf*) of the lexicographer Abū 'Ubayd better than anyone else of his time. He is credited with several works, among which is a lexicon, *al-Muḥkam*[46] — so called because it was considered the most marvelous and soundest of lexicons. The lexicon was patterned after that of al-Khalīl, arranged alphabetically according to phonetic principle from *'ayn* to *alif*.[47] Each letter constitutes a section divided into chapters headed biliteral, triliteral, quadriliteral, and so forth. Each entry is explained — giving, for instance, the verb, its imperfect, verbal nouns, and derivatives. He often mentions his predecessors' opinion regarding the explanation of linguistic items. His purpose was to collect expressions from literary works and to present a comprehensive dictionary. It was followed by a large-scale lexicon entitled, *al-Mukhaṣṣaṣ*.[48] In the introduction, Ibn Sīdah explained that one reason prompting him to compose such a lexicon was that previous lexicons were incomplete and deficient, failing to do justice to the great wealth of the Arabic language and lacking full and lucid explanations of terms. He also provided a long discussion of various aspects of the language, mainly the question of the excellence and the origin of language. He takes a middle position between those who advocated divine origin of language and those who held that language resulted from human convention. He maintained that he had pondered this question for a long time and found that each of the opposing views had some convincing arguments, but he concluded that Arabic is so noble, perfect, and elegant that God must have helped to make it so through His teaching and inspiration.[49] The *Mukhaṣṣaṣ* was classified by subject matter for the benefit of poets, orators, and rhetoricians. It was divided into books, each of which concerned itself with a specific topic such as "horse," "camel," "birds," "plants," "vestments," "food," and "women," for which he supplies all the terms known to him and his leading predecessors (Sībawayhi, Ibn Durayd, Ibn Sikkīt, and others).

Of philological interest also were Ibn Sīdah's various commentaries on the poetical collection *al-Ḥamāsah*, the poetry of the great Easterner al-Mutanabbī, and the poems contained in the grammatical work of the tenth-century grammarian al-Zajjājī.

Another able philologist of the century was Abū 'Ubayd al-Bakrī,[50] who was also a poet, geographer, historian, and religious scholar. He lived in Cordova for a while, but moved to Seville and then to Almería. He distinguished himself as a commentator on a number of works, mainly *Sharḥ kitāb al-amthāl* of Abū 'Ubayd al-Qāsim b. Sallām and *al-'Ālī fī sharḥ al-āmālī* of al-Qālī. The aim of al-Bakrī was to expound on those works by filling the gaps in cases where the meaning was not clear, to explain rare expressions, and to make necessary corrections. In fact, he criticized the work of al-Qālī for its failure to provide sufficient illustrations to make the work more lucid and accurate.

There were other eleventh-century commentators[51] on Eastern works. Abū al-Ḥajjāj al-A'lam,[52] known as "the grammarian," was versatile in the art of prosody and was an able commentator on pre-Islamic poetry. Ibn Sarrāj[53] is credited with a number of commentaries. Another prominent commentator was Ibn Sayyīd,[54] who was born in Badajoz in 1048. His family was forced out of the city and went to Cordova. Owing perhaps to the unsettled situation there, he moved to Valencia. He became known as the leader (*imām*) in language and lexicography; students sought him out for training. Some of his important works were an explanation (*sharḥ*) of the *Saqṭ al-Zand* of the famous Syrian poet Abū 'Alā' al-Ma'arrī; the work has come down to us in five volumes.[55] He also explained with profuse example the *Adab al-kātib* of Ibn Qutaybah[56] and the *Jumal* of al-Zajjājī.

The thirteenth century had its best representatives in Abū 'Alī al-Shālūbīn (d. 1247) and Ibn Mālik (1208–1274). Al-Shālūbīn was a teacher of poetics and a talented grammarian whose principal interest lay in phonetics. However, he had a speech defect which often proved embarrassing. It is reported that he pronounced the letter *s* and the emphatic *ṣ* like *th*. Thus when he wished a ruler Godspeed before a forthcoming expedition, with the saying *Sallamaka al-lāhu wa-naṣṣaraka* (May God protect you and grant you victory), he would say *Thallamaka al-lāhu wa-naththaraka* (May God split you, and scatter you all over).[57] Al-Shālūbīn left a number of able pupils, one of whom was Aḥmad Ibn Yūsuf al-Lablāh,[58] who resided for a time in Morocco and then settled in Tunis, where he became a well-known teacher. In the words of al-Maqqarī, "Nothing ever escaped al-Lablāh from the eloquent speech of the Arabs."[59] He was known for his commentaries on the *Jumal* of al-Zajjājī and the *Ṣaḥīḥ* of Tha'lab.

Undoubtedly the most influential man of the century in linguistic studies was Ibn Mālik, a native of Jaén.[60] He received solid training in the language and travelled extensively in the East. He spent most of his life teaching in Aleppo, Ḥamāh, and Damascus; he was widely known as the most erudite grammarian. His merit lies in the simplification and versification of Arabic grammar in a work of one thousand verses, the *Alfiyyah*.[61] This work enjoyed a great popularity during his lifetime and up to modern times. It is a compendium of a larger work in three thousand verses called *al-Kāfiyah al-shāfiyah*. In addition, he wrote numerous works which dealt with grammatical and lexical topics and which exerted no small influence on his pupils and later generations.

A near contemporary of Ibn Mālik was Abū Ḥayyān (1256–1344),[62] a poet, grammarian, and commentator on the Qur'ān. He was born in Granada where he received his early training. Subsequently, he studied in Málaga and Almería up to about 1281. Because of some differences with one of his teachers, he left his homeland and went afterward to Ceuta, Tunis, Cairo, Alexandria, Ethiopia, and Mecca. He also taught at Cairo. He was described as the "Leader of Grammarians." Al-Ṣafadī called him "The Commander of the Faithful in Grammar," and proclaimed, "Had he been contemporary to the scholars of Baṣrah he would have enlightened them," and would have been a match for any grammarian or school of grammarians.[63] In addition to composing a number of *Muwashshaḥāt*, he was a prolific writer, having been credited with some sixty-six works on a variety of subjects. As a linguist his interest went beyond Arabic and Arabic grammar and led him to the study of Turkish, Persian, and Ethiopic, for each of which he wrote a grammar. He also commented on the works of his predecessors, such as the *Kitāb* of Sībawayhi, the *Alfiyyah* of Ibn Mālik, and others.[64]

As long as Muslim predominance lasted, interest in the language and the process of Arabization made headway, reaching a peak of development in the tenth and eleventh centuries. However, both declined gradually with the advances of the Reconquista from 1085 onward. Although Arabic and Arabic learning still had some gifted advocates, their hold on the Andalusian population was dwindling drastically as early as the thirteenth century. Except for the kingdom of Granada, Arabic ceased to be the language of diplomacy and culture. It lingered longer at the oral level, but it had to compete with the national Spanish languages, which were making great strides both at the written and oral level. Already in the eleventh century the Romance epic of the Cid was enjoying great popularity, and in the thirteenth century Spain had its own educational institutions in Palencia (f. 1214), Salamanca (f. 1215), and other places. Alfonso X gave depth and dimension to Romance through his publications and the sponsorship of many translations from Arabic into that language. From this time on, Spain began to acquire a linguistic consciousness that finally ended in the re-Latinization of the Peninsula by the early part of the sixteenth century when the systematic purges of the religion, customs, and language of the Arabs were successfully consummated.

However radical and systematic those purges may have been, it was impossible to erase the traces of several centuries upon succeeding generations. These traces can be seen in the arts and architecture, in early Spanish literature, and, especially, in the Spanish language. In this connection, a host of Arabic expressions were absorbed into Spanish to cover a wide range of terms in the sciences, literature, military affairs, administration, commerce, industry, produce and drugs, art and architecture, agriculture, and so forth. Ordinarily, most words of Arabic origin start with *al*, corresponding to the definite article in Arabic. There are hundreds of these words,[65] of which a few appear in the accompanying list of Arabic or arabized words which made their way into Spanish.

Arabic or Arabized Words in Spanish

Arabic	Spanish	English
al-amīr	almirante	admiral
al-bannā'	albañil	builder
al-birkah	alberca	pool
al-dalīl	adalid	guide
al-diwān	aduana	customhouse
al-fakhkhār	alfarero	potter
al-farīḍah	alfarda	a duty paid on irrigation
al-fāris	alferez	horseman
funduq	fonda	inn
al-Ḥamrā'	Alhambra	Alhambra (red)
Jabal Ṭāriq	Gibraltar	Gibraltar
al-jabr	algebra	algebra
al-jubb	aljibe	well
al-kāfūr	alcanfor	alcanfor
al-kuḥl	alcohol	alcohol
laymūn	limón	lemon
al-makhzin	almacén	magazine
al-muḥtasib	almotacén	inspector
al-mukhaddah	almohada	pillow
al-munādah	almoneda	sale by auction
al-nā'ūrah	noria	an irrigation wheel
naẓīr	nadir	nadir
al-qāḍī	alcalde	judge
al-qā'id	alcaide	commander
al-qantarah	alcántara	bridge
quintār	quintal	hundredweight
qitār	guitarra	guitar
al-qubbah	alcoba	alcove
al-quṭn	algodón	cotton
al-ruz	arroz	rice
Ṣāhib al-madīnah	zalmedina	watchman
al-ṣuffah	sofa	sofa
al-sukkar	azúcar	sugar
sūq	zoco	market
al-ṭirāz	altiraz	embroidery
al-'ūd	laúd	lute
yāsmīn	jasmín	jasmine
al-za'frān	azafrán	saffron
zakāt	azaque	charity tax
zaytūna	aceituna	olive
al-zuhr	azahar	flower

But the Arabic influence on Spanish extends beyond extensive borrowing of words. It includes a number of morphological and phonetical changes,[66] as in the use and sound of the Spanish *j*, which often came to replace the initial *s* of a number of Latin words. In addition, a host of expressions were incorporated into Spanish either in their original Arabic form (*ojalá* = *inshā' allāh*) or in literal translations of such expressions as "si Dios quiere," "vaya con Dios," "Dios te guarde."[67]

All in all, philological studies in al-Andalus occupied the forefront in the education of a scholar, and Arabic had a prominent place in the life of the country for nearly eight centuries. Andalusian scholars were great teachers with vast erudition. They loved books and wrote on a variety of subjects, contributing thereby to the creation of an enormous literature in the Arabic language. This literature encompassed all the disciplines known to the time and came to exert no small influence on Spanish and other European literatures. By and large, it was written in an easy style and a lucid language comparable with and often superior to anything written in the East. In fact, al-Andalus produced a number of literary giants who, by virtue of their literary productions, quality of language, and content, could be placed on the par with the great masters of the East. *The Ring of the Dove* of the theologian Ibn Ḥazm, the *Ḥayy Ibn Yaqẓān* of the philosopher Ibn Ṭufayl, and the tender and beautiful poetry of al-Andalus can be cited as great Arabic classics deserving a place of honor in world literature.

11

Prose and Belles Lettres (Adab)

THE full development of the Arabic language along with its pre-eminent position would not have been possible had it not been for the parallel evolution of an extensive literature written in it. Arabic remained not only the instrument of religion, but developed into the language of state and that of culture. In consequence, one can hardly separate the stages of development of the language from those of the literature. It is because of this relationship that prose and belles lettres written by Andalusians cannot be studied without reference to their Eastern background, from which they were inspired and derived. Andalusians borrowed, assimilated, and slavishly followed Eastern literary productions in form and content; they do not appear to have established literary genres or schools of their own. Andalusian literature developed as a consequence of the growth of Eastern literature and evolved from a simple and direct prose into a more ornate form.

Early prose writing in Arabic is represented by oratory (*khiṭābah*) and epistolary writing (*inshā'*), both of which arose in response to the political, religious, and administrative needs of the Islamic community. Preachers, rulers, secretaries, and litterateurs left an enormous body of material in these two genres. Many epistles (*rasā'il*, sing. *risālah*) and orations (*khuṭab*, sing. *khuṭbah*) were recorded in all sorts of works if only to show their skillful use of language and the technique of producing them. In fact, many became famous models of elegance and were attributed to Islamic leaders.

The origin of oratory may be traced to pre-Islamic times. It seems to have occupied an important place in Arabic society, as important, perhaps, as the position of poetry. It consisted of maxims, proverbs, and allusions. Politico-religious orations at public gatherings pleased the ear and emotions of the audience. They were simple and direct and uttered in a rhymed and rhythmical language. During the rise of Islam, oratory gained significance and evolved into unaffected language serving as a unifying factor among a large number of converts. It dealt with political, religious, and social matters and became an integral part of the politico-religious process of the nascent Islamic community. It was lucid and clear, with more attention paid to meaning than to form. Although we cannot be certain about the authenticity of many of the early orations, belletrists and others living almost two centuries after the events collected and preserved a large number of them. These orations consisted of religious sermons, exhortations, admonitions, political speeches, expressions of congratulation and condolence, and so forth. They were committed to memory and became the models of eloquence for orators and litterateurs throughout the Islamic empire.

Although in pre-Islamic times the orator (*khaṭīb*) had played an important role in the affairs of his tribe, he emerged to a position of leadership during the rise and expansion of Islam in his capacity as preacher (*wā'iẓ*), politician, ruler, general of an army, polemicist, missionary, storyteller (*qaṣṣās*), and so forth. In fact, he became more important than the poet, who had occupied the limelight for a long time. He continued to enjoy an enviable position of influence in society and remained a major representative of his culture. In early Islamic times, the names of orators who followed the rules of eloquence and presentation became household names in Muslim society. Of course, the Prophet Muḥammad gave "the best and most eloquent orations," as did his companions. The theologian Ḥasan al-Baṣrī (d. 718), and al-Ḥajjāj, the schoolteacher and viceroy of the caliph 'Abd al-Malik (685–705), among many others, became famous for their eloquent orations.

In the course of time oratory developed into a discipline with rules governing its form and content. Those rules imposed on the orator the requirements of a good appearance, proper intonation of the voice, and the use of gestures appropriate to the mood and occasion. It was one of the early manifestations of prose writing, along with contracts, deeds, treaties, correspondence, and other transactions.

Concurrent with the development of oratory there emerged the important genre known as epistolary writing (*inshā' al-rasā'il*). At first epistles were simple, brief, and direct, but they evolved into ornate forms with increasing attention to style and expression rather than to content. They became flowery and verbose and abounded in epithets, exaggerations, and plays on words. The use of rhymed prose (*saj'*) became the rule. Many epistles were collected by belletrists to serve as models for the secretary (*kātib*, pl. *kuttāb*). Secretaries were considered the alter ego of the ruler and were among the most important individuals at the court because their writings were considered a reflection of the stature of the court in which they served. It was through this elaborate writing that many secretaries became famous. Many treatises were written concerning the requirements demanded of secretaries. They were expected to have a broad education and a good command of the Arabic language, to take dictation, to know the rules and techniques of writing an epistle, to improvise according to the needs of the occasion, to be able to express themselves clearly and eloquently, to possess a handsome handwriting, and to have a good appearance.

Along with the development of oratory and epistolary writing there emerged a large amount of literary composition encompassing many disciplines and at the same time reflecting the nature and extent of an Arab education (*adab*) or the would-be educated man (*adīb*). The content of such an education can be gauged from the extant works dealing with that broad spectrum of disciplines often found in treatises known as *adab* works. The word *adab* has several connotations in Arabic. It may mean education or the broad knowledge ordinarily expected from a cultured man — ruler, vizier, chamberlain, secretary, boon-companion, and the like. In this connection, the term *adab* appears generally with *'ilm* (knowledge), the combination indicating the form and content of an education. By and large, this education comprises the religious disciplines, knowledge of Arabic grammar and lexicography, poetry, history, wisdom literature, epistolary writings, anecdotes, stories, games, sports, and some knowledge of the speculative and natural sciences. Philologists have been responsible for developing the *adab* genre through collecting the best of prose and poetry for the purpose of increasing linguistic dexterity and eloquence. *Adab* is defined as the "expert knowledge of the poetry and history of the Arabs as well as the possession of some knowledge regarding every science."[1] Aside from its educational connotation, *adab* also refers to the etiquette of eating, drinking, dressing, and other behavior.

It seems that belles lettres developed as a consequence of the social need for a smattering of knowledge about everything for every occasion. In fact, *adab* works became indispensable manuals for educated men, mainly public officials. As such, these works came to occupy an important place in Arabic literature and constitute a valuable source of information concerning the socio-intellectual conditions and mores of the Arabs.

Belles lettres had its first manifestation in the early part of the eighth century and reached its full development in the ninth and tenth centuries. It is difficult to judge an *adab* work by its content since this varies from one work to another. Thus, an *adab* work may be concerned for the most part with a particular topic — such as epistolary writing and wisdom sayings; sermons; historical events; grammatical, poetical, and lexical explanations; and edifying stories — or with a combination of these topics. While they were simple in content at the beginning, *adab* works came to include something on every conceivable subject. The major *adab* works produced in the ninth and tenth centuries became a model for many generations of writers.

Orators and epistolary writers made their influence felt in *adab* works. They contributed to the establishment of a set of requirements expected of the educated man. A great exponent of epistles was ʿAbd al-Ḥamīd (d. 750), known as the *kātib*. He studied under Sālim, a leading scribe of the day, becoming a schoolteacher and eventually a secretary (*kātib al-dawāwīn*) under the last Umayyad rulers of Damascus. He was considered "the most eloquent" (*ablagh*) secretary of the Umayyad period and left a number of epistles which became the model of this genre. In one epistle, he shows the importance of the secretary and the kind of education expected of him.

Of far-reaching importance were the writings of ʿAbdallah Ibn al-Muqaffaʿ. Ibn al-Muqaffaʿ is justifiably considered the originator of a smooth Arabic prose. He was born around the year 724 to a Zoroastrian family in a small village in Persia. He emigrated to Baṣrah, where he received an Arabic education from the leading men of the time. He served as secretary to various governors and became known for his ability in the art of epistolary writing which was in great demand at the time. He knew Arabic and Persian well, a qualification that enabled him to translate into Arabic the famous book of fables *Kalīlah wa-Dimnah*,[2] a work of Indian origin. He is credited with writing a number of works, among them two in *adab*: the *Adab al-ṣaghīr*[3] and the *Adab al-kabīr*.[4] The outlook of Ibn al-Muqaffaʿ is quite evident in these works as well as in his translation of *Kalīlah wa-Dimnah*. He is mainly concerned with moralizing, particularly with respect to the conduct of the ruler and the relationship between government and society. In all this, Ibn al-Muqaffaʿ centers his attention on how the government and the community should cooperate for attaining the ultimate good. This topic found ample space in subsequent and more comprehensive *adab* works. The fame of Ibn al-Muqaffa‘ did not rest on his outlook, but on the fact that he wrote in a simple and lucid style avoiding rare expressions, verbosity, and rhymed prose.

‘Abd al-Ḥamīd and Ibn al-Muqaffa‘ belonged to the Umayyad period (661–750). They set the stage for further development of prose writing, which reached its golden age under the ‘Abbāsids (750–1258) in the ninth and tenth centuries. It was particularly under the ‘Abbāsids that many elements influenced the form and content of Arabic literature. This literature became more and more sophisticated and comprised many sciences drawn from Greek, Sanskrit, and Persian. Writing took on a more elaborate and artistic form. Epistolary writings in particular were not meant to convey intents and ideas only, but to create wonderment and elation among readers and listeners by virtue of their eloquence, choice of wording, and the sonority and musicality of the words. This tendency gained momentum from the tenth century on owing to a life of elegance and luxury.

Ibn al-Muqaffa‘ was followed by a host of belletrists; the most outstanding of them were al-Jāḥiẓ (d. 866), Ibn Qutaybah, al-Mubarrad, and al-Qālī, who in the words of Ibn Khaldūn (d. 1406) set in their works the basic principles and pillars of *adab*.[5] The influence of these men was enormous in the eastern and western parts of the Islamic world and was acknowledged widely by their contemporaries and successors.

Al-Jāḥiẓ was the leading ninth-century *adab* writer and influenced both his contemporaries and successors. He was born in Baṣrah in 775, where he received his education in Arabic, poetry, and other disciplines. He moved to Baghdād to continue his training under leading authorities. After some travel he returned to his native city, where he died in 868–869. He wrote profusely and is credited with some 170 works on a variety of subjects. His *al-Bukhalā’* (*Misers*)[6] and *Ḥayawān* (*Animals*)[7] were used widely, and the topics treated in them were integrated literally or paraphrased in later *adab* works. But of great significance is his *al-Bayān wa-l-tabyīn*,[8] which was composed late in life. Although the work lacks a thematic organization, it appears evident that al-Jāḥiẓ was concerned with eloquence (*balāghah*) and correct speech because he makes profuse use of poetry, anecdotes, historical information, proverbs, wisdom sayings, and other material. As outlined, the work comprises style and eloquence, correct versus faulty speech, origination of sounds, mispronunciations, oratory illustrated by famous orations, poetry (which he considers the means for eloquence), rhymed prose, samples of testaments and correspondence, ascetics and storytellers with sketches of their lives, and fools and weak-minded persons.

Al-Jāḥiẓ was known for a good and smooth style in which both elegance and clarity were of the essence. He was equally concerned with both form and content, with the purpose of satisfying the ear as well as the mind without affectation. A contemporary of al-Jāḥiẓ was Ibn Qutaybah (828–889), a belletrist and literary critic whose *Adab al-kātib*[9] and *'Uyūn al-akhbār*[10] became very influential in *adab* literature. The *Adab al-kātib* is mainly concerned with linguistic matters; the *'Uyūn* comprises ten sections (*abwāb*, sing. *bāb*) which deal with the following subjects:

1. On the ruler (*sulṭān*): the conduct of the ruler, his policies, aides, companions, advisers, and secretaries.
2. On war: its nature, strategy, the qualities of good and bad soldiers, weapons, horses, camels, mules, donkeys.
3. On leadership: good conversation, nobility, poverty, acquisition of livelihood, praise of poverty, condemnation of wealth, commerce, humility, self-praise, clothes, the company of others, and buildings.
4. On the good and bad qualities of man: instinct, envy, anger, etc. It ends with a section on the nature of animals, birds, and reptiles.
5. On knowledge and style (*bayān*): books, the Qur'ān and Prophetic Traditions, religious disputations, refutations of heretics, poetry, good speech, and sermons of leading men.
6. On asceticism: its nature, outstanding ascetics, and some of their exhortations.
7. On friendship: its needs, loyalty, neighborliness, visits, gifts, condolences, congratulations, enmity, hatred, insults, etc.
8. On personal effects.
9. On food: its kinds, etiquette, hunger, fasting, feeding, hospitality, avarice; the care of the body; good, harmful, and appetizing food.
10. On women: their character, what is desirable and undesirable in them, marriage, beauty, ugliness, association with them, offspring, divorce, love, and passion.

Another important figure was al-Mubarrad (826–898), who often refers to al-Jāḥiẓ.[11] Al-Mubarrad, born and reared in Baghdād, was considered one of the leading scholars in lexicography and *adab*. These interests are evident in his *al-Kāmil* (*The Perfect*). It has fifty-four sections, each of which contains miscellaneous, unrelated items. However, the aims of al-Mubarrad become clear by virtue of the great attention paid to explaining rare terms as they occur in the Qur'ān, Prophetic Traditions, proverbs, poems, correspondence, orations, sayings of leading men, and other literary genres. It is not always easy to determine whether al-Mubarrad's use of literary texts in prose and verse are intended for their artistic and meaningful value, are intended to explain difficult linguistic problems, or both.

The authors discussed above exerted a great influence on Andalusian writing, as did their tenth-century followers. Among the latter were the poet and belletrist Ibn al-Mu'tazz (d. 908),[12] the secretary and prolific writer al-Ṣūlī (946),[13] Abū Faraj al-Iṣfahānī (d. 967), and others. Abū Faraj was the author of the voluminous and invaluable *Kitāb al-Aghānī* (*The Book of Songs*),[14] which reached al-Andalus when the work was still unknown in the East. It contains an enormous collection of poetry from pre-Islamic days up to the author's own time. It also includes anecdotes about the Arabs, their history and genealogy, and poets and musicians.

No sooner had the generation of al-Jāḥiẓ set the model for clarity and eloquence than affectation and embellishment began to spread, with more attention paid to form than to content. For instance, Ibn al-'Amīd (d. 971), the son of a secretary who himself became vizier-secretary, introduced many artifices into Arabic prose and extended a good and elegant style to the extremes of ornamentation. He was able to do so by combining refined rhymed prose (*saj'*) in patterns that resemble colorful mosaics. His writings were emulated by his pupil and companion al-Ṣāḥib Ibn 'Abbād (d. 997), who used *saj'* indiscriminately in his writings as well as in his daily conversation. His contemporary Abū Isḥāq al-Ṣābī (d. 996) made profuse use of *saj'*, forming a tapestry of colors and producing an embellished style with sonorous and melodious words. This excessive embellishment reached its apogee with Badī' al-Zamān (d. 1008), Abū 'Alā' al-Ma'arrī, and al-Ḥarīrī.

While this literary efflorescence was going on in the East, the Andalusians kept abreast of literary developments and studied them with keen interest. By the tenth century al-Andalus had an array of able and important writers. Belles lettres had its early and most eloquent representative in Ibn 'Abd Rabbihi (d. 940). He was born in Cordova in 860, where he received his education in religious studies, grammar, prosody, history, and other subjects required of the would-be courtier. He was a loyal client of the Umayyads and their panegyric poet. He served three of their emirs, mainly the great 'Abd al-Raḥmān III. Although he showed a great ability in various subjects, he became renowned as a belletrist and the author of the most comprehensive *adab* work of the tenth century, *al-'Iqd al-farīd* (*The Unique Necklace*),[15] consisting of twenty-five books which each bears the name of a gem. Although the work is based on Eastern sources — mainly, on the works of Ibn al-Muqaffa',[16] al-Jāḥiẓ,[17] Ibn Qutaybah,[18] al-Mubarrad,[19] Abū 'Ubaydah (d. 825),[20] al-Aṣmā'ī,[21] and others — Ibn 'Abd Rabbihi displays a great discernment and ability in the selection of his material. The work concerns itself for the most part with matters Eastern or with topics already dealt with by Eastern writers, but this does not diminish its value as a source for the social, political, moral, and literary aspects of tenth-century Islam. Moreover, in spite of his dependence on Eastern authors in form and content, Ibn 'Abd Rabbihi shows a great ingenuity in the arrangement of the work, making it a continuous whole. He achieved this goal by starting each book with an introduction relating it to the previous one. The *'Iqd* has the added virtue of being the most comprehensive *adab* work, containing something on every subject; its choice selection justified the author's calling it a "unique necklace."

In the introduction to the *'Iqd*, Ibn 'Abd Rabbihi states that people of different tongues throughout the ages compiled or selected the best and most eloquent expressions of their ancestors. It is in this spirit that "I composed this work and chose its jewels from the choicest jewels of letters, and made it the epitome of eloquence (*bayān*)." He points out that history had been omitted in works of this kind and feels the need of including it, leaving out the chain of transmitters (*isnād*) for simplicity. "I called it *The Unique Necklace* because it contains the various jewels of speech, a good and careful arrangement, and divided it into twenty-five books, each of which contains two sections and bears the name of a gem." In broad outline the *'Iqd* deals with: politics, government, the relationship between a ruler and his subjects, military affairs, good speech, the virtue of knowledge and the manner and content of education, biographical sketches of famous men, etiquette, anecdotes, sayings of the prophets, proverbs, religious duties, death and burials, orations and elegies, the superior genealogy of the Arabs, famous sermons, the post of secretary, a history of caliphs and Spanish rulers, biographies of leading Muslim statesmen, the excellence of poetry and its rules, songs and singers, women, women's qualities and defects, the home and vestments, geography, medicine, food and drinks, and jokes. A more detailed outline of the work follows.

1. *Al-lu'lu'ah* (pearl) deals with good and just government and the need for rendering it obedience; exemplary conduct for a ruler is prescribed. Wisdom sayings are cited to this effect. The ruler has need of assistants such as chamberlains, judges, advisers, and other aides, who ought to be loyal and capable; government is equated with justice, and the ruler is compared with a shepherd. The ruler should provide for the well-being of the community, preside over and correct cases of injustice, seek the advice of the learned and wise men, but never that of a teacher, weaver, shepherd, or companion of women.
2. *Al-farīdah* (the unique pearl) deals with war. War is defined as "strife whose shield is patience, its ax is deceit, its pivot is industry . . ."[22] Ancestral sayings are quoted concerning the manner in which it should be fought and a list of Arab knights and heroes and their accomplishments is given. Weapons, horses, strategy, and other details are discussed.
3. *Al-jabarjadah* (topaz) deals with generosity and gifts. A number of wisdom sayings and traditions support generosity and condemn avarice; bestowing of favors is praised by wisemen, the Prophet, and his companions; famous men of generosity, the best manner of asking for favors and fulfillment of promises are discussed.
4. *Al-jumānah* (pearl, or silver bead) concerns itself with delegations. On delegations to Persian kings and Muslim rulers; the manner of asking audience or seeking favors; how to excuse oneself, ask for forgiveness; how witty remarks can save the life of a condemned man; and how to correspond with a ruler.
5. *Al-marjānah* (small pearl) deals with the art of addressing a ruler. Addressing the ruler should be done with clarity and eloquence and not without formality and reverence. It is customary to kiss his hand, although some rulers are not enthusiastic about the practice. How often an intelligent and witty answer may result in handsome reward and in saving the life of a condemned person; praising the ruler, asking forgiveness; and correspondence among rulers.
6. *Al-yāqūtah* (sapphire) deals with knowledge (*'ilm*) and education (*adab*).The virtue of knowledge and how knowledge should be acquired and disseminated; how the scholar should use it and how he should be regarded with deference and respect. There are two kinds of knowledge: that of the body and that of religion; rulers should know genealogy and history. "He who

wants to be a scholar, let him seek one discipline, and he who wants to be an educated man (*adīb*), let him pursue all the sciences.'' [23] And among the prophetic traditions is the saying of the Prophet: ''A man is learned as long as he seeks knowledge; and if he thinks that he knows it all, he is ignorant.'' Another saying: ''Let knowledge be your possession and education (*adab*) your ornament.'' [24]

7. *Al-jawharah* (jewel) deals with proverbs. Proverbs ''are the ornament, the substance, and the jewels of speech.'' [25] Throughout the ages Arabs and non-Arabs made use of them; they are more lasting than poetry and better than oration. God used them in the Qur'ān, so did prophets and scholars. He gives a good selection of proverbs attributed to leading men of pre-Islamic and Islamic times. Proverbs in their good or bad connotations vividly describe human qualities and are ordinarily coined as the result of individual experience or observation; they may also be coined around animals and natural phenomena.
8. *Al-zumurrudah* (emerald) deals with religious exhortations and asceticism. This book mentions a host of men who became known for their spiritual counsels and austere behavior — prophets, scholars, religious men; exhortations of fathers to sons; famous sermons. Exhortation and asceticism are defined: the best exhortation is that which comes from a sincere man and is addressed to a fair-minded individual.[26] Asceticism is to restrain the soul from appetite, and not to allow patience to be overwhelmed by what is permissible.[27] Next are considered fear, hope, repentence, pestilence, crying, excessive laughter, tribulations of the faithful, temperance, seclusion, boastfulness, God's determinism, invocation to Him, and the asking of forgiveness.
9. *Al-durrah* (pearl) deals with condolences and elegies. Elegies are meant to soften the heart and make the stagnant tears flow during death and other calamities; lamentation at death and burials; famous elegies to renowned men; obituaries and epitaphs; elegies of fathers and mothers to sons, wives to husbands, brothers to brothers; and elegies to concubines.
10. *Al-yatīmah* (the unique pearl) deals with genealogy and the virtues of the Arabs. ''He who does not know genealogy does not know people and he who does not know people should not be considered from among them,'' [28] says Ibn 'Abd Rabbihi. He traces the origin of mankind to the three sons of Noah and deals at length with the origin of the Quraysh tribe and its subdivision into various tribes; he points to the excellence of each one of them and to their leading men in pre-Islamic and Islamic times. He makes the usual distinctions between Northern

and Southern Arabs; he calls attention to the claim of the Shu'ubiyyah for equality with Arabs and to Ibn Qutaybah's refutation of it.

11. *Al-'asjadah* (golden gem) deals with the speech of the Arabs. This book consists of famous invocations, sayings, exhortations, praise, satire, love, and other items which are intended to represent the choicest, clearest, and most eloquent Arab speech.
12. *Al-mujannibah* (frontal pearl) deals with the art of conversation. Ibn 'Abd Rabbihi says that conversation is the most difficult form of speech since it requires swift, witty, and intelligent answers according to the occasion. He gives a number of illustrations showing the degree of intelligence and sagacity required for the various occasions.
13. *Al-wāsiṭah* (the central pearl) deals with sermons and orations. It consists of selections of famous sermons and orations possessing the best eloquence delivered from pulpits, at fairs, and in courts of rulers. Included are the sermons of the Prophet and his successors, caliphs, governors, and eloquent men.
14. *Al-mujannibah al-thānyah* (the second frontal pearl) deals with writing and its tools and history of secretaries. In this book Arabic script is traced to Adam, and the development of Arabic writing and the manner of writing a book are discussed. It includes praise of secretaries and writers and mention of the most famous of them; the requirements expected of a secretary, such as vestment and good handwriting "which is the tongue of the hand, the beauty of the conscience, the ambassador of the intellect, the voice of thought, and the armor of knowledge."[29] The best secretary is he who states his intention at the beginning and writes eloquently but clearly; other requirements are that he should have a good education in poetry, history, biography of leading men, grammar, and religious studies, because a secretary is "the eyes of the king, his listening ear, and uttering tongue."[30] The rest of the book deals with the implements of writing: pen, ink, inkstands, paper, seals of rulers; it ends with sample correspondence for expressing a wish, making invitations and recommendations, and conveying thanks, praise, etc.
15. *Al-'asjadah al-thānyah* (the second golden gem) deals with the history of caliphs. This book is a political history which begins with Muḥammad and ends with the author's own time. It includes the orthodox caliphs, the Umayyads of Damascus, and the Umayyad rulers of al-Andalus. He concludes the works with his own poem which celebrates year by year the military expeditions of his patron 'Abd al-Raḥmān III. His treatment consists

of giving a biographical sketch of the ruler with a description of his physique, time of his succession, virtues, and death; he also includes the names of the ruler's wives, sons, secretaries, chamberlains, viziers, and judges.

16. *Al-yatīmah al-thānyah* (the second unique pearl) deals with history of Ziyād, al-Ḥajjāj, ʻAlīds, and the Barmacids. This book is actually a continuation of the preceding book on caliphs, but with main concentration on Ziyād and al-Ḥajjāj, the two able governors of ʻIrāq under the Umayyads; the ʻAlīds, and the famous Barmacid family that served the ʻAbbāsids. He explains his heading by stating that these people were "the axis of rulership upon which rested the pivot of policy; the source of administration, the fountain of eloquence and epitome of clarity."[31] The book concludes with a survey of the ʻAbbāsid caliphs up to and including the caliph al-Muṭīʻ (946–974).[32]
17. *Al-durrah al-thānyah* (the second pearl) deals with the days of the Arabs. Ibn ʻAbd Rabbihi considers the pre-Islamic period important by virtue of the memorable events. He deals with inter-tribal wars and the major participants with special reference to heroes and poets and some of their deeds; his accounts of the major events of the period start ordinarily with the heading of *Yawm* (day) of such and such a tribe.
18. *Al-zumurrudah al-thānyah* (the second pearl) deals with the excellence of poetry. This book is devoted to the choicest of poetry with reference to the famous *Muʻallaqāt*, to an evaluation of poets, and to the excellence of poetry. The most prominent poets are singled out from among the companions of the prophets and succeeding generations, and some of their poems on praise, satire, love, and other themes are included.
19. *Al-jawharah al-thānyah* (the second jewel) deals with prosody. This book deals with the art of versification with a detailed explanation in both verse and prose; the poetical meters and rhymes are explained, and the rules for composing verses are given. Each step is illustrated with examples.
20. *Al-yāqūtah al-thānyah* (the second sapphire) deals with singing and the opinion of people concerning it. Contrary to the opinion of those who attribute to singing an adverse effect, such as disturbing the mind and shattering the heart, Ibn ʻAbd Rabbihi justifies the inclusion of singing by saying that this art is "the pasture of the ear, the prairie of the soul, the spring of the heart, the field of love, the solace of the sad, the companion of the lonely, and the provision of the traveller."[33] He further reproduces the opinions of philosophers and leading Muslims who praise the excellence of a good voice and a good song in that

the latter is related to poetry, which had been praised in Islamic society. After stating the pros and cons, he supplies a great number of singers and songs.

21. *Al-marjānah al-thānyah* (the second small pearl) deals with women and their qualities. This book relates numerous opinions concerning the virtues and defects of women. Al-Aṣma'ī is supposed to have said, "After the confession of faith, no one elevates himself more than in a good marriage; and after unbelief, no one lowers himself more than in a bad marriage." Solomon said, "A level-headed woman builds her home while the evil-tongued woman destroys it."[34]
22. *Al-jumānah al-thānyah* (the second pearl) deals with false prophets, insane people, misers, and cheats. This book offers amusing stories concerning these peoples which are meant to entertain.
23. *Al-zabarjadah al-thānyah* (the second topaz) deals with nature of man and animals and the excellence of countries. This book takes into consideration the salient characteristics of man and animals and ponders on their natural disposition: the rational soul pursues the sciences and the truth, while the bestial soul aims at indulgence in food, drink, and sex. The opinions of physicians and philosophers are cited concerning the nature of the living, and the characteristics of individual animals and birds are discussed. A brief description of some of the Islamic provinces and mosques, especially those of Mecca and Jerusalem, is given. The last part is on miscellaneous topics, ranging from angels to the length of the earth, magic, poison, evil eye, and the bestowing of gifts.
24. *Al-farīdah al-thānyah* (the second unique pearl) deals with food and drink. This book deals with a classification of foods according to whether they are useful or harmful; names of foods and the manner of partaking them; and advice for a good health; nutrition and sleep in connection with meals; and the proper time of eating. The various drinks are discussed, discerning between those which are permissible and those which are forbidden.
25. *Al-lu'lu'ah al-thānyah* (the second pearl) deals with jesting and anecdotes. Jests and anecdotes are "the recreation of the soul, the springtime of the heart, the pasture of the ear, the source of leisure, and the mine of joy."[35] They are condoned by the prophets and leading Muslims. The book includes a large number of stories, jokes, anecdotes, and riddles.

One can readily see that *The Unique Necklace* contains something on virtually everything and for everyone. It is perhaps the best compendium of *adab* ever written. Ibn ʻAbd Rabbihi was not exaggerating when he set out to bring together the choicest of materials from the leading works of his predecessors. This he accomplished with great success, adding to it an excellent organization and coherent treatment not found among his predecessors. Moreover, he showed a great ability in the use of the language and a remarkable discernment in the balanced choice of materials on a variety of subjects, thus making *The Unique Necklace* an invaluable source for the litterateur, philologist, historian, sociologist, and political scientist. More important still, the work is a priceless document for gaining an insight into the literary and intellectual perspective of al-Andalus during the tenth century.

No doubt, Ibn ʻAbd Rabbihi set the framework of the form and content of an education expected from the cultured man of al-Andalus. When he died in 940 at eighty, his position at the court was filled by the Eastern emigré al-Qālī,[36] who most probably was brought to al-Andalus to continue the tradition of Ibn ʻAbd Rabbihi. Al-Qālī, who had received his training under leading scholars of the East, proved himself an able scholar whom the Andalusians later preferred to consider proudly as one of their own. An able teacher and philologist, he wrote *al-Amālī*.[37] Although the *Amālī* may be classified under *adab*, it is limited in scope to selections of poetry, proverbs, anecdotes, and stories, which were used mainly for lexical explanations. Inasmuch as al-Qālī was attached to the court, it is plausible that he tried to avoid duplication of subjects treated by Ibn ʻAbd Rabbihi and concentrated on linguistic matters. As a result, the work is often associated with the *Kāmil* of al-Mubarrad rather than with the works of Ibn Qutaybah and al-Jāḥiẓ.

In the introduction al-Qālī states the purpose of the work and includes laudatory statements about his patrons, ʻAbd al-Raḥmān III and al-Ḥakam II.[38] He proceeds to explain difficult lexical terms as they occur in his selections and on the authority of the major Eastern scholars who had left works behind or with whom he had come into contact. Among these were Abū ʻUbaydah, Thaʻlab, al-Aṣmaʻī, and Ibn Durayd. He often gives further elucidation on the basis of passages from the Qur'ān, Prophetic Traditions, proverbs, poetry, and anecdotes. His headings start with a query (*maṭlab*) concerning various expressions: the various names of a person who associates himself with women, names of young men in love, descriptions of women by a bedouin, meetings of poets with rulers and their poems, queries on various poetical wits between two rival poets, strife between a bedouin and his wife, praise and damnation of grey hair and its dyeing, speeches, advice and council of wisemen, letters, stories, poems of eulogy and praise, farewells, and commentaries on some verses.

Al-Qālī was imitated as widely in his *adab* work as in other disciplines in which he was renowned. His *Amālī* was closely followed by his successors, and a supplement or continuation (*dhayl*) of it was made after his death. Moreover, the work was widely studied and commented on and even criticized. For one, al-Bakrī (d. 1094) wrote his *Tanbīh 'alā awhām Abī 'Alī fī Amālīhi* (*A Reminder Concerning the Presumptions of Abī 'Alī in His Dictions*),[39] in which he criticized *al-Amālī*, calling attention to what al-Qālī had neglected or failed to explain and identify.

The importance of Ibn 'Abd Rabbihi and al-Qālī cannot be underestimated in both Eastern and Western parts of the Islamic world. In fact, many authors followed in their footsteps, to study, comment on, and emulate their works.[40] Although none of their successors attained their remarkable achievements, one can find a number of works with a limited scope which could be classified under the rubric of *adab*. While Ibn 'Abd Rabbihi makes an indiscriminate use of spiritual and profane topics, his followers would limit themselves to one or the other. For example, the prolific thinker Ibn Ḥazm wrote a socio-ethical treatise bearing the title of *Akhlāq* (moral character) and consisting of a prologue and twelve chapters.[41] The work is partly autobiographical and contains Ibn Ḥazm's opinions on a variety of subjects: human experience, praise, the sciences, relations with others, the giving of advice, justice, vanity, friendship, love, moderation, virtue, avoidance of bad habits, and correct behavior in a literary meeting. Although the book lacks organization and the chapter headings do not conform to their content, Ibn Ḥazm appears as a practical moralist and concentrates on questions affecting human conduct. He is particularly interested in the ultimate good and in the finality of human actions. After thanking God for giving him the gift of writing and being able to offer his work for the benefit of the reader, he makes certain generalizations about all sorts of men — for example, the pleasure experienced by an intelligent person, a scholar, an ascetic, or a prudent man is far more lasting and superior to that experienced by a glutton, a merchant, or a gambler. He asserts that all human actions aim at avoiding preoccupation and pain. After realizing this sublime truth he attempted to find a way to eliminate all kind of worries, but he found that this can be done only by addressing oneself to God with useful pursuits for the life after death.[42]

Equally important was the jurist Abū Bakr al-Turtūshī (1059–1130), who was born at Tortosa and studied in Saragossa and Seville. He made the pilgrimage to Mecca and travelled to Syria. He settled in Jerusalem where he attracted a number of students. Among his works is the *Sirāj al-mulūk* (*The Lamp of Princes*),[43] which contains the virtues and qualities a ruler ought to have; biographical sketches of many kings and savants among the Arabs, Persians, Greeks, Indians, and others; numerous charming and amusing anecdotes; and miscellaneous accounts concerning battles, the army, the administration of justice, and so forth. Finally, one may mention al-Mawā'īnī (d. 1168), a native of Cordova who lived and worked in Granada. He is the author of *Rayḥān al-albāb wa ra'yān al-shabāb* (*The Comfort of the Hearts and Protection of Youth*),[44] which consists of seven parts and deals with the general sciences, explanation of lexical terms and ambiguous expressions, eloquence, elegant style, poetics, genealogy, and history.

Adab works cover a wide spectrum of Arabic prose writings. They had two important functions: first, instructing, moralizing, and entertaining and, second, producing an excellence of language, elegance of style, and aesthetic effect. After the full development of Arabic literature, literary artifices and ornate rhymes were used frequently and became a primary consideration in prose writings. Their most significant manifestations are found in the *maqāmāt* (assemblies, or episodes), a genre originally consisting of witty and dramatic stories told to an audience in beautiful, elegant rhymed prose. They were best represented by the *Maqāmāt*[45] of the Eastern author al-Ḥarīrī (1054–1122) which, after the Qur'ān, has been considered the finest Arabic prose. Al-Ḥarīrī, who had come under Persian influence, popularized an elegant and ornate style that was characterized by its rhymes. His influence soon spread in East and West.

Al-Ḥarīrī patterned his work after the *Maqāmāt* of al-Hamadhānī (969–1008), known as the "wonder of the time" (*badī' al-zamān*), who attempted to produce a dramatic effect in his work. Badī' al-Zamān had a fantastic memory and knew Persian and Arabic. He wrote some two hundred thirty treatises employing rhymed prose with abundant use of paronomasia (*jinās*), rare expressions, proverbs, Qur'ānic verses, and poems. Besides epistles, he composed some four hundred *maqāmāt* of which perhaps fifty are extant. They are stories with two main central characters: one is a wandering scholar who travels from place to place entertaining his audience and impressing them with his eloquence and verbal dexterity;

the other is the storyteller (*rāwī*), who always recounts the scholar's adventures with the use of tricks, thus producing the desired suspense and dramatic effect.

The influence of Badī' al-Zamān on the form of Arabic literature was enormous, perhaps as great as that of Abū 'Alā' al-Ma'arrī (d. 973–1059), the poet-philosopher of Syria. If Badī' al-Zamān indulged in excessive ornamentation, thereby presenting difficulties in understanding his writings, al-Ma'arrī complicated the form of rhymed prose by further embellishment and by an abundance of rare expressions that tended to obscure the meaning. It was against this background of ornate style and difficult language that al-Ḥarīrī formulated his *Maqāmāt*, which was to have a great impact on literary form.

Al-Ḥarīrī was born near the city of Baṣrah. He had a broad education and displayed a great talent in the use of rare expressions and literary artifices. He wrote numerous treatises, in one of which he made use of the letter *s* in each word of the whole treatise. But al-Ḥarīrī's fame rested on his *Maqāmāt*, which consists of anecdotes from which some morals are drawn. Each of its fifty *maqāmāt* takes place in a different location in the Muslim world. The author's avowed purpose is to offer a serious language; to combine refinement with dignity of style, brilliance with jewels of eloquence, and the beauties of literature with its rarities. "Besides I have adorned them with verses of Koran and goodly metonymies, and studded them with Arab proverbs, and scholarly elegance, and grammatical riddles, and decisions dependent on the meaning of words, and original addresses, and ornate orations, and tear-moving exhortations, and amusing jests."[46] It is a narrative done by a *rāwī* named al-Ḥārith concerning Abū Zayd, the central hero who fascinates his audience by his eloquence and clever deeds. Each *maqāmah* centers on one of two devices: a verbal feat showing superb mastery of the Arabic language, or a scheme to create wonderment, amusement, or a moralizing effect. However, the main purpose is to gain wealth by these devices. As a rule, al-Ḥārith plays the dupe and is often outwitted by Abū Zayd, who is always unpredictable and eloquent and assumes the role of a satirist collecting alms for his preaching, that of a devoutly religious man, or that of a rascal using all forms of deceit for personal gains.

Already widely known during al-Ḥarīrī's lifetime, the *Maqāmāt* became one of the most popular classics of Arabic literature. It was considered unique in style and eloquence, and its form was imitated profusely even to the point that authors gave more attention to form than to content. The *Maqāmāt* of Badī' al-Zamān and that of al-Ḥarīrī were introduced in al-Andalus and became an important part of the curriculum. Subsequently, numerous *Maqāmāt* were composed in al-Andalus[47] and circulated widely.[48] However, Andalusians remained faithful to al-Ḥarīrī's *Maqāmāt* with its elegance of style, eloquence, and *saj'*. The content became diversified to include episodes describing a journey, soliciting favors, or relating one's experience. As a rule, authors would write one, two, or more *maqāmāt*. An exception was Muḥammad al-Saraqusṭī (d. 1143), who composed fifty *maqāmāt* but preferred the use of the linguistic embellishment of the Syrian poet al-Ma'arrī (d. 1057) in his *Luzumiyyāt*.[49] Several commentaries or critiques were made of al-Ḥarīrī's *Maqāmāt* by Andalusians, principal among them the *Sharḥ al-Maqāmāt*[50] of Aḥmad al-Sharīshī (d. 1222).

The influence of the *maqāmāt* form and content on Andalusian literature was profound, as was their impact on the Hebrew *maqāmāt*. They seem also to have had strong relationship to Spanish picaresque literature, especially *Lazarillo de Tormes*.[51] Here the *pícaro* Lazarillo is equated with Abū Zayd of al-Ḥarīrī; he practices deception for money like Abū Zayd, besides sharing such other characteristics as contempt for society, love of freedom, and ridicule of other people.[52]

Andalusian writers emulated their Eastern peers such as 'Abd al-Ḥamīd, al-Jāḥiẓ, and Badī' al-Zamān, considered the paragon of excellence in prose writing.[53] No doubt, the *Maqāmāt* of al-Ḥarīrī exerted an enormous influence on Andalusian prose writing in general and on epistolary composition in particular. Like their Eastern counterpart, the subjects of Andalusian epistles were varied, including rulers' instructions to public officials, requests, congratulations, condolences, greetings, descriptions of nature or a journey, anecdotes, stories, satire, polemics, requests for clemency, or the merits of al-Andalus and its outstanding men.[54]

Along with the philologists and authors mentioned in Chapter 10, there was an array of prose writers who mastered epistolary composition and other literary genres. Although many of them will be referred to in the discussion of the various disciplines in which they attained distinction, the following authors deserve special mention here. Although Ibn Darrāj al-Qasṭallī (d. 1030) was considered one of the best poets of al-Andalus, he also distinguished himself as a master of epistolary composition during his tenure as a secretary under al-Ḥakam II and the 'Āmirid rulers.[55] Two epistles[56] of the great poet Ibn Zaydūn became famous for the choice of language, style, and content. One epistle (*al-risālah al-hazliyyah*)[57] consisted of a venomous satire addressed to his rival Ibn 'Abdūs, who had been flirting with Ibn Zaydūn's beloved Wallādah. In it, Ibn Zaydūn caricatures Ibn 'Abdūs as stupid, uncouth, conceited, and the lowest of creatures (a fly, a mosquito), a ridiculous and comical figure who could not possibly be a suitor to an average lady, let alone to the beautiful princess Wallādah. He forged Wallādah's name on the treatise, causing her great anger and the eventual severance of their liaison. The treatise was written in an ornate style and rhymed prose. In it, Ibn Zaydūn displays great familiarity with the sciences, history, religion, and law. He tells Ibn 'Abdūs that Ptolemy, Hippocrates, Galen, and other sages could not possibly have arrived at their discoveries and knowledge without the inspiration and tutelage of Ibn 'Abdūs — a man who lacked any erudition. He satirizes Ibn 'Abdūs' assumed powers over the course of great historical events, revelation, and law. This epistle aroused the anger of Ibn 'Abdūs, a man of wealth and influence, and led to Ibn Zaydūn's imprisonment. In jail, he pleaded for clemency in a lengthy epistle (*al-risālah al-jiddiyyah*),[58] arguing his case and pleading his innocence against Ibn 'Abdūs' charges of mismanagement while serving Ibn Jahwar, ruler of Cordova.

There are too many prose writers to name them all in this section. However, one cannot omit mention of certain key works: *al-Tawābi' wa-l-zawābi'* of the poet Ibn Shuhayd (d. 1034); *al-Ṭawq al-ḥamāmah* of the erudite Ibn Ḥazm; and *Ḥayy Ibn Yaqẓān* of the philosopher Ibn Ṭufayl. Ibn Ṭufayl's philosophical novel narrating the evolution of man from his primitive state to the highest rational attainment will be discussed in Chapter 17.

Al-Tawābi' wa-l-zawābī'[59] (*Spirits and Demons*) describes a journey to a supernatural realm where the author meets the spirits of leading pre-Islamic and Islamic poets and rhetoricians. *Al-Tawābi'* gives an insight not only into the literary situation in al-Andalus, but into the character, claims, prejudices, and literary and poetical ability of the author. Abū 'Āmir Ibn Shuhayd[60] witnessed the prosperity and glory of Cordova under the 'Āmirids, and the decline and pillage of the city after 1009. His father was vizier under the dictatorship of Ibn Abī 'Āmir al-Manṣūr and served as governor of Valencia and Tudmīr. Al-Manṣūr had great affection for the young Ibn Shuhayd and showered him with gifts. After the fall of the

'Āmirids Ibn Shuhayd, like many others used to high living and influence, was faced with the predicament of the unsettled affairs in Cordova. He hoped for the resurgence of Umayyad power but was greatly disappointed, as was his close friend Ibn Ḥazm. Unlike this austere and serious-minded scholar, Ibn Shuhayd led a life of pleasure and displayed pride and conceit.

These qualities are evident in his *al-Tawābi'*, which is apparently meant to show his literary talent vis-à-vis leading pre-Islamic and early 'Abbāsid poets such as Imru' al-Qays, Ṭarafah, al-Buḥturī, Abū Nuwās, and al-Mutanabbī. He also matches wits with the great prose writers al-Jāḥiẓ, 'Abd al-Ḥamīd, and Badī' al-Zamān. In his imaginary journey accompanied by his faithful companion and guide Zuhayr, Ibn Shuhayd meets the spirits of all these people in different settings and asks them to recite their poems or pieces of their prose; he then recited his own in order to show his equality to and even his superiority over them. It is only in the presence of the poet al-Mutanabbī that Ibn Shuhayd admitted some shortcomings. In the process, Ibn Shuhayd displays, no doubt, a great talent and a marked sense of literary criticism. He concludes the work with a discussion of the virtue of poetry by a mule and a donkey, and with a story by a goose satirizing some unidentified Cordovan enemies of Ibn Shuhayd. All in all, Ibn Shuhayd proved himself an excellent poet of eulogy, satire, and praise, and a prose writer who felt confident in comparing himself with the great Eastern rhetoricians al-Jāḥiẓ and Badī' al-Zamān.

The imaginary journey of Ibn Shuhayd resembles that of the Syrian poet al-Ma'arrī in his *Risālat al-ghufrān* (*The Epistle of Forgiveness*), but all indications are that Ibn Shuhayd's work antedates that of al-Ma'arrī by a few years. Both works are concerned with literary questions but the settings are different — the underworld in the treatise of Ibn Shuhayd and Paradise in that of al-Ma'arrī. Their purposes are also different — Ibn Shuhayd is concerned with poetical and literary questions with a view to prove his own merits, whereas al-Ma'arrī delved into philosophical and religious matters, defending poets who had been killed on charges of heresy.

The main purpose of the *Tawābi'* seems to be to show the author's poetical dexterity and his ability to write excellent prose. In the process he emerges as a literary critic with an aversion for pedantic philologists. In statements attributed to him, Ibn Shuhayd argues that eloquence and clarity are not dependent on the memorization of rare expressions and hair-splitting answers to grammatical questions, but on the kind of relationship between the body and the soul — that is, the stronger the hold of the soul over the body, the better is the artistic production. Literary productions depend on environmental conditions, political circumstances and other factors. He conceives the good writer as the one who aims at lucidity and smoothness with respect to the choice of words, who uses good grammar, avoids deceitful and obscure expressions, and aims at achieving artistic unity.

While Ibn Shuhayd attempted to show his own poetical and literary gifts, his contemporaries al-Ḥimyarī (d. 1049) and Ibn Ḥazm had great praise for their Andalusian compatriots vis-à-vis leading talents of the East.[61] This self-awareness meant that Andalusians had already digested the Eastern disciplines, and were able to discern a good literary piece or poetical composition on the basis of certain criteria transcending mere feeling or taste. As a result, literary criticism[62] was in the making and was influenced, no doubt, by the criteria used by poets, philologists, belletrists, theologians, and philosophers in the East. There as well as in al-Andalus, certain poets, writers, and orators became the model of excellence. These models still had their critics, matched by vocal defenders. Even the great poets Abū Tammām, al-Mutanabbī, and al-Ma'arrī had their critics and defenders. The modernist poets (*muḥdathūn*) and the ancient poets had also advocates and opponents. All this led to heated controversies expressed in literary sessions and books in both East and West. The criteria often used for determining the poetical or literary talent of an individual consisted of linguistic purism, correct grammar, and eloquence; expressions in relation to clear meaning, style, brevity, and conciseness; avoidance of verbosity; and the problem of plagiarism.[63]

In this connection, Ibn Ḥazm gives us his views on the merits and demerits of poetry[64] and on rhetoric (*balāghah*). He considers poetry as an art adorned with lies,[65] and rhetoric as an artifice which is good so long as it is used in the "path of God"[66] and so long as it conveys clear meaning for both the notables and the masses.[67] Rhetoric ought to possess clarity — brevity for those who are able to grasp the meaning and repetition for those who are not. For him, the language of the Qur'ān is the clearest expression, unique and beyond the ability of rhetoricians to imitate.[68]

No doubt, Ibn Ḥazm paved the way to literary criticism as did his good friend Ibn Shuhayd. He was followed by his able pupil al-Ḥumaydī (d. 1098), author of various important works among which is *Facilitating the Way of Learning the Art of Correspondence*.[69] In it, al-Ḥumaydī ponders the various aspects of rhetoric (*balāghah*), eloquence (*faṣāḥah*), and the manner of attaining them. His near contemporary Ibn Abī al-Khiṣṣāl (d. 1146), a leading poet and prose writer, took issue with a colleague who had put Badī' al-Zamān above the belletrist al-Ṣābī.[70] Ibn Abī al-Khiṣṣāl considers al-Ṣābī superior to Badī' al-Zamān because of his great facility with words and ability to convey meanings as contrasted with the trickery and contrived situations found in the writing of Badī' al-Zamān.

Perhaps the most articulate defender of prose in al-Andalus was Abū al-Qāsim al-Kulā'ī (d. ca. 1150), author of five works in which he criticizes or praises leading authors.[71] His *Iḥkām ṣan'at al-kalām*[72] deals with Arabic prose with reference to its leaders and stresses its importance over poetry. After pointing to the various opinions concerning prose and poetry, he maintains that poetry is beautiful by virtue of its meters and rhymes but prose is more reliable for conveying meaning. Moreover, poetry has a corrupting influence, leads to distortion, and is done for profit.[73] On the whole, the *Iḥkām* is concerned with the education of a secretary and the manner of writing correspondence and oratory. Al-Kulā'ī emphasizes eloquence and clarity, and warns against rare expressions, verbosity, rhymed prose, and ornate style — all of which could lead to obscurity.

Finally, Ḥāzim al-Awsī (d. 1286)[74] wrote perhaps the most comprehensive work of literary criticism. Born in Cartagena, reared and educated in al-Andalus, al-Awsī emigrated to Tunisia; he displayed great interest in literature, grammar, and literary criticism. His *Minhāj al-bulaghā' wa-sirāj al-udabā'* (*Road of the Rhetoricians and the Lamp of the Erudite*)[75] offers a great insight into literary criticism. It deals with various kinds of prose profusely illustrated with passages from the works of leading authors. He pays due attention to poetry and the manner of composing it, and to meanings (*ma'ānī*), oratory, and criticism of leading poets and authors.

What emerges from this brief chapter is the fact that al-Andalus displayed a unity in language and literature vis-à-vis the rest of the Muslim world. Andalusian writers adopted not only the literary genres of the East, but their mode of expression and stylistic innovations. At first they proved to be good pupils who borrowed, commented on, and adapted all sorts of Eastern works; but from a slavish dependence on the East, they emerged with self-awareness of their talents and displayed a great ability in producing works of their own, becoming discerning critics of a good or bad literary piece. They also reflected on the purpose of prose and poetry and on the question of the respective merits of the two. Moreover, they achieved parity with their Eastern peers and, in some instances, surpassed them. An enormous amount of literature was written on Andalusian soil, in all Arabic literary genres: orations, epistolary writings, *maqāmāt*, stories, legends, proverbs, wisdom sayings, and so forth. Although Andalusian literature does not differ much from its Eastern counterpart in form and content, it does point, by virtue of its quality and quantity, to a brilliant culture transplanted from the East to European soil.

12

Poetry: The Classical Tradition

THE enormous amount of prose writing in al-Andalus was matched by an equally enormous amount of poetical composition. In pre-Islamic times, poetry ruled supreme over the hearts and minds of the people, overshadowing both oratory and prose writings. Only after the rise and expansion of Islam did the orator and scribe gain importance owing to the religious, political, social, and administrative needs of the Islamic community. They were able to compete with the pre-eminent position of the poet, whose mode was no longer viable for expressing the multifarious concepts of a rapidly growing society. This notwithstanding, the poet was able to hold his own against the strong competition of the scribe and continued to occupy an important place in Islamic society in spite of the fact that his poetry remained, by and large, worldly and profane. In consequence, if al-Andalus was united with the East in language and literature, it was also united with it in poetry. And if the orator, scribe, and storyteller were important figures in Islamic society, so was the poet. In fact, the poet was a permanent figure at the court of rulers and was admired for his art of versification and excellence of language. He often occupied a high post and received ample rewards from his patrons. It was against this background that the scribe strove for excellence in his writings and aimed at innovating and embellishing his style to create artistic effect as well as wonderment and suspense. No doubt he attempted to please the ear and the mind through the use of elegant language in expectation of high rewards. But in doing so, the scribe could hardly displace the poet and had instead to learn the art of versification, which enabled him to assume the role of both a scribe and a poet.

Poetry in al-Andalus had a development parallel to that of prose writing. In consequence, Hispano-Arabic poetry cannot be studied without due consideration of the poetry which developed in the East. From pre-Islamic times up to the present, poetry has occupied a prominent place in Arabic literature.[1] It constitutes the earliest literary and artistic manifestation of Arabic culture. In pre-Islamic as in Islamic times, it played an important role in Arabian society and represented the most eloquent expression. It preserved Arabic deeds, values, and vices. The poet, who was said to be possessed by a *jinn* (spirit), was a leader of his tribe and, as such, exerted great influence on it. He sang its glory, praised its virtues, encouraged it in war to defend cherished values such as honor, bravery, loyalty, and hospitality.

Arabic poetry (*shi'r*) falls under the heading of the science of prosody (*'ilm al-'arūḍ*). It is designated by the term *naẓm* (ordering) as opposed to *nathr* (scattering), which is applied to prose. It contains both rhyme (*qāfiyah*) and meter (*wazn*, or *baḥr*). There are sixteen Arabic meters.[2] An Arabic verse or line is called *bayt* (plural *abyāt*), and consists of two halves or hemistichs (*miṣrā'*).

Poetry was highly developed in pre-Islamic times. It may have started with a rhymed form without a meter (*saj'*). One may assume that from this rhymed prose a poetical form with meters evolved. This form, known as *rajaz*, consists of four to six feet to the line; the lines rhyme.

On the basis of these two forms, poetry reached a high development with strict laws for rhyme, quantity, and manner of introduction. Although no fixed date is agreed upon regarding this development, it is best represented by the *qaṣīdah* (ode), which had already matured in the sixth century. The meaning of the word *qaṣīdah* is not clear. Some Arab grammarians explain it as meaning a poem with an artistic purpose; others suggest that it means "aiming at," for instance, reward in return for praise and flattery; and still others associate it with a form of *qaṣada* meaning "to break," since the *qaṣīdah* consists of verses, each one of which is divided into hemistichs.[3]

The *qaṣīdah* has a complicated meter and preserves the same rhyme throughout. As a rule, the poet stands with his companion at a deserted campsite and reminisces about bygone days, recalling his intense feeling for his beloved and the anguish of his separation from her, and the detailed hardship of a journey by horse or camel. He ends the poem by vilifying the enemy or praising the hearer in expectation of reward.

The classical *qaṣīdah* of pre-Islamic times is represented in the famous seven *Mu'allaqāt*[4] (the Suspended Ones). The term is supposed to have originated when the pre-Islamic bards entered a contest at 'Ukāẓ; and the best poem was suspended on the Ka'bah for all to see. It is also suggested that such poems were written on cloth with golden letters — hence, their other appellation as *Mudhahhabāt*. It is unlikely that either of these meanings was the actual one inasmuch as writing, on the whole, was scarce in the sixth-century Arabia, let alone writing in gold. On the other hand, *mu'allaqah* also means "necklace" and was used, perhaps in a figurative sense, to imply that the poem had an artistic unity and was self-contained.

Although Muḥammad attacked the poetry of his time, its form and content continued to be popular not only in the early Islamic period but also in centuries afterward, despite great changes in environmental, social, and religious conditions. Umayyad and 'Abbāsid poets had long taken the pre-Islamic poet as a model for their inspirations. This was true also among Hispano-Arabic poets of the Iberian Peninsula. However, here as elsewhere, poetry in its old garment was influenced by the changed environment and new perspectives.

The Arabic-speaking people have a great fascination for and love of poetry. It has been regarded as the highest artistic attainment of the Arab and the mark of his culture, and as such has occupied a prominent place in the Arabic curriculum. Rulers, princes, scholars, and women have tried their hand at it, either as versifiers or reciters. At parties and public gatherings extemporaneous compositions or recitation of the works of leading poets were common. Arabic poetry has a great wealth of vocabulary, similes, and metaphors. Although its content is often vaguely understood or not understood at all, poetry has an impact on the audience as great as that of music. In essence, Arabic poetry appeals more to the ear and heart than to the mind. More often than not it caters to the vanity of a patron and the emotion of the hearer.

It would be harsh to suggest that Arabic poetry as a whole lacks sincerity and substance. It possesses great artistry, and often conveys intense and noble feelings. This is true, perhaps, more in al-Andalus than elsewhere in the Arabic-speaking world. This may be due to the fact that the Andalusian enjoyed life intensely and was uninhibited, expressing his feelings about his favorite subjects — love and nature — in beautiful and moving poems. In another context, Arabic poetry offers valuable insight into the history of Arab-Muslim society. Moreover, early Arabic poetry served as a valuable means for codifying the language and was considered second only to the Qur'ān as a medium for the most eloquent expression. As a consequence, poetry has been preserved with care in the oral tradition as well as in the writing throughout the centuries. The enormous number of poetical collections (sing. *diwān*) that have come down to us from pre-Islamic and Islamic times attest to the pride the Arab took in poets and poetry.

On the other hand, Arabic poetry was in some measure dissociated from life itself, and, as such, it remained formal: rigid and austere in form, artificial and stereotyped in content. This was due principally to the role of the poet in society. He was often a tool of the patron or a captive of the audience. In such a capacity, the poet's task was to impress and please; he was compelled to indulge in insincere imitation, particularly when he was asked to compose poems of praise, satire, or elegy. Under the circumstances, the lot of the professional poet was not an easy one. His success depended as much on his willingness to accommodate his audience as on his artistry. He depended on his patron for a livelihood and, unless he was a wealthy man, he had to succeed in affluent circles through a great deal of tribulation and hardship. He began his career wandering from one place to another reciting his poems to anyone who was willing to listen and in expectation of some reward. The poet hoped eventually to reach the court of a ruler. Once at court, he was given generous stipends and even land in fief. He was ordinarily provided with special vestments befitting his rank at the court. And, depending upon his educational preparation, he might be appointed to an important office.[5]

Both the form and content of Arabic poetry were standardized to the point of rigidity. Due regard for these requirements was observed among the Hispano-Arabic poets, although they introduced new images and metaphors drawn from the Spanish soil. Whereas 'Abd al-Raḥmān I had sung nostalgically to a palm tree in the manner of the old bards, his successors in al-Andalus addressed themselves to gardens, brooks, rivers, and monuments. Moreover, whereas the pre-Islamic poet had sung the saga of inter-tribal wars, the Andalusian poet celebrated the victories of Islam in its wars against Christian rulers. This notwithstanding, the language remained essentially akin to the classical or "pure" Arabic. However, new popular forms known as *zajal* and *muwashshaḥ* began to appear in the tenth century and differed substantially from the classical in form, language, and even content. These new forms will be treated in Chapter 13.

Arabic poetry in general and Hispano-Arabic poetry in particular contain the following major themes:

Love (*nasīb*, or *ghazal*), in which the poet sings the joy of a reciprocal love, the thrill of a rendezvous, or the beauty of the beloved. The poet laments the suffering of an unhappy love and separation from the beloved.

Praise (*madḥ*), in which the poet indulges in praise for his patron's superior qualities, which often are imaginary.

Satire (*hijā'*), in which the poet depicts, often with exaggeration, the blemishes and evil qualities of an enemy.

Elegies (*marāthī*), in which the poet emphasizes the deceased's qualities, such as generosity, courage, nobility, and wisdom.

War poems (*ḥamāsah*), in which the poet laments reverses at the hand of the enemy or celebrates the victory of his benefactor.

Ascetic (*zuhd*) and mystical poetry, in which the poet dwells on the transitory character of this world; on fate, virtue, or the merit of knowledge; on union with God.

Descriptive poetry (*waṣf*), in which the theme of love found the most eloquent expression among the Hispano-Arabic poets. Here the poet showed his intense feeling for and love of nature. Cities, rivers, mountains, valleys, palaces, monuments, gardens, promenades, fruits, and flowers were favorite themes. The night, dawn, sunset, wind, snow, the planet, animals, and plants were also objects of his attention, as were ruins, which reminded the poet of bygone greatness.

Wine poetry (*khamriyāt*), in which the poet extolls wine and its effects.[6]

Hispano-Arabic poetry depended for a long time on that produced in the East. Eastern poets, from pre-Islamic times down to the tenth century, were the models and sources of inspiration for the Hispano-Arabic poet, or lover of poetry. More often than not the Hispano-Arabic poet was considered successful if his poetry closely imitated that of leading Eastern poets. Among the latter were Shanfara, Samaw'al, Ḥātim al-Ṭayy', and Imru'-l-Qays of pre-Islamic times; Ibn Abī Rabī'ah (d. 719), Jarīr (d. 728), al-Farazdaq (d. 728), and al-Akhṭal (d. ca. 710) from the Umayyad period; and Bashshār Ibn Burd (d. 783), Abū Nuwās (d. 810), Abū al-'Atāhiyah (d. 828), al-Buḥturī (d. 897), al-Mutanabbī (d. 965), and al-Ma'arrī, to mention only a few, from 'Abbāsid times. All of these men were well known in al-Andalus and were considered consummate poets. Their poetry was widely studied, commented on, and recited.

Despite its dependence on the East, Hispano-Arabic poetry reached its full development in the eleventh century when the Andalusians became fully conscious of their own poetical gift and were not satisfied with comparison with Eastern poets. At this point, the Andalusian desired to be equal or even superior to the Easterner, as is evidenced by the several treatises of Ibn Ḥazm,[7] Ibn Bassām,[8] Ibn Khāqān,[9] and al-Shaqundī,[10] who extolled the poetical talents of their compatriots.

The development of Hispano-Arabic poetry may be analyzed according to the following major periods: the formative period, which extended from 711 to 1031, or the rule of the Umayyads; the flowering of poetry or its golden age, particularly under the party-kings (1031–1090) and shortly thereafter; the eventual decline and ultimate disappearance of such poetry from Spanish soil, which was completed by the sixteenth century.

It is hardly possible to do justice to the enormous number of poems written by a staggering number of individuals from all walks of life. The sample of the poetical compositions included here falls short of conveying both the actual content and the form of the original Arabic.

The Umayyad rulers, not to mention the poets who came to Spain during and after the conquest, had considerable knowledge of poetry and even composed poems in the best classical tradition of the *qaṣīdah*. For one, ʻAbd al-Raḥmān I (756–788)[11] is said to have composed various poems, outstanding among which is one addressed to a palm tree. He gives the tree personalized human feelings not unlike his own and he expresses a strong feeling of nostalgia for his Syrian homeland:

> A palm tree I beheld in Ar-Ruṣāfa,
>   Far in the West, far from the palm tree land:
> I said: You, like myself, are far away, in a strange land;
>   How long have I been far away from my people!
> You grew up in a land where you are a stranger,
>   And like myself, are living in the farthest corner of the earth:
> May the morning clouds refresh you at this distance,
>   And may abundant rains comfort you forever![12]

He had a passion for hunting, and his companions tried to tempt him at the sight of herons to go hunting instead of pursuing a campaign against the enemy. But ʻAbd al-Raḥmān, who had been driven from his homeland to taste the hardship and bitterness of exile, did not fall to the temptation. He reminded his companions that his task was to hunt felons and he admonished his companions that the path to glory is attained only through hardship and effort; following are the last two verses of the poem:

> Tell those who like to sleep on cushions
> That glory is forged by effort, nought else!
> So ride toward it through hardships' straits,
> Else will you be the lowest of all beings![13]

To the emir al-Ḥakam I also are attributed a number of poems — one celebrating his crushing a revolt at Toledo and another appeasing five rebellious members of his harem![14] Also 'Abd al-Raḥmān II, who "orientalized" his court in the fashion of Baghdād, composed some verses, as did some of his immediate descendants. It was during his reign that the famous singer-musician Ziryāb came to Spain from Baghdād. Ziryāb seems to have aroused the jealousy of many, among them the poets Ibn Ḥabīb and al-Ghazāl.[15] Ibn Ḥabīb also sought reward from 'Abd al-Raḥmān II through praise but the satirical vein of his poetry reminded the ruler that he, as a scholar, was more deserving of munificence than the musician Ziryāb:

> I am hard pressed, yet what I wish
> Is an easy thing for the Merciful's power
> One thousand red ones, or even less, would accept
> A scholar, whose wish may have been too great:
> Ziryāb was given this sum, no more, no less
> Yet my profession is surely nobler than his.[16]

Likewise, the satirist Yaḥyā b. al-Ḥakam, known as al-Ghazāl by virtue of his extreme beauty, composed venomous satire against Ziryāb. These satires earned him exile: he went to Iraq, where he met leading poets. As a poet, he had great ability to charm ladies by flattery — especially those whom he encountered on his diplomatic missions to the Normans and Byzantines. His poetry of wine strongly resembled that of the famous Baghdādi poet of wine, Abū Nūwās (d. 810).

Sa'īd b. Jūdī[17] is an example of the knight poet. Appearing during the rebellion of 'Umar b. Ḥafṣūn, he composed war verses[18] and others expressing his tender feelings for a certain Jayḥān, a fictitious name for the Umayyad prince's songstress, with whom he was madly in love. Some of his verses are:

> My ears refused to leave my soul in my body:
> Because of them, my heart was filled with sadness;
> I gave Jayḥān my soul merely because
> I recalled her song, without having seen each other:
> It seems that I and her *name* — while the tears flow
> From my eyes — are like a *monk* who prays to his idol.[19]

The fame of Ibn Hānī al-Andalūsī (b. ca. 932–937/d. 973)[20] rests on his *adab* work. He first led a licentious life in Seville; he was banished from the city and went to North Africa, where he received the patronage of the Fāṭimid ruler. Ibn Hānī preferred to return with his family, but he died en route under obscure circumstances. In honor of the Fāṭimid Mu'izz (952–975) he composed a famous *qaṣīdah*, which by its quality could be compared with the best poetry in East or West, according to the evaluation of the biographer Ibn Khallikān. However, it is an example of panegyric which lacks both sincerity and a sense of proportion. Following is a part of the poem praising the Fāṭimid ruler:

> By God, if equinoctial rains were like him,
> Despair of famine would never arise in the world:
> In the light of his person Time made appear
> An empire free from weaknesses and baseness!
> An *imām* just and honest in every respect,
> Such as a just *imām* should be and is expected to be:
> He surpassed in glory all past and present eras,
> Like a necklace whose center excels its ends in worth:
> He finds not enjoyment in accumulating wealth,
> Nor does he take pleasure in this world's joys:
> Lions are trembling with fear in their dwellings
> Before his sword which, once unsheathed, is bound to win:
> When all the kings together are compared to thee,
> Thy greatness equals a sea, they are mere drops![21]

From the tenth century onward Hispano-Arabic poets became numerous, and the list of eleventh-century poets is staggering indeed. "Everybody," says García Gómez, "from the poorest farmers to kings, is a poet and every thing serves and is put into poetry."[22] One may single out some of the leading poets such as al-Ramādī, Ibn Darrāj, Ibn Shuhayd, Ibn Ḥazm, Ibn Zaydūn, al-Mu'tamid, Ibn 'Ammār, Ibn Labbāna, and Abū Isḥāq of Elvira. Some of these poets are mentioned in connection with courtly love.[23] By and large, their poetical talent went beyond love poems, and comprised the various contents of Arabic poetry: panegyrics, satire, elegies, wine poems, description of nature and so forth.

Al-Ramādī (d. 1015)[24] was born in a village in the Algarve and studied in Cordova, where he later taught. He became the leading poet at the court of the caliph al-Ḥakam II. However he was imprisoned on charges of having ridiculed his patron in a poem. While in prison, he composed a number of poems and gave them the title of the "Book of the Bird" in which he praised the ruler and pleaded for mercy. Subsequently he served at the court of Ibn Abī ʻĀmir al-Manṣūr for a time but seems to have fallen into disfavor. His poems include panegyrics to his patrons, lamentations, wine poetry, satire, and love poetry.

Ibn Darrāj al-Qasṭallī has been mentioned along with Ibn Shuhayd in connection with epistolary compositions.[25] Ibn Darrāj was the secretary and court poet of Ibn Abī ʻĀmir al-Manṣūr and earned the surname of al-Mutanabbī by virtue of his excellent poetry. Ibn Shuhayd, an able poet, equated himself with leading poets of pre-Islamic and early ʻAbbāsid times.[26]

These poets flourished in the city of Cordova at a time when Seville began to emerge as the important political and intellectual center of al-Andalus. In Seville as elsewhere in al-Andalus, an array of poets served at the courts of petty rulers. The most important and colorful poets were, perhaps, Ibn ʻAmmār and his patron al-Muʻtamid, the poet-king of Seville.

Ibn ʻAmmār (1031–1086)[27] was of Arab origin, belonging to a humble family. He received literary training in Silves and Cordova and showed a great inclination for poetry at an early age. He started as a vagabond poet and composed poems of praise for whomever paid for them. His fame must have been widespread when he was introduced to the ʻAbbādid al-Muʻtaḍid, ruler of Seville, for whom he composed a *qaṣīdah* of praise on the occasion of the latter's victory over the Berbers. Ibn ʻAmmār soon became the intimate friend of al-Muʻtaḍid's son, al-Muʻtamid, himself an accomplished poet of wine and song. Both young poets enjoyed a good time and an adventurous life, a relationship that caused al-Muʻtaḍid to exile Ibn ʻAmmār. However he was reinstated to the ʻAbbādid court at the accession of his companion, and was appointed governor of Silves.

Because of his humble origin, perhaps, and a life of deprivation, Ibn ʻAmmār tended to skepticism and certain feeling that he would sooner or later lose the friendship of al-Muʻtamid. This conscious awareness may have been the result of his own behavior, which was often radical and indiscreet. For instance, he was prone to pomposity and showmanship; he appeared to arrogate to himself functions that actually belonged to his benefactor. This situation led to suspicion and ended in tragedy when Ibn ʻAmmār made the fatal mistake of inciting the people of Valencia to rebellion. The hitherto tolerant al-Muʻtamid composed a poem to Ibn ʻAmmār reminding him of his low origin and baseness. To make matters worse, Ibn ʻAmmār, in turn, composed a venomous satire against al-Muʻtamid and his family. This destroyed once and for all the old friendship. Ibn ʻAmmār had to flee to the North and finally was sold to the highest bidder; al-Mu'tamid bought him and brought him to Seville. Ibn 'Ammār asked the ruler's pardon in a poem that became famous, but to no avail. The enemies of Ibn 'Ammār were pressing for his death, and al-Mu'tamid, in a fit of anger, seized an ax and killed his former friend with repeated blows.

The poet-king al-Mu'tamid (1040–1091)[28] was one of the most renowned poets of Muslim Spain. He was the poet of nostalgia, love, gaiety, and suffering. As a ruler he assumed first the governorship of Silves in the name of his father al-Mu'taḍid, and he then succeeded to the throne of Seville at the age of twenty-nine. He was an able ruler and he could have become a great one had it not been for difficult circumstances beyond his control — namely, the internal struggle among the party-kings, the successful inroads of the Christians, and finally the emergence of the African kingdom of the Almoravids, who put an end to his kingdom and humiliated him. It was he who invited the Almoravid ruler to check the victorious Alfonso VI. The final outcome was that the proud ruler was taken captive from Spanish soil to the desert at Āghamāt in Morocco, where he lived his last days in poverty and humiliation. Al-Mu'tamid ceased to be a king, but he remained a great poet with an outlook quite different from that of his youth when he led a life of joy and splendor.

On the whole, al-Mu'tamid's poetry may be divided into two periods: that composed during a time of prosperity and ease, and that composed during exile and suffering. In many respects, his poetry has an autobiographical character pertaining to his youth, adventures, reminiscences, and the like. His merit as an outstanding poet has been widely recognized in the East and West.

When he was in trouble as the result of a military fiasco, he composed flattering verses to soothe his father's anger; he sang passionate and tender verses to his beloved I'timād; and he composed many other love verses, some celebrating his victories. In captivity, his various elegies were marked with nostalgia, sorrow, and a deep feeling of humiliation. At times he complained about his state of inactivity, and at others he reminisced about the good old days, expressed his concern for the conditions of his family, or lamented his suffering.

He lived a life full of contrast: a seemingly lasting and sincere friendship with Ibn 'Ammār ended in violence by his own hand; a relatively strong kingdom was taken away because of an invitation he had made and for which he blamed himself later on. All of these sad and dramatic situations were food for poetry. Aside from them, his poems addressed to his wife I'timād, whom he had bought from a muleteer, are quite famous. He had a strong attachment to I'timād, who appears to have been beautiful and gracious, but witty and capricious. If she wanted to see snow in the hot days of summer, al-Mu'tamid planted almonds to simulate a snow setting.

A famous poem was addressed to his friend Ibn 'Ammār on the occasion of the latter's nomination to the governorship of Silves. Here al-Mu'tamid recalls the days he had spent there as governor. He wonders if the dwellings and castle remember the young man who longs for them and sighs for the nights spent with round-hipped maidens: with a girl who poured out wine for him from her bewitching glances, "from her glass and from her mouth"; who thrilled him by the tunes of her lute; and who resembled a blossoming rose when she let fall her mantle!

In contrast to a life of luxury, parties, and passion is the life of exile, humiliation, and suffering which he describes in moving poems. He bemoans his lamentable condition as a captive in chains which clasp him "like serpents and bite like lions." In one poem he nostalgically reminisces about his beloved Seville — its flower gardens, pools, groves, and palaces — and he ponders his fate:

A stranger, a captive in the Maghrib: over there,
  The throne will mourn him and the pulpit also,
Sharp, cutting swords, and the lances likewise,
  Will shed, profusely, bitter tears of grief!
There was a time when power was his friend,
  A very close one, but today it eschews him,
By the decree of a misguided, corrupt Fate:
  Has Fate e'er dealt justly with those who're just?
Mā as-Samā's sons, destiny has humbled them;
  Great, indeed, is the shame of Mā as-Samā's sons!
Her waters, made of tears shed o'er their misery,
  Flow over all regions of the sky like oceans!
I wonder whether I ever shall spend a night,
  With flower gardens and water pools around me,
Where green olive groves, far famed, are planted,
  Where the doves sing, the warbling of birds resounds,
In the Zāhir on the heights, refreshed by soft rain,
  The Thurayyā pointing at us, we pointing at it,
The Zāhī looking at us with its round Sa'd as-su'ūd,
  Jealous of each other, like a beloved and a lover!
All this is now hard, not easy to attain:
  Yet, whatever God wishes to pass, is easy to bear![29]

In another poem, an epitaph, he asks the stars to dampen with their tears the tomb that encloses his remains and describes his qualities of wisdom, mercy, generosity, bravery, and justice:

Tomb of a stranger, my evening and morning dew refresh thee!
  Truly, thou has won the mortal rests of Ibn ʻAbbād:
Wisdom and knowledge, and munificence, all in one,
  Opulence for the poor, the water stream for the thirsty,
The lance, the sword, the arrow in fierce affray,
  The giver of death to the enemy lion,
One who was like Fate in vengeance, a sea of generosity,
  A moon in the darkness, the leader of courtly gatherings!
Yes, it is true, God's decree thus has attained unto me,
  Heavenly decree thus has brought me to my appointed time.
And before seeing this bier I never could imagine
  That high mountains could be placed on wooden boards!
Do not ask for more: be kind to the nobility entrusted to thee,
  And may the storm-laden clouds pour rain amidst lightnings
Over thee, who hidest their brother, whose streams now rest
  Under the stone slab; each evening, each morning,
Let the tears of the dew fall upon thee, descending
  From the eyes of the bright stars that failed to help him!
May the blessings of God be poured without number
  Upon him who lies here, fore'er and fore'er! [30]

Many were the poets at the court of the ʻAbbādids of Seville. Prominent among them were Ibn Labbāna (d. 1113),[31] who, having received the favors of al-Muʻtamid, remained faithful to his patron and visited him in exile at Āghamāt. In one poem, he describes with verses that touch the heart the departure of al-Muʻtamid from al-Andalus. He ponders on the inevitability of destiny; he pictures the unforgettable sorrowful scene of departure with unveiled girls sobbing and giving their last farewell to the sons of ʻAbbād.

The eleventh century produced other outstanding poets who received the patronage of the party-kings of Toledo, Murcia, Badajoz, Almería, Granada, and others. Mention should be made of Abū Isḥāq al-Ilbīrī (Sp. *Elvira*) of twelfth-century Granada,[32] who is famous for his ascetic poetry and a long poem written about 1066 inciting the people to rise against the Jews, who he believed had arrogated to themselves too much power and wealth. In other poems he reflects on the transitory character of this life, finds solace in seclusion, and condemns the conceit and vanity of rich people.

The poet-king al-Muʻtaṣim (1051–1091)[33] of Almería surrounded himself with great poets of the time, such as Ibn al-Ḥaddād (d. 1087),[34] a poet of love and praise, who fell in love with a Christian girl and composed tender verses for her. His daughter Umm al-Kirām[35] is known for her passionate verses addressed to the handsome youth al-Sammār.

At this juncture, it is important to mention that, at the coming of the Almoravids in 1090, Arabic poetry in its classical form began to decline. This may be due to the lack of appreciation by the Berber rulers for poetry and to the gradual and steady decline of Muslim power in the Peninsula. Moreover, new poetical forms as represented by the *zajal* and *muwashshaḥ* were making inroads, and the pre-eminent position of classical poetry was challenged. Nevertheless, the deeply rooted poetical tradition did not suddenly halt. The philosopher Ibn Bājjah[36] from Saragossa composed a number of poems; Ibn 'Abdūn (d. 1134)[37] from Badajoz is famous for his elegy, the *'Abdūniyyah*, and for his prodigious memory; the exiled poet Abū al-Ṣalt (d. 1134),[38] author of an anthology of Andalusian poets, was known for his poems of the descriptive (*waṣf*) and love (*ghazal*) types.

Perhaps the leading poet of the first half of the twelfth century was Ibn Khafājah (d. 1139).[39] In his youth he was a poet of love and pleasure. He later became the great poet of nature, for which he received the appellation of *al-jannān* (the Gardener); he composed many poems describing flowers, gardens, rivers, and mountains. Late in life he turned to asceticism (*zuhd*) and wrote several poems on that subject.

The classical tradition was continued by the grammarians Ibn Mālik[40] and Abū Ḥayyān,[41] and by the great thinker and statesman Ibn al-Khaṭīb, who composed a number of *zajals* and *muwashshaḥāt*.[42] But the great poetical talent of the fourteenth century was Ibn Zamrak (1333–1392),[43] called "the poet of Alhambra." He was born to a poor family in eastern Spain and moved to Granada, where he became the pupil of Ibn al-Khaṭīb. Ibn Zamrak distinguished himself as a poet, scholar, and prose writer. Like his master, he served the Naṣrid rulers of Granada, gaining prominence in state affairs through the help of his teachers. He composed a number of panegyric and lyric poems in eloquent and polished language which must have earned the admiration of his patron since he chose to have some of them inscribed on the walls of the Alhambra as a testimony of Ibn Zamrak's poetical genius.

In conclusion, the contribution of al-Andalus to Arabic poetry in general can hardly be overstated. In addition to popular innovations, al-Andalus remained faithful to the classical poetry with respect to poetical forms and language, thereby preserving the integrity of the *qaṣīdah*. On the other hand, Andalusian poets drew their themes and raw material from the resources of al-Andalus, without the artificiality and obscurantism of the neo-classicist poets of the East. Their poems could stand a favorable comparison with the best compositions produced in the East. Ibn Zaydūn, al-Mu'tamid, Ibn Khafājah — to mention only a few — rank among the leading Arab poets. Their lyrical compositions as well as their poems describing nature have enjoyed great popularity among the Arab-speaking people and have been anthologized in both the eastern and western parts of the Arab world. Their proper use of similes and metaphors, besides genuine sentiments, contribute to the greatness of their poetry, which remains urbane and sophisticated, drawing its inspiration from the fauna and flora of al-Andalus as well as from the fascination for and attachment to the fair sex.

13

Poetry: The Popular Forms

ALONG with the wide cultivation of classical poetry there emerged from about the tenth century onward a popular poetry, which did not conform to the classical pattern in meter, rhyme, or even in language. It was frowned upon by the neoclassicists or purists, who argued that it was vulgar and artless, not deserving the name of poetry. On the other hand, the new poetry was regarded by its advocates as alive, vigorous, and spontaneous without the formality and artificiality of the classical compositions. Thus, the dichotomy between the old and the new, or the classical poetry and the new popular poetical forms, was in some respects similar to the one which took place between the neo-classic poets and the modernists in Baghdād from the eighth century.[1] However great the dichotomy between the popular and the classical, social circumstances and currents in al-Andalus dictated their coexistence for a long time.

Whether the popular tendency as represented by the *muwashshaḥ* and *zajal*[2] originated on Spanish soil or was inspired by an Eastern model, as was the case for classical poetry, remains a major point of contention among scholars. All considered, indications are that the new poetical forms began in Spain itself, where they reached full development in a manner unparalleled elsewhere in the Arabic-speaking world. This notwithstanding, the Eastern model as seen in the *mawālīyā* (*mawwāl*) might have played some role in their development.[3] Another question remains as to whether the *muwashshaḥ* and *zajal* emerged simultaneoulsy or one was an offshoot of the other.[4] They do resemble each other in form and content, although they differ considerably in language and often in rhymes, which are more consistently adhered to in the *muwashshaḥ*.

The following paragraphs provide some observations on the nature of *zajal* and *muwashshaḥ*, their relationship, components, development and dissemination with reference to some leading poets, and their possible impact on European lyrical compositions. The *zajal* often refers to that poetical composition in which a spoken Arabic dialect along with some non-Arabic expressions is used. As for the *muwashshaḥ*, it is considered a more artistic production containing — except for the *kharjah*, or concluding verses — literary Arabic expressions only. Ibn Quzmān (d. 1160), a leading *zajal* poet, commends his predecessor, a certain Ibn Numāra, "for not having committed the error of using popular language in *qaṣīdah* and *muwashshaḥ*, or classical Arabic in *zajal*."[5] This statement indicates that *muwashshaḥ* and *zajal* existed side by side and often overlapped. To be sure, both of them constituted a definite departure from the tradition represented by classical poetry. They remained for a long time at the oral level, and it was only after their acceptance by a wide circle that they were committed to writing. The nature of the Arabic script and the long-standing tradition against writing in the vernacular suggest that compositions in the literary language found space in anthologies and poetical collections, while compositions in the vernacular were omitted. Under the circumstances, a parting of the way between *muwashshaḥ* and *zajal* took place, the one considered worthy of preservation while the other remained at the oral level. This may explain the fact that the number of *muwashshaḥāt* that has reached us is by far much greater than that number of *zajal*. This situation compounds the problem of relationship between *muwashshaḥ* and *zajal* and the question of which preceded the other. Ibn Khaldūn simply says: "*Muwashshaḥ* poetry spread among the Spaniards. The great mass took to it because of its smoothness, artistic language, and the [many] internal rhymes found in it [which made them popular]. As a result, the common people in the cities imitated them. They made poems of the [*muwashshaḥ*] type in their sedentary dialect, without employing vowel endings. They thus invented a new form which they called *zajal*. They have continued to compose poems of this type down to this time. They achieved remarkable things in it. The [*zajal*] opened a wide field for eloquent [poetry] in the [Spanish-Arabic] dialect which is influenced by non-Arab [speech habits]."[6]

The popular character of *muwashshaḥāt* can be gauged by the attitudes of classical authors, who either made passing or cryptic references to the new form or ignored it completely. At first, they considered *muwashshaḥāt* either outside the field of classical poetry or not poetry at all since the *muwashshaḥāt* did not conform to the classical meters and often oscillated between the rather primitive poetical meter of *rajaz* and the faultless classical poem (*qaṣīdah*). The two twelfth-century Andalusian anthologists, Ibn Bassām and Ibn Khāqān, who aimed in their works to demonstrate the great poetical genius of al-Andalus, say next to nothing about the *muwashshaḥāt*. Ibn Bassām explains their exclusion from his work simply by saying that the meters of the *muwashshaḥāt* are outside the objective of his *Diwān* (anthology) since most of the *muwashshaḥāt* are composed in meters different from those of the classical poetry of the Arabs.[7] Even the thirteenth-century historian al-Marrākushī (d. 1247), who lived during the flowering of these compositions, admired them but felt that they did not merit inclusion in a scholarly work.[8] However, the Egyptian Ibn Sanā' al-Mulk (d. 1211) considered the *muwashshaḥāt* as poetry (*manẓūm*) having numerous meters far and above the sixteen meters of the classical poetry.[9] He was followed by al-Ṣafadī (d. 1363)[10] and al-Muḥibbī (d. 1699)[11] who pondered on the meaning, structure, and components of *muwashshaḥ*. According to al-Muḥibbī, "It is like poetry with respect to vowel ending (*i'rāb*) but differs from it by the abundance of meters (*awzān*) conforming sometimes to the standard poetical meters and differing from them at others."[12] Furthermore, he considers the *muwashshaḥ* a form of *naẓm* (ordering), the term applied to poetry, as opposed to *nathr* (scattering), the term for prose. He suggests that it was derived from *wishāḥ*, meaning an ornamental belt of a double band worn by women, because the relationship of its concluding lines (*kharjah*) and branches (*aghṣān*) are like alternating ornaments of a *wishāḥ*. The form of the *muwashshaḥ* is also compared with a band of leather ornamented with alternating jewels and pearls and worn by women; and the versifier of this kind of poetry (*washshāḥ*) is the one who bases his composition on imitation of the shape of the ornamental belt or band of leather (*shakl al-wishāḥ*) — that is, alternating between the "refrains" and stanzas. As for the meaning of *zajal*, it is derived from the Arabic root *z-j-l*, the first verbal form of which, *zajala*, means "to make a sound" or "cry"; "to prolong one's voice" or "to modulate it sweetly." The verbal noun *zajal* may also mean "play," "sport," or "pleasure."[13] All this indicates that *zajal* was that kind of poem which was sung ordinarily in festive occasions and, like the *muwashshaḥāt*, came to be used for all purposes and social situations.

It was only after the full development of the *muwashshaḥ* and its wide dissemination and acceptance that authors pondered its nature, objective, forms, and various components. The fourteenth-century thinker Ibn Khaldūn considers that the *muwashshaḥ* was easy to grasp and understand[14] and free from artificiality.[15] It seems that the term was limited at first to erotic and laudatory poetry,[16] but in the process of its development its themes included wine, descriptions of nature, panegyrics, elegy, satire, asceticism (*zuhd*), and other subjects of classical poetry.[17] In many respects, its content was almost identical with that of *zajal*, whose avowed purpose was: "to obtain and to thank for gifts, money, or provisions. . . . to please and praise his companions in a life of pleasure of the 'wine, women and songs' variety amidst beautiful spring scenery during clear nights of full moon and glittering stars."[18]

This amounts actually to the conclusion that *muwashshaḥāt* and *zajal* are almost identical in form and content and differ from each other in the choice of language, since the *muwashshaḥāt* make use of classical Arabic whereas the *zajal* make free use of colloquial Arabic and Spanish dialect. In consequence, the technical terms referring to their components are the same; the remaining requirements of good and acceptable *muwashshaḥ* and *zajal* are also the same.

The technical terminology that has come down to us for the various components of a *muwashshaḥ* is rather confusing. Although the rules governing the compositions of both *zajals* and *muwashshaḥāt* seem to have been formulated during the eleventh century, there is no reliable information from the period. The type of information in twelfth-century sources leaves us guessing what certain expressions actually mean. We are not even sure about the actual meaning of *muwashshaḥ* or *zajal*, except that they were applied to a poetry different from the classical poetry. Ibn Bassām refers cryptically to the terms *marākiz* (sing. *markaz*) and *aghṣān* (sing. *ghuṣn*).[19] He refers to Yūsuf Ibn Harūn al-Ramādī (d. 1013), considered an author of *muwashshaḥāt*, as the first one who made profuse use of *marākiz* ensuring thereby a pause at each *markaz*. And when he refers to 'Ubādah Ibn Mā' al-Samā' (d. ca. 1032), reportedly a leading *washshāḥ*, he says that he was the one who effected a change consisting of making a pause at the *aghṣān*. Ibn Quzmān, the leading contemporary *zajjāl*, says that he improvised his poems on the basis of a *markaz* ordinarily devised himself or supplied him by a friend.[20] It should be indicated here that the *kharjah* was also supplied in advance for the composition of a *muwashshaḥ*.[21] Ibn Khaldūn (d. 1406) mentions *aghṣān*, *asmāṭ*, and *bayt* by simply saying: "The *muwashshaḥāt* consist of 'branches' (*ghuṣn*) and 'strings' (*simṭ*) in great number and different meters. A certain number [of 'branches' and 'strings'] is called a single verse [stanza]. There must be the same number of rhymes in the 'branches' [of each stanza] and the same meter [for the branches of the whole poem] throughout the whole poem. The largest number of stanzas employed is seven. Each stanza contains as many 'branches' as is consistent with purpose and method."[22]

It is not clear here what is meant by *aghṣān* (branches) and *asmāṭ* (strings), although it appears that they refer to the various parts of the poem — that is, *asmāṭ* representing the lines of the poem and the *aghṣān* the "refrains" and the "strophes." So far, there is a great deal of ambiguity concerning the actual meaning of *markaz, aghṣān*, *asmāṭ*, and *bayt*. Only with the treatment of Ibn Sanā' al-Mulk is one able to infer the meaning of some of these terms. Ibn Sanā' al-Mulk (1115–1211) of Egypt was an able *washshāḥ* who attempted in his *Dār al-ṭirāz* to explain the rules, characteristics, the meters, rhymes, and the various components of a *muwashshaḥ*.[23] He was followed by the Palestinian al-Ṣafadī (d. 1363) who reproduced Ibn Sanā' al-Mulk's analysis.[24] Both authors describe a good *muwashshaḥ* as consisting of six *aqfāl* (sing. *qufl*) and five *abyāt* (sing. *bayt*). They give examples showing that the *aqfāl* are those lines which may appear at the beginning of the poems but which occur with certainty after each *bayt* or strophe. They also specify that in cases where a poem begins with *qufl*, it is called complete (*tāmm*), and if it does not begin with it, it is called bald (*aqra'*). In other words, a poem should have six *aqfāl* or five *abyāt*, or a minimum of five *aqfāl* and five *abyāt*.[25] They also refer to *ajzā'* (sing. *juz'*), which refer to all the lines of a poem. A *qufl* may consist of as many as twelve lines; the *bayt* may consist of three, four, or more lines. These lines may be simple (*mufrad*) or compound (*murakkab*). If they are compound lines, they may consist of two, three, four, or more sections (*fiqar*, sing. *fiqrah*), each of which rhymes vertically with its correspondent lines. Thus, a *bayt* may consist of two, three, or four sections each having three, four, or five lines. Reference is also made to the *kharjah*, or the concluding lines of a poem.

Ibn Sanā' al-Mulk gives numerous examples to illustrate the enormous varieties of the structure of the *muwashshaḥāt*. Here are two of them; the first by Ibn Baqī:

'abitha sh-shawqu bi-qalbī fa-shtakā
alama-l-wajdi fa-labbat admu'ī

This is an opening *qufl* consisting of two lines (*juz'ayn*). It is followed by a simple strophe (*bayt basīṭ*) made up of three lines (*ajzā'*):

ayyuhā n-nāsu fu'ādī shaghifu
wa-hu fī baghy l-hawā lā yunṣifu
kam udārīhi wa-dam'ī yakifu

This, in turn, is followed by a *qufl* of two lines, which is followed by another *bayt* of three lines. This arrangement is followed throughout the poem.

The following poem by Ṭuṭīli has a *qufl* of four lines and a compound strophe (*bayt murakkab*) made up of three lines, each of which has two *fiqar*:

ḍāḥikun 'an jumāni
safirun 'an badri
ḍāqa 'anhu al-zamānī
wa-ḥāwahu ṣadrī

āh mimmā ajid | shaffanī mā ajid
qamā bī wa-qa'ad | bāṭishun mutta'id
kullamā qultu qad | qāla li ayna qad[26]

The following three paragraphs attempt to explain the various components of a *muwashshaḥ* on the basis of the terminology used by Ibn Sanā' al-Mulk, comparing them with terms alluded to by Ibn Bassām, Ibn Quzmān, Ibn Khaldūn, and some modern writers:[27]

Qufl (pl. *aqfāl*) seems to correspond to the *markaz* of Ibn Quzmān or to *maṭla'* of al-Karīm. Its general meaning in Arabic is "lock," a word perhaps used here in a figurative sense to indicate the closing of a stanza, or the beginning of another one. It may be designated "refrain," (Sp. *estribillo*). It constitutes the opening lines of a *muwashshaḥ*. Ordinarily, it describes the theme of a poem and, in this case, would correspond to the *kharjah*.[28] As already pointed out, it makes the *muwashshaḥ* complete if it occurs at the beginning and bald (*aqra'*) if it does not. The *qufl* should consist of at least two lines (*juz'ayn*), although it may contain as many as eight or even twelve lines. It is indispensable that a *qufl* follow a stanza and that the various *aqfāl* agree with respect to meters (*awzān*), rhymes (*qawāfī*), and lines (*ajzā'*). Finally, the *qufl* may or may not rhyme with the various *abyāt* of a poem.

Bayt (pl. *abyāt*) is also used by Ibn Sanā' al-Mulk and Ibn Khaldūn to connote stanza or strophe.[29] On the other hand, al-Ibshīhī (d. 1448) uses the term *dawr*,[30] which may mean "turn" or "alternation" in that a stanza together with a *qufl* is followed by another combination of stanza-*qufl* in a rotating basis. It corresponds to the Spanish *mudanza*. A poem may have five *abyāt* according to Ibn Sanā' al-Mulk, seven according to Ibn Khaldūn, and a higher number depending on the ability of the *washshāḥ*, or *zajjāl*, according to Ibn Quzmān.[31] They need not have the same rhymes, but should conform to each other with respect to meters and number of lines. As already pointed out, a *bayt* could be simple (*mufrad*) or compound (*murakkab*). In this case the lines of a poem consist of sections called *fiqar*; in each *fiqrah* portions of the lines rhyme vertically. This structure continues throughout the poem. Finally, the last *bayt* of a poem should be followed by a *qufl*, called *kharjah*.

Kharjah (exit), the concluding lines of a poem, is identical to the rest of the *qufl* or *markaz-maṭla'* in meter, rhyme, and number of lines. For the *muwashshaḥ*, it is the one part of the poem that admits either colloquial Arabic or foreign expressions. Its presence is as indispensable as that of the strophes. "The *kharjah*," says Ibn Sanā' al-Mulk, "is the distinctive mark of the *muwashshaḥ*, its salt and sugar; its musk and ambergris. In spite of the fact that it occurs at the end, it ought to be laudable, for it is the seal and the precedence."[32]

In conclusion, *qufl, bayt-dawr*, and *kharjah* are the principal components of a *muwashshaḥ*. *Ajzā'* and *asmāṭ* are terms applied to all the lines of a poem, and *aghṣān* refers to the refrains and strophes of a poem. Thus, a standard *muwashshaḥ* may be represented as follows:

aa *Qufl, markaz,* and *maṭla'*, the opening lines corresponding to *refrain* or Spanish *estribillo.* Each word may represent a branch of the poem.

bbb *Bayt*, corresponding to stanza or strophe, or Spanish *mudanza*. Each *bayt* may represent a *ghuṣn* made up of lines.

aa *Qufl*, following a *bayt* and consisting of lines having the same meter, rhyme, and parts as the first *qufl*.

This order may be repeated five or more times, ending with the *kharjah*.

aa *Kharjah,* ending the poem and its most distinctive characteristic.

The various components of a *muwashshaḥ* can be seen by the English-speaking reader in this translation of a *dawr* (*qufl* and *bayt*) followed by a *kharjah*:

aa Come, hand the precious cup to me,
And brim it high with a golden sea!

bbb Let the old wine circle from guest to guest,
While the bubbles gleam like pearls on its breasts,
So that night is of darkness dispossessed.

aa How it foams and twinkles in fiery glee!
'Tis drawn from the Pleiads' cluster, perdie.[33]

The tenth century is ordinarily suggested as the time when *muwashshaḥāt* began to find an audience. Their invention is attributed to a certain Muqaddam Ibn Mu'āfā al-Qabrī (d. ca. 900), a blind man who is said to have composed a number of short poems. He was followed by the belletrist Ibn 'Abd Rabbihi (d. 940), who is also said to have perfected this type of poetical composition, and by al-Ramādī, Ibn Mā' al-Samā' (d. 1033), and Ibn 'Ubādah al-Qazzāz.[34] It is not clear what these men actually contributed to the invention or creation of this type of popular poetry, but one cannot discount the possibility that attempts at composing something resembling the *muwashshaḥ* and the *zajal* were made at that early date, although a haphazard manner characterized the use of language, meters, and rhymes. Such compositions had little or no chance of success as long as the classical traditions remained supreme among the literati in the tenth and eleventh centuries, times of great literary productivity in the classical language. As a result, whatever popular compositions existed were limited to oral transmission; little or no attempt was made to commit them to written form. It was only after the political disintegration in the Peninsula and the decline of the classical traditions that they began to make considerable inroads among the masses and high circles as well. Both *muwashshaḥāt* and *zajal* were less rigid in form and language and more spontaneous and comprehensible in content than classical poetry. These characteristics may have contributed to their acceptance and dissemination within a wide circle. It may be assumed that the *muwashshaḥ* was preferred by the educated class whereas the *zajal* attracted both the masses and the elite, as is the case today with Arabic songs.

Both *muwashshaḥ* and *zajal* came into general vogue in the twelfth century and had their best representatives in the great *zajjāl* Ibn Quzmān,[35] al-A'mā al-Ṭuṭīlī (d. 1126),[36] the philosopher Ibn Bājjah,[37] Yaḥyā Ibn Baqī

d. 1145),[38] the physician Abū Bakr Ibn Zuhr (d. 1198),[39] and others who composed a great number of *muwashshaḥāt* and elevated this type of poetry to a respectability never attained before. In the following centuries there appeared a large number of *washshāḥūn*, such as the great mystic Muḥyy al-Dīn Ibn ʻArabī (d. 1240),[40] Ibrāhīm Ibn Sahl al-Isrā'īlī (d. 1251),[41] Ibn al-Khaṭīb,[42] and his pupil Ibn Zamrak.[43] A large number of these men's *muwashshaḥāt* are preserved for study and analysis, but the same is not true of *zajal*. This genuinely popular poetry may be assumed to have equalled or even surpassed the *muwashshaḥāt* in quantity, but only fragmentary *zajals* and an incomplete *dīwān* by Ibn Quzmān have reached us and provide a basis for understanding the nature of these compositions.

For an insight into the *zajal* composition, we are fortunate to possess the *Dīwān* or *Cancionero* of Ibn Quzmān, which consists of 149 *zajals* of lengths ranging from five to eleven strophes, although the majority (114) average five to nine.[44] Ibn Khaldūn[45] considers Ibn Quzmān to be the first person to create the *zajal* method, although Ibn Quzmān himself points to its existence before his time. Notwithstanding this and Ibn Quzmān's boastfulness about his unusual ability, he was widely acclaimed the best *zajjāl* of his time. He was, in the words of Nykl, "the most conspicuous exponent of the art of composing *zajal* in the spoken Arabic of al-Andalus, particularly in the Cordovan dialect."[46] Ibn Quzmān tells us that his *zajals* were improvised and that a refrain (*markaz*) was ordinarily proposed to him by a friend.[47]

Ibn Quzmān's biographical data are scanty. He was born and educated in Cordova. It seems clear from some of his *zajals* that he had to earn his living reciting poems in all sorts of places with the hope of reward, travelling to Seville, Granada, Málaga, Almería, and other cities. He was a cultured man who knew the best in Arabic poetry and was conversant in philosophy, jurisprudence, and rhetoric, but his best talent lay in composing *zajal*. The preface to his *Cancionero* states his preference for this composition, but not without a great deal of boastfulness:

When I acquired a perfect freedom in the art of composing *zajals*, and when my natural talent responded easily to its strange charms, the foremost leaders in this art became my suite and my attendants, because I reached in it a mastery which no one had reached before me, and a technical virtuosity whose fame was spread far and wide. I established the principles of the art and made it difficult for dull brains to engage in it. At the same time I removed all roughness from it and polished it so that it became smooth, free from grammatical inflections and technicalities; yet, while apparently easy, it became difficult, and while apparently vulgar, it was full of *finesse*, and while apparently obvious, it was difficult to understand, so that now, when someone hears the abundance of its hemistiches and its verses, he is induced to imitate it; but if he wished to follow in my footsteps and emulate my natural talent, which bursts forth spontaneously and never tarnishes, he would discover that he is trying to reach something unattainable . . .[48]

Ibn Quzmān mentions as his predecessor a certain Ibn Numāra who, if he were still alive, would certainly acknowledge Ibn Quzmān's superiority.[49] Following is the first part of Ibn Quzmān's *Zajal* XCIX with its various components:

Qufl-maṭla'-markaz	*aa*	Yā melīh ad-dunyā, qūl: 'A lā's ent, yā'bni, malūl?
Bayt	*ddd*	Ey anā 'indak wajīh, Yatmajjaj minnu wafīh Thumma f'aḥlā mā tatīh
Qufl	*a*	Tarja' anasak waṣūl!
Bayt	*eee*	Mur ba'ad, jīd hu saraf, Lam yurā mithlu naṣaf Wa les et illā ṭaraf
Kharjah	*a*	W'alladhī qulnā fuḍūl![50]

Following is the translation as given by Nykl:

Oh you, the world's most graceful, tell me:
Why do you grow fickle so easily?
Now you hold me in great esteem
And I, loyal to you, am moved by it:
Then, at once, haughty you grow,
And then again become kind?
Never mind, let him go to extremes;
One like him is never just:
You will always want to go to the limit,
And whatever I may have said, is mere teasing.[51]

Ibn Quzmān was witty and loved wine, women, and song. It is related that on one occasion he became so drunk that, to sober him, it was necessary to throw him into a pool of cold water. When he emerged with his clothes drenched, he improvised the following verse:

Oh Abū Bakr, there is no way of repelling the
  onslaught of (malicious) glances and mockery!
My clothes are in a pitiful condition indeed!
My lord, you have drowned me in water; now
Please make it good by drowning me in money![52]

All in all, Ibn Quzmān's *Cancionero* gives us glimpses of the author's life and outlook. His *zajals*, like other compositions of this type, were sung accompanied by musical instruments such as the lute, flute, or drum.

Judging from Ibn Quzmān's *Zajal* LXV, in which the poet boasts that his excellent *zajals* are heard in Iraq, one may assume that this popular composition was already widely disseminated in both West and East as early as the twelfth century. This is further attested by reports of a great number of poets whose *zajals* and *muwashshaḥāt* have not come down to us. Ibn Quzmān's contemporaries and his successors up to the fourteenth and fifteenth centuries constitute an impressive list. From among a galaxy of poets are: al-Madghalīs (twelfth century),[53] Abū 'Abdallah al-Lūshī (d. 1351),[54] and Ibn al-Khaṭīb.

The aforementioned poets and many others did not totally abandon the classical poetry; they cultivated it and composed *muwashshaḥāt* and *zajals* as well. Ibn al-Khaṭīb is a good example. He is credited with a number of *zajals*, such as the following one:

Bayn ṭulū' wa-bayn nuzūl
Ikhtalaṭat al-ghuzūl
Wa maḍā man lam yakun
Wa baqā man lam yazūl!
(Between sunrise and sunset
A mingled chorus of lovesongs resounded
Those who were not eternal, departed
He who is eternal, remained!)[55]

Muwashshaḥāt and *zajals*, which Andalusian emigrés carried to North Africa and the East, seem to have been readily accepted and emulated by Eastern scholars. In the twelfth century the *zajals* of Ibn Quzmān were heard and appreciated in Baghdād. As already mentioned, it was an Egyptian, Ibn Sanā' al-Mulk, who left ample explanations of the various components of the *muwashshaḥ* in his invaluable work *Dār al-ṭirāz fī 'amal al-muwashshaḥāt.* Ibn Sanā' al-Mulk, who had great appreciation of this type of poetry, composed a number of *muwashshaḥāt* and compiled many others by leading *washshāḥūn* of al-Andalus. He was followed by the Palestinian scholar al-Ṣafadī, who tells us in his *Tawshī' al-tawshīḥ* about his fascination for his predecessors' *muwashshaḥāt* which he tried to emulate and even surpass. His work contains 61 *muwashshaḥāt*, 28 of which are his own compositions and the rest are by leading composers from al-Andalus, North Africa, and the East. In addition to Ibn Sanā' and other Egyptians,[56] he names the two Syrian poets, Sirāj al-Muḥār (d. 1301) and Aḥmad Ibn Ḥasan al-Mawṣilī (fourteenth century), along with a sample of their *muwashshaḥāt*.[57] Another famous Eastern *washshāḥ* was Ṣafi al-Dīn al Ḥillī (d. 1349) of Iraq, who left *muwashshaḥāt* and *al-'Āṭil al-ḥālī*, which contains useful information about *muwashshaḥāt* and *zajals* as well.[58]

The question of the impact of *muwashshaḥ* and *zajal* on Spanish and European lyrical compositions has been the object of divergent views among scholars, some admitting their influence and others discounting it altogether. The controversy is tied up with the problem of origin of this kind of composition. Those who attribute to them an Andalusian, Galician, or Roman origin discount any Arabic influence. In his *Fann al-tawshīḥ*,[59] the Sudanese scholar al-Karīm sums up the controversy and advocates a non-Arabic origin on the ground that they flourished in al-Andalus first and not in the East; and that when they made their way to the East, poets there produced affected poems only. Moreover, they were built on songs set to music rather than on the poetical model of the classical poetry. He also holds the view that the *kharjah*, which admits foreign expressions, may be the link between the *muwashshaḥ* and its non-Arabic origin. This is so because it often occurs in Hebrew versions.[60]

Research in this area is still in its early stages and does not allow for a definite conclusion. However, the immense material in Arabic and the lack of it in Romance tends to tip the balance in favor of Arabic. For one thing, medieval authors from Ibn Bassām to Ibn Sanā' al-Mulk and Ibn Khaldūn do concede the supremacy of al-Andalus over the East in the composition of *muwashshaḥāt* and *zajals*.[61] However, it should be emphasized that they were composed in an Andalusian and Arabic context — that is, through the interaction of Arabic and Romance. Consequently, it would be reasonable to assume that the Andalusian temperament and outlook produced such a literary development at a time when the classical tradition was gradually declining.

After the discovery of the *Cancionero* of Ibn Quzmān, Julián Ribera called attention to important points of contact and the possible influence of the *zajal* on European lyrics. He pointed out that the *Cancionero* offers "the key for explaining the poetical forms of the various lyrical systems of the civilized world in the Middle Ages."[62] He was followed enthusiastically by González Palencia, who pointed to its influence in France, England, and particularly Spain.[63]

In the past two decades, a great number of *zajals* and *muwashshaḥāt* have become available to supplement the *Cancionero*. The most important works on the subject on influence are those of Nykl. He has attempted, on the basis of a large amount of material, to show the influence of Arabic lyrical compositions on the troubadours.[64] In his *Hispano-Arabic Poetry*, Nykl points to the Arabic influence on the form and content of works by the troubadours of Aquitaine. He refers particularly to Guillaume IX, Cercamon, and Marcabru.[65] He sees striking similarities between the *zajal* and Provençal poetry in the following important aspects: the rhyme *aaab* in Ibn Quzmān's poems and those of the Provençal poets are similar; the Arabic *markaz* or *maṭla'* (Sp. *estribillo*) corresponds to the *finada* of Provençal poems; the number of strophes, ordinarily five to nine, is a common feature of both Arabic and Provençal compositions; the theme is often strikingly similar, as is the use of fictitious names in the songs; they share the use of a messenger between the lover and the beloved, and the same attitude about duty of the lover toward his beloved.[66]

These elements do, in the light of the available material, point to the intimate relationship between the *muwashshaḥ* and *zajal* compositions and the lyric poetry of the Provençal and early Spanish poets. Interaction or even one-way influence is not altogether impossible. In fact, it would have been a logical and natural development owing to geography, social intercourse, and the borrowing of a higher culture by a less cultured society. This interdependence and the indebtedness of Europe to Hispano-Arabic culture in general is attested by the large number of Arabic works which were translated into Latin and Romance.

With respect to Spain in particular, there is ample evidence to point to the influence of the *zajal* on early Spanish lyrical composition. González Palencia has amply illustrated the dependence of early Spanish poets on Arabic models. The *Cantigas* of Alfonso X takes the form of *zajal*, as can be seen in the following poem:

aa Omildades con pobreza quer a Virgen Coroada
mas d orgullo con requeza e ela muy despegada
e desta razon vos direi un miragle muy fremoso
bbb que mostrou Santa Madre do Rey grorioso
a un crerigo que era de a servir deseioso
a e por en grau maravilla le foe per ela mostrada[67]

Likewise, *El Libro de Buen Amor* of Juan Ruiz — known as the Arcipreste de Hita — contains fables, moral digressions, and allegorical fragments in addition to numerous lyric poems spread throughout his voluminous works.

The author appears to know some Arabic. The content of the work, not to mention the use of *zajal*, is reminiscent of the Arabic model. In this connection, González Palencia states that Arabic influence on the Arcipreste de Hita is beyond doubt and that the Arcipreste knew Arabic, as attested by the frequent use of Arabic terms and references to Arabic musical instruments and to Moorish dancers.[68] The following composition of the Arcipreste belongs to the *zajal* type:

aa Sancta María, luz del día,
tu me guía todavía
Gáname gracia e bendición
bbb et de Jesus consolación
que pueda con devoción
a cantar de tu alegría[69]

In the light of the data available, one can ascertain that the *zajal* and *muwashshaḥ* originated and flourished in al-Andalus, and that Arabic-speaking Andalusians were the creators of these two poetical forms. The question remains to what extent they were influenced by an "Arabic" or "Roman" background. The decisive factor in such a determination lies in language and cultural milieu, which are predominantly Arabic, but not without non-Arabic elements. The fact that the *kharjah* may contain some Romance words and that the *zajal* may be a mixture of both colloquial Arabic and Romance does not offer a strong argument in favor of "Roman" origin. There is no evidence of works preceding the Arabic compositions. Eastern poets of the so-called modernist school such as Abū Nuwās and Abū-l-'Atāhiyah made use of both colloquial and Persian words in their poems, but one can hardly conclude that their poetry had its origin in ancient Iran. By the same token, it would be farfetched to trace *zajal* and *muwashshaḥ* to a "Roman" origin by virtue of mere occurrence of Romance words in poems ordinarily composed by people who knew both Arabic and Romance.

Al-Andalus contributed *zajal* and *muwashshaḥ* to the body of Arabic poetry in the same manner that Arabia contributed its classical poetry. Through these two popular poetical forms, al-Andalus was able to emancipate itself from the formalism of classical poetry, producing thereby a kind of poetry that was spontaneous and simple and at the same time akin to the personality and temperament of the Andalusian.

14

Courtly Love

LOVE and lust are as old as man and common to all societies. They are natural biological and psychological expressions that manifest themselves in all seasons. Left unbridled, they could well lead not only to promiscuity but to the demolition of the whole social edifice: the home, tribe, or any organized society. Thus, when we speak about the practice and conception of love, particularly courtly love, we are referring to an institutionalized love which has its own norms, rules, and its own form of expression. It always conforms to the values and code of a particular society.

In the case of Arab-Muslim society, woman, love, and marriage have received wide attention throughout the centuries. The merits and defects of the fair sex have been described profusely in all types of literature. In some contexts a woman may appear cunning, unreliable, deceitful, a gossiper, the cause of division between brothers and friends, unfaithful, and the source of all sorts of calamities. We are not concerned with these aspects, and it suffices to mention two traditions transmitted by Ibn 'Abd Rabbihi which reveal some of the negative and positive qualities of female companions. To King Solomon is attributed the remark, "A level-headed woman builds her home while the evil-tongued one destroys it." Another tradition says, "After the confession of faith, no one is more happy than in a good marriage and after unbelief, no one is more damned than in a bad marriage." [1]

The fair sex occupies a central place in lyric compositions. This type of poetry has been abundant, and the love theme, known as *ghazal* or *nasīb*, was a common feature in pre-Islamic and subsequent Islamic poetry. From the sixth century onward, Arab poets composed tender verses praising the supreme qualities of and expressing deep feelings for their beloved ones. There is a great deal of sensualism in Arabic poetry. For instance, the great poet 'Umar Ibn Abī Rabī'ah (d. 719)[2] charmed the ladies of Mecca and Medina with his poetry which was so sensual and erotic that it made the religious scholars blush, but they nevertheless could not help reciting and admiring it because of its beauty.

However, though part of this enormous poetic genre can be called sensual, erotic, and mundane, a good portion of it expresses tender feelings for and idealizes the fair sex. This aspect of the love theme, the spiritual love (*al-ḥubb al-'udhrī*), concerns us here. The lady is the principal object. She is the beloved not in a subordinate sense. On the contrary, her lover is the one who is subordinated, submissive, obedient, and always willing to endure pain and all sorts of vicissitudes for her sake. In the pre-Islamic sixth century, 'Antarah, a freed slave, became a great warrior and performed extraordinary deeds in order to gain the hand of his beloved 'Ablah. His lyric poems expressing his deep love for 'Ablah and his saga are still being recited in the Arab world. A certain Qays Ibn al-Mulawwaḥ (d. ca. 699) became infatuated with his Layla to the point of madness, hence his surname *majnūn* (crazy). His poetry conveys intense and tender feelings for Layla, who reciprocated his love but married another at the insistence of her father. This drove Qays to madness and for the rest of his life he wandered, half-naked, in the hills and valleys of northwest Arabia, singing the beauty of his beloved, yearning for a sight of her, and bemoaning his miserable condition. His moving story became the model for Arabic, Persian, and Turkish romances which extoll the power of undying love. Jamīl al-'Udhrī (d. 701), to whom the tradition of spiritual love (*'udhrī*) is ordinarily traced, immortalized innocent and pure love. He composed many tender verses to his beloved Buthaynah which still enjoy great popularity.[3]

In Muslim Spain in particular, lyric compositions found fertile ground and reached a high degree of development. They were expressed in both the classical poetry as well as in the popular *muwashshaḥāt* and *zajals*. In fact, the Andalusians were great poets and lovers. A number of famous pairs of lovers appeared in al-Andalus: the ruler-poet 'Abd al-Raḥmān II and Ṭarūb; the scholar-caliph al-Ḥakam II and Ṣubḥ; the colorful poet-ruler al-Mu'tamid of Seville and I'timād; and the poet Ibn Zaydūn and princess

Wallādah — all of whom contributed enormously to the perpetuation of a poetic tradition concerned with deep, noble and undying love.

It was perhaps in Andalusian soil more than any other place in the Muslim world that the fair sex appeared in all splendor. Ladies were relatively free, gay, and more accessible than in other parts of the Muslim world. The beloved was an important part of nature, equal and even superior to anything ever created; she was seen as a lovely creature, tender, delicate, and beautiful. She was a shining sun capable of eclipsing the sun at dawn; a moon, a bright star that was responsible for bringing light into darkness, or darkness into light. She was a delicate and aromatic flower, or a garden of flowers to be contemplated and enjoyed, but never touched or eaten because this would make of it a pasture fit only for beasts. She was elegant and swift like a gazelle, a jewel to be admired and beheld, and so on.[4]

That was not all; belletrists,[5] philosophers,[6] and mystics,[7] among others, delved into the subject of love (*ḥubb, maḥabbah*, and *'ishq*). The term *'ishq* (passion) seems to refer to genuine and true love. It is defined as a noun exceeding ordinary love (*maḥabbah*) in the same manner that prodigality is a noun exceeding liberality.[8] It begins with a glance in the same manner a fire begins with sparks.[9] It manifests itself in many ways and affects the whole personality and character of those who are afflicted by it. It changes the whole complex of both the beloved and lover: their color changes — red as a sign of the beloved's bashfulness, yellow as a sign of the lover's restlessness. The lovers lose weight, and their manner of walk is affected considerably. The lover becomes attached to anything belonging to the beloved and forgiving to relatives even if they had humiliated him. It is related that the famous lover Jamīl was once with his beloved Buthaynah and was humiliated by the latter's brother, Shubayb. While in Mecca, Jamīl was told that Shubayb was coming and he should avenge himself. To which Jamīl retorted in a verse:

> They said, O Jamīl, her brother has come
> And I replied, the beloved has come who is
> the brother of the beloved.[10]

There is submissiveness in love — a submissiveness of the lover to the beloved. This should not be construed as a humiliation. There are many stories in which the lover submits to the will and even the whims of his beloved. Al-Mu'tamid, the proud ruler of Seville, humbled himself before his beloved I'timād. Once she looked through the window of the palace and saw some old ladies mixing mud in the street. She exclaimed to al-Mu'tamid, "If they could do that, why couldn't I?" And it was for al-Mu'tamid to order that dirt be mixed with perfume so that his beloved could play in the mud.[11]

Falling in love could mean death or the will to die for it. When a Bedouin was asked, "Who are you?" he replied, "From a people who die if they love." Then the hearers exclaimed that he must be of the 'Udhrah tribe.[12] Ibn Qutaybah[13] relates the dramatic story of a youth who inflicted death upon himself when he learned that he mistakenly killed his beloved:

> The youth was with his companions on a mountain where he spotted a girl and fell in love with her. He decided to stay behind after his companions pleaded with him to go back with them. He finally met the girl and one night entered her dwelling and woke her up. She warned him to go away before her brothers awoke and killed him. He defiantly retorted that death was easier for him than his condition, and told her that he would leave immediately if she gave him her hand to put on his chest. She did and then he left. He met her a second time under similar conditions, and insisted that he would leave only if she gave him her lips. He kissed her and she felt the effect like a fire. This became known to her tribe, which decided to chase him away. The girl warned him that they would attack him that day, but torrential rain intervened and they were not able to go through with their plans. At night she left to meet him, accompanied by a servant. Seeing them, and believing that they were his enemies, the lover aimed an arrow and hit his beloved, who fell dead while her companion wailed. The youth rushed to the awful scene and then committed suicide. The pair were given a joint burial.[14]

In its purest and mystical form, love means chastity. Ibn Ḥazm considers the effect of the union of the soul a thousand times more beautiful than that of the union of the body.[15] An instance of chastity is the love of Jamīl for his Buthaynah. An early Eastern story tells of a man who passed by a house where there was a girl singing. He stopped, and the master of the house invited him in. He was reluctant to meet the girl at first, but they finally met and were attracted to each other. One day, the singer told him, "I love you"; he retorted, "So do I." She said, "I wish to put my lips on your lips"; he replied, "So do I." Then she said, "I wish to put my chest against yours"; he replied, "So do I." He was hesitant, which prompted the girl to say, "What is the matter? No one is around." He paused for a little while, recited a verse of the Qur'ān, and said, "I detest that the friendship that exists between us will become an enmity in the day of judgment." And he left![16]

Numerous other illustrations concerning love, its nature, and manifestations can be cited from Eastern literature. However, one can hardly add much to the treatise on love written by Ibn Ḥazm, who late in life stated that love poetry should be avoided at all costs in the education of youth.[17] This would appear paradoxical from a man who composed the most comprehensive work in Arabic on love and lovers. But the statement may perhaps be understood within the context of the life of Ibn Ḥazm and his time — that is, the youthful Ibn Ḥazm as opposed to the elderly, austere theologian who lived in a period of turmoil and moral decadence.

Ibn Ḥazm of Cordova (944–1064)[18] was the greatest prose writer of the eleventh century. A man of great erudition, he had much to say on many subjects, and knew how to say it. Like Ibn Shuhayd, Ibn Ḥazm belonged to the ruling aristocracy and felt the brunt of the *fitnah* and the political disintegration of al-Andalus after 1009. His father was a cultured man highly esteemed by the ʿĀmirids, whom he served in various official capacities. Whether the Banū Ḥazm was of Persian or Spanish stock cannot be ascertained. The assertion of the great Dutch scholar Dozy[19] that Ibn Ḥazm was the most Christian of the Islamic poets and possessed on that account something delicate and spiritual which cannot be called Arabic is quite misleading. Ibn Ḥazm, himself an able genealogist, believed himself to be of Persian origin, blended well into the current cultural environment of al-Andalus, and defended with great conviction the beliefs, values, and way of life of Islam.

Ibn Ḥazm received an Islamic education, attending literary sessions in his father's home and spending a good deal of time in the harem among concubines who taught him the Qur'ān, poetry, and some writing. He grew to be quiet and bashful, especially in the company of men, and became infatuated with a blonde girl in his youth. However, he married another girl who died shortly thereafter, and mourned her seven months with such a deep grief that he did not change his clothes. He was an ardent follower of the Umayyad cause, and all indications are that he aspired to a political career, following in the footsteps of his father. As the Umayyad cause became hopeless, Ibn Ḥazm decided to concentrate on his studies; he travelled to Almería, Játiva, Málaga, Majorca, Seville, and other cities. Disappointed and bitter, he became a nonconformist and an ardent intellectual rebel in polemics and acid criticism of both rulers and religious scholars. This confrontation did not endear him to the powerful circles, who charged him with heresy and caused his books to be burned.

What interests us here is the youthful Ibn Ḥazm who wrote the charming *Dove's Ring*,[20] an essay on love, its nature, and its manifestation in joy and suffering. In time he stands between Ovid and Andreas Capellanus. Unlike Ovid,[21] who stresses sensuality and aims to show man the art of deceiving and seducing women, Ibn Ḥazm emphasizes the spiritual aspects of love, condemns sexual excesses, and recommends continence. There are neo-Platonic elements in Ibn Ḥazm as well as a number of parallels with *The Art of Courtly Love*[22] of Andreas Capellanus. Ibn Ḥazm wrote the *Dove's Ring* at the request of a friend when he was about twenty-seven years old and at a time of disillusionment and misfortunes. Realizing that his enemies, mainly the religious scholars, would criticize him for a seemingly trivial undertaking, he excused himself on the basis of a tradition permitting people overburdened with grief to distract themselves with things which may appear mundane. Although the work is heavily indebted to and inspired by *Kitāb al-Zahrah*[23] of Abū Dāwūd al-Iṣfahānī (d. 910) and other Eastern writers,[24] it contains many elements reflecting not only neo-Platonic and Ṣufī ideas, but also the amorous life of Ibn Ḥazm and his fellow Andalusians. The *Dove's Ring* is a prose work containing a large number of Ibn Ḥazm's own poems. It consists of thirty chapters: ten dealing with the origin of love and the manner of effecting it; twelve with the accidents of love, its praiseworthy and blameable qualities; six with calamities occurring in love; and the concluding two on illicit practices and on the virtue of continence. Following is an outline of the various chapters:

Chapter 1 is an introduction explaining the nature of love, its definition, causes, and various kinds. He points out that love (*ḥubb*) is not forbidden by religion or the religious law. Many Muslim rulers, saints, and religious scholars were in love, and al-Andalus had numerous pairs of lovers who became famous. He points out that love was defined by philosophers, but to us "it is the reunion of parts of the soul separated in this creation." True love takes possession of the soul and never passes away except through death. It should be distinguished from other types of love: love of secrecy, love of pleasure, love of fame, love of work, etc., all of which vanish upon the cessation of their causes or the desires inspiring them. Moreover true love (*al-'ishq al-ṣaḥīḥ*) is the only love that causes preoccupation, madness, sighing, emaciation, sorrow, and other symptoms. It is a "mutual spiritual appreciation and commingling of the soul (*istiḥsān rūḥānī wa-imtizāj nafsānī*)"; the soul of the lover is free, knows the place of its companion, inquires about, searches for it, and gravitates toward it like iron to a magnet; two persons are truly in love only when they are bound by accord and share natural qualities, and the greater the likeness of these qualities, the stronger the affinity. A similar but opposite phenomenon occurs in hatred when those natural qualities are different and tend to collide, thereby causing two people to detest each other without a rational cause. In sum, love is not caused by physical beauty or likeness of character, but is something which constitutes an integral part of the very essence of the being. It is a fusion of two souls. He emphasizes the point in a poem saying that love is eternal by virtue of its very essence and cannot diminish or grow:

> My affection for you is permanent in accordance with
> Its *being*: It attains its utmost limit, and [then]
> Does not decrease nor increase in any way;
> There is no cause for it, except *will*, and there is
> No other cause but this that anyone could know;
> When we find a thing to be its own cause,
> Such an existence does not pass away in all eternity:
> And if we do find in something to have its cause in
> Something different from it,
> The coming to naught of that thing will be caused by our
> Being bereft of that to which it owed its existence![25]

It is something from the higher spheres:

> Are you of the world of angels or merely human?
> Make it clear to me, for fatigue has weakened by understanding!
> I see a human form, but when I think more deeply
> [It seems] to be a body from higher spheres![26]

Ibn Ḥazm concludes the chapter by saying that love is an incurable disease containing its own remedy; it is a delightful condition, a malady which a person longs for and from which he does not seek cure; it causes the person to accept as pleasant what he used to dislike; it makes the difficult easy to the point of changing all his personal traits and general outlook.

Chapter 2 deals with the signs of love. These signs consist of a continuous look with the eye, which is the "wide gate of the soul, the explorer of its secrets, the interpreter of its hidden thoughts, and the translator of its inward meanings." The continuous look is followed by conversation, careful listening, agreeing, and believing in what is said; attempting to be near the beloved and reluctance to depart from her side; surprise and thrill upon meeting the beloved unexpectedly; conscious attempts to show one's best qualities such that a stingy man becomes generous, a sad one becomes gay, a coward becomes brave. Other signs are getting close to each other, touching the hand; becoming sensitive to what is said; quarrels followed by reconciliations; provoking the mention of the beloved's name; preference for solitude; loss of weight, manner of walk and motions of the body; and sleeplessness, which makes of lovers, in the language of poets, "the shepherds of stars":

> I guard the stars as if I had been commissioned
> To guard all the fixed stars and the planets:

And they and the night resemble the fires of passion,
Which have been kindled in my thoughts coming from the dark night,
And it seems as if I had started in the evening as the watchman of a green garden,
And its green plants had girt themselves with white narcissus:
If Ptolemy were living he would have been certain that I am
The strongest of men in the observation of the orbits of stars![27]

Chapters 3 to 7 are devoted to the causes of love. For Ibn Ḥazm, every love must have a cause which constitutes its origin. Falling in love in dreams (Ch. 3) is strange and unreal, and he says that he would not have mentioned it had it not been for an actual case of a friend who experienced it. It is followed by a chapter dealing with falling in love as a result of description (Ch. 4). This cause he considers one of the strange origins and causes of love. However, he says that it has happened to many persons and has led to all the signs of love, but he considers such love to have a weak foundation since the person involved builds for himself an image which may or may not be faithful to the idealized person. These occurrences happen frequently among secluded ladies in castles who are more prone than men, owing to their weakness and natural disposition, to respond quickly to this kind of appeal. Another cause is love at first sight (Ch. 5), which also lacks foundation since things that grow the fastest are quickest to vanish. Yet, he relates the story of a poet who became madly in love with a girl whom he saw once and whom he never met again. To Ibn Ḥazm, this kind of love is nothing but a passionate infatuation and could not possibly penetrate into the deepest corners of the heart. After presenting these weak causes with some details he passes on to love resulting from prolonged association (Ch. 6), which he considers the most lasting. He refers to his own experience: love never overpowered him except after a long time during which he shared with his beloved frivolous and serious things, experienced tender memories, and suffered the pain of separation:

True love is not the daughter of a moment,
And its flintstone does not make the fire come out at will:
But it is generated and propagated slowly
By a long intermingling, and thus its pillars will become firm;
The absence and decrease of it does not approach it,
And its permanence and increase cannot be removed from it:
This is confirmed by our seeing that everything
Which is quickly accomplished will also perish shortly.[28]

He emphasizes that prolonged association could or ought not to be construed as a contradiction of his early thesis that "love is the reunion of souls as they were originally in their higher world." On the contrary, he maintains that it corroborates it. Love is one, the heart is one, and the true religion is one; thus, it is not possible to love passionately two different persons:

He who pretends that the love of two
    is irrevocably ordained, lies;
  This, according to the fundamental laws,
    is more false than Mānī:
There is not in the heart room enough for two dear friends,
  Nor can the most favorite thing have there a second;
And just as Reason is one and knows no other Creator,
    except One, the Merciful,
  Thus heart is one and does not love except one,
    whether far away or nearby;
The contrary, according to the law of affection,
    is very doubtful,
  Far removed from true belief!
Thus also there is but one, straight religion,
  And he who pledges loyalty to two religions
    is a great heretic![29]

He mentions a final cause — that is, loving certain qualities which result in exerting decisive power on the soul (Ch. 7). These qualities may be arbitrary and even unacceptable among the great majority of people. He illustrates this by his preference for blonde girls, a taste which resulted from his falling in love with a blonde girl during his adolescence.

Chapters Eight through Eleven concern themselves with the manner of communication between the two lovers. This may begin with allusion in speech (Ch. 8) which is the first means which people in love use in order to convey their feelings; it is followed by glances of the eye (Ch. 9), which convey a number of messages and take the place of a messenger. Hints with the eye may mean coming together, promise, threats, warning, laughter, grief, etc. For instance, a sign from the end of one eye conveys prohibition, while its slackening indicates acceptance, and staring shows suffering and sadness. But the most important means of communication consists of correspondence (Ch. 10), which takes the place of the tongue and of a personal interview. Letters cause joy in writing, sending, and receiving. They are almost equal to a rendezvous. This is why the recipient presses the letter of the beloved to the eye and chest. They are so significant that some lovers write them with their own blood. In the eleventh chapter, he discusses the messenger, who plays a key and delicate role. The messenger must be chosen carefully, for on him depends the life, death, and honor of the lovers. He must be clever and capable of predicting and avoiding problems, of keeping secrets, and observing agreements; and he must be faithful and loyal. He may be a servant whom no one notices, or a person of high standing who would not arouse any suspicion. Ordinary messengers are women: old ladies with crutches and prayer beads, hairdressers, singers, fortune-tellers, and others of similar occupations. This type of messenger, who is cunning and deceitful, betrays striking similarity to the *alcahueta* as portrayed in the *Libro de buen amor* and the *Celestina*.

Ibn Ḥazm proceeds at this juncture to contrast the joys and tribulations of love which result from the actions of the lovers themselves. The keeping of secrets (Ch. 12) is an indispensable prerequisite for preserving love and avoiding danger. It is so much so that the lover should deny having any relationship with the beloved; in fact, he should appear as a woman-hater, notwithstanding his deep love, and however overwhelmed he may be under its strong influence. This praiseworthy quality is contrasted with the misfortune resulting from divulging secrets (Ch. 13), which is abominable and leads to untold embarrassments. Divulging of secrets is done ordinarily, says Ibn Ḥazm, for notoriety, out of desire for revenge, or because of a lack of self-control.

Submissiveness or obedience (Ch. 14) of the lover to his beloved is a highly desirable quality, although it may lead to unsavory situations if carried to extremes. On the whole, it makes obstinate and proud men humble, pliable, and easygoing when with the beloved:

> Submission in love is not odious,
> For in love the proud one humbles himself:
> Do not be surprised at the docility of my condition,
> For before me al-Mustanṣir has suffered the same lot![30]

In contrast to submissiveness is the lover who uses the beloved as an outlet for satisfying his pleasure and whims (Ch. 15).

In the next two chapters, he deals with the faultfinder (Ch. 16) and the helping friend (Ch. 17). The faultfinder may be of the sympathetic and well-meaning kind, whose warnings and admonitions are useful; but there is also the chiding faultfinder who blames and criticizes everything. The help of a good friend is most desirable. But to be effective, the friend must be correct, well spoken, and tactful, inspiring confidence and capable of keeping secrets; he should console the lover in moments of crisis and distress. This kind of help can be found most effectively in ladies, especially old women, who may prove harmless.

There are two other upsetting characters who make the lovers uncomfortable and unhappy, the watcher (Ch. 18) and the slanderer (Ch. 19). The watcher is like hidden fever and recurrent pleurisy. There are different kinds of watchers. One makes himself obnoxious, sitting in a place where the lovers come together and want to be alone. Another watcher is the ill-intentioned one who wants to find out what is going on between the two lovers. And finally, there is the guardian of the beloved who cannot be avoided; it is up to the lover to bring him to his side. But a more dangerous and vicious character is the slanderer, who attempts to break up the relation between the lovers through carrying tales or accusing the lover of divulging secrets. This may happen for gossip's sake, or because the slanderer wants the beloved for himself.

The most pleasurable condition of love is union (Ch. 20). Union of the lovers constitutes "renewal of life, perfect existence and permanent joy" almost approximating Paradise itself. It is indescribable and may consist of a rendezvous or of a promise of a visit which is regarded with high expectations. In a true love, the longer the duration of the union the better. In contrast to this bliss is avoidance (Ch. 21), which takes various forms: because of the presence of a watcher; feigning censure of the lover on account of some fault; making false accusation; boredom; or other causes. Loyalty (Ch. 22) is the most praiseworthy aspect of love and carries with it mutual trust, forgiveness, and fidelity; its anathema is betrayal (Ch. 23), which may result from a messenger or other outsider or one of the lovers:

> Little faithfulness on the part of the beloved
> is considered much,
> And great faithfulness on the part of lovers
> is considered small:
> Thus a rare fit of bravery in a coward
> is considered greater
> Than what is done by a brave man
> who stands proudly alone! [31]

Separation (Ch. 24), which is cruel and the "sister of death," may occur temporarily and cause deep grief; it may be the outcome of forced seclusion of the beloved, a journey, avoiding gossips, or death. Depending on the situation, it is marked by farewell signs, pain, and weeping:

> The proof of pain is the fire which burns in the heart,
> And tears which flow and are shed on both cheeks:
> If the passionate lover hides the secret of his bosom,
> The tears of his eyes will show and disclose it:
> Whenever the tear ducts of the eyelids
> send forth their streams,
> Then surely there is an illness in the heart,
> afflicted with ardent desire! [32]

In ordinary separations, the lovers must find contentment and resignation in whatever they can get (Ch. 25): a visit, a greeting, a promise, or possession of some belongings such as locks of hair, and the like, contemplating the walls that enclose the beloved, or talking to someone who had seen her.

The next three chapters deal with illness (Ch. 26), oblivion (Ch. 27), and death (Ch. 28). Love produces illness and even leads to insanity:

> This is an illness the healing of which
> has worn out the physician,
> It will no doubt bring me to the tomb on my battlefield:
> I have agreed to become the victim of my affection for him,
> Like him who swallows poison well mixed in good wine! [33]

It ends only in death or oblivion. Oblivion may take the form of complete forgetfulness or conditions which make the soul forget — because of another love or because of other aspects thereof. But love causes death, also, and Ibn Ḥazm relates a number of deaths caused by it. However, he relates a tradition saying, "He who falls in love, abstains, and then dies, shall die as a martyr."

With this sober thought, Ibn Ḥazm devotes the last two chapters to the ugliness of illicit practices (Ch. 29) and the excellence of continence, respectively. He points to the struggle facing man — the struggle between reason and sensual desires. It is for this reason that reward and punishment is recommended for licit and illicit relationships and that religion is here to refrain man from his unbridled desires. In consequence, adultery, which is the profanation of woman and corruption of progeny, is punished severely. He emphasizes chastity (Ch. 30) and relates a story of a man visiting a friend who was called away. The visitor was tempted by the wife and was at the point of succumbing to the temptation when it occurred to him to place his finger on the flame of the lamp until it was burned red. He then exclaimed, "Oh, my soul, taste this, and what is this compared to the fire of Hell." [34] And the work ends with an apologetic and devout note.

In summary, the *Ṭawq* represents the most comprehensive anthology on love in Arabic literature. It has the virtue of being a synthesis of Eastern and Western elements. In form and content, it deserves to be called not only an Arabic, but a world classic. It may very well have been instrumental in preserving and disseminating the conception of love in the Mediterranean basin, serving thereby as one of the links between Islamic practices and those of the troubadours. There are, indeed, many striking similarities which are reinforced further by the poetical forms *muwashshaḥāt* and *zajals*.

It is difficult to measure the impact of the *Ṭawq* either during the lifetime of Ibn Ḥazm or in subsequent generations owing to its linkage with his controversial stand vis-à-vis rulers and religious scholars. But the subject of love was dear to the hearts of the Andalusians, and it is inconceivable that the *Ṭawq* could have been relegated to oblivion. It must have been widely used by Andalusian lovers. As for its impact on Western, mainly Spanish, literature, the question is both interesting and challenging. As of now, the Arabist would tend to see much influence, while the Romance scholar would be prone to deny anything Arabic. This professional prejudice borne out of one's specialty in the single field of Arabic or Romance would cease only when serious and thorough research is done to determine the extent and means of transmission from Arabic to Western languages. In the present state of research, one can only make certain generalizations about the Arabic influence which may be justified geographically, by virtue of a long history of brilliant Arabic culture in al-Andalus, intercourse of people and ideas, and the prevalent bilingualism in the country up to and even after the fall of Granada in 1492. One may add the conscious attempts to commit Arabic works of all sorts into Latin and Romance — a process that was on the increase from the twelfth century onward.

One might not be unjustified in making broad comparisons between some elements of the *Ṭawq* and those occurring in the *Libro de Buen Amor*[35] of the fourteenth-century Juan Ruiz. Although the works differ enormously in organization, they have striking similarities with respect to their treatment of love and its effects, the use of autobiographical data, and anecdotes. Moreover, comparisons of some similar passages in both works have been made by Américo Castro[36] and García Gómez.[37] No light has been shed on the manner in which the Arcipreste de Hita derived his information — that is, whether through the oral folklore of Spain or through literary means. But this should not obscure the fact of the strong relationship between Arabic lyric compositions and those of the troubadours.[38]

No treatment of courtly love would be complete without reference to the lyrical compositions of Ibn Zaydūn and the poet-king al-Mu'tamid, both famous lovers. They lent lustre to lyrical composition, sang the beauty of the beloved, the suffering of separation and the pain of betrayal and rejection.

Ibn Zaydūn (1003–1070)[39] represents the best traditional classical Arabic style in al-Andalus. He is often compared with the great Eastern poet al-Mutanabbī (d. 915–965). The son of a religious scholar, he received a general education and displayed a remarkable talent for poetry at an early age. His love poem rhyming in *nūn* is considered "the most beautiful love poem of the Muslims of Spain, and one of the most famous in general Arabic literature."[40] It was one of many addressed to the Princess Wallādah (d. 1087), daughter of the caliph al-Mustakfī. Wallādah, a beauty, rebelled against tradition after her father's death and made her house the meeting place of scholars and poets. She was an accomplished poetess; she is reported to have had two verses of hers embroidered on the two hems of her robe — which may reveal her character. The one on the right side said:

> I am, by God, fit for noble things
> And walk with pride!

and the one on the left side:

> I allow my lover [to touch] my cheek,
> And bestow my kiss on whoever craves for it.[41]

Ibn Zaydūn fell madly in love with Wallādah in his twenties. She responded in like manner, it seems, telling him in verse to visit her:

Be ready to visit me as darkness gathers,
  For I believe that night keeps all secrets best:
The love I feel for you — did the sun feel it thus —
  It would not shine, moon would not rise,
    stars would cease travelling![42]

The lovers met, and had an enchanted evening. But the time of separation had to come, and it was for Ibn Zaydūn to comfort his beloved:

Patience has departed from the parting lover,
  Who divulged the secret, confiding it to you;
He is embarrassed because of not having been able
  To take more steps along with you when taking his leave:
Oh, brother of the full moon in high rank and splendor,
  May God protect the time which caused thee to rise!
If your absence made my nights seem long,
  I spent this night with you complaining of its shortness![43]

Ibn Zaydūn again expresses his strong feelings for her and suffering for being away from her; food has become insipid, wine tasteless:

When shall I unfold what I feel for you
  Oh my delight and suffering?
When shall my tongue take the place
  Of a letter to explain my love?
God knows what
  Has become of me because of you:
My bedroom has become void
  And my drink tasteless.[44]

He tells her that his heart could withstand what other hearts could not bear and that he would always be responsive to whatever she might ordain:

Between you and me — if you wished — there could exist
  What cannot be lost: a secret undivulged,
    if other secrets are:
Oh you, who are selling your love for me, know that I
  Would not sell my love for you even at the price of my life!
Know that if you imposed on my heart what those
  Of other people could not bear, mine can withstand:
Disdain me, I'll bear it; postpone, I'll be patient;
    be haughty, I'll be humble;
  Turn back, I shall follow; speak, I shall listen;
    order, I shall obey![45]

This submissiveness to Wallādah became more intense when Ibn Zaydūn committed the indiscretion of either flirting with a maiden or divulging a secret. Wallādah was infuriated and admonished him in a poem saying that if he had been faithful to the love binding them, he would not have yearned for or chosen her maiden; nor would he have exchanged a beautiful and fruitful branch for a sterile one, thereby forgetting that she was a heavenly moon and could not be traded for an inferior creature.[46] In a poem, he pleaded to hear from her and hoped that patience might eventually result in the bliss of seeing her. He assured her that he would be careful not to rouse the attention of the watcher or talebearer.[47]

In other poems, he describes the anguish of separation at a time when Wallādah seemed determined to forego her love for him. This situation increasingly worsened to a point of no return, but Ibn Zaydūn persisted, hoping to reactivate the lost love. Meanwhile, Wallādah was encouraging Ibn 'Abdus, to whom Ibn Zaydūn directed his vituperative epistle in her name. This violent reaction did not help matters: it antagonized Wallādah, and besides her suitor conspired with Ibn Zaydūn's enemies and charged him with misconduct, for which he was jailed. In a desperate move, he escaped and roamed Cordova and elsewhere, still with the ardent hope of regaining Wallādah's love. Hidden in the ruins of al-Zahrā' built by 'Abd al-Raḥmān III, he bemoaned in tender verses the ruin of his love.

It was at this juncture that he composed his famous *Qaṣīdah* of fifty verses rhyming in *nūn*. In it, he expressed the anguish of separation and fixed the date of his "death" as the end of their last rendezvous; smiles resulting from proximity to her had changed to tears; the enemy was pleased at seeing them separated; neither despair nor oblivion could soothe his suffering; neither absence, wine, or lute could change his love or distract him; without her his days turned black, when nights with her were bright; mutual love made life cloudless and joyous; he asks the breeze to transmit his greeting to the one whom God fashioned of musk rather than clay and crowned with the purest gold for rare beauty.[48]

Al-Mu'tamid of Seville[49] was famous for his love of I'timād. His passion may be represented in the following verses addressed to her while he was away on military expeditions:

I am pining because of being separated from you,
  Inebriated with the wine of my longing for you;
Crazed with the desire to be with you,
  To sip your lips and to embrace you!

These eyelids of mine made a solemn oath
  Not to meet each other until they meet you!
Come to me, dear, fully trusting me,
  Believe me: my heart is in your bond!

Oh you, whose person is absent from my eye,
  But is ever present in the deepest of my heart:
My greetings to you, equal in number to my pains,
  And to my eyes' tears, and to my sleepless nights!
You mastered the recalcitrant rein
  Of my soul, and made it docile to your lead;
My wish is to be always with you,
  How I wish I were granted that wish of mine!
Be faithful to the pact that is between us,
  And do not swerve from it in my long absence!
I put your sweet name into this message,
  And spelled out all the letters of: I'timād![50]

Reminiscent of the Wallādah–Ibn Zaydūn love affair was the case of Ibn Sa'id (d. 1164) and Ḥafṣa (d. 1190), both able poets, who were deeply in love and sang of love's tribulations. Their love, too, had a tragic end. Ḥafṣa had a powerful suitor in the governor of Granada, who ultimately caused the execution of Ibn Sa'id to the remorse of Ḥafṣa.[51]

Finally, brief reference must be made to the love theme as it appears in *zajal* composition. In several of his poems, Ibn Quzmān, the leading *zajjāl* of al-Andalus, refers to love and its various aspects: "Love is a heavy burden . . . The very victims of love are grateful for their sufferings and sing the praises of the power that anguishes them . . . Love takes its origin from sight. Let my eyes meet a pair of charming eyes that are replete with sorcery, and I am forthwith deprived of calm and reason." "O joy of love! In thee is life, in thee is death. Since my eyes met thine, I am like to die, and no pang equals what I endure."[52]

15

History, Geography, and Travel

HISTORY and geography occupied a prominent place in Arab-Muslim society. More often than not, an historical work was replete with geographical information concerning countries, their peoples, resources, topography, rivers, mountains, and roads. For religious, administrative, and military reasons, these works were among the early manifestations of Arabic literature. In fact, history was in many ways ancillary to Islam and its subsequent success over an enormous territory. A historical consciousness that can be traced to pre-Islamic times was perpetuated first by word of mouth and later in writing. The noble deeds, legends, and sagas of the pre-Islamic Arab gained added dimension with the rise of Islam, which gave the Arab ascendancy in the Islamic state. When oral transmission proved unsatisfactory for bridging the historical process, written words became a matter of course. Profane and religious histories were combined into one historical form, which found great acceptance among religious scholars and rulers. As a consequence, pre-Islamic times, the rise and endurance of Islam, the life, deeds, and sayings of Muḥammad and of his early companions, the conquest (*fatḥ*), and genealogy captured the attention of the historian and characterized early Muslim historiography.[1] Although interest in those matters never diminished throughout the centuries, other topics were added, including general political and military histories, literary histories, local histories of a city or region, world histories that ordinarily began with the creation of the world and ended with the author's own time, contemporary histories, histories of dynasties and their rulers, comprehensive biographical dictionaries of men accomplished in all fields of endeavors, and histories of individuals classified according to their fields — such as secretaries, poets, grammarians, jurists, and judges. Also a number of autobiographies and memoirs are extant. All of these constitute the core of Muslim historiography.

These general remarks concerning Muslim historiography are relevant to the historical writings in al-Andalus. Here, as in the East, history was abundantly cultivated; its form and content conformed to an Eastern model. Judging from the ample biographical references to Hispano-Arabic historians and their works, one must conclude that the historical literature in al-Andalus was indeed enormous. Unfortunately, the bulk of this literature has been lost. The small fraction of such literature which has escaped wanton destruction or negligence remains largely in manuscripts in the libraries of the Escorial, Madrid, Toledo, in the Zaytuna Mosque in Tunis, in Fez, Cairo, and several European cities. Dozy, Moreno Nieto, Pons Boïgues, Codera, Ribera, González Palencia, Lévi-Provençal, 'Abdallah 'Inān, Mu'nis, Iḥsān 'Abbās, and others [2] have attempted to uncover these manuscripts. However, many works remain unavailable to the historian and the general scholar.

In spite of its political isolation from the East after 711, and in spite of its independence in 756, al-Andalus continued to receive the attention of Eastern historians and biographers. In fact, they paid as much attention to the Peninsula as they did to other regions of the Muslim world. One may single out Ibn al-Athīr (d. 1234), [3] al-Nuwayrī (d. 1332), [4] Yāqūt (d. 1229), [5] and Ibn Khallikān (d. 1282), [6] who paid no small attention to the history and important men of al-Andalus. But while the works of these authors are still valuable for important information on al-Andalus, they could not serve as substitutes for works written by Andalusians, who closely observed and even participated in the events of their times.

The Andalusian historian wrote in great detail. His historical accounts often included long poems and valuable geographical data about rivers, bridges, canals, topography of cities, mosques, palaces, and other monuments.

As in the East, history in al-Andalus was considered useful as a means of instruction for secular and religious life. In his *Marātib al-'ulūm*, [7] Ibn Ḥazm considered the study of history, in all its good and bad aspects, an important part in the education of the individual, providing instructive examples to be emulated or avoided. Moreover, history, according to Ibn Ḥazm, is one of the sciences pursued by all peoples and as such constitutes a mark of distinction among the various nations. The science of history (*'ilm al-akhbār*) may be classified as dynastic or annalistic, according to countries or categories (*ṭabaqāt*).[8] The science of genealogy (*'ilm al-nasab*) is also part of history.[9]

The Hispano-Arabic scholar was not a professional historian in the strict sense of the word but rather a man of erudition and diversified learning. He was more often than not a religious scholar, grammarian, poet, jurist, scientist, or statesman. As such, he was a prolific writer who tried his hand at writing on the various disciplines. Thus, it is a matter of accident, perhaps, that one is labeled a historian rather than a jurist. Be this as it may, an interest in history was related to politico-religious questions, and to the man of accomplishments.

Al-Andalus was, by and large, the main concern of the Hispano-Arabic historian. He seems to have depended largely on Eastern authors for information concerning the rest of the Muslim world, although some Andalusian writers attempted to abridge the works of Eastern historians or to construct a universal history from the Creation. As a rule, however, the Hispano-Arabic historian was concerned with the general history of the Peninsula. Fortunately, several histories that bear upon the major periods of Andalusian history have survived. Historical content thus may be summarized as follows:

1. The conquest (*fatḥ*), which is recounted with some bare facts but also with legends and fanciful stories. The latter may have been perpetuated by Eastern writers who were quite removed in time and space from the events. Perhaps *The Conquest of Egypt*[10] by Ibn 'Abd al-Ḥakam may have been partly responsible for the dissemination of legends concerning the conquest of al-Andalus.
2. The Umayyad emirate and caliphate (711–1031), which often starts as a general history and ends with the author's own time.
3. The party-kings (*Mulūk al-Ṭawā'if*) (1031–1090).
4. The Almoravids (1090–1147).
5. The Almohads (1147–1248).
6. The Naṣrid Kingdom of Granada (1232–1492).
7. Biographies of single individuals and biographical dictionaries of outstanding men by field of endeavor.
8. Genealogy.
9. Autobiographies and memoirs.
10. Histories of particular cities or regions.

There was an impressive array of Andalusian historians, from among whom one can only mention a few. Their extant works constitute the primary sources for the history of al-Andalus.

Among the early historians of al-Andalus was ʿAbd al-Malik Ibn Ḥabīb (d. 845),[11] a man of wide learning and the author of many works in various disciplines. He is known to have written a work entitled *Ta'rīkh* (history). The work starts with the creation of the world and ends with the author's own time. It deals with early prophets, the Prophet Muḥammad and his successors, the conquest of Spain, Umayyad emirs, and the natural resources of the Peninsula. It also contains chapters on jurisprudence and other disciplines. The account may have been continued by a disciple of Ibn Ḥabīb, since it goes beyond the latter's death.[12] Among some thousand works attributed to him, there is one dealing with the categories of jurists and another with traditionists.

One may assume that contemporaries of Ibn Ḥabīb interested themselves in history, but nothing has reached us concerning these men. However, the Banū al-Rāzī, three in number, are associated with historical writings. Muḥammad Ibn Mūsā al-Rāzī (d. 886),[13] came originally from the East and is known to have written a work dealing with the entry of Mūsā Ibn Nuṣayr into Spain and with the composition of his troops. Muḥammad's son, Aḥmad (d. 936), is reported to have written several historical works: one dealing with the emirs of al-Andalus; a second with the genealogy of famous Andalusians; a third with the Muladies; a fourth with a description of the capital city of Cordova; and a fifth with a description of roads, the major cities of al-Andalus, and their characteristics. Only the first work has reached us, but in the Spanish version. It deals with the country under the Visigoths up to the time of Roderick and the Arab conquest up to the time of al-Ḥakam II. Aḥmad had a worthy successor in his son ʿĪsā, who is credited with a general history of al-Andalus and a biographical dictionary of chamberlains (*ḥājib*). Although the bulk of the works of the Banū al-Rāzī did not come down to us, they appear to occupy a prominent place in Andalusian historiography because they were cited profusely by later historians.[14]

Alongside the works of the Rāzīs is the *Akhbār majmūʿah*,[15] a collection of information from multiple but unknown authorship. The date of its composition is uncertain, though suggestions have been made that it was written in the late tenth or early eleventh century. The work consists of scattered notes without any specific organization by chronology or subject matter. It is valuable not so much for its content as for the light it sheds on the historical writing of the period and as a source for later historians. Aside from these considerations, the work deals with the conquest according to the usual legends, the early governors, civil wars, and the Umayyad emirs from 'Abd al-Raḥmān I to early in the reign of 'Abd al-Raḥmān III. Although the author is critical of 'Abd al-Raḥmān III, probably for his preference for non-Arabs in the administration, it does, on the other hand, display pride in Arab aristocracy in general and the Qurayshite genealogy in particular.[16]

Equally valuable is *The History of the Conquest of al-Andalus*[17] by the versatile scholar Ibn al-Qūṭiyah. The work is made up of notes and is suspected to have been written by a pupil. It supplements the *Akhbār* in showing concern for non-Arabs, although it remains at the same time essentially sympathetic to the Umayyad dynasty which Ibn al-Qūṭiyah served. Like the *Akhbār* it deals with the history of al-Andalus from the time of the conquest to the reign of 'Abd al-Raḥmān III. It starts with a brief account of the internal situation in the Peninsula before the conquest and refers to the legendary Julian and other heroic tales. The book describes the conquerors Ṭāriq and Mūsā, their squabble and recall to Damascus; their successors in al-Andalus and the unsettled situation; the appearance and ultimate success of 'Abd al-Raḥmān I and his policies; the introduction of *al-Muwaṭṭa'* of Mālik Ibn Anas; 'Abd al-Raḥmān's successor and his judges; the policies and major events of al-Ḥakam I's reign; 'Abd al-Raḥmān II and his organization of the administration, his patronage of learning, the enlarging of the mosque of Cordova, the eclipse of the sun, the appearance of the Norsemen, revolts, the arrival of Ziryāb in al-Andalus; the reign of the emir Muḥammad, with details concerning the question of succession to the rule and other information about officials; severe famine; the revolt of Ibn Ḥafṣūn; and the days of the emirs al-Mundhir and 'Abdallah.

In the eleventh century, a number of historians are worthy of mention. Ḥusayn Ibn 'Āṣim wrote a biography of Ibn Abī 'Āmir entitled *al-Ma'āthir al-'āmiriyyah*.[18] But the most prominent historian of the century was Abū Marwān Ibn Ḥayyān. He was born in Cordova in 987 and served the 'Āmirid as a secretary. He witnessed the fall of the 'Āmirid, revolts in Cordova, and the rise of the party-kings. He was a prolific scholar on various subjects, but his fame rests mainly on his historical works, which were written with discernment and great attention to detail. He wrote a monograph on the 'Āmirids and another dealing with judges. But he is known for his two voluminous histories: *al-Matīn*, consisting originally of some sixty volumes, and *al-Muqtabis*, originally in ten volumes. Unfortunately, only scattered fragments from the *Matīn* have survived. Of *al-Muqtabis*, there remain only the third volume and fragments dealing with the reign of 'Abd al-Raḥmān II and part of al-Ḥakam II's rule.[19] Both works dealt with the history of al-Andalus from the time of the conquest. Based mostly on the works of his predecessors, they became standard references for later historians.

On the basis of the extant portion dealing with the reign of al-Ḥakam II for the year 970–974, Ibn Ḥayyān sheds a great deal of light on court life. He pays special attention to court protocol, ceremonials, embassies to Cordova, and the North African wars with al-Andalus. He follows the annalistic arrangement and lists the major events in great detail. For instance, he records the following under the year 360 A.H.: a call for the capture of a thief; the arrival of an embassy with an elaborate description of the ceremonies; distribution of alms-giving in the month of Ramaḍān; the Norse intrusion; the death of Zīrī in North Africa; the feast at the breaking of the fast of Ramaḍān with minute description of the court ceremonials; the feast of the sacrifice (*'īd al-aḍḥā*), also with elaborate description of court ceremonials; and the reception given to two North African leaders who come to recognize al-Ḥakam's sovereignty over their territories. Ibn Ḥayyān inserts long poems recited at those court receptions, and often acknowledges his indebtedness to the sources of his information.

The prolific writer Ibn Ḥazm is the author of some four hundred works (eighty thousand folios) on nearly all conceivable subjects: philosophy, theology, morals, jurisprudence, poetry, literary works, and history. Among his historical sections are: the names of caliphs and governors and duration of their reigns; the names of companions of the Prophet and reciters of the Qur'ān; the imamate and politics; and *Fiṣal*,[20] a critical and comparative history of the various religions, which is intended to demonstrate the superiority of Islam over all others. The *Fiṣal* has come down to us, as have his *Tārīkh al-khulafā'*,[21] *Jamharah*,[22] and a few other treatises.

The *Jamharah*, which deals with the genealogy of the Arabs, is the most detailed book of its kind that remains. Ibn Ḥazm was not the first Andalusian who dealt with this topic; in fact, the *Jamharah* is based on earlier works. However, this volume is noteworthy for its clear and coherent presentation. It includes the genealogy of prominent men, including the relatives of the Prophet, his companions, caliphs and their sons, and others. He places them in historical context and mentions important events and religious and literary information. Moreover, he attempts to establish a relationship among the tribes which had come to the Maghrib and al-Andalus and between their leaders and the areas in which they settled. He justifies his work by saying that the science of genealogy (*'ilm al-nasab*) is indispensable for knowing that Muḥammad was a Qurayshite, that the caliphate should belong to the Quraysh through the descendants of Fihr Ibn Mālik Ibn al-Naḍr Ibn Kināṇah, and that a person should know his father, mother, and close kinship for the purpose of marriage and inheritance and should also know the mothers of the faithful and the companions,[23] etc. Thus, "It is false for the one who says that the knowledge of genealogy is a useless pursuit, and an ignorance that does not hurt."[24]

Ṣā'id[25] is the author of an extensive history of various nations entitled *Jāmī' akhbār al-umam*, and the *Ṭābaqāt al-umam* (*Categories of Nations*).[26] As mentioned in Chapter 9, the *Ṭābaqāt* deals with Indians, Greeks, Romans, Egyptians, Persians, Arabs, and Israelites, with special reference to the sciences in which they distinguished themselves. He also includes information about their customs, characters, and religions. The work is concise and to the point, and it is unusual in that it was written at the time of the party-kings, when there was a tendency among historians to limit themselves to histories of the dynasties to which their patrons belonged.

Of extreme interest and value is the *Memoirs*[27] of the emir 'Abdallah, the last ruler of the Zīrid dynasty of Granada. The work provides first-hand information about the interplay of politics, military engagements, and the unsettled situation during the last days of the party-kings. 'Abdallah was born in 1056 and succeeded to the throne at the age of eight. He reveals the problems of his nation — the presence of a personally ambitious vizier at a time when the Christian rulers were making great inroads into Muslim territories and other Muslim rulers coveted his kingdom. In moving terms he describes how in 1090 all seemed hopeless: his kingdom was captured by the Almoravids, and he and his mother were subjected to untold humiliations. He remained in captivity at Āghamāt in Morocco, where he wrote his *Memoirs* and spent his last days.

Equally important for the Almoravid and Almohad periods are contemporary writings by policymakers and eyewitnesses, besides official documents. Ibn Tūmart, the founder of the Almohad dynasty, wrote a number of tracts explaining his religious ideas. His works, known as the *Book of Ibn Tūmart*,[28] were collected by order of his successor 'Abd al-Mu'min, and constitute a valuable source of information about the dynasty. Ibn Tūmart's works are enhanced by the *Memoirs* of al-Baydhaq, who accompanied Ibn

Tūmart on his travels and witnessed many contemporary events. These writings, along with official documents,[29] the works of Ibn al-Qaṭṭān,[30] Ibn Ṣāḥib al-Ṣalāh,[31] Ibn Abī Zar',[32] al-Zarkashī,[33] and the *Ḥulal al-mawshiyyah*[34] of unknown authorship, constitute some of the main sources of information about the Almoravids and the Almohads.

Of wider scope are the works of 'Abd al-Wāhid al-Marrākushī (1185–1224), 'Alī Ibn Sa'īd al-Maghribī (ca. 1201–1274), and Ibn 'Idhārī (d. ca. 1295). Al-Marrākushī was born in Marrākush, received his early training at Fās, and travelled to al-Andalus, where he met the Almohad governor of Seville. He also resided in Cordova and joined the classes (*ḥalaqah*) of the scholar al-Ḥimyarī.[35] He went to his native city and back in 610/1213. From al-Andalus, he decided to go to the East, stopping in Egypt, al-Ḥijāz, Syria, and finally, Baghdād. It was in this city that he composed his *al-Mu'jib fī talkhīṣ akhbār al-Maghrib*[36] at the urging of a vizier who wanted to know more about the geography, politics, and leading men of the Maghrib. Al-Marrākushī begins his work with the conquest of al-Andalus, and describes the country, its early governors, emirs, and caliphs. He often interrupts his account to discuss prominent men of letters, to whom he often devotes more space than that allotted to the rulers. For instance, he describes the reign of 'Abd al-Raḥmān III in one page, while he devotes nearly four pages to the scholar Mundhir Ibn Sa'īd al-Ballūṭī. He treats the reign of al-Ḥakam II in a like manner and gives ample space to the belletrist al-Qālī, the chamberlain-poet al-Muṣḥafī, the grammarian al-Zubaydī, and the poet al-Ramādī. The work offers valuable information about the Almohad dynasty, with which al-Marrākushī was quite familiar. His sources of information, ordinarily acknowledged, consist of data transmitted to him by eyewitnesses or derived from old sources, mainly the works of Ibn Ḥayyān and Ibn Ḥazm.

Ibn Sa'īd al-Maghribī was a historian, poet, and man of letters. He was born near the city of Granada, where he received his education. He travelled extensively in the East, visiting North Africa, Syria, and Iraq. He wrote a number of historical works, most of which are extant in manuscript. Of special interest are his works dealing with his family's genealogy and his travel books. He is frequently quoted by contemporary and later authors. His best-known work is his fifteen-volume *al-Mughrib fī ḥulā al-Maghrib*,[37] two volumes of which have survived. This work is a contemporary history of the period 1135–1243.

Ibn 'Idhārī was born in Marrākush to a family who had emigrated from al-Andalus. Little is known about his life, but his fame rests on his historical work *al-Bayān al-mughrib*,[38] which is one of the most important sources for the history of North Africa and al-Andalus. It is a comprehensive history of the conquest up to the author's time (667/1270), arranged chronologically according to important topics. As he tells us in the introduction, he wrote the work at the behest of friends aware of his interest in the history of caliphs, countries, and emirs of both East and West. Of the three surviving volumes, Volume 1 is wholly devoted to North Africa and includes the major dynasties that appeared there; Volume 2 deals specifically with al-Andalus and gives special attention to its rulers, revolts, and dynasties up to the year 478/1086; and Volume 3 documents the Almoravids and then the Almohads until the rise of the Marīnids in North Africa. Ibn 'Idhārī recognizes his indebtedness to such earlier historians as al-Ṭabarī, al-Bakrī, al-Raqīq, Ibn Ḥabīb, and Ibn Ḥayyān.

The fourteenth century produced two great statesmen and thinkers: Lisān al-Dīn Ibn al-Khaṭīb and Ibn Khaldūn (d. 1406). Both were civil servants and active participants in the affairs of a time beset by political intrigues and confusion.

Ibn al-Khaṭīb[39] was born in 1313 in Loja, a town west of Granada; his family was originally from Cordova. He received his early education from his father and other scholars of the day, and he was exposed to the traditional, diversified learning of religious sciences, grammar, poetry, and the natural sciences. His father, who served the Naṣrids in various capacities, was killed by invading Christians in 1340. The Naṣrid ruler invited the twenty-seven–year–old Ibn al-Khaṭīb to occupy the post of secretary in the Department of Correspondence (*Diwān al-inshā'*). He soon excelled in the writing of epistles and was promoted to the office of vizierate; he then became the ruler's confidant, advisor, and trusted emissary to foreign potentates. He earned the title of the "double vizierate" (*Dhū al-wizāratayn*), traditionally conferred upon people of executive powers. His influence at the court and his wealth aroused the jealousy of both the court entourage and his pupil, the poet Ibn Zamrak, who plotted to have him charged with heresy. Ibn al-Khaṭīb was exiled to Fās, returned to his post, and was exiled again to North Africa. There he was strangled in prison as the result of continued intrigues from his enemies at home.

In spite of court intrigues and other political preoccupations, Ibn al-Khaṭīb excelled as physician, philosopher, poet, and historian, as well as maintaining a distinguished career as a statesman. He is credited with more than fifty works on music, medicine, poetry, Ṣūfism, politics, travel, and history.

Although most of his works are lost, enough have survived to consider him one of the great Muslim scholars of all ages. He was the historian par excellence of the contemporary history of Granada, whose topography, monuments, men of learning, and rulers were the principal subjects of his writings. In fact, most of his prose writings are concerned with historical themes which he regards as highly valuable in the context of the meaning and purpose of history. He recognizes the nobility of history (*sharaf al-tārīkh*),[40] even if limited to writing the biography of Muḥammad, his conditions, his call to believe in one God, his relation with the Arabs, his raids, and the biography of his relatives and companions. Aside from its religious significance as the means of collecting Prophetic Traditions and as the source of commentaries of the Holy Book, he considers history beneficial as a means for gaining experience and for showing good example, besides being the source of people's pride. He concludes by saying that were it not for history, virtue would die with its possessors.

Ibn al-Khaṭīb left a number of historical works which constitute an invaluable source of information for the history of al-Andalus in general and that of Granada in particular. Some of these works are still in manuscripts in the Escorial and other libraries. Among those available is his diplomatic correspondence on behalf of the Naṣrid rulers.[41] Ibn al-Khaṭīb also wrote several histories of varying lengths on the kingdom of Granada; a work dealing with biographical sketches of poets, orators, jurists, and secretaries;[42] and an autobiography.[43] But his most impressive works that have been edited are the *A'māl al-A'lām*[44] and the *Iḥāṭah*.[45]

The *A'lām* was written during the last years of Ibn al-Khaṭīb's exile in North Africa. It was composed as the result of the death of the Marīnid ruler 'Abd al-'Azīz and the subsequent enthronement of the latter's minor son. The object of the work is to find precedents for the practice of nominating and enthroning minors. The end result was a general history of the Muslim world in three parts: the first dealing with Eastern history; the second with al-Andalus with reference to the Umayyads, party-kings, Almoravids, Almohads, revolts, the establishment of the Naṣrid kingdom and its rulers up to the author's own time, an account of his tenure as vizier, and a list of the various Christian rulers of northern Spain; the third part of the work deals with North Africa from the time of the Aghlabids of Tunis up to the author's time.

The *Iḥāṭah* begins with a justification for writing it. Ibn al-Khaṭīb states

The Mosque of Cordova; red-and-white naves built by ʿAbd al-Raḥmān I, 8th century.
Courtesy Foto Mas, Barcelona

The Mosque of Cordova; Chapel of the Lucernario. Courtesy Foto Mas, Barcelona

The Mosque of Cordova; dome of antechamber of the Miḥrāb. Courtesy Foto Mas, Barcelona

The Mosque of Cordova, western façade. Courtesy Foto Mas, Barcelona

Madinat al-Zahrā'; partial restoration of the great salon, built by
'Abd al-Raḥmān, 10th century. Courtesy Foto Mas, Barcelona

Madinat al-Zahrā'; partial view of the foundations. Courtesy Foto Mas, Barcelona

Bronze sculpture of a deer, from a fountain at Madinat al-Zahrā'.
Courtesy Museo Arqueológico, Cordova, and Foto Mas, Barcelona

The Giralda Tower, Seville; once the minaret of the Almohad Mosque, 12th century, now Cathedral Tower. Courtesy Foto Mas, Barcelona

Palace of Alcázar, Seville; Hall of Ambassadors, Mudéjar workmanship. Courtesy Foto Mas, Barcelona

Arabic inscriptions woven in silk. Courtesy Instituto Valencia de D. Juan, Madrid, and Foto Mas, Barcelona

Small wooden chest enlaid with silver, from cathedral at Gerona. Courtesy Foto Mas, Barcelona

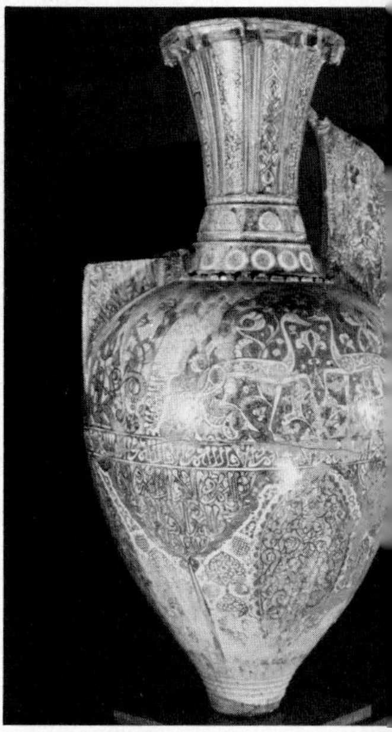

Glazed ceramic vessel from the Alhambra. Courtesy Museo Alhambr and Foto Mas, Barcelona

Marble water basin from the Alhambra. Courtesy Museo Alhambra and Foto Mas, Barcelona

Bronze lamp, 18 cm high and 42 cm in diameter. Courtesy Museo Arqueológico, Cordova

Astrolabe. Courtesy Instituto Valencia de D. Juan, Madrid, and Foto Mas, Barcelona

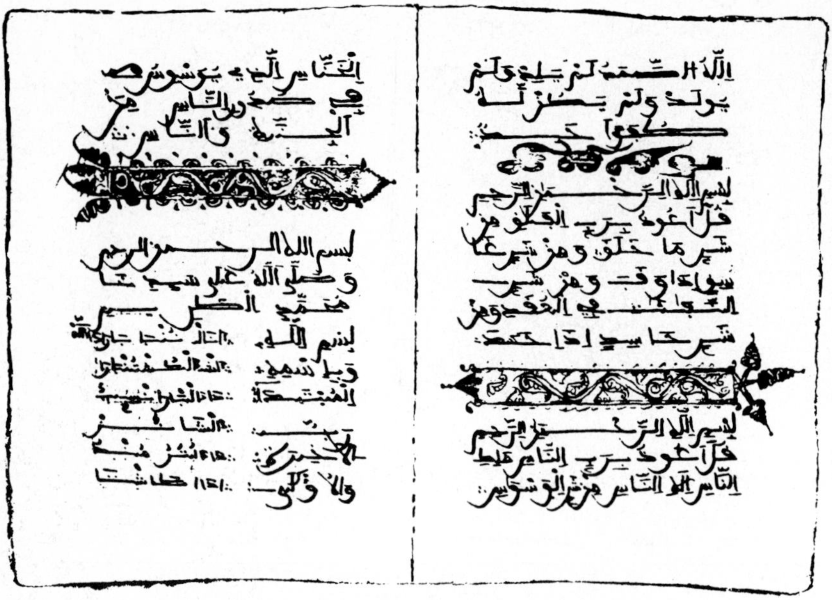

Bilingual manuscript of prayer in *aljamiado* and Arabic.
Courtesy Biblioteca Central de Barcelona

Bilingual document of sale in Latin and Arabic, 1167.
Courtesy Foto Mas, Barcelona

Indi noie. Ego heça fili de muça alazeiri uendo. iiij. alholder
de uinea cu sua intrada et exita. ub don heiz de phitero p. iiij.
morab lopis de peso bonos. et fu pacato de auer et de aliala. Sun iste
alholde in pradiela iuxta uinea de heiz de firero metipse. et ex par
te montecadi iuxta la cequa de pdiela. et dono ub fidanza de saluetate
ad foz tutele sine ulla mala uoce. Mofferriz peletero. Sun testes
uisores et auditores. Bernard de monthaio. Unecho de anselmer. Alpelmi
alcadi. Abdala auenlup.
Facta carta mse noub In. era. m. cc. v. Regnante rege Sancio in tutela
et in nauarra. Senior in tutela pet daraguri. Dauj iusticia. Fortunio
fortunones alcalde. Al chaiet in castelhi Sancio aluiz de ualtra.

The Alhambra; Hall of Ambassadors, 14th century. Courtesy Foto Mas, Barcelona

The Alhambra; Court of the Lions. Courtesy Foto Mas, Barcelona

that many local histories had been written in both East and West, and he lists a large number of them. Thus, he feels amply justified in writing the history of Granada with special reference to its leading men and to all those who passed through, even if only for a day. Ibn al-Khaṭīb explains the two main categories (*ṭabaqāt*), which distinguish individuals as residents or visitors in Granada. After a description of the country, he proceeds with biographical sketches of prominent men in alphabetical order and with a further classification into rulers, notables, virtuous men, judges, Qur'ānic readers, religious scholars, traditionists, jurists, secretaries, poets, provincial governors, ascetics, pious people, Ṣūfīs, and poor men. Each entry includes the full name of the man, his genealogy, relatives, date of birth, school or denomination, specialty, teachers, writings, and date of death. If the individual happens to be a ruler, reference is made to his children, viziers, secretaries, judges, other contemporary rulers, major events of the reign, and the dates of his birth and death. He concludes the work with an autobiography.

The man who has earned the admiration of Western and Eastern scholarship is Ibn Khaldūn,[46] the philosopher of history and the inventor of a science which he called *'umrān al-basharī*, human civilization or sociology. He may not have been the most brilliant figure in Islamic culture, but he definitely was the last intellectual giant. The lessons and reflections embodied in his work were heeded only long after his death, and such lessons changed the course of events in a declining Muslim society. He was born in Tunis in 1332 to a family which had emigrated from Seville, where they had enjoyed a prominent position in the political and social affairs of the city. The family maintained this prominence in their adopted land. In Tunis Ibn Khaldūn received his education — at home, in the mosque, and at the feet of Andalusian refugees. He seems to have had a good acquaintance with logic, metaphysics, and the religious sciences.

In 1345, his parents succumbed to the plague, and soon afterward Ibn Khaldūn found employment as "seal bearer" at the court of the Ḥafṣids. This inaugurated a political career marked by intrigues and shifting loyalties between the warring Ḥafṣid and Marīnid dynasties — the two great powers in the fourteenth-century Maghrib. He always chose the victor, but this dangerous game made life precarious and resulted in imprisonment. In 1362, Ibn Khaldūn decided to go to Granada. Here he was cordially received by the Naṣrid ruler and his friend, the vizier Ibn al-Khaṭīb, who gave him employment at the court and even sent him on a diplomatic mission to Peter the Cruel in Seville. However, things did not work out to Ibn Khaldūn's satisfaction, and he returned to Tunisia. There he again enjoyed the favor of the ruler and became a *ḥājib* (chamberlain), but he soon found himself in the same intrigue and insecurity. To avoid further imprisonment and unsavory situations, he decided on a voluntary retirement in the oasis of Baskarah, in present-day Algeria. However, circumstances compelled him to return to politics, though he foresaw and experienced the dire consequence of such a pursuit.

In 1375, he took advantage of an offer to retire in a castle in Oran, where he devoted himself to study and scholarship, and where in the next five years he wrote a work which was to immortalize him for all times. Afterward, he was drawn back into politics and was again victimized by intrigues. Under the circumstances he beseeched the ruler to allow him to make a pilgrimage; he left his native land in 1382 and never returned.

For the next twenty-four years, Ibn Khaldūn found a home and a more peaceful career in Egypt. He became a Mālikite judge several times, a lecturer at al-Azhar University and other institutions, and in 1401 an emissary to Tamerlane, the harsh, destructive conqueror of Syria, who then was threatening Egypt itself.

The fame of Ibn Khaldūn does not lie in his checkered career, nor in the vast literary works which typify the great majority of Muslim scholars. Rather it rests on the introduction (*al-Muqaddimah*) to his universal history entitled *The Book of Examples and Collections from the Early and Subsequent Information Concerning the Days of Arabs, Non-Arabs, and Berbers.*[47] The work has reached us in seven stout volumes and consists of three books, each of which is a self-contained unit. The first book is *al-Muqaddimah*, and the other two are the universal history. To the work is attached his autobiography, entitled *Ta'rīf*.

Al-Muqaddimah has earned for Ibn Khaldūn a place of honor among the leading thinkers of the world. Ibn Khaldūn divides the work into six sections:

1. On human civilizations in general, its various kinds, and the portion of the earth that is civilized.
2. On desert civilization, including a report on the tribes and savage nations.
3. On dynasties, the caliphate, and royal authority, including a discussion of government and ranks.

4. On sedentary civilization, countries, and cities.
5. On crafts, ways of making a living, gainful occupations, and their various aspects.
6. On the sciences, their acquisition and study.[48]

In his opening remarks to *al-Muqaddimah*, Ibn Khaldūn expounds his views of society, with its cycles of growth from primitive to sedentary patterns, and finally to a highly sophisticated urban structure characterized by a level of luxury that ultimately leads to its decay and downfall. In this process of growth and decline, Ibn Khaldūn emphasizes environment, politics, economics, and religion as influencing society in its stages of development.

Important too are his reflections and views on what constitutes history, the method of historical research, and historical criticism. Echoing Ibn Ḥazm, Ibn Khaldūn says that history is cultivated among all nations and races and is pursued by kings and common people alike. It is highly instructive and useful. It is not mere information about political events and dynasties "elegantly preserved and spiced with proverbs," or a means to entertain and enable us to understand human affairs and changing conditions, but it has a deeper meaning: "The inner meaning of history . . . involves speculation and an attempt to get at the truth, subtle explanations of the causes and origins of existing things, and deep knowledge of the how and why of events. [History] is, therefore, firmly rested in philosophy. It deserves to be accounted a branch [of philosophy]."[49]

According to Ibn Khaldūn, the historian should have a clear knowledge of customs, facts of politics, the nature of civilization, and the conditions governing social organization. Furthermore, he should use critical judgment in dealing with the past, duly regarding changes that occur in the course of time; and he should be fully aware of accounts not properly verified, partisan, or ignorant of the true nature of various conditions arising in a civilization.[50]

There are many other things in *al-Muqaddimah* that deserve mention, but for these the reader is referred to the reliable English translation by Rosenthal.

The universal history is the bulk of the work, almost six volumes: "The Second Book deals with the history, races, and dynasties of the Arabs, from the beginning of creation down to this time. This will include references to such famous nations and dynasties contemporaneous with them as the

Nabateans, the Syrians, the Persians, the Israelites, the Copts, the Greeks, the Byzantines, and the Turks. . . . The Third Book deals with the history of the Berbers and of the Zanatah who are part of them; with their origins and races, and, in particular, with the royal authority and dynasties in the Maghrib.''

This long history has been overshadowed by the importance of *al-Muqaddimah* and thus neglected by modern scholarship, except for the portion dealing with North Africa, which has been translated into French.[51] The work is for the most part a political history and is arranged around individuals, dynasties, rulers, and important events. For instance, Volume 2 contains such items as the history of the Arabs from the time of the creation; an introduction to the various nations of the world; the Arab periods or generations (*ajyāl*); Abraham, Ismā'il, and other prophets; the Arabized Arabs; Israelites, Perisans with their four eras; Greeks, Romans, and Goths; the third generation of Arabs and their successors (the kingdoms of al-Ḥīrah, Kinda, etc.), the coming of Islam; the Prophet Muḥammad, his raids; the early caliphate apostasy up to the death of 'Alī. Volume 3 takes up the Umayyad dynasty: its rulers, civil wars, appointments and dismissals of governors, conquests, and the coming of the 'Abbāsids. The latter is treated in a similar fashion, with reference to religious denominations, caliphs and other civil and military leaders up to the appearance of the Saljūqs, Ghaznavids, and Tartars. Volume 4 is devoted to the various dynasties in the Maghrib, al-Andalus, and petty states in the East, such as the dynasties of the Ḥamdānids, Ṭulūnids (of Egypt), Ṣaffārids, Ṣāmānids, Buwayhids, and others. Volume 5 continues with the Saljūqs, Ghaznavids, Tartars, Crusades, Ayyūbids, Mamlūks, Mongols, and others. Volumes 6 and 7 are entirely devoted to North Africa: its conquests; Berbers; the various tribes and dynasties, Almoravids, Almohads, Ḥafṣids, Zanātah, Marīnids, and others about which he gives first-hand information not found elsewhere.

His *Ta'rīf* covers the gamut of his career. It begins with his genealogy, which he traces to Yemen; his upbringing and teachers; his political career in North Africa; his two trips to al-Andalus; and his stay in Egypt.

A general survey of the historical literature would not be complete without a mention of the major anthologies, biographical, or bibliographical works which are invaluable for the intellectual and social history of al-Andalus. For instance, the *'Iqd al-farīd*[52] of Ibn 'Abd Rabbihi contains a mine of information about government, social and intellectual history, and the history of Eastern and Andalusian rulers. Similar Eastern works made their appearance in the tenth century and seem to have enjoyed great popularity, which explains the large-scale continuation of literary histories in the form of biographical dictionaries in the following centuries.

Among the early anthologists was Ibn Mughīth (898–963),[53] who enjoyed the favor of al-Ḥakam II. He was known for his asceticism, yet he appears to have held the office of judge in Cordova and to have acquiesced to his patron's request for a book on the poetry of caliphs from both the East and al-Andalus, similar to the work of the Eastern litterateur al-Ṣūlī.[54] Similarly his contemporary, Ibn Faraj al-Jayyānī (d. 970),[55] dedicated to al-Ḥakam II his *Kitāb al-ḥadā'iq* (*The Book of Gardens*), which was inspired by and patterned after *Kitāb al-zahrah* (*The Book of the Flower*) of the Easterner Ibn Dāwūd al-Iṣfahānī. The *Ḥadā'iq*, which exists today only in scattered excerpts in later biographies, reportedly contained 200 chapters of 200 verses each and was limited to Andalusian poets. The work became the model for subsequent authors.

Ibn Faraj al-Jayyānī was followed by Abū al-Walīd al-Ḥimyarī (d. ca. 1048),[56] a native of Seville and author of *al-Badī' fī waṣf al-Rabī'* (*The Marvellous Things Concerning the Descriptions of Spring*).[57] Here al-Ḥimyarī extolls Spanish talents in a tone described by Pérès as "un véritable manifeste de nationalisme littéraire."[58] The work contains a large number of poems by Andalusian poets who concerned themselves specifically with the description of spring and flowers.

Setting forth Andalusian talents in the form of literary histories was a tendency that continued in the twelfth century, with Ibn Bassām[59] and Ibn Khāqān[60] as the most outstanding representatives. They left two works which constitute an invaluable source of information about leading men of al-Andalus who excelled in various fields, particularly poetry, linguistics, and rhetoric.

Ibn Bassām was born about 1069 to a wealthy family in Santarem, Portugal, where he received his education. Around 1100, he was forced to emigrate to Cordova and earn his livelihood by his pen. He is credited with several works, the most important of which is *al-Dhakhīrah*.[61] This anthology, composed around 1106–1109 in Seville, contains the best examples of poetic and prose composition by representative Andalusians. He may have used the works of Ibn Faraj al-Jayyānī and al-Tha'ālibī for models. The work has four parts, according to region, and contains 126 entries of leading men from the various regions of al-Andalus and from foreign lands. Ibn Bassām avoids chronological and alphabetical arrangements, and lists the authors by region and by his judgment of their importance. He gives a biographical sketch of each author, an evaluation of his literary qualities, and excerpts from his prose or verse.

The *Qalā'id*[62] of Ibn Khāqān is a work similar to the *Dhakhīrah*. Its author was born in a village not far from Granada. His youth was, for the most part, spent in dissipation. His frequent travels to various cities of al-Andalus enabled him to collect material for his anthology of the poems and anecdotes of 66 prominent men of al-Andalus, particularly those who flourished under the party-kings. The work is written in an embellished rhymed prose and appears to be directed to the general public. Unlike Ibn Bassām, Ibn Khāqān omitted a great deal of biographical information, a practice that is apparent also in his other work, *Maṭmaḥ*.[63] The *Qalā'id* is divided into four parts; each lists first those persons whom the author considers to be the most outstanding of the group. Part 1 concerns itself with the noble qualities of rulers and their sons; Part 2 with poetry of viziers, secretaries, and rhetoricians; Part 3 with judges and scholars; and Part 4 with literati and poets.

The works of Ibn Bassām and Ibn Khāqān are concerned with leading poets and the best of their poetry, and are intended to complete and bring up to date the works of their predecessors. Similar attempts were undertaken by their near contemporaries and successors, who drew heavily from their works. These lesser works are permeated by a nationalistic and apologetic tone, a tendency quite discernible in the treatises of Ibn Ḥazm,[64] Ibn Sa'īd al-Maghribī,[65] and al-Shaqundī.[66]

In addition to anthologies, the Andalusians concerned themselves with biographical dictionaries of outstanding men according to their professions — grammarians, physicians, secretaries, judges, and the like. But the biographical dictionaries of outstanding men of al-Andalus itself were perhaps the most important contribution. Some biographical dictionaries were limited to a class of professionals, whereas others were more comprehensive and included Andalusians who excelled in various disciplines or professions. The information in an entry is rather brief and includes, as a rule, the man's full name, *kunyah* (patronymic), his dates of birth and death, education, teachers, and place of residence. Some specialized dictionaries dealt with the teachers of a scholar or with his pupils and followers. Significant also was a chain of works which supplemented one another.

Only brief reference can be made to some of these authors and works. Al-Zubaydī wrote on the categories of grammarians and lexicographers,[67]

Ibn Juljul (ca. 1000) on physicians,[68] and Ibn 'Abd al-Barr[69] on the jurists *(fuqahā')* of Cordova. Muḥammad Ibn Ḥārith al-Khushanī (d. 971) wrote a work on jurists and traditionists and another called *The History of the Judges of Cordova.*[70] The latter, which was preserved, is of inestimable value for its account of many social and legal matters from the time of the conquest down to the year 968, shortly before the author's death. It sheds much light on the office of judge for over two and a half centuries.

There were other specialized works which are of great interest for their form and content. Abū 'Alī Ibn Sukkarah al-Ṣadafī (d. 1121)[71] of Saragossa became the object of adulation by his contemporaries and successors. He was a famous traditionist and judge, and known for his virtue and austerity. He fell in the Battle of Kutandah, becoming a "martyr" and the subject of biographical works. His contemporary Ibn 'Iyāḍ (d. 1149) — to whom al-Maqqarī devotes a three-volume work[72] — wrote on the teachers of al-Ṣadafī, and Ibn al-Abbār wrote a dictionary (*mu'jam*) which dealt with the pupils and followers of al-Ṣadafī. Equally significant is the *Fahrasah*[73] of Ibn Khayr. Ibn Khayr was born in Seville in 1109 and died in Cordova in 1180. He received his early education in his native city and continued it for most of his life in the major cities of al-Andalus where he studied the most important works under leading scholars of the day. In essence, the *Fahrasah* is a catalogue of some 1,040 books which he studied under numerous teachers. Those books comprise Qur'ānic studies, Prophetic Traditions, law, grammar, lexicography, and literature. The work is unique; it is valuable not only for its insight into the content and extent of an education during the twelfth century, but also into the manner of acquiring it.

More comprehensive biographical works were written by al-Ḥumaydī, al-Ḥijārī, and al-Ḍabbī. Al-Ḥijārī is known for his six-volume *Book of the Loquacious Concerning the Extraordinary Qualities of the People of the Maghrib*,[74] giving biographies of prominent men of the Maghrib from the time of the conquest up to 1135. Although the work is lost, it was widely used and was later continued by Ibn Sa'īd al-Maghribī. Al-Ḍabbī, who was born in a town west of Lorca and spent most of his life in Murcia, left us his valuable *Bughyah*[75] based on al-Ḥumaydī's biographical dictionary dealing with the rulers, traditionists, jurists, and poets of al-Andalus.[76]

Of great interest is Ibn al-Faraḍī (962–1013), whose *History of the Scholars of al-Andalus*[77] became the model of biographical dictionaries for generations. He was not only emulated but had a number of followers who supplemented or completed his work by bringing it up to their own times.

Among them were Ibn Bashkuwāl, Ibn al-Abbār, Ibn 'Abd al-Malik, Ibn al-Zubayr, Ibn al-Khaṭīb, and others who constituted a dynasty of *mudhayyilūn* (continuators) of the work of Ibn al-Faraḍī.

Ibn al-Faraḍī [78] was born and educated in Cordova. He assumed the office of judge in Valencia and in 992 he went on a pilgrimage to Mecca, spending almost two years in the East. At his return, he resided in Cordova until 1013, when he was murdered in his home during the great revolt. As traditionist and historian, he wrote several works, one dealing with the poets of al-Andalus and another with its traditionists. Neither is extant, although later authors refer to them. However, his fame rests on his biographical dictionary, which remains in two volumes. In the introduction, Ibn al-Faraḍī says that he had intended to write a large work which would contain extensive information about each scholar, but he decided on brevity — still making the work unprecedented according to him. He arranges the work alphabetically giving the full name of the scholar, his patronymic, relatives, teachers, place of residence, travels, and dates of birth and death. The work is quite comprehensive and done with care; it includes a large number of jurists, learned men, transmitters of Traditions, poets, and other leading men.

Ibn al-Faraḍī had a worthy successor in Ibn Bashkuwāl (1101–1182), [79] who was born in Cordova to a family originally from Sorrion near Valencia. He received his education in his native city and Seville. He is credited with some fifty works, such as his *History of the Conditions of al-Andalus*, another on reciters (*ruwāh*) of the *Muwaṭṭa'*, and other biographical works. His extant and important work is *al-Ṣilah* [80] (continuation, or addendum). As its name indicates, the *Ṣilah* follows the work of Ibn al-Faraḍī and includes some 1,541 entries of literati, traditionists, and imams of al-Andalus up to Ibn Bashkuwāl's own time. In the introduction, he says that the *Ṣilah* was undertaken at the behest of colleagues desiring him to bring Ibn al-Faraḍī's *Tārīkh* up to date. He follows the format and method (*rasm wa ṭarīqah*) of Ibn al-Faraḍī.

The *Ṣilah* was esteemed as much as the *Tārīkh*. Many attempted addenda to the *Ṣilah* (*dhayl al-ṣilah*) but none have survived except Ibn al-Abbār's thirteenth-century completion (*takmilah*) of Ibn Bashkuwāl's *Ṣilah*. Ibn al-Abbār (1199–1260), [81] traditionist, belletrist, and historian, was born in a small town in the province of Valencia and received his education under leading scholars of the day. He lived in Valencia, but after the capture of the city by the Aragonese in 1238, he was compelled to emigrate to Tunisia where he served its ruler. He fell victim to court intrigues and was put to death in 1260. He is the author of some forty-five works on Traditions, belles lettres, and history, most of which are lost. From his surviving historical works,[82] Ibn al-Abbār emerges as an able and distinguished historian. *Takmilah li-kitāb al-ṣilah* (*The Completion of the Book of Continuation*) by Ibn Bashkuwāl brings Ibn al-Faraḍī's *Tārīkh* up to his own time, and follows it in format and method. His other major work, *Mu'jam*, deals with the pupils and followers of al-Ṣadafī and was perhaps a continuation of the work of the jurist Ibn 'Iyāḍ. The *Mu'jam* is arranged alphabetically, giving the full name, place of residence, teachers, travels, dates of birth and death, and the field in which each individual excelled. It consists of 315 entries, each of which contains much more information than found in the works of Ibn al-Faraḍī or Ibn Bashkuwāl. Important too is his *al-Ḥullah al-siyarā'* (*The Garment with Golden Lines*), collecting the biographies of princes with poetical talents. He gives samples of their poetry with a discernment that justifies the title of the work.

The *Takmilah* of Ibn al-Abbār was continued by Ibn 'Abd al-Malik al-Anṣārī (d. 1303), author of the *Supplement and Completion* (*al-Dhayl wa-l-takmilah*) in ten volumes, most of which are scattered in manuscript in various libraries.[83] The aim of the author was to continue (*tadhyīl*) the *Tārīkh* of Ibn al-Faraḍī and the *Ṣilah* of Ibn Bashkuwāl, and to include and complete (*takmīl*) what they had neglected. A contemporary of Ibn 'Abd al-Malik was Ibn al-Zubayr (d. 1308), who was born in Jaén and resided in Málaga and Granada. He is the author of *Ṣilat al-ṣilah* (*Link of Link*),[84] a continuation of Ibn Bashkuwāl's *Ṣilah*. Finally, Ibn al-Khaṭīb concluded the series of "supplement and completion" in his work entitled *'Ā'id al-ṣilah*, which has not survived.

In any survey of anthologies and biographical works one can hardly omit reference to some of the works by Ibn al-Khaṭīb. In this connection, it is of particular interest to mention the seventeenth-century author al-Maqqarī (d. 1631), who was born in Tlemcen. Al-Maqqarī was compelled to leave his native town and resided in Fez, then Damascus, and later Cairo, where he died. Al-Maqqarī left two invaluable works, *Nafḥ al-ṭīb* and the *Azhār al-riyāḍ*.[85] The *Nafḥ*, often mentioned in this study, contains a mine of information about the history and culture of al-Andalus and was written at the behest of Damascene scholars. Although the work was intended to be a biography of the great statesman and thinker Ibn al-Khaṭīb, al-Maqqarī devotes almost half of it to the history of al-Andalus: its description, conquest by the Arabs, history of the various dynasties; minute description and history of Cordova; Hispano-Arabic scholars who travelled to the East and Easterners who visited or settled in al-Andalus; biographical sketches and miscellaneous extracts; and the reconquest by Christians and expulsion of Muslims. The second portion of the work is devoted to the life, career, and literary works of Ibn al-Khaṭīb. All in all, the *Nafḥ* is an invaluable source of information about the history of al-Andalus and its leading men.

Equally valuable is al-Maqqarī's *Azhār al-riyāḍ* (*The Flowers of Meadows*), a work devoted to the twelfth-century religious scholar and jurist Ibn 'Iyāḍ. Only a portion of the work was edited, in three volumes.[86] It follows an arrangement similar to the *Nafḥ* and includes a wealth of information about the general history of al-Andalus and its outstanding men. The work is divided into eight "meadows," each of which is concerned with one aspect of Ibn 'Iyāḍ's physical and cultural environment long before and after the death of Ibn 'Iyāḍ. For instance, ample space is given to cities and the life and time of Ibn al-Khaṭīb. The eight "meadows" also correspond to the various stages of Ibn 'Iyāḍ's life: his early surroundings, upbringing, teachers, poems and prose writings, unique writings, wisdom and sayings, death, and his influence on succeeding generations.

As already mentioned, geography and history were interdependent in many respects. *Geography* (*jughrāfiyā*) is a term borrowed from the Greek. Although this science was greatly influenced by the Ptolemaic conception, it made no small strides through Muslim geographers, who added to their geographical knowledge from books by means of their own study and observation. Geographical studies had their inception in the East and were pursued throughout the Muslim world at both the theoretical and the practical levels. No doubt the field arose out of religious, military, and administrative needs, as well as out of intellectual curiosity to know the Earth, its form, positions, longitude, and latitude. This wide interest is reflected in the surviving works, which may be classified into, first, descriptive geography and, second, mathematical or theoretical geography.[87]

Descriptive geography was immediately useful for religious, military, and administrative purposes. It was written by roving scholars who gathered the necessary information for the benefit of rulers, officials, and the public. Inasmuch as the Muslim had to face Mecca five times a day during his prescribed prayers, it was imperative to determine his position in relation to the Holy City. Moreover, as Islam dictates that the faithful should pilgrimage to both Mecca and Medina once in a lifetime, if at all possible, the need for geography became even more important. These needs increased enormously as the Muslim empire expanded over a vast territory. Thus many geographical works were written for practical use or even for entertainment. Some of the early works dealt with specific topics such as topography, climate, and natural resources. An early representative work bore the significant title of *al-Masālik wa-l-mamālik* (*Roads and Countries*), a title that was adopted by many generations of writers. This type of work proved very useful for the postal service (*barīd*) as well as for government officials and secretaries. Other works dealt with the characteristics of countries and were entitled *'Ilm 'ajā'ib al-buldān* (*The Knowledge of the Marvels of Countries*). At first these works were limited in scope, but they were followed by more comprehensive works in the form of compendia, geographical dictionaries, and travel accounts (*riḥlah*).

On the other hand, the mathematical or theoretical geography was inspired by and based on the Ptolemaic geographical notions as they became known to the Arabs in translation sometime during the ninth century. The early works dealt with the form of the Earth (*ṣūrat al-arḍ*), longitudes and latitudes (*'ilm al-aṭwāl wa-l-'urūḍ*), and the positions of countries (*'ilm taqwīm al-buldān*).

Muslim geographers gained their information through written data, informants, or their own travels. Some of them wrote on geography at their own initiative; others were commissioned by rulers. Their interest did not lie in Muslim countries alone, but extended as far as China, Russia, India, the Balkans, and other countries. The content of their works depended upon the proclivity of a particular author; it might include stories, anecdotes, legends, historical information about peoples, their customs and religion, itineraries of merchants, agricultural products and clothing, cosmography, description of cities, rivers, mountains, monuments, bizarre things, or marvels. In this connection, Eastern geographers did not fail to mention important data about al-Andalus and its marvels.[88]

At first, Andalusians emulated the works of Eastern geographers. Among those who appear to have exerted an influence are the mathematician al-Khuwarizmī (d. 847) and Ibn Kurdādhbih (d. ca. 900), who were among the pioneers to write about geography in its theoretical and practical aspects. Al-Khuwarizmī composed a work entitled *Ṣūrat al-arḍ* (*The Form of the Earth*), in which he included a map of the heavens and the earth. Ibn Khurdādhbih wrote his *al-Masālik wa-l-mamālik*[89] for the use of officials; it contained Ptolemaic cosmological notions with respect to the position of the Earth in the universe, Baghdād as the center of the world; itineraries to Iran, India, China, Syria, Egypt, the Maghrib, Armenia, and the Arabian Peninsula; and the division of the world and its marvels. Al-Khuwarizmī and Ibn Khurdādhbih had worthy contemporaries and successors in Ibn Rustah (d. 903), Ya'qūbī (d. ca. 897), al-Mas'ūdī (d. 956), Ibn Ḥawqal (d. 977), al-Muqaddisī (d. ca. 1000),[90] Yāqūt,[91] and others.

In al-Andalus proper,[92] an early geographer was the historian Aḥmad Ibn Muḥammad al-Rāzī (d. 936), who concerned himself with the roads, provinces, and cities of al-Andalus.[93] His contemporary, Muḥammad b. Yūsuf al-Warrāq (d. 973), is often referred to as writing several geographical and historical works at the behest of al-Ḥakam II. Among these was a treatise entitled *al-Masālik wa-l-mamālik*, which deals specifically with North Africa. The work is lost, as are several others on the rulers and cities of North Africa.[94] They all became basic sources for later geographers and historians. Aḥmad al-Rāzī and al-Warrāq were pioneers in the field of geographical writings — the interest of the former being the topography of al-Andalus, and that of the latter the roads and regions of North Africa. Another contemporary was Ibrāhīm Ibn Ya'qūb (d. 900's), a Jewish slave trader from Tortosa. He travelled widely in Germany, the Balkans, and northern Europe, and made an itinerary of his trips that became valuable to merchants as well as contributed to the knowledge of non-Muslim countries and their people.

The influence of Aḥmad al-Rāzī, al-Warrāq, and Ibrāhīm Ibn Ya'qūb on geographical writing cannot be overstated. They were quoted profusely by generations of geographers. Aḥmad Ibn 'Umar al-'Udhrī (d. ca. 1084)[95] depended on them for writing a seemingly comprehensive work on roads and countries.[96] He was born in a small village of the province of Almería, and emigrated to the East in 1016, where he studied literature and religion for almost a decade. He arranged his geographical work into chapters, each dealing with a district (*kūrah*). He describes districts with reference to their capitals, towns, and villages; their characteristics; and the distances separating them.

It would seem that geographical writing in al-Andalus reached the peak of its development in the eleventh century with al-'Udhrī and his contemporaries, mainly his disciple, the poet and philologist al-Bakrī (d. 1094), who elevated geographical writing to a height previously unknown in al-Andalus. Al-Bakrī relied heavily on his predecessors, mainly al-Rāzī and al-Warrāq. Little is known about his life. He was born about 1014 at Saltes to a noble family. In 1001, his grandfather had secured the governorship of Huelva and Saltes in the southwest of the Iberian Peninsula and became independent from the central government of Cordova in 1011. In 1051, al-Bakrī's father was forced to emigrate to Cordova after his domain had been absorbed by the 'Abbādids of Seville. It is probable that the young al-Bakrī stayed in Cordova until his father died in 1064 and then moved to Almería, where he served its ruler and wrote his important works. In 1085, he was sent on a diplomatic mission to the 'Abbādid court of Seville, and decided afterward to settle there, where he died in 1094.

Al-Bakrī was a prolific scholar as belletrist, philologist, poet, botanist, historian, and geographer. He is considered the outstanding geographer of al-Andalus. He wrote two important works: *Mu'jam mā ista'jam*,[97] an extant geographical dictionary which explains place-names related to the Arabian Peninsula; and *Masālik wa-l-mamālik*, probably in several volumes. The *Mu'jam* has a long description of the Arabian Peninsula; it is arranged alphabetically and contains numerous geographical terms for dwellings, villages, towns, mountains, rivers, and monuments as found in the Traditions and historical works. His explanations of those terms are ordinarily checked against those contained in the works of his predecessors. The arrangement appears to be the first of its kind among Arab geographers. The *Masālik* is a general geography which starts with the Creation and treats the countries of the world with sketches of their history, climate, natural resources, customs, roads, cities, provinces, and monuments. Only the portion dealing with North Africa and fragments dealing with al-Andalus, Europe, and other parts of the world have reached us.[98]

Al-Bakrī is known not to have left al-Andalus. Therefore, his geographical information was based on documents and works of his predecessors from East and West such as Ibn Rustah, al-Mas'ūdī, Muḥammad Ibn Yūsuf al-Warrāq, al-Rāzī, Ibrāhīm Ibn Ya'qūb al-Isrā'īlī, al-'Udhrī, and others.

On the basis of the extant material, one is able to gain an insight into al-Bakrī's approach to geographical writings. Grouping his material by countries, he describes locations with information about people, customs, and climate; some distinctive features of the country, historical data, description of roads, cities and the distances separating them; information about resources; and some interesting stories. The portion on al-Andalus and Europe starts with al-Andalus, discussing the various names under which the Peninsula was known — Iberia, Baetica, España, and al-Andalus. This is followed by a reference to six political and administrative provinces including the major cities. He then takes up Galicia and mentions some of its kings and their relations with the Muslims. He characterizes the Galicians as inhabitants of an "arid land; they are treacherous, dirty, and bathe once or twice a year, even then with cold water. They never wash their clothes until they are worn out because they claim that the dirt accumulated as the result of their sweat softens their body . . ."[99] He dismisses Brittany in northwest France by simply saying that the people have a language which is unpleasant to the ear; they are ugly, have bad character, and count among them many thieves who steal from the French, who put them to the cross when apprehended.[100] He passes on to discuss the mountains of al-Andalus and its various cities: Toledo with its fortifications; Talavera; Tudela, which had a woman with a long beard like that of a man;[101] Bobastro; Barcelona with mention of its rulers; Cordova with description of its great mosque; Seville with a sketch of its history, walls, main mosque, and revenue; Algeciras; Merida; and Badajoz. The part dealing with al-Andalus concludes with a section on forestry, minerals, and precious stones.

The remainder of the text, roughly more than half the total, deals with foreigners and their countries: Spaniards, Turks, Khazars, Lombards (al-Mukbard?), English, Russians, Bulgars, Poles, and the *Ṣaqālibah*, to whom he devotes relatively ample space.[102] The work proceeds with a brief sketch of the "country of the Romans" and of the various islands in the Mediterranean. He describes the parades of the Byzantine Emperor to the main church in Constantinople; and passes on to the city of Rome, referring to its location and to the Basilica of St. Peter. He has a few words about the Romans, their history, and religions, pointing out that they shaved their beards and labeled those who didn't as Christians! Cyprus is said to have extolled idol worship in antiquity; its people are famous for their wealth. Crete took its name from a Magian (but he does not mention its occupation by Andalusians). Sicily is rich in agriculture, has an awesome, horrifying volcano and phosphorus mines, and was inhabited in antiquity by cannibals; it is a land torn by strife and was conquered by the Muslims. Malta is famous for its port and pine trees; Cossyra is one of many islands around Sicily; Macedonia was the home of Aristotle, who was the teacher of Alexander; and Thrace is the land where reins for horses were said to have been used for the first time.

A near contemporary of al-Bakrī was the anthologist al-Ḥimyarī who in *al-Rawḍ al-mi'ṭār*[103] included a description of al-Andalus. Geographical information continued to occupy the attention of subsequent writers. 'Abdallah al-Ḥijārī (d. 1155) was a belletrist and historian-geographer. His

Mushib, originally in six volumes, can be described as a work of cultural geography and contains, besides information about men of letters, a general description of al-Andalus, its wonders, cities, and political divisions. Although the work is not extant, it was the model and the basis for the *Mughrib* of the historian Ibn Sa'id al-Maghribī, author of a work dealing with the length and width of the Earth.[104] Outstanding among the geographer-travellers are al-Idrīsī (d. 1166), Abū Ḥamīd al-Māzinī, Ibn Jubayr, and Ibn Baṭṭūṭah (d. 1377). But a truly professional geographer was al-Idrīsī (d. 1166).

Al-Idrīsī, called the Strabo of the Arabs, is one of the most important geographer-cartographers of the Middle Ages. He was born in Ceuta in 1100, and received his education in Cordova. He visited Spain, North Africa, and Asia Minor, and recorded his impressions, supplementing them from old sources and reports of his contemporaries. He settled in Sicily, where he worked under the auspices of the Norman king, Roger II, for whom he made a globe in silver showing the seven zones of the world, countries, seas, rivers, deserts, principal cities, and roads. He was commissioned by his patron to write a geography of the world. In this, al-Idrīsī not only used knowledge based on old sources and his own observations, but he availed himself of a group of geographers sent to survey the inhabited earth. Their findings were finally compiled into a book entitled *Nuzhat al-mushtāq fī ikhtirāq al-āfāq*. The work was dedicated to his benefactor and became known as the *Book of Roger*.[105] He also composed another geographical work, dedicated to Roger's successor. Of this work only an abridgement has survived.

The *Book of Roger* is a valuable source of information about Muslim and non-Muslim countries. It is profusely illustrated with maps. Al-Idrīsī deals first with the Western countries and concludes with those of the East. He gives a general view of a country and its conditions during al-Idrīsī's time. The section on Africa includes such countries as the Sudan and the surrounding area bordering the Nile, Nubia, and Abyssinia. He discusses its topography and resources, including lakes, mountains, rivers, plants, animals, and minerals. He also gives useful data about the customs of the people, their commercial activities, agricultural products, and cultural standing.

The greatest contribution of al-Andalus and the Maghrib to geography was, perhaps, in the field of travel. Andalusians travelled extensively within and outside their country. Many travellers must have gathered a great deal of information and many impressions. At first, travellers orally transmitted their impressions of the lands visited to relatives and friends, but subsequently they attempted to record their observations and experience. They would describe the difficulties experienced during their journeys by land or sea. They would also record all sorts of information about the lands visited, describing their cities, resources, and wonders, whether real or imaginary. In spite of intensive travel, however, the written data is scanty. It was not until the twelfth century that written documentation appears with some frequency. Some travellers wrote about a particular country, and others left more comprehensive works.

It appears that the jurist Abū Bakr Ibn al-'Arabī (1076–1148) was the first person who left records of his travel to the East. In his *Tartīb al-riḥlah* (*The Itinerary of a Journey*), he describes his impressions and observations in various North African and Eastern cities with particular emphasis on his meetings with teachers and notables.

While Ibn al-'Arabī was mostly concerned with his studies and teachers, his contemporary Abū Ḥamīd al-Māzinī (1080–1170) displayed keen interest in fanciful stories and wonders (*'ajā'ib*), besides useful information about what he saw, heard, or read in books. He travelled extensively in Sicily, Egypt, the region of the Caspian Sea, Russia, and the Balkans. He reached the Oxus River in the East and returned westward through Baghdād. Only excerpts of his two travel works have reached us.[106] They contain a great number of amazing and charming stories and other items that attracted his curiosity. Abū Ḥamīd's aim appears to be to inform and entertain. Thus, he mixes serious information with rare and bizarre things. In *al-Mu'rib*, he indicates that he saw in Cairo a watermelon weighing some 160 pounds; that a fish in Bulgaria had the weight of a man or even that of a camel; that the Sierra Nevada in Granada had a church near which was an olive tree whose fruit ripens in one day; that "spirits" built a "copper city" for Solomon; and the like. In a more serious vein, he describes cities, roaring volcanoes in Sicily, various fishes of the sea, monuments, latitude and longitude of the Earth, and the seven zones or climates of the Earth. In his *Tuḥfah*, he also mixes actual happenings with fanciful stories under the following main headings: general description of the inhabited world; marvels found in the various countries with special reference to buildings and monuments; seas and islands with mention of rare animals residing therein; and caves, sepulchres, fossils, and the like.

A contemporary of Abū Ḥamīd was Muḥammad al-Zuhrī, to whom is attributed a book on geography concerned mainly with al-Andalus — its major cities, resources, mountains, rivers, routes. The part dealing with Egypt, Syria, India, and China abounds in legends and fanciful stories.

A great traveller was Ibn Jubayr (1145–1219) who made travel a lively and interesting adventure, unequaled before or after his time. He was born in Valencia and received a broad education in Játiva. He became secretary to the Almohad governor of Granada. He made trips to Mecca and Medina in 1183, 1189, and 1217, leaving a record of the first. Some of the important places he visited were Alexandria, Cairo, Kūfah, Baghdād, Aleppo, Damascus, and Sicily. He recorded his impressions in a diary, which was later put in book form under the apt title *Riḥlah* (*Travel*).[107] He begins the work with his departure from Granada and gives a detailed account of his daily observations, describing cities and their monuments, peoples, and the difficulties he experienced because of the weather or people (such as the custom officials at the port of Alexandria). In concise and clear language he supplies important details about the precise time of departure and arrival, giving the dates in Gregorian and Muslim calendars; distances; atmospheric conditions; description of major towns along with their main features and attractions, represented by roads, bridges, mosques, and monuments.

A near contemporary of Ibn Jubayr was Muḥammad al-'Abdarī of Valencia, who in 1289 made a voyage to North Africa which he recorded in a work entitled *al-Riḥlah al-Maghribiyyah*.[108] He visited Fez, Tlemcen, Constantine, Tunis, and Alexandria, and found objections about people and conditions in general. Only in Tunisia did he find people who were amiable and cooperative; elsewhere they were crude and ignorant. One may also mention Muḥammad Ibn Rushayd al-Fihrī (d. 1321), who left a record of his trip to the East.[109]

But a truly world traveller was Ibn Baṭṭūṭah (1304–1377). Ibn Baṭṭūṭah was born in Tangier, where he received his education in law. At the age of twenty-one he travelled to the East, visiting North Africa, Syria, Mecca, and Iraq. In 1329, he performed his second pilgrimage to Mecca; from there he went to Yemen and then to East Africa. During his third pilgrimage he went via the Nile Valley and the Red Sea to the Holy Places; from there he travelled through Syria, Asia Minor, the Black Sea, Crimea to Constantinople; and then to the Crimea, Afghanistan, India, and China. Upon his return to North Africa, he passed through most of the above countries and finally ended in Granada.

Ibn Baṭṭūṭah put down his impressions of these extensive travels in his book *Tuḥfat al-nuẓẓār fī 'ajā'ib al-amṣār,*[110] which was written at the request of the Marīnid ruler with the assistance of a courtier of Fez, Ibn Juzā'ī (d. 1356). Although the work is based on notes taken by Ibn Baṭṭūṭah during his travels, or on his memory, it is greatly indebted to earlier geographical and travel works. Nonetheless, the work contains a wealth of information concerning the beliefs and customs of countries visited, in addition to numerous legends and amazing stories.

It is significant that numerous travel treatises were written in rhymed prose in emulation of the *Maqāmāt* of al-Ḥarīrī. This form seemed quite popular in al-Andalus.[111] Perhaps its best representative was Ibn al-Khaṭīb, who, in addition to including extensive geographical information in his historical works, mainly the *Iḥāṭah* and *al-Lamḥah al-badriyyah*, left us three treatises.[112] The first treatise deals with a description of cities of Granada[113] and North Africa; the second is concerned with the boastfulness of the cities of Málaga and Salé, each of which tried to show its superiority over the other;[114] and the third describes the journey of Ibn al-Khaṭīb's patron through the eastern part of Granada.[115]

16

The Religious Sciences

THE RELIGIOUS sciences, *'Ilm sharī'at al-islām*, an expression borrowed from Ibn Ḥazm, means literally "the science of the revelation of Islam." Ibn Ḥazm defines it as follows: "The Science of the Revelation of Islam is divided into four parts: the science of the Qur'ān, the science of Traditions (*ḥadīth*), the science of jurisprudence (*fiqh*), and the science of theology (*kalām*). The science of the Qur'ān is divided into the knowledge (*ma'rifah*) of its reading and meaning; the science of Traditions into the knowledge of its texts and transmitters; the science of jurisprudence into the exact knowledge (*iḥkām*) of the Qur'ān, Traditions, the consensus of agreement and disagreement of Muslims (*ijmā'*), and the procedures of demonstration with respect to what is valid and invalid; and the science of theology into the knowledge of the writings (of theologians), their arguments, and what is true or false through scientific demonstration (*burhān*)."[1]

This statement by the most prolific author of al-Andalus not only sums up what the religious sciences are, but shows their intimate interdependence. Of course, the Qur'ān — the divinely revealed Book — is in theory the fountainhead and the guiding principle of both Traditions and jurisprudence, which are essentially supposed to elaborate rather than contradict the Qur'ānic precepts. In actuality, however, many moral concepts emerged in the Traditions and the law which are not specifically spelled out in the Holy Book, and which remained for a long time a point of contention among early Muslims. Moreover, basic questions related to God and His attributes, free will and human action, sins, salvation and damnation, and others, were equally objects of divergent views and heated controversies; these questions led to the establishment of a theology which took several centuries for its final formulation and crystalization. It was then that this theology was incorporated into the Qur'ān, the Traditions, and the law and became inseparable from them.

The impact of the religious sciences on Muslim culture can hardly be underestimated. They have formed the base of education in Muslim society and have constituted the noblest objective in the pursuit of knowledge. All sciences are not only subordinated to them but would prove futile if they were not directed to their attainment. Ibn Ḥazm, for one, recognizes the validity of all the sciences and crafts; he considers them intertwined and useful, but he adds that they would be useless if isolated from the religious sciences, which alone aim at attaining reward in the Hereafter and enable the individual to be righteous and at peace with the ruler, nobles, and masses alike.[2] "In sum, were it not for the quest of salvation in the Hereafter, the pursuit of any of the sciences would be meaningless, because such pursuit would be a waste of time; besides, it prevents one from enjoying the pleasures of the transitory world such as food, drink, amusement, foolishness, ambition for promotion (*i'tilā'*), and the following of one's desires. Moreover, were it not for the Hereafter which leads to the pursuit of the sciences, no one would be in a worse lot than the one devoted to knowledge. If this is the case, then all the sciences are related to each other as we have demonstrated before and each one requires the knowledge of the other. They do not have any aim other than the knowledge that leads to the Hereafter alone, that is, to the knowledge of the science of revelation (*'ilm al-sharī'ah*)."[3]

No doubt, Ibn Ḥazm reflects a universal conviction among Muslims, regarding the superiority and primacy of the religious sciences over other disciplines. It is because of this conviction that Muslim scholarship was heavily permeated by religious thinking. Moreover, one can hardly find a scholar of consequence — be he philosopher, mathematician, astronomer, physician, or philologist — who did not delve deeply into the religious sciences. In consequence, those sciences were abundantly cultivated in both the East and the Islamic West, the Maghrib and Spain. The amount of religious literature is staggering, and so is the number of religious scholars. A mere listing of religious scholars and their works in Spain alone would be lengthy indeed, not to mention the production of the rest of the Muslim world.

The religious scholars exerted a portentous influence in Muslim society in both the spiritual and secular spheres, affecting the mental outlook of the people and their way of life: the scholars contributed to the existence of a universal religiosity and became the arbiters of human conduct in its multifarious aspects. Islam has been to the believer a way of life, having as much bearing on the well-being of the individual in this world as in the Hereafter. This conviction has been nourished from birth to death. A child begins his formal education with the memorization of the Qur'ān and continues to study it along with the Traditions and Islamic practice in their dogmatic and ritualistic forms. This was true in the East and in Muslim Spain. The western part of the Muslim world adopted an orthodox path (*sunnah*) from the outset and continued its espousal with staunch faithfulness to the text of the Qur'ān, the sayings and deeds of the Prophet Muḥammad as handed down by the early and conservative schools of the East. In consequence, Muslim Spain spared itself the hair-splitting religious deliberations and strife that long shook the very foundations of Islamic polity in the East. The main reason, perhaps, for this conservatism lies in the considerable distance of al-Andalus from the main religious centers and in its political isolation from the heartland at an early period when religious speculations were still of little or no consequence. The early Muslims of Spain continued the practices of the Umayyads of Damascus. As a result, Muslim Spain did not have the preoccupation of formulating a theology or of establishing a legal rite. Politico-religious movements such as the Shī'ah, the Khawārij, Murji'ah, Mu'tazilah, and their respective offshoots — all of which took inception in the East and were powerful forces to contend with — never attained a foothold in al-Andalus as organized and coherent entities.

A deeper appreciation of the posture of Muslim Spain with respect to the religious sciences and religious life can be gained by exploring the subject under four main categories, which conform to Ibn Ḥazm's divisions: Qur'ānic studies, Traditions, jurisprudence, and theology.

Qur'ānic Studies

From the inception of Islam in the seventh century up to the present, the Qur'ān has been considered the Book of God. Except for the Mu'tazilah, a theological school that appeared in the eighth century, it has been conceived as uncreated or co-eternal with God Himself. As such, it has been the supreme and most revered document in the Arabic language and has permeated Muslim thinking throughout the ages.[4] It has been regarded as the pillar of the language as well as the fountainhead of law and all sciences. It is no wonder then that Qur'ānic studies occupied a prominent place in Muslim culture.

The Qur'ān has been the core of the spiritual and temporal life of Muslims wherever they may be. In it, God speaks in the first person plural. It consists of 114 chapters (*sūras*), each consisting of verses (*āyah*, pl. *āyāt*). Except for the opening chapter (*fātiḥah*), it is arranged according to the length of the chapters, the longest at the beginning and the shortest at the end. It is written in a rhymed prose (*saj'*).

The chapters are divided into Meccan and Medinese, according to whether they were revealed in Mecca or Medina. This division is important since it reflects the mental and religious orientation of the Prophet Muḥammad. The 90 Meccan *sūras* are short, full of religious inspiration, and deal for the most part with God: His Oneness, His Attributes, and constant exhortations to believe in Him. On the other hand, the 24 Medinese *sūras* are lengthy and deal for the most part with social and political matters, and with ordinances concerning marriage, divorce, inheritance, treatment of slaves, orphans, the oppressed, and other legislative matters. They also concern themselves with dogmas related to prayer, fasting, pilgrimage, almsgiving, and other duties incumbent upon a Muslim.[5]

It is significant to note that the Qur'ān is filled with Judeo-Christian traditions. The great prophets of the Bible are not only recognized as recipients of a divine revelation, but they are also revered because they constitute an unbroken chain of prophecy ending with Muḥammad himself.[6]

When Muḥammad died on June 8, 632, the Qur'ān was not yet committed to writing. A group of people called *ḥuffāẓ* specialized in committing it to memory. Shortly afterward, the memorizers were at variance among themselves concerning the faithful reproduction of certain passages, and the need for preserving the true Word of God became increasingly urgent. The first caliph is reported to have attempted to collect the Qur'ān in book form, but the collection lent itself to various readings, and it was for the third caliph 'Uthmān in 651 to make the necessary revision. However, owing to the nature of Arabic script, some variant readings remained, and a final fixation of the text was not made until the tenth century by two viziers, Ibn Muqlah and Ibn ʿĪsā.[7]

Along with the codification of the Qur'ān in book form in the seventh century, there arose the pressing need for explaining and expounding the Revealed Book in all its detail — its origin, its vocabulary, its correct reading, its intended meaning, and the like — so as not to allow any room for ambiguity or ambivalence. This was done with devotion, zeal, and meticulous care. It suffices here to mention some of the leading authorities in the two major fields of Qur'ānic exegesis, and Qur'ānic reading.

Qur'ānic Exegesis. The first exegesis appears to have been made by 'Abdallah b. 'Abbās, a cousin of the Prophet, and one of the most respected religious authorities in Islamic traditions. Although his writings and those of his immediate followers did not come down to us, many oral traditions attributed to them were disseminated and committed to writing. The major commentary (*tafsīr*)[8] was that of the prominent historian al-Ṭabarī (d. 922), who in his monumental thirty-volume work gives the gist of an enormous body of traditions. Al-Ṭabarī's work came to exert much influence, and was closely followed for a long time by succeeding commentators in the East and West. Among the outstanding Eastern commentators are al-Zamakhsharī[9] (d. 1144), al-Bayḍāwī[10] (d. 1286), and al-Suyūṭi[11] (d. 1505).

Andalusians shared the Eastern perspective on Qur'ānic explanation. The early Andalusian commentators had sought their education in the East and when they returned to al-Andalus they remained faithful to the orthodox way of thinking. The early and most influential representative was al-Bāqi b. Makhlad (d. 886), a man of integrity and independent judgment. This posture made him unpopular among his colleagues, who tried to accuse him of certain tendencies to heresy. Notwithstanding, his commentary (*tafsīr*)[12] was highly esteemed, even more than that of al-Ṭabarī. It fell upon the Granadine Muḥammad b. 'Aṭiyyah (d. 1152), a judge of Almería y Granada, to abridge existing commentaries and select the likely interpretations in his *tafsīr* that became renowned.[13] He was followed and emulated by the Cordovan Muḥammad b. Aḥmad b. Faraḥ al-Qurṭubī (d. 1273) and others.

Qur'ānic Readers. The Qur'ān was not an ordinary book and, therefore, should be read and recited in a manner befitting its supreme quality. This realization led to an early development of a specialized reading of the Holy Book. Special care was taken in pronunciation, enunciation, intonation, and other aspects. These were standardized to such an extent that they required training from professional readers (*Qurrā'*). These readers at first transmitted their teaching orally, but they soon codified the general rules governing the proper reading. There emerged seven readings that received the sanction of Muslim scholars.[14]

The Qur'ānic readers were those who could repeat the Qur'ān by heart according to certain fixed norms. Because of the great demand for their services as reciters and teachers, they were respected and influential in the religious community. Some of the readers became well known in that they succeeded in explaining the seven accepted readings in book form, thereby perpetuating an almost unbroken tradition of reading that was handed over from generation to generation and from place to place throughout the Muslim world.

Al-Andalus had from the outset inherited those readings which were disseminated by the conquering army. The neophites adhered to them faithfully up to the very end. They kept up to date in this respect by going to the East for training or through books and imported teachers. Thus, reading the Qur'ān according to norms established in the East was considered a worthy undertaking. Some of the many readers became famous. Al-Mujāhid (d. 1044), who became the ruler of Denia, earned great fame as an authority in Qur'ānic reading rather than as a statesman. His compatriot Abū 'Amr al-Dānī (d. 1053) achieved, in the words of Ibn Khaldūn, "the greatest perfection in the reading of the Qur'ān"[15] and came to exert a considerable influence through his various works on the subject. Notable among his works is *Kitāb al-taysīr*, a manual dealing with the seven readings that came to supersede all the existing texts.[16] He was followed in popularity by Abū al-Qāsim b. Firrūḥ of Játiva (d. 1194), who abridged the work of Abū 'Amr and undertook the task of putting the material in a poem that became famous.[17]

Prophetic Traditions (*Ḥadīth*)

At the death of Muḥammad in 632, many an issue needing solution arose because no single man could substitute for the Prophet, nor could anyone give answers either to daily pressing problems or to the complicated questions of dogma and rituals. The Qur'ān itself contained precepts, but the details for a workable solution had to be supplied if the Islamic community was to continue as an organized body. Thus arose the *ḥadīth* and the *sunnah*, of which the former implied hearing the Prophet say something and the latter indicated seeing him do something.[18] As a rule, the *ḥadīth* (Tradition) was traced to the source, the Prophet, or to his companions, and/or his immediate successors. By and large, the *ḥadīth* came to supplement the Qur'ān and had to be learned like the Holy Book. Originally, a huge body of traditions was transmitted orally, and much of it was contradictory or even irreconcilable. This was due mainly to forgeries or fabrications on the part of the emerging politico-religious parties, who produced their own *ḥadīth* to meet vested interests. As a result, the need for verifying and ascertaining the truth of a tradition arose and led to a study with rigorous methods. First, in order to be true or sound, a *ḥadīth* must have an unbroken chain of authorities (*isnād*) and a text (*matn*). The authorities must be fully identified as to the dates of birth and death, their travels, relationships with one another, and most important, their probity.

By the ninth century and even before, the number of traditions became overwhelming. They were in need of codification and careful screening to distinguish between the true and reliable and the false and spurious. The task of the codifiers was, indeed, an enormous one. Men like al-Bukhārī (d. 870) and Muslim (d. 875) attempted with some measure of success to sift from thousands of traditions what they believed to be valid or nearly valid traditions. Their work bore the suggestive title of *ṣaḥīḥ* (sound). Their findings were accepted by orthodoxy and became an integral part of the religious life of the Islamic community. Less ambitious collections were made by Abū Dāwūd in his *Sunan*, by al-Tirmidhī (d. 892) in his *Jāmi'*, and by Ibn Māja and al-Nisā'ī (d. 915) in their books, both entitled *Sunan*. All these collections constitute the Six Canonical Books (*al-kutub al-sittah*).[19]

The Prophetic Traditions comprise a variety of subjects — all that pertains to the faith and the duties of a Muslim toward his Creator and his fellow men: faith, God and the Holy Qur'ān, purification, prayer, funeral, almsgiving, fasting, pilgrimage, business transaction, marriage, emancipation of slaves, retaliation, punishments, the office of the qāḍī (judge), Holy War (*Jihād*), games, foods, clothing, medicine and spells, visions, general behavior, words which soften the heart, and life after death.[20]

By virtue of its great significance, the *ḥadīth* was widely pursued and venerated. *Ḥadīth* scholars approached their task with meticulous care, and played an important role in Islamic society. The Six Canonical Books were objects of careful study and constituted the framework for future compilations and abridgements. Early Andalusian scholars trained by the masters of the

East became, in turn, teachers and compilers in their native land. Their large number is amply attested by the numerous biographies of *ḥadīth* scholars. Only some of the most prominent can be mentioned here: Muḥammad b. Waḍḍāḥ (d. 900), Qāsim b. Aṣbagh, Ibn al-Futays (d. 1011), Abū 'Abdallah al-Jawlanī (d. 1075), Ibn 'Abd al-Barr, the Qāḍī 'Iyāḍ (d. 1149), among others.[21] For one, the works of Ibn 'Abd al-Barr on Tradition and Law according to the Mālikite rite are unequalled according to the dictum of Ibn Ḥazm.[22]

Jurisprudence (*Fiqh*)

No less important was the study of jurisprudence[23] in Islamic society for the obvious reason that it had immediate bearing on practically all aspects of daily life. As such, its practice opened an immense opportunity for lucrative posts and influence. The Arabic term *Fiqh* has the connotation of knowledge, theology, and law, and jurisprudence is intimately based on the Qur'ān, the Prophetic Traditions, the consensus of the Islamic community (*ijmā'*), and in some instances, on personal opinion (*ra'y*) and analogy (*qiyās*). This, however, did not exclude the incorporation of a great variety of customary laws which may go back to the ancient Middle East and to Roman law.

In the course of the eighth and ninth centuries there developed four legal schools that have exerted an immense influence on the life of Muslims up to the present time. The first, the Ḥanīfite school, was founded by Abū Ḥanīfah (d. 767), a moderate man of great virtue, who flourished in Kūfah and Baghdād. He reasoned that if the Qur'ān and Traditions did not give a clear answer, then the principle of *qiyās* (analogy) or *istiḥsān* (preference) should be the guiding criteria. His system was adopted in Turkey, India, and Central Asia. The second, the Mālikite school, was established by Mālik b. Anas (d. 795) of Medina, whose *al-Muwaṭṭa'* is the earliest great Muslim legal corpus that survives. Mālik's system advocated a strict adherence to the Qur'ān and Traditions, and also recognized the decision of *ijmā'* as valid and binding. It became the only recognized system in al-Andalus and in Northwest Africa. The third, the Shāfi'ite school, was founded by al-Shāfi'ī (d. 820) of Baghdād. He elaborated the principle of *ijmā'*, and gave validity to personal opinion (*ra'y*). His system was adopted in Egypt and East Africa. The fourth, the Ḥanbalite school, was established by Aḥmad b. Ḥanbal (d. 855) who, in reaction to the rationalism of his days, displayed a great conservatism in his system by his strong advocacy of Qur'ānic interpretation by letter rather than reason. He was the pupil of al-Shāfi'ī, and seceded from his school on this account. His system, as perpetuated by Ibn Taymiyyah (d. 1326) and Muḥammad b. ʻAbd al-Wahhāb, is still the law of Saudi Arabia.

Although these four schools have been recognized by orthodoxy throughout the Muslim world, only that of Mālik Ibn Anas received official recognition in al-Andalus to a point that the other schools were banished as though they sanctioned heresy. The exact date of the introduction of Mālikism into Spain is uncertain, but it was probably at the turn of the eighth century during the reign of Hishām I. Mālikism rapidly replaced the juridic school of al-Awzāʻī (d. 774), a Syrian Imām and follower of Abū Ḥanīfah. The doctrine of al-Awzāʻī persisted for a while through the efforts of the staunch disciple, Ṣaʻṣaʻ b. Sallām al-Shāmī (d. ca. 800), who discharged the functions of Muftī and leader of prayer in Cordova.[24]

Al-Awzāʻī was highly esteemed in Syria, but with the fall of the Umayyad dynasty of Damascus in 750, his influence declined and he settled in Beirut, where he continued his teaching. In the meantime, Andalusians flocked to Medina and studied under Mālik Ibn Anas, who opposed the tyrannical policy of the ʻAbbāsid ruler al-Manṣūr. Mālik is said to have expressed the hope that the Umayyad rulers of al-Andalus would eventually "adorn our sanctuary,"[25] and upon learning this, the Andalusians began to follow the Mālikite rite and to make legal decisions (*fatwā*) according to the opinion of Mālik as early as the reign of Hishām I.[26]

The introduction of Mālikism into Spain and its ultimate success were undoubtedly due to the rather cautious and unsophisticated perspectives of the early settlers, who were not given to philosophic and theological speculation. Moreover, the importance given to Mālikism owed much to the zeal of Andalusian students, who increasingly fell under the influence of Mālik b. Anas and his followers. Among those students who gave currency and vigor to Mālikism in al-Andalus were ʻĪsā Ibn Dīnār (d. 827), Yaḥyā Ibn Yaḥyā (d. 847), Ibn Ḥabīb, and Muḥammad Ibn Aḥmad al-ʻUtbī (d. 868).

ʻĪsā Ibn Dīnār, known as the "jurist of al-Andalus,"[27] introduced into al-Andalus several works on Mālikism and wrote a twelve-volume work entitled *al-Hidāyah* (*The Right Course*). The work deals with the school of Mālik, and was highly regarded by his contemporaries and Ibn Ḥazm.[28] Perhaps the most influential proponent of Mālikism was Yaḥyā Ibn Yaḥyā al-Laythī,[29] a Berber who came to exert powerful influence at the court of the Umayyad emirs, especially under the reigns of al-Ḥakam I and ʻAbd al-Raḥmān II. Although he was slighted under their reigns first during the

Suburb Revolt and second by the preferential treatment of the musician Ziryāb by 'Abd al-Raḥmān II, he remained all powerful, influencing state policy and the general conduct of the people within and without the court. Yaḥyā was initiated into Mālikism at home, and completed his education in that school under Mālik himself in Medina. During his travels in the East, he also came into contact with leading Mālikites. He returned to al-Andalus with great enthusiasm for the school of his master, becoming its leading advocate. In addition, he asserted himself as traditionist, jurist, and reciter (*rāwī*) of the *Muwaṭṭa'* of Mālik. His students were numerous and disseminated Mālikism throughout al-Andalus.

Ibn Ḥabīb,[30] known as the "scholar of al-Andalus," is credited with hundreds of works. Important among them is the *Wāḍiḥah*, which expounded on Mālik's rite. He travelled to the East, where he may have met the aging Mālik or some of his prominent followers. Ibn Ḥabīb had a worthy follower in al-'Utbī, who became renowned for his work the *'Utbiyyah*, which came to supersede the *Wāḍiḥah* as the major textbook on Mālikism.

These men strongly influenced religious life in al-Andalus throughout Umayyad rule. Their influence began to dwindle at the beginning of the eleventh century when the religious scholars (*'ulamā'*) and jurists (*fuqahā'*) could no longer control the rulers in the midst of revolts and political disintegration. However, Mālikism continued as the universal doctrine of the land. Many scholars were responsible for perpetuating Mālikism through their teaching and writings. Only a handful can be mentioned here: Ibn 'Afīf (d. 1029), author of a biographical dictionary of judges and jurists of Cordova; Abū al-Walīd al-Bāqī (d. 1081), author of various works on religious subjects, including a study of *al-Muwaṭṭa'*; Abū al-Walīd Muḥammad Ibn Rushd (d. 1126), the grandfather of the philosopher and prominent jurist Averroës.

Although Mālikism was recognized as the only official doctrine in al-Andalus, nonetheless the other legal schools — Ḥanifite, Shāfi'ite, and Ḥanbalite — were certainly known to the Andalusians and attracted followers. Andalusians who went to the East for their education must have acquired familiarity with the other legal schools and must have made them known to their students in al-Andalus. Moreover, the influx of books into al-Andalus was never hampered. Under the circumstances, it is known that a number of scholars displayed strong inclinations for schools other than Mālikism. There was Bāqī Ibn Makhlad, a great commentator of the Qur'ān, who was accused of Shāfi'ism. Both Mundhir Ibn Sa'īd al-Balluṭī (d. 966)[31] and the leading theologian of Muslim Spain, Ibn Ḥazm, became followers of the Ẓāhirite school, which advocated strict adherence to the textual explanation of the Qur'ān and Traditions in conformity with their literal (*ẓāhir*) meaning. Ibn Ḥazm wrote four long juridical works. In his eleven-volume *al-Muḥallā* Ibn Ḥazm expounds his juridical system including all aspects and practice of law: its origin, beliefs, almsgiving, rituals, family affairs, marriage and divorce, wills, food, drink, clothes, and other items. He discusses 2,308 problems and introduces each one by giving his opinion on the basis of the Qur'ān, Prophetic Traditions, and *ijmā'*. He also refers to the views of other legal schools and refutes them whenever they are not in conformity with his Ẓāhirite system. Ibn Ḥazm had a number of followers among his pupils. Among these were Ṣā'id of Toledo, the author of the *Categories of Nations*, the jurist and traditionist Abū 'Umar Ibn 'Abd al-Barr (d. 1071), and Abū 'Abdallah al-Ḥumaydī (d. 1095) of Majorca, author and renowned jurist.[32]

Theology (*kalām*)

Owing to its complete reliance on the East in matters of dogma, ritual, and law, al-Andalus may be said to have contributed very little to the formulation of a theology or to dogmatic speculation. In other words, al-Andalus acquiesced to its position of recipient and follower rather than that of contributor and innovator. This is generally admitted by the Andalusians themselves. In his treatise praising the great talents of al-Andalus, Ibn Ḥazm, who may justifiably be called the country's greatest theologian, stated that the study of theology did not flourish in al-Andalus for the simple reason that religious conflicts were lacking there. However, that the country was not indifferent to theology is attested by a number of individuals, including Ibn Ḥazm, who had different leanings (*i'tizāl*), pondered on its origins (*uṣūl*), and composed works dealing with it.[33]

The development of an orthodox Islamic theology was accomplished in the East after almost four centuries. During this long period, the East was torn by hair-splitting dissensions concerning God, His nature and attributes, reward and punishment, the question of sin, duties of the worshipper, good and abominable deeds, the question of authority, succession to rule, and others. Agreement on these and other issues was achieved to some degree by al-Ash'arī (d. 935) and consummated by the great theologian al-Ghazālī

(d. 1111), who compressed in his monumental work *The Revivification of the Religious Sciences*[34] all important theories and issues affecting the worshipper in this world and in the Hereafter.

Theological speculation began soon after Muḥammad's death. Certain political events, such as the assassination of ʻUthmān in 656, followed by the battles of the Camel and of Ṣiffīn in 659, led to the formation of politico-religious movements, each of which came to be identified with a political stand or religious view. Those events had grave repercussions in both the political and theological spheres. Thereafter, a number of sects arose holding conflicting views; the resulting strife was serious enough to shatter the very foundations of the nascent Islamic community. The first sect in Islam was the Shīʻah,[35] meaning "party," which advocated the exclusive right of ʻAlī, a cousin and son-in-law of Muḥammad to the rulership succession. The partisans of ʻAlī were uncompromising in this respect. When ʻAlī compromised his stand at the battle of Ṣiffīn by agreeing to arbitration with Muʻāwiyah, a mere governor of Syria, some of ʻAlī's partisans became indignant and seceded from his ranks, charging him with betraying the cause and God, the arbiter of all decisions. These were the Khawārij,[36] against whom ʻAlī had to fight. This faction rebelled repeatedly against the Establishment for a long period of time, alleged that they and they alone were the true Muslims, and charged anyone who was not from among them with being a sinner deserving death and the Hell fire in the Hereafter. In the course of time, they split into several groups, some of which continued to adhere to extremist views while others tended to moderation. However, they all held staunchly to the concept of community as the core of their doctrine. As for the Shīʻah, it also split in the course of time into some twelve sects, each of which had a great attachment to a charismatic leader (usually called *Mahdī* or *Imām*) who is endowed by God with divine attributes and who would appear some day to fill the earth with justice and righteousness. In sum, the Shīʻites turned to the charismatic leader for the fulfillment of their objectives, while the Khawārij turned to the charismatic community.[37]

Of different inclination from the Shīʻah and the Khawārij were the Murji'ah and the Muʻtazilah.[38] Both were known by their moderation and neutrality on the burning political questions facing early Islam. They developed their theology in the calm and urbane setting of Baṣrah, the home of early Islamic theology. The Murji'ah, whose name literally means "suspension," was a group that objected to the extremism of the Khawārij concerning the question of sin, and advocated a suspended judgment on the subject in the belief that God alone is the Ultimate Judge who determines whether or not a sinner would cease to be a Muslim and whether he would deserve the punishment of Hell or the reward of Paradise. This type of thinking could be seen in the views of Ḥasan al-Baṣrī, a pious and ascetic man, who held that the believer had sole responsibility for his acts and that a sinner was not an outcast but a misguided Muslim. These views seem also to constitute the foundation of Mu'tazilism,[39] which came to advocate free will, the absolute oneness of God, and denial of God's attributes and the createdness of the Qur'ān.

Each one of the aforementioned sects — Shi'ah, Khawārij, Murji'ah, and Mu'tazilah — were at variance among themselves with respect to important questions that led to the establishment of numerous schools (*madhhab*). These schools were known under the names of their founders, who often took uncompromising stands not only toward the other major sects but also toward the sect from which they split. Conflicts ranging from heated controversies and polemics to persecution and wars characterized their relationships. At the same time, an "orthodox" theology was developing in the midst of intense speculation and acrimonious debate. This theology, in its ritualistic and dogmatic aspects, embodied the whole of religion: beliefs and observances, the nature of God, salvation and damnation, and so forth. The Qur'ān, the Traditions as provided in the Six Canonical Books, and the law as formulated by Abū Ḥanīfah, Mālik, al-Shāfi'ī, and Ibn Ḥanbal became the pillars of orthodox theology. Even with the establishment of these codices, orthodox theology remained cloudy until it was finally rescued by two great theologians: al-Ash'arī and al-Ghazālī. They upheld the uncreatedness of the Qur'ān, the divine attributes, and the necessity for the Islamic community's having at all times a spiritual and temporal leader in an *imām* or a caliph. However, they left the question of free will vacillating between divine will and individual action and human volition.

Al-Ash'arī[40] was born at Baṣrah in 873 and became a staunch Mu'tazilite. Late in life, about 915, he changed position and attempted to reconcile Mu'tazilism with orthodox dogmatism. He defended the superiority of revelation against philosophical theology and devoted himself to the study of Traditions and the Qur'ān. Concerning the question of free will, al-Ash'arī formulated the doctrine of *iktisāb*, which held that God creates the acts of a man and that a man "acquires" them. Al-Ash'arī had many followers and was succeeded by a number of theologians. Important among them were al-Bāqillānī (d. 1013), who emphasized the miraculous nature (*i'jāz*) of the

Qur'ān; al-Baghdādī (d. 1037), who refuted the various schools in his valuable book on sects; and al-Juwaynī (d. 1085), the teacher of al-Ghazālī, perhaps the greatest theologian of Islam.

Abū Ḥāmid al-Ghazālī[41] was born in 1058 at Ṭūs in northeastern Iran, where he received his early education. In 1091, he became professor at the Niẓāmiyyah College in Baghdād, which was founded by the Saljūq vizier Niẓām al-Mulk, a staunch supporter of orthodoxy. After four years of teaching, writing, and studying philosophy on his own, al-Ghazālī left his post and joined the Ṣūfī movement through which he hoped to satisfy his ardent desire for answering the great religious questions of his day. When he did not find the answers in philosophy, he wrote an acid criticism of the philosophers in *Tahāfut al-falāsifah* (*The Incoherence of the Philosophers*). He found in Ṣūfism solace and peace, and he remained an avowed Ṣūfi for the remainder of his life. He attempted to reconcile Ṣūfi practices and observances with those of orthodoxy. The attempt at producing a pious life is embodied in his *Revivification of the Religious Sciences*, a stout work in four volumes which consists of some forty books dealing with all aspects of an upright and religious life. In some respects it is the epitome of theological formulations and religious duties, the faithful adherence to which would secure a blissful life in this world and in the Hereafter.

Islamic theology for nearly four centuries was marked by vicissitudes and tribulations. The Andalusians were all aware of this situation but never allowed themselves to succumb to it. They held staunchly to Mālikism and followed the content of the recognized corpus of Tradition, Qur'ānic commentaries, and Qur'ānic readings.

However, in their capacity as students, the Andalusians who sought their education in the East or received it at the feet of Eastern scholars on their own soil could not possibly avoid Eastern influences even in theological matters. Ibn Masarrah (d. 931),[42] the first philosopher of Muslim Spain, had been imbued with Mu'tazilite thinking in the East. Upon his return to Cordova, his views proved unpopular and he was pressured to seek refuge in the mountains around Cordova, where in seclusion he developed mystical tendencies. He was an example of many scholars who were attracted by schools other than that of Mālik Ibn Anas. No doubt the best representative of this tendency was Ibn Ḥazm, the greatest theologian of Muslim Spain. He received the traditional education in the Qur'ān, Traditions, grammar and lexicography, and other disciplines. Ibn Ḥazm covers the gamut of the religious sciences. In addition to his *Fiṣal*, a voluminous work on sects and denominations, Ibn Ḥazm wrote a number of works having theological interest: one dealing with the refutation of heretics "who are inspired by the devil and infidels,"[43] a second demonstrating that the Qur'ān is beyond human eloquence,[44] a third dealing with the Jews' and Christians' interpolations in the Old and New Testaments, and a fourth consisting of counsels against the abominable errors of the major Muslim sects.

In his youth, he showed a great interest in a political career, but after a series of disheartening experiences, he turned to religious studies at the age of twenty-four. It was then that he devoted himself wholly to the study of jurisprudence and theology. He began with *al-Muwaṭṭa'* of Mālik, but after some four years his inquisitive mind became disenchanted with Mālikism. He turned to Shāfi'ism, which he soon abandoned for Ẓāhirism,[45] and he became its staunch exponent for the rest of his life. The Ẓāhirī school was founded in the East by Dāwūd Ibn Khalaf (d. 883) and advocated the principle that the texts of the Qur'ān and Traditions should be viewed in their literal or external sense (*ẓāhir*) as opposed to either their hidden, internal meaning (*bāṭin*) or the principle of analogy. This Ẓāhirī literalism would seem to restrict reasoning, which Ibn Ḥazm strongly advocates. But Ibn Ḥazm argues that the individual is able by virtue of reason to arrive at the conclusion that the world exists and that it must have a creator. Beyond this, reason is unable to grasp the finality of divine will or God's essence by means of analogy, personal opinion, preference, or any other means. The Qur'ān and the authentic traditions are the only sources of revelation and must be adhered to and understood on the basis of the strict rules of grammar, syntax, and stylistic forms of the Arabic language. Care must be taken to follow the chronological order of the texts within a particular or general context. In the event that the literal meaning of a given text contradicts human reason, it should be rejected.[46] In the process, personal endeavor (*ijtihād*) for seeking the truth is required. This interpretation offered great latitude for individual Muslims to study the texts and arrive at conclusions on the basis of reasoning. This fitted very well with the restless temperament of Ibn Ḥazm, who objected to the blind adherence to established authority by the *'ulamā'* of his day. The reaction of the *'ulamā'* was such that Ibn Ḥazm was ostracized, but he continued relentlessly to defend his position with all the vigor and eloquence of his tongue. Although this principle was applied to legal questions, Ibn Ḥazm expanded on it and applied it to theological matters as well.

Ibn Ḥazm adhered to the precept that the Qur'ān and Traditions are the sole basis of law and that the individual should interpret them on the basis of lexical and grammatical structure alone. Consequently, other criteria used by the other legal schools such as personal opinion (*ra'y*), analogy (*qiyās*), preference (*istiḥsān*), and submission to authority (*taqlīd*) do not find room in his system,[47] since they are an affront to Divine Wisdom. This uncompromising attitude was reflected in a number of his writings. The theology of Ibn Ḥazm is essentially an extension of his Ẓāhirī views. It is best illustrated in his valuable work *Sects and Denominations*, in which Ibn Ḥazm not only shows the superiority of Islam over all other religions, mainly Judaism and Christianity, but of his own brand of orthodoxy over all other Muslim denominations and schools.

To Ibn Ḥazm the untutored mind needs faith alone to grasp the truth of Islam.[48] This faith inspired by Divine grace is so strong that it does not need reinforcement, even with the study of logic. This helps the individual only to reject false conceptions; he criticizes those who devote themselves to the natural sciences, pretending that they know it all and neglect the religious disciplines.[49] In the same manner he criticizes those who concentrate upon the religious sciences without paying due attention to the secular sciences. To him, the religious and secular sciences are complementary and thus enable the individual to forge an alliance between faith and reason.

Ibn Ḥazm perceives God as all perfect, eternal, self-sufficing, and Creator of all things; revelation is not only possible but necessary and conforms to the dictate of reason, and so is the existence of prophets who received revelation from God in the same manner that the sciences and crafts are acquired through teaching. He accepts the miracles of the prophets and the divine nature of the Qur'ān. Of course a better idea can be gained through a careful reading of the *Fiṣal*, of which only a brief analysis can be given here. The work is not, as Asín Palacios maintains,[50] the first of its kind in Islam. Several heresiographies were written in the East before the time of Ibn Ḥazm. But by sheer volume, it is perhaps the largest work on heresiography having a distinct plan to refute doctrinal adversaries whether they were Muslims or non-Muslims, polytheists or agnostics such as the Sophists; the atheism of the philosophers, and deism of others for not admitting that God is the Creator of all existing things; the dualism of the Zoroastrians and Manichaeans; the polytheism of the Trinitarian Christians; the Brahmans who deny the concept of prophetic revelation; the Jews who recognize only some prophets and deny others.[51] To all these he adds acid refutation of the various Muslim denominations such as the Mu'tazilah, Murji'ah, Shī'ah,

Khawārij, and the fanatical attitude of those who express orthodoxy with a narrow mind and blind imitation. His treatment of the Islamic sects is similar to his discussion of other religions; he first expounds the essential aspects of a religion or a sect as understood by the followers and then proceeds to refute its tenets, point by point. He objects to the allegorical interpretation of the Qur'ān as applied by some sects, and adheres to his literal and outward (*ẓāhir*) explanation. He takes up the following principal questions: God, His nature and attributes; free will and predestination, faith; life after death, the *Imamate*,[52] and other theological issues.

At the time of Ibn Ḥazm's death in 1064, the influence of the religious scholars on the life of the Andalusians had diminished considerably. However, a spirit of intolerance remained much alive and resulted in the burning of Ibn Ḥazm's books. This was followed by the burning of the *Revivification of the Religious Sciences* of al-Ghazālī, which comprised the Summa Theologica of orthodox Islam. Under the circumstances, a quest for a new theology was in the air, and manifested itself in the revival of philosophy on Andalusian soil at a time when this discipline had been discredited in the East as harmful to religion. Already al-Ghazālī had sounded his objections to philosophy in *Tahāfut al-falāsifah*, which was bitterly attacked by the Andalusian philosopher Averroës (Ibn Rushd).

It was the search for a new theology, perhaps, that led to the upsurge of philosophy under the Almohad dynasty (1130–1269), which rose on a religious platform. Ibn Tūmart (c. 1080–1130), the founder of the dynasty was a theologian himself who had objected to the religious practices of his day and had gone to the East, where he became imbued with the theological views of the various schools, mainly those of al-Ash'arī and al-Ghazālī. He proclaimed himself Mahdī, and conceived himself as an infallible *imām* (*al-imām al-ma'ṣūm*). He emphasized the unity of God (*tawḥīd*), from which the word *Muwaḥḥid* is derived and under which his followers were known. More important, he revoked the ban which had been imposed on the books of al-Ghazālī, and some of his writings show his theological inclination.[53] One of his successors, Abū Yūsuf Ya'qūb (1184–1199) had at his court the two great philosophers of al-Andalus: Ibn Ṭufayl and Averroës, who came to the defense of reason as a sure means of perceiving the truth.[54]

In conclusion, al-Andalus adopted orthodoxy from an early stage. It remained thereafter not only staunchly conservative, but highly intolerant of any form of heresy or sectarianism. For this reason, it remained practically free from the internecine religious wars which occurred in the East. Spain's wars, and there were many, were politico-ethnic wars: squabbles among the Arabs themselves, Arabs against Berbers and vice versa, and Muslims against the independent or semi-independent Christians. Thus, early Islamic religio-political movements such as Shi'ism, Khārijism, Murji'ism, Mu'tazilism, and their offshoots never attained a foothold in Spain as organized and coherent entities. Each of these developed its own outlook, theology, and philosophy of life which often conflicted with the established order and led to long and bloody wars in the East. The role of these movements in Spain was insignificant, simply because Spain was insulated from them from the beginning. If and when heresy appeared, it was crushed immediately. In consequence, many individuals suffered ostracism and persecution. On the whole, orthodoxy as interpreted and understood by Mālikism reigned supreme on Spanish soil in a manner not unlike Catholicism today. Moreover, Mālikism, like the Catholic Church, exerted an enormous influence in state affairs. The Spanish scholar Asín Palacios summarized the situation of the time as follows:

> One can actually say that during its long history, Muslim Spain was the most conservative region of the Muslim world in spite of the fact that it was the most distant from the center of the faith. Although its literature and theology were a replica of the East, the innumerable heresies of the East could not find there more than an insignificant echo. The Orthodox-Mālikite clergy understood instinctively, perhaps, that the political life of Spanish Islam rested on its dogmatic unity — or inspired by preserving it safe and sound through a traditionist and anti-philosophical attitude, succeeded in repressing all sorts of innovations with the most violent intolerance. Especially at the beginning, the state supported with its moral authority and repressive measures this policy of the Orthodox clergy.[55]

The alert vigilance of church and state against religious nonconformists may have secured a religious unity in Muslim Spain, and may also have avoided compounding an already tense and complicated sociopolitical structure. However, it may have played havoc in the process of intellectual freedom. Under the circumstances, suspicion prevailed in many a mind that was fertile and capable of producing the highest form of thought. Ibn Masarrah, like many of his compatriots, was exposed at an early age to Eastern thought. He could not give bent to his intellectual pursuits and chose to live a secluded life in a mountain not far from Cordova. His books remained clandestine, and eventually disappeared, leaving us with excerpts attributed to him but often prejudicial to his actual thinking. He appears to have been a philosopher-theologian of great talent and of great intellectual persuasion, but unfortunately little has survived concerning his system that would place him in a position of greatness.

Many an outstanding individual may be added to the list. Bāqī b. Makhlad, a respectable jurist and traditionist, was persecuted principally for having introduced the books of the Jurisconsult al-Shāfiʿī, himself staunchly orthodox and recognized by orthodoxy[56] in a large sector of the Muslim world.

Even during the period of great splendor in Muslim Spain, those who did not wholly conform were victims of persecution and ostracism. The towering figure of Ibn Ḥazm may be added to the list of those who had endured some form or another of persecution. For all intents and purposes, Ibn Ḥazm was orthodox in the fullest sense of the word. Yet, some of his views earned him the place of persona non grata among his colleagues, the *fuqahā*ʾ (jurists). The great Averroës, philosopher, physician, and statesman did not escape the milieu inhospitable to free thought. In spite of the fact that much of Christian Scholasticism was indebted to him, he was the object of attack from both Muslim scholars and Christian clerics. The same may be said of the equally talented Ibn Maymūn (Maimonides), a Jew by religion and an Arab by culture. Maimonides was not fully appreciated by either his coreligionists or the Muslims of his time. To escape the intolerance of his Spanish homeland, he had to go to Cairo, where his talents were fully appreciated at a Muslim court. On the whole, Andalusian contributions to the religious sciences may be said to be nil and for very obvious reasons. On the other hand, the religious scholars remained faithful to the traditions embodied in the works of the great masters of the East. Moreover, inasmuch as a considerable number had travelled to the East for religious training, they tried to reproduce as faithfully as possible the thoughts of their early teachers as embodied in books they had brought back. By and large, the line was distinctly drawn for the would-be religious scholar. If he went to the East for training, he specifically sought the teacher that he knew would introduce him to the ideas that would most fit the needs of his country. Thus, he would avoid entanglements with "heretics" or those inclined to heresy. However, he was not completely unaware of the various religious shades prevalent in the East, or of the often bloody consequences engendered by them.

In consequence, the Andalusian religious scholar was a mere reproducer of Eastern dogmatism. Furthermore, he went one step further by limiting himself to a single school instead of drawing from the various schools in the East. He chose Mālikism and adhered to it to the very end. The legal schools of al-Shāfi'ī, Abū Ḥanīfah, and Aḥmad Ibn Ḥanbal — although recognized by orthodoxy on par with the school of Mālik b. Anas — were in al-Andalus almost as far removed from him as the schools of recognized heresies.

Moreover, the Andalusian religious scholar could not add anything to what had been agreed on in the East. Because he was far removed from the source, he — as a traditionist for instance — could not produce a Tradition based on what he heard from so-and-so on authority of so-and-so who heard it from a companion of the Prophet who heard it from the Prophet himself. This would have been untenable. Instead, he took the *Muwaṭṭa'* of Mālik as his single guide, and supplemented it with the corpus of Traditions as codified by al-Bukhārī, Muslim, Abū Dāwūd, and others.

The Andalusians had a deep commitment to Islamic orthodoxy and viewed any deviation from it as tantamount to heresy. As a result, there was no room for sectarianism from within or without al-Andalus. Eastern heresies received outright condemnation, so did other religions. Ibn Ḥazm represents the general attitude of the Andalusian. In fact, he offers in his *Fiṣal* acid refutations of Islamic heresies as well as other world religions known to him: Zoroastrianism, Hinduism, Judaism, Christianity, and other non-Islamic sects. The *Fiṣal* is a significant study by a man with an unswerving faith in Islam.

Ibn Ḥazm starts with the premise that Islam is the true faith and has superseded the two revealed religions: Judaism and Christianity. He argues that Islam came to complement and abrogate Christianity in the same manner that the latter appeared to supplement and replace Judaism. To prove his point, Ibn Ḥazm bases his criticism on passages drawn from the Old and New Testaments and other Jewish and Christian writings. He also bases his arguments on polemics he had had with Jews and Christians. Ibn Ḥazm argues that both Judaism and Christianity degenerated into various sects and came to possess falsified scriptures full of contradictions, inaccuracies, and insults. He says that the Jews lived in ghettoes, took a free hand with the Divine Scripture to a point that it is next to impossible to determine its authenticity. Likewise, Christian scriptures were corrupted owing to the vicissitude of early Christianity.

In the process, both Jews and Christians allowed interpolations into the scriptures, thereby altering the original texts and permitting false attributions to God, angels, and prophets. In essence, the Old and New Testaments are apocryphal following traditional fanaticism. Most of the Old Testament was forged by liars, malicious and treacherous people who indulged in inaccuracies and contradictions.[57] They had the audacity of attributing doubt to Sara and Abraham when God promised them a child in their old age![58] Worse still, they made Lot have intercourse with his two daughters to perpetuate the race. As for the Christians, they followed the errors of the Jews and added to them unspeakable errors of their own. In their division, they make of Christ all things,[59] human, incarnation of the deity, both human and divine; father, son, and spirit in one, or the son of God at times, the son of Joseph at others, and what have you.[60] To demonstrate his allegations, he takes up seventy passages of the four Gospels and shows the great discrepancy found in them. He considers the Gospels less authentic than the Old Testament; they contain many abominable things attributed to God and His Prophets. For instance, the genealogy of Jesus in St. Matthew has a serious gap and is in contradiction to the Jewish writings.[61] The version in St. Luke does not conform with it at all, and he concludes that one or all of the authors of the Gospels are liars. Moreover, both Matthew and Luke have Jesus being manipulated by the devil,[62] to which Ibn Ḥazm says how could this be possible if they regard Him God or how can it be possible that such idiots could conceive or have the audacity to suggest that the devil would propose that God worship him. More abominable is the fact that the Gospels admit that Jesus had a father, mother, brothers, and sisters and yet they called him God; to which Ibn Ḥazm exclaims saying thank God for having brought forth Islam, the pure, true, and splendid religion without blemish or error.[63]

17

Philosophy and Mysticism

THIS and the following chapter deal for the most part with what are commonly known among Muslim scholars as the "foreign sciences" — that is, those disciplines which were transmitted into Arabic from Greek and, to some extent, Sanskrit.[1] These include such subjects as philosophy, metaphysics, logic, medicine, mathematics, astronomy, and music. These sciences, too, as they appeared in al-Andalus were, like the traditional or "Arabic" sciences, dependent on Eastern models.

In pre-Islamic times, the Arabs of the Arabian Peninsula did not possess "sciences" in the Greek or modern conception of the term *science.* Whatever conceptions they may have had concerning the universe and the world and institutions around them, these were not coordinated into a system, nor were they well articulated into a system of thought. The Arabs of the desert were practical men who had little predilection for abstractions and theorizing. They had some notions about the stars and diseases, but these hardly constituted sciences. They worshipped numerous idols which personified forces of nature or heavenly bodies, and they had hazy notions about the soul and its fate after death. Predestination permeated their lives. By the time of Muḥammad, they had been exposed to the external influences of Judaism, Christianity, and Zoroastrianism — all of which brought them closer to the outside world and its multifarious ideas.

It was only after the expansion of Islam in the seventh and eighth centuries in a wide area of the Near East, North Africa, and al-Andalus that the sciences began to be cultivated in earnest, reaching full development in the ninth and tenth centuries. This intellectual efflorescence owed its impetus to the conquered populations who pursued intellectual activities under enlightened Muslim leadership. The process was facilitated by a great reservoir of human talent which came into a vast and fecund legacy. Hellenism, the amalgamation of Greek and Near Eastern thought, spread widely in the area from the time of Alexander the Great. Moreover, at the coming of Islam Hellenistic culture was much alive, with its major centers in Alexandria, Edessa, Antioch, Jundīshāpūr, and Ḥarrān (Mesopotamia). The influence of these centers on the development of Hellenistic culture can hardly be underestimated; it began long before the process of translating foreign works into Arabic. The Syriac-speaking people of the Near East were imbued with the Greek sciences and knew Greek well. They served as intermediaries between Hellenism and the nascent Arab culture.[2]

This transmission was accomplished through the medium of translation, which started in the eighth century and continued unabated through the tenth. Greek manuscripts were sought even in Byzantine territory and were committed into Arabic. We are told that the 'Abbāsid caliph al-Manṣūr (754–775) encouraged those activities, which culminated under al-Ma'mūn (813–833). Al-Ma'mūn displayed a great interest in philosophy, particularly the works of Aristotle, whom he saw in a dream. One can only make passing reference to some of the prominent translators. Yaḥyā Ibn Baṭrīq (d. 800) is said to have translated for al-Manṣūr the works of Galen, Hippocrates, Ptolemy, and Euclid. Early translations were faulty and cumbersome, but they improved enormously with Ḥunayn Ibn Isḥāq (d. 873), Thābit Ibn Qurrah (ca. 836–901), and their descendants. Ḥunayn was the dean of translators. He not only translated numerous works, but he also took charge of training new translators who, under his supervision, began translating new Greek works into Arabic and improving upon earlier translations. Similar functions were discharged by Thābit, who continued making known to the Arabs the works of the Greek sages, who were held in high esteem. Aristotle was regarded as the first teacher (*al-mu'allim al-awwal*), having prepared a valid way to attain the truth.

The Arabic term *al-falsafah* (philosophy)[3] is from the Greek *philosophia*, meaning "love of knowledge." This connotation was familiar to the Arabs. What such knowledge comprises has never been clearly specified. Greek philosophy in a Muslim context comprised both the speculative and the natural sciences. In its new setting, philosophy at first was ancillary to religion. Thus, it is often difficult to distinguish between theology and philosophy, except that the philosophers sought to rationalize or give proofs of religious questions in conformity with, or independent of, revelation. Thus, it would seem that the goal of both was one and the same, although the procedures were different.

No doubt the interests of early Muslim scholars in philosophy arose from their desire to forge a coherent religious system or theology satisfying the heart and mind, faith and reason. Many questions preoccupied them: God, His nature, and attributes; the world — whether it was created or not; man, free will, and human actions; the soul and its faculty, vision, prophecy, and intellect; virtue, perfection, happiness, and so on. Some of the theological sects, such as Mu'tazilah, Khawārij, Murji'ah, and Shi'ah, have been alluded to.[4] It suffices here to single out some of the views of leading Eastern philosophers who exerted an enormous influence on, and molded the course of, Andalusian philosophy.

Al-Kindī (ca. 800–865),[5] known as "the philosopher of the Arabs," was born in Baṣrah, where he received his early training. He moved to Baghdād, where he served the court of the 'Abbāsid caliphs as tutor of princes. He was a Mu'tazilite when Mu'tazilism was the state doctrine, and he was ostracized and physically punished by al-Mutawakkil in 856 when the caliph had a change of heart and outlawed Mu'tazilism in favor of an ill-defined orthodoxy. However, al-Kindī's fame rests on the fact that he was the earliest outstanding Muslim philosopher. He is credited with some two hundred seventy works and treatises on a wide range of subjects: philosophy, logic, psychology, astronomy, astrology, mathematics, atmospheric phenomena, geography, music, politics, preparation of perfume, cooking, and horse breeding.[6] This broad perspective was reflected in his pupils, the most outstanding of whom was al-Sarakhsī,[7] who followed in his master's footsteps and wrote profusely about most of the same subjects.

To al-Kindī, philosophy is the most sublime, noblest human art and "is defined as the knowledge of things in their realities to the limit of human power. The purpose of the philosopher in his knowledge is to arrive at the truth and in his action to act in accordance with the truth."[8] In another context, al-Kindī gives other definitions[9] of philosophy, one of which says: "Philosophy is the science of sciences and the wisdom of wisdoms." Sooner or later this exalted position of philosophy was apt to collide with the pre-eminent position of the revealed religion. The conflict was already apparent during the time of al-Kindī, who was quite aware of it and of its grave implications. As a result, he attempted to dress philosophy in an Islamic garb and to show the harmony between philosophy and revelation, or between faith and reason. In this connection, he was the precursor of later Muslim philosophers in both East and West. He attempted with some measure of success to explain in scientific or philosophical terms God, man, and the universe — but in a manner conforming, as humanly as possible, to the revealed religion. That the attempts of the philosophers were often sincere, leading some of them to extremes suggestive of heresy and even cynicism, can easily be seen in their systems.

To al-Kindī, God is one, eternal, omnipresent, wise. He is the first cause (*'illah ūlā*) of the world, motion and law, hence, creator and ruler (*mudabbir*) of all things — all of which had been created in time and will have an end. The soul (*nafs*) is eternal and knowing in its pure state, incorporeal and descendant from the world of intelligence. It has the faculties of anger, appetite, and reason, and it is able through the senses, images, and reason to attain comprehension. Virtue is the avoidance of extremes; it consists of abstinence, avoidance of appetite, and pursuit of wisdom and justice. Philosophy and religion aim at the same thing, the former seeking the truth through investigation and the latter through divine light. That is, both aim at knowledge of God and pursuit of virtue. In fact, al-Kindī includes theology as part of philosophy.[10] All in all, he places philosophy on a par with religion, although in a second thought, perhaps, he considers prophecy a surer way for attaining the truth than philosophy.

Al-Kindī's philosophical stand is quite conciliatory with religion on the question of the creation of the world and divine attributes. However, this harmonization had its vicissitudes in the course of more than two centuries, when al-Fārābī, Ibn Sīnā, and the Andalusian philosophers outwardly put revelation and philosophy on the same plane but often covertly gave precedence to reason over faith.

The philosophical system of al-Kindī received wide attention. Although al-Rāzī (865–925) was considered a physician more than a philosopher, he wrote some two hundred works which dealt with philosophy, astronomy, alchemy, medicine, and other disciplines. He emphasized the pre-eminent place of reason for knowing God and for distinguishing between good and evil. It appears that he relegated religion to a secondary place. This tendency was followed by al-Fārābī (870–950), who was born in Transoxania, educated in Baghdād, and served the Shi'ite Ḥamdānid of Aleppo. Like al-Kindī and al-Rāzī, he was conversant with all the known branches of the sciences, which he classified.[11] He attempted to reconcile Aristotelianism and Platonism. His philosophical system became so popular that he was considered second to Aristotle and, as such, was known as the second teacher (*al-mu'allim al-thānī*). His influence was so great that he was referred to by his surname Abū Naṣr as far as al-Andalus.[12]

Al-Fārābī wrote a number of philosophical works, the most important of which are the *Ideal City* (*al-Madīnah al-fāḍilah*)[13] and *City Government* (*al-Siyāsah al-madaniyyah*),[14] both of which betray strong neo-Platonic influence. In these, as in other works, al-Fārābī was mainly concerned with an ideal government and the manner of attaining it. To him, this is possible when the soul achieves such a perfection that it no longer needs matter for its subsistence. It then attains ultimate virtue and happiness, which are the aim of an ideal city. Within this conception, al-Fārābī views the state as resting on the strict cooperation of its members, all of whom have defined roles and functions not unlike those characterizing the organs of the human body. For its ruler the state requires a leader (*ra'īs*) whose role is like the heart in the body; to this ruler the rest of society looks for inspiration and guidance. Such a man must be divinely inspired, wise, virtuous, courageous, healthy, and fearless. It is only under the leadership of a philosopher-king that ultimate perfection and happiness can be reached. Here intellect and wisdom play the decisive role. Al-Fārābī chose not to mention whether a prophet would qualify to discharge the function of the *ra'īs*. Moreover, he explains God as the first existing-being (*al-mawjūd al-awwal*), who is one, self-existing, self-knowing, eternal, wise, and powerful. All existing things (*mawjūdāt*) are derived from Him in ten stages, decreasing in perfection from the second to the tenth stage. This doctrine of emanation (*fayḍ*) precludes the religious conception of creation through time by divine volition.

Al-Fārābī did not neglect the question of matter and its relation to form, nor did he overlook the subject of the soul and its various faculties (*quwwah*) of nutrition, sensation, imagination, and reasoning. These subjects were also pursued by later philosophers, most outstanding of whom was Ibn Sīnā (980–1037), known in the West as Avicenna. Ibn Sīnā became renowned as both philosopher and physician. As a philosopher, he was able to codify most of the philosophical system of the Greeks and to express it with smooth, intelligible language in his *al-Shifā'*[15] and in an abridgment of the same under the title *al-Najāt*.[16] Both works exerted an enormous influence on Muslim philosophy in both East and West.[17] Introduced to logic at the tender age of fourteen, Avicenna pursued other philosophical branches with such devotion that by the age of eighteen he had acquired a great facility. To Avicenna, God is one, all-powerful, and the source from which all things emanate. The soul has three faculties: vegetative, animal, and rational. The vegetative faculty is common to plant, animal, and man; it has the function of nutrition, growth, and procreation. The animal faculty comprises movement, emotion, sense, imagination, and memory. Only the rational faculty has the power of reasoning — that is, of distinguishing between right and wrong. More importantly, the rational faculty has as its goal the search for the truth.

To conclude this general background for Andalusian philosophy, mention should be made of the Brethren of Purity (*Ikhwān al-Ṣafā'*), a secret group of intellectuals which flourished in Baṣrah during a time of political turmoil and moral decadence, from 946 to 1055. The Brethren endeavored to harmonize authority with reason and to devise a universal system of religious philosophy. This system, which was introduced to al-Andalus about the beginning of the eleventh century, was preserved in fifty treatises (*rasā'il*)[18] of multiple but unknown authorship. The *Rasā'il* include most of the natural and speculative sciences. They indicate that the Brethren were eclectic, attempting to combine religious morality with philosophical speculation in order to please God and thereby attain perfection.

Their philosophy may be summed as follows: God is existing and the creator of the world, all-powerful and free to do as He chooses; the active intellect emerges from Him. From the Universal Soul (*nafs kulliyah*) emerges the first matter in a spheric form, which is the highest form, and with a circular movement, which is the most perfect — thereby constituting the heavenly bodies. These were followed by less perfect forms of animals, plants, and minerals. Man has free will and cognitive faculties in the senses, imagination, reflection, memory, and reason. He is a small part of a large universe. His morality depends on climate, the stars, religion, and education. He will attain the desired perfection when he fully realizes that God is one, the Universal Soul is one, the world is one, humanity is one, religion is one, truth is one, and philosophy is one.

The works and philosophical systems of these philosophers were widely known in al-Andalus. However, there are ample indications that the study and pursuit of philosophy was discouraged and even forbidden. Philosophy was not part of the curriculum. Moreover, there is no evidence that the Andalusians took any initiative in translating available foreign works, mainly from Greek and Latin, into Arabic. Neither did they attempt to improve on Eastern translations, relying instead upon works brought to al-Andalus from the East. Such works were studied, but their readers, fearing ostracism by the staunchly conservative religious authorities, offered no public commentary. If an individual were suspected of philosophical pursuits, he was declared heretic and persecuted, and his books were burned. There are many instances of this antagonism to philosophy. Ibn Masarrah, the first philosopher of al-Andalus, was ostracized and his books were prevented from circulating. To placate the feelings of the religious scholars, Ibn Abī 'Āmir (d. 1002), the powerful *ḥājib* and actual ruler of al-Andalus, ordered that the famous library of the scholar-king al-Ḥakam II be purged of books on ancient sciences, including those on logic and astrology.[19] Ibn Ḥazm of Cordova, a man of independent judgment and great learning, was ostracized and his books set on fire. The books of al-Ghazālī and of Averroës were also burned.

It is no wonder that Andalusian philosophers, perhaps as a reaction to these restrictions, became staunch defenders of philosophy and its preeminent role in ascertaining the truth. In this connection, they explicitly placed it equal to revelation and implicitly gave it supremacy over religion. Even logic had its staunch defenders in Ibn Ḥazm and Ibn Ṭumlus, both of whom give a clear insight into the general apathy and opposition to philosophy in general and logic in particular. Ibn Ḥazm's *al-Taqrīb li-ḥadd al-manṭiq wa-l-madkhal ilayh* (*Simplification of Logic*)[20] is a treatise based on Aristotle's eight books[21] of logic but with juridical and linguistic examples for elucidation.[22] In this work he shows his concern for the wanton negligence of philosophy and logic among his contemporaries and their opposition to them. He does not see any conflict between philosophy and revelation;[23] he considers logic a sound tool for determining whether an opinion is true or false. In fact, he urges the student to pursue logic[24] to arrive at the proofs of any given situation. He reiterates this recommendation in his *Marātib al-'ulūm* (*Categories of the Sciences*).[25] It appears that Ibn Ḥazm had the student in mind when he wrote *al-Taqrīb*. He says that those who befriend knowledge and know its merit should make it as palatable as humanly possible to others.[26] He vehemently objects to those who maintain, without any knowledge, that the books of the ancients contain only unbelief (*kufr*) and lead to heresy (*ilḥād*).[27] On the contrary, he says: "We have found these books [on logic] as a strong medicine. If it were taken by anyone who has a strong health, sound nature, firm composition, good mixture, it would profit him, purify the form of his body, chase away his mixture (*ikhlāṭ*), strengthen his senses, and make him more wholesome. However, if it were taken by a sick man whose mixture is disturbed, whose composition is weak, it would do him harm; his misfortune will increase; and perhaps it may lead to his ruin and death."[28] No doubt Ibn Ḥazm implies, as his successors explicitly pointed out, that philosophy is not a subject that could be undertaken by anyone, mainly, by those who do not have sufficient preparation and knowledge.[29]

In sum, Ibn Ḥazm says: "Let it be known that he who reads this book of ours will find that the usefulness of this kind of work is not limited to one single discipline but includes the Qur'ān, Traditions, and legal decisions concerning what is permissible and what is not, and what is obligatory and what is lawful."[30]

Ibn Ṭumlus (d. 1225), who lived more than a century after Ibn Ḥazm's death, argues that the negligence of logic by the scholars of his time too was appalling. Born in the principality of Valencia, he received his education in the traditional sciences. He emigrated to the south of al-Andalus and must have studied under the great philosopher Averroës. In his *Kitāb al-madkhal li-ṣinā'at al-manṭiq* (*Introduction to the Art of Logic*),[31] he provides a long introduction concerning the state of the subject in al-Andalus, its importance, and how he had to learn logic without help or guidance from his colleagues, who were not only oblivious to the subject, but highly prejudiced against it. He says that the religious sciences, grammar, lexicography, rhetoric, prosody — and to some degree medicine, physics, geometry, mathematics, astronomy, and music — had received such great scholarly attention that these subjects were overworked. He argues that writing on them would only mean repeating what others have said.

There remain two crucial subjects, metaphysics and logic. Although metaphysics did receive some attention because of its relation to theology, logic remained wholly neglected. Ibn Ṭumlus complains that this negligence arises from the fact that people considered it useless[32] and feared being accused of unbelief and heresy. He expresses his amazement at the ignorance of logic by scholars who learned things by heart, and who were passionate followers of the Mālikite rite. Under the circumstances, he had been informed that logic was an illicit subject, which prompted him all the more to acquaint himself with it, yet he could find no writing on it except the works of al-Ghazālī,[33] which he studied avidly and complemented with the work of al-Fārābī. He discovered that logic was not only harmless to religious belief but also highly useful. Moreover, he did not find that logic contradicted revelation, and this prompted him to compose an introduction on the subject in order to make it available to his brethren.[34]

Ibn Ṭumlus defines logic as the art which gives the rules that straighten the intellect and lead to ascertaining the truth in all situations where mistakes are apt to take place.[35] Those rules are similar to those used for grammar, prosody, and drawing.[36] It alerts the individual against untruth,[37] and prevents him from suspecting those who utter the truth or from following blindly those who are in the wrong. Those who allege that mathematics and geometry are a good substitute for logic in determining the truth or falsity of a thesis resemble those who maintain that mere exercises and memorization are just as good for that purpose; and those who maintain that its study is a waste of time are like those who consider the study of grammar superfluous.[38] All in all, logic supplies the rule for the right use of expressing ideas in the same manner that grammar supplies rules for the right use of expressions. But while the rules of grammar change from language to language, the rules of logic are universal.

It is significant that Ibn Ṭumlus does not refer to the numerous works on philosophy and logic by his near contemporary Averroës, or other Andalusian works on logic. Could it be possible that the works of Averroës were removed from circulation, as had occurred before, or did Ibn Ṭumlus choose to ignore his master and arrogate to himself the sole credit for reviving such a useful and neglected subject? It is plausible that Averroës was still discredited after his disgrace under the Almohad ruler Abū Yūsuf and that Ibn Ṭumlus used discretion to avoid grave repercussions. The dangers of undertaking the study of philosophy can be illustrated by the career of Averroës himself.[39]

Of course, opposition to philosophy was rampant elsewhere in the Muslim world and was not peculiar to al-Andalus, notwithstanding the extreme religious intolerance there. The statement of Ibn Khaldūn is illuminating in this respect: "The early Muslims and early speculative theologians greatly disapproved of the study of this discipline [logic]. They vehemently attacked it and warned against it. They forbade the study and teaching of it."[40] The attitude that logic was harmful to religion was applicable to philosophy as a whole.[41]

Philosophy in al-Andalus had its golden age despite the heavy restrictions imposed on it. Comparing its size with the rest of the Muslim world, al-Andalus fared very well in the cultivation of a nearly forbidden science.

Ibn Masarrah, Ibn Ḥazm, Ibn Bājjah, Ibn Ṭufayl, Averroës, and the two Jews Ibn Gabirol and Ibn Maymūn (Maimonides) constitute no small list of outstanding philosophers.

To be sure, the Andalusians were fully aware of the different schools of thought which flourished in the East. Although they were often inhibited from openly airing their views, they were nonetheless highly knowledgeable in the speculative sciences. In the tenth century, Muḥammad Ibn Ismā'īl (d. 331/943), known as the *ḥakīm* (wiseman, or philosopher), was conversant in mathematics and logic.[42] But the philosopher of the century was Ibn Masarrah.[43] He travelled to the East, where he was influenced by Mu'tazilism, mainly with regard to the createdness of the Qur'ān and the question of free will. He returned to al-Andalus full of enthusiasm and attempted to disseminate his unorthodox views. He soon found himself in trouble with the religious scholars, who accused him of heresy. Ibn Masarrah fled to the mountains near Cordova, where he led an ascetic life surrounded by devoted pupils and developed pantheistic ideas foreshadowing Hispano-Arabic mysticism. He is credited with two works which were suppressed during his lifetime and for a period after his death.

In spite of the chaotic conditions in the eleventh century, a number of outstanding talents made their appearance in completely intellectual pursuits. Sa'īd Ibn Fattūḥ (d. 1029) of Saragossa, known as "the donkey," wrote a number of philosophical treatises under the enlightened reigns of 'Abd al-Raḥmān III and al-Ḥakam II. One of his treatises, *Shajarat al-ḥikmah* (*The Tree of Knowledge*), was an introduction to philosophy. However, he was jailed by Ibn Abī 'Āmir, and after his release he left al-Andalus for Sicily.[44]

Two contemporaries of Ibn Fattūḥ had similar interests in philosophy. 'Abd al-Raḥmān Ibn Ismā'īl Ibn Zayd, "the Euclid," emigrated to the East, where he died. He was an outstanding mathematician who also displayed a keen interest in logic. His work on logic was well known.[45] Ibn al-Kattānī wrote a number of treatises on philosophy which, according to his pupil Ibn Ḥazm, were well known, of high quality, and very useful.[46]

But the most outstanding man of the eleventh century was Ibn Ḥazm, some of whose four hundred works dealt with philosophy. Nowhere did Ibn Ḥazm show himself averse to philosophy; he considered it a tool to be used in harmony with revelation. In spite of his great attachment to Islam, which he considered superior to all religions, Ibn Ḥazm displayed always such a methodical and lucid mind that one can hardly fail to admire him.

It is for these and other reasons that Ibn Ḥazm's position as a philosopher should not be overlooked — in fact, further study will no doubt place him among the giants in the intellectual history of Islam. His works cover the religious sciences with all the hair-splitting polemics and speculation, but also many aspects of philosophy and the remaining sciences. His *Categories of the Sciences* and *Simplification of Logic* have been alluded to above. His *Fiṣal* (Ch. 16) gives a great insight into Ibn Ḥazm's approach to philosophic and theological questions pertaining to God and His attributes. It attacks all sorts of religious denominations within and outside Islam. Important here are his views concerning the harmony between faith and reason.[47] His *Book of Conduct* (*Kitāb al-akhlāq*)[48] is an ethical treatise prescribing norms of behavior for righteous living. It also contains a mine of information concerning its writer and his thinking. In addition, he criticizes the work on metaphysics[49] by the great Eastern philosopher al-Rāzī. Ibn Ḥazm refutes al-Rāzī's dualism as influenced by Zoroastrianism.

A contemporary of Ibn Ḥazm was Ibn Gabirol of Málaga, who espoused a neo-Platonic philosophy as evidenced in his work *Yambū' al-ḥayāt* (*The Fountain of Life*),[50] which was translated by Gundisalvus into Latin in 1150. In it Ibn Gabirol maintains that spiritual beings, including angels, are composed of matter and form. Like Ibn Ḥazm, he holds that philosophy is capable of grasping the truth and that the principle behind all phenomena requires a knowledge which is hidden from the ignorant but revealed to the philosopher. This doctrine of knowledge as a differentiating factor among philosophers, theologians, and the masses became more pronounced in the systems of Ibn Bājjah, Ibn Ṭufayl, Averroës, and Maimonides.

The twelfth century marks the flowering and golden age of philosophy in al-Andalus. Ibn Bājjah, known in the West as Avempace, attempted to separate traditional theology from philosophy as such. His near contemporary and follower Ibn Ṭufayl said of Ibn Bājjah that he was more perceptive and closer to the truth than the three intellectual giants of Islam: al-Fārābī, Ibn Sīnā, and al-Ghazālī; Ibn Khaldūn[51] concurs with him and places Ibn Bājjah among the great philosophers of Islam (al-Fārābī, Ibn Sīnā, and Averroës). Ibn Bājjah was born in Saragossa at the end of the eleventh century. He discharged the office of vizier, but he was forced to flee when the city fell to Alfonso I of Aragón. He went to Valencia, Seville, Granada, and finally to Fez in northwest Africa, where he was fatally poisoned, either by a jealous enemy or because of his heretical views. He had a broad education and wrote on a number of subjects: medicine, music, mathematics, astronomy, and philosophy; he also composed fine *muwashshaḥ* poetry.

However, Ibn Bājjah's fame rests on his philosophy and the probable influence it exerted on such contemporaries and successors as Ibn Ṭufayl, Averroës, and Maimonides. He is credited with numerous treatises on logic, metaphysics, and on the works of Aristotle. However, little remains of these works. His *Tadbīr al-mutawaḥḥid*[52] (*The Regime of the Solitary*) has been preserved, but it is not certain that the work is complete. This notwithstanding, the *Tadbīr* shows Ibn Bājjah's familiarity with the philosophical systems of his Greek and Muslim predecessors — Plato, Aristotle, Galen, al-Fārābī, Ibn Sīnā, and al-Ghazālī. Ibn Bājjah frequently refers the reader to these authors. Moreover, the *Tadbīr* reveals Ibn Bājjah's own philosophy, which considers man capable of reaching perfection and happiness if his life conforms to nature and is based on contemplation. This goal of perfection can be attained only when the individual reaches the pure intellect not through society, wealth, honors, or even virtues, but through austerity and renunciation of all worldly things. In this regard, he seems to differ with al-Fārābī and al-Ghazālī in major areas. Whereas al-Fārābī thought that ultimate perfection could be realized in a social group — that is, in the *Ideal City* — Ibn Bājjah aims at the government of the solitary man (*tadbīr al-insān al-mutawaḥḥid*) for the purpose of attaining the best of his existence (*afḍal wujūdātih*).[53] He criticizes the Ṣūfī path and al-Ghazālī by saying that the Ṣūfīs claim ultimate happiness not in learning the spiritual essence and grasping it but rather in a state of isolation and reverie (*tafarrugh*).[54]

Ibn Bājjah begins his work with the various connotations of the term *tadbīr*,[55] which may mean the ordering of various actions, but never one single action, toward an intended goal. It is for this reason that God is called *mudabbir* (ruler) of the universe. This implies the use of faculty and reflection, which is characteristic of man, though it may be particular (*khuṣūṣ*), having to do with the management of a particular trade or agency. Ibn Bājjah then turns to the political regime, on which he had already composed a treatise,[56] and refers to Plato's political ideas. He contrasts al-Fārābī's four defective cities, established by convention (*waḍ'*), with the virtuous city, founded in conformity with nature (*ṭab'*). Government based on nature is the most perfect, most noble of governments because it resembles God's government of the universe, whereas government based on convention resembles a disease.[57] The perfect city does not need a physician nor a judge; it is bound by love without strife, and its actions are always righteous.[58] Only in the defective cities do doctors and judges become rich while everyone else is poor;[59] the actions of their inhabitants are misguided and their opinions are false. When a person who possesses wisdom and truth emerges in a defective city, he is considered a ''weed'' and is opposed according to the intensity of the inhabitants' false opinions.[60] Such ''weeds'' do not spring up in the virtuous city for the obvious reason that all its inhabitants possess wisdom or perfection. In the four imperfect cities they lead a solitary life; they are often called strangers (*ghurabā'*) by the Ṣūfīs, having attained certain stations (*marātib*) that remove them from the rest of the people. It is with this ''weed,'' or solitary individual, that Ibn Bājjah is concerned. Such a person should govern himself in order to reach his most perfect existence and happiness.

This intended objective leads Ibn Bājjah to a detailed discussion of existing beings — inanimate things, animals, and human beings. He classifies them by similarities and differences. He contrasts necessary actions, common to man and beast, and strictly human actions, performed by volition (*ikhtiyār*) on the basis of reasoning, which is the distinctive quality of man. Moreover, actions performed by volition must have a purpose. For example, a person may break a stone accidently because it scratches him, and this is an animal action; if he breaks the stone because it may scratch someone else, then this is a human action.[61] Most actions in the imperfect cities are categorized as being both animal and human actions. Actions of a perfect man are performed only through reasoning, without regard for the animal soul responsible for animal actions.[62]

Existing things are either corporeal or incorporeal. Corporeal beings are those having length, width, and depth, which the incorporeal lack. The incorporeal include such things as nobility, knowledge, and all those concepts that are perceived by reason. This is followed by a discussion of spiritual forms. Ibn Bājjah considers that matter cannot exist without form, yet form does exist independently of matter. Forms have a hierarchy from low to high — that is, from material forms to the universal spiritual or intellectual form (*ṣūrah 'aqliyyah*), which man should strive to perceive. The soul has six faculties (*quwat al-nafs*): rational, spiritual, sensory, generative, nutritive, and rudimentary. In the first four faculties there is room for reason and volition.[63] But the highest faculty of man is the intellect (*'aql*), by means of which true knowledge and happiness can be attained in a gradation from the sensory world to imagination to intellectual contemplation and ultimate happiness. This is achieved when the human intellect (*al-'aql al-insānī*) links itself with the higher active intellect (*al-'aql al-fa' 'āl*) and eventually with the universal intellect (*al-'aql al-kullī*), which is God. It is through this knowledge and identity with the Supreme Being that man attains ultimate happiness. Only the solitary "weed" is able to reach this coveted goal.

This conception of the solitary man was elaborated with consummate detail by Ibn Ṭufayl in his charming *Ḥayy Ibn Yaqẓān* (*Alive, Son of the Awake*).[64] Ibn Ṭufayl was born at Guadix in 1106 and lived for a time in Granada. Although we know little about his early life and education, he apparently was widely versed in astronomy, mathematics, poetry, philosophy, and the religious disciplines. Whether or not he studied under Ibn Bājjah is not clear, but it is certain that he was acquainted with him and certainly with his works. Ibn Ṭufayl's adult life coincided with the Almohad arrival in al-Andalus. The early Almohad rulers showed great proclivity to philosophico-theological speculations, and it was the fortune of Ibn Ṭufayl to serve Abū Ya'qūb Yūsuf (1163–1184) as court physician and vizier. The enlightened Abū Ya'qūb allowed Ibn Ṭufayl to form an intellectual court circle which attracted the best talents of the day, including Averroës,[65] whom Ibn Ṭufayl commissioned to write a commentary on the works of Aristotle.

Unlike Ibn Bājjah and other scholars of his time, Ibn Ṭufayl does not seem to have written a large number of works, although many poems are attributed to him. His fame rests on *Ḥayy Ibn Yaqẓān*, which has become a classic. In it, Ibn Ṭufayl narrates the evolution of man from birth to infancy, adolescence, and adulthood. He characterizes the processes and human experiences which correspond to each major stage of man's development. The work is divided into three parts:

Part 1, in four chapters, states the purpose of the work as uncovering the secrets from Wisdom, whose leaders he mentions: Ibn Bājjah, who was inclined to self-effacement (*fanā'*); al-Fārābī, who concerned himself with the soul; Ibn Sīnā, who stated the truth according to Aristotle; and al-Ghazālī, who devoted himself to Ṣūfism and reproached the philosophers.[66]

Part 2, in six chapters, deals with Ḥayy on a deserted Indian island, presumably Ceylon;[67] Ibn Ṭufayl gives the various opinions concerning spontaneous generation (*al-tawallud al-dhātī*), or birth without mother or father, and considers Ḥayy as having had a natural birth (*wilādah ṭabi'iyyah*),[68] without parents. An alternative account for the incredulous is given and makes the child the offspring of a lovely princess and Yaqẓān, whom she had married secretly. Because of the secrecy, the princess placed Ḥayy on a little ark and set him afloat. When the ark reaches the island, the cries of the infant attract a doe which supplies him the necessary nourishment. Ḥayy grows to be a strong boy, but when the doe dies, he is saddened and must take care of himself. By the time he is seven years old, he acquires his first knowledge on the basis of senses and personal experience. His life continues to be enriched. He becomes aware of some of the soul's faculties, such as memory and observation. He begins to know the parts of the body and the difference between the body and that which moves it. He discovers fire and learns how to control it for use; he inquires whether or not that which moves the body has the same nature as fire. He uses animal skins and tree leaves for clothes, and he domesticates birds and animals. By now he is twenty-one years old.

He passes from the knowledge acquired by the senses to that gained from experience. He differentiates between matter and form; sees that bodies may be light or heavy and have dimensions. He realizes the meaning of causation and concludes that there is a first cause to all causes. Ḥayy progresses from knowledge of worldly existence to the contemplation of the heavens and the universe. He arrives at mathematical calculation of the spheric bodies and then inquires whether the world is created (*ḥādith*) or primeval (*qadīm*). He then ponders the Creator of the world (*fā'il al-'ālam*) and deprives him of any attributes. Ḥayy is now thirty-five years old.

Through reasoning (*tafkīr*) and contemplation (*ta'ammul*)[69] he learns that he has a spiritual soul which is different from his body. It is this soul that attains the spiritual truth. He now yearns for a life of contemplation by which he will be able to comprehend existence, thereby achieving happiness and immortality. He becomes prone to asceticism and begins to believe that his self is part of the Supreme Truth. He has reached the mature age of forty-nine.

It is at this juncture, in Part 3, that Ibn Ṭufayl introduces two new characters, Salamān and Asāl, who had lived on an island inhabited by a religious community. Salamān is a worldly man who pursued the path of the common people; Asāl has a grasp of religious law, but continues to search for its esoteric meaning. Asāl comes to the island and finds that Ḥayy on his own had discovered truth by virtue of his rational faculty and knowledge of the first cause, the existence of the soul, immortality, happiness, and the inner meaning of the law (*bāṭin al-shar'*).[70] Ḥayy and Asāl find out that the way of philosophy as pursued by Ḥayy and the formal religion taught to Asāl are merely forms of the same eternal truth. Ḥayy and Asāl decide to go to the inhabited island to teach the religious community the way of truth and contemplation, but their attempts fail to persuade indisposed and ignorant people. The two become convinced of the weakness of men living in society, and decide to return to Ḥayy's uncorrupted isolation to spend the rest of their lives contemplating the Eternal Truth. The worldly Salamān remained in the inhabited island.

As a Muslim, Ibn Ṭufayl concedes that Islam as revealed by Muḥammad is a valid, sure path to the truth and that philosophy can achieve the same end. However, one wonders whether he actually gives primacy to philosophy since his story climaxes with the characters emerging triumphantly in contemplation rather than in formalistic religion. No doubt he brought to the fore the solitary "weed" of Ibn Bājjah. At any rate, Ibn Bājjah and Ibn Ṭufayl agree that knowledge, perfection, and happiness are attained through the intellect and in conformity with the nature of man. Of course, the theme of the story was borrowed from Eastern sources,[71] although turned to a different purpose.

It is very difficult to determine with any degree of accuracy the extent of the dissemination of *Ḥayy Ibn Yaqẓān*. However, considering its easy language and smooth style, it is likely that the story became a part of the folklore within and without al-Andalus among the people and the literati. The story is easy to follow, however great its philosophical implications. Moreover, its written form must have been known in the Maghrib and the East. In the thirteenth century, the brilliant Egyptian physician Ibn al-Nafīs (d. 1288) used the theme of *Ḥayy Ibn Yaqẓān* in *The Treatise Relating to Kāmil on the Life-History of the Prophet.*[72] There are many points of similarity between the two works: "several points of detail in the story of spontaneous generation; the description of the working of the sense organs; the idea of the helplessness of individual man as compared with the animals which are provided with natural covering and weapons; the hero's arriving at the knowledge of anatomy by dissecting the bodies of dead animals with primitive instruments; his proceeding from the observation of animals to that of plants, then that of the meteorological phenomena, then that of the celestial bodies; and finally, by the same reasoning in both books, to the knowledge of the Creator and His attributes; his feeling the obligation to conform to the commands of the Supreme Being. . . ."[73]

Another important question is the influence of *Ḥayy Ibn Yaqẓān* upon European literature and thought. The subject of harmony between reason and faith passed to the West through the works of Averroës, who, no doubt, was influenced by the ideas of Ibn Bājjah and Ibn Ṭufayl. Moreover, the story of Ḥayy must have been known to Westerners of the thirteenth century. This may explain the reappearance of the theme in seventeenth-century Spain and England. The *Criticón* of the Spaniard Baltasar Gracián (1601–1658) is a philosophical novel consisting of three stages of man's development: childhood, adolescence, and old age; each stage of knowledge and experience is a progression from rudimentary to highest form. The main characters of the novel are Critilo, a wiseman, who lands on an island and meets Andrenio, who had lived there in nature's surroundings. After Critilo teaches Andrenio language, they depart for Spain. In Madrid, Andrenio falls victim to a woman's deceit; this causes Critilo to reflect on the evils of women. In the second stage, they journey to France, where they discover the arts and sciences, find a true friend, visit various places including madhouse — all of which give them a glimpse of humanity at large. In the final stage, they travel to Rome, where they attend an academy located on a hill; from this hill they contemplate the wheel of time, the transitory existence of man, death, and other human foibles. They finally attain immortality and virtue.

Robinson Crusoe by Daniel Defoe (1660–1731) betrays a striking similarity to the theme developed by Ibn Ṭufayl. Defoe, who was educated for the Presbyterian ministry, published *Robinson Crusoe* in 1719, not long after the translation of *Ḥayy Ibn Yaqẓān* into English.[74] The basic idea of both works is that man is not only capable of overcoming his environment, but he also can attain material and spiritual sufficiency independent of society. However, the two works differ basically in that Ibn Ṭufayl advocates strict seclusion and reason while Defoe concludes with social experience and the search for God through biblical revelation as the ultimate goal of man — that is, Ibn Ṭufayl's characters attain their goal with the intellect, while Crusoe experiences fear and emotion.

Of greater impact on Western thought were the works of Ibn Rushd, known in Europe as Averroës.[75] Averroës (1126–1198) was born in Cordova to a distinguished family. His grandfather was a Mālikite judge of Cordova and his father also was a learned man. As was the custom of the day, the young Averroës received his education within the family, studying the religious sciences — Qur'ānic studies, Traditions, jurisprudence, and theology, in which he excelled. But his most outstanding accomplishments were in the area of medicine and philosophy. He composed a number of philosophical works, some of which became known in the West in Latin versions. In fact, he left a great legacy, known as Averroism in thirteenth-century Europe, which provoked heated debate in learned circles for centuries.[76] He is often known as "the commentator" (*shāriḥ*) by virtue of having abridged, explained, and commented on the works of Aristotle. Like his Muslim predecessors, Averroës greatly admired Aristotle and considered him a giant who had attained the truth. This enthusiasm contributed to keeping Aristotelianism alive at a juncture of history when Aristotle was being relegated to oblivion in the rest of the Muslim world.

The "revival" of philosophy in al-Andalus coincided with the appearance of enlightened Almohad rulers who displayed great interest in philosophy. However, scholars in al-Andalus were traditionally timid about discussing philosophy openly. Averroës himself displayed this inhibition when in 1169 he was introduced by his friend Ibn Ṭufayl to Abū Ya'qūb Yūsuf. This ruler was conversant in philosophy and was interested in adding Averroës to his learned entourage. The historian al-Marrākushī relates the tense moments at that meeting and Averroës's reactions as he recounted them to his friends:

When I entered into the presence of the Prince of the Believers, Abū Ya'qūb, I found him with Abū Bakr Ibn Ṭufayl alone. Abū Bakr began praising me, mentioning my family and ancestors and generously including in the recital things beyond my real merits. The first thing that the Prince of the Believers said to me, after asking me my name, my father's name and my genealogy was: 'What is their opinion about the heavens?' — referring to the philosophers — 'are they eternal or created?' Confusion and fear took hold of me, and I began making excuses and denying that I had ever concerned myself with philosophical learning; for I did not know what Ibn Ṭufayl had told him on the subject. But the Prince of the Believers understood my fear and confusion, and turning to Ibn Ṭufayl began talking about the question of which he had asked me, mentioning what Aristotle, Plato, and all the philosophers had said, and bringing in besides the objections of the Muslim thinkers against them; and I perceived in him such a copious memory as I did not think could be found [even] in any one of those who concerned themselves full time with this subject. Thus he continued to set me at ease until I spoke, and he learned what was my competence in that subject; and when I withdrew he ordered me a donation in money, a magnificent robe of honor, and a steed.[77]

This kind of encouragement inaugurated a brilliant career for Averroës in philosophy. Clearly, Averroës had sufficient training to understand philosophy, but it was the ruler's patronage which allowed his philosophical thinking to be publicized through thirty-eight philosophical works. Moreover,

Averroës enjoyed favors from Abū Ya'qūb; he became a judge in Seville in 1169, chief judge of Cordova in 1171, and court physician in 1182. After the death of Abū Ya'qūb, Averroës received patronage and enthusiastic support from his successor Abū Yūsuf (1184–1199) until 1195, when, under the pressure of the religious scholars within a rather precarious political context, Abū Yūsuf disavowed philosophy and philosophers, ordered Averroës's books burned, and accused Averroës of heresy. Averroës went into exile and spent the last three years of his life utterly disillusioned.

Averroës covered all aspects of philosophy and was indebted to his Muslim predecessors, though he often criticized them. To Averroës, the world has been moving from eternity and has an Eternal Mover (*muḥarrik*), which is God. Matter and form are inseparable except in the mind; there is a hierarchy of existing beings and forms. Matter is always in motion, whereas the intellect is motionless and perceives itself. The soul is one in all men, but it is maintained separately by bodies, and its relation to the body is like the relation between form and matter.[78] In these and other respects, he closely follows Aristotle, whose views he paraphrases as he understands them. However, his most important contribution to philosophy lies in its defense with unprecedented conviction and articulation. Philosophy had been defended before — by al-Kindī, al-Fārābī, and Ibn Sīnā in the East, and by Ibn Ḥazm, Ibn Bājjah, and Ibn Ṭufayl in al-Andalus — but never with the certainty or lucidity of Averroës. To him, "Philosophy is the friend and milk-sister[79] of religion. It does not contradict the *sharī'ah* (revelation) but confirms it. As such, philosophy is as valid for attaining the supreme truth as the *sharī'ah* itself." These views are crystalized in his *Faṣl al-maqāl*,[80] *Tahāfut al-tahāfut*,[81] and other treatises.[82] He says, "Now since this religion is true and summons to the study which leads to knowledge of the Truth, we the Muslim community know definitely that demonstrative study does not lead to [conclusions] conflicting with what Scripture has given us; for truth does not oppose truth but accords with it and bears witness to it."[83]

Faṣl al-maqāl begins with a confirmation that the *sharī'ah* requires the study of philosophy and that philosophy contains nothing opposed to the *sharī'ah*. However, he qualifies these assertions by stating that the *sharī'ah* is available to all people and is meant to teach them true science and right practice,[84] whereas philosophy is limited to the few — that is, to those individuals who have the capacity for demonstrative reasoning. For the ignorant majority religious belief can be sustained by faith alone. This leads

Averroës to discern three classes of people: the masses, who belong to the rhetorical class; the theologians, who are dialecticians, and the elite or philosophers, whose interpretations ought not to be expressed to the dialecticians-theologians and certainly not to the masses.[85] For them such discussion would only lead to division and confusion. He thus criticizes the Mu'tazilah, who, lacking the basic requirement of demonstration, introduced division and hatred in Islam through their false allegorical interpretations.

Those who allege that the study and use of philosophy is an innovation (*bid'ah*), because it was not current among the early believers, must admit that the use of analogy (*qiyās*) in jurisprudence is also an innovation, or heresy: "For just as the lawyer infers from Divine Command to him to acquire knowledge of the legal categories that he is under obligation to know the various kinds of legal syllogisms, and which are valid and which invalid, in the same way he who would know [God] ought to infer from the command to study beings that he is under obligation to acquire a knowledge of intellectual reasoning and its kind."[86]

Averroës had in mind the religious scholar and particularly al-Ghazālī, the greatest Islamic theologian, whose books were once banned in al-Andalus but were then reinstated by the Almohads. Almost a century earlier, al-Ghazālī wrote *Tahāfut al-falāsifah*[87] in which he attacked the pretensions of the philosophers to disciplines beyond their competence. He also criticized those who attributed things to religion which actually belonged to the speculative sciences, such as mathematics and logic. The work marked a milestone in the thinking of al-Ghazālī, from receptivity to philosophy at one stage of his career to rejection of it in preference for a mystic path. In spite of the esteem which al-Ghazālī enjoyed among the Almohads, Averroës, perhaps oblivious to the prevailing religious sensitivity, took issue with the venerable theologian in *Tahāfut al-tahāfut*, which consisted of systematic refutation of al-Ghazālī's *Tahāfut*. Whereas al-Ghazālī gave precedence to revelation over reason for attaining the truth, Averroës placed revelation and philosophy (or faith and reason) on an equal plane and insisted that philosophy, like the *sharī'ah*, is a sure means for grasping the truth of both physical and metaphysical worlds.

In this and other respects, Averroës's views endeared him neither to his fellow Muslims nor to thirteenth-century Christians, who often misunderstood him. To Christians, Averroism was thought to mean that philosophy was true and revealed religion was false. This notwithstanding, Averroës played a dominant role in the development of Christian Scholasticism through his commentaries on the work of Aristotle. These commentaries were translated into Hebrew and Latin by such men as Moses Ibn Tibbon (d. 1283), Michael Scot (d. 1232), Herman the German, Kalonymus ben Kalonymus (d. 1328), and others.[88] Averroës became the object of controversy among Christians, some supporting his views and others were staunchly opposed. His school remained much alive until the seventeenth century.

The influence of Averroës was also felt among the Jews, who were the great transmitters of Arabic writings into their own language as well as into Latin. One eminent Jewish theologian-philosopher was Mūsā Ibn Maymūn (1135–1204),[89] or Moses Maimonides, an Arab by culture and a Jew by religion, who tried to reconcile Greek philosophy with Judaism in the same manner as his Muslim predecessor tried to reconcile philosophy with Islam. Maimonides was born in Cordova, where he received his early education from his father in both Hebrew and Arabic and became acquainted with the various disciplines taught at that time to people aspiring to scholarly positions. He may have learned philosophy under Averroës, who was nine years his senior. At the age of twenty-three, he published a book on logic, a subject which he considered a prerequisite to scholarship. In 1160 Maimonides was forced under harsh Almohad policies to leave al-Andalus for more tolerant environment. He finally settled in Cairo, where he became the court physician of Ṣalāḥ al-Ḍīn (Saladin), who had wrested Jerusalem from the Crusaders.

Most of Maimonides's writings were in Arabic. His major work, *Guide to the Perplexed*,[90] was written in Arabic but with Hebrew characters. Its stated object is to explain certain terms occurring in the prophetic book and other obscure figures. An analysis of the *Guide* shows that Maimonides concerned himself with the same subjects which had preoccupied Muslims for centuries and which remained burning issues in his time. The *Guide* consists of three main parts: an exposition of the esoteric ideas in the Bible; a treatment of metaphysical problems; and an examination of Muslim theology (*kalām*), which he dismisses as illogical in the light of Aristotelian philosophy. He argues that the apparent conflict between science and religion arises from misinterpretation of the scriptural language with respect to questions of anthropomorphism, divine attributes, and other properties of God. To him, God is the primal cause, one, incorporeal, free from emotion and privation, and not comparable to any of His creatures. Anything contradicting this creed should not be applied to God. Following thus in the footsteps of the Mu'tazilah, he deprives God of other attributes because they would implicitly or explicitly limit His perfection. He asserts that the attribution of other physical and pictorial properties to God should be taken metaphorically. He rejects four classes of attributes: those which include a definition, a partial definition, a quality, or a relation. For instance, definition would include efficient cause, and since God is the primal cause, He cannot be defined or described by a partial definition. Some of the language of the Bible, Maimonides explains, is allegorical and cannot be taken literally. The "account of creation" signifies the "natural science," and the "description of the chariot"[91] denotes "metaphysics." Adam, Eve, and the serpent in Genesis represent the intellect, the body, and the imagination, respectively. He explains numerous terms in this way.

He speaks of the limit of human intellect; the study and teaching of metaphysics; attributes; the twenty-six propositions employed by the philosophers to prove the existence of God, mainly, the arguments of Aristotle; prophets and prophecy; man as having a free will and a choice of decision; law as reflecting the ordinary condition of man; the fear of God, love, righteousness, and true wisdom, which is more than a knowledge of the law, but demonstrates by proof those truths which Scripture teaches us by way of tradition.[92] Wisdom is the highest of all the perfections, whether pursued for wealth and honor, the building of the body, or moral perfection. Although moral perfection is the highest degree of excellency in man's character, it concerns only the relation of man to his neighbor. The ultimate perfection is that by which man will attain the highest intellectual faculties which will lead to true metaphysical opinions of God. "With this perfection man has obtained his final object; it gives him immortality, and on its account he is called man."[93] Finally, the one who worships God best and is in direct communion with Him is the one who has gone beyond studying the Scripture and has learned the mathematical sciences and logic, physics, natural philosophy and metaphysics.[94]

The *Guide* may be considered the *Summa Theologica* of Judaism. It had staunch adversaries at first from among the conservative rabbis,[95] but Judaism reconciled itself with the allegorical explanations of the Bible through Maimonides, who was held by his contemporaries and succeeding generations in high regard as one of the greatest Jews, in the popular saying: "From Moses to Moses there was none like Moses." His *Guide* and other works were translated into Hebrew during his lifetime. When Samuel Ibn Tibbon told Maimonides of his desire to translate the *Guide*, Maimonides said that the translator ought to know both Aristotelian philosophy and the Bible in order to do a good job. Ibn Tibbon went ahead with the task and proved himself competent in making the *Guide* available to a large audience of Jews, some of whom admired the author's genius while others condemned him as a falsifier of their traditional religion. Another translation was made later by Jehudah al-Ḥarīzī. When this controversy over the *Guide* subsided among the Jews in the fourteenth century, the work came to play an important role in the development of Christian Scholasticism,[96] as did the works of Muslim authors with whom Maimonides shared methods and views of God, the world, man, prophecy, and the harmony between faith and reason.

All in all, philosophy in a Muslim context did not disavow revelation (*sharī'ah*). On the other hand, the philosophers, in their enthusiasm for placing reason as the highest endowment of man and a sure means for attaining the ultimate objective of religion, had emphasized that human intellect, as a derivative of the Pure Intellect, deserves to be on a par with Revelation, if not higher, as a method for attaining the Supreme Truth. They were fully aware of the grave ramifications of such a position, and they attempted to minimize the problem by asserting that revelation is for all to believe and practice, while philosophy is restricted to the domain of the few, beyond even the dialectician-theologians, who lack ability in demonstrative reasoning. Under the circumstances, the relationship between faith and reason remained a tenuous one, and a solution to the problem was sought in Ṣūfism, the mystical path which emphasized intuitive experience and knowledge in a life completely devoted to the ideals of revelation, that is, to attaining God.

The words *mystic* and *mysticism* are represented by the Arabic expressions of *ṣūfī* and *ṣūfism*, respectively. The origin of the term *Ṣūfism (al-taṣawwuf)*[97] is rather obscure, although several suggestions have been given for its etymology: from Greek *sofous* meaning "wise," Arabic *ṣafw*, "purity," or *ṣūf*, "wool," since early Ṣūfīs wore woolen garments.[98] Because of the vastness of the Islamic empire, which came face to face with Christian, neo-Platonic, Gnostic, and Buddhist mystical ideas,[99] there is the temptation to assume that Ṣūfism was inspired by, and based upon, these movements. It is clear that there are several elements common to all these mystical movements, but to determine the extent of borrowing is difficult, if not impossible. It is also evident that Ṣūfism in Islam, as with mysticism in other religious movements, developed as the result of a strong and genuine concern with the best means to serve God, whether in a social setting or in a life of seclusion. This urge was often accompanied by spiritual crisis and sociopolitical turmoil as well. In its development, Christianity was faced with these crucial problems, and had sincere and devout adherents who chose to divorce themselves from the world with the hope of attaining spiritual contentment and the maximum goal of eternal salvation. Likewise, Islam was torn by ideological, dogmatic, political, and social conflicts from the outset, despite its sweeping success and acceptance among millions of people. Sects sprang up in large numbers, and the issues confronting and dividing them remained irritating and insoluble for long periods of time. Under the circumstances, Ṣūfīs developed a religious philosophy and preferred to call themselves the people of the Truth (*ahl al-ḥaqq*).

It is difficult to date the emergence of the first Ṣūfī movement in Islam. All indications are that it appeared sometime in the eighth century. Like other Islamic sects, Ṣūfism found its raison d'être in the Qur'ān and the Prophetic Traditions. Moreover, Ṣūfīs received their inspiration from the Prophet, his companions, and other great religious leaders of Islam — all of whom are said to have been the model Ṣūfīs. In fact, the Qur'ān became the base and the pillar of their doctrine. It was quoted profusely and its passages were given esoteric meanings. Verses such as "Whithersoever you turn, there is the face of God" (Q2:109) and "He loveth them, and they love Him" (Q5:50) became enough justification and guidance for Ṣūfism. The Ṣūfīs also drew from the Traditions and had their own corpus of Prophetic Traditions concerning poverty, humility, disavowal of wealth, reliance on God, and all things pleasing to Him which will lead to love and knowledge, as in the saying "Whoso knows himself knows his Lord." Moreover, they claim that the Prophet Muḥammad not only approved of Ṣūfism but was himself the first Ṣūfī and the Perfect Man (*al-insān al-kāmil*).

The core of the Ṣūfī doctrine and its pillars are light, knowledge, and divine love.[100] The would-be Ṣūfī must endure rigorous initiation under the supervision of a peer. He is considered a traveller (*sālik*) who goes through several stages (*maqāmāt*) along a path (*ṭarīqah*) with the ultimate goal of union with God (*fanā' fī-l-ḥaqq*).[101] The stages should lead to various psychological states (*ḥāl*, pl. *aḥwāl*) until the traveller attains the high plane of gnosis (*ma'rifah*), truth (*ḥaqīqah*), and the full realization that knowledge, knower, and known are One.[102] The stages are seven to some Ṣūfīs: repentance, abstinence, renunciation, poverty, patience, trust in God, and satisfaction; they may be followed by various states, such as meditation, nearness to God, love, fear, hope, longing, intimacy, tranquility, contemplation, and certainty.[103] In sum, the Ṣūfī aims, through complete self-effacement, to love and know God and become near or part of Him, thereby acquiring supernatural powers. "If ye know God as he ought to be known, ye would walk on the seas, and the mountains would move at your call." [104]

Ṣūfism went through several stages of development. It began as an ascetic movement which incorporated gnostic elements, then developed pantheistic tendencies. Thus, from quietism and a practical form of religion, it developed into a philosophical system with a terminology which is not readily understood and which often requires a commentary for grasping its hidden meaning. Like other sects in Islam, Ṣūfism became divided, some factions being considered "orthodox," while others the Ṣūfīs themselves labeled heretical. This notwithstanding, the movement spread throughout the Muslim world from beyond continental India to al-Andalus. It attracted prominent leaders everywhere; these leaders committed their doctrines to writing and thus contributed to making Ṣūfism one of the Islamic sciences. [105]

One of the outstanding early Ṣūfīs was Ḥārith Ibn Asʿad al-Muḥāsibī (ca. 781–837), considered the actual founder of Ṣūfism. He was a native of Baṣrah and wrote on the various aspects of Ṣūfism. [106] He developed the concept of *muḥāsabah* (self-scrutiny), from which his name was derived, and which is meant to distinguish between what God likes and dislikes. Dhū al-Nūn (d. 861) of Egypt is credited with numerous treatises and poems which portray the lover's intense feeling for the beloved. He is also credited with having introduced the ideal of gnosis (*maʿrifah*), which became one of the main pillars of Ṣūfism. The Persian Bāyazīd of Bistam (d. 875) was one of the first "intoxicated" Ṣūfīs, [107] whose mystical fervor led him to consider himself identical with God, according to the saying attributed to him, "Glory to me! How great is My Majesty." With him the concept of *fanāʾ* (self-effacement), or the attainment of union with God, had reached its full development. He was followed, among others, by al-Junayd (d. 910) of Baghdād, who elaborated on the idea of *fanāʾ* and the concept of union (*tawḥīd*).

Ṣūfism reached its apogee in the tenth century, and produced many intoxicated Ṣūfīs who claimed to have reached union with God and identified themselves with Him. Al-Ḥallāj (d. 922) [108] was a cause célèbre. He was crucified for blasphemy, having claimed that he was reunited with God and having boasted, "I am the truth" (*anā al-ḥaqq*) and "I am whom I love and the one I love is I." In spite of the indignation of orthodoxy over this claim, al-Ḥallāj became a martyr and saint among his followers. Likewise, writing on the subject of Ṣūfism became abundant. Abū Saʿīd Ibn al-

'Arabī (d. 952) wrote *Categories of Pious Men* (*Ṭabaqāt al-nussāk*), which is lost, but it was followed by many other works such as the *Luma'* [109] of Abū Naṣr al-Sarrāj (d. 988); *The Categories of Ṣūfīs* [110] by Abū 'Abd Raḥmān al-Sulamī (d. 1021), and the *Risālah* [111] of Abū Qāsim al-Qushayrī (d. 1074) — all of which give ample information concerning Ṣūfī doctrine and its most outstanding leaders.

Al-Ghazālī (d. 1111) was a Ṣūfī who avoided the extremes of Ṣūfism in favor of the Golden Mean, which enabled him to reconcile the religious devotion and dedication of Ṣūfism with the Islamic precepts of avoiding evil and espousing good for the sake of salvation. The blueprint expressing this goal is contained in his writings, mainly in *Iḥyā'* [112] and *al-Munqidh min al-ḍalāl*.[113]

It was from this background that Andalusian Ṣūfism emerged. Ascetic tendencies in al-Andalus, we are told, were apparent as early as the conquest. A number of individuals who frowned upon worldly things are said to have spent a good portion of their life in prolonged fasting and prayers and to have disdained honors and women.[114] However, it is doubtful that they constituted an organized body or developed a school of thought. It was not until the tenth century that a semblance of organization was initiated by Ibn Masarrah, often referred to as the first philosopher of al-Andalus.[115] He had a number of followers who carried the banner of their dead master, but it is not certain to what extent they influenced Hispano-Arabic mysticism. Except for the material collected by Asín Palacios, which is not altogether authentic,[116] little is known about the mystical system of Ibn Masarrah and his followers or its relation to the fully developed Ṣūfī doctrine in the East. This does not imply that the Andalusians were unaware of the existence of Ṣūfism or of its main leaders and their writings, but it may be assumed that the religious scholars imposed stringent measures on any movement that appeared to deviate from the established dogma. Under the circumstances, the ascetic tendencies in al-Andalus were often expressed by a display of religiosity and piety, avoiding the extremes of self-identification with God. However, as the power of the religious scholars began to decline in the eleventh century, their hold on al-Andalus became less restrictive. Political dislocation, continuous internal wars, rampant insecurity, and decline in morals must have influenced many sensitive souls to withdraw from the daily turmoil and to seek solace in religious exercises and contemplation beyond ordinary devotion and seclusion.

Thus, by the twelfth century, collective movements, each of which identified itself with a leader, made their appearance. The first group of Ṣūfis appears to have had its nucleus in Almería; from there the movement spread to Cordova, Seville, and other southern towns. The first prominent leader was Abū-l-ʻAbbās Ibn al-ʻArīf (1088–1141).[117] Ibn al-ʻArīf was born in Almería. His poor father forced him to go to work at a tender age, but the boy showed a great dedication to the study of religious and philological books and became a respected authority on various disciplines. His erudition permitted him to teach in his native town and in such faraway places as Saragossa and Valencia. But Ibn al-ʻArīf's fame rests on his role as a mystic and on the great influence he exerted upon the formulation and dissemination of Ṣūfism in al-Andalus. He was highly respected and admired, yet he was persecuted by the judge of Almería, who exiled him to Ceuta and then to Marrākush, where he gained the ruler's favor and later died, reportedly of poison. Among Ibn al-ʻArīf's writings is his *Maḥāsin al-majālis*,[118] which is frequently mentioned in Ibn ʻArabī's *Futuḥāt*.[119] The work describes the various stages of the mystical path: gnosis, wishes, abstinence, trust, patience, sorrow, fear, hope, gratitude, and love, to which, in a second thought perhaps, he adds repentance and proximity to God. The gnostic comes to the realization that God and only God exists in reality and that all which is not God ought to be rejected.

The leading contemporaries of Ibn al-ʻArīf were Abū al-Ḥakam Ibn Barrajān (d. 1142) of Seville, Abū Bakr al-Mayurqī (twelfth century) of Cordova, and Ibn Qasī (d. 1152) of Silves. Both Ibn Barrajān and Abū Bakr al-Mayurqī were exiled with Ibn al-ʻArīf to North Africa, where they influenced the course of Ṣūfism in both al-Andalus and North Africa. They are credited with some works on Ṣūfism based on Eastern Ṣūfism, mainly on the works of al-Ghazālī. However, it was such men, with different worldly and spiritual outlooks, who were instrumental in disseminating Ṣūfism under unfavorable conditions in the twelfth century, and who were responsible for creating an environment that was later to produce Ibn ʻArabī, one of the great mystics of Islam.

It is interesting, however, that the conduct of some of the Andalusian Ṣūfis hardly satisfied the rigorous discipline of a devout Ṣūfī. For instance, Abū-l-Qāsim Ibn Qasī (d. 1152) was a Ṣūfī shaykh (*shaykh min mashāyikhat al-ṣūfiyyah*) and the leader of the Murīdīn sect in western al-Andalus. From his monastery (*rābiṭah*) in a town near Silves he spread his views, and became a Mahdi, claiming to be inspired and able to fulfill any material request. People both inside and outside his sect flocked around him for material rewards. He was thus able to launch a revolt and threaten the last remnant of the Almoravids.[120] Moreover, the Ṣūfis seem to have been recognized as a political faction; they are mentioned among orators, pious men, the poor, and scholars attending the inauguration of a ruler.[121]

Of course, this worldly display does not conform to the puritan and spiritual pursuits of a devout Ṣūfī, though of course the Ṣūfī movement in the East also included people who exploited the sincere and devout. However the Andalusians had devout Ṣūfis in Yūsuf Ibn Khalaf al-Kūmī (d. 1181), Abū 'Amrān al-Mirṭuli, and others whose devotion and austerity[122] Ibn 'Arabī admired. Unfortunately, information concerning these devout Ṣūfis and their doctrine is limited. The only major Andalusian who formulated a Ṣūfī doctrine and became a leading Ṣūfī in the thirteenth century was Muḥyy al-Dīn Ibn 'Arabī, who was influenced by his Islamic background, the Eastern Ṣūfis, Muslim sects and philosophy, and non-Islamic sources.[123]

Ibn 'Arabī[124] was born at Murcia in 1165 and moved in 1172 to Seville, where he was educated in the religious sciences and other disciplines. Here he came into contact with leading scholars, including prominent leaders of Ṣūfism. Because of the tenuous situation in al-Andalus he went east in 1201, visiting Egypt, the Ḥijāz, Iraq, and Syria. He died in 1240 in Damascus, where his tomb is still venerated by admirers from all over the Muslim world.

In his youth Ibn 'Arabī led a licentious life, but he was influenced by some Ṣūfis who initiated him into the path of ascetism and self-examination. This transformed his thinking, and he became a true mystic after following the Ẓāhirite and the Bāṭinite (esoteric) schools. He chose a life of seclusion, during which he devoted most of his time to reading Ṣūfī books. He felt inspired by what he considered to be a divine light descending upon him and illuminating his mind with knowledge.

Unfavorable political and social conditions in al-Andalus and northwest Africa may have contributed to Ibn 'Arabī's decision to leave his native homeland permanently. During his journeys, he enjoyed great popularity and, often, much enmity. He was threatened with assassination in Egypt, but this did not distract his followers from revering him as the great master (*al-shaykh al-akbar*).

Ibn 'Arabī was a prolific writer and an able poet. His biographers credit him with some four to five hundred works, which include poems[125] with mystical content. As a rule, his language is ambiguous and complex, containing a terminology that needs to be explained before the purpose and trend of his thought can be understood. His love poems to a Meccan lady appeared so erotic to the average pious man that Ibn 'Arabī felt the need to explain them. He insisted that the poems were far from worldly or sensual, but instead pointed to "divine knowledge and light, spiritual secrets, intellectual apperceptions, and lawful exhortations." [126] His fame rests on his numerous mystical writings in prose, most outstanding of which are *Fuṣūṣ al-ḥikam*,[127] *al-Futuḥāt al-makiyyah*,[128] and other treatises that have been made available.[129] Both *Fuṣūṣ* and *Futuḥāt* embody Ibn 'Arabī's mystical philosophy with encyclopedic detail of the various aspects of Ṣūfism: its stages and states, the Ṣūfi path; the categories of mystic perfection; the mutual union of the souls with God; and the ultimate ecstatic state. His doctrine is a mixture of earlier ideas, but it contains the stamp of his genius and his own interpretation of dogmatic Islam as well as the Ṣūfi outlook.

To Ibn 'Arabī, God is the Absolute Being, yet all-embracing; the source of all existence, transcendent, and immanent; One Reality as the all-prevailing Love and Beauty.[130] The Universe of First Intellect is the Reality of Muḥammad, who is the Perfect Man, the *Logos*,[131] and the greatest of Prophets — all of whom he regards as saints and he himself the Seal of Saints.[132] The Perfect Man is a miniature of the One Reality (God), the microcosm reflecting all perfect attributes of the macrocosm. He advocates a pantheistic monism (*waḥdat al-wujūd*); to him there is One Reality in existence and all created things are manifestations of that Reality, or "the One and the Many are only names for two subjective aspects of One Reality." [133] 'Afifi paraphrases his thinking as follows: "Owing to our finite minds and our inability to group the *Whole as a Whole*, we regard it as a plurality of beings, ascribing to each one characteristics which distinguish it from the rest. Only a person possessed of the vision of a mystic, Ibnul 'Arabī would say, can transcend, in a supramental state of intuition, all the multiplicity of forms and 'see' the Reality that underlies them." [134]

It is in this context that Ibn 'Arabī views divine attributes as subjective and relative.[135] Human intellect is capable neither of knowing God nor of studying theology, whereas the way of the mystic, invested with divine light, leads toward knowing Him.[136] It is through ecstatic experience and the mystical state of *fanā'* (self-effacement) that the individual finds the full realization of himself in God. This final stage is attained only through two types of knowledge — *al-ma'rifah* or "knowledge by acquaintance," acquired by the soul, and *'ilm*, an intellectual knowledge achieved by reason.[137] He says that ordinarily all knowledge is acquired by the five senses and the intellect, but the most important and reliable means of acquiring the truth is the intuitive or esoteric knowledge, born of experience and as the result of inner experience. This kind of knowledge is often called taste (*dhawq*), or knowledge of secrets (*'ilm al-asrār*), and knowledge of the unseen (*'ilm al-ghayb*).[138] This kind of knowledge is innate; it is not the outcome of any discipline, but rather, it "lies dormant in the deepest recesses of the human heart." It is beyond reason, which cannot even be invoked to test its validity. "On the contrary, if reason and intuition should conflict, the former should always be sacrificed for the latter"; it manifests itself in the form of light which floods every part of the heart of the Ṣūfī, and materializes itself in certain men; it perceives Reality itself, which speculative knowledge is not able to achieve; it is one and identical with God's knowledge. It is infallible, and through it the mystic gains perfect knowledge of the nature of Reality.[139]

The realization of this knowledge is achieved through *fanā'*, for which Ibn 'Arabī's interpretation differs from the traditional Ṣūfī conception. To Ibn 'Arabī, *fanā'* is not self-effacement, but the passing away from sin, all actions, attributes, one's own personality, the whole world, all divine attributes — that is, the passing away from all ignorance and appearances to the attainment of true knowledge. In its various stages, *fanā'* is complemented by *baqā'*[140] (remaining or continuing).

To Ibn 'Arabī, neither philosophy, nor theology, nor a particular religion is a good substitute for the mystical path. He describes the journey of a mystic and philosopher to the seven heavens in emulation of the ascension (*mi'rāj*) of Muḥammad. This passage illustrates the shortcomings of the philosopher and the distinct advantages of the mystic-believer. In the course of the journey, the mystic gains infallible truth while the philosopher is beset by skepticism and confusion. Even when the philosopher relinquishes all his speculations and joins the path of the mystic, he is able to perceive only the phenomenal and the apparent things, while the mystic attains the spiritual and the real. Although both pursue the same goal, the methods are different and the results uneven. For instance, the philosopher is able to know causality on the basis of observation alone, while the mystic "sees" for himself how the One Cause operates in all causes. Moreover, the philosopher's knowledge cannot go beyond the seven spheres, whereas the mystic continues his spiritual ascension and enters other spheres, wherein he is taught eschatological and mystical subjects.[141]

Ibn 'Arabī had a great number of followers, and his influence was strongly felt among both Muslims and Christians.[142] Asín Palacios, an ordained cleric who often placed scholarship over religious and national prejudices, showed Dante's indebtedness in the *Divine Comedy* to Ibn 'Arabī. One of Ibn 'Arabī's able disciples was Ibn Sab'īn (1218–1269) of Murcia. Ibn Sab'īn received his education in the religious sciences and philology and emigrated to Ceuta, where he attracted many followers. He wrote a number of treatises and a manual for the Ṣūfī.[143] His influence on subsequent mystical thinking was enormous. It appears in the saintly conduct of Ibn 'Abbād, and in the work of 'Abd al-Karīm al-Jīlī (d. 1428), who wrote a work with the appropriate title of *The Perfect Man* (*al-Insān al-kāmil*).

The last outstanding Ṣūfī of al-Andalus was Ibn 'Abbād (1332–1389).[144] He was born in the rather secluded mountains of Ronda to a wealthy, prominent family that might have originally come from Seville. He received his education in his native town and seems to have been exposed to Ṣūfī literature at an early age. He travelled to Tangier, Tlemcen, and Fez. It was in Fez that he spent the rest of his life as preacher and *imām* of the main mosque. He was highly regarded by the ruler and the people. His ascetic, exemplary life earned for him the reverence of his followers and even the religious scholars, who ordinarily frowned on Ṣūfīs. His writings consisted for the most part of sermons and homilies which were recited in mosques for generations after his death. Equally important is his *Commentary of the Maxims of 'Atā'allah* (d. 1309, of Alexandria), which explains the ascetic life and the mystical path. His influence was felt beyond northwest Africa; it appears to permeate the writings of the great Spanish mystic San Juan de la Cruz (d. 1591).[145]

In sum, it appears that neither the *sharī'ah* in its literal sense, nor theological speculation according to *ijtihād*, nor philosophy based on investigation and demonstrative reasoning satisfied the innermost feelings of the Ṣūfīs. The ascetics were even horrified at both excessive intellectual and theological speculation. The mystic, therefore, seems to have overlooked the fact that Islam is an instrumentality for attaining the well-being of the community both on earth and in Heaven. Instead, they concentrated on individual well-being and relied heavily on emotionalism and on what they labeled "inner perception" transcending the literal sense of the *sharī'ah*, the endless speculation of the theologians, and the rather limited capability of philosophy in perceiving the ultimate truth, which is God. In this posture, the Ṣūfīs were apt to have confrontations with both the theologians and philosophers. They looked into the esoteric meaning of the religious texts and often gave their own interpretations which did not conform to those of the dogma. The crux of the problem was the relation of man to his Creator. Whereas the orthodox world sees this relation in terms of worshipper and worshipped, the Ṣūfīs would prefer it to be between a lover and the beloved.[146] They viewed the philosophers as perplexed skeptics whose tools, mainly reason, for attaining the truth fall far short of the ''inner perception'' (*dhawq*, or divine love) of the Ṣūfī, which is the basis for a life of devotion and the attainment of God.

18

The Natural Sciences

THE Muslim conception of the natural sciences [1] distinguishes them as natural to man and not restricted to any particular religious group.[2] These intellectual sciences (*al-'ulūm al-'aqliyyah*) include the sciences of philosophy and wisdom, including logic, physics, metaphysics (*al-'ilm al-ilāhī*), and the mathematical sciences (*ta'ālīm*), including geometry, arithmetic, music, and astronomy. According to Ibn Khaldūn,[3] these are the seven basic philosophical sciences, each of which has subdivisions. For instance, physics includes medicine; arithmetic includes calculation, inheritance laws, and business; astronomy includes astronomical tables (*zīj*) and astrology. Even in practice, Muslim philosophers like al-Kindī, al-Rāzī, and Ibn Sīnā deal with all or most of these sciences — which makes it difficult to determine where philosophy begins and where the natural sciences end. More often than not, these men were astronomers, mathematicians, music theorists, alchemists, physicians, metaphysicists, and botanists, in addition to their general familiarity with the religious sciences and Arabic philology.

The foreign origin of these sciences as opposed to the so-called Arabic sciences is universally recognized by Muslim writers. For one, Ṣā'id of Toledo [4] characterizes nations by their contributions to the various sciences. Ibn Ḥazm [5] admits the universality of astronomy, mathematics, medicine, and philosophy, and Ibn Khaldūn [6] credits Persians, Greeks, Chaldeans, and other pre-Islamic people with contributions to the various secular sciences. Moreover, Muslim writers acknowledge their indebtedness to those pre-

Islamic peoples and the extensive borrowing through translation, which began in the eastern Islamic empire, mainly in Baghdād.

Al-Andalus depended heavily on the East for the incorporation and cultivation of the "intellectual sciences." The Andalusians may have had a late start in those sciences, but once they became interested, they were able to perpetuate a scientific tradition and to produce a large number of scientists in medicine, astronomy, mathematics, and related subjects. More important still, they were responsible for transmitting those sciences to the West through the process of translation from Arabic into Latin.[7]

By the nature of things, the natural or intellectual sciences, unlike the religious or Arabic sciences, made a tardy entry into al-Andalus. The reason is that they came into vogue in the East only after the translation of foreign works into Arabic. There is no evidence that the Andalusians had taken the initiative in translating Greek or Latin works into Arabic; rather, they cautiously awaited the result of scientific experimentation in the East. Once successful under the patronage of the 'Abbāsid rulers of Baghdād, the scientific wave was hard to halt even in so ultraconservative a region as al-Andalus. Although the religious scholars of al-Andalus kept a watchful eye on this development and often showed their intolerance to innovation, they were eventually overwhelmed by the current of ideas spreading all over the Muslim world. A cult around the person of Aristotle, the "first teacher," was emerging in the East and finding great acceptance among intellectuals and rulers. Al-Kindī, al-Fārābī, Ibn Sīnā, and other Muslim philosophers enthusiastically followed the broad intellectual perspective of the Greek sage. It is no wonder then that the Andalusians, who were dazzled by the wisdom of the East, sooner or later participated actively in the intellectual experiment. This was accomplished through travel between East and West and through an intensive process of education and borrowing.

To be sure, those natural sciences having a practical application for daily transactions and religious significance found their way easily into al-Andalus at an early stage. Mathematics, astronomy, and medicine may be said to be among those sciences. Mathematics had many uses in figuring prices, inheritance, and distances, besides being a necessary adjunct to other sciences. Astronomy served for determining the position of the Ka'bah vis-à-vis any geographical point, the exact hour of the day for the purpose of prayer, the seasons of the year, and the calendar. As for medicine, it had immediate bearing on the health of the body, just as religion was conceived to have the function of preserving the health and purity of the soul.

A rationalistic distinction was often made between legitimate sciences and pseudosciences in terms of utility. Astrology was often confused with astronomy, and it was common to find astronomers and astrologers equally regarded at court. In fact, the astrologer often outranked other courtiers, since he was considered able to predict future events on the basis of a knowledge of the stars and their influence on birth, growth, death, the outcome of wars, the end of dynasties, and other events. Similarly, chemistry, which deals with the elements and their compounds, was confused with alchemy, whose practitioners had the obsession of making silver and gold out of base metals. This popular confusion of the scientific with the pseudoscientific led authors to point to their differences in terms of the soundness of astronomy and chemistry on the one hand and the baselessness of astrology and alchemy on the other.

The views of Ibn Ḥazm and those of Ibn Khaldūn are worth noting in this respect. They pertain to astronomy, astrology, and alchemy. Ibn Ḥazm [8] says that the influence of the stars on people and events is an absurdity and defies the nature of things. To Ibn Ḥazm, talisman, magic, music, and alchemy fall under the same category, for their pursuers are liars and shameless. To these abominable qualities may be added those of the alchemist, namely taking away people's money and falsifying it.[9] These points were taken up by Ibn Khaldūn [10] of Tunis three and a half centuries later. He says that the astrologers' claims to predict the future through their knowledge of the stars' power and influence is preposterous; that their knowledge is the result of experience and revelation is also untenable, since the whole discipline is based on conjecture and guesswork. In fact, both reason and prophecy deny the influence of the stars. "In addition, astrology does harm to human civilization" [11] since it misleads people and, for this reason, it should be totally forbidden. Ibn Khaldūn is likewise critical of alchemy and alchemists. While he considers alchemy a science and devotes a whole section [12] to it, he refutes it [13] as devoid of any scientific value. He points out that producing silver and gold from lower metals is both impossible and harmful. It is, for him, an undertaking pursued by greedy people who are not able to earn a living and who consider it a craft to accumulate wealth in a devious manner. Some alchemists devised a technique with the expectation of converting silver into gold, and copper and tin into silver. This failed utterly. Others simply indulged in forgery by covering silver with gold, copper with silver, or mixing the two metals in a ratio of one to two. They even forged money, and thus were guilty of stealing. "They are thieves, or worse than thieves."[14] Although he considers these extreme cases, Ibn Khaldūn still views all alchemists as people who are "infatuated with something and taken by fanciful stories about the subject of the infatuation."[15]

On the other hand, astronomy is highly regarded as a legitimate science. Ibn Ḥazm[16] and Ibn Khaldūn[17] consider it a noble art. Ibn Khaldūn says that it deals with the motion of the stars and planets; it deduces by geometrical methods the existence of certain shapes and position of the spheres; it determines the motions and the time of their occurrence through the aid of an astrolabe.[18] It has a subdivision known as astronomical tables (*zīj*), which deal with the course of motions peculiar to each star, and which serve to show the position of the stars at any given moment.

With an early start in the eighth century, mathematics and astronomy[19] developed into full-fledged sciences. They appear to have gone hand in hand. As a rule, a mathematician was an astronomer, or vice versa, and often wrote on both subjects. Euclid's *Book of Basic Principles* (*Kitāb al-uṣūl wa-l-arkān*) was translated into Arabic and became the basis for geometry. Subsequently, Muslim scholars made great strides in the field of mathematics in both transmission and original contributions. Arabic numerals were transmitted to the West by the Arabs. "The Arabs have really achieved great things in science; they taught the use of ciphers, although they did not invent them, and thus became the founders of the arithmetic of everyday life; they made algebra an exact science and developed it considerably and laid the foundations of analytical geometry; they were indisputably the founders of plane and spherical trigonometry which, properly speaking, did not exist among the Greeks."[20]

Among the outstanding mathematicians in Islam is al-Khuwārizmī, who not only compiled astronomical tables but also is credited with having written the oldest work on arithmetic and algebra, entitled *Ḥisāb al-jabr wa-l-muqābalah* (*Calculation of Integration and Equation*).[21] It deals with equations, algebraic multiplication and division, measurement of surfaces, legal questions pertaining to division of estates, and the like. Al-Khuwārizmī's works became the foundations of Arabic mathematics and astronomy; they were studied and commented upon in both East and West (mainly in al-Andalus), and they were widely emulated.

Astronomy was inspired by Indian and Greek works. The *Sindhind*, an Indian work on astronomy, was translated into Arabic by Ibrāhīm al-Fazārī (d. ca. 777) who is credited with the construction of the first astrolabe on a Greek model. It was followed by the translation of Ptolemy's

Quadripartitum, which became known in several versions. The *Sindhind* and *Quadripartitum* became the pillars of astronomy and the objects of intense study leading to fresh observations (*raṣd*) and discoveries, to the construction and wide use of the astrolabe, and to the establishment of observatories in the major cities of the Muslim empire in both East and West. A number of astronomers left works which became standard references. Most were translated into Latin by Gerard of Cremona and others via al-Andalus — which also produced its own astronomers. Among the leading early astronomers were Māshā'allah (d. 815), who wrote on the astrolabe and meteorology, and al-Farghānī (d. ninth century), who wrote on the forms of the stars. The Banū Shākir, father and sons, were outstanding astronomers and teachers who left a brilliant legacy consisting of works dealing with measurement of plane and spherical surfaces. They were followed by Abū Ma'shar of Balkh (d. 886) and by al-Baṭṭānī (d. 929), who made emendations on the work of Ptolemy and determined with precision the eclipses of the sun and the coming of the new moon. He also wrote a work on the astronomical tables.[22]

The astronomical and mathematical traditions established in the East found their way into al-Andalus[23] through students who were educated in the East. Among these were Ibn Abī 'Ubaydah (295/908) of Valencia, who was an expert in the motions and influence of the stars;[24] Yaḥyā Ibn Yaḥyā, known as Ibn Taymiyyah (d. 346/928), who emigrated from Cordova to the East and became versatile in both astronomy and medicine.[25] They were followed by others, among them Abū Bakr al-Anṣārī, who taught arithmetic, geometry, and astronomy under al-Ḥakam II.[26] But the great exponent of the natural sciences in al-Andalus was Maslamah al-Majrīṭī (d. 398/1008),[27] justifiably called "the Euclid of Spain." He excelled in mathematics, astronomy, and related sciences and can favorably be compared with Eastern scholars: "Many [scientists] restricted themselves to cultivating the mathematical disciplines and the related sciences of astrology, sorcery, and talisman. The most famous practitioners of these sciences were Jābir b. Ḥayyān in the East and the Spaniard Maslamah b. Aḥmad al-Majrīṭī, and his pupils."[28] "He was the leading mathematician of his time in al-Andalus and more knowledgeable in astronomy than any one before him."[29]

He wrote a number of works bearing on mathematics and astronomy, merchant mathematics, a commentary on the work of the Eastern mathematician al-Khuwārizmī, the astrolabe, and other topics. He had a great grasp of Ptolemy's *Almagest.* His book on astronomical tables is, according to the dictum of Ibn Ḥazm, unequaled anywhere.[30] He not only took into consideration the work of al-Khuwārizmī on the subject, but he also corrected, emended, and enlarged it. Among his changes were the addition of new tables and the conversion of the Persian calendar into Arabic dates using the Hijrah as the point of departure for calculations.[31] Aside from being a leading mathematician and astronomer, he is credited with abridging a number of books on magic, sorcery, and alchemy; principal among them is his *Rutbat al-ḥakīm* on alchemy, which is compared with the *Seventy Treatises* of Jābir Ibn Ḥayyān on the subject.[32] His *Kitāb al-ghāyah*, mentioned frequently by Ibn Khaldūn,[33] deals with sorcery and talisman. He is said to have considered alchemy and sorcery the result and fruits of philosophy and science and to have reasoned that those who were not acquainted with them would miss the fruits of scholarship and philosophy altogether.[34]

Al-Majrīṭī left an array of pupils who interested themselves in mathematics, astronomy, and related subjects. Among his successors were Abū Bakr Ibn Bashrūn (eleventh century) who wrote a treatise on alchemy,[35] Abū Muslim Ibn Khaldūn (d. 1057),[36] Ibn al-Samḥ (d. 1035),[37] Ibn al-Ṣaffār,[38] al-Kirmānī (d. 1066),[39] and 'Alī Ibn Sulaymān al-Zahrāwī (d. 1036).[40]

Abū Muslim Ibn Khaldūn wrote mathematical works dealing with business arithmetic for sale of merchandise, measurement of land, figuring charity taxes, and other business transactions.[41] But al-Majrīṭī's ablest pupil was Ibn al-Samḥ, who excelled in practically all the natural sciences: mathematics, geometry, the form and motion of the stars, and medicine. His astronomical tables were a quality equal to those of his master.[42] In addition, he wrote a commentary on the work of Euclid and two works on the astrolabe, one dealing with its manufacture and the other with its functioning and uses.[43] He was perhaps equaled by Ibn al-Ṣaffār, who left a number of works on the natural sciences, mainly an abridgment of astronomical tables and another on the use of the astrolabe. These men not only kept alive the school of their master Maslamah, but they also perpetuated it through many pupils of their own, such as Ibn Burghūth (d. 1053), al-Wāsiṭī (eleventh century), Ibn Shahr (d. 1043) and Ibn 'Aṭṭār (eleventh century).[44]

Moreover, the mathematical and astronomical sciences found acceptance in the major cities of al-Andalus. Two princes of the Banū Hūd of Saragossa distinguished themselves in these studies. Al-Zarqālī (Arzachel)[45] of Toledo was an outstanding astronomer-mathematician. He was born in Toledo; following its conquest by Alfonso VI in 1085, he moved to Cordova, where he died in 1100. He constructed excellent astronomical instruments and was greatly admired for his wide knowledge of astronomy. Ṣā'id of Toledo, who wrote an astronomical work,[46] describes him as the most knowledgeable in the motion of the stars, astronomical observation, preparation of tables, and construction of instruments.[47] He built a water clock that was capable of determining the hour of day and night and the days of the lunar months.[48] His name is associated with the Toledan tables, which were based on the doctrine of the *Sindhind* and the works of his predecessors, mainly al-Khuwārizmī. However, he added his own observations and studies.[49] His astronomical legacy was enormous, as attested by his numerous works. Among these is the *Book of Tables*[50] (*jadwal*), done in the form of an almanac and containing various tables: some determining what day marks the beginning of each lunar, Coptic, Roman, and Persian month; others describing the position of the sun, moon, and other stars; and others predicting the eclipses of the moon and sun. Another work[51] deals with determination of the position of the sun on the bases of tables, position of the planets, longitude and latitude, and eclipses of the moon and sun. He also improved a type of astrolabe called al-Ṣafīḥah, and wrote a treatise on it which was translated into Romance at the order of Alfonso X.[52] The Toledan astronomical tables were translated into Latin by Gerard of Cremona.

Jābir Ibn al-Aflaḥ (d. ca. 1150) of Seville also made a contribution to astronomy through his work entitled *Kitāb al-Hay'ah*, which was translated into Latin. Of equal stature was Abū Isḥāq al-Biṭrūjī (d. ca. 1204), known to the West as Alpetragius. Al-Biṭrūjī promulgated a new theory concerning the movement of the stars, and his work entitled *Kitāb al-Hay'ah* (*Book of Form*) was translated into Latin by Michael Scot in 1217. It was also rendered into Hebrew by Moses ben Tibbon in 1259 and into Latin by Kalonymous ben David in 1529. In sum, "Arab astronomers have left on the sky immortal traces of their industry which everyone who reads the names of the stars on an ordinary celestial sphere can readily discern. Not only are most of the star names in European language of Arabic origin, such as Acrab (*'aqrab*, scorpion), Algedi (*al-jadī*, the kid), Altair (*al-ṭā'ir*, the flyer), Deneb (*dhanab*, tail), Pherkard (*farqad*, calf), but a number of technical terms including *azimuth* (*al-sumūt*), *nadir* (*naẓīr*), *zenith* (*al-samt*), are likewise of Arabic etymology. . . ."[53]

In the field of medicine[54] and its various subdivisions, including pharmacopea, the Arabs inherited the rich legacy of the Near East and that of the Greeks and, in turn, made their own contribution. The Greek legacy was represented by the works of Hippocrates (d. 360 B.C.) and Galen (d. A.D. 210) who were considered the leading medical authorities. By and large, it was through Galen that the Arabs became acquainted with Greek medicine in its fictitious, theoretical, and experimental aspects. To this legacy was added the pre-Islamic medical conceptions and the so-called prophetic medicine (*al-ṭibb al-nabawī*) of early Islamic times. The Prophet is said to have maintained that God provided a suitable remedy for every illness and that one should avoid going to an area inflicted by pestilence. He recommended three principal remedies: administration of honey, cupping, and cautery. In the course of time, however, medicine was emancipated from superstitions, witchcraft, and the belief that illnesses were the results of demons, anger of the dead, or the ill will of an enemy. In fact, from about the eighth century, a time when old beliefs and superstitions were prevalent in the West, medicine among Muslims emerged as a science based on experimentation (*tajribah*), reasoning (*qiyās*), and observation.

Not only did the practice of medicine follow a scientific method, but its functions became the object of deliberation. Medicine was conceived as a science. Ibn Ḥazm divides the science of medicine into the medicine of the soul (*ṭibb al-nafs*), which is the result of logic and aims at correcting or curing the moral character and avoiding the extremes, and the medicine of the body, which deals with the knowledge of the bodily characteristics, the composition of the organs, diseases and their causes, and preparation of drugs.[55] It aims at healing through drugs, cauterization, surgery, and other methods required by the nature of things. As such, medicine was recognized as a highly technical profession requiring thorough training and a code of conduct. The candidate was expected not only to fulfill the academic requirements demanded of the profession but also to possess certain qualities and qualifications such as being a free man, good, kind, understanding, unselfish, friendly, a keeper of secrets, and able to endure insults and adverse criticism. Even his physical appearance was regulated: he was required to have short hair and fingernails; to wear clean, white clothes; and to walk with poise. He had to pass an examination which entitled him to have a licensed practice. Once he became a practitioner, he had to abide by certain rules within the framework of the Hippocratic oath, the neglect of which would result in his dismissal from the profession.

Along with the study and practice of medicine there developed the institution of hospitals (*bīmāristān*), which appeared in a large number in the major cities of the empire: Baghdād, Damascus, Cairo, Cordova, and elsewhere.

They were well organized and provided with baths, running water, and good food. They had various pavillions for the different diseases, and were headed by a chief physician. A hospital was open twenty-four hours a day to all citizens, rich and poor, residents and nonresidents. Drugs and food were available at all times.

Although Arabic medicine dervied its mainstay from Greek medical knowledge, the Arabs made noteworthy contributions to the field not only by preserving and transmitting it to the West, but by fresh discoveries, such as the recognition of the degree of putrefaction, the differences between measles and smallpox, and circulation of the blood, to mention only a few. From the eighth century onward, there appeared an array of physicians who were at first mostly Syriac-speaking. There was the Bakhtīshū' family, which produced distinguished physicians for generations. Yuḥannā Ibn Masāwayh (d. 857) and Ḥunayn Ibn Isḥāq, among others, served at the court of caliphs and princes. Ḥunayn was not only an able physician but the dean of translators in his time. Among his translations were the medical works of Galen, the *Aphorism* of Hippocrates, and *De Materia Medica* of Dioscorides.[56] Moreover, he wrote numerous medical works, including one on diseases of the eye.[57] He and some of his contemporaries left a great medical legacy that bore fruit in the tenth century which produced al-Rāzī, the greatest physician of Islam.

Al-Rāzī (865–925) was the natural scientist par excellence, and wrote about two hundred works,[58] which deal with medicine, astronomy and astrology, chemistry and alchemy, logic, metaphysics, and psychology. He started his medical training at the age of thirty, came to excel in the profession, and deservedly is called the Galen of the Arabs. He served the rulers in Khurāsān and Baghdād. When invited to build a hospital in Baghdād, he placed pieces of meat in different parts of the city in order to determine the degree of putrefaction, and, thus, to choose the best spot. His medical works covered the gamut of the medical sciences: diseases of the bladder, kidney, and other organs; anatomy, drugs, and a work on smallpox and measles which distinguishes between them. But his most comprehensive and important work is *al-Ḥāwī*, which was based on the medical knowledge of his predecessors and on his own observations and experiences. It was translated into Latin in 1279 under the title of *Continens* and was reprinted several times for use in European universities.

Al-Rāzī was followed by the Persian Haly 'Abbās (d. 994), author of an encyclopedic work that enjoyed great popularity in the West, where it was known as the *Liber Regius*. The work of 'Abbās was soon superseded by *al-Qānūn fī-l-ṭibb* of the great philosopher Ibn Sīnā. This comprehensive work became known to the West in the twelfth century and gained wide acceptance there. It embodied all the medical knowledge of the time, and dealt with general medicine, drugs, and all sorts of diseases. It is described by an authority as "the culmination and masterpiece of Arabic systematization. . . . Probably no medical work ever written has been so much studied and it is still in current use in the East."[59] Ibn Sīnā made use of psychoanalysis for determining ailments. For instance, while keeping his finger on the pulse of a young woman with whom he could not find anything physically wrong, he asked her some general questions first and then more personal ones. From her answers and her pulse reactions he was able to determine that the young lady was in love, but not with the young man selected by her father.

Al-Rāzī, Haly Abbās, and Ibn Sīnā are a few important names whose impact was felt quite strongly in al-Andalus particularly and in the rest of Europe generally. The works of these men, as well as those of other Eastern physicians, were widely studied and emulated. Andalusian physicians appeared early on the scene and were readily accepted at the court of rulers and princes. In fact, they were important functionaries at the court, and were respected and relied upon. The tenth-century physician and botanist Ibn Juljul served at the courts of al-Ḥakam II and Hishām II.

Ibn Juljul was born in Cordova in 943, studied Arabic and the religious sciences in early youth, and became deeply interested in medicine at the age of fourteen. When he was twenty-four years old, he was one of the leading physicians. Moreover, he composed a commentary on the names of the simple drugs found in *De Materia Medica* of Dioscorides; a treatise on drugs not mentioned by Dioscorides, including those found in al-Andalus; another on antidotes; and another on the mistakes of some physicians.

Of particular interest is Ibn Juljul's *Categories of Physicians*,[60] written at the behest of an Umayyad prince. It is divided into nine categories (*ṭabaqāt*) tracing the history of the sciences from the supposed founders Hermes and Aesculapius to Ibn Juljul's time. Biographical sketches are given of pre-Islamic and Islamic physicians and sages; Hippocrates, Dioscorides, Plato, Aristotle, Ptolemy, Euclid, Galen, leading Syriac-speaking physicians, al-Kindī, al-Rāzī, and fellow Andalusians. Ibn Juljul derived his information from Arabic sources, Paulus Orosius (fifth century A.D.), St. Jerome, Isodore of Seville, and oral information from his contemporaries.

In turn, the *Categories* served as a basic source for Andalusian writers and other Eastern writers such as al-Qifṭī and Ibn Abī Uṣaybiʿah. Important too is the fact that Ibn Juljul contributed to the translation of *De Materia Medica* from Greek into Arabic when the work was sent to ʿAbd al-Raḥmān III by the Byzantine emperior. The *Ṭabaqāt* is extremely valuable for shedding light on the extent of the knowledge and propagation of the sciences in both the East and al-Andalus.

Ibn Juljul says that medicine in al-Andalus was in the hands of Christians at first, who relied heavily on the *Aphorism* of Hippocrates. They lacked insight into the profession as well as in philosophy and geometry.[61] On his part, Ṣāʿid of Toledo says that people considered medicine without validity and did not interest themselves in its pursuit or in the study of medical works.[62] However, the profession began to gain acceptance and prominence as early as the ninth century. Both Ibn Juljul and Ṣāʿid give an impressive list of those whom they considered the most prominent physicians up to their own times.[63] Aḥmad Ibn Iyyās, who lived during the reign of the emir Muḥammad (852–886) is said to have been the first Andalusian to become famous in medicine.[64] He probably served at the court of Muḥammad I and was joined by the physician al-Ḥarrānī, originally from Ḥarrān, Mesopotamia.[65] At first, al-Ḥarrānī sold a beverage for bellyache which proved successful and contributed to his success. He also had a medication extracted from a nasturtium plant (*ḥurf*), but sold it under a different name (*al-thuffā'*). The Christian physician Ibn Malūkah was known for bleeding the veins and for his practice of medicine. He kept visiting hours and had some thirty chairs in front of his house for patients.[66] His coreligionist Isḥāq was an able practitioner to whom many useful and marvelous things are attributed.

It was in the tenth century that a large number of physicians appeared at the court of the caliphs ʿAbd al-Raḥmān III and al-Ḥakam. Saʿīd Ibn ʿAbd Rabbihi (d. 951), the nephew of the belletrist Ibn ʿAbd Rabbihi, was a physician-poet who composed a poem in *rajaz* dealing with medicine[67] and is said to have invented a special cure for fevers. Yaḥyā Ibn Isḥāq[68] was the son of a Christian physician. He became a Muslim and served as physician and vizier at the court of ʿAbd al-Raḥmān III (912–961). He was the author of a medical work in five volumes. The Ḥarrānī brothers — Aḥmad and ʿUmar[69] — emigrated to the East and studied the works of Galen under Thābit Ibn Sinān and Thābit Ibn Qurrah in Baghdād. They returned to al-Andalus in 963 and became al-Ḥakam II's favorite physicians; he accommodated them in the government complex, al-Zahrā'. Moreover, the caliph befriended Aḥmad and took him to his own palace. Aḥmad took charge of a dispensary which distributed food to the poor and patients. Muḥammad Ibn 'Abdūn also emigrated to the East in 347/959, visited Baṣrah and Egypt, where he administered a hospital (*bīmāristān*), and became an expert in medicine. Upon his return to al-Andalus in 971, he served al-Ḥakam II and wrote a standard work on fractures.[70] Ḥasdai ben Shaprūt (d. 990), minister and court physician, is said to have helped in the translation of the *Materia Medica* of Dioscorides into Arabic. The *Materia Medica* served as a model and helped considerably in the study of botany and pharmacy.

The Ḥarrānīs, Ibn 'Abdūn, and Ben Shaprūt were followed by other Andalusians who received their training in al-Andalus proper. Ibn al-Kattānī (d. 1029) was a prominent scientist who served the 'Āmirids in Cordova, then went to Saragossa. He was a teacher of the sciences and produced a number of students, among whom was Ibn Ḥazm. Ibn al-Kattānī is credited with a number of works on medicine.[71] Ibn 'Abd al-Raḥmān Ibn Shuhayd[72] was famous in medicine and the manner of curing diseases. He was familiar with the books of Galen, Aristotle, and other philosophers, and he was an expert in the disciplines (*'ulūm*) of simple drugs, which he grasped better than anyone else of his time and on which he composed an "important book," which was unequaled. It included the works of Dioscorides and Galen on the subject of simple drugs and gave the name and property of each drug with respect to its potential and limitation. He argued that there was no need for drugs if food would suffice, and if drugs were needed, simple drugs should be used. Compound drugs should be reserved for extreme cases and given in moderate dosage.

The reputation of Ibn 'Abd al-Raḥmān Ibn Shuhayd seemed to equal that of Abū-l-Qāsim al-Zahrāwī (936–1013), known to the West as Abulcasis. He, too, was a court physician of al-Ḥakam II and excelled as a surgeon. His fame rests on *al-Taṣrīf*, an encyclopedia of medicine and surgery. It consists of two parts, each in fifteen sections. On the whole, the work is based on the medical knowledge of his predecessors, mainly al-Rāzī. Of great significance, however, is the surgical section, which contains numerous illustrations of surgical instruments and is divided into three books: the first on cautery; the second on surgery, which describes lithotrities, amputations, ophthalmic and dental surgery, and treatment of wounds; and the third on fractures. The work is written with lucidity. It was translated into Latin by Gerard of Cremona and came into vogue in Europe.[73] Another work is *Liber servitoris*, describing drug preparations from plants, minerals, and animals.

The Zuhr family produced a number of eminent scientists. The founder of the family was Muḥammad Ibn Marwān Ibn Zuhr (d. 1030), a jurist of Talavera. His son, 'Abd al-Malik, went to Qayrawān and Egypt, where he received his medical training. Upon his return to al-Andalus, he settled in Denia and acquired great fame as a physician. It is reported that he forbade bathing in the belief that it upset the body and corrupted the "mixture."[74] He was succeeded in the profession by his son and pupil Abū-l-'Alā', who settled in Cordova. Abū-l-'Alā' wrote his *Mujarrabat al-khawāṣṣ*, a manual of medical instruction. But the most prominent member of the family was his son, Abū Marwān Ibn Zuhr (d. 1162), known to the West as Avenzoar. He was born in Seville and learned medicine from his father. He enjoyed great popularity in al-Andalus and North Africa as an authority in medicine and pharmacy. He made original experiments in therapeutics and described mediastinal tumors and abscesses. He served as a court physician of the Almoravids and Almohads and wrote a medical guide entitled *Kitāb al-iqtiṣād fī iṣlāḥ al-anfus wa-l-asjād* and another dealing with the cure and preservation of health entitled *Kitāb al-taysīr fī-l-mudāwāt wa-l-tadbīr,* translated into Latin under the title of *Theisir* in 1280. This work, a manual on practical medicine, describes methods of preparing drugs and diets.

One may conclude by mentioning the well-known philosophers Ibn Bājjah, Ibn Ṭufayl, Averroës, and Maimonides, who were excellent physicians. Aside from their philosophical works, they wrote on medicine and the natural sciences. Ibn Bājjah wrote on the natural sciences, astronomy, medicine, and music. Likewise, Averroës displayed this general interest, and wrote *Kulliyāt fī-l-ṭibb* (*The Comprehensive Book on Medicine*), which was translated into Latin in 1255 as *Colliget*. Widely known in the West, the work deals comprehensively with anatomy, physiology, diseases, their symptoms and cures, drugs, food, and the preservation of health. In addition, he wrote some fourteen works bearing on medicine, eight of which consist of abridgements of Galen's works on mixture, natural faculties, diseases, fevers, simple drugs, cures, and so forth.

The most prominent scientist of the thirteenth century was, perhaps, Ibn Bayṭār, who was born in 1197 at Málaga.[75] He received his early education in his native town, and resided for a while in Seville. He became an outstanding student of botany, a science he learned from books as well as from his observation and experiments. In 1219, he left his homeland and travelled through North Africa, the Arabian Peninsula, Syria, and Mesopotamia, where he continued his investigation of plants, studied, and taught. Among his pupils was Ibn Abī Uṣaybi'ah, author of the authoritative history of leading physicians. Ibn Bayṭār died in Damascus in 1248.

Ibn Bayṭār's merit rests on his valuable work entitled *Collection of Simple Drugs and Food*,[76] in which he discussed drugs and food and the manner they are made of animal, vegetable, and mineral. He arranged the work alphabetically, describing each drug and its various names. He mentions predecessors, from Dioscorides to Arabic authors, who concerned themselves with drugs and their preparation. He often corrected their mistakes and pointed to their differences of opinion, which he tried to reconcile. The work became extremely popular in both East and West, and was abridged in chapters to facilitate its use by physicians.

These were followed by other physicians and natural scientists, the last and most important among them, Ibn al-Khaṭīb, the historian, poet, and statesman, who wrote among other medical works a treatise advocating the theory of contagion. "The fact of infection," says he, "becomes clear to the investigator who notices how he who establishes contact with the afflicted gets the disease, whereas he who is not in contact remains safe, and how transmitting is effected through garments, vessels, and earrings."[77] Ibn al-Khaṭīb may also be considered the last medical encyclopedist. His *al-Yūsufī* was a general medical work in two volumes with a companion volume that became the standard work in medicine. In addition, he wrote another work on medical questions[78] and a poem in *rajaz* meter on simple food.

On the whole, the sciences in Islam lost their vitality with the death of Ibn al-Khaṭīb at a time when Europe had become fully aware of the importance of the scientific achievement of the Muslims.[79] It should be recalled that the Arabic-speaking world was in ascendance from the eighth to the thirteenth centuries while Europe was indifferent to scientific inquiry. The Muslims had delved into all the sciences and composed numerous works. In the medical sciences in particular, they trained their physicians, wrote standard medical works, practiced surgery, prepared drugs, and built numerous hospitals and dispensaries. In the meantime, Europeans relied on charms and amulets; the clergy frowned on and repressed medicine, leaving the whole field in the hands of quacks, barbers, and untrained women.

The religious enthusiasm among Christians in the eleventh century, which was responsible for a number of inroads into Muslim territory, would have been futile had it not been followed by intellectual inquiry and eventual cultivation of the sciences. Inroads into Muslim Spain, Syria-Palestine, and Sicily proved successful in the long run because of the Christians' willingness to live among and learn from the "infidels." With this receptive attitude, all began to change. Christians respected, depended on, and eventually emulated the great achievement of the Muslims. Spain, Syria-Palestine, and Sicily were the major centers of interaction of ideas and people. Translation of Arabic books into Latin came into vogue, gained momentum in the twelfth and thirteenth centuries, and eventually led to the cultural independence of the West from Arabic tutelage.

Constantinus Africanus (1020–1087)[80] set the stage for the process of translation and was instrumental to some degree in sparking the tide of Arabism in the intellectual life of Europe. He was followed by a large number of translators in Toledo, southern Italy, and Sicily. Among the major translators were Gundisalvus,[81] Gerard of Cremona, Mark of Toledo,[82] Michael Scot,[83] and Juan Hispano (Ibn Dāwūd).[84] By 1140, Roger of Sicily had set regulations for the study and practice of medicine and decreed that everyone who desired the practice of medicine must, under penalty of imprisonment and confiscation of property, present himself before a magistrate and obtain authorization. These measures found echoes throughout Europe. Moreover, the works of Muslim scientists and philosophers such as al-Rāzī, Ibn Sīnā, Ibn Zuhr, and Averroës were translated into Latin and became the standard works among scholars. Some of their works remained in use at European universities as late as the sixteenth century. No doubt, they influenced the thinking of men like Alexander of Halle, Thomas Aquinas, Albertus Magnus,[85] Roger Bacon, Peter of Abano,[86] and Arnold de Villanova, among many others. These men cited Arabic works which dealt with the philosophical and natural sciences. It is only as late as the sixteenth and seventeenth centuries that Arabic influence can no longer be traced, when men like Copernicus, Vesalius, Michael Servetus, Nicolaus Massa, Galileo, and others gave new insight and direction to the sciences.

19

Architecture, the Minor Arts, and Music

ARCHITECTURE, the minor arts, and music in Islam [1] were not unlike literary activities in their inception, growth, and development. They were likewise the product of cross-cultural interaction and adaptation. Artistic expression, which in Islam achieved sublime beauty, constituted a synthesis of elements from widely divergent regions of the world. In turn, Islamic artistic expression left its stamp on an equally large area — West Asia, North Africa, and southern Europe. This notwithstanding, the attitude of Islam toward some aspects of these arts has been ambivalent if not altogether negative. The notion exists that Islam condoned neither pictorial and sculptural representation, nor music and singing. No doubt this attitude is influenced by religious considerations in that pictorial representations would compromise God's exclusive role as creator, and would distract the faithful from true worship of God, who alone is the *bārī'* (creator) and *muṣawwir* (painter). It would be a blasphemy to apply these surnames to mere mortals. Prophetic Traditions condemn painters and sculptors as the "worst of men" and the "owning of pictures with figures is put on the same level with the keeping within one's house of a dog, a despised unclean animal which likewise impedes the entry of the angel of mercy; or it is compared with other low practices such as tattooing or the taking of interest." [2] However, pictures may be allowed on carpets, pillows, and similar objects since stepping, sitting, or leaning on them are deprecatory acts.[3] This attitude has led to the absence of both sacred iconography and church music and has contributed to the rise and cultivation of the secular aspects of architecture, art, and music. As a result, calligraphy, floral and geometrical designs, and paintings with figures of animals became the most distinctive features of architecture and the arts. The same may be said of music, where the sensual and the mundane appear to constitute its distinctive features.

Nevertheless, architecture, the minor arts, and music evolved with a distinctive Islamic personality in spite of the diverse elements from which they were derived and inspired: "The remarkable and incontrovertible fact about Muslim architecture is that in all countries and in all centuries it retained an unmistakable individuality of its own although its origin was so diverse."[4]

Wherever the Muslims went, they founded new cities or improved old ones. Kūfah, Baṣrah, and Baghdād in the East and Qayrawān and Cairo in North Africa are only a few of many cities they established. Particularly in al-Andalus, a number of cities were founded[5] and provided with mosques, palaces, marketplaces, public baths, surrounding walls pierced by enormous gates, and other facilities. Whether in old or new cities, the mosque and the government palaces constituted the nerve center of the city and the point to which all roads and activities converged. Around this center shops, baths, and lodgings were built, and major functions — prayer, education, distribution of alms, and various sociopolitical activities — were performed.[6] Possibly because of these multiple functions, attempts were made to beautify the mosques, sparing neither expense nor effort. The best talent — whether Muslim or non-Muslim — was put to work in construction and decoration, as if to compete with the luxurious dwellings of rulers and princes, whose palaces were extravagant, beautiful, and elegant. Decorative art became an essential ingredient of the new taste and developed into a form which could satisfy the innermost feeling for the ideal and the beautiful.

This was as true in al-Andalus as elsewhere in the Islamic world. The Andalusians were highly urbane yet they had a great love for nature and beauty. These two qualities are quite evident in their arts and architecture. If their rulers prided themselves in having the best poetical and literary talents at court, they also took pride in erecting mosques, palaces, canals, bridges, promenades, gardens, and fortresses. These great monuments became the raw material for poets, who composed tender verses to them in the same manner as they did to beautiful women, flowers, trees, mountains, brooks, rivers, stars, the sky, or the moon.[7] Hispano-Arabic monuments were both magnificent and beautiful. Likewise, the rulers encouraged the manufacture of luxuries such as ornate utensils, cosmetics, jewelry, textiles, fine robes, jewelry boxes, and caskets. To this extent, the arts and architecture went hand in hand with the great literary activities which the rulers sponsored; as with literature, the visual arts were inspired and influenced by Eastern models. From their inception in the eighth century until their peak of development under the Umayyads, art and architecture continued to flourish, though with less intensity, under the party-kings, Almoravids, Almohads, and the Naṣrids of Granada. It was the Naṣrid dynasty which left the beautiful Alhambra as an eloquent example of the artistic genius of Muslim Spain.

The elegance of the Andalusian building lies not so much in its exterior as its interior. The profuse decorations made use of the fauna and flora of al-Andalus, many intricate geometrical designs, and fanciful Arabic inscriptions. The artists did not slavishly follow any particular school or technique; they looked to the experience of their contemporaries and predecessors for models, to which they added their own ingenuity and genius and thereby gave their works an Andalusian-Islamic stamp. The synthesis and the eclecticism of their monuments and crafts achieved universal appeal.

It is interesting to note that from the eleventh century onward, the Andalusians were quite conscious of their artistic and architectural talents. Authors rarely failed to note what al-Andalus offered in the fine arts, architecture, and urbanity. In his *Nafḥ al-ṭīb* the seventeenth-century author al-Maqqarī devotes ample space to the excellence and wonder of al-Andalus as witnessed by an array of authors from the eleventh century onward. He devotes an entire section to Cordova and describes with great detail its location, extent, suburbs, mosques, palaces, its recreational palaces (*muntazihāt*), public baths, bridges, and canals. He compares Cordova's dominance in al-Andalus to the head of the body[8] and notes the fame of Cordova and its wonders: the sciences, the Umayyad mosque, al-Zahrā' palace, and al-Zāhirah palace.[9] For instance, at the turn of the tenth century, Cordova had some 1,600 mosques; 900 public baths; 60,300 mansions for notables, viziers, secretaries, commanders of the army; 213,077 houses for the people; and 80,455 shops.[10] Other cities had distinctive attractions. Al-Shaqundī refers to them in *Risālah*,[11] which is intended to show the superiority of al-Andalus over North Africa. Seville is famous for its magnificent buildings; its musical instruments; and its surrounding villages, which are well constructed and carefully tended, making them look like "stars in a sky of olive groves."[12] The minaret of Seville's great mosque, built by Ya'qūb al-Manṣūr, is the "greatest minaret ever built in the Muslim world."[13] Jaén is referred to as "silk city" (Jayān al-ḥarīr), known also for its great fortifications.[14] Ubeda, not far from Jaén, is famous for its places of entertainment and dancers;[15] Granada for its splendid buildings, gardens, and baths;[16] and Málaga for its mansions that look like stars in the sky.[17]

Cities were also famous in and beyond al-Andalus for their fine products made of wood, marble, ivory, leather, textiles, and precious metals. Cordova was famous for its leather shoes, jackets, belts, shields, bookbindings, and boxes, and for the clear white and reddish-brown marble cut in its mountains.[18] The musical instruments and fine steel tools of Seville were noted. Málaga was renowned for its admirable gilded pottery[19] and multicolor silk vestments bordered with gold.[20] These beautiful garments, sold to rulers and notables for thousands of dinars, were also produced in Almería and Murcia.[21] Almería was also known for its superior *dībāj* (silk embroidery),[22] for its iron tools, copper, and glassware.[23] Glassware was also produced in Murcia.[24] Valencia excelled in its brocades.[25]

Medieval authors were quite justified in singling out the artistic talents, skills, and urbanity of the Andalusians. Although many works of art and architecture have vanished, the few remaining provide eloquent testimony to the artistic and architectural genius of the Andalusians. In spite of the fact that their works contain various foreign elements and bear great similarity to Islamic models, they possess individuality, and a unique style known as "Hispano-Mauresque."[26] Architecture found its best expression in mosques, palaces, and towers. Although many great monuments have been ravaged by time, the remains constitute great tourist attractions. Among these are the Great Mosque of Cordova, the Alcázar and the Giralda in Seville, the Generalife and the Alhambra in Granada. These monuments were built in different periods, but they preserve a continuity of architecture from the eighth to the fourteenth century. These, among others, exerted a great influence on both Spanish and European architecture. In Spain especially, this architectural tradition continued through the Muslim presence in al-Andalus and was carried on by Mozarabs and Mudejars, who built churches, palaces, and houses for their Christian contemporaries. In the minor arts, al-Andalus produced beautiful pieces in metal, leather, textile, ivory, and wood — all decorated profusely with intricate designs and motifs drawn from the fauna and flora of the country.

The use of Arabic calligraphy was perhaps one of the most outstanding artistic features. Arabic inscriptions were drawn from the Qur'ān, the Traditions, wisdom literature, and poetry. Bearing the name of the craftsman and the owner, these inscriptions in intricate, fanciful Arabic script appeared on buildings, tiles, pottery, ivory, silver, gold, brass, and textiles. Although human representations were frowned upon, they were frequently used in paintings. Hunting scenes, musicians, flowers, fruits, birds, and animals were also depicted often. Mosaics were widely used in mosques, palaces, and bathhouses. They included floral motifs, river landscapes, vases, trees, birds, and animals. Painting was also used for illustrating books. This practice led to the "art of the book," which included profuse illustrations of the fables of *Kalīlah wa-Dimnah*, the *Maqāmāt* of al-Ḥarīrī, *De Materia Medica* of Dioscorides, and other works.[27] Many of these items were not only marketed throughout the Mediterranean basin, but they were also closely copied in other countries.

Although painting and sculpture were by and large limited in Islamic society, Muslim artisans and craftsmen excelled in other areas. They were great carvers and engravers, indulging in lavish ornamentation which was considered to be "the outstanding minor art evolved by Muslim genius."[28] Gold, silver, bronze, copper, brass, iron, and steel were used for manufacturing a great variety of objects. Gold and silver was demanded for decorating thrones and for amulets, necklaces, earrings, bracelets, caskets, inkstands, birds, figurines, and jewel cases. Inlaying designs, consisting of Arabic inscriptions and geometric and floral patterns, were used profusely. Iron was used for swords and other implements, and bronze for sculpture of lions, gazelles, and other animals. "In Venice Muslim metal works inspired native craftsmen so profoundly that a distinct Venetian Oriental school arose in which Muslim technique and designs were adapted to Italian Renaissance taste."[29] Woodwork had its finest expression in the construction of the *minbar* (pulpit), *miḥrāb* (prayer niche), carved ceilings, doors, windows, boxes, and furniture; the wood was often inlaid with ivory. From earthenware came profusely painted jars, dishes, cups, and tiles. Glassware ornamented with colored enamel, foliage, and inscriptions was formed into bottles, vases, lamps, bowls, and other items. Ivory carved and engraved with intricate birds, animals, scrolls, and Arabic inscriptions was used for rectangular or cylindrical caskets, boxes, and jewel cases. This ornamentation flourished in Cordova during the tenth century and was much in vogue in Spain, Sicily, and Egypt.

Textile industries, especially silk factories, were abundant in various cities; brightly colored materials carried various geometric figures and intricate birds, animals, and foliage. Embroidery (*ṭirāẓ*) was perhaps the best form of textile decoration. It was used for silken garments worn by rulers and notables. The profuse decoration included Arabic inscriptions in gold and silver thread. Wool carpets were also made in al-Andalus, but they never surpassed those manufactured in the East. Textiles found ample market in the Mediterranean basin; their impact on Europe is attested by Arabic terms in Western languages, such as *grenadine* from Granada.[30] Book decoration and binding flourished with elaborate designs; gold tooling and lettering were impressed upon books by means of metal dies.[31] Finally, the astrolabe, of Greek invention, was adopted by the Muslims and used for nautical observations and determining the hour of prayer. Manufactured widely and engraved with skill and care, it became important not only for its utility but for its beauty.

Illustrations of Andalusian crafts should give an idea about their individuality. This individuality in the minor arts can also be seen in the architecture. No doubt, it owes its raison d'être to Islam, a religion that moved from desert surroundings at first to urban and sophisticated centers. This change can be seen in the evolution of the mosque, considered the base of Muslim architecture. The mosque, which has been the center for religious, social, and educational activities of Muslims throughout the centuries, evolved from a simple square enclosure with an almost barren interior to an architectural complex attractive both internally and externally. Some of its major features — such as an open court (*ṣaḥn*) surrounded by arcades, *minbar*, screens of wood (*maqṣūrah*), *miḥrāb* indicating the direction to Mecca, minarets, domes, interior columns, colorful mosaics, and windows of colored glass — were refined as time went on. These developments took place in the East; they appear in full splendor in the Dome of the Rock in Jerusalem and in the Great Umayyad Mosque at Damascus. These two mosques were erected in the seventh and eighth centuries, respectively. They increased in sophistication and artistry, becoming the models of mosques everywhere in the Muslim world, including al-Andalus.

An early mosque, perhaps the best representative of those in Andalusia, is the Great Mosque of Cordova.[32] Al-Maqqarī[33] supplies a large number of quotations from his predecessors admired the mosque as the best and the greatest ever built. To them, its beauty was so dazzling that it defied any description. Its construction was begun by ʻAbd al-Raḥmān I in 786 on the site of the Church of St. Vincent. The land was bought for ten thousand dinars.[34] It was originally a simple rectangular structure consisting of a roofed section for prayer and an open court containing trees and surrounded by arcades. Its marble columns were linked by horseshoe arches.

From a rather modest building, the Great Mosque was enlarged, improved, and beautified in the ninth and tenth centuries and became a large and complex structure. One of the successors of 'Abd al-Raḥmān provided it with a section for women. 'Abd al-Raḥmān II added two aisles to the existing nine. 'Abd al-Raḥmān III and his immediate successors introduced major alterations. In 950, he ordered the construction of a new minaret, 80 yards high, and enlarged the mosque. Al-Ḥakam II enlarged it further, built a dome for the *miḥrāb*, and placed the *minbar* near it. He brought water to the mosque in canals made of stone, and on the west side he erected a house for the distribution of alms (*dār al-ṣadāqah*). Other houses for the poor were located in front of the west wing.[35] Ibn Abī 'Āmir added eight arcades and employed Christian captives to carry stones from their destroyed churches on their shoulders.[36]

In its final shape, the mosque contained the finest artistic expressions of the Andalusians. Some say it had 360 arches, each receiving the rays of the sun every day of the year.[37] It had 1,445 lamps and 224 candlesticks.[38] One of its copper chandeliers held 1,000 lights. It had 1,293 marble columns supporting its roofs.[39] Its many ample doors were covered with finely decorated copper.[40] The *maqṣūrah*, a compartment screened with wood — 56 yards long, 22 yards wide, and 8 yards high — had three profusely decorated doors,[41] one made of gold. Also of gold were the walls of the *miḥrāb*,[42] which was 8 yards long, 7½ yards wide, and 13½ yards high.[43] Its *minbar* was carved from teak and ebony;[44] and its minaret reached 108 feet high with two staircases, one for ascending and the other for descending. During the time of Ibn Abī 'Āmir, 159 persons were required to run and maintain it.[45] It is said that it housed an 'Uthmānī copy of the Qur'ān.

The Great Mosque of Cordova was the major religious and educational center.[46] It became the model for Andalusian and North African mosques and came to influence the architecture of the Christian churches.[47] Many cities of al-Andalus attempted to emulate the mosque and monuments of the capital city under the Umayyads. A large number of mosques appeared in each of the major cities: Seville,[48] Toledo, Tudela, Valencia, Saragossa, Badajoz, Granada, Almería, Murcia, and others. All of those mosques were either pillaged and destroyed or converted into Christian churches and monasteries. The Great Mosque of Cordova was converted into the Church of Santa María right after the conquest of the city by Fernando II in 1236. However, proper care was taken to preserve its beauty. In 1263, Alfonso X ordered all the Moorish servants in Cordova to work two days every year in the Mosque so that nothing pertaining to it might suffer damage or destruction. Queen Isabella would not allow a part of it to be demolished so that a cathedral could be erected on its site as the clergy insisted. As a compromise, Charles V allowed a chapel to be built in the center in 1523, a decision which he regretted when he saw the building. With neglect, the building lost much of its grace and beauty. In the nineteenth century, Spanish authorities ordered that the Mosque become a national monument, and have kept it fairly well as a tourist attraction. The chapel also remains; it is misplaced in time and space, and does a gross injustice to the Mosque.

Al-Andalus was also famous for its secular buildings, inspiring many poets to describe their dazzling beauty.[49] In addition to military architecture, consisting of fortresses and huge walls around the cities for protection, there were abundant bridges, canals, promenades, and resorts.[50] But the most refined feature of this secular architecture can be found in the palaces and castles.[51] The palaces were quite numerous in Cordova, as elsewhere in al-Andalus. The most glorious examples were al-Zahrā' and al-Zāhirah,[52] which can actually be called government cities. Their beauty and magnificence dazzled the imagination of medieval authors.

The construction of al-Zahrā' was begun in 936 by ʻAbd al-Raḥmān III, who spent one-third of the state budget on public construction.[53] He chose a site northwest of Cordova on the slope of the Sierra Morena overlooking the Guadalquivir River. He reportedly named it al-Zahrā' after a favorite concubine.[54] It consisted of several palaces, a mosque, gardens, a zoo, a compound for birds, and a number of manufacturies for weapons and tools. It took some twenty-five years to complete the complex, rightly referred to as a city (*madīnah*). We are told that ʻAbd al-Raḥmān used some 10,000 workers, some 1,500 beasts of burden, and some 6,000 carved stones every day during its construction and spent some 300,000 dinars per year.[55] White marble was brought from Almería, and rose and green marble from Carthage. Engraved basins were brought from Constantinople and Syria. The tiles of the roofs were covered with gold and silver, and water was brought to it from the neighboring mountains.

It was richly decorated with colorful paintings, carved wood, and floral and geometric designs. It contained twelve busts of animals and birds made of gold and decorated with precious stones. It had a number of spacious halls and conference rooms. One of these rooms (*majlis*) was provided with pure crystals, which, when lit by the sun-rays, produced a rainbow. It had eight doors of ivory and ebony inlaid with gold and jewels.

Al-Zāhirah[56] was built by Ibn Abī ʻĀmir al-Manṣūr to equal or even surpass al-Zahrā'. Al-Manṣūr ordered its construction in 368/979 and completed it within two years. Having provided it with several palaces, gardens, shops, and mosques, he moved into it with his family, entourage, and government ministries. He gave land in fief in the surrounding area to his viziers, secretaries, generals, and other partisans — all of whom built ostentatious mansions. The complex was so much the center of activities that people competed with each other to live around it.

However, the gorgeous palaces of al-Zahrā' and al-Zāhirah were not destined to endure. They were pillaged and destroyed by mobs during the great rebellion (*fitnah*) of 1010, and only scattered sections remain. After the fall of the Umayyads in 1031, the party-kings as well as the Almoravids and Almohads tried to capture their magnificence and built palaces that were equal in splendor to those of the great Umayyad rulers. Meanwhile, the Mozarabs and Mudejars who fell under Christian rule continued the architectural traditions in churches, mansions, and palaces.

Al-Zahrā' and al-Zāhirah were not the only notable palaces in al-Andalus. Among the extant ones are the Alcázar of Seville and the Alhambra of Granada — the most beautiful remaining monuments of al-Andalus. The Alcázar was built under the Almohads at the turn of the twelfth century. It was altered and restored by Mudejar architects, ultimately becoming the palace of Pedro the Cruel in 1353. Among its beautiful features are colorful mosaics, marbled columns, profuse decorations, and abundant Arabic inscriptions. Its many beautiful halls and chambers include the Hall of Ambassadors, the Maiden's Court (Patio de las Doncellas), and the Dolls' Court (Patio de las Muñecas). The Alcazar is surrounded by well-kept gardens which abound in orange and lemon trees and the fragrance of jasmine and other flowers.

Equaling it in splendor and majesty is the Giralda Tower, also in Seville. A product of the Almohads, it took about twenty-five years to complete (1172–1195), and served at first as a minaret and observatory. It is 300 feet tall and has a base of 43 square feet. It originally had four copper spheres on top which could be seen from miles away. An earthquake demolished them and a *giraldillo* pointing to the direction of the wind was erected in their place in 1568. It is now a cathedral tower from which one can contemplate a panoramic view of Seville and the Guadalquivir River.

The culmination of Hispano-Arabic architecture was reached with the Alhambra[57] built by the Naṣrid dynasty. The Alhambra is one of the few monuments which escaped wanton destruction and the erosion of the elements. It may be seen erect and graceful on a hilly terrace southeast of Granada. The site was originally a fortress called *al-Ḥamrā'* (The Red). Its construction was started by the first Naṣrid ruler, Muḥammad Ibn al-Aḥmar (1232–1272). Originally it must have been a modest palace, but in the course of time it was enlarged and embellished to become the permanent residence of the Naṣrid dynasty until its fall in 1492. A government city in the manner of al-Zahrā' and al-Zāhirah, it was surrounded by vast walls flanked by towers. It was supplied with running water. A number of palaces around courtyards, linked by corridors, join the main palace. Some of the gorgeous parts of the Alhambra are the Hall of Abencerrajes, the Hall of the Two Sisters, the Court of the Myrtles, the Court of Lions, and the Hall of Ambassadors, overlooking the Generalife. The interior is profusely decorated with geometric figures, floral motifs, paintings of hunting scenes, and Arabic inscriptions in beautiful Kufi and Nashki scripts. Some of the inscriptions consist of panegyric verses of the fourteenth-century poet-statesman Ibn Zamrak. Not too far from it to the northwest is the beautiful palace of the Generalife surrounded by a garden appropriately called the "Architect's Paradise" (*Jannat al-'arīf*, Sp. *Generalife*).

The Alhambra is still one of the great architectural monuments of the world and represents the nature of Andalusian genius and culture. "And so Naṣrid art has left us the chef d'oeuvre of its classical age, the greatest testimony of its architecture and art decoration. And the Alhambra has naturally become nothing less than a place of pilgrimage for all who wish to know, and for all who love, the arts of Spanish Islam in their final flourishing."[58]

To the visual arts, may be added singing and music, in which the Andalusians displayed great interest. The Arabic word *mūsīqā* is of Greek origin; yet Arabic music developed an individuality that differentiates it from Western music.[59] Like other artistic and intellectual manifestations, it had its roots in the Near East, owing much of its practical and theoretical aspects to Persia, Byzantium, and Greece. In fact, a number of Greek works bearing on music were translated into Arabic and became objects of study and commentary among Muslim scholars.

No doubt music and its ancillary fields have formed an integral part of the social life of various peoples throughout the ages. In pre-Islamic times, Arabic women sang war songs and laments; they were accompanied by instrumentalists at nuptials, festivals, and other occasions. The lute, reed pipe, vertical flute, drum, tambourine, and other instruments were in use. These musical traditions survived to Islamic times, were enriched by new techniques, and enjoyed great popularity among the nobility and the common people. However, it seems paradoxical that a popular and flourishing art should have been considered unpraiseworthy in Islamic tradition. In this connection, it is not clear whether the censure of music can be attributed to Muḥammad himself, or to his followers who were jealous of their roles as torchbearers of social values and public morality. Traditions are contradictory with respect to the nature, lawfulness, or unlawfulness of music and singing. Some praise such pursuits, while others condemn them on the ground that they disturb the mind and dissipate the emotions. Some of the traditions which consider listening to music unlawful are:[60] "Iblis [Satan] was the first who wailed and the first who sang"; "No one lifts up his voice in singing, but Allah sends to him two devils to his shoulders"; "Music and singing cause hypocrisy to grow in the heart as water makes corn grow." Still another tradition asserts that singing girls and stringed instruments are signs of the end of the world and the most powerful means by which the devil seduces men.

On the other hand, music and singing had their strong advocates according to certain traditions which condone the playing of instruments and singing. One tradition says: "Allah has not sent a prophet except with a beautiful voice." This notwithstanding, legists decided that music in its various aspects is undesirable, and instituted stringent measures against its practitioners. Musicians were denied ordinary justice in courts and regarded as unfit witnesses. Musical instruments were not considered property and as such their theft would not — as in other cases — be punishable by amputation of the hand.

This seemingly contradictory situation conforms to historical reality with respect to attitudes and practice. At an early stage, Muslim authors tried to explain this conflict or reconcile the contradiction. Western Muslim authors — Ibn 'Abd Rabbihi of Cordova and Ibn Khaldūn of Tunis, among others — concerned themselves with both the negative and positive attitudes toward singing and music and their practice. Ibn 'Abd Rabbihi, in *The Unique Necklace*, says that it would be distasteful not to include the art of singing in a book containing all the arts, wisdom sayings, anecdotes, and proverbs.[61] He gives the pros and cons for the permissibility of singing and music from a wide range of people — religious men, philosophers, physicians, rulers, and others. He says:

People had opposing views concerning singing; the majority of the people of Ḥijāz condoned it while the majority of the 'Irāqis disapproved it. Those who condoned it argue that its source lies in poetry which was allowed by the Prophet, may peace be upon him, who urged people to use it, eulogized his companions with it, and armed himself with it against the polytheists . . ."[62]

. . . And those who disapprove of singing argue that it shatters the heart, disturbs the mind, makes the forebearing light-witted, leads to pasttime, incites the people to excitement (*ṭarab*), and for this reason, it is false from the outset."[63]

This notwithstanding, Ibn 'Abd Rabbihi appears to be more inclined to favor singing and music, as evidenced by his numerous quotations praising those arts. In fact, a full section is devoted to the praise of the lute (*'ūd*) and includes some of his own poems.[64] Ample space is given to statements supporting a beautiful voice: "Physicians claim that a beautiful voice flows into the body and runs into the veins making the heart limpid and happy, the soul cheerful, the limbs shaky, the movements soft . . .[65] Even the beasts take delight in a beautiful voice and know its excellence."[66]

Centuries later, Ibn Khaldūn wrote that the arts of singing and music are concerned with the setting of poems to music.[67] Moreover, he includes music among the sciences.[68] One of the reasons he gives for Muslim concern with singing and music is the fear of confounding Qur'ānic cantilation, which has certain fixed rules not allowing for melodies.[69] In addition, the recitation of the Qur'ān is an occasion of reverence and awe incompatible with the pleasure and amusement produced by singing and music.[70] However, a beautiful voice is highly desirable for the recitation of the Qur'ān in addition to proper articulation and enunciation of letters.[71]

In spite of legal restrictions on and religious ambivalence, music and singing became part and parcel of entertainment at all levels of society. They were cultivated widely in both the Eastern and Western Muslim world. War, battle, and love songs were sung and were accepted, however grudgingly, by the religious scholars. Music, singing, and dancing became common features at festivals, weddings, births, and circumcisions. Even the spiritual effects of music were widely recognized among the mystics, who came to accept music as an elixir and a means to ecstasy. The great Egyptian mystic

Dhu-l-Nūn says "Listening (*al-samā'*) is a divine influence which stirs the heart to see Allah; those who listen to it spiritually attain to Allah; and those who listen to it sensually fall into heresy."[72]

Rulers in both East and West vied for the best talents in these areas, and musicians, singers and dancers — male and female — became an integral part of court entourage. They had great passion for music and singing, patronized them, and encouraged their study. It is perhaps for these reasons and out of a natural attraction to music and singing that the study of music was allowed at the practical and theoretical levels. There emerged an abundant literature which dealt with the various aspects of music and singing and its leading figures. The lexicographer al-Khalīl b. Aḥmad (d. 791) is credited with two works, the *Kitāb al-nagham* (*The Book of Notes*)[73] and the *Kitāb al-iqā'* (*The Book of Rhythm*).[74] The philosopher al-Kindī wrote seven treatises on arrangement of notes, rhythm, composition, introduction to the art of music, art of lute, and so forth.[75] He was followed by his able pupil al-Sarakhsī, who is credited with a number of treatises. The great philosopher al-Fārābī was an able instrumentalist as well as a theorist of music. He was able to play the lute in such a manner as to cast his hearers into a fit of laughter or draw tears from their eyes.[76] He wrote three works on music. These men were followed by al-Rāzī, Ibn Sīnā, the Brethren of Purity, and others who considered music one of the sciences and wrote numerous works about it. In addition, Abū Faraj al-Iṣfahānī wrote his famous *Book of Songs*[77] in twenty-one volumes which reached al-Andalus before its circulation in the East. Although these authors were inspired by Greek music as learned in translation, they were also concerned with the various musical instruments. All of these preoccupations became known to the Andalusians, who, in turn, emulated and assimilated the musical lore of the East. Moreover, leading Eastern instrumentalists, singers, and dancers were known to the Andalusians. There was the Meccan Siyyāṭ (d. 785), a famous singer and lute player, who left an array of pupils — Ibrāhīm and Isḥāq al-Mawṣili, Ibn Jāmi', al-Ḥakam al-Wādī (d. ca. 800) — all of whom were accomplished singers and musicians.

By and large the musical traditions of the East passed on to al-Andalus and became part of the culture in spite of the avowed conservatism and protest of the religious scholars. The Andalusians loved poetry, songs, music, and dancing. These arts suited their temperament and permeated their lives.

As among the 'Abbāsids in the East, the Andalusian rulers introduced singers, musicians, and dancers into their courts. At first, they imported both male and female singers and dancers from the East. The Eastern singers 'Alwan and Zarqūn[78] entered al-Andalus during the reign of the emir al-Ḥakam I and were followed by others. Among the female singers was Faḍl al-Madīnah, originally from al-Andalus, who received her musical training in Baghdād and Medina. The songstress Qamar was brought from Baghdād[79] and became famous for composing melodies at the court of Seville.

But the most important emigré was 'Alī Ibn Nāfi', known as Ziryāb (789–857).[80] He was probably a client (*mawlā*) who was brought up and educated in Baghdād. According to Ibn 'Abd Rabbihi,[81] he was a black slave of the famous musician Ibrāhīm al-Mawṣilī, the leading musician of the day, who trained him in the arts of music and singing. He was so gifted that his special talents attracted the attention of the caliph Hārūn al-Rashīd (786–808), who requested Isḥāq al-Mawṣilī to have Ziryāb perform for him. We are told[82] that the caliph was so pleased that his master became jealous and advised Ziryāb in unmistakable terms either to leave the country immediately and settle in a distant land or to remain and suffer anguish and enmity. The story has an element of exaggeration, and Ziryāb's departure may have been prompted by the unsettled conditions during the civil wars between the brothers al-Amīn (808–813) and al-Ma'mūn (813–833). At any rate, he left for North Africa, where he spent some time in Qayrawān at the court of the Aghlabid ruler Ziyādat Allah I (816–837). Here Ziryāb is said to have incurred the displeasure of the ruler, to have been whipped and given three days to leave the country.[83] However, the displeasure may have been caused by Ziryāb's decision to go to al-Andalus at the invitation of al-Ḥakam I.

Ziryāb travelled with his family to Algeciras and had reached al-Andalus in 822 when his patron-to-be died. However, he was received by a delegation sent by the new emir 'Abd al-Raḥmān II. His arrival coincided with the inauguration of this ruler, who bestowed a furnished mansion and expensive gifts. He also gave Ziryāb a salary of 200 dinars per month, and 20 dinars to each of his four sons, a bonus of 3,000 dinars a year, and 500 to 1,000 dinars for special religious festivals. Ziryāb's influence at the court grew rapidly, and he was soon one of the ruler's favorites. Ziryāb became the boon-companion of his patron, and introduced new fashions in hair styles, culinary arts, table etiquette, and dresses for every season and occasion. However, Ziryāb's greatest talent lay in singing, playing the lute, and instructing and training students. He is credited with knowing one thousand songs from memory. He composed numerous songs and claimed that the *jinn* (spirits) had inspired them at night. As an instrumentalist, he excelled at the *'ūd* (lute), which he improved by adding a fifth string. The color of the string was red, representing the soul, and was placed between the second and third strings.[84] He also used plectras which were made of eagles' talons rather than those hitherto made of less durable wood; this innovation assured longer life to the strings and improved the tone.

Perhaps Ziryāb's greatest contribution to the art of music was in the field of instruction. He founded a conservatory of music in Cordova, the first of its kind. He introduced a curriculum consisting of three stages: first, the study of rhythm, meter, and words of songs taught to the accompaniment of musical instruments; second, the mastery of melody; and third, an introduction to *zā'idah* (gloss). He had an ingenious method of training singers. He would have the student sit down on a round cushion and make him use the full power of his voice. If he found that the voice of the student was weak, he would tie a turban around the waist to increase the voice. If the student stammered or clenched his teeth, Ziryāb would put in his mouth a small piece of wood in order to expand his jaws, and he would then order him to utter certain words, which if done clearly would gain admission for the student.[85] It was in this conservatory that a great number of students, including his concubine Mut'ah and his daughter Ḥamdunah, were trained who became famous for their singing, dancing, and musical compositions.[86]

Ziryāb's position was so high that he was able to accumulate a fortune valued at some 300,000 dinars in addition to several villages that were given to him in fief. His affluence aroused the resentment of poets and religious men alike, for different reasons. This notwithstanding, his influence on the taste of Cordova was felt strongly and spread to the capital cities of the provinces and eventually to North Africa.

The musical legacy of Ziryāb was kept alive by his pupils who were natives of al-Andalus. Thus, from the ninth century onward, the Andalusians began to make their own contributions to the field of singing and music. Ibn Firnās (d. 888) is said to have been the first teacher of music in al-Andalus. He was followed by a group of teachers who dealt with the theoretical and practical aspects of music. We owe to Ibn 'Abd Rabbihi[87] a collection of songs. He was followed by Yaḥyā al-Khudujj of Murcia (twelfth century) who wrote a *Book of Songs*.[88] Ibn Fatḥūn (eleventh century) wrote treatises on music,[89] as did his near contemporary Ṣā'id of Toledo. Perhaps the greatest musical theorist of al-Andalus was the philosopher Ibn Bājjah, whose book on music was "as popular in the Maghrib as was that of al-Fārābī in the East."[90] He was followed by Averroës and by the two great Andalusian mystics, Ibn 'Arabī and Ibn Sab'īn, who dealt with some aspects of music.

Cities prided themselves in possessing the arts of music, singing, and dancing. Seville became famous as the center of music and the major producer of musical instruments. Al-Shaqundī[91] recognizes this fact as the major merit or wonder of Seville and gives an impressive list of musical instruments manufactured there. Among these instruments[92] disseminated throughout al-Andalus, some of which found their way into Europe, are:

al-khayyāl
al-karrij (Sp. *carrigo*)
'ūd (Sp. *laud*, Eng. *lute*)
rūta (Sp. *rota*)
rabāb (Sp. *rabeb*, Eng. *rebec*)
qānūn (Sp. *arpa*, a string instrument resembling the harp)
mūnis
kanīra (Sp. *citara*)
qitār (Sp. *guitarra*, Eng. *guitar*)
zulāmī (a woodwind instrument)
shagira (Sp. *flauta*, some sort of organ)
nūra (Sp. *flauta*)
būq (Sp. *albogue*, trumpet of copper)
duff (Sp. *adufe*, tambourine)
aqwāl (Sp. *tambor*)
jarā (Sp. *citela*)
abū qarūn
dabdaba
ḥamāqī

Likewise, al-Shaqundī singles out Ubeda, a town near Jaén famed for its places of entertainment and for its dancers, who are the best female manipulators of swords.[93]

In sum, music, singing, and dancing were widespread both in high circles and among the general populace. These arts were so deep rooted that the judge Ibn al-'Arabī of Seville defended music against the strictures of the religious scholars. More significantly still, it was in al-Andalus that popular poetry as embodied in the *zajal* and *muwashshaḥāt* was set to music and sung in all places and for every occasion.

20

Aljamiado Literature

DURING the progress of the Reconquista from the late eleventh century onward, bilingualism in al-Andalus became less prevalent, with Romance gradually displacing Arabic at the spoken and written levels. Thus, the military conquest of Christians was followed by a linguistic conquest of the Arabic-speaking population. It was natural for the Mozarabs, the arabized Christians, to make a rapid adjustment to the language of their conquering coreligionists. The same could not be said of the Mudejars, Muslims living under Christian rule. Their adjustment to the status of a subject people with the fresh memories of their political, military, and intellectual ascendance was not easy. As their hopes of regaining their pre-eminent role in the affairs of al-Andalus became dimmer, they had to resign themselves. Although they enjoyed a modicum of tolerance at first because of their number, skill, and know-how, they became in the course of time the object of intolerance and abuse. In the process and in spite of their bitter opposition and disappointment, they became gradually romanized until they possessed only vague memories of their past. The hope for a day of deliverance from their Christian masters came to an end with the fall of Granada in 1492. The Inquisition could not tolerate them unless they became Christians. Many were forced to acquiesce, while others secretly remained Muslims but outwardly were Christians. They were known as Moriscos who were despised and distrusted. They were forbidden to speak Arabic in public, to continue their customs, and to practice their religion.

It was under these circumstances that the Mudejars and Moriscos wrote *aljamiado* literature[1] in the language they knew best, a Spanish dialect, using Islamic themes concerned with the religion and the heroic deeds of their ancestors. Probably this literature was written by religious scholars and teachers whose aim was to keep alive the great traditions of Islam. In this connection, a religious scholar complains that his coreligionists were forced to use the language of their Christian enemies because they no longer remembered Arabic or knew much about their religious obligations unless they were stated in a foreign language.[2] This is further corroborated by Rabadan, a Morisco emigré to North Africa, who in 1603 wrote a book in Spanish dialect explaining the Islamic doctrine to his fellow Moriscos exiled in North Africa. The following pages survey the writings of the Moriscos which are known as *aljamiado* or *aljamía* in the hope that insight will thereby be gained into their attitudes and intellectual perspective.

The Spanish term *aljamiado* or *aljamía* is a corruption of the Arabic *'ajamiyyah*, meaning "foreign." In general, the Arabic expression *'ajam* and its derivative *'ajamiyyah* were applied to people of non-Arabic ancestry. In its present connotation, *aljamiado* is that literature written by Moriscos in their own Spanish dialects — Castillian, Galician, Catalan, Aragonés, Portuguese, and others — using Arabic characters. *Aljamiado* literature represents an interesting development. It was written for the most part during the fifteenth and sixteenth centuries, when Arabic culture was in decline and when Muslims in the Iberian Peninsula were subjected to all sorts of restrictions and persecution. Judging by its religious overtones, *aljamiado* literature was written by staunch devotees to Islam who wanted to preserve their Islamic legacy and to teach it to those who had forgotten the Arabic language. It seems that they wrote in defiance of the stringent measures imposed upon them by the Spanish inquisitors.[3]

In spite of the lack of artistic value, vigor, and variety, *aljamiado* literature is significant not only for philological, sociological, religious, and psychological reasons, but for gaining insight into the intellectual perspective of a minority living in a hostile environment. It has a further importance as a link between Arabic writings and early Spanish literature, particularly with respect to a number of legends and stories which appear in both. As such, Gayangos, Saavedra, and Guillén Robles recognize its importance. Guillén Robles states that the linguist will find in it a good foundation for the formation of the Spanish language besides idiomatic expressions, expressive terms, and Arabic expressions used among the Spaniards; that the archaeologist will find enough data for explaining the symbols and mythology used among the Muslims; that the artist will find beautiful and original vestiges and even grandiose inspirations; and that the historian will find enough documentation for the understanding of the moral, religious, and the intellectual life of thousands of Spaniards over a long period of time.[4]

Aljamiado literature offers enormous possibilities for both the Arabist and the Hispanist. The Arabist will find in it not only the Arabic script but Arabic themes permeated by Islamic thought and Islamic beliefs. The Hispanist will find that the language of the Moriscos was Romance, which contains valuable data for gaining an insight into the phonetics, syntax, and morphology of Old Spanish or a dialect thereof.[5] Considering the adverse conditions under which the Moriscos lived and the peculiarity of the *aljamiado* literature, it is surprising that a large amount of that literature survives needing editing, transliteration, and analysis. One single item of a religious, novelistic, or legendary nature would constitute an interesting study not only linguistically but from the vantage point of its origin against a Christian-Islamic background. A most interesting aspect would be to determine the technique of translation from Arabic sources into *aljamiado*. On the basis of an examination of some manuscripts, it would seem that translations were, by and large, standardized in vocabulary and idioms. This implies that there was a school which prevailed and regulated translations. It is equally surprising that the Arabic system of transliteration was consistent and standardized, implying again a general consensus in the use of the Arabic script for writing in a Spanish dialect.[6]

When the Arabic script began to be used for writing in Romance cannot be determined with accuracy. Perhaps it began as early as the eleventh century among the Mozarabs and Jews, who like the Persians, and later the Turks, Afghani, and Muslim Indians, used it for writing in their own languages. (One should also mention the Jews who used the Hebrew script to write in Arabic, Spanish, or Yiddish.) But for the Moriscos, the Arabic script was perhaps associated with Islam and the great Arab past and, thus, was sacrosanct to them. As long as they had some traces of Islam, they must have received a rudimentary education in Arabic — mainly memorizing and reading the Qur'ān and some daily prayers. In Granada, in particular, where Arabization lingered after 1492, Christian doctrine had to be translated into Arabic.[7] To the north, however, they became more and more latinized until they had in all probability abandoned the use of Arabic, even Arabic script in some cases and used roman characters instead.[8]

But if they were forced to forget the language of their ancestors, they remained staunchly attached to their traditions and memories of the glorious past. The use of the Arabic script for writing in their own dialects symbolized something dear to their hearts and emotions in time of distress and grave injustice. In this way they could communicate among themselves without being subjected to the whims of the inquisitors, who forbade their possessing Arabic books, and to express their innermost thoughts concerning their beliefs and hopes. In fact, their libraries, which were often hidden, contained a good number of classical Arabic texts dealing with religious matters. In 1884, a large number of manuscripts were discovered when destroying or repairing a house in Almonacid de la Sierra in the province of Saragossa. They had been hidden by the erection of an artificial wooden ceiling. Many of the manuscripts were destroyed or burned by children, but the bulk was salvaged by Pablo Gil,[9] himself a collector of *aljamiado* texts.

It could be argued that the use of Arabic script for writing in a Spanish dialect would not only serve the purpose of educating the young people in the religion and mores of their ancestors, but would at the same time help to overcome the many obstacles in an intolerant environment. However great the limitations imposed on them, the Moriscos continued to concern themselves with Islamic themes using the Arabic script as the symbol of their identity. More often than not, texts of the Qur'ān and theological material appear in both Arabic and *aljamiado*, frequently side by side. This implies bilingualism and/or careful consideration for the original meaning. Moreover, that there were scholars among the Moriscos who knew Arabic well is attested by a number of works translated from Arabic into *aljamiado*. For instance, the book of the Eastern religious scholar al-Samarqandī[10] was translated into a Spanish dialect and must have been popular owing to its comprehensiveness on religious questions. The work was translated by an Aragonese Morisco in the sixteenth century and consists of some 330 folios and 96 chapters dealing with religious practices, law, and right conduct.[11] Quite significant is the translation of the Qur'ān, often by injecting the Spanish between lines of the Arabic text. Also historical[12] and juridical[13] works were committed into *aljamiado*.

It should be emphasized that the bulk of *aljamiado* literature has religious overtones and was mostly translating or paraphrasing of Arabic texts. Arabic themes were carefully chosen to fit into the perspective, emotional needs, and temperament of the Moriscos. Those themes were often elaborated and embellished and given an Andalusian setting, as is the case of the *Bath of Zarieb*.[14] The Moriscos also used themes from their Christian environment, such as the translation of *Paris and Viana*[15] from Spanish into *aljamiado*. Although most of the literature is in prose, there are a number of poems, such as the story of Joseph, the work of Muḥammad Rabadan, the poem in praise of the cloak of Muḥammad, and numerous poems expressing bitterness against their treatment by Christians. From the sizable number of manuscripts found in the Biblioteca Nacional and in the Biblioteca de la Junta of Madrid (the latter manuscripts are now in the Escuela de Estudios Arabes in Madrid), it is easy to ascertain that the Moriscos were first and foremost preoccupied with religious questions pertaining to the knowledge of Islam, beliefs and rituals, contracts, inheritance, marriage, divorce, reward for the faithful, and punishment of those who are removed from the true faith. There are abundant materials on orations and the manner of performing one's religious duties. In spite of the grave consequences, the Moriscos appear to have had an undaunted conviction in their Islamic faith. Not only did they expose themselves to the risk of practicing their faith, but they displayed considerable courage in refuting both Judaism and Christianity with all the passion of a devotee. That was not all. As far as the extant literature indicates, the Moriscos remained true to the historical traditions of Islam. Consequently, historical tracts, legends, and stories about prominent biblical and Islamic figures and major historical events were some of their major concerns. Some notions of medicine and astronomy as handed down from the great sages of the past were known, but they were intermingled with quackery, superstition, astrology, horoscopes, magic, and divination.[16] In sum, one may discern the following categories in *aljamiado* literature: religious and juridical texts; history, legends, and polemics; and the ''sciences'' and miscellanea.

Religious and Juridical Texts

Of course, the Qur'ān was the most precious possession of the Moriscos. There are an enormous number of copies of it in the libraries of Spain, most of which belonged to Moriscos. An extant treatise[17] deals with the rewards accruing from reading, copying, and carrying certain verses of the Holy Book. More often than not, copies of the Arabic text of the Qur'ān contained annotations of various kinds — devotional items, exaltations at the excellence of the Qur'ān — all of which were written in a Spanish dialect.[18] Likewise, the Qur'ān was frequently translated into *aljamiado*, as were the attributes and excellent names of God.[19] Translations of the Qur'ān were ordinarily interlinear, with the *aljamiado* text above or beneath the Arabic original. Commentaries of some chapters of the Qur'ān were also made.[20] Next in importance to the Qur'ān were certain Prophetic Traditions and a large number of catechisms (devocionario).[21] One treatise[22] is meant to guide the ignorant to the true faith, to show him the best way of serving God, practicing what is lawful, and avoiding the unlawful. Another treatise[23] urges the faithful to comply with his religious duties for which he will attain eternal rewards, but includes extraneous items such as the seasons of the year, prescriptions, and medical advice taken from the works of Galen, Hippocrates, al-Rāzī, and Ibn Sīnā. There are other catechisms. The *Devocionario morisco*[24] contains formulas with respect to the unity of God as demonstrated by Qur'ānic verses, the beautiful names of God, exaltation of God and praise of Muḥammad and a number of biblical figures, formulas used before and after eating, performance of ablution, and praise of the Qur'ān. The *Devocionario musulman*[25] is similar, but also includes a poem in praise of the *Burdah* (cloak) of Muḥammad. This poem was composed by the thirteenth-century al-Būṣīrī (d. 1294)[26] and became popular and the object of commentaries.[27] The *Devocionario* also contains thanks for the revelations handed down by the angel Gabriel to Muḥammad, famous orations, praises of the Prophet, and prayers for seeking help. In the field of religious practices[28] there are directions on how to perform prayers, ablutions, fasting, and how to know the tenets of Islam. A similar work[29] contains items on orations, Prophetic Traditions connected with rewards and punishment, advice, and two stories about the caliph 'Umar — when God made him see the souls of the dead, and when he was coverted to Islam.

But the most comprehensive work for the guidance of the faithful is the *Book of al-Samarqandī* already mentioned.[30] It deals with such problems as death in its frightening and fortifying aspects, confronting the Day of Judgment, how people look in Hell and Paradise, doing good deeds and avoiding bad ones; repentance; obedience due to parents, the rights of the son vis-à-vis the father, the rights of the neighbor; the bad things attending the drinking of wine, lies, and excessive laughter; virtue of silence and abstinence from worldly things; ablutions, prayers, and the fulfilment of other religious duties; treatment of captives and servants, piety, fear of God, wisdom, humility, the rights of husbands and wives, and so forth.

The Mufti of Segovia wrote a work that became known as the *Book of Segovia* (*Alquiteb segoviano*).[31] It is a treatise of moral and legal precepts, enumerating the religious duties of a Muslim. In the prologue the author states that he wrote the book in the language of the infidels for the simple reason that Moriscos had forgotten the language of their ancestors. Finally, two more works should be mentioned here. The first[32] contains traditions about the birth of Muḥammad and his revelations, and traditions about Abraham, Moses, and others. It also includes an essay about Islam and the opinion of the jurist Mālik on the fundamentals of Islam. The other work[33] is meant as a cure for the soul to love the Hereafter and abhor this world.

Although the above-mentioned works refer to legal questions pertaining to the religious duties expected of a Muslim, one cannot overlook the *Juridical Treatise*,[34] which summarizes all the duties and obligations of a Muslim to his Creator and fellow men. The work, which is quite comprehensive, gives minute details on what to do in case of an emergency during prayer (for instance, if the nose bleeds); it also supplies information about the amount of the almsgiving (*zakāh*) and the manner of doing it, whether in cattle, silver, or gold; it has sections on loans, sales, and other transactions.

History, Legends, and Polemics

History and legends could hardly be separated from the religious writings, and in fact, they constitute an integral part of them. On the basis of the extant literature, the Moriscos seem to have lost a secular historical consciousness. The great moments of the Islamic past appear to be unknown to them. This was due in great measure to their deficient education and to the stringent measures imposed on them by their Christian peers. Instead, their historical consciousness was limited to Islam the religion, Islamic and biblical figures, traditions, apologetics, and legends.

However, those historico-legendary writings derived for the most part from Arabic are both entertaining and moralizing. Invariably, they point to the adversity and ultimate triumph of the true religion, Islam, over evildoers and idolatry; to the miraculous feats of Muḥammad; to the role of the angel Gabriel, who always appears to Muḥammad in times of crises and helps rescue the Muslims from evil men and demons. Muḥammad's birth, his revelations, deeds, and sayings, and his ascension to the seven heavens (*mi'rāj*)[35] permeate *aljamiado* literature. His son-in-law 'Alī emerges as the personification of chivalry and heroism; he defeats the great champions of his day and often single-handedly defeats thousands of men.[36] Muḥammad depended on him heavily whenever the Muslims were overwhelmed by powerful forces.[37] There is also 'Umar, the staunch supporter and companion of Muḥammad, who was known for his austerity and stern justice.[38] Pre-Islamic figures were singled out either for their evil deeds or for their virtues and religiosity;[39] in fact, a considerable part of the pseudohistorical writings consist of legends and stories around them. The story of Alexander the Great,[40] containing his legendary and extraordinary deeds, was translated from Arabic into *aljamiado* and seems to have enjoyed great popularity among the Moriscos.

Alexander, known to the Arabs as Dhu-l-Qarnayn (The Two-Horned One),[41] was endowed with great power. He was a man of great courage, a founder of a vast empire, and builder of bridges, palaces, and great walls. His prowess and saga were known to Greeks, Christians, and Muslims. He was a man who wrestled with the question of good and evil, and emerged as the arbiter of goodness, punishing the evildoers and rewarding the righteous ones. He is pictured as a believer who performed great deeds and defeated the mischievous Gog and Magog, who were half human and half beast. He was an invincible hero who was magnanimous to friends and stern with enemies. In his childhood, the devil tried to poison him but failed. He was educated by Aristotle, who taught him the merit of love and sweetness. He was thus able to conquer many nations and subjected the people to the belief in one God. After many astonishing successes, the angel of death surprises the great hero, who surrenders to him realizing, perhaps, the transitory character of human power.

No less interesting and popular is the legend of Joseph,[42] which survives in both prose and verse. The story is based on the biblical account, but inspired by the Qur'ānic version,[43] which had been elaborated and embellished by Muslim traditionists, commentators, and storytellers.

Joseph is portrayed as the personification of virtue and beauty. He was the favorite of his father Jacob, causing the envy of his brothers who threw him in a pit. The brothers disavowed any guilt, claiming that a wolf had devoured him. When Joseph was rescued by a caravan, the brothers claimed and sold him to the caravan people, who, in turn, sold him to a high official in Egypt. While his father grieved, Joseph endured hardship, but ultimately attained the highest success. At first, Zulaykhah, the wife of his master, made advances, and though he was inclined to respond, an angel appeared and rescued him. Angered by such rejection, Zulaykhah accused him of trying to dishonor her, and Joseph was imprisoned to be freed later on when the truth was unfolded. He became an influential figure at the court of the pharaoh, whom Joseph warned about seven years of abundance which would be followed by another seven years of drought. In the meantime, he finds

Zulaykhah, old and decrepit, begging for alms; he rejuvenates her to her former beauty and marries her. The rest of the story deals with the coming of his brothers to Egypt and eventual reunion of the family, including his father Jacob, who regained his sight after many years of blindness.

Although the stories of Alexander and Joseph have received ample attention by scholars, the same is not true of many other stories waiting critical edition, transliteration, and study with reference to their Islamic and non-Islamic backgrounds. Fortunately, in his *Leyendas Moriscas*, Guillén Robles made a popular transliteration of thirty-five stories from the collections of Don Pascual de Gayangos. References to those stories, conforming to Guillén Robles's arrangement, are made below with brief remarks about their nature and the message they try to convey.

Volume I of the *Leyendas* consists of ten stories which are devoted to pre-Islamic personalities. Three stories [44] deal with Christ: his birth, death, and the events of his time. They are significant in that they reveal the general attitude of the Muslims toward Christ.[45] His birth from the Virgin Mary, a beautiful and chaste woman, is a miracle. The angel Gabriel appears and breathes on her breast, thus causing his birth. His phenomenal birth was followed by numerous miracles and by an equally phenomenal death, but without the suffering and humiliation attributed to it by Christian traditions. Interestingly enough, Christ will appear on the Day of Judgment and fuse Christianity and Islam into a single religion — a hope the Moriscos entertained for coexistence with their Christian countrymen.

The story of Carcayona [46] reveals how the belief in one God led a beautiful girl from tragedy to ultimate happiness. It is a charming and moving novel that has great dramatic effect. Carcayona's father was a king and idol worshipper, and became infatuated with her. Her filial affection for him never diminished, but she was adamant about not giving in to her father's carnal desire. One day while she was worshipping the idol, she observed a dove on its head, commanding her to repeat the formula "there is no God but God." After an interesting dialogue in which the dove explained the Muslim doctrine with a full description of life in the Hereafter, the dove flew away and the idol fell into pieces. The girl found solace in the new belief to the great astonishment of her father, who insisted that she desist from such an unholy doctrine. When she refused to listen, he cut off her hands and sent her to a remote mountain where a deer conducted her to a cave and cared for her. Although disheartened, she never lost faith. One day a prince-hunter who had been chasing the deer appeared on the scene. Astonished at the sight of the beautiful girl, he inquired about her fate, fell in love with her, took her along to his kingdom, and married her against the vehement protest of the queen mother. They lived happily and had a child. However, the prince was compelled to go on a military expedition.

During his absence the queen mother plotted against the girl and sent her away with the child. Desperate and helpless, but remaining faithful to the belief in one God, she was cared for by the deer until one day God made her dream come true by returning her hands. Of course, her faith was reinforced. In the meantime her husband returned victorious from war and was informed that his wife had left him on her own. He set out in search of her and the deer led him to her again. Rejoiced at seeing her, they returned home; the queen mother was ordered to live in a distant palace, and the couple lived happily thereafter.

Although it does not conform wholly with the biblical account, the story of Job[47] relates in a colorful and poetical manner the place of Job among the people chosen by God. He is a prophet who endured great pains. Since he did not succeed in spreading God's message, he resorted to arms and subdued several tribes. After a life of great affluence, he became poor, desolate, and afflicted by horrible diseases to the point that he became an outcast cared for by his beautiful wife, who remained faithful and chaste. She is portrayed as the paragon of virtue and perfect spouse in spite of the persistent temptations of devils. In spite of his suffering and humiliation, Job remained faithful to God, who ultimately sends him the angel Gabriel. Gabriel submerges Job in a fountain of pure water and brings back his youth, health, and wealth.

From the vantage point of Moriscos living in a Christian environment, the story of a devout Muslim scholar[48] is both interesting and revealing. It relates how the pious life of the scholar was ruined by the charms of a Christian lady with whom he fell in love and ultimately married after she had compelled him to abandon his own religion. Furthermore, it reveals a noble and true love involving great sacrifice in this world and the Hereafter. However, the story has a happy ending; the man was forgiven his capital sin by returning to the true faith along with his wife. All this was done by Divine Grace.

The story of Solomon[49] describes in great detail the power, wealth, and wisdom of the man. Solomon is almost superhuman, but devout and obedient in spite of his extravagances. He never missed a prayer; he converts and marries the Queen of Sheba. His power extended over nature, man, and beasts; he understands the noises of nature, the singing of the bird, and the voices of beasts; lions kneel before him and the wings of eagles shelter him in the blazing sun. He possessed gorgeous palaces; his sword was unique; his ring had the power to predict the future and recreate the past; even demons were tamed and served him. But in moments of vainglory, God made his ring disappear and compelled him to walk forty days as a mendicant. When he died, he was buried on an island, and his tomb was guarded by a horrible serpent so that no demons could approach it.

To Moses, who is regarded as the communicant with God (*kālim Allah*) and the possessor of the secrets of nature, are devoted three stories.[50] One deals with a certain Jacob, a butcher from Damascus, who was despised by everyone but nevertheless became a close companion of Moses. The second story relates the events in Sinai between Moses and God, how Moses was taken to the summit of Mt. Sinai and how he listened to God with an overwhelming fear; it describes at the same time, God's power, the dialogue between Moses and God, and several moral, social, and religious questions. It also describes the return of Moses to Egypt, where he appears before the pharaoh and performs miracles in his presence so that he may free his people. The third story deals with a dove and a falcon, and shows how Moses preferred to sacrifice part of himself rather than to hurt an ant.

Volume II of *Leyendas Moriscas* contains Islamic themes. It starts with an idealized biography of Muḥammad,[51] a hero who played a great role in the history of his own people and in that of mankind at large. Muḥammad also appears prominently in the rest of the stories in his role as active participant, adviser, and admonisher.

The story of Tamīm[52] is full of human and religious elements. Muḥammad had predicted the happy end of the adventure of one of his companions, Tamīm, in a mysterious world of demons and spirits. Tamīm went to perform the ablution while his wife was waiting in bed. After long waiting, his wife searched for him and could not find him anywhere. The search went on for days and weeks, and no trace of Tamīm was found. The demons had taken him away to a cave where he lived, ate, and drank with his undesirable hosts, but he continued to believe in one God and read the Qur'ān to the annoyance of the demons, who often ridiculed and threatened him. This had gone on for almost four years when a good geni passed by the cave. The geni inquired about Tamīm's fate and his religion, and became interested in him as a tutor for his children. The chief demon would not allow him to take Tamīm, and a war ensued between the two bands of spirits, numbering in the millions. The good geni triumphed and took Tamīm to his land, where he was esteemed and lived in comfort for the next three years. Meanwhile, Tamīm's wife was celebrating her nuptials in the quietness of her home when suddenly Tamīm appeared to demand recognition and possession of his home and wife. A quarrel between the two husbands was averted by the wife's suggestion to have 'Umar, a companion of the Prophet, decide the case in the morning. The wife slept by herself while the two husbands stayed in an adjoining room. The following day, they appeared before 'Umar, who asked Tamīm to identify himself. Tamīm relates his saga at great length with an emphasis on his journey back home. He describes a world of fantasy in which he witnessed many marvels: spirits, saints, great cities and palaces, believers, unbelievers, and other creatures with which he had dialogues concerning the virtue of the Islamic doctrine. He also tells about the wonder of travelling over a cloud on his way home. The account is exciting and full of suspense. Tamīm gave ample proof of his faith and knowledge of Islam, but this was not much of an identification until 'Alī, the son-in-law of Muḥammad, ordered a barber to shave Tamīm to facilitate his identity. Once this was done, the basic problem of right to the wife remained. However, the opinion was given that had Tamīm left his wife voluntarily, he would have forfeited his right and the second marriage would be valid, but inasmuch as he did not leave her of his own free will, his marriage to her was still valid. But given the circumstances of the case — long lapse of time and so forth — the wife should have the choice of the man she wanted. She chose Tamīm, alleging that she never knew a man except Tamīm and that she would continue to be his wife. Her second husband was given back the expenses incurred in the marriage, and Tamīm and his wife lived happily thereafter by the grace of God.

While the story of Tamīm attempts to illustrate the rewards accruing from unshaken belief, the story of the supposed founder of Medina[53] shows the ultimate triumph of Islam against overwhelming forces and the religious significance of the Ka'bah in pre-Islamic and Islamic times. The founder of Medina, a powerful king with a huge army, decided to besiege Mecca and destroy the Ka'bah, the holy shrine of Muslims. During the siege, the king became alarmed when a fetid liquid ran from his nose. He summoned his ministers, astrologers, and physicians for advice, but could not determine the cause of his illness. One wiseman of the audience confided to the prime minister that he would find a cause if the ruler would tell him whether he intended to destroy the Ka'bah. When the ruler revealed that he intended to destroy it, the wiseman told him that that was the cause of his illness, which could be cured if he desisted from his plans. The king not only gave up his plans but embraced the religion of Abraham and proceeded from there to the north and founded Yathrib, which the wiseman predicted would become the city of Muḥammad (Medina). The king died the day Muḥammad was born, willing the city to Muḥammad.

But the triumph of Islam under Muḥammad was yet to come. It is shown in bold relief in the account of the conquest of Mecca by Muḥammad,[54] who tore down its idols with his own sword. As his enemies gathered a huge force for attack, the angel Gabriel warned him in advance and the contenders met in the battlefield, resulting in the false announcement that Muḥammad was killed. This news created havoc among his partisans until they heard from 'Abbās, the uncle of Muḥammad, that their leader was much alive. Finally, the battle was decided by 'Alī, the hero of all battles.

Claimants to prophecy during the time of Muḥammad are treated with ridicule, as in the story of a prophetess and a prophet.[55] These two prophets had their followers and contended for power. The prophetess had an edge over the prophet in that she was wiser, more knowledgeable, and had stronger forces. She marched against her enemy, but he was advised to erect a pavilion and provide it with decoration, singing, and music, after which he should invite her for a private conference in the midst of soft music and perfumed surroundings. In this seductive environment he endeared himself to her with amorous words and asked her hand in marriage. She fell for these advances and announced to her followers that the angel had appeared and commanded her to surrender to the prophet. However, the new prophet had to prove his claims to prophecy. Muḥammad put his hand on the head of a scaldheaded man and cured him, but when the false prophet did the same, the patient caught leprosy; Muḥammad made a blind man see, while the false prophet made him blind again; Muḥammad made saltwater sweet, while the false prophet made the sweet water salty. The prophetess, being a woman, was not asked to do anything.

In the "Battle of Muhalhil," [56] Khālid Ibn al-Walīd, who won many victories in the expansion of Islam, and 'Alī, son-in-law of Muḥammad and the fourth caliph, are singled out by virtue of their courage, heroism, and triumph over overwhelming odds. Muḥammad announced from the pulpit the coming of Muhalhil at the head of 100,000 cavalrymen, 50,000 infantrymen, and 40,000 blacks — an overwhelming force, indeed. Muḥammad's followers decided to sacrifice their lives on the battlefield, but were restrained by advice to contact the enemy first and invite him to embrace Islam; if he refused, they would fight him to the end. The fearless general Khālid was selected to deliver the message. On the way Khālid's horse fell and would not go on; Khālid had to carry the saddle and walk. After walking two miles, he returned to the horse and reminded it of the Prophet's letter; suddenly the horse rose up and continued the journey through a huge mountain from which a beautiful valley could be seen. The valley was inhabited by incredulous people who intercepted Khālid by the thousands. He defeated them all. He then met the servant of Muhalhil, a giant with hands like windmills and legs like walls. The servant fought Khālid, but the Muslim general overcame him and went on. He met Muhalhil who was praying before an idol, but refused to deliver the letter until the idol was removed from sight. When Muhalhil stretched his left hand to receive the message, Khālid rebuked him and insisted on his stretching his right hand instead. Muhalhil read it and became infuriated. Khālid warned him that the Prophet had five knights who could dispose of Muhalhil's army. This angered Muhalhil further, and he ordered that Khālid's horse be skinned and Khālid be put in the skin ready for the fire the following day. In dire distress, Khālid asked the wind to relay his fate to Muḥammad, who instantly heard the angel Gabriel asking him to send 'Alī to rescue the captive Khālid. 'Alī rushed to the scene, covering in one night a distance which took Khālid twenty days. He freed Khālid and both faced and inflicted terror on Muhalhil's army. 'Alī killed its champions and then Muhalhil himself and all who fought him, sparing only those who accepted Islam. At this juncture, a contingent of Muslims appeared on the scene and joined in the celebration of victory in the name of the Creator.

The bravery and fearlessness of 'Alī is shown in other stories. In the

"Legend of the Girl and the Arab,"[57] 'Alī fetched against heavy odds a Syrian man who had buried his beautiful daughter to avoid a disgrace in the family when she told him that "the true god is Allah and not the goddesses Allāt and 'Uzzah." The sweetness and gracefulness of the girl are described in moving terms. When her father was digging her grave, she cleansed off his sweat. After the burial, the father was surrounded by a huge fire from which a voice was heard telling him that the should go to Muḥammad if he wanted to be saved. Muḥammad visited the tomb and brought the girl to life; she greeted him by name. When Muḥammad inquired how she knew his name, she said that she learned about it in Heaven.

A battle with a Meccan leader[58] is concluded with an indecisive duel with 'Alī, but the Meccan leader adopts Islam after his father and sister had done so. This quasi-miraculous end is matched by the "Miracle of the Moon,"[59] in which Muḥammad was told by a Meccan leader that if he performed a miracle he would adopt Islam. With the help of the angel Gabriel, Muḥammad changed the course of the moon and split it in halves.

Another interesting story is the *Mi'rāj*,[60] or the ascent of Muḥammad to the seven heavens. The story was very popular among Muslims and made its way into Latin, Spanish, and French. A comparison of the *aljamiado* version with various Arabic recensions and translations into European languages should reveal interesting variations. For one thing, the *aljamiado* version is embellished with colorful descriptions and details not found in old Arabic versions. It begins with the angel Gabriel descending upon Muḥammad in a dark night. He put Muḥammad on a beast called Burāk which was made of gold, silver, and precious jewels. Burāk established a dialogue with Muḥammad and headed for Mecca. On the way, they heard a voice ordering them to stop, but Gabriel interceded and asked them not to do so. The callers were Christians and Jews and a woman representing the world. Had Muḥammad listened to them, his people would have become Christians, or Jews, or worldly people. They continued the journey and reached a green valley where Muḥammad dismounted and prayed; then headed for Jerusalem where Gabriel offered Muḥammad wine, honey, and milk. Muḥammad chose milk and took a little of it; then a voice was heard telling him that had he drunk all of it, none of his people would enter Paradise. Muḥammad entered the mosque and found three hundred prophets who greeted him cordially and invited him to conduct the prayer. From Jerusalem, Muḥammad and Gabriel ascended toward the seven heavens on a staircase made of gold, rubies, bronze, and other precious jewels, leaving Burāk behind. The heavens were separated from one another by five hundred years' journey, and the width of each is equal to that number. Each heaven is described in detail. Muḥammad was greeted cordially in each one of them, put at ease, and established dialogues with their guardians.

In the first heaven, Muḥammad found Ismā'īl at the gate sitting on a chair of light and surrounded by angels. He was greeted as "the most honored of God's creatures.'' He saw an old man, Adam, who smiled whenever he looked to the right where Paradise was located, and cried when he looked to the left where Hell was. Muḥammad made the oration and left for the second heaven, guarded by a porter who was sitting on a chair of light, snow, and fire. There he saw two youths, John and Jesus. In the third heaven an old man, Abraham, watched its gate, surrounded by angels. In the fourth heaven, a gigantic angel — the angel of death — was at the gate seated on a resplendent chair with a tablet on his right and with a large tree at his left. In the tablet are written all the names of Adam's children; and on the tree's leaves are inscribed all the names of people indicating the date of their death. There he found Idrīs. Looking through the gate of the fifth heaven, Muḥammad sees Hell, where some of his people — cheaters and drunkards — were being eaten by the fire. The sixth heaven has an angel with 70,000 heads, each having an equal number of mouths and tongues. The seventh heaven is the abode of Gabriel, from which one cannot advance one step without being blinded by the intense light of God. There Muḥammad was accompanied by a beautiful angel who took him through an ocean of light, passing angels, each of which could swallow heaven and earth. They continued their journey through an ocean of green light, then a black ocean. He saw the angel Michael measuring and weighing water. Then he saw the throne of God, which was made of gold and surrounded by angels singing God's praise in all languages. He went through several circles separated by massive walls and saw files and files of angels. He heard a voice, the voice of the Lord commanding him to come near. He was asked to state his wishes. Muḥammad then asked God to aid the poor, to help him defeat the enemy. God exalted Muḥammad over all prophets, and instructed him to require fifty prayers a day from his followers. Grateful and acquiescent, he turned back, only to be questioned by Moses about the excessive number of prayers; after debate, the number of prayers was reduced to five at the insistence of Moses, who felt that five prayers a day is a reasonable number.

The legend of Guara[61] deals with the deceit of an Arabian idolater who, meeting Muḥammad, appeared to be impressed with the Islamic doctrine and asked Muḥammad to send missionaries to teach his subjects. Missionaries were sent, but the idolaters had no intention of learning a new doctrine, planning to burn the Muslims. As usual, the angel Gabriel alerted Muḥammad, who sent his son-in-law 'Alī to the scene. 'Alī freed the Muslims from chains, fought thousands, and put many to death until the rest submitted to Islam.

The story of Muḥammad and a Yemenite ruler, al-Ḥārith,[62] shows once more the determination and success of Muḥammad against adversaries and unbelievers. After the fall of Mecca, Muḥammad wrote to the Yemenite leader calling on him to embrace Islam or else. Muḥammad's messenger reached the capital of Yemen, and was led through many halls and luxurious palaces to the Yemenite ruler, who was surrounded by a large entourage. The king rejected conversion, summoned his ministers, and sought their advice; but an old man warned him of the consequences. This notwithstanding, war ensued, and the Muslims emerged victorious, succeeding in gaining large booty and converting the people to Islam.

Notwithstanding his successes and miraculous deeds, Muḥammad, as a mortal, had to die. His death[63] was replete with family situations in which his daughter Fāṭimah, wives, and companions expressed their deep feeling for him and their wish to die instead, but the final hour arrived and the angel of death, accompanied by the angel Gabriel, took him to Heaven.

Although the previous stories deal with Muḥammad and the role of ʻAlī in the great battles threatening Islam and Muslims, others deal with some of his companions. The conversion of ʻUmar[64] was a great moment for Islam. ʻUmar, the actual founder of the Islamic empire, was a man who opposed Islam and even made attempts on the life of Muḥammad, especially when ʻUmar's brother-in-law and sister had embraced the faith. He was so angered at them that he wounded his brother-in-law, but felt such remorse afterward that he asked them to allow him to read the Qurʻān. He was so overwhelmed by the wording and content of the Holy Book that he rushed to Muḥammad, not with the intent to kill but to make the confession of the faith to the surprise and delight of Muḥammad and his followers.

Once he embraced the faith, ʻUmar had the merit of bringing the Islamic movement to a success undreamt of even by Muḥammad himself. The Battle of Yarmūk[65] in Palestine takes heroic and even miraculous proportions under the leadership of Khālid Ibn al-Walīd, called the "Sword of God." The Battle of Yarmūk marks the victory of the faith over the tyranny, injustice, and abuses of the powerful Byzantines, who in spite of overwhelming military power, fell because of demoralization and treason.

ʻUmar was also known for his austerity and strong sense of justice. He executed the law with great impartiality without consideration to noble lineage or high social status. In the story of his son and a Jewish woman,[66] he flogged his own son in public for dishonoring her, in spite of pleas for mercy from companions and other leaders. It is also mentioned that he prevented his son's succeeding him to the throne, and asked a governor to pay his debt to a Jew or to resign.

ʻAlī emerges as a hero who not only defeats proved champions, but "spirits" and strange creatures as well. In the legend "The Golden Castle,"[67] an Arab embraces Islam, but complains that in a castle there is a serpent that devours everything. ʻAlī sent a group of people to the castle made of gold and fine marble. They found it in smoke that emerged from the mouth of the horrible snake. They were horrified and returned. ʻAlī then marched against the castle shouting as if "heaven was falling and earth splitting." He knocked at the gate and a thunderous voice came out. He was taken for lost; attempts at rescuing him proved fruitless. In the meantime, his wife Fāṭimah dreamt that he was surrounded by giants and demons, and informed her father, Muḥammad, about it. Muḥammad waited for the angel Gabriel to appear, who informed Muḥammad that 'Alī was also surrounded by angels and would return safely. Muḥammad then rushed to the scene, urged 'Alī to kill the dragon first, then the demons, which he did. He emerged victorious after killing some 17,000 demons.

In the story " 'Alī and the Forty Girls,"[68] the physique of 'Alī and his poverty were ridiculed by an old lady, who, accompanied by forty well-groomed girls, asked Fāṭimah why she wanted to marry 'Alī, who is almost bald with a big stomach, thin legged, and poor. When informed about it, 'Alī prayed and hoped for the opportunity to fight in order to show that handsome appearance and wealth were not that important. Muḥammad's messenger Bilāl soon summoned him to appear before Muḥammad, who informed him that 80,000 invaders were at the gate of the city. 'Alī volunteered to fight them alone on condition that the old lady, her entourage, and Fāṭimah should watch the battle from the tower. The poorly dressed Fāṭimah was given a beautiful dress, brought to her by Gabriel from Heaven. They watched 'Alī defeat the champions of the enemy and many men. 'Alī got out of battle drenched in blood, and went to Fāṭimah and the girls, who were so impressed that Fāṭimah became his bride and the girls Muslims; the old lady was put to death. Similarly, 'Alī shows his military prowess and heroism in two other battles launched against two Arabian chieftains,[69] both of which marked the triumph of Islam over unbelievers.

The death of Bilāl,[70] the faithful messenger of Muḥammad, was caused by the grief felt at the death of his master in Medina. He even left the city and lived among tribes to which he taught the Qur'ān. Once in a dream he saw Muḥammad, who admonished him for leaving Medina. He returned to find that Fāṭimah had died. He fainted at the news, left the city again, and died after he converted a Jewish lady.

Abraham, known as the "friend of God," was shown many miracles and marvels.[71] He was sent on a journey and was recognized by a man with whom he walked on water to an island where a lamb fell from heaven. They roasted the lamb and ate it; then took the bones together and ordered that the lamb get up, which it did by the grace of Allah. Pursuing his journey, he was also recognized by a frog and a bird as the friend of God, and he found a new city whose inhabitants were dead for having ruled themselves without reason. A black lad supplied him with water extracted from a stone and so forth.

"The Legend of the Two Friends"[72] deals with the request of two believers who wanted to know the language of the dead. When one of them died, the other became anxious to know what happened to him. His dead friend told him how his body was surrounded by good angels on the right, and bad angels on the left, each group trying to pull it to their side. The bad angels made threats, but he, although frightened, made the confession of faith to the good angels. Then he was taken to Heaven and led to palaces of pleasures, from which he was taken to Paradise where he faced the lord.

"The Legend of the Antichrist" [73] is the prelude to the day of judgment. The Antichrist, who was the son of a prostitute, will deceive people, but Christ will emerge and strike him with his sword; everyone then will become Muslim. Jesus will get married and will have a son who will live to be forty years old and will conduct the pilgrimage. All this will foretell the Day of Judgment.

The Day of Judgment [74] was preceded by unbelief, injustice, lies, wars, and chaos. Israfil, the angel of death, blew the horn announcing doomsday. In the Hereafter, people went to their spiritual leaders and asked for intercession on their behalf, but their leaders refused to help. The people were passed from Adam to Noah, to Abraham, to Moses, to Jesus. Jesus sent them to Muḥammad, who, instead of giving an excuse, prostrated himself before God, who told him that he would receive all that he requested. At that juncture, the fire is being started, and the scales and measures are prepared. Prophets appeared and asked forgiveness for themselves. But Muḥammad asked not for himself nor his daughter but for his people. The rest of the story deals with the way the final judgment is made and the results announced as to whether a man should go to Heaven or Hell. Those in Hell were devoured by the fire, but some among them still uttered the formula "there is no God but God and Muḥammad the Messenger of God." God sent the angel Gabriel for an inspection, after which Gabriel rushed to Muḥammad crying to tell him about the suffering of his people. Muḥammad, who was in a place made of emeralds and rubies and surrounded by damsels, appealed to God on their behalf. He was instructed to pull out from Hell anyone who had as much faith as a grain of mustard. He did this, and the gates of Hell and Heaven closed forever.

The religious overtone of these stories is quite obvious. Islam emerges as the best of religions and its prophet Muḥammad as the prophet most favored by God. Figures who antedated Islam by many centuries were true Muslims, including Alexander the Great, whose power, prowess, and mission were the manifestations of a divine will. Faithful to the Muslim traditions, the biblical figures Adam, Noah, Abraham, Moses, and Jesus had a single mission — to bring man under the divine will. Muḥammad was the seal of that chain of prophecy and, as such, discharged a role of a great consequence. He came to fuse Judaism and Christianity into one religion for all mankind. The Moriscos believed in Christ, but lost faith in what was done by clerics under his name.

The Moriscos also interested themselves in worldly topics pertaining to love and its tribulations. The two novels *El Baño de Zarieb* (*The Bath of Zarieb*)[75] and *Paris and Viana*[76] are cases in point. *The Bath of Zarieb*, which may have been derived from a simple Eastern model,[77] has its setting in tenth-century Cordova. The theme of the story is as follows:

A wife of a wealthy man went to one of the public baths of Cordova and was not properly taken care of by the attendants, who were busy with the wives of high public officials. She complained to her husband about not having a bath of her own. The husband then built for her the most gorgeous bath in the city, which attracted the attention of nobility and officials, including the wife of the powerful chamberlain al-Manṣūr. Only Zaynab, the daughter of one of al-Manṣūr's ministers, was prevented by her jealous father from going until one day he consented on the condition that she be accompanied by her servants. On the way to the bath, Zaynab got lost in a huge crowd and wandered until she found an attractive home at whose entrance stood a man who had squandered great wealth. When she inquired whether that building contained the bath of Zarieb, she was told yes and conducted inside. She soon discerned that the young man had bad intentions, lifted her veil, and kissed the young man with the declaration that she had been madly in love with him for months. In consequence, she would like to enjoy his company with food and drink. Not having provisions or money, he was given one of her jewels to purchase food; when he returned with it, the girl had gone. He searched for her, asking if anyone saw a girl looking for the bath of Zarieb. His search continued for days as he became half mad. Zaynab's father, who had known him when he was rich, felt sorry for him and tried to find out what was ailing him. The young man told the father that he was searching for the owner of the jewel, which the minister took. The minister went home with great apprehension and asked his daughter for an explanation of how a piece of her jewelry came into the hands of the young man. The father so marvelled at the conduct of his daughter that he told the story to al-Manṣūr, who summoned the young man to give him an explanation. Love at first sight had maddened the young man, he was given employment and a happy nuptial ceremony.

Paris and Viana, probably of French origin, was translated into Italian, Catalan, Spanish, and *aljamiado*. The *aljamiado* version was based on a Spanish text.[78] The novel, which resembles chivalrous accounts familiar to the Muslims, deals with the intense love of the knight Paris for Viana, the daughter of a count.

Paris, who won many trophies, loved Viana in secret and sang tender songs to her. His love was reciprocated by Viana, whose father threatened to kill Paris. They decided to flee, but were pursued. Paris managed to escape to Genoa, but Viana was taken back home by one hundred knights and put in prison along with Paris's father, whose property was confiscated. In the meantime, Paris was suffering the pain of separation and knew about the fate of his beloved. He devised a strategem by which he went to the East to learn Arabic in order to appear as a Moor and thereby disguise his identity. Coincidentally, Viana's father went in the East as a spy for the Crusades, but was discovered and put in jail. Paris, who had established good contacts in the East, managed to release his would-be father-in-law without revealing his identity to the count. The count promised to make Paris his favorite knight and heir to his domain. He fulfilled his promise upon their return home. Paris's identity was then revealed; he was forgiven and allowed to marry Viana, who had been in prison until that time.

By and large, the preceding works represent the historical consciousness of the Moriscos of the fifteenth and sixteenth centuries. Their belief in their faith led them to defend themselves against the attacks on it by Jews and Christians. In a treatise [79] written by a certain 'Abdallah al-Kātib there is a refutation of the religious and historical arguments of the Jews against Islam; it also contains arguments against Christianity, with the main concentration on the circumstances attending the birth of Christ.

The "Sciences" and Miscellanea

Scientific inquiry among the Moriscos was at a standstill. The Moriscos appear to have resigned themselves to certain traditional concepts, clichés, and formulas for all seasons and every occasion. They possessed some scientific knowledge that had been handed down to them, but this knowledge was intermingled with superstition, magic, and horoscopes. However, medical knowledge appears to have occupied a pre-eminent position. The *Memoria*, [80] which deals with the four seasons of the year, comprises invocations for the four seasons, discussion of the days of the week and the propitious hours of the day, amulets, and divinations. In addition, it contains medical recommendations for the woman who cannot bear children; remedies for people bitten by mad dogs; and cures for sleeplessness, fever, headache, and other ailments. Hippocrates, Galen, al-Rāzī, and Ibn Sīnā are mentioned with high praise. Similarly, a work [81] dealing with the true doctrine, punishment, and good behavior contains, in addition to rewards accruing from fulfilling religious obligations, a number of prescriptions derived from the works of Hippocrates, Galen, al-Rāzī, and Muslim physicians.

There are numerous texts which deal with divination and formulas for every situation. Two texts [82] contain formulas for rain. The *Book of Marvel-*

ous Sayings[83] contains a large number of superstitions, formulas, and amulets used for causing the devil to flee the house, for making married people love each other, for knowing the secrets of the wife, for curing animals, for seeing others without being seen, for having one's desires seen in dreams, for getting what one wants, for finding out the result of an enterprise, and so on. It also contains discussions of the effect of each lunar day on human acts and the days and hours of each month which are propitious for acting. In addition, there are numerous magical prescriptions and orations for every heart's desire. Similarly, the *Book of Divination*[84] makes use of Qur'ānic verses for every conceivable activity: walking, hunting, and every wish, and ends with a formula for making black ink.

The miscellaneous texts contain a hodgepodge of many things: items pertaining to the Islamic faith and its practices, historical tracts about biblical, New Testament, and Islamic figures; magical prescriptions, stories and legends, contracts, petitions, and so on. The *Book of the Moriscos*[85] contains various crude illustrations: one representing a Muslim with a beard and a crown reading a book and surrounded by several people; another of two black men facing a tomb; a third represents an eagle with two heads; and so forth.

One set of documents and fragments in the Biblioteca Nacional[86] includes prayers in Arabic, orations to God for every day of the week, and a discourse on the pronunciation of the Arabic letters. A second set of documents and fragments[87] contains such items as a memorandum to an individual stating the price of a home bought from so and so. It also includes excerpts from the *Book of al-Samarqandī*, medical notes, the draft of a petition, a receipt, a marriage license, a contract of dowry, and passages from the Qur'ān and from other religious texts. A third set of documents[88] contains letters of dowry (dated February 9, 1503) and from an individual to his cousin; the importance of jurists; a list of medical terms in Arabic and notes on some drugs; a list of expressions in both Arabic and *aljamiado*; a request for a book, a petition for a mortgage; legal decisions and a court minute of two litigants who had a fight because the one accused the other of being of Jewish extraction; a contract obliging a man to teach a trade to another; and fragments of poetry about Eastern figures and cities. A fourth set of documents[89] contains testimonies of two litigants, one over a mule and the other over an inheritance. It also includes contracts of sale, dowry, and inventory of property, and fragments on religious questions. A fifth[90] includes magical formulas for curing any wound and for protecting the house;

orations; exercises on the Arabic alphabet, grammatical questions, and the usual Qur'ānic and religious excerpts.

In conclusion, this chapter makes some broad remarks about a literature which is extensive in size and in scope, limited but which nevertheless is valuable for an understanding of the intellectual perspective and the hopes of a minority living under unfavorable circumstances. In this literature the Moriscos reminisce about their great past, ponder their present, and hope for a day of deliverance wherein they will regain their land and dignity. There is some inkling of hopes for reconciliation between Christianity and Islam, since both are revealed religions; however, the practice of discrimination was so obvious that the Moriscos expressed in poems their bitterness and disgust at the malpractices of fanatical clerics.[91] They found an outlet in contemplating the extraordinary triumph of Islam, which was aided by divine will and carried out by the angel Gabriel. If those triumphs were achieved against heavy odds beyond human power, then there are hopes for the future. The Mancebo of Arévalo felt despondent when he visited the lost southern al-Andalus in the fifteenth century. He could not help feeling sad at the sight of what he called sweet and beautiful land, rich in bread and olive, sweet water and gold.[92] All in all, *aljamiado* literature deserves more study and evaluation and waits competent hands with good knowledge of Arabic and Arabic literature, Spanish and Spanish philology. However great its deficiencies may appear to be, *aljamiado* literature is important for the simple reason that it offers enormous possibilities for unraveling interesting and revealing data about the Moriscos in general, and in particular about their posture and treatment at a critical juncture in their history.

21

The Islamic Legacy

THE impact of Arabic culture on the West has come to light largely through Western scholarship. By the eighteenth century, the Jesuit Juan Andrés, in his *Origin, Progress, and Present State of World Literature* [1] had pointed to various elements of Arabic culture in European literature. In the nineteenth century, Western Orientalism began to discover and bring to the fore the Islamic legacy which, by its great dimension and quality, earned the admiration of scholars. As research advanced and more material was made available, students became increasingly aware of Arabic contributions to the West and of cultural interaction in the various disciplines of philosophy, literature, astronomy, medicine, art, and architecture. In his monumental work, *Introduction to the History of Science*, [2] Sarton conveys the quality and quantity of these contributions; the works of Asín Palacios, [3] Ribera, [4] González Palencia, [5] Farmer, [6] Nykl, [7] and the *Legacy of Islam*, [8] written by leading Western specialists, also discuss various aspects of Arabic cultural influence.

In looking at the world map of today, one cannot fail to see the enormous influence Islam has had in an immense area of the world. This area stretches from Indonesia in the East to the Atlantic Ocean in the West and includes portions of China, India, the Soviet Union, Afghanistan, Iran, and the entire Arab world. Islam left its mark on the culture and institutions of those areas in varying degrees. The adherents of Islam number more than half a billion. The Arab world alone — Iraq, Syria, Jordan, the Arabian Peninsula, and the North African states of Egypt, the Sudan, Lybia, Tunisia, Algeria, and Morocco — has a population of some hundred million people who speak the Arabic language and are deeply influenced by Islam and Islamic culture.

The question of influence is difficult to gauge. Therefore, we ought to determine its meaning. In broad terms it may mean the contact and ascendance of a society vis-à-vis another society. For this influence to become perceptible or visible there are certain prerequisites — especially, first, a geography that would facilitate human intercourse, and second, contact among people which may be of political, commercial, or cultural nature. When these prerequisites are established, one can speak of osmosis, that is, of giving and receiving. In a sense, the process becomes a confrontation between two societies in which one side gains ascendancy over the other in some respects and, at the same time, is itself influenced. This can be illustrated by the Greek and Roman confrontations with other peoples in antiquity, and by the Arab confrontation with the West in medieval and modern times. In all three instances, great empires comprising enormous territories were established by minorities which came into contact with peoples of different cultures and languages. The outcome was invariably that the conquering minority succumbed in many ways to the majority, but preserved certain features of its own which became the distinctive mark of its civilization. By these processes, composite cultures were born under what may be called Pax Hellenica, Pax Romana, or Pax Arabica.

The Arabs of the seventh century A.D. were in a minority, a primitive and backward minority to be sure. However, during the seventh and eighth centuries, they succeeded in establishing a vast empire, which stretched from the Indus River to the Atlantic Ocean, and from the Arabian Sea to the confines of Turkey and the Caucasus. This empire included Spain, which was held for almost eight centuries; Sicily, for over 200 years; and Crete, for 125 years. This area was larger than the empire established by Alexander the Great or the Roman Empire at its height. Although the conquerors succumbed to the native cultures of the conquered areas, they adhered staunchly to their language, Arabic, and to their religion, Islam. These two elements became the distinctive features of their culture and have had a great impact on life and thought among the Arab-Muslim peoples throughout the centuries.

Arabic has enjoyed in medieval and modern times a universalism that can be compared favorably with the world's great languages — Greek and Latin in ancient times; French, English, Spanish, and Russian in modern times. This is true not only because its modern speakers number about a hundred million but also because of its place in history and its important role in Arab-Muslim society.[9] It has not only accompanied Islam, which has been gaining influence in many regions of the world, but it also preserves one of the world's great literatures. In medieval times, Arabization went hand in hand with Islamization and often transcended it, since non-Muslims — mainly Jews and Christians — used Arabic as the instrument of intellectual expression. As for Islam, it was a continuation of the Judeo-Christian tradition. To the Muslim, Islam is the fulfillment and culmination of the divine revelation; it is a religion, a state, a culture, and a way of life. We need here to take up the cultural aspects, their formation into a distinctive unit, and their subsequent impact on the West.

In the first place, Muslim culture is a composite culture. It emerged in the ninth and tenth centuries as a mighty river which owed its very existence to the amalgamation and fusion of many tributaries — that is, to many Eastern and Western elements. It had its origin in the Arabian Peninsula with Arabic and Islam as its earliest and most distinctive features. Although modest and primitive at the beginning, it gained dimension and depth during the expansion of Islam in the seventh and eighth centuries and became one of the great cultures of the world. Its constituents stemmed from various sources:

1. The Ancient Near East, a background which comprises the cultures of the Egyptians, Sumerians, Akkadians, Phoenicians, Hebrews, Aramaic- and Syriac-speaking peoples, and others. These peoples left many things to posterity, important among which are the alphabet, the concept of monotheism, codified law, and other literary and scientific manifestations.
2. Greece, whose influence was felt in the sciences and philosophy, which were translated from Greek into Arabic beginning in the eighth century and ending by about the tenth century. The great works of the ancient sages became known in Arabic: Plato and Aristotle in philosophy, Galen in medicine, Ptolemy in geography, and Euclid in mathematics, among others.
3. Persia, a background that was felt through direct contact and found its expression in historical tracts and wisdom literature pertaining to government and the conduct of the ruler.
4. India, which contributed the famous book of fables, *Kalīlah wa-Dimnah*, and other stories that came to have a great popularity in world literature. It also contributed astronomical treatises, wise

sayings, many agricultural products, and the so-called Arabic numerals.

5. China, which contributed paper and the techniques for manufacturing it.
6. Byzantium, which, though at war with Islam, contributed many features of its institutions.

Some scholars emphasize foreign elements in Islamic culture and are inclined to deny the culture itself any distinct merit or value. Others who are willing to grant it some merit single out the intellectual giants of Islam and argue that they were not Arabs. But arguing that there is nothing new under the sun, or this or that person did not possess this or that kind of blood, is futile and leads nowhere. The important thing is that a cultural and intellectual environment under the aegis of Islam enabled all components of society to participate and give vent to their talents. In this climate there prevailed a unity of mind and a uniform intellectual perspective that transcended ethnic and religious boundaries. This situation was like that created before by the Greeks and Romans, under whose aegis the Mediterranean basin became a fecund ground for acculturation and the interaction of ideas. Before the Greeks and Romans, other peoples had risen to prominence in the area and had their confrontations, not only in a military sense but in a cultural sense as well. They had imposed their stamp on the conquered and at the same time had received from them many elements, thus giving rise to a new culture whose success depended always on its universal appeal. This was exactly the nature of Islamic culture. It was universal in character and appealed to many people of different linguistic and cultural backgrounds. The mere fact that the Arab-Muslim people borrowed extensively and knew how to make good use of their borrowing is of utmost significance. They were able to forge a cultural synthesis which they dressed in Islamic garb. Important too is the fact that the Arab-Muslims proved themselves avid students who had a great appreciation for and love of knowledge. They were fully aware of their indebtedness to other peoples (for example, Aristotle was highly regarded and revered as the first teacher).

By the ninth and tenth centuries, the sciences in the Arabic language became so numerous that Arab scholars felt the need for classifying them into two main categories: the Arab sciences and the foreign sciences introduced into Arabic by translation. Their contributions were thus enormous — if not in terms of great creativity, then indeed in terms of cultivating and preserving the sciences of the ancient sages and of transmitting them to the West. Moreover, the Arab-Muslim scholars worked in the important urban centers of a great and sophisticated civilization. New cities such as Baghdād and Cairo were founded and became known for their splendor. In the tenth century, Cordova surpassed the splendor of Constantinople, with its hospitals, universities, gorgeous mosques and palaces, public libraries, public baths, and beautiful gardens and promenades. Those facilities were all present in the major cities of Muslim Spain, and helped to create the intellectual environment that produced the greatest Andalusian minds.

It is significant to point out that while this great civilization was enjoying intense intellectual activities and cultural efflorescence, Europe was going through the so-called Dark Ages, or period of transition, and was indifferent to the voices of great thinkers from the past and to methodical and scientific approaches. This attitude prevailed from the time of Augustine to about the thirteenth century. Western man was preoccupied with the theocentrism of the Church to the extent that he negated the anthropocentrism of the Classical period and considered it lacking in Supreme Truth. For centuries, truth could — within the framework of Church policy — be conceived by faith alone, as opposed to reason. Furthermore, the validity of reason as a means capable of perceiving the truth did not gain ascendance until the thirteenth century, when the conflict between faith and reason was virtually reconciled by Thomas Aquinas, who was greatly indebted to Muslim philosophers, chiefly Averroës.

The process of change in the West started at the turn of the eleventh century. While the Muslim peoples were undergoing a general recession in their endeavors, the European countries were making considerable strides in the political, social, and intellectual fields. The Westerner emerged in his role of conqueror and embarked on the road to secularism. The Italian merchants of Pisa, Venice, and Genoa developed their own commercial fleet and thus broke the monopoly of the Muslims in the Mediterranean. The long confrontation between the Muslims and Christians began to be resolved, in favor of the Christian West. In Spain Alfonso VI not only conquered the important city of Toledo in 1085, but succeeded in making tributaries of all the Muslim rulers of the Peninsula. Sicily fell to the Normans in 1091, and a Crusade called in 1096 wrested the coast of Syria-Palestine from the Muslims. Although these conquests were made in the name of religion, Christian rulers displayed remarkable freedom from the hitherto strict control of the Church. They befriended people imbued with Arabic culture and made use of their services in the transmission of Arabic lore to the

West. Westerners began to look into the factors responsible for past successes of Islam and to enter into a dialogue of inquiry. This led to the translation of Arabic books in the various disciplines into Latin and to the subsequent foundations of universities where Arabic books in translation were studied and commented on.

The Crusades contributed little to the transmission of the sciences to the West, but their impact on the mode of thinking of Western man and his manner of living can hardly be underestimated. The long contact between Eastern Muslims and Western Christians resulted in extensive borrowing. Pilgrims were constantly going back and forth and carried with them souvenirs of all sorts in the form of gold-work, textiles, tapestry, seeds, and the like. One fact little noted is that Ṣalāḥ al-Dīn, the conqueror of Jerusalem, became the personification of chivalry in the West; Dante even spares him hellfire in the *Divine Comedy*.

On the other hand, Sicily [10] and Spain served to bridge the East and West, with the main centers of transmission in Palermo and Toledo, respectively. In the eleventh century Constantinus Africanus, a Tunisian renegade and a monk, spent some seven years in Salerno. In 1070 he began the translation of various Arabic works into Latin, thereby inaugurating a process that continued under the Norman kings, mainly Roger II (1101–1154) and Frederick II (1215–1250). These two rulers, because of their fascination for Arab culture, are referred to as the "two baptized sultans of Sicily." [11] They surrounded themselves with Jewish, Muslim, and Christian scholars who devoted themselves to translating Arabic works into Latin. More important still, Frederick founded the University of Naples in 1224 and gave it a royal charter. He provided it with a program of Oriental studies and encouraged scholars to pursue their research and studies. It was at that university that Thomas Aquinas studied and became acquainted with the content of Arabic works.

Simultaneously, similar activities were taking place in Spain. In this arabized country, under Muslim occupation for centuries, the processes of transmission and cultural exchange had their best and most effective manifestations. Although Muslim power was in the decline after the eleventh century, Spain remained the center of attraction for scholars from England, France, Germany, and Italy. These scholars came to learn Arabic or to engage in translation. Christian rulers such as Alfonso VII (1126–1157) and his successors encouraged intellectual activities and more often than not patronized them. In this connection, the city of Toledo occupied the place of honor in the process of transmission.[12] Its archbishop, Raymond[13] (1130–1150), recruited a group of translators, thereby initiating an institution not unlike *Bayt al-Ḥikmah* (the House of Wisdom) established by the caliph al-Ma'mūn in Baghdād in the ninth century. It was in this school that all sorts of Arabic works in mathematics, astronomy, medicine, alchemy, physics, natural sciences, and philosophy were translated into Latin or Romance. A number of translations were undertaken by Dominic Gundisalvi[14] and Gerard of Cremona, among others. Gundisalvi discharged the function of director of the Bureau of Translation founded by Raymond, and Gerard of Cremona (1114–1184),[15] who was born in Italy, is credited with having translated into Latin some seventy works in the various disciplines. There were also other translators, such as Juan Hispano,[16] a convert from Judaism.

Toledo became the Mecca of scholars. Residing there were Abelard of Bath and Michael Scot from England, and Peter the Venerable,[17] the Abbot of Cluny. Their and others' activities ushered in a period of great intellectual interest that had immense repercussions on the development of Western thought. They were followed by Alfonso X;[18] Raymond Martin (1230–1286), "whose knowledge of Arabian authors has probably not been equalled in Europe until modern times";[19] and Raymond Lull[20] (1235–1315), who mastered Arabic at the spoken and written level and founded a school of Oriental studies.

By the thirteenth century, Classicism had nearly been revived through the medium of Arabic. Aristotle regained his deserved place in Western thought, and became an authority second only to the Bible. This acceptance of Classicism and of Arabic elements in philosophy, medicine, astronomy, mathematics, and other disciplines is extremely interesting and represents a new perspective on the Classical legacy and Arabic learning.

It is significant to point out that the attitude of the thirteenth-century Westerner toward Islam as a religion remained bitter and negative[21] while his attitude toward Arabic learning became more and more positive. This change meant the acceptance of the Classical legacy hitherto outlawed by the Church but now made available mainly through the translation of Arabic books into Latin and other European languages. These two seemingly conflicting attitudes — antagonism toward Islam and sympathy toward Arabic learning — are quite evident in the writings of three great representatives of the thirteenth century: Alfonso X (1226–1288), Thomas Aquinas (1225–1274), and Dante (1265–1321).

These men were above all Christians who conceived Islam as a false religion perpetrated by an ignorant and unscrupulous man. Yet their indebtedness to Arabic writings was enormous. Alfonso X was born in Toledo, long an important center of Arabic culture even after its fall into Christian hands. He came into contact with Muslims, Jews, and Christians who had a good grasp of Arabic culture and who undertook the task of translating Arabic works into Romance or abridging them. It is in these efforts that the process of transmission reached its apogee. Alfonso X established a school in Seville where Arabic studies occupied a prominent place in the curriculum. But his outstanding accomplishment rested on the translation of Arabic works not only into Latin, but into Romance and French as well. Among the principal works translated under his auspices, one may mention the book of fables *Kalīlah wa-Dimnah*, astronomical works, and the *Mi'rāj* (ascension of Muḥammad to the seven heavens).[22]

Moreover, the intellectual perspective of Alfonso X is clearly manifested in his writings and in works done under his auspices, which reflect the encyclopedic Arabic knowledge of the time and which include history, astronomy, mineralogy, astrology, poetry, games, and horsemanship. His dependence on Arabic works is evident in his *Cantigas*[23] and books on astronomy, astrology, chess, and other subjects.[24]

In his *Summa contra gentiles*, Thomas Aquinas casts grave doubt on the prophecy of Muḥammad and describes the Arabs as "brutish men dwelling in the desert."[25] However, he consciously referred to Arab authors and unconsciously incorporated their views. He was definitely influenced by Muslim philosophers in the attempt to reconcile faith and reason — a subject that was dealt with in the East as early as the ninth century by al-Kindī and in al-Andalus by the eleventh-century Ibn Ḥazm and later by Averroës[26] and Maimonides.

Dante reflects both antagonism to Islam and sympathy to Arabic thought in the *Divine Comedy* and his other works.[27] On the one hand, he places Muḥammad in the *Inferno*[28] among those who had caused discord and strife in a place full of blood where the sinners display their wounds. He deprives the Prophet of all dignity: "When a cask loses from its head the middle piece or one of the cants, it does not gape so wide as one I saw who was split from chin to farting place. Between his legs were hanging his entrails: his heart and the organs about it were visible, and the loathsome sack that makes what is swallowed into turd. While I was all intent on seeing him, he looked at me, and with his hands opened his breast, saying: 'Now see how I split myself; see how Mohammed is ravaged.'"[29]

On the other hand, though Dante is also harsh with some of Muḥammad's followers, he shows a particular regard for others, such as Ṣalāḥ al-Dīn [30] and the two great Muslim philosophers, Ibn Sīnā (Avicenna) [31] and Ibn Rushd (Averroës), [32] whom he places in Limbo, "a noble town" for virtuous souls whose only fault was lack of baptism. Here these "virtuous" Muslims are among the great thinkers of antiquity such as Thales, Anaxagoras, Heraclitus, Democritus, Socrates, Plato, Zeno, Ptolemy, Galen, and others.[33]

This tolerance of the great men of antiquity in general and of certain Muslim thinkers in particular is definitely a departure from the former complete rejection. For one thing, it recognized the merit of Arabic learning. In fact, Dante himself must have been aware that the theme of his *Divine Comedy* was inspired by an Arabic legend describing the *Mi'rāj*.

In this connection, it is interesting to mention that the able Spanish scholar Asín Palacios created an uproar in academic circles with the publication in 1919 of his *La escatología musulmana en la Divina comedia*. Asín Palacios suggested that the key to the *Divine Comedy* can be found in Arabic literature, especially in the *Mi'rāj*. The controversy engendered by this suggestion dragged on for almost a decade and subsided only when two scholars Muñoz Sendino [34] of Spain and Cerruli [35] of Italy produced more evidence in support of what Asín Palacios had argued originally. The probability of such a link between the work of Dante and the Muslim legend was far from remote.[36] The *Mi'rāj* in an embellished form was in vogue in Spain and Sicily, two areas with which Dante had direct or indirect contact. Dante himself visited Sicily and was familiar with leading Muslim figures; his teacher Brunetto Latini was for a time at the court of Alfonso X, who translated and included the *Mi'rāj* in his *Crónica general*. Moreover, Asín Palacios pointed to the close parallel between the two works: Both Muḥammad and Dante wake up from deep sleep and undertake their journeys accompanied by a guide; they both narrate their adventure in the first person. There are also similarities in the punishment for identical sins and in descriptions of places and situations. Other details resemble many details found in *al-Futuḥāt* by the great mystic Ibn 'Arabī.[37]

Alfonso X, Aquinas, Dante, Roger Bacon, and Albertus Magnus are only a few among many Western thinkers who from the thirteenth to the seventeenth century made profuse references to Arabic authors and Arabic themes. In fact, many Arabic works which have been lost in the original still exist in Latin or Hebrew versions. All this suggests a wide familiarity with Arabic learning, the effect of which could be shown in the social and intellectual spheres. There is no doubt that it was through the Arabic culture that Europe received the necessary impetus for reviving Classicism, and for embarking on the continuing road of scientific development. This transfusion was achieved at a time when the Muslim world was plunging into a state of lethargy not unlike that which Europe experienced before the thirteenth century. Now the positions were reversed. The Near East remained dormant until the nineteenth century, when it began to revive and to confront the West by imitating its progress.

Although the state of research concerning the impact of Islamic culture on that of the West is still untapped in many areas, one may discern various elements in medieval Western thought. The Arabic language is, perhaps, the best place to trace the transmission and interaction of ideas. It contains an enormous amount of material which shows the great cultural osmosis that took place in medieval times and is still taking place. The language shows the extent of its indebtedness as well as its contributions to a number of languages. Spanish and Portuguese, for instance, contain an enormous number of words which either originated in Arabic or were handed down through the medium of Arabic.[38] English has many words of common usage — such as *coffee, sugar, rice, lemon, syrup, soda, alcohol, alkali, cypher, algebra, arsenal, admiral, alcove,* and *magazine* — which have relevance to human endeavor in the arts and the crafts.

Arabic linguistic elements did not find their way into European languages by mere chance, but as the result of social intercourse and of conscious attempts to emulate a higher culture. This was accomplished by translating Arabic works into Latin, a process that revolutionized the thinking of the Western man and his approach to the sciences. One may mention a few instances in this connection. At a time, before the twelfth century, when diseases were considered a diabolic curse in Europe, for which a priest was needed to chase out the devil, medicine developed into a science among the Arabs. It required careful training and licensing and was freed from superstition by virtue of experimentation and observation. Hospitals were built in the major cities of the empire. The medical literature was varied and comprehensive. Such books as the *Canon* of Ibn Sīnā and the *Continens* of al-Rāzī were translated into Latin and were used in some European universities as textbooks as late as the seventeenth century.

In philosophy, the works of al-Kindī, al-Fārābī, Ibn Sīnā, Ibn Bājjah, Ibn Ṭufayl, and Averroës became known in Europe and exerted a considerable influence on both Christian Scholasticism and the revival of the study of philosophy.

In geography, the Arab contributions cannot be underestimated.[39] Although some of the geographical conceptions can be traced to those of Ptolemy, many new insights were added to geographical knowledge. Aside from theoretical geography, Muslim geographers compiled vast new information about distant places, peoples, and their customs. They illustrated their works with maps and gave detailed descriptions of roads, rivers, mountains, and monuments. In the twelfth century, Roger II of Sicily commissioned al-Idrīsī to compile for him the geographical knowledge of the day. Al-Idrīsī produced a book illustrated with some seventy maps, which he dedicated to his patron. The Muslims recognized and accepted the sphericity of the Earth, which was compared to the "yolk of an egg"; this fact may have played an important role in the discovery of America.

The Arab influence was also felt in mathematics and astronomy. The Arabic numerals, which should be called Indo-Arabic, and algebra, which is a corruption of the Arabic word *al-jabr*, are still used in all Western languages. Many astronomical terms can be traced to Arabic origin such as Betelgeus (*bayt al-jawzā'*), *zenith* (Ar. *al-samt*), and *nadir* (Ar. *naẓīr*).

In poetry and that branch of literature known as belles lettres (*adab*) the influence of Arabic is evident in Spanish literature in particular and in several other European literatures. The popular poetry known as *zajal* or *muwashshaḥ*,[40] which may have been an Andalusian invention, betrays a form and content which greatly resemble that of Spanish, French, and Italian troubadours. Courtly love found eloquent expression in the *Ṭawq al-ḥamāmah*[41] (*Dove's Ring*) of the talented Ibn Ḥazm. Various elements of the work occur in early Spanish literature: pure love, a procuress, the suffering of separation, and the submission of the lover to the beloved.

Perhaps the most conspicuous Arabic influence in early Spanish literature lies in fables, anecdotes, wise and moralizing sayings, proverbs, and stories of novelistic, epic, and picaresque character.[42]

In this connection, *Kalīlah wa-Dimnah*,[43] a work of Indian origin, consists of fables, each of which conveys an admonition or moral lesson. It was translated into various European languages (Hebrew, Latin, Spanish, French, etc.) and appears to have exerted a profound influence on European literature in general and Spanish literature in particular. This influence can be seen in *Libre de les marvilles* of Raymond Lull; *Conde Lucanor*[44] of

Juan Manuel (1282–ca. 1349); *Libro de los gatos*[45] and *Libro de los exemplos*[46] of Sánchez de Vercial; and *Libro de buen amor*[47] of Juan Ruiz. It also influenced the *Disciplina clericalis*[48] of Peter Alfonso, which consists of proverbs and admonitions.

Important too is the *Sindbār*,[49] also of Indian origin, known in Spanish under the title *Libro de los engannos y assayamientos de la mugeres* (*Book of the Wiles and Deception of Women*). The oldest Spanish translation was made in 1253 by Don Fadrique, a brother of Alfonso X. Subsequently, it appeared in various Spanish versions and in Hebrew, Persian, Turkish, Latin, Italian, German, English, and French. It was often known under the title *Book of the Ten Wisemen* or *Ten Viziers*. The *Sindbār* consists of twenty-six stories showing the deceit and cunning of women. The framework for the stories centers around a king who had no children. One night, he dreamt that he would have a son who would be fortunate after a grave misfortune. The dream came true; and the son was entrusted to Sindbār, who pledged to teach the young man everything in seven weeks, provided that the king would act justly toward his subjects and would consult his viziers before making decisions. Sindbār proceeds with the boy's education. He foresees a grave danger to the boy and orders him not to utter a word no matter what. The misfortune happened when the boy passed through the *harem* and was being tempted by an infatuated stepmother. The boy shunned her advances, but she accused him of dishonoring her. He was brought to justice and condemned to death. The king's viziers interceded and pleaded for postponement of the execution. They began to tell him about the deceit of women until the truth was unraveled. The boy emerged innocent and was given the power to rule while the concubine was exiled or put to death. The moral of the story is that women cannot be trusted.

The story of Barlaam and Josaphat,[50] dealing with the legend of Buddha, appears to have influenced Juan Manuel in his *El libro de los estados*.[51] It is a legend consisting of parables and aiming at spiritual love and self-abnegation. Buddha's father was a king who predicted that his son would become a famous man and a hermit. He attempted to avoid the occurrence of the latter and put his son in the beautiful garden of the palace in the midst of all sorts of pleasantries and distractions, making him thereby oblivious to all human sufferings and miseries. But one day, Buddha left his enclosure and found a sick man, a dead man taken to burial, and a mendicant. Upset by these findings, he pondered life and its tribulations, becoming a hermit who hoped to penetrate into the true meaning of life.

One cannot omit mention of the One Thousand and One Nights, which came into vogue in Europe, nor overlook the many legends and stories translated from Arabic into *aljamiado* which were common among the Spanish-speaking Moriscos.

In sum, there is a great deal to be done in the field of Hispano-Arabic studies, and the present work is merely an attempt to give a descriptive account of the history and culture of Muslim Spain, in the hope that it will lead to further studies of many important aspects of medieval Spain. Special attention has been paid to basic facts which, it is hoped, will enable the reader to have a clear idea about the dimension and depth of Hispano-Arabic studies and their significance for the history of Spain in particular and that of Europe in general. For obvious reasons, speculations, interpretation, and theorizing are beyond the immediate objective of this work and have been kept to a minimum. However, one cannot fail to mention the divergent views of Spanish Arabists regarding the Arab past of their country. Monroe's work[52] supplies ample information about Spanish scholarship in this area and the diversity of opinions regarding the Arab period. Some would say that if al-Andalus produced anything worth recording it was done by the Spanish element to the exclusion of everyone else. Some who are willing to credit the Muslims with something bemoan the evil consequences of the Arab presence on Spanish character and on the subsequent course of Spanish history. Religion and nationalism seem to obscure the facts of history among those scholars who tend arbitrarily to exalt one historical period over the other in order to accommodate their preconceived ideas. On the other hand, Spanish Arabists who belong for the most part to the school of Codera have made distinct contributions to the field with a sympathy and objectivity that have earned for them the gratitude of scholarship. They recognize that the Arab period of Spanish history is not sterile after all, and that it had enormous consequences, influencing the literature and culture and the very character of Spain.

Al-Andalus produced a brilliant culture to which many ethnic elements and imposing figures gave shape and dimensions. The 'Abd al-Raḥmāns, al-Ḥakam II, and Ibn Abī 'Āmir were great statesmen who were cultured and sophisticated and had no equal at that time in any other European country. They were men of destiny who played an important role in the history of al-Andalus. Their drive was inspired by Islam and Arabic and by the epoch-making events of their Muslim counterparts in the East. In consequence, northern Spain and southern France had little to offer for them. Moreover,

Muslim Spain produced intellectual giants who would do honor to any culture or country. Their genius had nothing to do with their Arabness or Spanishness, but owes its inspiration and guidance to the mainstream of Islamic culture — which, in spite of all its variety, enjoyed a remarkable unity throughout the length and breadth of the Muslim world. Those men were the net product of that culture transcending any consideration of ethnicity or biology. Putting it differently, one may ponder what caused the development of great urban centers such as Cordova, Seville, and Granada, which had their counterparts elsewhere in the Muslim world in cities like Cairo and Baghdād, at a time when one can hardly find anything comparable in France, Germany, or other European countries. Or, was there any figure in northern Spain or southern France that could be compared with Ibn Ḥazm, Ibn Ṭufayl, or Averroës?

The facts of history are that there was an ascendant Islamic culture in Muslim Spain which was nurtured by the spirit of Islam and the magic of the Arabic language. It had the capacity of absorbing and integrating many elements from many peoples and cultures. A look at the Alhambra reveals to the observer three basic things: it is Andalusian from a certain distance, Islamic at a closer range, and universal by the multiplicity of magnificent details inspired by and drawn from non-Islamic sources. In many ways, it is a microcosm of al-Andalus.

This brings us to the question of identity and personality. Al-Andalus had both, yet it remained intrinsically Muslim in outlook for most of the duration of the Muslim presence there. Although politically independent from the main Islamic polity, it never revolted against Islamic ideals and values in a religious or intellectual sense. Even when it became culturally independent from the East during the eleventh century, al-Andalus never ceased to be an integral part of Islamic society. Andalusians continued to travel to the East and settled in many parts of the Muslim world. They were pioneers in North Africa and brought with them the skill and know-how of their brilliant Andalusian culture. This posture was not very different from that of many independent or semi-independent states that existed elsewhere in the Muslim world. In spite of its vulnerability to Christian attacks, it remained staunch to an ideal and struggled to the very end against overwhelming odds. Long after the Reconquest, its Moriscos defied the harsh measures of the inquisitors.

But the identity and personality of al-Andalus can be seen in various areas: in the facility and expressiveness of its men of letters and poets, who more often than not were superior to their Eastern peers; in lyricism and love of nature, which were expressed in beautiful and heartwarming poetry, whether in its classical or popular forms; in the individuality of its arts and architecture, which inspire awe and reverence for something earthly yet majestic and sublime; and in a spirit of freedom amounting to rebelliousness. But this individuality was the product of diversity. Arabs, Berbers, Mozarabs, and Jews contributed to its formation, making of al-Andalus an important cultural center on European soil and, at the same time, a bridge between the Islamic East and Christian West. In varying degrees, they were the bearers and carriers of a great culture, in spite of the constant animosity that marked the relationship of Western Christianity and Islam. Recurrent wars within and without al-Andalus did not prevent more constructive interaction between the two contending religions. In fact, they learned a great deal from each other in their almost uninterrupted interaction over a long period of time. Travel to and from al-Andalus did not require passports, nor was it obstructed by the watchful eyes of border guards or the whims of foreign ministries. Such interaction was the result of social, economic, commercial, diplomatic, and cultural relations. Christianity was a reluctant disciple when Islam was in ascendance and vice versa. Finally, in the light of the wide cultivation of geography among the Muslims, the prevalent notion of the sphericity of the earth, extensive travel throughout the then known world, the developed technique of map making, the profuse use of the astrolabe, and the intense commercial activities in the Mediterranean and Atlantic, one may justifiably inquire about the reasons behind the success of the Portuguese and Spanish explorers, or behind the exploits of a Magellan (ca. 1480–1521), or Columbus (1446–1506). It was in this and other areas of transmission that al-Andalus played a most significant role — a role that can hardly be overlooked by people in the fields of history, comparative literature, art history, music, and the sciences in general.

Appendix

Some Christian Rulers of Spain

THE history of the Christian kingdoms is marked by uncertainty and confusion. From 718 to 1479, they lacked unity and fought among themselves as bitterly as against their Muslim enemies to the south. There were periodic political alignments which were often broken by dynastic wars, rivalries, and division of territories among a ruler's heirs. The earliest kingdom was that of the Asturias (718–909), which comprised the area between the Atlantic Ocean and Cantabric Mountains. It kept the spirit of reconquest much alive, particularly after the discovery of the tomb of the apostle Santiago at Compostela in 813. Taking advantage of the internal wars in al-Andalus, the kingdom expanded eastward. It then gave rise to the kingdom of León (909–1027), which merged with Castile (1035–1157), which was soon separated into the kingdoms of León (1157–1232) and Castile (1157–1217) to be united again into the kingdom of Castile and León (1217–1479) which was finally united to the kingdom of Aragón (1035–1479) through the marriage of Isabel of Castile and Fernando II of Aragón. In the meantime, there were the kingdoms of Navarre (840–1304), Portugal (1138–1383), and other earldoms. For more detailed information see:

Pedro Aguado Bleye. *Manual de Historia de España*. 2 vols. 10th ed. Madrid, 1967.

Rafael Altamira. *Historia de España y de la Civilización española*. 4 vols. Barcelona, 1900–1911.

Antonio Ballesteros y Beretta. *Historia de España y su influencia en la historia universal*. Barcelona, 1919–1936.

F. de Almeida. *Historia de Portugal*. 3 vols. Coimbra, 1922–1925.

R. Menéndez Pidal, ed. *Historia de España.* Vols. 3 and 4. Madrid, 1950–1957.

C. Sánchez Albornoz. *España, un enigma histórico.* 2 vols. Buenos Aires, 1956.

List of Rulers

Asturias

- Pelayo, 718–737
- Alfonso I, 739–757
- Alfonso II, el Casto, 791–842
- Ramiro I, 842–850
- Ordoño I, 850–866
- Alfonso III, 866–909

Navarre

- Iñigo Arista, 840–860?
- Sancho Garcés, 925–970
- Sancho Garcés II, 970–994
- García Sánchez II, 994–1000
- Sancho Garcés III, 1000–1035
- García, 1035–1045
- Sancho IV, 1054–1076
- Under Sancho Ramírez, Navarre was united to Aragón; this union lasted until 1134
- Sancho, 1194–1234
- Teobaldo I, 1234–1253
- Teobaldo II, 1253–1270
- Enrique I, 1270–1274
- Juana, 1274–1304

León

- García I, 909–914
- Ordoño II, 914–924
- Ramiro II, 931–951
- Ramiro III, 967–984
- Bermudo II, 984–999
- Alfonso V, 999–1027

Castile and León

- Fernando I, 1035–1065
- Sancho II, 1065–1072
- Alfonso VI, 1072–1109
- Doña Urraca, 1109–1126
- Alfonso VII, 1126–1157

Portugal

- Alfonso Enriquez, 1138–1185
- Sancho I, 1185–1211
- Alfonso II, 1211–1223
- Sancho II, 1223–1248
- Alfonso III, 1248–1279
- Dionis, 1279–1325
- Alfonso IV, 1326–1356
- Pedro, 1357–1367
- Fernando I, 1367–1383

León

- Fernando II, 1157–1188
- Alfonso IX, 1188–1230

Castile

- Alfonso VII, 1126–1157
- Sancho III, 1157–1158
- Alfonso VIII, 1158–1214
- Enrique I, 1214–1217
- Doña Berenguela, 1217

Castile and León

- Fernando III, 1217–1252
- Alfonso X, el Sabio, 1252–1284
- Sancho IV, 1284–1295
- Fernando IV, 1295–1312
- Alfonso XI, 1312–1350
- Pedro I, 1350–1369
- Enrique II, 1369–1379
- Juan I, 1379–1390
- Enrique III, 1390–1406
- Juan II, 1406–1454
- Enrique IV, 1454–1474
- Isabella, 1474–1504

Aragón

- Ramiro I, 1035–1063
- Sancho Ramírez, 1063–1094
- Pedro I, 1094–1104
- Alfonso I, el Batallador, 1104–1134
- Ramiro II, 1134–1137
- Jaime I, el Conquistador, 1213–1276
- Pedro III, 1276–1285

Alfonso III, 1285–1291
Jaime II, 1291–1327
Alfonso IV, 1327–1336
Pedro IV, 1336–1387
Juan I, 1387–1395
Martin I, 1395–1410
Fernando I, el de Antequera, 1412–1416
Alfonso V, 1416–1458
Juan II, 1458–1479
Fernando II, el Católico, 1479–1516

Aragón and Castile

Carlos V, 1516–1555
Felipe II, 1555–1598

Notes

LIST OF ABBREVIATIONS

AHDE. *Annuario de Historia del Derecho Español*
AI. *Ars Islamica*
AIEO. *Annales de l'Institut d'Études Orientales* (Faculté des Lettres de l'Université d'Alger)
AJSLL. *American Journal of Semitic Languages and Literature*
AMG. *Annales du Musée Guimet* (Bibliothèque d'Études)
AOS. American Oriental Society
AR. *Archivum Romanicum*
BAE. *Biblioteca de Autores Españoles*
BAF. *Bibliothèque arabe-française*
BAH. *Biblioteca Arábico-Hispana*
BAS. *Bibliotheca Arabo-Sicula*
BCB. Biblioteca Central de Barcelona
BEA. *Bulletin des études arabes* (Algiers)
BELOV. *Bibliothèque de l'École des Langues Orientales Vivantes*
BEO. *Bulletin d'études orientales*
BGA. *Bibliotheca Geographorum Arabicorum*
BH. *Bulletin Hispanique*
BHS. *Bulletin of Hispanic Studies*
BNM. F. Guillén Robles, *Catálogo de los manuscritos árabes existentes en la Biblioteca Nacional de Madrid* (Madrid, 1889)
BPT. Biblioteca Provincial de Toledo
BRABL. *Boletín de la Real Academia de Buenas Letras de Barcelona*
BRAE. *Boletín de la Real Academia Española*
BRAH. *Boletín de la Real Academia de Historia de Madrid*
BSOAS. *Bulletin of the School of Oriental and African Studies*
Casiri. M. Casiri. *Biblioteca Arábico-Hispana Escurialensis* (2 vols.; Madrid, 1760–1770)
CT. *Cahiers de Tunis*
EEAM. Escuela de Estudios Arabes de Madrid
EI. *Encyclopedia of Islam* (4 vols.; Leiden, 1913–1914; 2nd ed., Leiden, 1954–)
Escorial. H. Derenbourg et al., *Manuscrits arabes de l'Escurial* (3 vols.; Paris, 1884–1941)

Études d'Orientalisme. Études d'Orientalism dédiées à la mémoire de Lévi-Provençal (2 vols.; Paris, 1962)
GAL. C. Brockelmann, *Geschichte der arabischen Literatur* (2 vols., 3 sups.; Weimar & Leiden, 1898–1942)
IC. *Islamic Culture* (Hyderabad)
IEIM. *Manuscritos en el Instituto de Estudios Islámicos en Madrid* (for the most part, on microfilm)
IL. *Islamic Literature*
IO. *Islam et l'Occident*
JA. *Journal asiatique*
JAOS. *Journal of the American Oriental Society* (New Haven)
JNES. *Journal of Near Eastern Studies*
JPHS. *Journal of the Pakistan Historical Society* (Karachi)
JRAS. *Journal of the Royal Asiatic Society*
Junta. J. Ribera and M. Asín, *Manuscritos árabes y aljamiados de la Biblioteca de la Junta* (Madrid, 1912)
JWH. *Journal of World History*
Majma'. *Majallat al-majma' al-'ilmī al-'arabī* (Damascus)
MAO. *Mélanges africains et orientaux* (Paris)
MEAH. *Miscelánea de Estudios Árabes y Hebraicos*
MEJ. *Middle East Journal* (Washington, D.C.)
MRAH. *Memorias de la Real Academia de la Historia*
MW. *Muslim World*
NBAE. *Nueva Biblioteca de Autores Españoles*
OM. *Oriente Moderno*
PIHEM. *Publications de l'Institut de Hautes Études Marocaines*
Rabat. E. Lévi-Provençal, et al., *Les manuscrits arabes de Rabat* (Paris, 1921)
RABM. *Revista de Archivos, Bibliotecas y Museos*
RBPH. *Revue belge de philologie et d'histoire*
RCEH. *Revista del Centro de Estudios Históricos de Granada y Su Reino*
REI. *Revue des études islamiques*
RES. *Revue des études sémitiques*
RFE. *Revista de Filología Española*
RH. *Revue hispanique*
RIEEI. *Revista del Instituto Egipcio de Estudios Islámicos* (Madrid)
RIEI. *Revista del Instituto de Estudios Islámicos* (Madrid)
RO. *Revista de Occidente*
RT. *Revue tunisienne*
SEI. *A Shorter Encyclopedia of Islam* (Cornell, 1953)
SI. *Studia Islamica*
Zaytūnah. 'Abd al-Ḥāfiẓ Manṣūr, *Fihris makhṭūṭāt al-maktabah al-aḥmadiyyah bi-Tūnis* (Beirut, 1969)
ZDMG. *Zeitschrift der Deutschen Morgenländischen Geseltschaft*

Notes

1. The Conquest of Spain and the Emirate

1. For a general history of the Islamic peoples, see P. K. Hitti, *History of the Arabs* (6th ed.; London, 1958); C. Brockelmann, *History of the Islamic Peoples* (New York, 1960); and B. Lewis, *The Arabs in History* (London, 1954).

2. On the Visigoths, see vol. 3 of R. Menéndez Pidal, ed. *Historia de España* (Madrid, 1950); A. K. Ziegler, *Church and State in Visigothic Spain* (Washington, D.C., 1930); E. A. Thompson, *The Goths of Spain* (Oxford, 1968).

3. On the conquest of North Africa, see Ḥ. Mu'nis, *Fajr al-Andalus* (Cairo, 1959), pp. 34–49, and *Fatḥ al-'Arab li-l-Maghrib* (Cairo, 1947); 'Abd al-'Azīz Sālim, *Ta'rīkh al-muslimīn wa-āthāruhum fī-l-Andalus* (Beinut, 1962), pp. 132–148; C. A. Julien, *Histoire de l'Afrique du* Nord (Paris, 1951). See also Mu. 'A. 'Inān, *Dawlat al-Islām fī-l-Andalus* (3rd ed.; Cairo, 1960), vol. 1, pp. 14ff.; E. Lévi-Provençal, *Histoire de l'Espagne musulmane* (Paris, 1950–1953), vol. 1, pp. 8ff.

For the general history of Spain, I have relied mainly on the following important works: *Akhbār majmū'ah*, ed. E. Lafuente y Alcántara (Madrid, 1867); Ibn al-Qūṭiyah, *Tārīkh iftitāḥ al-Andalus*, ed. 'Abdallah A. al-Ṭabbā' (Beirut, 1957); Ibn 'Idhārī, *Kitāb al-bayān al-mughrib fī akhbār mulūk al-Andalus wa-l-Maghrib*, ed. Lévi-Provençal et al. (Paris, 1930); al-Marrākushī, *al-Mu'jib fī talkhīṣ akhbār al-Maghrib*, ed. M. S. al-'Iryān (Cairo, 1963); *Ibn al-Abbār, al-Ḥullah al-siyarā'*, ed. Ḥ. Mu'nis (Cairo, 1963); Ibn al-Khaṭīb, *A'māl al-a'lām*, ed. E. Lévi-Provençal (Beirut, 1956); Ibn Khaldūn, *Kitāb al-'ibar wa-dīwān al-mubtadā wa-l-khabar* (hereafter *'Ibar*; Beirut, 1956); al-Maqqarī, *Nafḥ al-ṭīb min ghuṣn al-Andalus al-raṭīb*, ed. M. Muḥyy al-Dīn 'Abd al-Ḥamīd (Cairo, 1949).

For modern Arabic works, the most comprehensive and reliable history is that of 'Inān, *Dawlat al-Islām fī-l-Andalus*, covering the whole period from the conquest to the fall of Granada. This impressive work was followed by a number of studies such as *Tārīkh al-Muslimīn wa-āthārahum fī-l-Andalus* by Sālim, *Tārīkh al-'Arab fī-Isbāniyah* (Aleppo, 1963) by Khālid al-Ṣūfī, and *al-Andalus wa-ḥaḍārātuha* (Damascus, 1969) by Aḥmad Badr.

As for Western sources, a number of attempts at a comprehensive history of Muslim Spain, dating from the eighteenth century, have been made. One may mention Denis D. Cardonne, *Histoire de l'Afrique et de l'Espagne sous la domination des Arabes*

(Paris, 1765); Thomas Bourke, *A Concise History of the Moors in Spain* (London, 1811); George Power, *The History of the Empire of Musulmans in Spain and Portugal* (London, 1815); J. A. Conde, *Historia de la dominación de los árabes en España* (Madrid, 1820–1821); Joseph Aschbach, *Geschichte der Ommaÿaden in Spanien* (Frankfurt a.M., 1829) and *Geschichte Spaniens und Portugals zur Zeit Herrschaft der Almoraviden und Almohaden* (Frankfurt a.M., 1833); P. de Gayangos, *The History of the Mohammedan Dynasties in Spain* (London, 1840–1843), being a translation of the first part of al-Maqqarī's *Nafḥ al-ṭīb*; F. Codera, *Estudios críticos de la historia árabe-española* (Saragossa, 1903–1917); S. P. Scott, *History of the Moorish Empire in Europe* (Philadelphia, 1904); S. Lane-Poole, *The Story of the Moors in Spain* (New York, 1911). But the most reliable works are those of R. Dozy, *Histoire des musulmans d'Espagne*, ed. E. Lévi-Provençal (Leiden, 1932), English trans. by F. G. Stokes, *Spanish Islam* (New York, 1913); Lévi-Provençal, *Histoire de l'Espagne*, Spanish trans. E. García Gómez constituting vol. 4 of R. Menéndez Pidal, ed., *Historia de España*; A. González Palencia, *Historia de la España musulmana* (2nd ed. Barcelona, 1932); C. Sánchez-Albornoz, *La España musulmana* (Buenos Aires, 1946); S. M. Imamuddin, *A Political History of Muslim Spain* (Dacca, 1961); Américo Castro, *The Structure of Spanish History*, trans. E. L. King (Princeton, 1954); W. M. Watt, *A History of Islamic Spain* (Edinburgh, 1965).

4. Ibn Khaldūn, *'Ibar*, vol. 4, p. 398, places the appointment of 'Uqbah in A.H. 45 (A.D. 665), while Ibn al-Abbār, *Ḥullah*, vol. 2, p. 323, places it in 46. According to *Akhbār majmū'ah*, p. 3, 'Uqbah took Tangier shortly before his death.

5. Ibn Khaldūn, vol. 4, p. 399; Ibn al-Abbār, vol. 2, pp. 324 ff.

6. Ibn Khaldūn, vol. 4, p. 401; Ibn al-Abbār, vol. 2, pp. 331ff.

7. Ibn Khaldūn, vol. 4, p. 401.

8. Arab medieval authors give ample space to the prominent role played by Julian. See Ibn al-Qūṭiyah, *Iftitāḥ*, pp. 33ff. *Akhbār majmū'ah*, pp. 4ff., mentions that the conquest was definitely prompted by Julian, who had submitted to the authority of Mūsā Ibn Nuṣayr. Ibn 'Abd al-Ḥakam, *Futūḥ Miṣr wa-l-Maghrib wa-l-Andalus*, ed. Ch. Torrey (New Haven, 1922), pp. 90ff.; Ibn 'Idhārī, *Bayān*, vol. 2, pp. 4ff. Cf. Mu'nis, *Fajr*, pp. 52ff.

In addition to the figure of Julian, there is the legend of the "haunted house." Al-Maqqarī, *Nafḥ al-ṭīb*, vol. 1, pp. 227–232, relates a lengthy story concerning it. He calls it the "House of Wisdom" (*bayt al-ḥikmah*), supposedly built by a Greek king as a forbidden area to prevent the coming of the Berbers. It was supposed to remain closed for the desired effect. However, Roderick made the capital mistake of opening it against the warning of his advisers, who had told him that such an act would surely bring him disaster.

9. *Akhbār majmū'ah*, p. 6; Ibn 'Idhārī, *Bayān*, vol. 2, pp. 4ff.

10. For one, Ibn Khaldūn, *'Ibar*, vol. 4, p. 254, places the strength of the Visigothic army at 40,000 men; while *Akhbār majmū'ah*, pp. 7–8, places it at 100,000, and the number of Ṭāriq's army at 12,000 men.

11. *Akhbār majmū'ah*, pp. 14ff.; Ibn 'Idhārī, *Bayān*, vol. 2, p. 19, describes the Table of Solomon as having three circles: one of pearls, the second of saphires, and the third of chrysolythe. He also mentions the gems of Alexander the Great, the beautiful robes of Gothic kings, and the staffs of Solomon and Moses. Cf. al-Maqqarī, *Nafḥ al-tīb*, vol. 1, pp. 254ff., who also gives an extensive description of the Table and other trophies. See also P. de Gayangos, who translated extracts of al-Maqqarī's work as *The History of the Mohammedan Dynasties in Spain* (London, 1840), vol. 1, pp. 282ff.

12. On the conquest of Mūsā, see *Akhbār majmū'ah*, pp. 15ff.; Ibn al-Qūṭiyah, *Iftitāḥ*, p. 35. Invariably, Arabic sources tell us that Mūsā chastised Ṭāriq severely but that they soon became reconciled and marched together to the north. However, upon their return to Damascus, Ṭāriq appears to have stolen Mūsā's glory in the eyes of the caliph by taking sole credit for the capture of the Table of Solomon. See *Akhbār majmū'ah*, pp. 19 and 29ff.

13. Gayangos, *History of the Mohammedan Dynasties*, vol. 1, p. 288; Ibn Khaldūn, *'Ibar*, vol. 4, p. 255.

14. *Akhbār majmū'ah*, p. 19; Ibn Khaldūn, *'Ibar*, vol. 4, p. 255.

15. Ibn Khaldūn, *'Ibar*, vol. 4, p. 255, says that Mūsā left his son in Cordova, which he made his capital (*fa-t-takhazahā dār al-imārah*). Cf. *Akhbār majmū'ah*, p. 19.

16. E. Saavedra, *Estudio sobre la invasión de los árabes en España* (Madrid, 1882), p. 127; Mu'nis, *Fajr*, p. 117; and Sālim, *Tārīkh*, p. 110.

17. Al-Marrākushī, *Mu'jib*, p. 35, says that 'Abd al-'Azīz was killed by the order of the caliph and that his head was sent to the caliph, Sulaymān, in Damascus. Ibn al-Qūṭiyah, *Iftitāḥ*, p. 37, also mentions the sending of his head to Sulaymān. In addition, he refers to 'Abd al-'Azīz's marriage to a Gothic woman. *Akhbār majmū'ah*, p. 20, also mentions that the influence of his Christian wife was the cause of his death. Cf. Ibn 'Idhārī, *Bayān*, vol. 2, p. 24. F. J. Simonet, *Historia de los mozárabes de España* (Madrid, 1897–1903), p. 147, is inclined to think that 'Abd al-'Azīz intended secession.

18. On the various governors, see Ibn 'Idhārī, *Bayān*, vol. 2, pp. 23ff.; *Akhbār majmū'ah*, pp. 22ff.; Ibn al-Qūṭiyah, *Iftitāḥ*, pp. 38ff. Also, Lévi-Provençal, *Histoire*, vol. 1, pp. 34ff.

19. Edward Creasy, *The Fifteen Decisive Battles of the World* (New York, 1918), pp. 159ff.

20. *Akhbār majmū'ah*, pp. 37ff.; Lévi-Provençal, *Histoire*, vol. 1, pp. 34ff.

21. On 'Abd al-Raḥmān I see Ibn al-Qūṭiyah, *Iftitāḥ*, pp. 45ff.; *Akhbār majmū'ah*, pp. 46ff. and 67ff.; Ibn 'Idhārī, *Bayān*, vol. 2, pp. 40ff.; Ibn al-Abbār, *Ḥullah*, vol. 1, pp. 35ff.; al-Marrākushī, *Mu'jib*, pp. 40ff.; Ibn al-Khaṭīb, *A'lām*, pp. 7ff.; Ibn Khaldūn, *'Ibar*, vol. 4, pp. 262ff.; al-Maqqarī, *Nafḥ al-ṭīb*, vol. 4, pp. 26ff.; Mu'nis, *Fajr*, pp. 658 ff.; Sālim, *Tārīkh*, pp. 183ff.; P. K. Hitti, *The Makers of Arab History* (New York, 1968), pp. 59–75; Lévi-Provençal, *Histoire*, vol. 1, pp. 91ff.; Thomas Irving, *Falcon of Spain* (Lahore, 1954).

22. Ibn 'Idhārī, *Bayān*, vol. 2, p. 48. Ibn al-Abbār, *Ḥullah*, vol. 1, pp. 35ff., says that 'Abd al-Raḥmān continued for a while to mention the name of the 'Abbāsid caliph in the Friday prayer.

23. Ibn 'Idhārī, *Bayān*, vol. 2, pp. 78 and 88–89; cf. Sālim, *Tārīkh*, pp. 198ff. Cf. Ibn al-Qūṭiyah, *Iftitāḥ*, pp. 57ff.

24. For details concerning the withdrawal of Charlemagne and the attack on his army at Roncesvalles, see R. Menéndez Pidal, *La Chanson de Roland y el neotradicionalismo* (Madrid, 1959); cf. 'Inān, *Dawlat al-Islām*, vol. 1, pp. 166ff.

25. Ibn 'Idhārī, *Bayān*, vol. 2, p. 61, reports this unlikely arrangement. On the other hand, Ibn al-Abbār, *Ḥullah*, vol. 1, p. 43, and Ibn al-Khaṭīb, *A'lām*, p. 11, say that he succeeded his father, and Ibn Khaldūn, *'Ibar*, vol. 4, p. 270, says that he succeeded 'Abd al-Raḥmān by previous nomination (*wa kāna qad 'ahada lahu bi-l-amri*), which is more likely.

26. Ibn al-Khaṭīb, *A'lām*, p. 11.

27. *Ibid*., p. 12, dismisses the charge as unfair criticism by citing the story of an old man who was ridiculed for riding his donkey with his son, for having his son ride it alone, for riding it himself, and for not riding it at all. In *Akhbār majmū'ah*, pp. 120ff., Hishām is described as virtuous and generous. Cf. Ibn al-Qūṭiyah, *Iftitāh*, pp. 65ff.

28. Ibn 'Idhārī, *Bayān*, vol. 2, p. 79; Ibn al-Khaṭīb, *A'lām*, p. 14.

29. *Akhbār majmū'ah*, p. 130; Ibn Khaldūn, *'Ibar*, vol. 4, p. 277. They were called mute (*khurs*), probably for speaking Arabic incorrectly.

30. Ibn al-Qūṭiyah, *Iftitāḥ*, pp. 68ff.; Ibn al-Khaṭīb, *A'lām*, p. 15.

31. Ibn al-Qūṭiyah, *Iftitāḥ*, pp. 72ff.; Ibn al-Abbār, *Ḥullah*, vol. 1, p. 44ff. On the other hand, Ibn Khaldūn, *'Ibar*, vol. 4, p. 274, places it in A.H. 190 (A.D. 806).

32. Ibn al-Khaṭīb, *A'lām*, p. 16.

33. Ibn al-Qūṭiyah, *Iftitāḥ*, p. 73; Ibn al-Abbār, *Ḥullah*, vol. 1, p. 45.

34. Ibn 'Idhārī, *Bayān*, vol. 2, p. 91; cf. Ibn al-Khaṭīb, *A'lām*, p. 20; *akhbār majmū'ah*, pp. 135ff.; and Ibn al-Qūṭiyah, *Iftitāḥ*, p. 83.

35. Ibn al-Qūṭiyaḥ, *Iftitāḥ*, pp. 89ff.

36. See one of the poems addressed to Ṭarūb in Ibn al-Abbār, *Ḥullah*, pp. 114–115. On the machinations of Ṭarūb with the eunuch to poison 'Abd al-Raḥmān so that her son 'Abdallah would succeed him, see Ibn al-Qūṭiyah, *Iftitāḥ*, pp. 96ff.

37. Ibn 'Idhārī, *Bayān*, vol. 2, pp. 87ff.; Ibn al-Qūṭiyah, *Iftitāḥ*, p. 88; Ibn al-Khaṭīb,

A'lām, p. 20; al-'Udhrī, *Nuṣūs 'an al-Andalus*, ed. 'Abd al-'Azīz al-Ahwānī (Madrid, 1965), pp. 98ff. and 118ff.

38. For more details see Simonet, *Historia de los mozárabes*, pp. 413ff.; Dozy, *Histoire*, vol. 1, pp. 317ff.

39. Ibn 'Idhārī, *Bayān*, vol. 2, p. 90.

40. See E. Lévi-Provençal, "Un échange d'ambassades entre Courdoue et Byzance au IXe siècle," *Byzantion*, 12 (1937), 1–24. Cf. his *Histoire*, vol. 1, pp. 249ff.

41. Ibn al-Khaṭīb, *A'lām*, p. 21; cf. *Akhbār majmū'ah*, pp. 141ff.

42. On the several revolts, see Ibn al-Qūṭiyah, *Iftitāḥ*, pp. 107ff.; al-'Udhrī, *Nuṣūs*, pp. 25ff., 101ff., and 112ff; Ibn Khaldūn, *'Ibar*, vol. 4, pp. 288ff.; Ibn 'Idhārī, *Bayān*, vol. 2, pp. 133ff. Cf. Lévi-Provençal, *Histoire*, vol. 1, pp. 279ff.

43. Ibn 'Idhārī, *Bayān*, vol. 2, pp. 100 and 102. Ibn al-Qūṭiyah, *Iftitāḥ*, p. 106, says that A.H. 260 was a year in which "no single grain was cultivated in al-Andalus."

44. Ibn 'Idhārī, *Bayān*, vol. 2, p. 114. On Ibn Ḥafṣūn's revolt, see Ibn al-Qūṭiyah, *Iftitāḥ*, pp. 109ff.; Ibn 'Idhārī, *Bayān*, vol. 2, pp. 117ff. and 131ff.; Ibn al-Khaṭīb, *A'lām*, pp. 31ff.; Dozy, *Histoire*, vol. 1, pp. 253ff.

45. Ibn 'Idhārī, *Bayān*, vol. 2, pp. 114–115.

46. Ibn Khaldūn, *'Ibar*, vol. 4, p. 293.

47. Ibn al-Khaṭīb, *A'lām*, p. 27.

48. On Banū Ḥajjāj, see Ibn al-Qūṭiyah, *Iftitāḥ*, pp. 126ff.; Ibn 'Idhārī, *Bayān*, vol. 2, pp. 125ff.; Ibn al-Khaṭīb, *A'lām*, pp. 34ff.; Ibn Khaldūn, *'Ibar*, vol. 4, pp. 294ff.

49. On the emir 'Abdallah, see Ibn al-Qūṭiyah, *Iftitāḥ*, pp. 121ff.; *Akhbār majmū'ah*, pp. 150ff.; Ibn al-Abbār, *Ḥullah*, vol. 1, pp. 120ff.; Ibn al-Khaṭīb, *A'lām*, pp. 26ff.; Ibn Khaldūn, *'Ibar*, vol. 4, p. 288; Ibn 'Idhārī, *Bayān*, vol. 2, pp. 152ff. But the most valuable source is the extant portion of Ibn Ḥayyān's work, *Kitāb al-muqtabis fī-tārīkh rijāl al-Andalus*, ed. P. Melchor Antuña (Paris, 1937). See also, Lévi-Provençal, *Histoire*, vol. 1, pp. 329ff.

50. On the conquest and occupation of Sicily, see M. Amari, *Storia dei Musulmani di Sicilia* (2nd ed.; Catania, 1933–1939).

51. See Archibald R. Lewis, *Naval Power and Trade in the Mediterranean, A.D. 500–1000* (Princeton, 1951).

2. The Caliphate, 929–1031

1. Ibn Khaldūn, *'Ibar*, vol. 4, p. 297; Ibn al-Khaṭīb, *A'lām*, p. 29; *Akhbār majmū'ah*, p. 153.

On 'Abd al-Raḥmān III, see the important anonymous work entitled *Una crónica anónima de 'Abd al-Raḥmān III al-Nāṣir* (Madrid, 1950); Dozy, *Histoire*, vol. 2, pp. 115ff. 'Inān, *Dawlat al-Islām*, vol. 2, pp. 367ff.; Lévi-Provençal, *Histoire*, vol. 2, pp. 1ff.

2. Ibn al-Khaṭīb, *A'lām*, p. 29; cf. Ibn 'Idhārī, *Bayān*, vol. 2, p. 157; Ibn Khaldūn, *'Ibar*, vol. 4, p. 298.

3. On Banū Ḥajjāj, see Ibn al-Khaṭīb, *A'lām*, pp. 34ff.; Ibn Khaldūn, *'Ibar*, vol. 4, pp. 301–302; cf. Ibn Ḥayyān, *al-Muqtabis*, p. 84.

4. Ibn Khaldūn, *'Ibar*, vol. 4, p. 303.

5. On the last days of the Ḥafṣūnids, see Ibn al-Khaṭīb, *A'lām*, pp. 33–34; Ibn 'Idhārī, *Bayān*, vol. 2, p. 196; Sālim, *Tārīkh*, pp. 282ff.

6. Ibn Khaldūn, *'Ibar*, vol. 4, p. 294; cf. *Akhbār majmū'ah*, p. 154.

7. Ibn Khaldūn, *'Ibar*, vol. 4, p. 306; Ibn 'Idhārī, *Bayān*, vol. 2, p. 204.

8. Ibn 'Idhārī, *Bayān*, vol. 2, pp. 198–199; cf. Ibn al-Khaṭīb, *A'lām*, p. 30.

9. 'Abd al-Raḥmān's rule coincided with that of Ordoño II (914–924), Alfonso IV (925–951), Ramiro II (932–942), and others with whom he fought indecisive battles. On Christian Spain, see Lévi-Provençal, *Histoire*, vol. 2, pp. 33ff. Cf. Ibn al-Khaṭīb, *A'lām*, pp. 36ff.; al-Maqqarī, *Nafḥ al-ṭīb*, vol. 1, pp. 340ff.

10. Ibn al-Khaṭīb, *A'lām*, p. 37; Ibn Khaldūn, *'Ibar*, vol. 4, p. 309; al-Maqqarī, *Nafḥ al-ṭīb*, vol. 1, p. 341; see also 'Inān, *Dawlat al-Islām*, vol. 2, pp. 410ff.

11. Historians hardly fail to mention the fact that 'Abd al-Raḥmān III was a great builder. See Ibn al-Khaṭīb, A'lām, pp. 38ff.; Ibn Khaldūn, 'Ibar, vol. 4, pp. 311ff.; Ibn 'Idhārī, Bayān, vol. 2, pp. 229ff.

12. Ibn al-Khaṭīb, A'lām, p. 40.

13. Ibid., p. 39; Ibn Khaldūn, 'Ibar, vol. 4, p. 311.

14. Ibn al-Khaṭīb, A'lām, p. 40.

15. See below, Chapter 6.

16. Ibn 'Abd Rabbihi, al-'Iqd al-farīd, vol. 4, pp. 501–527, has a number of poems praising the expeditions and virtues of his patron.

17. On al-Ḥakam, see Ibn Ḥayyān al-Muqtabis; Ibn 'Idhārī, Bayān, vol. 2, pp. 233ff.; al-Marrākushī, Mu'jib, pp. 59ff.; Ibn al-Abbār, Ḥullah, vol. 1, pp. 200ff.; Ibn al-Khaṭīb, A'lām, pp. 41ff.; Ibn Khaldūn, 'Ibar, vol. 4, pp. 312ff.; Dozy, Histoire, vol. 2, pp. 176ff.; Lévi-Provençal, Histoire, vol. 2, pp. 165ff.

18. Ibn 'Idhārī, Bayān, vol., 2, p. 239.

19. Ibid., p. 241.

20. Ibid. However, Ibn Qannūn was eventually defeated and brought to Cordova (ibid., p. 244). Cf. 'Inān, Dawlat al-Islām, pp. 448ff.

21. Al-Marrākushī, Mu'jib, p. 62; Ibn al-Abbār, Ḥullah, vol. 1, p. 202. Ibn Ḥazm, Jamharat ansāb al-'Arab (Cairo, 1962), p. 100.

22. Ibn Khaldūn, 'Ibar, vol. 4, p. 317.

23. Ibn al-Abbār, Ḥullah, vol. 1, p. 201; al-Marrākushī, Mu'jib, pp. 61ff.; Dozy, Histoire, vol. 2, p. 184.

24. Ibn 'Idhārī, Bayān, vol. 2, p. 240; Dozy, Histoire, vol. 2, pp. 184–185.

25. Ibn 'Idhārī, Bayān, vol. 2, p. 242ff.

26. Ibn Ḥayyān, al-Muqtabis (ed. al-Ḥajjī), pp. 44ff., gives us detailed descriptions of these diplomatic receptions. Cf. Ibn 'Idhārī, Bayān, vol. 2, pp. 235 and 239. And see F. Codera, "Embajada de príncipes cristianos en Córdoba en los ultimos años de Alhaquem," BRAH, 13 (1888); 'Inān, Dawlat al-Islām, vol. 2 pp. 448ff.

27. Ibn 'Idhārī, Bayān, vol. 2, p. 241.

28. On al-Muṣḥafi, see Ibn 'Idhārī, Bayān, vol. 2, p. 254; al-Marrākushī, Mu'jib, p. 62; Ibn al-Abbār, Ḥullah, vol. 1, pp. 247ff.

29. On Ibn Abī 'Amir, see Ibn 'Idhārī, Bayān, vol. 2, pp. 251ff. and 256ff. 'Inān, Dawlat al-Islām, vol. 2, pp. 470ff.; also his al-Dawlat al-'āmiriyyah (Cairo, 1958).

30. Ghālib was known as the knight of al-Andalus and fought many battles. See Ibn 'Idhārī, Bayān, vol. 2, p. 246.

31. Ibid., p. 249.

32. Ibn al-Khaṭīb, A'lām, pp. 44ff.

33. Ibid., p. 41.

34. Ibid., p. 43.

35. Ibid., p. 48.

36. Ibn 'Idhārī, Bayān, vol. 2, pp. 259ff.

37. Ibn al-Khaṭīb, A'lām, p. 58.

38. Ibid., p. 65.

39. For instance, Ibn al-Khaṭīb, A'lām, 59 ff.; Ibn Khaldūn, 'Ibar, vol. 4, pp. 318ff. See n. 29 above.

40. Ibn 'Idhārī, Bayān, vol. 2, p. 251. al-Muṣḥafi was known as "the Chamberlain and the Sword of the Dynasty" (ḥājib wa-sayf al-dawlah; ibid., p. 234).

41. Ibn al-Khaṭīb, A'lām, p. 60.

42. Ibn 'Idhārī, Bayān, vol. 2, p. 251.

43. Ibid., p. 251.

44. Ibid., p. 252.

45. Ibid., p. 259.

46. On his successful raids, see ibid., pp. 264ff. Ibn Abī 'Āmir is said to have led some fifty expeditions against the Christians.

47. *Ibid*., p. 268.
48. *Ibid*., pp. 275ff.
49. *Ibid*., pp. 278ff.
50. *Ibid*., p. 279.
51. *Ibid*., pp. 287ff.
52. *Ibid*., p. 292.
53. *Ibid*., p. 293.
54. Ibn al-Khaṭib, *A'lām*, pp. 81–82.
55. On 'Abd al-Malik, see Ibn 'Idhārī, *Bayān*, vol. 3, pp. 3ff.; Ibn Khaṭib, *A'lām*, pp. 89ff.; Sālim, *Tārīkh*, pp. 336ff. It would seem that Ṣubḥ, who would oppose the new ruler, had died before 1002.
56. On 'Abd al-Raḥmān, see Ibn 'Idhārī, *Bayān*, vol. 3, pp. 38ff.
57. The text of the document may be found in Ibn al-Khaṭib's *A'lām*, pp. 91–92; Ibn 'Idhārī, *Bayān*, vol. 3, pp. 44ff.
58. Sālim, *Tārīkh*, pp. 343ff.; al-Ṣūfī, *Tārīkh*, pp. 161ff.; Ibn 'Idhārī, *Bayān*, vol. 3, pp. 66ff.; Ibn al-Khaṭib, *A'lām*, pp. 109ff.; Ibn Khaldūn, *'Ibar*, vol. 4, pp. 323ff.; Imamuddin, *Political History*, pp. 124ff.
59. On Muḥammad, known as Muḥammad II al-Mahdī, see Ibn 'Idhārī, *Bayān*, vol. 3, pp. 50ff.; al-Marrākushī, *Mu'jib*, pp. 88ff.; Ibn al-Khaṭib, *A'lām*, pp. 109ff.; Ibn Khaldūn, *'Ibar*, vol. 4, p. 323; Sālim, *Tārīkh*, pp. 347ff.
60. Ibn 'Idhārī, *Bayān*, vol. 3, p. 56.
61. *Ibid*., pp. 64ff.; Ibn al-Khaṭib, *A'lām*, p. 111.
62. Ibn 'Idhārī, *Bayān*, vol. 3, p. 77; Ibn al-Khaṭib, *A'lām*, p. 112.
63. Ibn 'Idhārī, *Bayān*, vol. 3, p. 81.
64. *Ibid*., pp. 91ff.; al-Marrākushī, *Mu'jib*, p. 90; Ibn al-Khaṭib, *A'lām*, pp. 113ff.; Ibn Khaldūn, *'Ibar*, vol. 4, pp. 324ff.
65. Ibn 'Idhārī, *Bayān*, vol. 3, p. 50.
66. Ibn al-Khaṭib, *A'lām*, p. 115.
67. *Ibid*., pp. 116–117.
68. *Ibid*., p. 117.
69 *Ibid*., p. 119.
70. *Ibid*., p. 128.
71. *Ibid*., p. 121.
72. On the Ḥammūdids, see Ibn 'Idhārī, *Bayān*, vol. 3, pp. 119ff.; al-Marrākushī, *Mu'jib*, pp. 98ff.; Ibn al-Khaṭib, *A'lām*, pp. 128ff.; Ibn Khaldūn, *'Ibar*, vol. 4, pp. 330ff. Also L. Seco de Lucena, *Los Hammudies señores de Málaga y Algeciras* (Málaga, 1955).
73. On 'Abd al-Raḥmān IX (al-Murtaḍā), see Ibn 'Idhārī, *Bayān*, vol. 3, pp. 121ff.; Ibn al-Khaṭib, *A'lām*, pp. 130ff.
74. Ibn 'Idhārī, *Bayān*, vol. 3, p. 121; Ibn al-Khaṭib, *A'lām*, p. 130.
75. Ibn al-Khaṭib, *A'lām*, p. 131.
76. On 'Abd al-Raḥmān V (al-Mustaẓhir), see Ibn 'Idhārī, *Bayān*, vol. 3, pp. 135ff.; al-Marrākushī, *Mu'jib*, pp. 105ff.; Ibn Khaldūn, *'Ibar*, vol. 4, pp. 328ff.
77. On Muḥammad III (al-Mustakfī), see Ibn 'Idhārī, *Bayān*, vol. 3, pp. 140ff.; al-Marrākushī, *Mu'jib*, pp. 107ff.; Ibn al-Khaṭib, *A'lām*, pp. 135ff.; Ibn Khaldūn, *'Ibar*, vol. 4, p. 329.
78. On Hishām III (al-Mu'tadd), see Ibn 'Idhārī, *Bayān*, vol. 4, pp. 145ff.; al-Marrākushī, *Mu'jib*, pp. 109ff.; Ibn al-Khaṭib, *A'lām*, pp. 138ff.; Ibn Khaldūn, *'Ibar*, vol. 4, pp. 329ff.

3. The Party-Kings, 1031–1090

1. On Mulūk al-Ṭawā'if, see Ibn 'Idhārī, *Bayān*, vol. 3, pp. 155ff.; al-Marrākushī, *Mu'jib*, pp. 111ff.; 'Abdallah, *Mudhakkirāt Emir 'Abdallah*, ed. E. Lévi Provençal (Cairo, 1955); al-Ḥimyarī, *Kitāb al-rawḍ al-mi'ṭār* (Cairo, 1948); Ibn al-Khaṭib, *A'lām*, pp. 144ff.; *Ibn Khaldūn, 'Ibar*, vol. 4, pp. 330ff.

The most comprehensive modern works on the subject are R. Menéndez Pidal, *La España del Cid* (Madrid, 1947); M. Gaspar Remiro, *Historia de Murcia musulmana* (Saragossa, 1905); A. Piles Ibars, *Valencia árabe* (Valencia, 1901); A. Campaner y Fuentes, *Bosquejo histórico de la dominación islamita en las Islas Baleares* (Palma, 1868); A. Prieto y Vives, *Los reyes de Taifas* (Madrid, 1926); M. 'A. 'Inān, *Duwal al-Ṭawā'if* (Cairo, 1960); 'Abd al-Salām A. al-Ṭūd, *Banū 'Abbād bi-Ishbīliyyah* (Tetuan, 1946). See also Imamuddin, *Political History*, pp. 136ff, and Ṣalāḥ Khāliṣ, *Ishbīlīyyah fī-l-qarn al-khāmis al-hijrī* (Beirut, 1965).

2. Ibn 'Idhārī, *Bayān*, vol. 3, p. 113; Ibn al-Khaṭīb, *A'lām*, p. 119; al-Ṣūfī, *Tārīkh*, pp. 235; al-Ṭūd, *Banū 'Abbād*, pp. 33ff.
3. 'Inān, *Duwal*, pp. 433ff., recognizes some twenty kingdoms; cf. Ibn al-Khaṭīb, *A'lām*, pp. 209–210 and 238–239.
4. M. Asín Palacios, in *al-Andalus*, 2 (1934), 35–37; cf. 'Inān, *Duwal*, pp. 404ff.
5. 'Umar 'Abd al-'Azīz was an Umayyad caliph (717–720) of Damascus known for his piety.
6. Ibn al-Khaṭīb, *A'lām*, p. 144.
7. *Ibid*., pp. 210ff.; 'Inān, *Duwal*, pp. 156ff.
8. See Gaspar y Remiro, *Historia de Murcia musulmana*.
9. Ibn 'Idhārī, *Bayān*, vol. 3, p. 121.
10. *Ibid*., p. 126.
11. Ibn al-Khaṭīb, *A'lām*, p. 193.
12. *Ibid*., p. 216.
13. On the checkered history of Valencia, see Piles Ibars, *Valencia árabe*; Menéndez Pidal, *España del Cid*, pp. 449ff.; 'Inān, *Duwal*, pp. 221ff.; C. D. Sarnelli, *Mujāhid al-'Āmirī* (Cairo, 1961); A Huici Miranda, *Historia musulmana de Valencia* (Valencia, 1970).
14. Ibn al-Khaṭīb, *A'lām*, pp. 217ff.; Ibn Khaldūn, *'Ibar*, vol. 4, pp. 353ff.; 'Inān, *Duwal*, pp. 183ff.
15. Campaner y Fuentes, *Bosquejo histórico*.
16. Ibn al-Khaṭīb, *A'lām*, p. 219.
17. *Ibid*., p. 221.
18. *Ibid*., pp. 222ff.
19. *Ibid*., p. 226.
20. *Ibid*., p. 189; cf. Ibn Khaldūn, *'Ibar*, vol. 4, pp. 350ff.
21. Ibn al-Khaṭīb, *A'lām*, p. 190.
22. 'Inān, *Duwal*, pp. 249ff.; Ibn 'Idhārī, *Bayān*, vol. 3, p. 127; Menéndez Pidal, *España del Cid*, p. 360.
23. On Banū Jahwar, see Ibn 'Idhārī, *Bayān*, vol. 3, pp. 185ff.; Ibn al-Khaṭīb, *A'lām*, pp. 145ff.; Ibn Khaldūn, *'Ibar*, vol. 4, pp. 342ff.; Prieto y Vives, *Los reyes de Taifas*, pp. 22ff.; 'Inān, *Duwal*, pp. 20ff.
24. Ibn al-Khaṭīb, *A'lām*, p. 151. He played the role of a peacemaker during the wars between the kingdoms of Seville and that of Badajoz.
25. On Banū 'Abbād, see al-Ṭūd, *Banū 'Abbād*; Ibn 'Idhārī, *Bayān*, vol. 3, pp. 193ff.; Ibn al-Khaṭīb, *A'lām*, pp. 152ff.; Ibn Khaldūn, *'Ibar*, vol. 4, pp. 336ff.; 'Inān, *Duwal*, pp. 31–79; Prieto y Vives, *Los reyes de Taifas*, pp. 69ff.; Imamuddin, *Political History*, pp. 147ff.
26. 'Inān, *Duwal*, p. 32.
27. Al-Ṭūd, *Banū 'Abbād*, p. 39.
28. *Ibid*., p. 42.
29. 'Inān, *Duwal*, p. 37.
30. *Ibid*., p. 52.
31. Ibn al-Khaṭīb, *A'lām*, p. 239; Ibn Khaldūn, *'Ibar*, vol. 4, p. 339.
32. On the Banū Hūd, see Ibn 'Idhārī, *Bayān*, vol. 3, 221ff.; Ibn al-Khaṭīb, *A'lām*, pp. 170ff.; Ibn Khaldūn, *'Ibar*, vol. 4, pp. 350ff.; 'Inan, *Duwal*, pp. 255ff.
33. Ibn al-Khaṭīb, *A'lām*, p. 170.

34. One may add the following Berber kingdoms: Banū Birzāl in Camona, Écija, and Almodar del Río; Banū Khazrūn in Arkash; Banū Yafran in Ronda; and Banū Dummar in Morón.

35. Ibn 'Idhārī, *Bayān*, vol. 3, pp. 276ff.; Ibn al-Khaṭīb, *A'lām*, p. 176; Ibn Khaldūn, *'Ibar*, vol. 4, pp. 347ff.; 'Abdallah, *Mudhakkirāt*, p. 56; 'Inān, *Duwal*, pp. 93ff.; Prieto y Vives, *Los reyes de Taifas*, pp. 51ff.

36. Ibn al-Khaṭīb, *A'lām*, p. 178.

37. Inān, *Duwal*, pp. 108ff.

38. Ibn 'Idhārī, *Bayān*, vol. 3, pp. 223ff.; Ibn al-Khaṭīb, *A'lām*, pp. 182ff.; Ibn Khaldūn, *'Ibar*, vol. 4, p. 344; 'Inān, *Duwal*, pp. 80ff.

39. Ibn al-Khaṭīb, *A'lām*, p. 185.

40. See also Ibn 'Idhārī, *Bayān*, vol. 3, pp. 262ff.; Ibn al-Khaṭīb, *A'lām*, pp. 227ff.; Ibn Khaldūn, *'Ibar*, vol. 4, pp. 345ff.

41. 'Abdallah, *Mudhakkirāt*, pp. 18ff.

42. *Ibid*., p. 22.

43. *Ibid*., p. 26.

4. Berber Dynasties

1. For a general history of al-Maghrib, see G. Marçais, *La Berbérie musulmane et l'Orient au Moyen Âge* (Paris, 1946); H. Terrasse, *Histoire du Maroc, des origines à l'établissement du protectorat français* (Casablanca, 1949); J. Charles-André, *Histoire de l'Afrique du Nord* (2nd ed.; Paris, 1952); R. Montague, *Les Berbères et le Makhzen dans le Sud du Maroc* (Paris, 1930); J. M. Abun-Nasr, *A History of the Maghrib* (Cambridge, 1971); A. Nāṣirī, *al-Istiqṣā'* (Casablanca, 1954–1956; French trans., Paris, 1923–1934).

On the Almoravids, see J. Bosch, *Los Almorávides* (Tetuan, 1956); F. Codera, *Decadencia y decaparición de los Almorávides en España* (Saragossa, 1899); J. Aschbach, *Geschichte Spaniens und Portugals zur Zeit der Herrschaft der Almoraviden und Almohaden* (Frankfurt, a.M., 1833); Mu. A. 'Inān, *'Aṣr al-Murābiṭīn wa-l-Muwaḥḥidīn* (Cairo, 1964); H. Monés, "Les Almoravides," *RIEI*, 14 (1967–1968), 49–102; Ibn 'Idhārī, *Bayān*, vol. 4, pp. 48ff.; al-Marrākushī, *Mu'jib*, pp. 200ff. and 225ff.; Ibn al-Khaṭīb, *A'lām*, pp. 241ff.; Ibn Khaldūn, *'Ibar*, vol. 6, pp. 373–389; Ibn Abī Zar', *al-Anīs al-ṭarab bi-rawḍ al-qirṭās fī akhbār mulūk al-Maghrib* (Upsula, 1843–1846); the anonymous work, *al-Ḥulal mawshiyyah fī dhikr al-akhbār al-marrākushiyyah* (Tunis, n.d.); al-Ḥimyarī, *al-Rawḍ*.

2. Ibn 'Idhārī, *Bayān*, vol. 4, p. 11.

3. *Ibid*., p. 12.

4. *Ibid*., p. 16.

5. *Ibid*., p. 15.

6. *Ibid*., p. 18.

7. *Ibid*., p. 20, has the year 463/1071, which is unlikely.

8. *Ibid*., p. 21.

9. It is reported by Ibn 'Idhārī (*ibid*., p. 26) that it was Yūsuf's wife, Zaynab, who instructed him to shower Abū Bakr with gifts; she also insisted that Yūsuf should continue to be the supreme leader.

10. It is uncertain when Ibn Tāshfīn assumed the title of "Commander of the Muslims." *Al-Ḥulal mawshiyyah*, pp. 16ff., and Ibn 'Idhārī, *Bayān*, vol. 4, p. 27, state that he assumed it in 466/1074, while Ibn Abī Zar', *Rawḍ al-qirtās*, p. 88, indicates that he assumed it following the battle of Zallāqah in 1086, and that he received a *fatwa* from the two great theologians of the day, al-Ghazālī and al-Ṭurṭūshī authorizing him to assume the title. 'Inān, *'Aṣr al-Murābiṭīn*, vol. 1, pp. 39ff., accepts the later date and inserts the text of al-Ghazālī's *fatwa* (*ibid*., pp. 41ff.).

11. Ibn al-Khaṭīb, *A'lām*, p. 245, reports that the warning came from al-Mu'tamid's son, who advised that al-Mu'tamid should settle his differences with the Christians rather than risk his domain, to which al-Mu'tamid retorted "O son, I prefer to die as a shepherd in the Maghrib rather than surrender al-Andalus to the abode of unbelief [*dār al-kufr*]."

12. Al-Ṭūd, *Banū 'Abbād*, p. 162; Ibn Khaldūn, *'Ibar*, vol. 6, p. 185.
13. As quoted by al-Ṭūd, *Banū 'Abbād*, from Ibn al-Khaṭib, *al-Ḥulal*, pp. 29–30.
14. Ibn al-Khaṭib, *A'lām*, p. 246.
15. Al-Marrākushī, *Mu'jib*, p. 190.
16. 'Abdallah, *Mudhakkirāt*, pp. 100ff.; al-Ṭūd, *Banū 'Abbād*, p. 172.
17. Al-Marrākushī, *Mu'jib*, p. 195. Muslim historians point to the deceit of Alfonso VI, who is said to have written on a Thursday to the Muslims informing them that the encounter should take place on Monday since Friday is a holiday to Muslims, Saturday to Jews, and Sunday to Christians.
18. Ibn al-Khaṭib, *A'lām*, p. 247.
19. 'Abdallah, *Mudhakkirāt*, p. 122.
20. Al-Ṭūd, *Banū 'Abbād*, p. 194. Cf. n. 10 above.
21. 'Abdallah, *Mudhakkirāt*, pp. 154ff.
22. *Ibid*., p. 164.
23. *Ibid*., p. 170.
24. Ibn 'Idhārī, *Bayān*, vol. 4, p. 59; al-Marrākushī, *Mu'jib*, p. 237.
25. Ibn al-Khaṭib, *A'lām*, p. 248.
26. *Ibid*., p. 248; al-Marrākushī, p. 281.
27. Ibn al-Khaṭib, *A'lām*, p. 252.
28. *Ibid*., p. 256.
29. Al-Marrākushī, *Mu'jib*, p. 278.
30. *Ibid*., p. 241.
31. The primary contemporary sources on the Almohads are Ibn al-Qaṭṭān, *Juz' min Kitāb naẓm al-jumān*, ed. Maḥmūd 'Alī Makkī (Tetuan, n.d.); Ibn Ṣāḥib al-Ṣalah, *al-Mann bi-l-imāmah*, partially published (Beirut, 1964); E. Lévi-Provençal, *Documents inédits d'histoire almohade* (Paris, 1928); also his edition of *Trente-sept lettres officielles almohades* (Rabat, 1941); al-Marrākushī, *Mu'jib*, pp. 245ff., has first-hand information about the dynasty. See also Ibn al-Khaṭib, *A'lām*, pp. 265ff., and his *al-Ḥulal*; Ibn Khaldūn, *'Ibar*, vol. 6, pp. 472–484; al-Ḥimyarī, *al-Rawḍ*; R. Le Tourneau, *The Almohad Movement in North Africa in the Twelfth and Thirteenth Centuries* (Princeton, 1969); A Huici Miranda, *Historia política del imperio almohade* (Tetuan, 1956–1957); 'Abdallah 'Alī 'Alām, *al-Da'wah al-muwaḥḥidiyyah bi-l-Maghrib* (Cairo, 1964); R. Millet, *Les Almohades, histoire d'une dynastie berbère* (Paris, 1923).
32. On Ibn Tūmart, see Huici Miranda, *Imperio almohade*, pp. 23ff.; al-Marrākushī, *al-Mu'jib*, pp. 245; *EI*, under Ibn Tūmart; J. D. Luciani, ed., *Le livre de Mohammed Ibn Toumert* (Algiers, 1903); H. Basset, "Ibn Toumert, chef d'état," *Revue de l'histoire des religions*, 2 (1925), 438–439; E. Lévi-Provençal, "Ibn Toumert et 'Abd al-Mu'min," in *Mémorial Henri Basset* (Paris, 1928), vol. 2, pp. 21–37; 'Inān, *'Aṣr al-Murabiṭīn*, vol. 1, pp. 156ff.; al-Baydhaq, *Akhbār al-Mahdī Ibn Tūmart wa-ibtidā' dawlat al-muwaḥḥidīn*, ed. and French trans. E. Lévi-Provençal (Paris, 1928); al-Zarkashī, *Tārīkh al-dawlatayn* (Tunis, A.H. 1289).
33. For more details on Ibn Tūmart's itinerary, see Huici Miranda, *Imperio almohade*, pp. 38ff.
34. Al-Marākushī, *Mu'jib*, pp. 246–247.
35. *Ibid*., p. 255; cf. Ibn 'Idhārī, *Bayān*, vol. 4, p. 68.
36. Al-Marrākushī, *Mu'jib*, p. 255.
37. Huici Miranda, *Imperio almohade*, pp. 32ff. and 95ff. Ibn Tūmart's doctrine is embodied in his *A'azz mā yuṭlab* (Algiers, 1903) and in his legal work, *al-Muwṭṭa'* (Algiers, 1905).
38. Ibn 'Idhārī, *Bayān*, vol. 4, pp. 68–69.
39. *Ibid*., p. 69.
40. Al-Marrākushī, *Mu'jib*, p. 259. In fact, he purged his followers by putting many to death. See Lévi-Provençal, *Documents inédits*, pp. 35ff.
41. Al-Marrākushī, *Mu'jib*, p. 255; cf. Huici Miranda, *Imperio almohade*, pp. 100ff.

See also J. F. P. Hopkins, *Medieval Muslim Government in Barbary until the Sixth Century of the Hijra* (London, 1958), pp. 85–111.

42. Ibn ʻIdhārī, *Bayān*, vol. 4, p. 75.

43. Al-Marrākushī, *Muʻjib*, p. 261; cf. al-Baydhaq, *Akhbār*, p. 28.

44. On ʻAbd al-Mu'min, see al-Marrākushī, *Muʻjib*, pp. 262ff.; al-Baydhaq, *Akhbār*, pp. 83ff.; anon., *al-Ḥulal*, p. 107; *EI*, under ʻAbd al-Mu'min; Huici Miranda, *Imperio almohade*, pp. 109ff.; ʻInān, *ʻAṣr al-Murābiṭīn*, vol. 1, p. 218ff.; Le Tourneau, *The Almohad Movement*, pp. 31ff.

45. Al-Marrākushī, *Muʻjib*, p. 281, says that many Almohads could be found in Algeciras, Ronda, Granada, Seville, Cordova, and other towns. Anon., *al-Ḥulal*, p. 111, mentions that Sevillian leaders came to Marrākush in 542/1148 and paid homage to ʻAbd al-Mu'min.

46. *Aʻlām*, p. 265; al-Marrākushī, *Muʻjib*, p. 282; cf. ʻInān, *ʻAṣr al-Murābiṭīn*, vol. 1, pp. 381ff.

47. ʻInān, *ʻAṣr al-Murabiṭīn*, vol. 1, p. 387.

48. Al-Marrākushī, *Muʻjib*, p. 306.

49. *Ibid.*

50. On Yūsuf, see *ibid.*, pp. 308ff.; Ibn al-Khaṭīb, *Aʻlām*, p. 269; Huici Miranda, *Imperio almohade*, pp. 219ff.

51. Al-Marrākushī, *Muʻjib*, pp. 308ff.

52. See below, chapter 17.

53. Al-Marrākushī, *Muʻjib*, pp. 316ff.

54. Huici Miranda, *Imperio almohade*, p. 317.

55. Al-Marrākushī, *Muʻjib*, p. 341.

56. On Yaʻqūb, see *ibid.*, pp. 336ff.; Ibn al-Khaṭīb, *Aʻlām*, p. 269; Huici Miranda, *Imperio almohade*, pp. 313ff.; Muḥ. Rashīd Mulīn, *ʻAṣr al-Manṣūr al-muwaḥḥidī* (Rabat, 1946).

57. Huici Miranda, *Imperio almohade*, p. 318.

58. On Banū Ghāniyah, see al-Marrākushī, *Muʻjib*, pp. 342–463; Huici Miranda, *Imperio almohade*, pp. 320ff. See also Alfred Bel, *Les Benou Ghanya, derniers représentants de l'empire almoravide et leur lutte contre l'empire almohade* (Paris, 1903).

59. Al-Marrākushī, *Muʻjib*, p. 359.

60. *Ibid.*, pp. 354ff.

61. *Ibid.*, pp. 384ff.

62. *Ibid.*, p. 370.

63. *Ibid.*, p. 364. On the cultural life under the Almohads, see Muḥ. Manūnī, *al-ʻUlūm wa-l-adab wa-l-funūn ʻalā ʻahd al-Muwaḥḥidīn* .(Tetuan, 1952).

64. Ibn al-Khaṭīb, *Aʻlām*, pp. 270ff.

65. *Ibid.*, p. 274.

66 *Ibid.*, pp. 275ff.

67. *Ibid.*, pp. 277ff.

68. The text of the document is to be found in Ibn al-Khaṭīb, *Aʻlām*, pp. 280ff.

69. Al-Maqqarī had in his *Nafḥ al-ṭīb*, vol. 6, pp. 82–307, an extensive section on the exodus of the Muslims from al-Andalus. See also A. Ballesteros, *Sevilla en el siglo XIII* (Madrid, 1913).

70. On the Crusades, see K. M. Setton, ed., *A History of the Crusades* (Madison, Wis., 1969).

71. J. D. Lathan, "Towards a Study of Andalusian Immigration and Its Place in Tunisian History," *CT*, 5 (1957), 203–252; M. de Espalza, "Recherches récentes sur les émigrations des 'Moriscos' en Tunisie," *CT*, 18 (1970), 139–147.

5. The Naṣrid Dynasty of Granada, 1231–1492

1. Our best sources of information concerning the Naṣrids are the works of Ibn al-Khaṭīb, mainly *al-Iḥāṭah fī akhbār Charnāṭah*, ed. Muḥammad ʻAbd Allah ʻInān (Cairo, 1955), and

A'lām, pp. 278ff.; and Ibn Khaldūn's *'Ibar*, vol. 4, pp. 366–384. The two were contemporaries and actively participated in the political affairs of the time. Of great significance is the work of al-Maqqarī, *Nafḥ al-ṭīb*, vol. 6, pp. 254ff., which is often mentioned in this work. Also an anonymous work entitled *Tuḥfat al-'asr fī-inqiḍā' dawlat Banī Naṣr*, ed. M. J. Müller (Munich, 1863); Ibn al-Khaṭīb, *al-Lamḥah al-badriyyah fī tārīkh al-dawlah al-naṣriyyah* (Cairo, A.H. 1347); M. 'Abdallah 'Inān, *Nihāyat al-Andalus* (Cairo, 1958).

For the kingdom of Granada, its conquest and subsequent Christian policies, see M. Lafuente Alcántara, *Historia de Granada* (Paris, 1913–1915); Fr. Henriquez de Jorquena, *Anales de Granada* (Granada, 1934); Imamuddin, *Political History*, pp. 173 ff.; F. J. Simonet, *Descripción del reino de Granada* (Granada, 1872); L. Eguilaz y Yanguas. *Reseña histórica de la conquista del reino de Granada* (Granada, 1894); P. Boronat, *Los moriscos españoles y su expulsión* (Valencia, 1901); C. H. Lea, *The Moriscos of Spain* (London, 1901); D. M. Dánvila y Collado, *La expulsión de los moriscos españoles* (Madrid, 1889).

2. See Ibn al-Khaṭīb, *A'lām*, pp. 272ff.

3. *Ibid.*, pp. 277ff.

4. On the founder of the dynasty, see Ibn al-Khaṭīb, *A'lām*, pp. 278ff.; Ibn Khaldūn, *'Ibar*, vol. 4, pp. 366ff.

5. *Ibid.*, p. 366.

6. 'Inān, *Nihāyah*, p. 35.

7. Ibn al-Khaṭīb, *A'lām*, pp. 294ff.; *al-Iḥāṭah*, vol. 1, pp. 385–412.

8. Ibn al-Khaṭīb, *A'lām*, pp. 295ff.; *al-Iḥāṭah*, vol. 1, pp. 540–542.

9. Ibn al-Khaṭīb, *A'lām*, pp. 296.

10. *Ibid.*, pp. 304ff.

11. *Ibid.*, p. 305.

12. *Ibid.*, p. 306. On Muḥammad V. see Mujṭār al-'Abbādī, "Muḥammad V, al-Ghānī bi-llāh, Rey de Granada," *RIEI*, 11–12 (1963–1964), 209–308; 13 (1965–1966), 43–102; and 14 (1967–1968), 139–192.

13. Ibn al-Khaṭīb, *A'lām*, p. 307.

14. *Ibid.*, p. 308.

15. It is important to indicate the lengthy diplomatic correspondence written by Ibn al-Khaṭīb and addressed to the Marīnid rulers imploring them to come and help the Granadine kingdom against the threat of the Christians. For some of the correspondence see al-Maqqarī, *Nafḥ al-ṭīb*, vol. 6, pp. 141ff.

16. See al-Maqqarī, *Azhār al-riyāḍ* (Cairo, 1939–1942), vol. 1, pp. 64–65.

17. 'Inān, *Nihāyah*, pp. 148 and 308; Lea, *The Moriscos of Spain*, p. 36.

18. In 1505, a Morisco addressed a long poem to the Turkish Sultan Bayāzid II calling his attention to the lamentable state of affairs of his fellow Moriscos. See text of the poems in al-Maqqarī, *Azhār al-riyāḍ*, vol. 1, 109–115. See also James Monroe, "A Curious Morisco Appeal to the Ottoman Empire," *al-Andalus*, 31 (1966), 281–303. For later communication between Moriscos and Ottomans, see A. C. Hess, "The Moriscos: An Ottoman Fifth Column in Sixteenth-Century Spain," *American Historical Review*, 74 (1968), 1–25.

19. See al-Maqqarī, *Nafḥ al-ṭīb*, vol. 6, p. 259.

20. 'Inān, *Nihāyah*, p. 191.

21. Al-Maqqarī, *Nafḥ al-ṭīb*, vol. 6, p. 259.

22. 'Inān, *Nihāyah*, p. 212. This and other treaties of surrender are contained in the Archivo General de Simancas.

23. On the fall of Granada, see al-Maqqarī, *Nafḥ al-ṭīb*, vol. 6, pp. 254ff.

24. *Ibid.*, p. 258.

25. Al-Maqqarī (*ibid.*, p. 277) says that the terms of surrender consisted of sixty-seven clauses. See also M. Garrido Atienza, *Las capitulaciones para la entrega de Granada* (Granada, 1910); A. Llorente, *Historia crítica de la inquisición de España* (Madrid, 1817); and 'Inān, *Nihāyah*, pp. 230–239.

26. Al-Maqqarī, *Nafḥ al-ṭīb*, vol. 6, pp. 277–278.

27. 'Inān, *Nihāyah*, pp. 262ff.

28. Al-Maqqarī, *Nafḥ al-ṭīb*, vol. 6, pp. 281–302 quotes the text of the lengthy letter; see also his *Azhār al-riyāḍ*, vol. 1, pp. 72–102.

29. 'Inān, *Nihāyah*, p. 308.

30. On the process of expulsion and religious intolerance, see Chapter 6.

6. Social Structure and Socio-Religious Tension

1. On the social structure of al-Andalus, see Lévi-Provençal, *Histoire*, vol. 1, pp. 87ff.; Mu'nis, *Fajr*, pp. 355ff.; Sālim, *Tārīkh*, pp. 119ff.; al-Sūfī, *Tārīkh*, pp. 73ff.; H. Pérès, "Les éléments ethniques de l'Espagne musulmane et la langue arabe, au Ve/XIe siècle" in *Études d'Orientalisme*, vol. 2, pp. 717–731.

2. For detail concerning their geographical distribution, see Mu'nis, *Fajr*, pp. 367ff.

3. *Ibid*., p. 358; cf. Sālim, *Tārīkh*, p. 161.

4. Mu'nis, *Fajr*, p. 360.

5. Ibn 'Idhārī, *Bayān*, vol. 2, p. 53.

6. See Aḥmad Mujtār al-'Abbādī, *Los eslavos en España* (Madrid, 1953).

7. S. D. Goitein, *Arabs and Jews* (New York, 1955), p. 62.

8. See W. J. Fischel, *Jews in the Economic and Political Life of Medieval Islam* (London, 1937); A. Neuman, *The Jews in Spain* (Philadelphia, 1948); I. Husik, *A History of Medieval Jewish Philosophy* (New York, 1916).

9. Goitein, *Arabs and Jews*, pp. 7–8.

10. Among the gifts sent by the Byzantine Emperior was a copy of Dioscorides' treatise on plants.

11. In addition to the designation of *ahl al-dhimmah*, the Mozarabs were known as *naṣārah*, or *mu'āhidūn*.

12. Isodoro de las Cagigas, *Los mozárabes* (Madrid, 1947), offers copious bibliographical data. See also F. Simonet, *Historia de los mozárabes de España* (Madrid, 1897–1903) and *Glosario de voces ibéricas y latinas usadas entre los mozárabes* (Madrid, 1888); F. Pons Boïgues, *Apuntes sobre las escrituras mozárabes toledanas existentes en el archivo histórico nacional* (Madrid, 1897)) M. Gómez Moreno, *Iglesias mozárabes* (Madrid, 1919); A. González Palencia, *Los mozárabes de Toledo en los siglos XII y XIII* (Madrid, 1926–1930) and *Moros y christianos en España medieval* (Madrid, 1945); F. Codera, "Mozárabes, su condición social y política" (doctoral thesis; Lérida, 1866).

13. See Simonet, *Historia*, pp. 381–386; Cagigas, *Los mozárabes*, pp. 195ff. and 211–221, where he gives a list of "martyrs." It should be indicated that San Eulogio, the ringleader of the "martyrs," defended in his *Memoriale Sanctorum* those suicidal acts; so did his contemporary biographer Alvaro in *Indiculo Luminoso*. They reproached the stand of moderate Christians, who thought that those acts were unjustified. Cf. Simonet, *Historia*, pp. 405 and 460ff.

14. Cagigas, *Los mozárabes*, pp. 235ff.

15. See Gómez Moreno, *Iglesias mozárabes*. On the other hand, Simonet claims that the Arabs did not contribute anything to the form and content of Spanish civilization (*Historyia*, p. xlvi; *Glosario*, xlvi.) He argues without much foundation that the Christians preserved their purity, heroism, originality, Christian spirit, and national character, and made all the worthy contributions to the culture of the Muslim infidels (*Historia*, pp. xlv and 349; see also his "De la influencia del elemento indígena en la civilización arábigo-hispana," *Ciudad de Dios*, vol. 4, pp. 5ff).

16. Cagigas, *Los mozárabes*, vol. 2, pp. 330ff. One may add that Naṣr was the eunuch under 'Abd al-Raḥmān II and that bishops and Christian judges assumed Arabic names. In 962, Walīd Ibn Khayzurān was the judge of the Christians in Cordova; Aṣbagh Ibn 'Abdallah, its bishop; and 'Ubaydallah Ibn Qāsim, the bishop of Toledo.

17. On Mudéjares and Moriscos, see Isidoro de la Cagigas, *Los mudéjares* (Madrid, 1948–1949); Julio Caro Baroja, *Los moriscos del reino de Granada* (Madrid, 1957); F. Fernández y

González, *Estado social y político de los mudéjares de Castilla* (Madrid, 1866); A. Delgado Hernández, *Memoria sobre el estado moral y político de los mudéjares de Castilla* (Madrid, 1864); J. Pedregal y Fantini, *Estado social y cultura de los mozárabes y mudéjares españoles* (Seville, 1878); F. Janer, *Condición social de los moriscos* (Madrid, 1857).

18. On the role and position of the Mudéjares in the national life of Spain, see Lea, *The Moriscos of Spain*, p. 57; Janer, *Condición social de los moriscos*, pp. 13–14; cf. 'Inān, *Nihāyah*, pp. 54–58.

19. N. Daniel, *Islam and the West* (Edinburgh, 1960); see also R. W. Southern, *Western Views of Islam in the Middle Ages* (Cambridge, Mass., 1962); J. T. Addison, *The Christian Approach to the Moslems* (New York, 1942); E. Doutté, "Mahomet Cardinal," *Mémoires de la Société d'agriculture, commerce, sciences, et arts de la Marne*, 2nd ser., vol. 1:2, 1898–1899, pp. 233–243; P. Khoury, "Jean Damascene et l'Islam," *Proche Orient Chrétien*, 7 (1957) and 8 (1958); J. E. Merril, "John of Damascus on Islam," *MW*, 41 (1951), 88–97; D. C. Munro, "The Western Attitude toward Islam during the Period of the Crusades," *Speculum*, 6 (1931), 338ff.

20. It should be pointed out that in Muslim tradition, the Qur'ān is the Word of God (*kalām Allāh*) and is co-eternal with Him.

21. Daniel, *Islam*, p.90.

22. Cagigas, *Los mudéjares*, vol. 1, p. 148, states: "Reyes, príncipes, eclesiásticos, vivían o trataban de imitar el facto de las cortes musulmanas. Armas, arreos, joyas, tapices, prendas de vestir, tejidos, ajuar de la casa, eran de origén musulman; los inventarios contemporáneos, que conocemos en gran cantidad y con variedades de fechas, no dejan lugar a duda; los descubrimientos que luego nos han ido haciendo arqueólogos e investigadores confirmaron lo que ya tenemos sabido. Reyes y arzobispos yacen aún en sus sepulcros con sus mantos y ropas orientales. De algunos reyes como Pedro I de Aragón — no conocemos más que sus firmas en árabe. De otros — Alfonso VIII de Castilla, Ramón Berenguer de Barcelona — nos consta que acuñaron sus monedas de oro a imitacíon de los tipos árabes y con inscripciones árabes."

23. *Ibid*., p. 153. Cagigas states: "los africanos se sorprendían y escandalizaban de la intensa hispanización de los *mulūk al-ṭawā'if* los europeos se escandalizaban y sorprendían de la islamización de los cristianos españoles."

24. Ibn al-Khaṭib, *A'lām*, p. 181.

25. *Ibid*., p. 203.

26. *Ibid*., p. 204.

27. *Ibid*., p. 245. Here Ibn al-Khatīb records that al-Mu'tamid of Seville retorted to the question of the Berber danger by saying that he preferred to be a mere camelherd in the Maghrib rather than making al-Andalus the abode of unbelief (*dār al-kufr*). No doubt, this acrimonious feeling had a religious base and was manifested in various polemical treatises written during the eleventh century and later. The Muslims were on the defensive and attempted to dispel charges launched against them and their faith. Ibn García was a neo-Muslim who became the secretary and court poet of Mujāhid (1010–1045), the ruler of Denia. He wrote a treatise in which he attempted to show the superiority of non-Arabs over Arabs. His treatise engendered a number of acid refutations by Arab sympathizers, who downgraded not only Ibn García's ancestors but their religious customs as well. See J. Monroe, *The Shu'ūbiyya in al-Andalus: The Risāla of Ibn García and Five Refutations* (Berkeley & Los Angeles, 1970); see also 'Abd al-Salām Hārūn, *Nawādir al-Makhṭūṭāt* (Cairo, 1953), which contains the Arabic text of Ibn Garcıa's *Risālah* along with refutations of the same. Cf. also Yūsuf Ibn al-Shaykh al-Balawī, *Kitāb alif bā'* (Cairo, A.H. 1287). Of interest also are two treatises in the corpus of miscellanea (Escorial 538 [Casiri 535], NOS. 11 and 12). One was written by a French monk and addressed to al-Muqtadir, ruler of Saragossa, and the other by Abū-l-Walīd al-Bājī (d. 1081), refuting it. See also Ibn Ḥazm's views, chapter 16 below.

28. J. B. Trend, in Th. Arnold and A. Guillaume, eds., *The Legacy of Islam* (Oxford, 1952), p. 10. It was also at this juncture that crusaders, or religious soldiers, constituted various societies that bore the names of saints, and made themselves available to serve Christian rulers.

29. *Ibid.*, p. 10.
30. Cagigas, *Los mudéjares*, vol. 1, p. 210.
31. *Ibid.*, vol. 2, p. 358.
32. See James Kritzeck, *Peter the Venerable and Islam* (Princeton, 1964), pp. 56ff.
33. *Ibid.*, pp. 51ff., and Daniel, *Islam*, pp. 17ff. and 68ff.
34. Published in Madrid in 1793.
35. See below; also cf. Cagigas, *Los mudéjares*, vol. 2, p. 358.
36. Daniel, *Islam*, p. 29.
37. *Ibid.*, p. 62.
38. Cagigas, *Los mudéjares*, vol. 2, p. 511.
39. *Ibid.*, p. 538.
40. See A. G. Solalinde, *Antalogía de Alfonso el Sabio* (Madrid, 1960), pp. 88–98; and Volverde J. Filgueira, ed., *Primera crónica general de España* (Madrid, 1949), pp. 103–117.
41. Filgueira, *Primera crónica general de España*, p. 104.
42. *Ibid.*, p. 107.
43. *Ibid.*, pp. 103–104: ". . . el diablo, que es enemigo dell' humana! Liñaje et que non queda con su envidia de buscarle mal cuanto él más puede, sembró la su mala simient et negra en el regno de España, e metió en los poderosos soberbia, e en los religiosos pereza et negligencia, e entró los que habien poz et amor discordia, e en ricos et abondados, luxuria, et muchodumbre de pecados, e en las sables et entendudos pereza de embotamiente, en manera que los oblispos et los clériges tornó tales como a los viles homnes del pueblo, e al rey et a los príncipes assí como a ladrones. Pues por esta guisa que habemos dicho fué el regno de los godos de España destroído, el que ante desto era grand et ancho ca tan gran era que el su señoría duraba et tenie de mar a mar, bien desde la cibdad de Tanjar, que es en Africa fastal río Ruédano."
44. *Ibid.*, pp. 116–117: "Los moros de la hueste todos vestidos del sirgo et de los paños de color que ganaran, las riendas de los sus caballos tales eran como de fuego, las sus caras dellos negras como la pez el más fremoso dellos era negro como la olla, assí lucíen sus ojos como candelas; el su caballo dellos ligero como leopardo e el su caballero mucho mas cruel et más dañoso que es el lobo en la grey de las ovejas en la noche. La vil yente de los africanos que se non solíe preciar de fuerca nin de bondat, et todos sus fechos facíe con art et a engaño, et non solíen amparar si non penchando grandes riquezas et grand haber, essora era exaltada, ca crebantó en una hora más aína la nobleza de godos que lo non podríe homne decir por lengua.

"España mexquina! Tanto fué la su muerte coitada que solamientre non fincó í ninguno que la llante lamanla dolorida, ya más muerta que viva."

45. *Ibid.*, pp. 116–117: "Aquí se remató la santidad et la religión de los obispos et de los sacerdotes; aquí quedó et minguó el abondamiento de los clérigos que sirvíen las eglesias; aquí perescíó ell entendimiento de los prelados et de los homnes de orden; aquí fallesció ell ensenamiento de la ley et de la sancta fe. Los padres et los señores todos perescieron en uno; los santuarios fueron destroídos, las eglesias crebantadas; los logares que loaban a Dios con alegría, esora le denostaban il maltraien; las cruces et los altares echaron de las eglesias; la crisma et los libros et las cosas que eran pora honra de la cristiandat todo fué esparzudo et echado a mala part; las fiestas et las sollemnias, todas fueron oblidadas; la honra de los santos et la beldad de la eglesia toda fué tornada en laideza et viltanca; las eglesias et las torres o solíen loar a Dios es ora confessaban en ellas et llamaban a Mohamat; las vestimentas et los calces et los otros vasos de los santuarios eran tornados en uso de mal et enlixados de los descreídos.

"Toda la tierra desgastaron los enemigos, las casas hermaron, los homnes mataron, las cibdades quemaron, los arboles, las viñas et cuanto fallaron verde cortaron. Tanto pujó esta pestilencia et esta cueta que non fincó en toda España buena villa ni cibdad o obispo hobiesse que non fuesse quemada o derribada o retenida de moros; ca las cibdades que los alarabes non pudieron conquerir engañáronlas et conquiríronlas por falsas pleitesias."

46. It has been generally accepted that Muḥammad was born ca. 570.

47. ''Un homme mucho esforzado et alzado et poderoso en regno et ley'' (Solalinde, *Antalogía de Alfonso el Sabio*, p. 88).

48. It has been generally accepted that the father of Muḥammad, 'Abdallāh, died shortly before Muḥammad's birth.

49. ''. . . e daqui Mahomat y tomó despues cosas, que metió en aquella mala secta que èl compuso por a perdicion de las almas daquellas que la creen, por facer creer a las yentes que era verdadera aquella predigacion'' (Solalinde, *Antalogía de Alfonso el Sabio*, p. 89).

50. The name Hadaya may be confused with Cadiga (Khadījah), whom he refers to as ''reina Cadiga.''

51. Solalinde, *Antalogía de Alfonso el Sabio*, p. 91.

52. *Ibid.*

53. *Ibid.* It is well established that Muḥammad began his revelations around 610 — that is, at the age of forty, almost fifteen years after his marriage to Khadījah.

54. ''Por sus encantamientos et sus artes magicas, et con la ayuda del diablo por quien se el guiaba de facer antella así çomo sennales et miraglos, e por que a las veces se torna el diablo así como diz la Escriptura en figura de angel de lux, entraba el diablo en ell a las veces et faciel decir algunas cosas daquellas que habien de venir, e por esta manera le habien de creer todas las yentes de lo que les dice'' (Solalinde, *Antalogía de Alfonso el Sabio*, p. 92).

55. It is interesting to note that some Western traditions make Muḥammad a cardinal from Rome, who, failing to be elected to the papacy, declared himself prophet. See Doutté, ''Mahomet Cardinal,'' and Kritzeck, *Peter the Venerable*, p. 18.

56. ''Arabo'' corresponds to Idrīs in the Arabic version.

57. Solalinde, *Antalogía de Alfonso el Sabio*, pp. 92–95.

58. There is no evidence to support the allegation that Muḥammad ever proclaimed himself king before, or after, his religious mission.

59. Solalinde, *Antalogía de Alfonso el Sabio*, p. 92.

60. *Ibid.*, p. 96: ''Daqui adelante comenzó Muḥammad a predigar su secta descubertamientre et de albozar los pueblos contra fe de Cristo.''

61. *Ibid.*, p. 97: ''E despues que se levantaban dalli predigábales et dábales leys que toviesen las que ellos llaman por su arabigo *zoharas* que son tanto como 'mandamientos,' a destas *zoharas* les fizo ell un gran libro departido por capitulos, al que ellos llaman *alcoran*; e tanta nemiga et tanta falsedat escribió ell en aquellas zoharas, esto es mandamientos, que verguenza es a homne decirlo nin de oirlo, et mucho más ya de seguirlo; e pero estas *zoharas* le recibieron aquellos pueblos malaventurados seyendo beldos de la ponzon del diablo et adormidos en el pecado de la luzuria, e hoy en dia los tienen et estan muy firmes en su porfia e non se quieren llegar nin acoger a la çarrera de la verdadera fe nin haber en si la ley de Dios nin el su ensenamiento. Así como ḥabemos dicho ensirió Mahomat los corazones de las yentes en aquella su porfiesa secta por sus enganos et su mal ensenamiento.''

62. *Ibid.*, p. 98: ''Aquí se acada la estoria de Mahomat. Ese ano tremío la tierra, et aparesció en el cielo un signo en manera de espada, bien por treinta dias, que demostraba el senorio que los moros habien de haber.''

63. To some degree, the Mudéjares were the object of suspicion and contempt on the part of their fellow Muslims living under Muslim rule. 'Inān, *Nihāyah*, pp. 52ff., found a manuscript in the Escurial (Casiri 1758) which consists of a *fatwa* on the status of Muslims under Christian rule. The *fatwa* states, among other things, that flight of Muslims from the land of unbelief to the land of Islam is a religious duty in the same manner as the flight from the land of falsehood, or from any forbidden act, such as eating dead animal, pork, or committing suicide. See Aḥmad al-Wansharīshī (d. 1508). *Asnā al-mutājir*, ed. H. Mu'nis, *RIEI*, 5 (1957), 129–191.

64. See Américo Castro, *History of Religious Intolerance in Spain*, trans. F. Parker (London, 1953), p. 7.

65. H. Kamen, *The Spanish Inquisition* (New York, 1965).

66. *Ibid.*, p. 168.

67. *Ibid.*, p. 181.

68. Brockelmann, *History*, pp. 220–221.

69. See above, Chapter 5. One may add the following important titles: D. Cabanelas Rodríguez, *El morisco granadino Alonso del Castillo* (Granada, 1965); J. Caro Baroja, *El Señor Inquisidor y otras vidas por oficio* (Madrid, 1968); M. S. Carrasco Urgoiti, *El moro de Granada en la literatura del siglo XV al XX* (Madrid, 1956); P. Dressendörfer, *Islam unter der Inquisition die Morisco prozesse in Toledo 1575–1619* (Wiesbaden, 1971); A. Gallego y Burín and A Gamín Sandoval, *Los moriscos del reino de Granada según el sínodo de Guadix de 1554*, ed. by D. Cabanelas (Granada, 1968); M. de Guadaljara y Xavier, *Memorable expulsión y justísimo destierro de los moriscos de España* (Pamplona, 1613); F. A. Roca Traver, *Un siglo de vida mudéjar en la Valencia medieval* (Saragossa, 1952).

It may also be relevant to point out that while the moriscos were forbidden the use of Arabic, manuals for learning the language were composed for the use of missionaries and clerics. For example, Pedro Alcalá wrote his *Arte para ligeramente saber la lengua arábiga* (Granada, 1501) which was followed in 1505 by the publication of his *Vocabulista arábigo en letra castellana*. Subsequently F. Cañes wrote *Gramática arábigo-española vulgar y literal con un diccionario arábigo español* (Madrid, 1775); and *Diccionario manual árabe y español* (Madrid, 1776).

7. Society and Administration

1. Lévi-Provençal, *Histoire*, vol. 3, pp. 188ff.

2. Ibn 'Abdūn, *Risālat Ibn 'Abdūn fi-l-qaḍā' wa-l-ḥisbah*, ed. by E. Lévi-Provençal along with two other treatises in *Thalāth rasā'il andalusiyyah* (Cairo, 1955), pp. 21ff.; French trans. by the same editor, *Séville musulmane au début du XII*^{e} *siècle* (Paris, 1947); Spanish trans. E. García Gómez, *Sevilla musulmana a cominenzos del siglo XII* (Madrid, 1948).

3. Ibn al-Ra'ūf, *Fī ādāb al-ḥisbah wa-l-muḥtasib*, ed. Lévi-Provençal in *Thalāth rasā'il andalusiyyah*, p. 86.

4. See Lévi-Provençal, *Histoire*, vol. 3, pp. 198ff.

5. *Nafḥ al-ṭīb*, vol. 2, pp. 79–80.

6. See al-Maqqarī, pp. 10–11, for the charming story regarding the fashionable use of libraries in homes.

7. Lévi-Provençal, *Histoire*, vol. 3, pp. 429ff.

8. See J. Ribera, *Historia de la música árabe medieval y su influencia en la española* (Madrid, 1927); also his *Las música de las cántigas de Santa María* (Madrid, 1922).

9. The games of chess and backgammon became very popular among the Christians; see F. M. Pareja Casañas, *Libro de ajedrez* (Madrid, 1935).

10. Lévi-Provençal, *Histoire*, vol. 3, pp. 441ff.

11. *Ibid*., p. 443.

12. Ibn al-Ra'ūf, *Fī ādāb al-ḥisbah*, p. 77.

13. 'Umar b. al-Jarsīfī, *Risālah fī-l-ḥisbah*, ed. E. Lévi-Provençal in *Thalāth rasā'il andalusiyyah*, p. 121.

14. Ibn 'Abdūn, *Risālah*, p. 32.

15. *Ibid*., p. 19.

16. *Ibid*., p. 48.

17. On Wallādah and Ibn Zaydūn, see below, Chapter 12.

18. On the *Dove's Ring* (*ṭawq al-ḥamāmah*), see below, Chapter 14.

19. Cf. A. R. Nykl, *Hispano-Arabic Poetry and Its Relations with the Old Provençal Troubadours* (Baltimore, 1946), p. 85.

20. See Chapter X of the *Dove's Ring*.

21. See Chapter XI of the *Dove's Ring*.

22. See Chapter XXIV of the *Dove's Ring*.

23. Gayangos, *Mohammedan Dynasties*, vol. 1, p. 30.

24. *Ibid*., pp. 55ff.

25. *Ibid*., p. 64.

26. For the early administration, see Mu'nis, *Fajr*, pp. 530ff. Also his "La división político-administrativa de la España musulmana," RIEI, 5 (1957), 79–135.

27. *Nafḥ al-ṭib*, vol. 2, p. 7.

28. *Ibid*., p. 9.

29. In fact, al-Maqqari devotes ample space to Cordova and its many attractions. See *Nafḥ al-ṭib*, vol. 2.

30. A. Chejne, *Succession to the Rule in Islam* (Lahore, 1960). Cf. Gayangos, *Mohammedan Dynasties*, vol. 1, pp. 30ff.

31. On various posts, see Lévi-Provençal, *Histoire*, vol. 3, pp. 1ff.; Ibn Khaldūn, *al-Muqaddimah*, trans. F. Rosenthal (New York, 1958), vols. 1 and 2. For an insight into the conception of political philosophy among Andalusian authors, see Ibn 'Abd Rabbihi, *al-'Iqd al-farid*, where he has a book on government (see below, Ch. 11); also Abū Bakr al-Ṭurṭūshī, *Sirāj al-mulūk*, Spanish trans. M. Alarcón, *Lámpara de los príncipes* (Madrid, 1930–1931).

32. See D. Sourdel, in *Études d'Orientalisme*, vol. 2, pp. 747–755.

33. Lévi-Provençal, *Histoire*, vol. 3, p. 18.

34. Ibn Khaldūn, *al-Muqaddimah*, vol. 2, p. 13.

35. On the office of the vizier in the East, see the exhaustive study of D. Sourdel, *Le Vizirat* (Damascus, 1959–1960).

36. Ibn Khaldūn, *al-Muqaddimah*, vol. 2, pp. 12ff. Also Gayangos, *Mohammedan Dynasties*, p. 103.

37. Ibn Khaldūn, *al-Muqaddimah*, vol. 2, p. 15.

38. *Ibid*., pp. 26ff.; cf. Lévi-Provençal, *Histoire*, vol. 3, pp. 22ff.

39. Gayangos, *Mohammedan Dynasties*, p. 103.

40. Lévi-Provençal, *Histoire*, vol. 3, pp. 28ff.

41. For more details concerning the organization and administration of justice in Islam, see E. Tyan, *Histoire de l'organization judiciaire en pays d'Islam* (Paris, 1938). For al-Andalus in particular, see Lévi-Provençal, *Histoire*, vol. 3, pp. 113ff. Hispano-Arabic authors have left a number of works containing valuable information about judges; among these is that of al-Khushani, *Quḍāt Qurṭubah*, ed. and Spanish trans. by J. Ribera, *Historia de los jueces de Córdoba de Aljoxani* (Madrid, 1914). Also, al-Nubāhi, *Tārikh quḍat al-Andalus*, ed. Lévi-Provençal (Cairo, 1948).

42. Gayangos, *Mohammedan Dynasties*, vol. 1, p. 104.

43. Lévi-Provençal, *Histoire*, vol. 3, pp. 132ff.

44. *Ibid*., pp. 153ff.

45. Gayangos, *Mohammedan Dynasties*, vol. 1, p. 104.

46. Ibn 'Abdūn, *Risālah*, p. 17.

47. *Ibid*., p. 20.

48. Al-Jarsifi, *Risālah*, pp. 119–120.

49. Ibn 'Abdūn, *Risālah*, pp. 37ff.

50. Gayangos, *Mohammedan Dynasties*, vol. 1, p. 104.

51. Lévi-Provençal, *Histoire*, vol. 3, pp. 55ff.

52. G. C. Miles, *The Coinage of the Umayyads of Spain* (New York, 1950).

53. Lévi-Provençal, *Histoire*, vol. 3, p. 39.

54. Al-Maqqari, *Nafḥ al-ṭib*, vol. 1, pp. 140ff. Cf. Lévi-Provençal, *Histoire*, vol. 3, pp. 33ff.

8. Acculturation and Self-Appraisal

1. In this connection, the Andalusians were like other independent or semi-independent Muslim states which had seceded at different intervals form the Islamic empire, and which took pride in belonging to the mainstream of Islamic culture. For the Eastern contributions to al-Andalus, see Muḥmūd 'Alī Makki, *Ensayo sobre las aportaciones orientales en la España musulmana* (Madrid, 1968); Muḥsin Jamāl al-Dīn, *Udabā' baghdādiyyūn fī-l-Andalus* (Baghdād, 1962–1963).

2. Ibn Khayr, *Fahrasah*, ed. F. Codera and J. Ribera (Saragossa, 1893).
3. al-Ḍabbī, *Bughyat al-multamis*, ed. F. Codera (Madrid, 1885).
4. Ibn al-Khaṭib, *al-Iḥāṭah*, vol. 1.
5. Al-Maqqarī, *Nafḥ al-ṭīb*.
6. Ibn al-Khaṭīb, *A'lām*, p. 185; cf. H. Pérès. *La poésie andalouse en arabe classique au XI*[e] *siècle* (Paris, 1953), p. 46.
7. Pérès, *La poésie andalouse*, p. 52. In fact, al-Ḥimyarī composed an anthology entitled *al-Badī' fī waṣf al-rabī'*, ed. H. Pérès (Rabat, 1940), which contains a large number of poems by Andalusian poets dealing with flowers, gardens, and so on.
8. Ibn Ḥazm's treatise is to be found in al-Maqqarī, *Nafḥ al-ṭīb*, vol. 4, pp. 154–170; see below, n. 49; French trans. C. Pellat, "Ibn Ḥazm: bibliographe et apologiste de l'Espagne musulmane," *al-Andalus*, 19 (1954), 53–102.
9. As translated by Nykl, *Hispano-Arabic Poetry*, p. 102; for a French translation of the poem in full, see Pérès, *La poésie andalouse*, p. 49.
10. Ibn Khāqān, *Qalā'id* (Būlāq, A.H. 1283); see also his *Maṭmaḥ al-anfus* (Constantinople, A.H. 1302).
11. Ibn Bassām, *al-Dhakhīrah* (Cairo, 1939–1945). This author, knowledgeable in both Eastern and Andalusian poetry, shows a remarkable preference for the poets of al-Andalus over those of the East.
12. Al-Shaqundī's treatise is to be found in al-Maqqarī, *Nafḥ al-ṭīb*, vol. 4, pp. 177–208; Spanish trans. E. García Gómez, *Elogio del Islam español* (Madrid, 1934). The motivation of al-Shaqundī, unlike that of Ibn Bassām, was to show the superiority of al-Andalus over Berber countries.
13. Ibn Sa'īd's treatise is to be found in al-Maqqarī, *Nafḥ al-ṭīb*, vol. 4, pp. 171–177.
14. See Pérès, *La poésie andalouse*, pp. 49ff. See S. M. Imamuddin, *Some Aspects of the Socio-Economic and Cultural History of Muslim Spain* (Leiden, 1965), pp. 127ff.; see also Makkī, *Ensayo*, pp. 11ff.
15. *Nafḥ al-ṭīb*, vol. 4, p. 4.
16. *Ibid*., pp. 6ff.
17. On Ziryāb, see al-Maqqarī, vol. 4, pp. 117–129; *EI*, under *Ziryāb*; see below, Chapter 19.
18. On al-Qālī, see al-Maqqarī, vol. 4, pp. 70–75; cf. below, Chapter 10.
19. Al-Maqqarī, *Nafḥ al-ṭīb*, vol. 4, p. 72.
20. Published in two volumes (Cairo, 1926). Ibn Khayr, *Fahrasah*, p. 323, calls it "unique," and al-Zubaydī, *Ṭabaqāt*, considers it the most useful work in the field.
21. The study of the *Amālī*, along with its Eastern counterpart *al-Kāmil* by al-Mubarrad, would be both interesting and profitable.
22. Al-Maqqarī, vol. 4, pp. 126ff. and 136ff., where he lists the singers Faḍl, Qamar, and al-'Ajfā'. Cf. Pérès, *La poésie andalouse*, pp. 40–41.
23. On Ẓafr al-Baghdādī, see al-Maqqarī, *Nafḥ al-ṭīb*, vol. 4, p. 108.
24. See *ibid*., p. 130.
25. See Pérès, *Poésie andalouse*, pp. 41ff. See also Ibn Khayr's *Fahrasah*, which contains an enormous list of works written by Eastern authors.
26. On Yaḥyā, see al-Maqqarī, *Nafḥ al-ṭīb*, vol. 2, pp. 214ff.
27. *Ibid*., pp. 217–220.
28. *Ibid*., p. 255.
29. *Ibid*., p. 254.
30. *Ibid*., vol. 3, p. 13.
31. *Ibid*., pp. 13ff.
32. *Al-Iḥāṭah*, vol. 1, pp. 122ff.
33. Al-Maqqarī devotes most of vol. 2 of his *Nafḥ al-ṭīb* to the opinions of his predecessors concerning the excellence of al-Andalus.
34. *Al-Iḥāṭah*, vol. 1, pp. 101ff.
35. *Nafḥ al-ṭīb*, vol. 2, pp. 7ff.
36. *Ibid*., pp. 10ff.

37. *Ibid*., p. 4.
38. Al-Ḥijārī (d. 1155) was a poet and author of the historical work *Kitāb al-mushib fī gharā'ib ahl al-Maghrib*, which is one of the main sources of Ibn Sa'īd al-Maghribī and al-Maqqarī.
39. Al-Maqqarī, *Nafḥ al-ṭīb*, vol. 2, p. 9.
40. He is Ibn Sa'īd al-Maghribī (d. ca. 1274), author of the historical work *al-Mughrib fī ḥulā al-Maghrib*. A continuation of al-Ḥijārī's *al-Mushib*, it is said to have consisted of fifteen volumes. Cf. Nykl, *Hispano-Arabic Poetry*, p. 361.
41. Al-Maqqarī, *Nafḥ al-ṭīb*, vol. 2, pp. 10–11.
42. *Ibid*., pp. 10–11.
43. *Ibid*., p. 11.
44. *Ibid*., p. 10.
45. The *Farḥat al-anfus* appears to be one of the main sources of al-Maqqarī.
46. Al-Maqqarī, *Nafḥ al-ṭīb*, vol. 4, pp. 146ff.
47. *Ibid*., pp. 146–147.
48. *Ibid*., pp. 148–149.
49. See above, n. 8.
50. Al-Rāzī (d. 995) was one of the early chroniclers of al-Andalus. See F. Pons. Boïgues, *Ensayo bío-bibliografico* (Madrid, 1897), no. 23.
51. 'Isā Ibn Dinār, an Andalusian jurist.
52. Ibn Makhlad (d. 893) is considered by al-Maqqarī, *Nafḥ al-ṭīb*, vol. 2, p. 253, as the author of many works the like of which had never before been composed in Islam. See also al-Marrākushī, *Mu'jib*, pp. 49ff., who says of him that he had no equal among his contemporaries. Cf. Ibn Bashkuwāl, *al-Ṣilah* (Cairo, 1966) vol. 1, p. 116.
53. Abū-l-Ajrab (d. 8th cent.). Cf. al-Ḍabbī, *Bughyah*, no. 626; Pérès, *La poésie andalouse*, p. 44; Pellat, "Ibn Ḥazm: bibliographe," *al-Andalus*, 10 (1954), p. 91.
54. Jarīr (d. ca. 729) was a leading satirical poet and panegyrist during the Umayyad period in Damascus.
55. Farazdaq (d. ca. 728) was also a leading satirical poet and panegyrist.
56. Al-Bukhārī (d. 870), is the author of a corpus of Traditions entitled *al-Ṣaḥīḥ*, which became one of the six canonical books on the subject on Prophetic Traditions (*ḥadīth*). The other five are by Muslim (d. 875), Abū Dāwūd (d. 888), al-Tirmidhī (d. ca. 892), Ibn Mājah (d. 886), and al-Nisā'ī (d. 915).
57. Muslim is also the author of a corpus of traditions entitled *al-Ṣaḥīḥ*, one of the canonical books.
58. Al-Sijistānī (d. 889).
59. Al-Nisā'ī is the author of a corpus of traditions entitled *Sunan*.
60. Qāsim Ibn Muhammad (d. 278/890). See al-Ḥumaydī, *Judhwat al-Muqtabis*, ed. M. T. al-Ṭanjī (Cairo, 1952), p. 310; al-Ḍabbī, *Bughyah*, no. 1293; cf. Pellat, *al-Andalus*, 19 (1954), 81.
61. Al-Qaffāl (d. 976), Muḥammad Ibn 'Alī, a leading Eastern religious scholar and philologist. Cf. Ibn Khallikān, *Wafayāt*, vol. 1, 458; *GAL*, sup. 1, p. 307.
62. Muḥammad Ibn 'Aqīl al-Faryābī (d. 928), a traditionist from Balkh or perhaps a Shāfi'ite jurist of Egypt, who died in 850; cf. Pellat, *al-Andalus*, 19 (1954), 92.
63. Al-Mazanī Abū Ibrāhīm (d. 878). He is Ismā'īl Ibn Yaḥyā, a Shāfi'ite from Egypt and author of various works. See al-Ziriklī, *Kitāb al-a'lām* (Cairo, 1954–1959), vol. 1, p. 327; *GAL*, sup. 1, p. 305.
64. 'Abdallah Ibn Qāsim Ibn Hilāl. Pellat, *al-Andalus*, 19 (1954), 92, suggests that he was 'Abdallah b. Muḥ b. Qāsim (d. 886), who was a Mālikite jurist and who studied in the Orient under Dāwūd (d. 884).
65. Mundhir Ibn Sa'īd (d. 966), known as the Ballūṭī; chief judge of al-Andalus and author of works on the Qur'ān and Tradition. See Ibn al-Faraḍī, *Tārīkh*, vol. 2, p. 17; al-Ḍabbī, *Bughyah*, no. 1357.
66. Abū-l-Ḥasan Ibn Muflis (?). Pellat has Mugallis, a Ẓāhirite jurist from Iraq.

67. Al-Khallāl (d. 923), Aḥmad Ibn Muḥammad b. Hārūn, a Baghdādī commentator and traditionist; *GAL*, sup. 1, p. 311.
68. Al-Daybājī — unable to identify.
69. Ruwaym Ibn Aḥmad (d. 942), a famous ṣūfī from Baghdad. Cf. Pellat, *al-Andalus*, 19 (1954), 92.
70. Muḥammad Ibn 'Umar Lubābah, a Cordovese traditionist and jurist (d. 926); see Ibn al-Faraḍī, *Tārīkh*, vol. 2, no. 1187.
71. Muḥammad Ibn 'Īsā b. Rifā'ah (d. 948), a traditionist; cf. Ibn al-Faraḍī, *Tārīkh*, vol. 2, no. 1243.
72. Fadl Ibn Salamah (d. ca. 931), a Mālikite jurist; see al-Ḍabbī, *Bughyah*, no. 1283. Pellat, *al-Andalus*, 19 (1954), 93.
73. Muḥammad Ibn 'Abdallah Ibn 'Abd al-Ḥakam (d. 882), an Eastern Mālikite jurist and author of juridical works; cf. *GAL*, sup. 1, p. 228.
74. Muḥammad Ibn Saḥnūn (d. 256/870), a Mālikite jurist of Qayrawān. He is the author of a commentary on the famous legal work, *al-Mudawwanah*.
75. Muḥammad Ibn 'Abdūs (260/874), a leading jurist from Qayrawān and author of a legal work entitled *al-Majmū'ah*.
76. Muḥammad Ibn Yaḥyā al-Riyāḥī (d. 968), a Cordovese grammarian; see al-Zubaydī, *Ṭabāqāt*, p. 335; Ibn al-Faraḍī, *Tārīkh*, vol. 2, no. 1290; al-Ḍabbī, *Bughyah*, no. 312.
77. Abū 'Abdallah Muḥammad Ibn 'Āṣim (d. 993), a leading grammarian. Cf. Ibn Bashkuwāl, *al-Ṣilah*, vol. 2, 478, no. 1034; al-Ḍabbī, *Bughyah*, no. 243; Ibn al-Faraḍī, *Tārīkh*, no. 1653.
78. Muḥammad Ibn Yazīd al-Mubarrad (d. 899), leading philologist of al-Baṣrah and author of the famous work entitled *al-Kāmil*.
79. Aḥmad Ibn Muḥammad Ibn Darrāj al-Qasṭallī (d. 1030) flourished under the 'Āmirids and is generally considered one of the great names in Arabic literature. Cf. Nykl, *Hispano-Arabic Poetry*, pp. 56ff.; R. Blachère, "La vie et l'oeuvre du poète-épistolier andalou Ibn Darrāg al-Qasṭalli," *Hespéris*, 16 (1933), 99–121.
80. Bashshār Ibn Burd (d. 783) was one of the great exponents of the modern school of poetry under the 'Abbāsids.
81. Ḥabīb refers to Abū Tammām (d. ca. 845), known for his *Dīwān* as well as by compilation of *Dīwān al-ḥamāsah*.
82. Al-Mutanabbī (d. 965) was one of the most gifted, if not the best, poets; his popularity has been great throughout the centuries.
83. Ja'far Ibn 'Uthmān al-Ḥājib (d. 978) served the caliphs 'Abd al-Raḥmān III and al-Ḥakam in the capacity of vizier and chamberlain (*ḥājib*), and was a competent poet of love and wine. See Nykl, *Hispano-Arabic Poetry*, p. 49.
84. Aḥmad Ibn 'Abd al-Malik Ibn Marwān (d. 10th cent.) was a poet at the court of 'Abd al-Raḥmān III; cf. al-Ḥumaydī, *Judhwah*, p. 123; al-Ḍabbī, *Bughyah*, no. 438.
85. Aghlab Ibn Shu'ayb (d. 10th cent.), also one of the poets at the court of 'Abd al-Raḥmān III; cf. al-Ḥumaydī, *Judhwah*, p. 165; al-Ḍabbī, *Bughyah*, no. 579.
86. Muḥammad Ibn Shukhayṣ (d. 1009) was the court poet of the caliph al-Ḥakam II. Cf. al-Ḥumaydī, *Judhwah*, p. 84.
87. Aḥmad Ibn Faraj (d. 970) flourished during the reign of al-Ḥakam II, to whom he dedicated his *Kitāb al-ḥadā'iq* (*Book of Gardens*). See Nykl, *Hispano-Arabic Poetry*, p. 43; al-Ḍabbī, *Bughyah*, no. 331.
88. 'Abd al-Malik Ibn Sa'īd al-Murādī, a court poet. Cf. al-Ḥumaydī, *Judhwah*, p. 266; al-Ḍabbī, *Bughyah*, no. 1067.
89. Ibn Ḥazm, *Risālah*, pp. 169–170.
90. See above, n. 13.
91. See above, no. 12.
92. Al-Shaqundī, *Risālah*, p. 178.
93. *Ibid*., p. 198.
94. *Ibid*., pp. 198ff.

95. *Ibid*., p. 206.

96. Attention should be called to the following studies: R. Blachère, "Un pionnier de la culture arabe orientale en Espagne au Xe siècle: Ṣā'id de Bagdad," *Hespéris*, 10 (1930), 15–36; E. García Gómez, "Bagdad y los reinos de Taifas," *RO*, 127 (1934), 1–22; E. Terés, "Préstamos poéticos en al-Andalus," *al-Andalus*, 21 (1956), 415–419.

For the influence of Arabic culture in the High March, see J. Vernet, "El valle del Ebro como nexo entre Oriente y Occidente," *BRABL*, 32 (1950), 249–286; J. Bosch Vilá, *El Oriente árabe en el desarrollo de la cultura de la Marca Superior* (Madrid, 1954).

9. The Sciences and Education

1. On Ziryāb, see Chapter 19.
2. On Yaḥyā, see Chapter 16.
3. On Ibn 'Abd Rabbihi, see Chapter 11.
4. On al-Qālī, see Chapter 11.
5. On al-Zubaydī, see Chapter 10.
6. On Ibn al-Qūṭiyah, see Chapter 15.
7. See Ṣā'id, *Ṭabaqāt al-umam* (Cairo, n.d.), pp. 88–89.
8. On al-Mu'tamid and Ibn 'Ammār, see Chapter 12.
9. On Ibn Zaydūn and Wallādah, see Chapter 12.
10. Al-Ḥajjāj was an able viceroy under the caliph 'Abd al-Malik and known to the historians as a blood-thirsty tyrant who put thousands of men to the sword while governor of al-'Irāq.
11. This one of several verses uttered by Ibn Ḥazm when al-Mu'taḍid, king of Seville, ordered Ibn Ḥazm's works committed to the fire. See Nykl, *Hispano-Arabic Poetry*, p. 102.
12. On Ibn Sīdah, see Chapter 10.
13. On Ibn Ḥayyān, see Chapter 15.
14. On Ibn 'Abd al-Barr, see below.
15. See Chapter 8.
16. On Ibn Bashkuwāl, see Chapter 15.
17. On al-Idrīsī, see Chapter 15.
18. On Ibn Jubayr, see Chapter 15.
19. On Ibn Zuhr, see Chapter 18.
20. On Ibn Bayṭār, see Chapter 18.
21. On Ibn 'Arabī, see Chapter 17.
22. On Ibn Sab'īn, see Chapter 17.
23. On those philosophers, see Chapter 17.
24. On the concept of knowledge in Islam, refer to the F. Rosenthal, *Knowledge Triumphant: The Concept of Knowledge in Medieval Islam* (Leiden, 1970).
25. On this work, see Chapter 11.
26. Ibn 'Abd Rabbihi, *al-'Iqd al-farīd*, vol. 2, p. 206.
27. *Ibid*., pp. 207–208.
28. *Ibid*., p. 208.
29. *Ibid*.
30. *Ibid*., p. 209.
31. *Ibid*., p. pp. 213–214.
32. *Ibid*., p. 215.
33. See A. Chejne, *The Arabic Language: Its Role in History* (Minneapolis, 1969), pp. 72ff.
34. Al-Kindī is credited with two treatises on the subject.
35. Al-Fārābī wrote an inventory of the sciences (*Iḥṣā' al-'ulūm*, ed. 'U. M. Amīn (Cairo, 1948).
36. Ibn Sīnā's work, entitled *Fī aqsām al-'ulūm al-ḥikmiyyah*, is still in manuscript form.
37. Al-Khuwārizmī's *Mafātīḥ al-'ulūm*, ed. G. van Vloten (Leiden, 1895).
38. The Arabic title of the work is *Jāmi' bayān al-'ilm wa-faḍluh* (Cairo, A.H. 1320).

39. The *Marātib al-'ulūm* is to be found in *Rasā'il Ibn Ḥazm*, ed. I. 'Abbās (Cairo, 1952), pp. 59–90. Cf. Asín Palacios, "Un codice inexplorado"; H. Monés, "Clasificaciones de la ciencias según Ibn Ḥazm," *RIEI*, 13 (1965–1966), 7–16.

40. The full title of the work is *Kitāb al-akhlāq wa-siyar fī mudāwāt al-nufūs* (Cairo, n.d.); Spanish trans. M. Asín Palacios, *Los caracteres y la conducta* (Madrid, 1916). The translation is referred to here.

41. Ibn Ḥazm, *Los caracteres y la conducta*, p. 17.

42. *Ibid*., p. 25.

43. *Ibid*., p. 23.

44. *Ibid*., p. 20.

45. *Ibid*., p. 19.

46. *Ibid*., p. 22.

47. *Ibid*., p. 24.

48. *Ibid*., p. 25.

49. Ibn Ḥazm, *Marātib al-'ulūm*, in *Rasā'vil*, p. 75.

50. *Ibid*., p. 77.

51. *Ibid*., p. 75.

52. *Ibid*., p. 76. And cf. Ibn Khaldūn, *al-Muqaddimah*, vol. 3, p. 288, who objects to the superabundance of books.

53. Ibn Ḥazm, *Marātib al-'ulūm*, p. 53.

54. *Ibid*., p. 61. He expresses the same thought in his *Akhlāq* (p. 18ff.) by saying that he who embraces an inferior science in preference to a higher one is like the one who sows one single grain of wheat in a fertile soil that is capable of abundant production; or like the one who sows wild trees in places suitable only for palms and olive trees.

55. *Ibid*., p. 63.

56. On Abū 'Ubayd, see Chapter 10.

57. On al-Zubaydī, see Chapter 10.

58. *Marātib al-'ulūm*, p. 68.

59. *Ibid*., p. 74; cf. his *Caracteres y conducta*, p. 20.

60. *Ibid*., p. 81.

61. *Ibid*., p. p. 89.

62. Ed. F. Codera.

63. Ibn Khayr, *Fahrasah*, p. 63.

64. *Ibid*., p. 8.

65. *Ibid*., p. 7.

66. *Ibid*., p. 6.

67. *Ibid*., p. 7.

68. *Ibid*., p. 11.

69. Undated Cairo edition is being used here. The *Ṭabaqāt* was translated into French by R. Blachère (Paris, 1935).

70. Ṣā'id, *Ṭabaqāt*, pp. 3–6.

71. *Ibid*., p. 7.

72. *Ibid*., p. 11.

73. *Ibid*., p. 12.

74. *Ibid*., p. 4.

75. *Ibid*., p. 14.

76. *Ibid*., p. 15.

77. *Ibid*., pp. 16ff.

78. *Ibid*., pp. 19–23.

79. *Ibid*., pp. 23–26.

80. *Ibid*., p. 26–43.

81. *Ibid*., p. 27.

82. *Ibid*., pp. 43–49.

83. *Ibid*., pp. 49–53.

84. *Ibid*., p. 49.
85. *Ibid*., pp. 53–113.
86. *Ibid*., pp. 53–62.
87. *Ibid*., pp. 62–83.
88. *Ibid*., pp. 83–113.
89. *Ibid*., p. 60.
90. *Ibid*., p. 64.
91. *Ibid*., p. 65.
92. *Ibid*., p. 92.
93. *Ibid*., pp. 83–113.
94. *Ibid*., pp. 114–118.
95. *Ibid*., p. 115.
96. Ibn Khaldūn, *al-Muqaddimah*. A good portion of vols. 2 and 3 is devoted to the sciences.
97. *Al-Muqaddimah*, vol. 3, p. 305.
98. *Ibid*., p. 307.
99. See above, n. 52.
100. *Al-Muqaddimah*, vol. 3, p. 288.
101. See Chapter 8, pp. 155, 158, and Abū-l-Ḥasan ʻAlī Ibn Muḥammad al-Ruʻaynī, *Barnāmaj shuyūkh al-Ruʻaynī* (Damascus, 1962), who gives insight into the curriculum and the manner of attaining it. One may add the names of Abū Muḥ. ʻAbd al-Ḥaqq b. Abī Bakr Ibn ʻAṭiyyah al-Muḥāribī (d. 1146) of Granada, who wrote the *Fahrasah* (Escorial 1753); cf. Pons Boïgues, *Ensayo*, no. 170, pp. 207ff. Al-Qāsim b. Yūsuf b. Muḥ. b. ʻAlī al-Qāsim al-Tujībī of Valencia composed his *Barnāmaj* in 1128, in which he lists the principal works studied by the author and the names of his teachers (Escorial 1756); cf. Pons Boïgues, no. 231, p. 274. Also, Abū ʻAbdallah al-Wādī Ashī (d. 1345) wrote a *Barnāmaj* in which he lists his teachers and the works studied under them (Escorial 1729). Of great interest is the *Taʻlīm al-mutaʻallim ṭuruq al-taʻlīm* (*The Instruction of the Teacher in the Ways of Teaching*) (Zaytūnah 5617), which was written by Barhān al-Dīn al-Zarnūjī (d. 1196).

On Muslim education in Spain, see J. Ribera, "La enseñanza entre los musulmanes españoles," in *Disertaciones y opúsculos* (Madrid, 1928).

102. Ibn Bashkuwāl, *al-Ṣilah*, vol. 1, p. 37.
103. Ibn ʻAbd al-Barr (Abū ʻUmar Yūsuf) left his *Bahjat al-majālis wa-uns al-majālis* in which he discusses literary clubs, their etiquette, and the conduct of the participant (*jalīs*), and describes the content of literary sessions. It is still in manuscript (Zaytūnah 4676; cf. Brockelmann, *GAL*, sup. 1, p. 629; microfilm in *IEIM*, C-16; *BRAH*, 16 (1890), no. 14, p. 384). In his *Miʻyār al-ikhtiyār* (Escorial 554), Ibn al-Khaṭīb has two literary sessions in the form of a dialogue.
104. On libraries, see S. M. Imamuddin, *Memoir of Hispano Arab Libraries* (Karachi, 1961), and J. Ribera, *Disertaciones y opúsculos* (Madrid, 1928), vol. 1, pp. 203ff.
105. See Chapter 8, p. 156. Treatises praising books are not hard to find. For instance, al-Jāḥiẓ (d. 869), *Risalah fī madḥ al-kutub* (MS., Zaytūnah 5682). Abū ʻAbdallah Muḥ. Ibn Nabātah (d. 1367) wrote an interesting treatise consisting of a dialogue between the pen and the sword, *al-Mufākharah bayn al-qalam wa-l-sayf* (*BRAH*, 16 (1890), no. 29, p. 389), in which each side boasts about its excellence.

10. Arabic and Linguistic Studies

1. On the place and role of Arabic in Arab-Muslim society, see Chejne, *The Arabic Language*.
2. For general works on Arab philology, see Ibn Fāris, *al-Ṣāḥibī fī fiqh al-lughah* (Cairo, 1910); al-Suyūṭī, *al-Muzhir* (Cairo, 1958); A. González Palencia, *Historia de la literatura arábigo-española* (Barcelona, 1928), Ch. 4; A. Darwīsh, *al-Maʻājim al-ʻarabiyyah* (Cairo, 1956); H. Naṣṣār, *al-Muʻjam al-ʻarabī* (Cairo, 1956); J. Haywood, *Arabic Lexicography* (Leiden, 1960).

For linguistic studies in al-Andalus in particular, see A. Muṭlaq, *al-Ḥarakah al-lughawiyyah fī-l-Andalus* (Sidon & Beirut, 1967); Chejne, *The Arabic Language*, pp. 46ff.

3. *Alvari Cordubensis opera. Indiculus luminosus* in *España Sagrada*, ed. H. Florex (Madrid, 1753), vol. 11, p. 273, as quoted by A. A. Vasiliev, *History of the Byzantine Empire* (Madison, Wis., 1964), vol. 1, p. 216. Cf. Chejne, *The Arabic Language*, pp. 15 and 181, n. 47. See also H. Pérès, "La langue arabe et les habitants de l'Andalousie au Moyen Âge," *Majma'*,19 (1944), 393–408.

4. Ed. and Spanish trans. by J. Ribera (Madrid, 1914), pp. 97–118; cf. J. B. Trend, in Arnold and Guillaume, eds., *Legacy of Islam*, pp. 7ff. See also A. Abel in G. E. von Grunebaum, ed., *Unity and Variety in Muslim Civilization* (Chicago, 1955), p. 207; also J. B. Trend, *The Language and History of Spain* (London, 1953), pp. 54ff.

5. *Al-Muqaddimah*, vol. 3, p. 357; cf. also, p. 364.

6. In addition to al-Maqqarī, *Nafḥ al-ṭib* (see Ch. 8), who gives ample information about migration to and from al-Andalus, there are the following other authors who supply valuable details about major grammarians and lexicographers and their contact with or dependence on the East: al-Zubaydī, *Ṭabaqāt al-naḥwiyyīn wa-l-lughawiyyīn* (*Ṭabaqāt*), ed. Muḥammad Abū-l-Faḍl Ibrāhīm (Cairo, 1954); Ibn al-Faraḍī, *Ta'rīkh*; Ibn Bashkuwāl, *al-Ṣilah*; al-Ḍabbī, *Bughyah*; Ibn Khayr, *Fahrasah*.

7. On Jūdī, see al-Zubaydī, *Ṭabaqāt*, p. 278; Muṭlaq, *al-Ḥarakah al-lughawiyyah*, pp. 69ff.

8. On al-Ghāzī, see al-Zubaydī, *Ṭabaqāt*, p. 277; al-Maqqarī, *Nafḥ al-ṭib*, p. 11.

9. Al-Maqqarī, *Nafḥ al-ṭib*, vol. 2, p. 214; al-Zubaydī, *Ṭabaqāt*, p. 282.

10. Al-Maqqarī, *Nafḥ al-ṭib*, vol. 2, pp. 255–256; al-Zubaydī, *Ṭabaqāt*, p. 309.

11. Al-Maqqarī, *Nafḥ al-ṭib*, vol. 2, pp. 253–255; al-Ḍabbī, *Bughyah*, p. 433.

12. For more details, see Muṭlaq, *al-Ḥarakah al-lughawiyyah*, pp. 73ff.

13. For one, Ibn Ḥazm discusses its various aspects in his juridical work, *Kitāb al-iḥkām fī uṣūl al-aḥkām* (Cairo, A.H. 1345–1348), vol. 1, pp. 29ff.; vol. 3, pp. 129ff.; vol. 4, 13ff., vol. 5, p. 126; vol. 8, pp. 76ff. See also R. Arnaldez, *Grammaire et théologie chez Ibn Ḥazm de Cordoue* (Paris, 1956).

14. See Ibn Khayr, *Fahrasah*, p. 305.

15. *Ibid*., p. 310.

16. *Ibid*., p. 333.

17. *Ibid*., p. 320.

18. *Ibid*., p. 329.

19. *Ibid*., p. 327.

20. *Ibid*., p. 308.

21. *Ibid*., p. 327.

22. For more details, see Muṭlaq, *al-Ḥarakah al-lughawiyyah*, pp. 313ff.

23. Al-Zubaydī, *Ṭabaqāt*, p. 278.

24. *Ibid*., p. 282.

25. See the following in al-Maqqarī, *Nafḥ al-ṭib*, vol. 4: Ibn Ḥazm, *Risālah*, p. 165; Ibn Sa'īd, *Risālah*, p. 178; al-Shaqundī, *Risālah*, p. 182.

26. See above. On al-Qālī, see al-Zubaydī, *Ṭabaqāt*, pp. 204–205; al-Marrākushī, *Mu'jib*, pp. 59ff.; Muṭlaq, *al-Ḥarakah al-lughawiyyah*, pp. 192ff.; al-Maqqarī *Nafḥ al-tib*, vol. 4, pp. 70ff.; Haywood, *Arabic Lexicography*, pp. 53ff. And see below Chapter 10.

27. Ibn Durayd is the author of the famous lexicon *Jamharat al-lughah* (Hyderabad, 1925), and Ibn al-Anbārī is the author of various grammatical and lexical works.

28. Cairo, A.H. 1324.

29. Al-Marrākushī, *Mu'jib*, p. 61; see below, Chapter 10.

30. Edited by A. S. Vloten (London, 1933). On the *Bāri'*, see Naṣṣār.

31. On Ibn al-Qūṭiyah, see Ibn al-Faraḍī, *Tārīkh*, vol. 2, p. 78; Ibn Khallikān, *Wafāyāt al-a'yān* (Cairo, A.H. 1299), vol. 4, pp. 4ff.; Yāqūt, *Mu'jam al-Udabā'* (Cairo, n.d.), vol. 18, pp. 272ff.; Muṭlaq, *al-Ḥarakah al-lughawiyyah*, pp. 165ff.

32. It bears the title of *al-Af'āl al-thulāthiyyah wa-l-rubā'iyyah*, ed. I. Guidi (Leiden, 1894).

33. On al-Zubaydī, see al-Ḍabbī, *Bughyah*, pp. 56ff.; al-Marrākushī, *Mu'jib*, pp. 62ff; Ibn Khallikān, *Wafāyāt*, vol. 4, pp. 7ff.; Yāqūt, *Mu'jam*, vol. 18, pp. 180ff.; Muṭlaq, *al-Ḥarakah al-lughawiyyah*, pp. 123ff.

34. As quoted by Haywood, *Arabic Lexicography*, p. 61.

35. Al-Zubaydī, *Ṭabaqāt*, p. 1, as quoted by A. Chejne, "Arabic: Its Significance and Place in Arab-Muslim Society," *MEJ*, 19 (1965), 457; also, Chejne, *The Arabic Language*, p. 14.

36. The work is in manuscript (Escorial 569 and 570; also *BNM* 5017) under the title *Mukhtaṣar kitāb al-'ayn*.

37. Edited by R. 'Abd al-Ṭawwāb (Cairo, 1964). Interestingly enough, the work was refuted by Abū 'Abdallah Muḥ. b. Aḥmad b. Hishām in his *Kitāb al-radd 'alā al-Zubaydī fī laḥn al-'awāmm* (Escorial 46).

38. *Kitāb al-istidrāq 'alā Sībawayhi*, ed. I. Guidi (Rome, 1890).

39. *Ṭabaqāt*, see above, n. 6.

40. A partial list of their pupils is to be found in Muṭlaq, *al-Harakah al-lughawiyyah*, pp. 237ff.

41. See above, Chapter 8.

42. Ibn Ḥazm, *Marātib al-'ulūm*, in *Rasā'il Ibn Ḥazm*, ed. I. 'Abbās (Cairo, 1952), pp. 64–65.

43. See Ibn Ḥazm, *Kitāb al-iḥkām fī-uṣūl al-aḥkām*, vol. 1, pp. 29ff., vol. 2, p. 127; vol. 8, p. 76ff. The chapter dealing with a discussion of the language was translated into Spanish by M. Asín Palacios, "El origén del lenguaje y problemas conexos," *Historia y filología árabe*, 2–3 (Madrid, 1948) pp. 377–378. See also Muṭlaq, *al-Ḥarakah al-lughawiyyah* 272ff.; Chejne, *The Arabic Language*, pp. 10ff.

44. *Qur'ān* 2:29.

45. On Ibn Sīdah, see Ibn Bashkuwāl, *al-Ṣilah*, vol. 2, pp. 396ff.; al-Maqqarī, *Nafḥ al-ṭīb*, vol. 4, pp. 351ff.; Naṣṣār, *al-Mu'jam*, vol. 1, pp. 238–246; Muṭlaq, *al-Ḥarakah al-lughawiyyah*, pp. 351ff.; Haywood, *Arabic Lexicography*, pp. 66ff.

46. The full title of the work is *al-Muḥkam wa-l-muḥīṭ al-a'ẓam* (Cairo, 1958).

47. Following is the alphabetical order of the dictionary: ', ḥ, h, kh, gh, q, k, j, sh, ḍ, ṣ, s, z, ṭ, t, d, ẓ, dh, th, r, l, n, f, b, m, ', y, w, alif.

48. *Al-Mukhaṣṣaṣ* (17 pts.; Būlāq, A.H. 1316–1321).

49. *Ibid*., pp. 3–6; cf. Asín Palacios, "El orígen del lenguaje," pp. 373–378; Chejne, *The Arabic Language*, p. 11.

50. On al-Bakrī, see Ibn Bashkuwāl, *al-Ṣilah*, p. 277; Ibn al-Abbār, *Ḥullah*, vol. 2, 180ff.; Muṭlaq, *al-Ḥarakah al-lughawiyyah*, pp. 525ff. See below, Chapter 15.

51. See Muṭlaq, *al-Ḥarakah al-lughawiyyah*, pp. 313ff. For more details on commentaries and commentators, see Muḥammad al-Dāyah, *Tārīkh al-naqd al-adabī fī-l-Andalus* (Beirut, 1968), pp. 69–230.

52. See Muṭlaq, *al-Ḥarakah al-lughawiyyah*, pp. 310ff. and 323ff.; cf. Ibn Khayr *Fahrasah*, p. 398.

53. See Muṭlaq, *al-Ḥarakah al-lughawiyyah*, pp. 307ff.

54. On Sayyid, see Ibn Bashkuwāl, *al-Ṣilah*, vol. 1, p. 282; Ibn Khallikān, *Wafayāt*, vol. 2, pp. 282ff.; Muṭlaq, *al-Ḥarakah al-lughawiyyah*, pp. 338ff. His commentary on Ibn Qutaybah's work is known under the title of *al-Iqtiḍāb fī sharḥ adab al-kātib*, which is extant (MS. Zaytūnah 4629; cf. *GAL*, sup. 1, p. 185).

55. Cairo, 1945–1948.

56. Beirut, 1901.

57. As quoted by Nykl, *Hispano-Arabic Poetry*, p. 324.

58. Al-Maqqarī, *Nafḥ al-ṭīb*, vol. 2, pp. 406–409.

59. *Ibid*., p. 407.

60. *Ibid*., pp. 421–433.

61. The *Alfiyyah* was edited by S. de Sacy in 1833, and was later translated into French by A. Goguyer (Tunis, 1888).

62. Al-Maqqarī, *Nafḥ al-ṭīb*, vol. 3, pp. 289–341; Nykl, *Hispano-Arabic Poetry*, pp. 358–359.

63. Al-Maqqarī, *Nafḥ al-ṭīb*, vol. 3, p. 290.

64. *Ibid.*, pp. 306–307. For one, Abū 'Abdallah Shams al-Dīn Ibn Jābir commented on the *Alfiyyah* MS. Escurial 74; *BNM* 225).

65. For further references, see R. Dozy, *Glossaire des mots espagnols et portugais dérivés de l'arabe* (Leiden, 1869); also his and H. W. Englemann's *Supplement aux dictionaires arabes* (Leiden, 1881); L. Eguilaz, *Glosario etimológico de las palabras españolas de origen oriental* (Granada, 1886); F. Fernández y González, *La influencia de las lenguas y literaturas orientales en la nuestra* (Madrid, 1894); Trend, in Arnold and Guillaume, eds., *Legacy of Islam*, pp. 181ff.; E. K. Neuvonen, *Los arabismos del español en el siglo XIII* (Helsinki, 1941).

See also, G. Díaz-Plaja, *Historia del español* (Buenos Aires, 1955); Wm. Entwistle, *The Spanish Language* (London, 1936, 1962); R. Lapesa, *Historia de la lengua española* (New York, 1965); R. Menéndez Pidal, *Orígenes del español* (Madrid, 1950); R. K. Spaulding, *How Spanish Grew* (Berkeley & Los Angeles, 1967); and J. B. Trend, *The Language and History of Spain* (London, 1953).

66. Diáz-Plaja, *Historia del español*, p. 44.

67. Lapesa, *Historia de la lengua española*, pp. 109ff.

11. Prose and Belles Lettres (*Adab*)

1. Ibn Kahldūn, *al-Muqaddimah*, vol. 3, pp. 339–341. On the various meanings of *adab*, see *EI* (1954) under *adab*. Cf. González Palencia, *Historia de la literatura arábigo-española*, Ch. 3; also G. E. von Grunebaum, *Medieval Islam* (Chicago, 1946), pp. 250–257. On prose writing, see Shawqī Ḍayf, *al-Fann wa-madhāhibuh fi-l-nathr al-'arabī* (Cairo, 1960); C. A. Nallino, *Raccolta di scritti editi e inediti* (Rome, 1939–1948); F. Rosenthal, *Orientalia*, vol. 4, sup. 11 (1942), 263–268.

2. *Kalīlah wa-Dimnah* was translated about 750 from Middle Persian (Pahlavi) into Arabic. The Arabic version became the basis for translations into Latin, Spanish, Italian, French, English, and other languages. See *EI* (1913–1914). See also the Spanish version, ed. J. E. Keller, *Calila e Degna* (Madrid, 1967).

3. The *Adab al-ṣaghīr* was edited by M. Amīn (Cairo, 1913).

4. The *Adab al-kabīr* was printed several times (Beirut, 1898).

5. Ibn Khaldūn, *al-Muqaddimah*, vol. 3, pp. 340–341.

6. The *Bukhalā'* was printed several times. It was edited for the first time by van Vloten (Leiden, 1900). In it al-Jāḥiẓ singles out a large number of misers and relates their conditions with profuse anecdotes reflecting their character; the ultimate purpose appears to be condemnation of avarice and praise of generosity.

7. The *Ḥayawān* was also published several times. A scholarly edition was done by 'Abd al-Salām Muḥammad Hārūn (Cairo, 1938). The purpose of the book is to describe the nature of animals vis-à-vis man.

8. Ed. 'Abd al-Salām Hārūn (Cairo, 1961).

9. Ed. Max Grunert (Leiden, 1900). *Adab al-kātib*, or *kuttāb*, received the attention of the Andalusians. For instance, 'Abdallah Ibn Muḥammad al-Sayyid al-Baṭalyūsī (d.1227) wrote a commentary on it entitled *al-Iqtiḍāb fī sharḥ adab al-kuttāb* (MS. Zaytūnah 4629; Escorial 503 and 222); cf. *GAL*, sup. 1, p. 185.

10. Published in 4 vols. (Cairo, 1925–1930).

11. Al-Mubarrad, *Kitāb al-kāmil fi-l-lughah wa-l-adab*, ed. Abū-l-Faḍl Ibrāhīm (Cairo, 1956), vol. 1, pp. 292, 301, 377; vol. 2, pp. 20, 93, 115. And see index to the work.

12. Especially his *Fuṣūl al-tamāthīl fi-tabāshīr al-surūr* (Cairo, 1925).

13. Mainly, his *Adab al-kuttāb* (Baghdād, A.H. 1341).

14. Edited by a board of scholars (21 vols.; Beriut, 1956–1957).

15. Ed. Aḥmad Amīn (Cairo, 1948–1953); J. Jabbūr, *Ibn 'Abd Rabbihi wa-'iqduh* (Beirut,

1933). Ibn 'Abd Rabbihi wrote a selection of the choicest of proverbs entitled *Jawharat al-amthāl* (MS. Zaytūnah 4792).

16. Ibn 'Abd Rabbihi often mentions Ibn al-Muqaffa'; see *al-'Iqd al-farīd*, vol. 1, pp. 11, 13; vol. 2, pp. 421, 478; vol. 3, pp. 5, 15; and index, vol. 7, p. 90. He also makes frequent references to *Kalīlah wa-Dimnah*, which he calls *Kitāb al-Hind* (*The Book of India*); see vol. 1, pp. 10, 15, 18, 43, 70, 123; and index, vol. 7, p. 20.

17. *Al-'Iqd al-farīd*, vol. 1, p. 250; vol. 2, pp. 172, 342, 422; index, vol. 7, p. 103.

18. *Ibid*., vol. 1, p. 36; vol. 2, p. 423; vol. 3, p. 408; index, vol. 7, pp. 89 and 204–205.

19. *Ibid*., index, vol. 7, p. 416.

20. *Ibid*., p. 140.

21. *Ibid*., p. 98.

22. *Ibid*., vol. 1, p. 93.

23. *Ibid*., vol. 2, p. 208.

24. *Ibid*., p. 209.

25. *Ibid*., vol. 3, p. 63.

26. *Ibid*., p. 141.

27. *Ibid*., p. 171.

28. *Ibid*., p. 312.

29. *Ibid*., vol. 4, p. 172.

30. *Ibid*., p. 179.

31. *Ibid*., vol. 5, pp. 3–4.

32. It should be pointed out that the inclusion of al-Muṭī' (946–974) must be considered a later interpolation if we accept that Ibn 'Abd Rabbihi died in 940, six years before the accession of al-Muṭī'.

33. *Al-'Iqd al-farīd*, vol. 6, p. 31.

34. *Ibid*., p. 82.

35. *Ibid*., p. 379.

36. On al-Qālī, see Chapters 8 and 10.

37. The full title of the work is *al-Amālī wa-dhayl al-Amālī* (Cairo, 1926).

38. *Al-Amālī*, vol. 1, p. 3.

39. Published as part of *al-Amālī*. See n. 37 above.

40. See Ibn Khayr, *Fahrasah*, p. 326.

41. The treatise is known under various titles. It was published in Alexandria at the beginning of this century under the title *Kalimāt fi-l-akhlāq* and later in Cairo under the title *Mudāwat al-nufūs wa-tahdhīb al-nufūs*. It was translated into Spanish by M. Asín Palacios as *Los caracteres y la conducta*, and into French by Nada Tomiche as *Epître morale*. An analysis of the work was made by A. R. Nykl, "Ibn Ḥazm's 'Treatise on Ethics,'" *AJSLL*, 40 (1923), 30–36.

42. Ibn Ḥazm, *Los caracteres y la conducta*, p. 5.

43. *Sirāj* was published in Būlāq (A.H. 1287); Spanish trans. M. Alarcón, *Lámpara de los príncipes* (Madrid, 1930). A compendium of the work is in manuscript (Zaytūnah 6795). Muḥammad Ibn 'Alī al-Azrafī al-Andalusī (d. 1491) also concerned himself with government in his *Badā'i' al-sulk fī ṭabā'i' al-mulk* (Zaytūnah 5068; cf. *GAL*, sup. 2, p. 962).

44. Excerpts of the work are to be found in R. Dozy's *Scriptorum arabum loci de Abbadidis* (Leiden, 1848–1853), vol. 2, pp. 1–10.

45. Published several times (e.g., Beirut, 1886). Ed. and English trans. *The Assemblies of al-Hariri*, pt. I by Thomas Chenery (London, 1867) and pt. II by F. Steinglass (London, 1898).

46. Chenery, *The Assemblies of al-Hariri*, pt. 1, pp. 105–106.

47. See A. Mujṭār al-'Abbādī, *Maqāmat*, in *RIEEI*, 2 (1954), 159–173; also I. 'Abbās, *Tārīkh al-adab al-andalusī: 'aṣr al-Ṭawā'if* (Beirut, 1962), pp. 305ff.

48. See González Palencia, *Historia de la literatura arábigo-española*, p. 316.

49. See Watt, *A History of Islamic Spain*, p. 125, see also 'Abbās, *Tārīkh al-adab al-andalusī*, p. 317.

50. Cairo, A.H. 1300.

51. González Palencia, *Historia de la literatura arábigo-española*, pp. 120–121.

52. There is a great need for research in order to determine the influence of Arabic on early Spanish literature. One good example of such research is F. Ayala, "Fuente árabe de un cuento popular en el Lazarillo," *BRAE*, 45 (1965), 493–495, found a story in the *Kitāb al-Māḥāsin* (Giessen, 1902) of the tenth-century al-Bayhāqī which was still current in sixteenth-century Spain during the time of the writing of the *Lazarillo*.

53. See Ibn Shuhayd, *Risālat al-tawābi' wa-l-zawābi'*, ed. B. al-Bustānī (Beirut, 1951), pp. 157ff.

54. See I. 'Abbās, *Tārīkh al-adab al-andalusī: 'aṣr siyādat Qurṭubah*, (Beirut, 1969), pp. 325; and his *Tārīkh al-adab al-andalusī: 'aṣr al-Ṭawā'if*, pp. 287ff., where there is a good sampling of epistles.

55. R. Blachère, "La vie et l'oeuvre," pp. 99–121; Nykl, *Hispano-Arabic Poetry*, pp. 56ff. See also his *Dīwān*.

56. Text of the two epistles are to be found in J. al-Rikābī, *Fī-l-adab al-andalusī* (Cairo, 1966), pp. 252–281.

57. It was commented on by Ibn Nabātah (d. 1366) and published under the title of *Sharḥ al-'uyūn fī sharḥ risālat Ibn Zaydūn* (Cairo, A.H. 1278).

58. It was commented on and published several times (Cairo, 1906, 1926).

59. Ed. with a long introduction by B. al-Bustānī (Beirut, 1951), English trans. J. Monroe (Berkeley 1971).

60. In addition to the introduction of al-Bustānī in the edition of *al-Tawābi'*, see Ibn Sa'īd, *al-Mughrib fī akhbār ahl al-Maghrib*, ed. Sh. Ḍayf (Cairo, 1954), vol. 1, pp. 78ff.; al-Ḍabbī, *Bughyah*, no. 437; 'Abbās, *Tārīkh al-adab al-andalusī: 'aṣr siyādat Qurṭubah*, pp. 270ff.; Nykl, *Hispano-Arabic Poetry*, pp. 103ff.; Pérès, *La poésie andalouse*, pp. 467–468.

61. See Chapter 8.

62. On literary criticism in general, see Abū Hilāl al-Askarī (d. 1005), *Kitāb al-ṣinā'aṭayn* (Constantinople, A.H. 1320); Ibn Rashīq, *al-'Umdah fī ṣinā'at al-shi'r wa naqdihi* (Cairo, A.H. 1344).

For modern works, see Sh. Ḍayf, *al-Naqd* (Cairo, 1954), and *al-Balāghah: taṭawwur wa-tārīkh* (Cairo, 1965); A. Amīn, *al-Naqd al-adabī* (Cairo, 1963); Ṭ. al-Ḥijārī, *Fī tārīkh al-naqd wa-l-madhāhib al-adabiyyah* (Alexandria, 1953); Mu. Zaghlūl Salām, *Tārīkh al-naqd al-'arabī ilā-l-qarn al-rābi' al-hijrī* (Cairo, 1964).

For al-Andalus in particular, see al-Dāyah, *Tārīkh al-naqd*. Al-Dāyah has gathered an enormous amount of material on the subject.

63. See Ibn 'Abd Rabbihi, *al-'Iqd al-farīd*, vol. 2, p. 123, who says that eloquence (*bayān*) is that which uncovers hidden meaning, is understood, and accepted by the intellect; *ibid*., vol. 4, p. 260; vol. 5, p. 338.

64. See Chapter 9.

65. Ibn Ḥazm, *Taqrīb*, p. 206.

66. Ibn Ḥazm, *Marātib al-'ulūm*, p. 80.

67. Ibn Ḥazm, *al-Taqrīb*, p. 204.

68. See al-Dāyah, *Tārīkh al-naqd*, p. 324.

69. *Ibid*., p. 332.

70. *Ibid*., pp. 338ff.

71. *Ibid*., pp. 401ff.

72. Ed. Mu. al-Dāyah (Beirut, 1966). Manuals for secretaries for the purpose of good writing are quite abundant. Mention can be made of *'Umdat al-kuttāb wa-'uddat dhawī al-albāb* of unknown authorship, which is in MS. (*IEIM*-C-18). Also Ibn al-Abbār's *I'tāb al-kuttāb* (*IEIM*-B-13; Escorial 1731), in which he deals with Andalusian secretaries and give examples of their writing.

73. *Iḥkām ṣan'at al-kalām*,. 36ff.

74. Al-Dāyah, *Tārikh al-naqd*, pp. 471ff.

75. Ed. Mu. Ibn Khawjah (Tunis, 1966). One may mention Ibn al-Khaṭib's *Riḥānat al-kuttāb wa-naj'at al-muntāb* (MS., Zaytūnah 6171; Escorial 1825; cf. *GAL*, sup. 2, p. 383, and Pons Boïgues, *Ensayo*, p. 343).

12. Poetry: The Classical Tradition

1. Following are some of the general works dealing with Hispano-Arabic literature: Juan Andrés *Dell' origine, progressi e stato attuale d'ogni letteratura* (Parma, 1782–1799), Spanish trans. Origen, *Progreso y estado actual de toda la literatura* (Madrid, 1784–1806); J. A. Conde, *Historia de la dominación de los árabes en España* (Madrid, 1820–1821); Jean Humbert, *Anthologie arabe* (Paris, 1819); J. B. von Hammer-Purgstalls, *Literaturgeschichte der Araber, von Ihrem Beginne bis zu Ende des Zwölften Jahrhunderts der Hidschret* (Vienna, 1850–1856); A. F. von Schack, *Poesie und Kunst der Araber in Spanien und Sizilien* (Berlin, 1865), Spanish trans. J. Valera, *Poesía y arte de los árabes en España y Sicilia* (Seville, 1881); R. Dozy, *Recherches sur l'histoire et la littérature de l'Espagne pendant le Moyen Âge* (Leiden, 1847); A. González Palencia, *Historia de la literatura arábigo-española* (Barcelona, 1928); R. A. Nicholson, *A Literary History of the Arabs* (Cambridge, 1956).

For poetry in particular the following works are important: H. Pérès, *La poésie andalouse en arabe classique au XIe siècle* (Paris, 1953); E. García Gómez, *Poemas arábigo andaluces* (Madrid & Buenos Aires, 1940), *Qasìdas de Andalucía* (Madrid, 1940), and *Cinco poetas musulmanes* (Madrid, 1944). A. R. Nykl, *Hispano-Arabic Poetry and Its Relations with the Old Provençal Troubadours* (Baltimore, 1946).

The following Arabic works, among many others, constitute an indispensable source of information: Abu-l-Walīd al-Ḥimyari, *al-Badī' fi-waṣf al-rabī'*, ed. H. Pérès (Rabat, 1940); al-Huṣri al-Qayrawānī, *Zahr al-ādāb* (Cairo, 1953–1954); Ibn 'Abd Rabbihi, *Kitāb al-'iqd al-farid*, ed. Aḥmad Amīn et al. (Cairo, 1948–1953); Ibn Bassām, *al-Dhakhīrah* (Cairo, 1939); Ibn Khāqān, *Qalā'id* (Būlāq, A.H. 1277); Ibn Khaldūn, *The Muqaddimah*, English trans. F. Rosenthal (New York, 1958),vol. 3; Ibn al-Kattānī, *Kitāb al-tashbīhāt*, ed. I. 'Abbās (Beirut, 1966); Ibn Khallikān, *Wafayāt*, several editions; Ibn Sa'īd al-Maghribī, *Kitāb rāyāt al-mubarrizīn wa-ghāyāt al-mumayyizīn* — ed. and Spanish trans. E. García Gómez, *Libro de las banderas y campeones* (Madrid, 1942), and English trans. A. J. Arberry, *Anthology of Moorish Poetry* (Cambridge, England, 1953); al-Maqarrī, *Nafḥ al-ṭib*; Yāqūt, *Irshād*, ed. D. S. Margoliouth (London, 1907–1927).

The following modern Arabic books are also important for Hispano-Arabic poetry: I. 'Abbās, *Tārīkh al-adab al-andalusī: 'aṣr siyādat Qurṭubah* (Beirut, 1969), and *Tārīkh al-adab al-andalusī: 'aṣr al-Ṭawā'if wa-l-Murābiṭīn* (Beirut, 1962); 'A. Kanūn, *al-Nubūgh al-Maghribī fi-l-adab al-'arabī* (Beirut, 1961); Muḥammad Khāfajah, *Qiṣṣat al-adab al-'arabi fi-l-Andalus* (Beirut, 1962); I. Abū-l-Khashab, *Tārīkh al-adab al-'arabī fi-l-Andalus (Cairo 1966);* K. Kīlānī, *Naẓarāt fī tā'rīkh al-adab al-andalusī* (Cairo, 1924); J. Rikābī, *Fī-l-adab al-andalusī* (2nd ed.; Cairo, 1966); Muḥammad R. al-Shabībī, *Adab al-maghāribah wa-l-andalusiyyīn* (Cairo, 1961).

2. These meters are called *mutaqārib, rajaz, hajaz, ramal, wāfir, kāmil, ṭawīl, sarī', basīṭ, muḥtathth, munsariḥ, khafīf, madīd, muḍāri', mutadārik, muqtaḍab*. For an explanation of these terms and an overall view of pre-Islamic poetry, see Charles Lyall, *Ancient Arabian Poetry* (Edinburgh, 1885), pp. xlv*ff.* See also Nicholson, *Literary History of the Arabs*, pp. 71ff.; A. J. Arberry, *The Seven Odes* (London, 1950).

3. Cf. Nicholson, *Literary History of the Arabs*, p. 73, n. 3.

4. Ed. C. Lyall, *A Commentary on the Ancient Arabic Poems* (Calcutta, 1894). Cf. Nicholson, *Literary History of the Arabs*, pp. 101ff.

5. For the position of the Andalusian poet, see H. Pérès, *La poésie andalouse*, pp. 55ff.; al-Rikābī, *Fī-l-adab al-andalusī*, pp. 63ff.

6. Nykl, *Hispano-Arabic Poetry*, pp. xix–xx; cf. Pérès, *La poésie andalouse*, pp. 115ff.; Rikābī, *Fī-l-adab al-andalusī*, pp. 114ff.

7. Ibn Ḥazm, *Risālah*, in al-Maqqarī, *Nafḥ al-ṭīb*, vol. 4, pp. 154–170.

8. Ibn Bassām, *al-Dhakhīrah*.

9. Ibn Khāqān, *Qalā'id* and *Maṭmaḥ al-anfus*.

10. Al-Shaqundī, *Risālah*.

11. On 'Abd al-Raḥmān and other rulers in their capaciy as poets, see Ibn al-Abbār, *al-Ḥullah*, vol. 1, pp. 35ff., 42ff., 113ff., 197ff.

12. Nykl, *Hispano-Arabic Poetry*, p. 18. Nykl''s translations have been used, unless otherwise indicated.

13. *Ibid*., p. 21.

14. See the Arabic text in Ibn al-Abbār, *al-Ḥullah*, vol. 1, p. 50.

15. On al-Ghazāl, see al-Maqqarī, *Nafḥ al-ṭīb*, vol. 1, p. 449; Nykl, *Hispano-Arabic Poetry*, p. 24; 'Abbās, *Tārīkh al-adab al-andalusī: 'aṣr siyādat Qurṭubah*, pp. 157ff.

16. Nykl, *Hispano-Arabic Poetry*, p. 23.

17. On Sa'īd b. Jūdī, see *ibid*., p. 30.

18. See the famous poem of Ibn 'Abd Rabbihi, *al-'Iqd al-farīd*, vol. 4, pp. 501–527, English trans. by J. Monroe in *JAOS*, 91 (1971), 67–95.

19. Nykl, *Hispano-Arabic Poetry*, p. 30.

20. On Ibn Hānī, see Nykl, *Hispano-Arabic Poetry*, p. 28; Ibn Hānī, *Dīwān* (Cairo, A.H. 1274); Munīr Nājī, *Ibn Hānī' al-andalusī: dars wa-naqd* (Beirut, 1962).

21. Nykl, *Hispano-Arabic Poetry*, p. 29.

22. *Qasīdas*, p. 8.

23. See Chapter 14 on Ibn Ḥazm and Ibn Zaydūn.

24. On al-Ramādī, see al-Maqqarī, *Nafḥ al-ṭīb*, vol. 2, p. 440; 'Abbās, *Tārīkh al-adab al-andalusī: 'aṣr siyādat Qurṭubah*, pp. 205ff. Nykl, *Hispano-Arabic Poetry*, p. 58; Pérès, *La poésie andalouse*, pp. 278ff.

25. See Chapter 11. On Ibn Darrāj, see 'Abbās, *Tārīkh al-adab al-andalusī: 'aṣr siyādat Qurṭubah*, pp. 237ff., and Ibn Darrāj, *Dīwān* (Damascus, 1961).

26. See Chapter 11.

27. On Ibn 'Ammār, see González Palencia, *Historia de la literatura arábigo-española*, pp. 73ff.; García Gómez, *Qasīdas*, pp. 55–71; Nykl, *Hispano-Arabic Poetry*, pp. 154–162; Pérès, *La poésie andalouse*, pp. 268ff. See also Ibn 'Ammār, *Dīwān* (Baghdad, 1957).

28. On al-Mu'tamid, see González Palencia, *Historia de la literatura arábigo-española*, pp. 71–83; García Gómez, *Qasīdas*, pp. 75–81; Pérès, *La poésie andalouse*, pp. 289ff.; Nykl, *Hispano-Arabic Poetry*, pp. 134–154. See also al-Mu'tamid, *Dīwān* (Cairo, 1951), and Ibn Khāqān, *Qalā'id*, pp. 4ff.

29. Nykl, *Hispano-Arabic Poetry*, p. 149; Ṣalāḥ Khāliṣ, *al-Mu'tamid Ibn 'Abbād* (Baghdād, 1958).

30. Nykl, *Hispano-Arabic Poetry*, p. 136; cf. García Gómez, *Qasīdas*, pp. 102ff.

31. On Ibn Labbānah, see Pérès, *La poésie andalouse*, pp. 301ff.; Nykl, *Hispano-Arabic Poetry*, pp. 163ff.

32. On Abū Isḥāq al-Ilbīrī, see Nykl, *Hispano-Arabic Poetry*, pp. 197ff.; González Palencia, *Historia de la literatura arábigo-española*, pp. 67ff.; García Gómez, *Abū Ishāq de Elvira* (Madrid, 1944).

33. On al-Mu'taṣim, see Nykl, *Hispano-Arabic Poetry*, pp. 183ff.; González Palencia, *Historia de la literatura arábigo-española*, pp. 67ff.

34. On Ibn al-Ḥaddād, see Pérès, *La poésie andalouse*, pp. 279ff.; Nykl, *Hispano-Arabic Poetry*, p. 194ff.

35. On Umm al-Kirām, see Pérès, *La poésie andalouse*, p. 429; Nykl, *Hispano-Arabic Poetry*, p. 186.

36. On Ibn Bājjah, see Nykl, *Hispano-Arabic Poetry*, pp. 251–254.

37. On Ibn 'Abdūn, *ibid*., pp. 175–179; Pérès, *La poésie andalouse*, pp. 106ff.

38. On Abū al-Ṣalt, see Nykl, *Hispano-Arabic Poetry*, pp. 238–240.

39. On Ibn Khafājah, *ibid*., pp. 227–231. mss. of his *Dīwān* are to be found in the British Museum, Paris, and the Escorial, microfilms of which are in IEIM: B-8, B-9, and B-10.

40. On Ibn Mālik, see Chapter 10.
41. On Abū Ḥayyān, see Chapter 10. See also his *Dīwān* (Cairo, A.H. 1286; Beirut, A.D. 1951).
42. In addition, Ibn al-Khaṭīb wrote *Prose and Poetry* (*al-Siḥr wa-l-shi'r*), which is extant (Escorial 455 and 456). It is of interest to mention here Ibn al-Aḥmar (d. A.H. 807), a contemporary of Ibn al-Khaṭīb and author of *Nathīr farā'id al-jumān fī naẓm fuḥūl al-zamān*, ed. Muḥammad Riḍwān al-Dāyah with a long introduction (Beirut, 1967). The work consists of an anthology of thirty-one Andalusian and Maghribī poets.
43. On Ibn Zamrak, see Nykl, *Hispano-Arabic Poetry*, p. 366; R. Blanchère, "Ibn Zumruk et son oeuvre," *AIEO*, 2 (1936), 291–312.

13. Poetry: The Popular Forms

1. For poetical trends in the East, classical versus modern, see Ibn Qutaybah, *Kitāb al-shi'r wa-l-shu'arā'*, ed. M. J. de Goeje (Leiden, 1904); Nicholson, *Literary History of the Arabs*, pp. 286ff.
2. The following books and articles are important for the study of *muwashshaḥ* and *zajal*: D. Alonso, in *RFE*, 33 (1949), 297–349, and *al-Andalus*, 8 (1943), 129–153; E. Asensio, *Poética y realidad en el cancionero péninsular de la edad media* (Madrid, 1957); E. García Gómez, in *al-Andalus*, 2 (1934), 215–222; 14 (1949), 409–417; 11 (1950); 157–177; 17 (1952), 57–127; 19 (1954), 43–54, 369–391; 21 (1956), 303–338, 406–414; 25 (1960), 287–311; 26 (1961), 253–321, 453–465; 27 (1962), 1–20, 21–104; 28 (1963), 1–60; also in *BRAE*, 27 (1957), 339–394 and in *RO*, 2 (1964), 129–145; *Una voz en la calle* (Madrid, 1933); *Las jarchas* (Madrid, 1963); *Todo Ben Quzmān* (Madrid, 1972).

A. González Palencia, *Historia de la literatura arábigo-española* (Barcelona, 1928), pp. 107ff., 329ff.; M. Hartmann, *Das arabische Strophengedicht* (Weiner, 1897); W. Hoenerbach and H. Ritter in *Oriens*, 3 (1950), 266–315; 5 (1952), 269–301; and in *al-Andalus*, 15 (1950), 297–334; R. A. Nicholson, *A Literary History of the Arabs* (Cambridge, 1956), pp. 417ff.; A R. Nykl, *Hispano-Arabic Poetry and its Relations with the Old Provençal Troubadours* (Baltimore, 1946); J. Ribera y Tarragó, *El cancionero de Abéncuzmán* (Madrid, 1912), *La música de las cántigas* (Madrid, 1922), and *La música andaluza medieval en las canciones de trovadores, troveros y minnesinger* (Madrid, 1922–1925).

S. M. Stern, *Les chansons mozárabes* (Palermo, 1953); various articles in *al-Andalus*, 13 (1948), 299–346; 14 (1949), 214–218; 15 (1950), 79–109; 16 (1951), 379–425; 23 (1958), 339–369; 28 (1963), 155–170; also in *Arabica*, 1 (1955), 150–192, and in *Hispanic Studies in Honor of I. González Llubera* (Oxford, 1959), pp. 367–386.

J. B. Trend, *The Language and History of Spain* (London, 1953); also in *Hispanic Studies in Honor of I. González Llubera* (Oxford, 1959), pp. 415–428.

The following Arabic works contain valuable information: I. 'Abbās, *Tārīkh al-adab al-andalusī: 'aṣr al-Ṭawā'if* (Beirut, 1962), pp. 216ff.; J. al-Rikābī, *Fī-l-adab al-andalusī* (Cairo, 1966), pp. 285ff.; I. 'A. Abū-l-Khashab, *Tārīkh al-adab al-'arabī fī-l-Andalus* (Cairo, 1966), pp. 267ff.; 'Abd al-'Azīz al-Ahwānī, *al-Zajal fī-l-Andalus* (Cairo, 1957), and "Kitāb al-muqtaṭaf min aẓāhīr al-ṭuraf de Ibn Sa'īd," *al-Andalus*, 13 (1948), 28–31; Ṣafī al-Dīn al-Ḥillī, *al-'Aṭil al-ḥālī*, ed. W. Hoenerbach (Wiesbaden, 1955); Ibn Khaldūn, *al-Muqaddimah*, English trans. F. Rosenthal (New York, 1958); Ibn Quzmān, *Dīwān*, transliterated into Latin characters and partial Spanish trans. by A. R. Nykl, *El cancionero de Aben Guzman*, (Madrid, 1933) and by García Gómez, *Todo Ben Quzmān;* Ibn Sanā' al-Mulk, *Dār al-ṭirāz fī 'amal al-muwashshaḥāt*, ed. J. al-Rikābī (Damascus, 1949); M. 'A. al-Karīm, *Fann al-tawshīḥ* (Beirut, 1959); al-Ṣafadī, *Tawshī' al-tawshīḥ*, ed. A. H. Muṭlaq (Beirut, 1966).
3. Although Eastern and Andalusian authors concede the supremacy to al-Andalus in this kind of composition, one cannot altogether discount the Eastern influence. In this connection, attention may be called to some of the short poems of Abū Nuwās (d. ca. 814), Abū-l-'Atāhiyyah (d. 826), and Ibn al-Mu'tazz (d. 908) — all of whom enjoyed great popularity in

al-Andalus. See E. García Gómez, "Un 'pre-muwaššaḥa' atribuída Abū Nuwās," *al-Andalus*, 21 (1956), 404–414.

It should be noted that Eastern innovations consisted of poems in *mukhammas* consisting of five rhymes, *murraba'* of four, and *mazdūj* (a mixture of rhymes) — all of which did not conform to the sixteen meters of classical poetry.

4. Nykl, *Hispano-Arabic Poetry*, pp. 339 — who was followed by 'Abbās, *Tārīkh al-adab al-andalusī: 'Aṣr al-Ṭawā'if*, pp. 221ff. and 257ff. — believes that the *zajal* precedes the *muwashshaḥ* on the grounds that *zajal* began as the result of popular songs.

5. See introduction to his *Dīwān*; also Nykl, *Hispano-Arabic Poetry*, p. 270.

6. Ibn Khaldūn, *al-Muqaddimah*, vol. 3, p. 454.

7. Ibn Bassām, *al-Dhakhīrah*, vol. 1, p. 2:2; cf. 'Abbās, *Tārīkh al-adab al-andalusī: 'aṣr al-Ṭawā'if*, p. 217.

8. Al-Marrākushī, *al-Mu'jib*, p. 145. However, this attitude did not prevent other people from paying due attention to them. In this connection, mention should be made of al-Ḥijārī (d. 1155), who dealt with *muwashshaḥāt* in his *al-Mushib*, which became the source of information for Ibn Sa'īd (d. 1274), who left us his *al-Muqtaṭaf min azhār al-ṭaraf*, which survives in manuscript form. Mention should also be made of Ibn Sa'd al-Khayr (d. 1131) of Valencia, who is reported to have composed *Jaysh al-tawshīḥ*, still in manuscript. See 'Abbās, *Tārīkh al-adab al-andalusī: 'aṣr al-Ṭawā'if*, 218ff. Muḥammad Ibn 'Asākir (d. 1168) composed *Tawāshī' al-tawshīḥ* (Escorial 438); cf. Escorial 369 and 439.

9. Ibn Sanā' al-Mulk, *Dār al-ṭirāz*, p. 35; Hartmann, *Das arabische Strophengedicht*, p. 199ff., recognizes as many as 146 meters. See Ibn Sanā' al-Mulk, *Dīwān*, ed. Mu. 'Abd al-Ḥaqq (Hyderabad, 1958).

10. Al-Ṣafadī, *Tawshī' al-tawshīḥ*, pp. 20ff.

11. Al-Muḥibbī, *Khilāṣat al-athar*, vol. 1, p. 108.

12. *Ibid.*, p. 108; al-Karīm, *Fann al-tawshīḥ*, p. 18.

13. E. W. Lane, *Arabic English Lexicon* (Edinburgh, 1867), vol. 2, p. 1217.

14. Ibn Khaldūn, *al-Muqaddimah*, vol. 3, p. 440.

15. *Ibid.*, p. 448.

16. *Ibid.*, p. 440.

17. Ibn Sanā' al-Mulk, *Dār al-ṭirāz*, p. 38; al-Rikābī, *Fī-l-adab al-andalusī*, pp. 302ff.

18. Nykl, *Hispano-Arabic Poetry*, pp. 270–271.

19. Ibn Bassām, *al-Ḍhakhīrah*, vol. 1, p. 2:2.

20. See introduction to his *Dīwān* (*Cancionero*); Nykl, *Hispano-Arabic Poetry*, p. 270.

21. Ibn Sanā' al-Mulk, *Dār al-ṭirāz*, p. 32; al-Ṣafadī, *Tawshī' al-tawshīḥ*, 29.

22. Ibn Khaldūn, *al-Muqaddimah*, vol. 3, p. 440.

23. *Dār al-ṭirāz*, pp. 20ff. See also E. García Gómez, "Estudio del *Dār al-ṭirāz*," *al-Andalus*, 27 (1962), 21–104.

24. Ibn Sanā' al-Mulk, *Dār al-ṭirāz*, pp. 20ff. al-Ṣafadī, *Tawshī' al-tawshīḥ*, pp. 20–30.

25. As seen in the previous quotation, Ibn Khaldūn conceives that the largest number of stanzas employed is seven. Nykl, in his transliteration of the *Cancionero* (X/vi–X/vii), made an inventory of Ibn Quzmān's *zajals* and found that they may range from two up to forty-two strophes, although the majority of them have from five to nine strophes. See also Nykl, *Hispano-Arabic Poetry*, p. 270.

26. Al-Ṣafadī, *Tawshī' al-tawshīḥ*, pp. 23ff.; al-Rikābī, *Fī-l-adab al-andalusī*, pp. 294ff.

27. Nykl, *Hispano-Arabic Poetry*, p. 273, uses *markaz* for *qufl*, *aghṣān* for *abyāt*, *simṭ* for both *qufl* and *kharjah*, al-Karīm, *Fann al-tawshīḥ*, pp. 21ff., uses *maṭla'* for *qufl*, but follows the usage of Ibn Sanā' al-Mulk with respect to the rest of the use of *qufl*. He also adheres to the *kharjah*. However, he prefers the term *dawr* for *bayt*, which he reserves for the combination of both *qufl* and *dawr* (p. 26). He uses the term *ghuṣn* (p. 27) for the various parts of *maṭla'*, *qufl*, or *kharjah*, and *simṭ* for the various parts of the *dawr* (stanza) (pp. 29ff). Finally, 'Abbās, *Tārīkh al-adab al-andalusī: 'aṣr al-Ṭawā'if*, pp. 235–238, uses *qufl* for the opening verses, *ghuṣn* for what follows it, or the stanza. *Dawr* is applied to the combination of *qufl* and *ghuṣn* and *kharjah* to the last *qufl*. 'Abbās overlooks *simṭ* or what it may mean.

Example of a *qufl* of four lines from a *muwashshaḥ* by Ibn Zamrak:
nasīm gharnāṭah 'alīl lākinnhu yubri' al-'alīl
wa rawḍuhā zāhir balīl wa rashfuhu yunji' al-ghalīl

28. In fact, al-Ṣafadī, *Tawshī' al-tawshīḥ*, p. 22, indicates that a *muwashshaḥ* should begin and end with it.

29. As already indicated in n. 27, Nykl uses *aghṣān*; al-Karīm *dawr*, and *bayt* for a combination of a stanza and a *qufl*.

30. Al-Ibshīhī, *al-Mustaṭraf* (Cairo, A.H. 1330), vol. 1, p. 174. This author does not go into any explanation of the term, but simply put the word *dawr* at the right side of a stanza, which also includes the *qufl*. See also al-Karīm, *Fann al-tawshīḥ*, p. 25.

31. See Chapter 13.

32. Ibn Sanā' al-Mulk, *Dār al-ṭirāz*, p. 32; al-Ṣafadī, *Tawshī' al-tawshīḥ*, p. 29.

33. This *muwashshaḥ* by Muḥammad Ibn Ḥasan al-Nawājī (d. 1455), is ably translated by Nicholson, *Literary History of the Arabs*, p. 417. It is reprinted here by permission of Cambridge University Press.

34. On the question of origin, see Ibn Bassām, *al-Dakhīrah*, vol. 1, p. 2:1; Ibn Khaldūn, *al-Muqaddimaḥ*, vol. 3, pp. 440ff.; al-Ṣafadī, *Tawshī' al-tawshīḥ*, pp. 20, 31; al-Karīm, *Fann al-tawshīḥ*, pp. 93ff.; 'Abbās, *Tārīkh al-adab al-andalusī: 'aṣr al-Ṭawā'if*, pp. 221ff.; González Palencia, *Historia de la literatura arábigo-española*, p. 105; al-Rikābī, *Fī-l-adab al-andalusī*, pp. 287ff. On Ibn 'Ubādah al-Qazzāz, who seems to have given impetus to *Muwashshaḥāt*, see S. M. Stern, "Muḥammad Ibn 'Ubāda al-Qazzāz: Un andaluz author de *'muwaššaḥs*,'" *al-Andalus*, 15 (1950), 79–109.

35. On Ibn Quzmān, see his *Dīwān (Cancionero)* transliterated by Nykl. See also Nykl, *Hispano-Arabic Poetry*, pp. 266ff.; García Gómez, *Una voz en la calle*; 'Abbās, *Tārīkh al-adab al-andalusī: 'aṣr al-Ṭawā'if*, pp. 266ff.; al-Ahwānī, *al-Zajal fī-l-Andalus*, pp. 76ff.; S. M. Stern, "Studies on Ibn Quzman," *al-Andalus*, 16 (1951), 379–425; W. Hoenerbach and H. Ritter, "Neue Materialien zum 'Zacal' I: Ibn Quzman," *Oriens*, 3 (1950), 266–315; E. García Gómez, "La jarya en Ibn Quzmān," *al-Andalus*, 28 (1963), 1–60, and his "Siete zéjeles de Ben Quzmān," *RO*, 2 (1964), 129–145.

36. On Tuṭīlī, see his *Dīwān*, ed. I. 'Abbās (Beirut, 1963); Nykl, *Hispano-Arabic Poetry*, pp. 254ff.

37. On Ibn Bājjah, see Nykl, *Hispano-Arabic Poetry*, pp. 254ff.

38. On Ibn Baqī, see Nykl, *ibid*., pp. 241ff.; cf. E. García Gómez, "La muwaššaha de Ibn Baqī de Córdoba: *Ma laday ṣabrun m'inu* con jarya romance," *al-Andalus*, 19 (1954), 43–54.

39. On Ibn Zuhr, see Nykl, *Hispano-Arabic Poetry*, pp. 248–251.

40. On Ibn 'Arabī, see Nykl, *ibid*., pp. 251.

41. On Ibn Sahl al-Isrā'īlī, see Nykl, *ibid*., p. 344; see his *Dīwān* compiled by A. Ḥusayn al-Qarnī (Cairo, 1926).

42. On Ibn al-Khaṭīb, see Nykl, *Hispano-Arabic Poetry*, p. 363.

43. On Ibn Zamrak, *ibid*., p. 366.

44. For further information on *zajal*, see Ibn Quzmān's *Dīwān*, published in 1896 in facsimile by D. Gunzburg. Cf. Nykl, *Hispano-Arabic Poetry*, p. 270; 'Abbās, *Tārīkh al-adab al-andalusī: 'aṣr al-Ṭawā'if*, pp. 252ff. A more comprehensive study is the work of al-Ahwānī, *al-Zajal fī-l-andalus*, which deals with its development, prominent *zajjālūn*, and the position of *zajal*.

45. Ibn Khaldūn, *al-Muqaddimah*, vol. 3, p. 455; for the history of *zajal*, see al-Ḥillī, *al-'Āṭil al-ḥālī*.

46. Nykl, *Hispano-Arabic Poetry*, p. 266.

47. *Ibid*., p. 270.

48. As quoted in *ibid*., pp. 269–270; see also Ibn Quzmān's introduction to his *Dīwān*.

49. *Ibid*., p. 270.

50. Ibn Quzmān, *Cancionero*, p. 239; also Nykl, *Hispano-Arabic Poetry*, p. 273. To the *markaz, aghṣān, simṭ* used by Nykl are added their equivalents: *qufl, bayt* and *kharjah*.

51. As translated by Nykl, *Hispano-Arabic Poetry*, p. 273.
52. *Ibid*., p. 301.
53. *Ibid*., pp. 309–311; see also W. Hoenerbach and H. Ritter, "Neue Materialien zum 'Zacal' II: Mugalis," *Oriens*, 5 (1952), 269–301.
54. Nykl, *Hispano-Arabic Poetry*, p. 343.
55. As translated in *ibid*., p. 364.
56. Al-Ṣafadī, *Tawshī' al-tawshīḥ*, p. 32.
57. *Ibid*., pp. 33, 39, 51.
58. Al-Karīm, *Fann al-tawshīḥ*, p. 161; W. Hoenerbach, "Teoría del 'zéjel' según Safi al-Dīn Ḥillī," *al-Andalus*, 15 (1950), 297–334.
59. Al-Karīm, *fann al-tawshīḥ*, pp. 107ff.
60. See F. Canteras, "Versos españoles en las muwaššaḥas hispano-hebreas," *Sefarad*, 9 (1949), 197–234; S. M. Stern, "Les vers finaux en español dans les muwaššaḥas hispano-hébraiques," *al-Andalus*, 13 (1948), 299–346; also *al-Andalus*, 14 (1949), 214–218.
61. For one, al-Ṣafadī, *Tawshī' al-Tawshīḥ*, p. 20, says "The *muwashshaḥ* is an art in which the people of the Maghrib were unique, superior to the people of the Orient, and increased its species, varieties and kinds."
62. Nykl, *Hispano-Arabic Poetry*, pp. 329–336.
63. *Ibid*.
64. Mainly in his translation of Ibn Ḥazm's *Ṭawq al-ḥamāmah*, in his transliteration of Ibn Quzmān's *Cancionero*, and in his invaluable *Hispano-Arabic Poetry*.
65. See his *Hispano-Arabic Poetry*, pp. 371ff.
66. See Nykl's introductory remarks to Ibn Quzmān's *Cancionero*, xvii; also his *Hispano-Arabic Poetry*, pp. 271ff.
67. As quoted by González Palencia, *Historia de la literatura arábigo-española*, p. 333.
68. *Ibid*., p. 69.
69. *Ibid*., p. 335.

14. Courtly Love

1. Ibn 'Abd Rabbihi, *al-'Iqd al-farīd*, bk. 6, p. 28. In fact, he devotes bk. 21 to the subject of women and their qualities. Cf. Chapter 11.
2. On Ibn Abī Rabī'ah, see J. Jabbūr, *'Umar Ibn Abī Rabī'ah* (Beirut, 1935–1939). For later representatives, see J. al-Rikābī, *La poésie profane sous les Ayyubides et ses principaux représentants* (Paris, 1949).
3. Dr. Perron, *Femmes arabes avant et depuis l'islamisme* (Paris, 1958); Hitti, *History of the Arabs*, p. 251.
4. For these points and further details, see Pérès, *La poésie andalouse*, pp. 397ff.
5. Mainly, al-Jāḥiẓ *Risālah fi-l-'ishq wa-l-nisā'*, in *Majmū'āt rasā'il* (Cairo, A.H. 1324), pp. 161–169; Ibn Qutaybah, *'Uyūn al-akhbār* (Cairo, 1925–1930), vol. 4, pp. 128ff.; Ibn 'Abd Rabbihi, *al-'Iqd al-farīd*, Bk. 21, and al-Ibshīhī, *al-Mustaṭraf fī kull fann musṭaẓraf* (Būlāq, A.H. 1330), vol. 2, pp. 134ff. *Uns al-'āshiq*, of unknown authorship, deals with love and lovers and the opinions concerning them. It is in prose and verse and still in manuscript form (*IEIM*-C-15). Al-Sarrāj Ibrāhīm Ibn 'Umar Ibn Ḥasan al-Buqā'ī (d. 1480) left his *Ikhtiṣār maṣārī' al-'ushshāq* (MS., Zaytūnah 4736), which is a compendium of a larger work, the second part of which is extant (Escorial 468).

One may add *Kitāb nuzhat al-mushtāq wa-rawḍat al-'ushshāq* (Escorial 471) by Muḥ. b. 'Alī b. 'Abdallah b. Aḥmad al-Ḥillī (d. 1116). Also the anonymous works *Nuzhat al-'āshiq wa-uns al-muyattam al-wāmiq* (Escorial 391); *Nuzhat al-muḥibb wa-l-aḥbāb* (Escorial 539); *Rushd al-labīb ilā mu'āsharat al-ḥabīb* (Escorial 563).
6. For instance, Ibn Sīnā (Avicenna). See E. L. Fackenheim, "A Treatise on Love by Ibn Sīnā," *Medieval Studies*, 7 (1945), 208–228. Also Ikhwān al-Ṣafā, *Rasā'il* (Bombay, A.H. 1305–1306), vol. 3, pp. 63–75.
7. See Ibn 'Arabī, *Tarjumān al-ashwāq* (Beirut, 1961), pp. 10ff.; English trans. R. A. Nicholson (London, 1911). Cf. M. Asín Palacios, *El Islam cristianizado* (Madrid, 1931).

8. Al-Ibshīhī, *al-Mustaṭraf*, vol. 2, p. 134.
9. *Ibid.*
10. *Ibid.*
11. In fact, the story appears in Juan Manuel's *El Conde Lucanor* (Madrid, 1968).
12. Ibn Qutaybah, *'Uyūn al-akhbār*, vol. 4, p. 131.
13. *Ibid.*, pp. 133ff.
14. For more cases of deaths caused by love, see al-Ibshīhī, *al-Mustaṭraf*, vol. 2, pp. 138ff.
15. *Ṭawq al-ḥamāmah*, ed. Bercher, p. 253; cf. Nykl's translation, *Hispano-Arabic Poetry*, p. 141. Cf. Pérès, *La poésie andalouse*, p. 424.
16. Ibn Qutaybah, *'Uyūn al-akhbār*, vol. 4, pp. 134–135. Cf. al-Ibshīhī, *al-Mustaṭraf*, vol. 2, pp. 135–136.
17. See his *Marātib al-'ulūm*, in *Rasā'il Ibn Ḥazm*, p. 66.
18. On Ibn Ḥazm, see al-Ḍabbī, *Bughyah*, no. 1204; al-Marrākushī, *Mu'jib*, pp. 93ff.; Ibn Sa'īd, *al-Mughrib*, vol. 1, p. 345; M. Asín Palacios, *Abenházam de Córdoba y su historia crítica de las ideas religiosas* (Madrid, 1927), vol. 1; Nykl, *Hispano-Arabic Poetry*, pp. 73ff.; 'Abbās, *Tārīkh al-adab al-andalusī: 'aṣr siyādat Qurṭubah*, pp. 303ff.
19. *Histoire* (2nd ed.), vol. 2, pp. 328ff. Cf. Asín Palacios, *Abenházam de Córdoba*, vol. 1, pp. 2ff.
20. *The Dove's Ring* (*Ṭawq al-ḥamāmah*) was first edited by D. K. Pétrof (Leiden, 1914) and has appeared in several versions in Arabic, such as Cairo, 1950. There are also translations of the work in several European languages: English A. R. Nykl (Paris, 1931) and the superior translation by A. J. Arberry (London, 1953); Russian A. Salil (Moscow & Leningrad, 1933); German Max Weisweiler (Leiden, 1941); Italian F. Gabrieli (Laterza, 1949); French L. Bercher (Algiers, 1949); and Spanish E. García Gómez (Madrid, 1952).
21. Ovid, *The Art of Love*, English trans. R. Humphries (Bloomington, Ind., 1962).
22. Trans. J. J. Parry (New York, 1964). Some of the rules of courtly love in Capellanus's work, pp. 184–186, find parallels in Ibn Ḥazm's *Ṭawq*; cf. Spanish trans. García Gómez, pp. 53, 85, 86, 128. The points of similarity are that love is a stranger in the house of avarice; love rarely endures when made public; lovers turn pale in the presence of the beloved; and love can deny nothing to love.
23. Ed. A. R. Nykl and I. Ṭūqān (Chicago, 1932). It consists of 100 chapters, each of which contains 100 verses. In the first 50 chapters, the author deals with the various manifestations of love: its essence and causes; its conditions such as avoidance, separation, fidelity, etc. Cf. Nykl, *Hispano-Arabic Poetry*, p. 401, n. 3.
24. See above, nn. 5 and 6.
25. Nykl, *Hispano-Arabic Poetry*, p. 79; cf. trans. García Gómez, p. 77.
26. Nykl, p. 8; García Gómez, p. 82.
27. Nykl, p. 82; García Gómez, p. 89.
28. Nykl, p. 86; García Gómez, p. 105.
29. Nykl, p. 86; García Gómez, p. 106.
30. Nykl, p. 89; García Gómez, p. 133.
31. Nykl, p. 95; García Gómez, p. 193.
32. Nykl, p. 82.
33. Nykl, p. 95.
34. García Gómez, p. 282.
35. Ed. J. Corominas (Madrid, 1967). Cf. *Coplas*, no. 438, 439, 440, etc., of the work and Ibn Ḥazm's *Ṭawq*, Spanish trans. García Gómez, p. 121.
36. *España en su historia* (Buenos Aires, 1958), pp. 396ff.
37. In his translation of the *Ṭawq*, pp. 53–54.
38. For further information on the relationship of Hispano-Arabic poetry to that of the troubadour see Nykl, *Hispano-Arabic Poetry*, and his "La poesía a ambos lados del Pirineo hacia el año 1110," *al-Andalus*, 1 (1933), 355–408; "L'influence arabe-andalouse sur les troubadours," *BH*, 41 (1939), 305–315; "The Latest Troubadour Studies," *AR*, 19 (1935), 227–235; and *Troubadour Studies* (Cambridge, Mass., 1944).

In addition, see H. Pérès, "La Poésie arabe de l'Andalousie et ses relations possibles avec la poésie des troubadours," *IO* (Marseilles, 1947), 107–130; E. Lévi-Provençal, "Les vers arabes de la chanson V. de Guillaume IX d'Aquitaine," *Arabica*, 1 (1955), 208–211, and "Poésie arabe d'Espagne et poésie d'Europe médiévale" in *IO* (Paris, 1948), 283–304; J. Cluzel, "Las jaryas et l'amour courtois," *Cultura Neolatina* (1960), pp. 1–18. P. LeGentil, *La poésie lyrique espagnole et portugaise à la fin du Moyen Age* (Rennes, 1949–1953); "A propos de la 'strophe zéjelesque,' " *Revue des Langues Romanes*, 70 (1949), 119–136; "La strophe zadjalesque, les khardjas et le problème des origines du lyrisme roman," *Romania*, 84 (1963), 1–27. E. García Gómez, "La lírica hispano árabe y la aparición de la lírica románica," *al-Andalus*, 21 (1956), 303–338; R. Menéndez Pidal, *Poesía árabe y poesía europea* (Madrid, 1963); L. Ecker, *Arabischer, provenzalischer und deutcher Minnesang* (Berne & Leipzig, 1934); R. Briffault, *The Troubadours* (Bloomington, Ind., 1965).

One may add A. J. Denomy, *The Heresy of Courtly Love* (Gloucester, Mass., 1965); "*Fin' Amors*: The Pure Love of the Troubadours, Its Amorality, and Possible Source," *Medieval Studies*, 7 (1945), 139–179; "Concerning the Accessibility of Arabic Influences to the Earliest Provençal Troubadours," *Medieval Studies*, 15 (1953), 147–158; "*Jovens*: The Notion of Youth among the Troubadours, Its Meaning and Source," *Medieval Studies*, 11 (1949), 1–22.

Denis de Rougemont, *Love in the Western World* (New York, 1966); T. Silverstein, "Andreas, Plato and the Arabs: Remarks on Some Recent Accounts of Courtly Love," *Modern Philology*, 47 (1949), 119–121; Jean-Claude Vadet, *L'espirit courtois en Orient* (Paris, 1968); G. E. von Grunebaum, "Avicenna's *Risāla fī'l-'išq* and Courtly Love," *JNES*, 11 (1952), 233–238.

On the other hand, A. Jeanroy, *La poésie lyrique des troubadours* (Toulouse & Paris, 1934), discounts any connection between the two.

39. On Ibn Zaydūn, see Nykl, *Hispano-Arabic Poetry*, pp. 106–120; García Gómez, *Qasīdas*, pp. 17ff.; A. Cour, *Un poète arabe d'Andalousie: Ibn Zaidoun* (Constantine, 1920); González Palencia, *Historia de la literatura arábigo-española*, pp. 59ff.; al-Rikābī, *Fī-l-adab al-andalusī*, pp. 161ff.; *Dīwān Ibn Zaydūn* (Cairo, 1932, 1957).

40. García Gómez, *Qasīdas*, pp. 18–19.

41. Nykl, *Hispano-Arabic Poetry*, p. 107; Arabic text in al-Rikābī, *Fī-l-adab al-andalusī*, p. 167.

42. Nykl, p. 108; cf. al-Rikābī, p. 167.

43. Nykl p. 108; cf. al-Rikābī, p. 169.

44. Cf. Nykl's translation, pp. 108–109; see Ibn Zaydūn's *Dīwān*, p. 264.

45. Nykl, p. 109.

46. See Arabic text in al-Rikābī, p. 171.

47. Cf. Nykl, p. 109.

48. See Ibn Zaydūn's *Dīwān*, p. 257.

49. For the translation of the poem see García Gómez, *Qasīdas*, pp. 18ff.; Nykl, pp. 115–117; al-Rikābī, pp. 207–211.

50. On al-Mu'tamid, see González Palencia, *Historia de la literatura arábigo-española*, pp. 71–85; García Gómez, *Qasīdas*, pp. 75–81; Nykl, *Hispano-Arabic Poetry*, pp. 134–154; *Dīwān al-Mu'tamid Ibn 'Abbād* (Cairo, 1951).

51. For more details on Ibn Sa'īd and Ḥafṣa, see González Palencia, *Historia de l literatura arábigo-española*, p. 93; Nykl, *Hispano-Arabic Poetry*, pp. 317ff.

52. On the *Cancionero* of Ibn Quzmān, see below, Chapter 13. See also Briffault, *The Troubadours*, p. 49; *Zajal* 117; *Zajal* 115.

15. History, Geography, and Travel

1. For a general account of Muslim historiography, see F. Rosenthal, *History of Muslim Historiography* (Leiden, 1952; 2nd ed., 1968). See also H. A. R. Gibb in *Supplement* to *EI* (1913–1914) under *ta'rīkh*, pp. 233–245; D. S. Margoliouth, *Lectures on Arabic Historians*

(Calcutta, 1930); E. Lévi-Provençal, *Les historiens de Chorfa* (Paris, 1922); B. Lewis and P. M. Holt, eds., *Historians of the Middle East* (Oxford, 1962); Maḥmūd ʻA. Makkī, "Egipto y los orígenes de la historiografía arábigo-española", *RIEI*, 5 (1957), 157–248; ʻAbd al-ʻAzīz al-Dūrī, *Baḥth fī nash'at ʻilm al-ta'rīkh ʻind al-ʻArab* (Beirut, 1960).

2. In addition to the editions of the works of al-Ḍabbī, Ibn al-Abbār, Ibn Bashkuwāl, and Ibn Khayr in *Bibliotheca arábico-hispana* (*BAH*) by F. Codera, J. Ribera, and others, one may mention the following important authors and their works in relation to Hispano-Arabic historiography:

M. Amari, *Biblioteca Árabo-Sicula* (Leipzig, 1957); M. Casiri, *Biblioteca arábico-hispaña escurialensis* (Madrid, 1760–1770); F. Codera, *Estudios críticos de la historia árabe-española*, ser. 2 (Saragossa, 1903); R. Dozy, *Scriptorum arabum loci de Abbadidis* (Leiden, 1848–1853); *Recherches sur l'histoire et la littérature de l'Espagne pendant le Moyen Âge* (Leiden, 1847); *Corrections sur les texts du Bayano 'l-Mogrib d'Ibn-Adhāri (de Maroc), des fragments de la chronique d'Arib (de Cordue) et du Hollato 's-siyara de'Ibno-'l-Abbar* (Leiden, 1883).

E. Fagnan, *Extraits inédits relatifs au Magreb. Géographie et histoire* (Algiers, 1924); A. González Palencia, *Historia de la literatura arábigo-española* (Barcelona, 1928), Ch. 5; E. Lévi-Provençal, *Les historiens de Chorfa* (Paris, 1922); J. Moreno Nieto, *Estudio crítico sobre los historiadores arábigo-españoles* (Madrid, 1864); M. J. Müller, *Beitrage zur Geschichte der Westlichen Araber* (Munchen, 1866); F. Pons Boïgues, *Ensayo bío-bibliográphico sobre los historiadores, y geógrafos arábigo-españoles* (Madrid, 1898); F. Wüstenfeld, *Die Geshichtschreiber der Araber und ihre Werke* (Göttingen, 1882).

3. A portion related to the Maghrib in general in Ibn al-Athīr's *al-Kāmil fi-l-ta'rīkh* (ed. C. J. Tornberg; Leiden, 1851–1876) was translated into French by E. Fagnan as *Annales du Maghreb et de l'Espagne* (Algiers, 1901).

4. Al-Nuwayrī was an Egyptian historian and author of the important encyclopedic work *Nihāyat al-arab* (Cairo A.H. 1345). The fifth part of the work is devoted to history in general, and chapters 5 and 6 deal with Spain. These two chapters were edited and translated into Spanish by M. Gaspar Remiro (Madrid, 1917–1919).

5. Yāqūt is also the author of a biographical dictionary entitled *Irshād*.

6. Ibn Khallikān is the author of the important biographical dictionary *Wafāyāt*.

7. *Rasā'il Ibn Ḥazm*, pp. 71–72.

8. *Ibid.*, p. 78. In fact, the form *Ṭabaqāt* was quite common among Andalusian writers. Examples are *Categories of Grammarians and Lexicographers* by al-Zubaydī (Cairo, 1954) and *Categories of Physicians* by Ibn Juljul (Cairo, 1955).

9. Ibn Ḥazm, *Marātib al-ʻulūm*, p. 79.

10. Ed. and English trans. by G. Torrey (New Haven, 1922).

11. On Ibn Ḥabīb, see al-Ziriklī, *al-ʻAlām*, vol. 4, p. 302, and *GAL*, sup. 1, p. 231.

12. Cf. González Palencia, *Historia de la literatura arábigo-española*, pp. 128ff. Ibn Ḥabīb's *Tārīkh al-kabīr* is in manuscript (Escorial *IEIM*-A-9). His biography of the Prophet entitled *Kitāb al-muqtafā min sīrat al-muṣṭafā* is extant (Escorial 1745, no. 8).

13. On Muḥammad, see al-Ziriklī, *al-ʻAlām*, vol. 8, p. 338.

14. It is known under the title of *La crónica denominada del moro Rasis*, ed. P. de Gayangos and R. Menéndez Pidal in *Catálogo de Crónicas* (Madrid, 1850). See also Pascual de Gayangos, "Memoria sobre la autenticidad de la crónica denominada del moro Rasis," *MRAH*, 8 (1852). Cf. Ibn Ḥazm, *Risālah*, in al-Maqqarī's *Nafḥ al-ṭīb*, vol. 4, pp. 156 and 166. The *Annals* of ʻĪsā al-Rāzī have been translated by E. García Gómez in the recension by Ibn Ḥayyān under the title of *Anales palatinos del califa de Córdoba al-Ḥakam II, por ʻĪsā Ibn Aḥmad al-Rāzī* (Madrid, 1967).

15. The full title of the work is *Akhbār majmūʻah fī fatḥ al-Andalus*, ed. and Spanish trans. by E. Lafuente y Alcántara (Madrid, 1867). For a critical study of the work, see Claudio Sánchez-Albornoz y Menduina, *El "Ajbar Maymuʻa," Cuestiones historiográficas que suscita* (Buenos Aires, 1944). It is of interest to point out that the work may have been collected over a long period of time.

16. See Alcántara's translation, p. 134, and Sánchez-Albornoz, *El "Ajbar Maymu'a"*, pp. 23ff.

17. Arabic title, *Tārīkh iftitāḥ al-Andalus*, ed. P. de Gayangos (Madrid, 1868); Spanish trans. J. Ribera (Madrid, 1926); French trans. O. Houdas (Paris, 1889). A more recent edition is that by 'Abdallāh Anīs al-Ṭabbā' (Beirut, 1957).

18. See Ibn Ḥazm, *Risālah*, in al-Maqqarī's *Nafḥ al-ṭib*, vol. 4, p. 167. In this connection, there is a biography of 'Abd al-Raḥmān III of unknown authorship entitled *Tārīkh 'Abd al-Raḥmān al-Nāṣir*, ed. E. Lévi-Provençal and E. García Gómez (Madrid, 1950).

19. The extant part is edited by P. Melchor Atuña under the title of *Chronique du règne du calife umaiyade 'Abdallah à Cordoue* (Paris, 1937). The portion on al-Ḥakam II was edited by 'Abd al-Raḥmān 'Alī al-Ḥajjī (Beirut, 1965); Spanish trans. E. García Gómez (Madrid 1967). See also E. García Gómez, "A propósito de Ibn Ḥayyān," *al-Andalus*, 11 (1946), 395–424.

20. Cairo, A.H. 1347–1348; Spanish trans. M. Asín Palacios, *Abenházam de Córdoba*.

21. The full title of the work is *Kitāb al-naqṭ al-'arūs fī tawārīkh al-khulafā' fī-l-Andalus* ed. C. F. Seybold in *RCEH*, 3 (1911), 160–180, and 4, 237–248. Of interest also is his *Ḥijjat al-wadā'*, ed. Mamdūḥ Ḥaqqī (Beirut, 1966), which deals with the pilgrimage of Muḥammad as related by his companions and followers, and his *Jawāmi' al-ṣīrah*, ed. I. 'Abbās (Cairo, 1970), a biography of Muḥammad.

22. *Jamharat ansāb al-'Arab*. And see J. Bosch Vilá, "Ibn Ḥazm, genealogista," *IX Centenario de Aben Hazam* (Córdoba, 1963).

23. *Jamharah*, p. 2.

24. *Ibid*., p. 3.

25. See above, Chapter 9.

26. Published in Cairo (n.d.) and Beirut (1912).

27. Ed. E. Lévi-Provençal (Cairo, 1955).

28. The collection of Ibn Tūmart's works is entitled *Kitāb a'azzu mā yuṭlab*, ed. J. D. Luciani (Algiers, 1903).

29. Lévi-Provençal, *Documents inédits* and *Trente-sept lettres officielles almohades*.

30. Ibn Qaṭṭān, *Juz' min kitāb naẓm al-jumān*.

31. Ibn Ṣāḥib al-Ṣalāh, *al-Mann bi-l-imāmah*.

32. Ibn Abī Zar', *Rawḍ al-qirṭās*.

33. Al-Zarkashī, *Tārīkh al-dawlatayn*.

34. Ed. I. S. Allouche (Rabat, 1936); Spanish trans. A. Huici Miranda (Tetuan, 1952).

35. See below, Chapter 15.

36. Ed. R. Dozy (Leiden, 1848); ed. Mu. Sa'īd al-'Iryān (Cairo, 1963); French trans. E. Fagnan, *Histoire des Almohades* (Algiers, 1893).

37. Two volumes of the work were edited by Sh. Ḍayf (Cairo, 1953).

38. The full title of the work is *Kitāb al-bayān al-mughrib fī akhbār mulūk al-Andalus wa-l-Maghrib*.

39. For abundant data on Ibn al-Khaṭīb, see the last four volumes of al-Maqqarī's *Nafḥ al-ṭīb* and Mu. 'Abdallah 'Inān, *Lisān al-Dīn Ibn al-Khaṭīb* (Cairo, 1968). See also Pons Boïgues, *Ensayo*, pp. 334–337.

40. His reflections on history appear in the introduction to his *Iḥāṭah* as well as at the end of his *A'lām*. 'Inān, *Lisān al-Dīn*, pp. 374–375, reproduces the passages from the *A'lām*.

41. See al-Maqqarī, *Nafḥ al-ṭib*, vol. 8, pp. 270ff.; also his *Azhār al-riyāḍ*, vol. 1, pp. 276ff. Cf. also 'Inān, *Lisān al-Dīn*, pp. 353–373, who edited some of the correspondence. See M. Gaspar Remiro, "Correspondencía diplomática entre Granada y Fez en el siglo XIV," *RCEH* (1912). Another work by Ibn al-Khaṭīb containing diplomatic correspondence is his *Kināsat al-dukkān ba'd intiqāl al-sukkān* (Escorial 1712). Other significant works of Ibn al-Khaṭīb are *al-Lamḥah al-badriyyah; al-Tāj al-muḥallā fī musājalat al-qadḥ al-mu'allā* (Escorial 554); and another general history of Granada, *Ṭarfat al-'aṣr fī tārīkh banū Naṣr*.

42. *Al-Katībah al-kāminah fī ahl al-mi'at al-thāminah*, ed. by I. 'Abbās (Beirut, 1963).

It is a biographical dictionary of 103 poets, viziers, orators, Qur'ānic readers, and secretaries of the eighth century of the *Hijrah*.

43. *Nufāḍat al-jirāb fī 'ulālat al-ightirāb* (Escorial 1755). He also gives us an account of himself in other works.

44. The part concerned with al-Andalus was edited by E. Lévi-Provençal (Beirut, 1956); part of the work was edited by Aḥmad M. al-'Abbādī et al. (Damascus, 1964). See 'Inān, *Lisān al-Dīn*, pp. 249ff. A similar general history of Muslim states is his *Raqm al-ḥulal fī naẓm al-duwal*, still in MS. (Escorial 1776; Qayrawīn 55449); Kattāniyyah Library (Rabat 3146); Zaytūnah 4507; published in Tunis A.H. 1316.

45. A complete edition of *al-Iḥāṭah fī akhbār Gharnāṭa* has not appeared as yet. Two volumes appeared in Cairo A.H. 1319); Mu. 'Abdallah 'Inān started a scholarly edition, the first volume of which has been published (Cairo, 1955). Partial manuscripts of the work are to be found in la Academia de Historia de Madrid; *IEIM* C-13.

46. For an up-to-date bibliography of Ibn Khaldūn, see W. Fischel in *al-Muqaddimah*, trans. Rosenthal, vol. 3, pp. 485–512.

47. *Kitāb al-'Ibar*.

48. Trans. Rosenthal, *al-Muqaddimah*, vol. 1, p. 85.

49. *Ibid*., p. 6.

50. *Ibid*., pp. 15ff.

51. Trans. W. McGuckin de Slane, *Histoire de berbères et des dynasties musulmanes de l'Afrique septentrionale* (Algiers, 1852–1856).

52. See above, Chapter 11.

53. On Ibn Mughīth, see Nykl, *Hispano-Arabic Poetry*, p. 45. He is the author of the *Book of Devotees to God* and the *Book of the Zealous*.

54. For instance, *Adab al-kuttāb* (Cairo, A.H. 1341).

55. On al-Jayyānī, see Nykl, *Hispano-Arabic Poetry*, p. 43.

56. *Ibid*., pp. 123ff.

57. Ed. H. Pérès (Rabat, 1940).

58. Pérès, *La poé*sie andalouse, p. 52.

59. See Nykl, *Hispano-Arabic Poetry*, pp. 219–223.

60. *Ibid*., pp. 223–237.

61. No complete edition of the work has appeared as yet. A portion of it was published in Cairo (1939–1945).

62. Būlāq, n.d.

63. *Maṭmaḥ al-anfus* (Constantinople, 1902).

64. See above, Chapters 14 and 16.

65. See above, Chapter 15.

66. See above, Chapter 8.

67. See above, Chapter 10.

68. See Chapter 15.

69. On Ibn 'Abd al-Barr, see above, Chapter 9.

70. *Ta'rīkh quḍāt Qurṭubah*, ed. and Spanish trans. J. Ribera, *Historia de los jueces de Córdoba* (Madrid, 1914; Cairo, A.H. 1372).

71. Al-Maqqarī, *Azhār al-riyāḍ.*

72. *Ibid*.

73. Ed. F. Codera (Saragossa, 1893; Baghdād, 1963).

74. See Nykl, *Hispano-Arabic Poetry*, p. 263.

75. The full title of the work is *Bughyat al-multamis fī tārīkh rijāl al-Andalus*.

76. *Judhwat al-muqtabis*. In this connection, one may mention 'Abdallah Ibn 'Alī al-Rishāṭī (d. 1147), who wrote a work on the genealogy of the Companions of the Prophet entitled *Iqtibās al-anwār wa-l-timās al-azhār fī ansāb al-ṣaḥābah wa-ruḥāt al-āthār* (MS., Zaytūnah 665), and Ibrāhīm Ibn 'Alī Farḥūn (d.1397), author of *al-Dībāj al-mudhahhab fī ma'rifat a'yān 'ulamā' al-Madhhab* (Cairo, A.H. 1351), dealing with jurists.

77. *Kitāb ta'rīkh 'ulamā' al-Andalus*. A similar work dealing with scholars, traditionalists,

and jurists of al-Andalus is in manuscript form under the title of *al-A'lām bi a'māl al-Andalus min al-'ulamā' wa-l-muḥaddithīn wa-l-muttaqīn wa-l-fuqahā'* (Zaytūnah 5033); cf. *GAL*, sup. 1, p. 578.

78. See al-Ḍabbī, *Bughyah*, p. 321; Ibn Bashkuwāl, *al-Ṣilah*, p. 248.

79. Al-Ziriklī, *A'lām*, vol. 2, p. 359; Ibn al-Abbār, *Mu'jam*, p. 82. Mention should be made of Ibn Bashkuwāl's compendium (*mukhtaṣar*) of the life of the Prophet, *al-Qurbah ilā rabb al-'ālamīn fī faḍl al-ṣalāh 'ala sayyid al-mursilīn* (Escorial 1745, no. 5). The work appears to be a compendium of an anonymous biography.

80. Ed. F. Codera (Madrid, 1882–1883; Cairo, 1955). It is of interest to point out that the practice of continuing, supplementing, or bringing a work up to date was common among Arabic authors. Ordinarily, these "supplements" or "addenda" bear the title of *dhayl*. In al-Andalus, the term *ṣilah* (continuation or link) was used. Also, the term *takmilah* (completion), or a combination of supplement and completion (*dhayl wa-takmilah*) was used. See C. Farah, *The Dhayl in Medieval Arabic Historiography* (New Haven, 1967).

81. On Ibn al-Abbār, see 'Abd al-'Azīz 'Abd al-Majīd, *Ibn al-Abbār* (Tetuan, 1951); Müller, *Beitrage zur Geschichte der Westlichen Araber*, pp. 161ff. For a more detailed bibliography, see Mu'nis's introduction to Ibn Abbār's *al-Ḥullah*.

82. *Al-Takmilah li-kitāb al-ṣilah*, ed. F. Codera (Madrid, 1887–1890); see also M. Alarcón and C. A. Gonzáles Palencia, *Apéndice a la edición Codera de Técmila de Aben al-Abbar*, in *Miselánea de estudios y textos árabes* (Madrid, 1915); M. Ben Cheneb, "L'introduction d'Ibn al-Abbar à su Técmila," *Revue Africaine* (1913), 300ff.; Ibn al-Abbār, *al-Ḥullah* and *al-Mu'jam*.

83. I. 'Abbās has edited three volumes of the work (Beirut, 1965–1966). They contain some 1,705 entries.

84. The extant portion of the work was edited by E. Lévi-Provençal (Paris, 1932).

85. See n. 69.

86. Ed. Muṣṭafā al-Siqā et al. (Cairo, 1939–1942).

87. For more details and bibliographical data, see S. Maqbūl Aḥmad in *EI* (1954) under *Djughrāfiyā*. Maqbūl Aḥmad recognizes eight broad categories in geographical literature: world geographical accounts, cosmological works, *ziyārāt* (visits), dictionaries, travel accounts, maritime, astronomical, and regional works. Cf. R. Blachère, *Géographes arabes du Moyen Âge* (Paris, 1958); I. I. Krachkovskii, *Istoria Arabiskoi geograficheskoi Literatury* (Moscow, 1957), Arabic trans. Ṣalāh al-Dīn 'Uthmān Hāshim (Cairo, 1963–1965).

88. For instance the geographers Ibn Faqīh (d. 903), Ibn Rustah (d. 903), and Ya'qūbī (d. 891). Cf. Blachère, *Géographes arabes du Moyen Âge*, pp. 83ff. and 125ff.

89. Ed. M. J. de Goeje (Leiden, 1889).

90. The geographical works of Ya'qūbī, al-Iṣṭakhrī, Ibn Ḥawqal, and al-Muqqadisī were edited by M. J. de Goeje in *Bibliotheca Geographorum Arabicorum* (Leiden, 1906).

91. Yāqūt's *Mu'jam al-buldān* was edited by F. Wüstenfeld (Leipzig, 1866–1878).

92. On geography and geographers of al-Andalus, see H. Mu'nis in *Majallat Ma'had al-Dirāsāt al-Islamiyyah*, 7–10 (1959–1961). These installments were put into book form under the title *Tārīkh al-jughrāfiyah wa-l-jughrāfiyyīn fī-l-Andalus* (Madrid, 1967).

93. See E. Lévi-Provençal, "La description de l'Espagne d'Aḥmad al-Razi," *al-Andalus*, 18 (1953), 51–108. Also Mu'nis, *al-Jughrāfiyah*, p. 57ff.

94. On al-Warrāq, see al-Ḥumaydī, *Judhwah*, no. 90; al-Ḍabbī, *Bughyah*, no. 304; Mu'nis, *al-Jughrāfiyah*, pp. 73ff.

95. On al-'Udhrī, see al-Ḥumaydī, *Judhwah*, no. 236; al-Ḍabbī, *Bughyah*, no. 446; Mu'nis, *al-Jughrāfiyah*, pp. 81ff.

96. The full title of the work is *Kitāb tarṣī' al-akhbār wa-tanwī' al-āthār wa-l-bustān fī gharā'ib al-buldān wa-l-masālik ilā jamī' al-mamālik*. Fragments about al-Andalus were edited by 'Abd al-'Azīz al-Ahwānī (Madrid, 1965).

97. Ed. F. Wüstenfeld (Göttingen & Paris, 1876; Cairo, 1945). Cf. Mu'nis, *al-Jughrāfiyah*, pp. 123ff.

98. The extant material on North Africa was edited by W. McGuckin de Slane, *al-*

Mughrib fī dhikr bilād Ifrīqiyah wa-l-Maghrib (Algiers, 1857); French trans. de Slane (Algiers, 1913). The fragments pertaining to al-Andalus and Europe were edited under the title of *Jughrāfiyat al-Andalus wa-Urubbā min kitāb al-masālik wa-l-mamālik* by 'Abd al-Raḥmān 'Alī al-Ḥajjī (Beirut, 1968). See A. Chejne's review of this work in *JAOS*, 89 (1969), 454–456, the substance of which is here reproduced. There are three microfilms of the *Masālik* in *IEIM* (A-6, A-7, and A-8).

99. *Jughrāfiyat al-Andalus wa-Urubbā*, p. 81.

100. *Ibid*., pp. 82–83.

101. *Ibid*., p. 90.

102. *Ibid*., pp. 154ff.

103. See above, n. 37.

104. Arabic title *Basṭ al-arḍ fī-l-ṭūl wa-l-'arḍ*, ed. Juan Vernet (Tetuan, 1958).

105. The work was edited several times, but only partially. See the edition and French translation by R. Dozy and M. J. de Goeje, *Description de l'Afrique et de l'Espagne* (Leiden, 1886). The description of the Mosque of Cordova was translated into French by Alfred Dessus Lamare under the title of *Description de la Grande Mosquée de Cordoue* (Algiers, 1949); see also the trans. of P. A. Jaubert (Paris, 1836–1840).

106. Abū Ḥāmid al-Gharnāṭī wrote two works about his travels: *Tuḥfat al-albāb wa-nukhbat al-a'jāb*, ed. G. Ferrand in *JA* (1925), and *al-Mu'rib fī 'ajā'ib al-Maghrib*, fragments of which were edited and translated into Spanish by C. E. Dubler as *Abū Ḥāmid el Granadino y su relación de viaje por tierras europeas* (Madrid, 1953). Cf. González Palencia, *Historia de la literatura arábigo-española*, p. 197; Mu'nis, *al-Jughrāfiyah*, pp. 303ff.

107. Ed. M. Wright (Leiden, 1852). Also ed. M. J. de Goeje (Leiden, 1917); French trans. Gaudefroy-Demombynes (Paris, 1949); English trans. J. C. Broadhurst (London, 1952).

108. Ed. Aḥmad Ibn Jadw (Algiers, 1965). Cf. Mu'nis, *al-Jughrāfiyah*, pp. 518ff.

109. Escorial 1680, 1732, 1735, 1736, 1737, and 1739.

110. Ed. and trans. C. Defremery and B. R. Sanguinetti (Paris, 1953); Arabic text (Beirut, 1960); English trans. H. A. R. Gibb (London, 1958); abridged version by S. Lee, *Travels of Ibn Batuta* (London, 1829).

111. See 'Abbās, *Tārīkh al-adab al-andalusī: 'aṣr al-Ṭawā'if*, pp. 303ff. Cf. above, Chapter 11.

112. See 'Inān, *Lisān al-Dīn*, pp. 261ff. They were reproduced by Müller, *Beitrage zur Geschichte der Westlichen Araber*, pp. 1–100; and published under the title *Mushāhadāt Ibn al-Khaṭīb fī bilād al-Maghrib wa-l-Andalus* (Fez, A.H. 1325).

113. The portion pertaining to Granada was translated into Spanish (Simonet, *Descripción del reino de Granada*). The *Maqāmah* bears the title *Maqāmāt mi'yār al-ikhtiyār fī dhikr al-ma'āhid wa-l-diyār*.

114. It is entitled *Mufākharāt Mālaga wa-Salā*, Spanish trans. E. García Gómez in *al-Andalus*, 2 (1934), 183–194. It would seem that Ibn al-Khaṭīb shows his preference for the Andalusian city of Málaga over the Maghribī city of Salā (Salé).

115. It is entitled *Khaṭrat al-ṭayf fī riḥlat al-shitā' wa-l-ṣayf*.

16. The Religious Sciences

1. Ibn Ḥazm, *Marātib al-'ulūm* in *Rasā'il Ibn Ḥazm*, p. 78; see above, Chapter 9.

2. *Ibid*., pp. 94ff.

3. *Ibid*., p. 90.

4. Chejne, *The Arabic Language*, pp. 8ff., 40.

5. J. Horovitz, *Koranische Untersuchungen* (Berlin & Leipzig, 1926); A. Jeffery, *The Foreign Vocabulary of the Qur'ān* (Baroda, 1928), *Materials for the History of the Qur'ān* (Leiden, 1937), *The Qur'ān as Scripture* (New York, 1952); Th. Noeldeke, *Geschichte des Qorāns* (2nd ed.; Leipzig, 1909–1838).

6. On this point see Tor Andrae, *Les origines de l'Islam et du christianisme*, trans. J. Roche (Paris, 1955); R. Bell, *The Origin of Islam in Its Christian Environment* (London, 1926); C. C. Torrey, *The Jewish Foundation of Islam* (Oxford, 1924).

7. It should be mentioned that recensions of the Qur'ān were made by Ibn Mas'ūd, Abū Mūsā al-Ash'arī, and Miqdād — all companions of Muḥammad.

8. *Tafsīr al-Qur'ān* (30 vols.; Cairo, various printings).

9. Al-Zamakhsharī's work bears the title *al-Kashshāf 'an ḥaqā'iq al-tanzīl*, ed. W. H. Lees (Calcutta, 1856).

10. Al-Bayḍāwī's work bears the title *Anwār al-tanzīl* (Cairo, A.H. 1315).

11. Al-Suyūṭī's work bears the title *Iqtān* (Cairo, A.H. 1279).

12. In the words of Ibn Ḥazm, the commentary of Ibn Makhlad is unique in Islam, even when compared with the great commentary of al-Ṭabarī (al-Maqqarī, *Nafḥ al-ṭīb*, vol. 4, p. 162); cf. González Palencia, *Historia de la literatura arábigo-española*, 249. One may mention the Cordovese Ibn Abī Ṭālib al-Qaysī (d. 1045), who wrote a commentary of the Qur'ān, *Tafsīr al-Qur'ān*, which is extant (*BNM* 4945); al-Qurṭubī, *al-Jāmi' li-aḥkām al-Qur'ān* (Cairo, 1933–1950); Muḥiyy al-Dīn Ibn 'Arabī, *Tafsīr al-Qur'ān al-Karīm* (Beirut, n.d.).

13. Al-Maqqarī, *Nafḥ al-ṭīb*, vol. 4, p. 171. Ibn 'Aṭiyyah's *Tafsīr* is in manuscript form (*BNM* 4874).

14. Ibn Khaldūn, *al-Muqaddimah*, trans. Rosenthal, vol. 2, pp. 440ff.

15. *Ibid*., p. 441.

16. See González Palencia, *Historia de la literatura arábigo-española*, p. 248. The work is extant (Escorial 65 and 1387). In this connection, one may add the name of Ibn 'Abd al-Quddūs of Cordova (1012–1068), who wrote *Kitāb al-miftāḥ fī ikhtilāf al-qirā'āt al-sab'ah* (*BNM* 5255).

17. In connection with Qur'ānic readings, there emerged the discipline of Qur'ānic spelling (*rasm*) in which Abū 'Amr of Denia excelled, and on which he wrote several works.

18. On the subject of *Ḥadīth*, see A. Guillaume, *The Traditions of Islam* (Oxford, 1924); I. Goldziher, *Muhammedanische Studien* (Halle, 1890); J. Robson, *An Introduction to the Science of Tradition* (London, 1953).

19. One should mention *Mishkāt al-maṣābiḥ*, a later collection translated into English by J. Robson (Lahore, 1965).

20. These are some of the major topics covered by *ḥadīth*. See *Mishkāt al-maṣābiḥ*.

21. Al-Maqqarī, *Nafḥ al-ṭīb*, vol. 4, p. 171.

22. *Ibid*., p. 163.

23. On Islamic jurisprudence see under *Fiḳh* in *EI* and under various schools mentioned in this essay. See also M. Khaddurī, *Law in the Middle East* (Washington, D.C., 1955); L. Milliot, *Introduction à l'étude du droit musulman* (Paris, 1953); J. Schacht, *The Origins of Muhammedan Jurisprudence* (Oxford, 1950) and *Introduction to Islamic Law* (Oxford, 1964); E. Tyan, *Histoire de l'organization judiciare en pays d'Islam* (Paris, 1938); N. J. Coulson, *Islamic Law* (Edinburgh, 1964).

24. See E. Lévi-Provençal, *España musulmana*, Spanish trans. E. García Gómez (Madrid, 1950). For a detailed account of the introduction and development of Mālikism in Spain, see P. J. López Ortíz, "La recepción de la escuela malequí en España," *AHDE*, 7 (1931), 1–169.

25. Al-Maqqarī, *Nafḥ al-ṭīb*, vol. 4, p. 215.

26. *Ibid*., p. 214.

27. *Ibid*., p. 215.

28. *Ibid*., pp. 161–162.

29. *Ibid*., vol. 2, pp. 217.

30. *Ibid*., pp. 214–217.

31. Asín Palacios, *Abenházam de Córdoba*, vol. 1, pp. 133ff.

32. For a list of the followers of Ibn Ḥazm, see *ibid*., pp. 280ff.

33. Al-Maqqarī, *Nafḥ al-ṭīb*, vol. 4, pp. 168–169.

34. The Arabic title of the work is *Iḥyā' 'ulūm al-dīn* (Cairo, 1933).

35. See D. M. Donaldson, *The Shī'ite Religion* (London, 1933).

36. For a general survey of the Khārijite movement, see A. Salem, *Political Theory and Institutions of the Khawārij* (Baltimore, 1956).

37. W. M. Watt, *Islamic Philosophy and Theology* (Edinburgh, 1962), p. 7.

38. On the various sects mentioned here see *EI* under the respective headings. See also the following works which cover not only the sects but general Islamic theology as well: D. B. MacDonald, *Development of Muslim Theology, Jurisprudence and Constitutional Theory* (New York, 1903); A. J. Wensinck, *The Muslim Creed* (Cambridge, 1932); L. Gardet and M. Anawati, *Introduction à la théologie musulmane* (Paris, 1948); A. S. Tritton, *Muslim Theology* (London, 1947); W. M. Watt, *Free Will and Predestination in Early Islam* (London, 1948) and *Islamic Philosophy and Theology*.

Attention should be called to the heresiographical works in Arabic, such as those of al-Ash'arī, *Maqālat al-islāmiyyīn w-ikhtilāf al-muṣallīn*, ed. H. Ritter (Istanbul, 1929–1930); al-Baghdādī, *Kitāb al-farq bayn al-firaq*, English trans. *Moslem Schisms and Sects*, pt. 1 by K. C. Seelye (New York, 1920), pt. 2 by A. S. Halkin (Tel-Aviv, 1936); al-Baghdādī, *al-Mukhtaṣar*, ed. P. K. Hitti (Cairo, 1924); Ibn Ḥazm, *al-Fiṣal fī-l-milal wa-l-ahwā' wa-l-niḥal* (Cairo, A.H. 1347–1348), Spanish trans. M. Asín Palacios, *Abenházam de Córdoba* (Madrid, 1927–1932); al-Shahrastānī, *Kitāb al-milal wa-l-niḥal*, ed. R. W. Cureton (London, 1842–1846).

39. On the Mu'tazilah, see A. N. Nader, *Le système philosophique de Mu'tazilah* (Beirut, 1956); al-Khayyāṭ, *Kitāb al-intiṣār* (Cairo, 1925), French trans. A. N. Nader, *Le livre de triomphe* (Beirut, 1957).

40. R. C. McCarthy, *The Theology of al-Ash'arī* (Beirut, 1953), and his English trans. of al-Ash'arī's *al-Ibānah* (New Haven, 1940). See also Watt, *Islamic Philosophy and Theology*, pp. 82ff.

41. On al-Ghazālī, see W. M. Watt, *Muslim Intellectual: The Struggle and Achievement of al-Ghazālī* (Edinburgh, 1963); M. Smith, *al-Ghazālī, the Mystic* (London, 1944); Watt, *Islamic Philosophy and Theology*, pp. 114ff.

42. See M. Asín Palacios, "Ibn Masarra y su escuela" in *Obras escogidas* (Madrid, 1946).

43. Asín Palacios, *Abenházam de Córdoba*, vol. 1, pp. 264 ff.

44. *Ibid*., p. 265.

45. On Ẓāhirism, see I. Goldziher, *Die Ẓāhiriten* (Leipzig, 1884).

46. Asín Palacios, *Abenházam de Córdoba*, vol. 1, pp. 176ff. On this point see Arnaldez, *Grammaire et théologie*; Ibn Ḥazm, *Iḥkām*, vol. 1, pp. 100 and 125; vol. 6, p. 103; Ibn Ḥazm, *al-Muḥallā*, vol. 1, p. 47.

47. Asín Palacios, *Abenházam de Córdoba*, vol. 1, pp. 140ff. Cf. Ibn Ḥazm, *Iḥkām*, vol. 6, p. 146, where he says that *taqlīd* (imitation) is a heresy (*bid'ah*); and that *qiyās* (analogy) is needless (*Iḥkām*, vol. 8, p. 17, and *Muḥallā*, vol. 1, p. 52. They represent abandonment of the *Sunnah* (*Muḥallā*, vol. 8, p. 46) and should be substituted by investigation (*ijtihād*), for "the researcher who errs is more virtuous in the eye of God than the imitator who is in the right" (*Muḥallā*, vol. 1, p. 62).

48. Asín Palacios, *Abenházam de Córdoba*, pp. 146ff.

49. *Ibid*., pp. 140ff.; vol. 2, pp. 91ff.

50. *Ibid*., vol. 2, p. 3.

51. *Ibid*., p. 35.

52. *Ibid*., p. 56.

53. I. Goldziher, *Le livre d'Ibn Toumart* (Algiers, 1903).

54. See below, Chapter 17.

55. See Asín Palacios, "Ibn Masarra y su escuela", p. 24; cf. Nicholson, *A Literary History of the Arabs*, pp. 408ff.

56. Asín Palacios, "Ibn Masarra y su escuela," p. 25.

57. Asín Palacios, *Abenházam de Córdoba*, vol. 2, pp. 41ff.

58. *Ibid*., p. 262.

59. *Ibid*., pp. 359ff.

60. Cf. *ibid*., vol. 3, 111, p. 69.

61. *Ibid*., pp. 21ff.

62. *Ibid*., pp. 30ff.

63. *Ibid*., p. 59.

17. Philosophy and Mysticism

1. See Chapter 9.
2. R. Walzer, *Greek into Arabic* (Oxford, 1962).
3. Some of the general works on Muslim philosophy are T. DeBoer, *The History of Philosophy in Islam* (London, 1903), Arabic trans. Muḥammad 'Abd al-Hādī (Cairo, 1957); S. Munk, *Mélanges de philosophie juive et arabe* (Paris, 1857)) R. Walzer, *History of Philosophy, Eastern and Western* (London, 1953); W. M. Watt, *Islamic Philosophy and Theology* (Edinburgh, 1962); M. M. Sharif, ed., *History of Muslim Philosophy* (Wiesbaden, 1963–1966); R. Lerner and M. Mahdi, *Medieval Political Philosophy* (Glencoe, Ill., 1963); M. Cruz Hernández, *Historia de la filosofía española* (Madrid, 1957) *La filosofía arabe* (Madrid, 1963).
4. See above, Chapter 16.
5. On al-Kindī, see G. N. Atiyeh, *al-Kindī: The Philosopher of the Arabs* (Rawalpindi, 1966).
6. *Ibid*., pp. 148ff. Most of al-Kindī's works are lost. However, a good number of them exist in Latin through the translations made by Gerard of Cremona and others.
7. F. Rosenthal, *Aḥmad b. aṭ-Ṭayyib as-Saraḥsī* (New Haven, 1943).
8. Al-Kindī, *Rasā'il al-Kindī al-falsafiyyah*, ed. M. A. Abū Riḍā (Cario, 1950–1953), vol. 1, p. 97; as quoted by Atiyeh, *al-Kindī*, p. 17.
9. Atiyeh, *al-Kindī*, p. 19.
10. Al-Kindī, *Rasā'il*, vol. 1, p. 104; Atiyeh, *al-Kindī*, p. 23.
11. Al-Fārābī, *Iḥṣā' al-'ulūm*, ed. A. González Palencia (Madrid, 1933).
12. I. Madkour, *La place d'al-Fārābī dans l'école philosophique musulmane* (Paris, 1934).
13. Ed. A. Nader (Beirut, 1959).
14. Ed. F. Najjār (Beirut, 1964).
15. The *Shifā'* has not been edited in full.
16. Ed. M. S. al-Kurdī (Cairo, 1944). A section of the *Najāt* was translated into English by F. Raḥmān under the title *Avicenna's Psychology* (London, 1952).
17. A. M. Goichon, *La philosophie d'Avicenne et son influence en Europe médiévale* (Paris, 1944); L. Gardet, *La pensée religieuse d'Avicenne* (Paris, 1951); A. M. Afnan, *Avicenna, His Life and Works* (London, 1958); H. Corbin, *Avicenna and the Visionary Recital* (London, 1961).
18. Ed. Khayr al-Dīn al-Ziriklī (Cairo, A.H. 1347). The *Rasā'il* is said (Ṣā'id, *Ṭabaqāt*, p. 94) to have been introduced to al-Andalus by al-Kirmānī (d. 458/1066). However, it may be possible that it was introduced by Maslama al-Majrīṭī — see *EI* and E. García Gómez, "Alusiones de los Ijwān al-Ṣafā' en la poesía arábigo-andaluza," *al-Andalus*, 4 (1936–1939), 462–465.
19. Ṣā'id, *Ṭabaqāt*, p. 88.
20. Ed. I. 'Abbās (Beirut, 1959). Ibn Ḥazm was followed by Abū al-Ṣalt (1067–1134) of Denia, who wrote a treatise on logic entitled *Taqwīm al-dhihn* (Escorial 646), ed. and Spanish trans. A. González Palencia (Madrid, 1915).
21. The eight books are *Categories* (*Maqūlāt*), *Hermeneutics* (*'Ibārah*), *Analytics (Qiyās)*. *Apodeictica* (*Burhān*), *Disputation* (*Jadl*), *Sophistici Elenci* (*Safasṭah*), *Rhetoric* (*Khiṭabah*), and *Poetics* (*Sh'ir*). Cf. Ibn Khaldūn, *al-Muqaddimah*, vol. 3, pp. 140–141.
22. Sā'id, *Ṭabaqāt*, p. 101; see also 'Abbās's introduction to Ibn Ḥazm's *al-Taqrīb*.
23. See Ibn Ḥazm's *Marātib al-'ulūm*, p. 71.
24. *Al-Taqrīb*, p. 71.
25. *Marātib al-'ulūm*, p. 72.
26. *Al-Taqrīb*, p. 8.
27. *Ibid*., p. 6.
28. *Ibid*., p. 9.
29. See below, this chapter.
30. *Al-Taqrīb*, p. 9.
31. Ed. and Spanish trans. M. Asín Palacios (Madrid, 1916).

32. *Kitāb al-madkhal*, p. 8[8]. The first number refers to the Arabic text; the bracketed number to the Spanish translation.
33. *Ibid*., p. 13[20].
34. *Ibid*., p. 15[26].
35. *Ibid*., p. 16[28].
36. *Ibid*., p. 16[29].
37. *Ibid*., p. 17[30].
38. *Ibid*., p. 20[34].
39. See below, this chapter.
40. Ibn Khaldūn, *al-Muqaddimah*, trans. Rosenthal, vol. 3, p. 143.
41. *Ibid*., pp. 246ff.
42. Ṣā'id, *Ṭabaqāt*, pp. 87–88.
43. See Asín Palacios, "Ibn Masarra y su escuela."
44. On Ibn Fattūḥ, see *Ibn Ḥazm, Risālah*, in al-Maqqarī, *Nafḥ al-ṭib*, vol. 4, p. 169; Ṣā'id, *Ṭabaqāt*, p. 92.
45. Ṣā'id, *Ṭabaqāt*, p. 91.
46. Ibn Ḥazm, *Risālah*, in al-Maqqarī, *Nafḥ al-ṭib*, vol. 4, p. 169.
47. Asín Palacios, *Abenházam de Córdova*, vol. 1, pp. 147ff., 159ff.; vol. 2, pp. 91–97; vol. 4, p. 38; vol. 5, p. 113.
48. See above, Chapter 11.
49. In his *Kitāb al-taḥqīq fī naqḍ kitāb al-'ilm al-ilāhī li-Muḥammad Zakariyā' al-ṭabīb;* cf. Asín Palacios, *Abenházam de Códova*, vol. 1, p. 252.
50. Abridged English trans. H. E. Wedeck (New York, 1962).
51. Ibn Khaldūn, *al-Muqaddimah*, vol. 3, p. 116.
52. The extant portion of the *Tadbīr* was edited and translated into Spanish by M. Asín Palacios, *El régimen del solitario* (Madrid, 1946). The first part of the work was translated into English by D. M. Dunlop in *JRAS* (1945), 61–81; and L. Berman in Lerner, *Medieval Political Philosophy*, pp. 122–133. Other philosophical treatises of Ibn Bājjah are in the Escorial 612, no. 3, 7, 8.
53. *Tadbīr al-mutawaḥḥid*, p. 11.
54. *Ibid*., p. 27. In a treatise which is extant (Escorial 612, no. 2) Ibn Bājjah criticizes al-Fārābī.
55. *Ibid*., pp. 3ff.
56. *Ibid*., p. 4; the work is entitled *'Ilm al-siyāsah*.
57. *Ibid*., p. 6.
58. *Ibid*., p. 8.
59. *Ibid*., p. 9.
60. *Ibid*., p. 10.
61. *Ibid*., p. 14.
62. *Ibid*., p. 16.
63. *Ibid*., p. 32ff.
64. English translations under the title of *Improvement of Human Reason* by S. Ockley (London, 1708) and by A. S. Fulton (London, 1929); English trans. P. Bronnle under the title of *Awakening of the Soul* (London, 1904); Spanish trans. A. González Palencia, *El filósofo autodidacto* (Madrid, 1934); French trans. L. Gauthier (Beirut, 1936); Latin trans. with Arabic text, E. Pococke (Oxford, 1671, 1700); German trans. G. Pritius (Frankfurt, 1726). See also Z. A. Siddiqi, *Philosophy of Ibn Tufayl* (Aligarh, 1965); 'Abd al-Ḥalīm Maḥmūd, *Falsafat Ibn Ṭufayl wa-risālatuh* (Cairo, n.d.).
65. See below, this chapter.
66. Reference to the Arabic text is made here: *Ḥayy Ibn Yaqẓān* (Beirut, 1962).
67. Antonio Pastor, *The Idea of Robinson Crusoe* (Watford, 1930), p. 85.
68. *Ḥayy Ibn Yaqẓān*, p. 19.
69. *Ibid*., pp. 59ff.
70. *Ibid*., pp. 83ff.

71. For instance, *The Tale of Alexander the Great*. See also Corbin, *Avicenna*, p. 225.
72. Ibn al-Nafīs, *al-Risālah al-kāmiliyyah fī-l-sīrah al-nabawiyyah*, ed. with English trans. M. Meyerhof and J. Schacht, *The Theologus Autodidacticus of Ibn al-Nafīs* (London, 1968).
73. *Ibid*., pp. 29–30.
74. In fact, three translations of the work of Ibn Ṭufayl were made in 1674, 1686, and 1708.
75. On Averröes, see L. Gauthier, *Ibn Rushd* (Paris, 1948); M. Fakhrī, *Ibn Rushd: faylasūf Qurṭubah* (Beirut, 1960).
76. E. Renan, *Averroès et l'averroisme* (Paris, 1852).
77. Al-Marrākushī, *Mu'jib*, pp. 314ff., trans. and quoted by G. Hourani, *Averroës on the Harmony of Religion and Philosophy* (London, 1961), pp. 12–13.
78. Fakhrī, *Ibn Rushd*, pp. 12ff.
79. Hourani, *Averroës*, p. 70.
80. Ed. G. Hourani (Leiden, 1959).
81. Ed. Sulaymān Dunyā (Cairo, 1964–1965); English trans. S. van den Bergh (Oxford, 1954).
82. Fakhrī, *Ibn Rushd*, p. 28. for instance, his *Kitāb al-jawāmi'* (MS., *BNM* 5000) contains six treatises and six commentaries on Aristotle.
83. As translated by Hourani, *Averroës*, p. 50.
84. *Ibid*., pp. 63ff.
85. *Ibid*., p. 65.
86. *Ibid*., p. 46.
87. Ed. M. Bouyges (Beirut, 1927).
88. Renan, *Averroès et l'averroisme*, p. 186; cf. Fakhrī, *Ibn Rushd*, pp. 139ff.
89. On Maimonides, see L. Roth, *The Guide for the Perplexed* (London, 1948); J. Melber, *The Universality of Maimonides* (New York, 1968).
90. The *Guide* was translated into English by M. Friedlander (New York, 1956). On Jewish philosophy in general, see Husik, *A History of Medieval Jewish Philosophy*.
91. Maimonides, *Guide*, p. 3.
92. *Ibid*., p. 394.
93. *Ibid*., p. 395.
94. *Ibid*., p. 384–385.
95. See D. J. Silver, *Maimonidean Criticism and the Maimonidean Controversy, 1180–1240* (Leiden, 1965).
96. J. Guttmann, *Der Einfluss der maimonidischen Philosophie auf das christliche Abendland* (Leipzig, 1908).
97. On Sufism, see *SEI*, under *Taṣawwuf*; T. Burckhardt, *An Introduction to Sufi Doctrine* (Lahore, 1959); D. B. Macdonald, *The Religious Life and Attitude in Islam* (Chicago, 1909); R. A. Nicholson, *The Mystics of Islam* (London, 1914, 1966), *Studies in Islamic Mysticism* (London, 1921), and *The Idea of Personality in Sufism* (Lahore, 1964); A. J. Arberry, *Sufism* (London, 1950); A. E. 'Afīfī, *al-Taṣawwuf* (Cairo, 1963); Ibn Qudāmah, *Kitāb al-tawwābīn*, ed. G. Makdisi (Damascus, 1961); L. Gardet and G. Anawati, *Mystique musulmane* (Paris, 1961).
98. Nicholson, *The Mystics of Islam*, pp. 3ff.
99. *Ibid*., pp. 10ff.
100. *Ibid*., p. 8.
101. *Ibid*., pp. 28ff.
102. *Ibid*., p. 29.
103. See Qushayrī, *Risālah* (Cairo, 1948).
104. As quoted by Arberry, *Sufism*, p. 28.
105. Ibn Khaldūn, *al-Muqaddimah*, vol. 3, pp. 76ff.
106. See his *Ri'āyah li-ḥuqūq allāh*, ed. M. Smith (London, 1940); cf. Arberry, *Sufism*, 46ff.
107. Arberry, *Sufism*, p. 54.
108. L. Massignon, *La passion d'al-Ḥallāj* (Paris, 1922).

109. Ed. R. A. Nicholson (London, 1914).
110. *Kitāb ṭabaqāt al-ṣufiyya*, ed. J. Pederson (Leiden, 1960).
111. Cairo, A.H. 1287, A.D. 1948.
112. Cairo, 1933.
113. Cairo, A.H. 1309.
114. M. Asín Palacios supplies a list of some eighteen ascetics who appeared from the time of the conquest to the ninth century; see his "Ibn Masarra y su escuela," pp. 185ff.
115. See above, same chapter.
116. In his "Ibn Massarra y su escuela."
117. M. Asín Palacios, "Biografía de Ibn al-'Arīf (1088–1141)," in *Obras escogidas*, pp. 219–234.
118. Cairo, A.H. 1315.
119. Asín Palacios reproduces various passages of the *Futuḥāt* where reference to the work is made; see his "Biografía de Ibn al'Arīf," pp. 235–242.
120. Ibn al-Khaṭīb, *A'māl al-a'lām*, pp. 248ff.
121. *Ibid*., p. 299.
122. A.E. 'Afifi, *The Mystical Philosophy of Muḥyid dīn Ibnul 'Arabi* (Cambridge, 1939). Lahore reprint of the work is used here. See also H. Corbin, *Creative Imagination in the Ṣūfism of Ibn 'Arabī* (London, 1969); M. Asín Palacios, *Ibn 'Arabī*, Arabic trans. 'Abd al-Raḥmān Badawī (Cairo, 1965).
123. 'Afifi, *The Mystical Philosophy*, pp. 183ff.
124. On Ibn 'Arabī, see *ibid*.; M. Asín Palacios, *La psicología según Mohidin Abenarabi* (Algiers, 1905), *El místico murciano Aben Arabi* (Madrid, 1925–1928), and *El Islam cristianizado*; R. Landau, *The Philosophy of Ibn 'Arabī* (London, 1959); R. P. Gómez Nogales, "Ibn 'Arabī eslabón cultural," *RIEL*, 13 (1965–1966), 25–42, and "La immortalidad del alma en Ibn 'Arabī," *RIEL*, 14 (1967–1968), 193–210.
125. *Diwān Ibn 'Arabī* (Būlāq, 1855).
126. *Tarjumān al-ashwāq* (Beirut, 1961), p. 10. This work was translated into English by R. A. Nicholson (London, 1911).
127. Būlāq, A.H. 1252; Cairo, A.H. 1309.
128. Cairo, A.H. 1295, A.D. 1946.
129. The *Inshā' al-dawā'ir*, *'Uqlat al-mustawfiz*, and *al-Tadbīrāt al-ilāhiyyah* — all of which were ed. by H. S. Nyberg under the title of *Kleiner Schriften des Ibn al-'Arabī* (Leiden, 1919).
130. 'Afifi, *The Mystical Philosophy*, p. 170.
131. *Ibid*., pp. 65ff.
132. *Ibid*., pp. 100ff. cf. Ibn 'Arabī's *Futuḥāt* (Cairo, A.H. 1293), vol. 1, p. 319.
133. *Ibid*., p. 10.
134. *Ibid*., p. 12.
135. *Ibid*., p. 45.
136. *Ibid*., p. 55.
137. *Ibid*., p. 103.
138. *Ibid*., p. 105; cf. Ibn 'Arabī's *Futuḥāt*, vol. 1, p. 38.
139. Afifi, *The Mystical Philosophy*, pp. 106–108.
140. *Ibid*., pp. 145–147.
141. *Ibid*., pp. 109ff.; cf. Ibn 'Arabī, *Futuḥāt*, vol. 2, pp. 359ff.
142. M. Asín Palacios, *La escatología musulmana en la Divina Comedia* (Madrid, 1919, 1943).
143. One of the major works of Ibn Sab'īn is his *Inshā' al-ḥikmah al-ilāhiyyah*, which is a commentary on and simplication of the language of the Qur'ān. Vol. 1 and 2 are in MS. (*IEIM* B-4 and B-5). See also his *Rasā'il*, ed. 'Abd al-Raḥmān Badawī (Cairo, 1956), and his *Kitāb al-iḥāṭah*, ed. 'Abd al-Raḥmān al-Badawī in *RIEI*, 6 (1958), 11–34.
144. See Abū-l-Wafā al-Ghunaymī al-Taftazānī, "Ibn 'Abbād al-Rundī," *RIEI*, 6 (1958), 221–258; Ibn 'Abbād, *Sharḥ Ibn 'Abbād al-Rundī li-ḥikam al-'Aṭā'iyyah* (Cairo, A.H. 1324).

145. M. Asín Palacios, "Un precursor hispanomusulmán de San Juan de la Cruz," in *Obras escogidas*, pp. 243–336; also in *al-Andalus*, 1 (1933), 7–79.
146. See G. Maqdisi, *Kitāb al-tawwābīn* (Damascus, 1961), p. xxv.
147. 'Afīfī, *al-Taṣawwuf*, pp. 111ff.

18. The Natural Sciences

1. On the meaning and conception of the sciences, see al-Khuwārizmī, *Mafātīḥ al-'ulūm*, ed. G. van Vloten (Leiden, 1895); Ibn al-Nadīm, *Fihrist*, ed. G. Flügel (Leipzig, 1871–1872); al-Fārābī, *Iḥṣā' al-'ulūm*, ed. 'U. M. Amin (Cairo, 1948); Ibn Sīnā, *Fī aqsām al-'ulūm* in MS.); Ibn Ḥazm, *Marātib al-'ulūm*, in *Rasā'il Ibn Ḥazm*, ed. Iḥsān 'Abbās (Cairo, 1952); Ibn Khaldūn, *al-Muqaddimah*, trans. Rosenthal (New York, 1958), particularly vol. 3.

One may add al-Qifṭī, *Ta'rīkh al-ḥukamā'*, ed. A. Müller and J. Lippert (Leipzig, 1903), and Ibn Abī Uṣaybi'ah, *'Uyūn al-anbā' fī ṭabaqāt al-aṭibbā'*, ed. A. Müller (Cairo, 1882–1884), which give valuable information about scientists and their works.

2. Ibn Ḥazm, *Marātib al-'ulūm*, p. 78.
3. Ibn Khaldūn, *al-Muqaddimah*, vol. 3, p. 112.
4. Ṣā'id, *Ṭabaqāt*; cf. above, Chapter 9.
5. Cf. above, n. 2.
6. Ibn Khaldūn, *al-Muqaddimah*, pp. 113ff.
7. The principal Western studies of the Arabic sciences and their transmission are F. Wüstenfeld, *Geschichte der arabischen Arzte und Naturforscher* (Göttingen, 1840); B. Carra de Vaux, *Les penseurs de l'Islam* (Paris, 1921–1926); G. Sarton, *Introduction to the History of Science* (Baltimore, 1927–1948); M. Plessner, *Die Geschichte der Wissenschaften in Islam* (Tübingen, 1931); C. H. Haskins, *Studies in the History of Medieval Science* (Cambridge, Mass., 1927); T. Arnold and A. Guillaume, eds., *The Legacy of Islam* Oxford, 1931); A. Mieli, *La science arabe et son rôle dans l'évolution scientifique mondiale* (Leiden, 1966).
8. Ibn Ḥazm, *Marātib al-'ulūm*, p. 68; cf. above, Chapter 9.
9. *Ibid*., pp. 60ff.
10. Ibn Khaldūn, *al-Muqaddimah*, vol. 3, pp. 258–267.
11. *Ibid*., p. 262.
12. *Ibid*., pp. 227ff.
13. *Ibid*., pp. 267–280.
14. *Ibid*., p. 270.
15. *Ibid*., p. 271.
16. Ibn Ḥazm, *Marātib al-'ulūm*, p. 67.
17. Ibn Khaldūn, *al-Muqaddimah*, vol. 3, p. 134.
18. *Ibid*., pp. 133ff.
19. See H. Suter, *Die Mathematiker und Astronomen der Araber und ihre Werke* (Leipzig, 1900); E. S. Kennedy, "A Survey of Islamic Astronomical Tables," *Transactions of the American Philosophical Society*, 46 (1956), 123–177.
20. B. Carra de Vaux, in Arnold and Guillaume, *Legacy of Islam*, p. 376.
21. Ed. and English trans. F. Rosen (London, 1831). It is probable that the Andalusian Ibn Badr of Valencia based his compendium entitled *Kitāb fīhi ikhtiṣār al-jabr wa-l-muqābalah* (Escorial 936) on al-Khuwārizmī's work. See Arabic text and Spanish trans. by Sánchez-Pérez (Madrid, 1916).
22. *Kitāb al-zīj*, ed. and Latin trans. C. A. Nallino (Rome, 1903).
23. J. Millás Vallicrosa, *Estudios sobre la historia de la ciencia española* (Barcelona, 1949).
24. Ṣā'id, *Ṭabaqāt*, p. 86; al-Maqqarī, *Nafḥ al-ṭīb*, vol. 4, p. 346.
25. Ṣā'id, p. 87; al-Maqqarī, vol. 4, p. 346.
26. Ṣā'id, p. 91.
27. On al-Majrīṭī, see *ibid*., p. 92; al-Qifṭī, *Ta'rīkh al-ḥukamā'*, p. 336; Ibn Abī Uṣaybi'ah, *'Uyūn al-anbā'*, vol. 2, p. 39.

28. Ibn Khaldūn, *al-Muqaddimah*, vol. 3, p. 116.
29. Ṣā'id, *Ṭabaqāt*, p. 92.
30. Ibn Ḥazm, *Risālah*, in al-Maqqarī, *Nafḥ al-ṭīb*, vol. 4, p. 168.
31. Ṣā'id, *Ṭabaqāt*, p. 92.
32. Ibn Khaldūn, *al-Muqaddimah*, vol. 3, p. 269.
33. *Ibid.*, p. 288.
34. *Ibid.*, p. 229.
35. Quoted in *ibid.*, pp. 230–245.
36. Ṣā'id, *Ṭabaqāt*, p. 95.
37. *Ibid.*, p. 93; al-Maqqarī, *Nafḥ al-ṭīb*, vol. 4, pp. 346–347.
38. Ṣā'id, p. 93; al-Maqqarī, vol. 4, p. 347.
39. Ṣā'id, p. 94; al-Maqqarī, vol. 4, pp. 347.
40. *Ibid.*
41. Ibn Khaldūn, *al-Muqaddimah*, vol. 3, pp. 126ff.
42. Ibn Ḥazm, *Risālah*, in al-Maqqarī, *Nafḥ al-ṭīb*, vol. 4, p. 160.
43. Ṣā'id, *Ṭabaqār*, p. 93; al-Maqqarī, *Nafḥ al-ṭīb*, vol. 4, pp. 346–347.
44. Ṣā'id, pp. 95–96. Cf. J. Millás Vallicrosa, *Estudios sobre Azarquiel* (Madrid, 1943–1950), pp. 30ff.
45. On al-Zarkālī, see Millás Vallicrosa, *Estudios sobre Azarquiel*; M. Steinschneider, "Études sur Zarakli, astronome arabe du XIe siècle, et ses ouvrages," *Bulletino di Bibliografia e di Storia delle Scienze Matematiche e Fisiche*, 14 (1881), 16 (1883), 17 (1884).
46. Ṣā'id's work corrects observations about the movements of the stars and errors of astronomers.
47. Millás Vallicrosa, *Estudios sobre Azarquiel*, pp. 3ff.
48. *Ibid.*, pp. 7ff.
49. *Ibid.*, pp. 23ff.
50. *Ibid.*, pp. 149ff.
51. *Ibid.*, pp. 74ff., where the Arabic text and Spanish translation are to be found.
52. Carra de Vaux, in Arnold and Guillaume, *Legacy of Islam*, p. 394.
53. Hitti, *History of the Arabs*, pp. 572–573.
54. The standard works on Arab medicine are L. Leclerc, *Histoire de la médecine arabe* (Paris, 1876); E. G. Browne, *Arabian Medicine* (Cambridge, 1921); Donald Campbell, *Arabian Medicine* (London, 1926); M. Üllman, *Die Medizin im Islam* (Leiden, 1970).
55. Ibn Ḥazm, *Marātib al-'ulūm*, p. 79.
56. M. Meyerhof, in Arnold and Guillaume, *Legacy of Islam*, pp. 316ff.
57. M. Meyerhof, *The Ten Treatises on the Eye by Ḥunain b. Isḥāq* (Cairo, 1928).
58. 151 according to Ibn al-Nadīm, *Fihrist*, pp. 299ff.; 135 according to al-Qifṭī, *Ta'rīkh al-ḥukamā*, pp. 271ff.; and 235 according to Ibn Abī Uṣaybi'ah, *'Uyūn al-anbā'*, vol. 2, pp. 309ff.
59. Meyerhof, in Arnold and Guillaume, *Legacy of Islam*, pp. 329–330.
60. The Arabic title of the work is *Ṭabaqāt al-aṭibbā' wa-l-ḥukamā'*, ed. F. Sayyid (Cairo, 1955). On Ibn Juljul, see the excellent introduction of F. Sayyid to the *Ṭabaqāt*; also al-Qifṭī, *Tārīkh al-ḥukamā*, p. 190; Ibn Abī Uṣaybi'ah, *'Uyūn al-anbā'*, vol. 2, pp. 46ff.
61. Ibn Juljul, *Ṭabaqāt*, p. 93.
62. Ṣā'id, *Ṭabaqāt*, p. 103.
63. Ibn Juljul, *Ṭabaqāt*, pp. 92–116, gives a list of twenty-three individuals who excelled in medicine. Ṣā'id, *Ṭabaqāt*, pp. 103–111.
64. Ibn Juljul, p. 93. The editor of Ibn Juljul's work points to the various readings of Ibn Iyyās' name, and chooses Ibn Abā. Ṣā'id, p. 104.
65. Ibn Juljul, p. 94; Ṣā'id, p. 104.
66. Ibn Juljul, p. 97.
67. *Ibid.*, pp. 104–105, quotes some of his poems; Ṣā'id, pp. 104–105.
68. Ibn Juljul, p. 100.
69. *Ibid.*, pp. 112–113; Ṣā'id, pp. 106–107.

70. Ibn Juljul, p. 107; also, al-Maqqarī, *Nafḥ al-ṭib*, vol. 2, p. 351.

71. Ṣā'id, *Ṭabaqāt*, p. 108; Ibn Ḥazm, *Risālah*, in al-Maqqarī, *Nafḥ al-ṭib*, vol. 4, p. 167.

72. Ṣā'id, *Ṭabaqāt*, p. 110; al-Maqqarī, *Nafḥ al-ṭib*, vol. 4, p. 348. One may add the name of Yūnis Ibn Isḥāq al-Isrā'ilī (11th cent.), who wrote his *Kitāb al-musta'īn* (*BNM* 5009) for Aḥmad Ibn al-Mu'tamin (1085–1109), ruler of Saragossa. The treatise, consisting of 139 folios, deals with simple drugs, their preparation, effect, and their different names.

73. Hitti, *History of the Arabs*, pp. 576ff. Some 257 folios of the *Taṣrīf* exist in *BNM* 5007.

74. Ṣā'id, *Ṭabaqāt*, p. 111.

75. F. Guillén Robles, *Málaga musulmana* (Málaga, 1880), pp. 387ff.

76. Ibn Bayṭār's work bears the title *al-Jāmi' li-mufridāt al-adwiyah wa-l-aghziyah* (Cairo, A.H. 1291).

77. As quoted by Hitti, *History of the Arabs*, p. 576; cf. Meyerhof, in Anrold and Guillaume, *Legacy of Islam*, p. 340. The treatise dealing with the causes and cure of epidemics is extant under the title of *al-Māqalah al-musammāh bi-muqna'at al-sā'il 'an al-maraḍ al-hā'il* (*BNM* 5067; cf. Escorial 1785, no. 50). A contemporary compatriot of Ibn al-Khaṭib wrote a treatise on epidemics (MS., Escorial, 1785, no. 7; *BNM* 5067). He was Abū 'Abdallah Muḥ. b. 'Alī al-Lakhmī (b. 1326). Another contemporary, Abū Ja'far b. 'Alī b. Muḥ. Ibn 'Alī b. Khātimah (d. 1369), wrote on the same subject (Escorial 1785, no. 6).

78. Al-Maqqarī, *Nafḥ al-ṭib*, vol. 4, pp. 304ff. An extant manuscript entitled *'Amal man ṭabba li-man ḥabba* (*BNP* 1070; *BNM* 4929) consists of 151 folios divided into two parts. The first part deals with general pathology in twenty chapters: diseases of the head, eyes, ears, nose, mouth, throat, respiratory organs, heart, lungs, stomach, liver, bladder, kidneys, and other organs. He defines each disease and gives its diagnostic, causes, symptoms, and treatment. The second part of the work concerns itself with fevers, "hot" tumors, "cold" tumors, ulcers, skin diseases, wounds, fractures, hair and baldness, poisons, snake bites, etc. For more details, see Leclerc, *Histoire de la médecine arabe*, vol. 2, pp. 287ff.

79. On the transmission and extent of Arabic sciences in the West, see D. M. Dunlop, *Arabic Science in the West* (Karachi, 1958); Sarton, *Introduction to the History of Science*; Haskins, *Studies in the History of Medieval Science*; and A. Mieli, *La science arabe* (Leiden, 1938.

See also A. A. Khairallah, *Outline of Arabic Contributions to Medicine and the Allied Sciences* (Beirut, 1946); D. M. Dunlop, "Arabic Medicine in England," *Journal of the History of Medicine and Allied Sciences*, 11 (1956), 166–182; J. M. Millás Vallicrosa, *Assais d'historia de les ideas fisiques i matematiques a la Catalunya medieval* (Barcelona, 1931), and *Nuevas aportaciones para el estudio de la transmision de la ciencia a Europa a través de España* (Barcelona, 1943); F. J. Carmody, *Arabic Astronomical and Astrological Sciences in Latin Translation* (Berkeley, 1956).

80. M. Steinschneider, "Constantinus und seine arabischen Quellen," *Virchow's Archiv*, 37 (1866), 352–354.

81. Manual Alonso, "Coincidencias verbales típicas en las obras y traducciones de Gundisalvo," *al-Andalus*, 20 (1955), 129–152, 345–380; "Hunayn traducido al latín por Ibn Dawūd y Domingo Gundisalvo," *al-Andalus*, 16 (1951), 37–48; "Juan Sevillano, sus obras propias y sus traducciones," *al-Andalus*, 18 (1953), 17–50; "Notas sobre los traductores toledanos Domingo Gundisalvo y Juan Hispano," *al-Andalus*, 8 (1943), 155–188; "Tecnicismos arábigos y su traducción," *al-Andalus*, 19 (1954), 102–128; "Traducciones del árabe al latín, por Juan Hispano (Ibn Dawūd)," *al-Andalus*, 17 (1952), 129–152; "Traducciones del arcediano Domingo Gundisalvo," *al-Andalus*, 11 (1947), 295–338; "El traductor y prologuista del 'Sextus Naturalium,' " *al-Andalus* 26 (1961), 1–36.

82. M. T. d'Averny and G. Vajda, "Mark de Tolède," *al-Andalus*, 16 (1951), 99–140, 259–308; and 17 (1952), 1–56.

83. See Dunlop, *Arabic Science in the West*, pp. 38ff. Also Haskins, *Studies in the*

History of Medieval Science, pp. 274ff. Michael Scot was responsible for translating a good part of Aristotle with Averroës' commentaries.

84. M. Alonso, "Traducciones del árabe al latín por Juan Hispano," *al-Andalus*, 17 (1952), 129–152. See also D. M. Dunlop, "The Work of Translation at Toledo," *Babel*, 6 (1950), 55–59.

85. Dunlop, *Arabic Science in the West*, pp. 61ff.

86. *Ibid.*, pp. 83ff.

19. Architecture, the Minor Arts and Music

1. The following works and articles are important for the study of Muslim architecture, minor arts, and music: K. A. C. Creswell, *A Bibliography of the Architecture, Arts and Crafts of Islam* (Cairo, 1961), *Early Muslim Architecture* (Oxford, 1932–1940), and *A Short Account of Early Muslim Architecture* (London, 1958); E. Diez, *Die Kunst der islamischen Volker* (Berlin, 1915); G. Marçaiś, *L'architecture musulmane d'Occident* (Paris, 1954) and *L'Art musulman* (Paris, 1927); D. T. Rice, *Islamic Art* (New York, 1965); E. T. Richmond, *Moslem Architecture* (London, 1926); A. H. Christie, "Islamic Minor Arts and their Influence upon European Works," in Arnold and Guillaume, *Legacy of Islam*, pp. 108–151.

For painting and decorative arts, see T. W. Arnold, *Painting in Islam* (Oxford, 1928); R. Ettinghausen, *Arab Painting* (London, 1962); M. S. Dimand, *A Handbook of Mohammedan Decorative Arts* (New York, 1958).

For al-Andalus and North Africa, see E. Sordo, *Moorish Spain* (London, 1963); H. Terrasse, *L'art hispano-muaresque des origines au xiii siècle* (Paris, 1932); L. Torrés Balbas, "Arte almohade, arte nazarí, arte mudéjar," *Ars Hispaniae*, 4 (Madrid, 1949), and "Los edificios hispano-musulmanes," *RIEI*, 1, (1953); E. Camps y Cazorla, *Arquitectura caliphal y mozárabe* (Madrid, 1929).

For music, see H. G. Farmer, *A History of Arabian Music to the Thirteenth Century* (London, 1929), "Music," in Arnold and Guillaume, *Legacy of Islam*, pp. 356–375, and "Clues for the Arabian Influence on European Musical Theory," in *JRAS*, 1929, pp. 119ff.; *The Ministrelsy of "The Arabian Nights"* (Bearsden, 1945); J. Robson and H. G. Farmer, *Ancient Arabian Musical Instruments as Described by al-Mufaḍḍal Ibn Salama* (Glasgow, 1958); J. Ribera y Tarragó, *La música de las cántigas* (Madrid, 1922); S. M. Imamuddin, "Music in Muslim Spain," *IC*, 33 (1959), pp. 147–150; B. R. d'Erlanger, *La musique arabe* (Paris, 1930–1959).

2. Ettinghausen, *Arab Painting*, pp. 12–13.

3. *Ibid.*, pp. 14–15.

4. M. S. Briggs, "Architecture," in Arnold and Guillaume, *Legacy of Islam*, p. 157; F. Chueca Goitia, *Historia de la architectura española* (Madrid, 1965).

5. L. Torres Balbás, "Ciudades — musulmanas de nueva fundación," in *Études d'Orientalisme*, vol. 2, pp. 781–803, lists a number of new cities, such as Caltayud, Elvira, Murcia, and Ubeda.

6. ʻAbd al-ʻAzīz Sālim, *Tārīkh al-muslimīn wa-āthāruhum fī-l-Andalus* (Beirut, 1962). p. 375.

7. Al-Maqqarī, *Nafḥ al-ṭīb*, vol. 2, pp. 35ff., supplies a number of poems in praise of Hispano-Arabic monuments.

8. *Ibid.*, p. 9.

9. *Ibid.*, p. 7.

10. *Ibid.*, pp. 79–80; cf. ʻAbd al-ʻAzīz Sālim, *Tārīkh*, pp. 292ff.

11. It is quoted in full by al-Maqqarī, *Nafḥ al-ṭīb*, vol. 4, pp. 177–208; Spanish trans. E. García Gómez, *Elogio del Islam español* (Madrid, 1934).

12. Al-Maqqarī, *Nafḥ al-ṭīb*, vol. 4, pp. 199ff.

13. *Ibid.*, vol. 1, p. 193.

14. *Ibid.*, vol. 4, pp. 203ff.; García Gómez, *Elogio*, p. 106.

15. Al-Maqqarī, vol. 4, p. 204; García Gómez, p. 107.

16. *Ibid.*
17. Al-Maqqarī, vol. 4, p. 205; García Gómez, p. 110.
18. Al-Maqqarī, vol. 1, pp. 187ff.
19. *Ibid.*, p. 145.
20. *Ibid.*, vol. 4, p. 207; García Gómez, p. 112.
21. Al-Maqqarī, vol. 1, pp. 187ff.
22. *Ibid.*, p. 53. The *dībāj* is a decorative silk brocade. Don Manuel Ocaña called my attention to the fact that the Spanish word *dibujo* (drawing) is derived from the Arabic *dībāj*.
23. Al-Maqqarī, vol. 1, p. 154.
24. *Ibid.*, p. 187.
25. *Ibid.*, vol. 4, p. 207; García Gómez, p. 116.
26. See Terrasse, *L'art hispano-mauresque*; A. van der Put, *Hispano-Moresque Ware of the XVth Century* (London, 1904); A. Wilson Frothington, *Lustreware of Spain* (New York, 1951).
27. See Ettinghausen, *Arab Painting*, pp. 67ff.
28. Christie, in Arnold and Guillaume, *Legacy of Islam*, p. 112.
29. *Ibid.*, p. 121.
30. *Ibid.*, p. 133.
31. *Ibid.*, p. 145.
32. See E. Lambert, "Histoire de la Grande Mosquée, de Cordoue au XIIe et IXe siècles," *AIEO*, 2 (1963); A.'Abd al-'Azīz Salem (Sālim), "Cronología de la mezquita mayor de Córdoba," *al-Andalus*, 19 (1954); L. Torres Balbás, "Nuevos datos sobre la mezquita de Córdoba cristianizada," *al-Andalus*, 14 (1949), and *La mezquita de Córdoba y las ruinas de Madīnat al-Zahrā'* (Madrid, 1952); K. Brisch, *Die Fenstergitter und Verwante ornamente der Hauptmosche von Cordoba* (Berlin, 1966); Christian Ewert, *Spanish-Islamische Systeme sich Kreuzender Bogen* (Berlin, 1968).
33. *Nafḥ al-ṭīb*, vol. 2, pp. 60ff.; cf. Sālim, *Tārīkh*, p. 377.
34. Al-Maqqarī, *Nafḥ al-ṭīb*, vol. 2, p. 84ff.
35. *Ibid.*, p. 92.
36. *Ibid.*, p. 84.
37. *Ibid.*, p. 60.
38. *Ibid.*, p. 89.
39. *Ibid.*, p. 84; Hitti, *History of the Arabs*, p. 594.
40. Al-Maqqarī, *Nafḥ al-ṭīb*, vol. 2, p. 84.
41. *Ibid.*, p. 88.
42. *Ibid.*, p. 85.
43. *Ibid.*, p. 88.
44. *Ibid.*, p. 95.
45. *Ibid.*, p. 87.
46. Torres Balbás, *La mezquita de Córdoba*.
47. Gómez Moreno, *Iglesias mozárabes*. See also his *El arte islámico en España y en el Mogreb*, vol. 5 of *Historia del Arte* (Madrid, n.d.), and *El arte árabe español hasta los almohades; arte mozárabe* in *Ars Hispaniae*, 3 (Madrid, 1951).
48. L. Torrés Balbás, "La primitiva Mezquita Mayor de Sevilla," al-Andalus, 11 (1946), 425–436; M. Ocaña Jiménez, "La inscripción fundacional de la la mezquita de Ibn Adabbas," *al-Andalus*, 12 (1947), 145–151.
49. Al-Maqqarī, *Nafḥ al-ṭīb*, vol. 2, pp. 35ff.
50. S. M. Imamuddin, "Gardens and Recreations in Muslim Spain," *IC*, 36 (1962), 159–166.
51. C. Sarthou Carreras, *Castillos de España* (Madrid, 1952).
52. R. Velázquez Bosco, *Medina Azzahara y Amiriya* (Madrid, 1912) and *Excavaciones en Medina Azzahara* (Madrid, 1923). See also B. Pavon Maldonado, *Memoria de la excavación de la mezquita de Medinat al-Zahra* (Madrid, 1966).
53. Al-Maqqarī, *Nafḥ al-ṭīb*, vol. 2, p. 105.

54. *Ibid.*, p. 65.
55. *Ibid.*, pp. 67ff.
56. *Ibid.*, pp. 112ff.
57. See A. F. Calvert, *The Alhambra* (London, 1907); M. Gómez-Morenco, *Alhambra y Generalife* (Coleccion Arte en España, nos. 15 and 17); L. Seco de Lucena, *La Alhambra como fué y como es* (Granada, 1935); M. Antequera, *La Alhambra y el Generalife* (Granada, 1959); A. Gallego y Burín, *La Alhambra* (Granada, 1963); Washington Irving, *Tales of the Alhambra* (Philadelphia, 1832); E. García Gómez et al., *The Alhambra* (*Forma y Color*, no. 10; Firenze, 1967); F. Prieto-Moreno, *Los jardines de Granada* (Madrid, 1962): J. Bermúdez Pareja, *La Alhambra: Alcazaba y Medina* (*Forma y Color*, no. 51).
58. H. Terrasse, in *EI* (1954), pp. 1020–1021.
59. Farmer, "Music," p. 356.
60. Farmer, *History of Music*, pp. 24ff.
61. *Al-'Iqd al-farīd*, vol. 6, p. 3.
62. *Ibid.*, p. 6.
63. *Ibid.*, p. 9.
64. *Ibid.*, p. 73ff.
65. *Ibid.*, p. 4.
66. *Ibid.*, p. 5.
67. *Al-Muqaddimah*, vol. 2, pp. 396ff.
68. *Ibid.*, p. 112.
69. *Ibid.*, p. 400.
70. *Ibid.*, vol. 2.
71. *Ibid.*, p. 401.
72. As quoted by Farmer, *History of Arabian Music*, p. 36.
73. *Ibid.*, p. 105.
74. *Ibid.*
75. *Ibid.*, pp. 127.
76. Ibn Khallikān, *Wafāyāt*, vol. 2, p. 501; Hitti, *History of the Arabs*, p. 372; al-Fārābī, *Kitāb al-mūsīqā al-kabīr*, ed. Ghitās 'Abd al-Malik Kashabah (Cairo, n.d.).
77. Būlāq, 1869.
78. Al-Maqqarī, *Nafḥ al-ṭīb*, vol. 4, p. 126.
79. *Ibid.*, pp. 136–137.
80. On Ziryāb, see H. G. Farmer, *EI*, under *Ziryāb*, sup., p. 266; Farmer, *History of Arabian Music*, pp. 128–130; al-Maqqarī, *Nafḥ al-ṭīb*, pp. 117–119.
81. *Al-'Iqd al-farīd*, vol. 6, p. 34.
82. Al-Maqqarī, *Nafḥ al-ṭīb*, vol. 4, pp. 118–119; Gayangos, *Mohammedan Dynasties*, vol. 1, p. 411.
83. Ibn 'Abd Rabbihi, *al-'Iqd al-farīd*, vol. 6, p. 34; Farmer, *History of Arabian Music*, p. 129.
84. Farmer, *History of Arabian Music*, p. 109.
85. Cf. S. M. Imamuddin, *Some Aspects of the Socio-Economic and Cultural History of Muslim Spain*, p. 179; al-Maqqarī, *Nafḥ al-ṭīb*, vol. 4, p. 125.
86. Al-Maqqarī, *Nafḥ al-ṭīb*, vol. 4, p. 127.
87. Ibn 'Abd Rabbihi devotes bk. 20 to the subject in *'Iqd al-farīd*; see above, Chapter 11.
88. Al-Maqqarī, *Nafḥ al-ṭīb*, vol. 4, p. 176; Farmer, "Music," p. 362.
89. Ṣā'id, *Ṭabaqāt*, p. 92; al-Ḍabbī, *Bughyah*, n. 813.
90. Al-Maqarrī, *Nafḥ al-ṭīb*, vol. 4, p. 176.
91. *Risālah*, in *ibid.*, p. 200; also García Gómez, *Elogio*, p. 98.
92. On some of these and other instruments, see Ibn Khaldūn, *al-Muqaddimah* vol. 2, p. 396; Farmer, "Music," pp. 360–361.
93. Al-Maqqarī, *Nafḥ al-ṭīb*, vol. 4, p. 204; García Gómez, *Elogio*, p. 107.

20. Aljamiado Literature

1. The most important works on *aljamiado* literature written in the nineteenth century were by Gayangos, Saavedra, Gil, and Guillén Robles, who were followed by Asín Palacios, Ribera, Menéndez Pidal, González Palencia, and Nykl. More recently, Galmés, Vernet, and Harvey have taken keen interest in the field and have come up with valuable editions and transliterations of texts.

It should be noted that Saavedra describes some 136 manuscripts, belonging for the most part to the collection of Gayangos. He was followed by Guillén Robles, who catalogued the Arabic manuscripts in the Biblioteca Nacional de Madrid, among which are a large number of *aljamiado* texts. Ribera and Asín Palacios catalogued the manuscripts of the Junta, now found in the Escuela de Estudios Árabes de Madrid. Gil et al. published very useful *aljamiado* texts. González Palencia describes ten manuscripts, four of which are aljamiado texts and proceed for the most part from the Biblioteca Provincial de Toledo.

Besides consulting a large body of manuscripts, I had occasion to examine the manuscript holdings of the Biblioteca Central de Barcelona and was able to find an *aljamiado* codex (BCB 680) of a religious character and a copy of a partial text of the Qur'ān containing various bilingual (Arabic and aljamiado) sections. According to Lévi-Provençal in the *EI*, a large number of manuscripts may also be found in the libraries of Paris, Algiers, Upsala, Morocco, and Tunisia. However, my search in the libraries of Morocco and Tunisia did not yield any material to justify his assertions. As of now, the bulk of the material is in the Biblioteca Nacional, the Escuela de Estudios Árabes, and the Real Academia de Historia, all in Madrid.

Following are the major works and articles dealing with *aljamiado*: *EI*, under *aljamía*; Pedro Alcalá, *Vocablulista arábigo en letra castellana* (Granada, 1505); M. Asín Palacios, "El original árabe de la novela aljamiada, 'el Baño de Zarieb,' " in *Homenaje de Menéndez Pidal*, vol. 1, pp. 378–388; J. Bosch Vilá, "Escrituras oscenses en aljamía hebraico árabe," in *Homenaje a Millás-Vallicrosa* (Barcelona, 1954), vol. 1, pp. 183–214; R. D. Cabanelas, "Juan de Segovia y el primer Alcorán trilingue," *al-Andalus*, 14 (1949), pp. 149–174; I. de la Cagicas, "Una carta aljamiada granadina," *Arabica*, 1 (1954), 271–275; A. Chejne, *Plegaria bilingue árabe-aljamiada de un morisco* (Madrid, 1973); M. Dánvila, "Ajuar de una morisca de Teruel en 1583," *BRAH*, 6 (1885), 410–439.

A. Galmés de Fuentes, ed., *El libro de las batallas* (Oviedo, 1967); *Historia de los Amores de Paris y Viana* (Madrid, 1970); "Interés en el orden lingüistico de la literatura española aljamiado-morisca," *Actes du X° Congres international de Linguistique* (Paris, 1965), pp. 542–543; and *Influencias sintácticas y estilísticas del árabe en la prosa medieval castellana* (Madrid, 1956).

P. de Gayangos, "Language and Literature of the Moriscos," *British and Foreign Review*, 8 (1839), 63–95, and "Tratado de legislación musulmana," *Memorial Histórico Español*, 5 (1853), 1–149.

P. Gil et al., *Colección de textos aljamiados* (Saragossa, 1888); A. Gonzáles Palencia, *Noticias y extractos de manuscritos árabes aljamiados* in *Miscelánea de estudios y textos árabes* (Madrid, 1915); F. Guillén Robles, *Leyendas moriscas* (Madrid, 1885–1888), *Leyenda de José y de Alejandro Magno* (Saragossa, 1888), and *Catálogo de los manuscritos árabes existentes en la Biblioteca Nacional de Madrid* (*BNM*) (Madrid, 1889).

L. P. Harvey, "Yusé Banegas, un moro noble de Granada bajo los Reyes Católicos" (MS., Extracto 3, *BNM* 245), *al-Andalus*, 21 (1956), 297–302; "The Literary Culture of the Moriscos (1492–1609)" (Ph.D. thesis, Oxford, 1958); W. Hoenerbach, *Spanish-islamische Urkunden aus der Zeit der Nasriden und Moriscos* (Bonn, 1965); P. Longàs, *Vida religiosa de los moriscos* (Madrid, 1915); D. Lópes, *Textos en aljamía portuguesa* (Lisbon, 1897); C. López Lillo, "Transcripción y notas a un manuscrito morisco del Corán" (MS. 18, *Junta*; now in EEAM) (M.A. thesis, University of Barcelona, 1966); M. Manzanares de Cirre, "Textos aljamiados," *BH*, 72 (1970), 311–327; R. Menéndez Pidal, "Poema de Yūçuf: materiales para su estudio," *RABM*, 8 (1902) (also Granada, 1952); J. Millás Vallicrosa, "Albaranes mallorquines en aljamiado hebraicoárabe," *Sefarad*, 4 (1944), 275–286; V. L.

Moraleda, "Edición de un manuscrito morisco del Corán" (M.A. thesis, University of Barcelona, 1965).

A. R. Nykl, "Aljamiado Literature," *RH*, 77 (1929), 448–465 and 587ff; J. Oliver Asín, "Un Morisco de Túnez," *al-Andalus*, 1 (1933), 409–450; J. Penella Roma, "Los moriscos españoles emigrados al norte de Africa después de la expulsión" (doctoral thesis, University of Barcelona, 1971); M. Rabadán, *Mahometanism Fully Explained*, English trans. J. Morgan (London, 1723; cf. British Museum, Harlow 7504); J. Ribera and M. Asín, *Manuscritos árabes y aljamiados de la Biblioteca de la Junta* (*Junta*) (Madrid, 1912); D. Romano, "Un texto en aljamía hebraico árabe," *Sefarad*, 29 (1969), 313–318.

D. E. Saavedra, *Discurso* (Address to the Real Academia de la Historia, delivered in 1878 and published in *MRAE*, 6 (1889), 141–328); "El alhadiz del baño de Zarieb," *Mundo Ilustrado*, 86 (1881); and "La historia de la ciudad de Alatón," *Revista Hispano-Americana*, 45 (1882).

G. Ticknor, *History of Spanish Literature* (Boston, 1866); J. Vernet, "Traducciones moriscas del Corán," in *Der Orient in der Forschung. Festschrift für Otto Spies* (Wiesbaden, 1967), pp. 686–705; J. Vernet and L. Moraleda, "Un Alcorán fragmentario en aljamiado," *BRABL*, 33 (1969–1970) 43–75.

2. See Saavedra, *Discurso*, pp. 144ff.

3. For the conditions of the Moriscos in general see Ferández y González, *Estado social y político de los mudéjares de Castilla.*

4. *Leyendas*, vol. 1, p. 13.

5. *Aljamiado* texts contain archaic expressions not found in contemporary literature. For instance, they preserve such words as *cibdad* (*ciudad*); *fazer* (*hazer*); *kerades* (*querays*). They also contain local expressions, dialectical variations, and a number of Arabisms of lexical and syntactical nature. In this connection, there are instances of literal translation of Arabic idioms, Arabic expressions, profuse use of the Arabic conjunction *waw* for the *que* often used in contemporary writings. For more details, see Galmés, *Historia de los Amores*, pp. 218ff., and his *Influencias sintácticas*.

6. The system of transliteration used in this work may be applied to aljamiado texts with the following exceptions and observations: The three Arabic vowels *u* (ـُ), *a* (ـَ), and *i* (ـِ), with the *u* and *a* above the consonant and *i* below it. In addition, a vowel *e* is used and written with *a* followed by an ālif (ا). The Arabic *u* (') expresses both the *o* and *u*.

Inasmuch as Arabic does not admit two joined consonants, the Moriscos used a vowel to separate them — as in *Gharan* for *ghran* (gran). For combinations such as *au* and *ia*, aljamiado writing inserts a *w* or *y* — as in *kuwando* for *kuando*.

As for the consonants:

ب invariably used for *b* and *v* and sometimes for *p*

بّ with *tashdīd* used for *p*

جّ with *tashdīd* used for ch

ش often used for *x* of Old Spanish, or *s* and *j*

لّ *ll*

نّ *ñ*

ق is often written with a dot above it

ف is written with a dot below it

For more details, see Menéndez Pidal, *Poema de José*, pp. 63ff.; Nykl, "Aljamiado Literature," pp. 448ff.; and Galmés, *Historia de los Amores*, pp. 149ff.

7. See MS. 4, BPT. And see González Palencia, *Noticias*, p. 126.

8. See Saavedra, *Discurso*, p. 276; *Alquiteb de la tafria* (BPT 336; González Palencia, *Noticias*, no. 8, p. 128; *BNM* 4908 and 4073; *Junta* 33). In all these manuscripts, Arabic and Latin scripts are used.

It is relevant in this connection to mention that the Arabic language was still common among the Mozárabs as late as the fourteenth century. In *Los Mozárabes de Toledo*, González Palencia edited some 1,151 documents dealing with contracts of sale, wills, loans, rental, guardianship litigation — all of which were written in Arabic among the Arabized Christians from 1083 to 1303. There are also documents using Hebrew and Arabic characters to write in the Arabic language which were used among the Jews of the same period. Colloquialisms, misspellings, and aljamiado expressions abound in those documents, some of which (nos. 981, 1098, etc.) state that the document was fully explained to the contracting parties in the language they understood best — whether Arabic or Romance. All this implies that bilingualism was still prevalent in Toledo, which fell to the Christians in 1085. See González Palencia, *Los Mozárabes de Toledo* (Madrid, 1930), vol. 1, pp. 129ff. It would seem also that the spelling of *aljamiado* terms was quite irregular and does not conform to later spelling, say of the fifteenth century, when spelling appears to have been standardized.

9. On this, see F. Codera, "Almacén de un librero morisco descubierto en Almonacid de la Sierra," *BRAH*, 5 (1884), 269–276.

10. Al-Samarqandī is Abū Layth Naṣr ibn Muḥammad ibn Ibrāhīm (d. 985). The full title of the work translated is *Tanbīh al-ghāfilīn wa-idāḥ sabīl al-murīdīn* (Cairo, A.H. 1326), which was known to the Moriscos as *Kitāb Samarqandī* and is completely extant (*BNM* 4871).

11. Likewise, the *Alquiteb de la tafria* by Abū-l-Qāsim 'Ubaydallah, was translated into *aljamiado*; see González Palencia, *Noticias*, no. 9, pp. 128ff. It deals with the performance of religious duties and legal questions.

12. For instance, *Shihāb al-akhbār* (*BNM* 5354) by Hakmūn ibn Abī 'Abdallah Muḥammad ibn Salamah. In connection with translation, it is relevant to indicate that Arabic-Spanish dictionaries were composed. Jean León of Granada, a convert to Christianity, composed such a dictionary in 1524 (Escorial 598). In the seventeenth century another stout dictionary, consisting of some 780 pages, was composed (Escorial 599).

13. The juridical work *Ta'rīf al-mukhtaṣar fī-l-fiqh* (*BNM* 4870) by Abū 'Abdallah al-Qāsim 'Ubaydallah ibn al-Ḥusayn ibn Shihāb (d. 1007).

14. See below, this chapter.

15. See below, this chapter.

16. See the introduction to the manuscript holdings in the Biblioteca de la Junta.

17. *BNM* 5081; cf. *Junta* 12, p. 1.

18. For instance, see manuscript copy of the Qur'ān in *BNM* 4983.

19. See *Junta* 18, 25, and 17, where there are numerous chapter with *aljamiado* lines, besides marginal annotations. López Lillo, "Transcripción y notas" (cf. *Junta* 17 and 25) consists of a transliteration from Sūrahs 41–56 inclusive. See also Vernet, "Traducciones moriscas del Corán"; Moraleda, "Edición de un manuscrito morisco del Corán"; Vernet and Moraleda, "Un alcorán fragmentario en aljamiado." Códice *aljamiado* (BCB 680) contains a number of Prophetic Traditions, besides a few passages in Arabic and aljamiado. BCB 1420, the Corán in 98 fols., contains a few chapters of the Qur'ān in Arabic, a bilingual section consisting of an exhortation to God (fols. 38–47), and various religious items dealing with Prophetic Traditions and rituals (fols. 80–98). Fols. 38–47 have been ed. by Chejne, *Plegaria bilingue árabe-aljamiado*.

20. *Junta* 47 and 62.

21. Numerous catechisms are extant (*BNM* 5223, 5346, 5377, 5383, 5384, 5385, 5389 etc.; *Junta* 55 and 56).

22. *BNM* 5252. Similarly, BPT no. 1 deals with admonitions, explanations of religious duties, good conduct, detachment from the pleasures of this world so that eternal salvation

will be attained. Cf. González Palencia, *Noticias*, pp. 120ff.; *Alquiteb de la Tafria* (*BNM* 4908); Saavedra, *Discurso*, p. 247; *Junta*, p. 131; González Palencia, pp. 128ff., where similar instructions are given for performing one's religious duties: ablution, prayer, fasting, burial, pilgrimage, and so on.

23. *BNM* 5273.

24. *BNM* 5378.

25. *BNM* 5377.

26. He is Sharaf al-Dīn Abū 'Abdallah Muḥammad ibn Sa'īd. A manuscript of the poem is in Escorial 248.

27. A commentary of the Burdah (*Sharḥ al-burdah*) was done by the Andalusian Abū 'Abdallah al-Ilbīrī (Escorial 282).

28. *BNM* 5374.

29. *BNM* 4953.

30. See above, this chapter.

31. The manuscript consists of 216 folios and sixty chapters. It was published in *Memorial Histórico Español*, 5 (1853).

32. It is the *Caxtigox para lax gentex*, consisting of 458 fols. (*Junta* 8).

33. It is the *Alquiteb de preicax y ejemplox* (*Junta* 53).

34. The *Tratado jurídico* (*BNM* 4987) has 153 fols. See also *Alquiteb de la tafria* (BPT 336); 286 fols.), which deals with ablution, prayer, almsgiving, fasting, burial, pilgrimage, Holy War (*jihād*), contracts, testimonies, drink, food, hunting, manumission, marriage, divorce, etc. Cf. González Palencia, *Noticias*, no. 8, p. 128; *al-Ta'rīf al-mukhtaṣar* (*BNM* 4870), which was translated from Arabic into *aljamiado*.

35. *BNM* 5053; see also *Miscelánea* (*Junta* 9), where the story of the *Mi'rāj* appears along with poems in praise of Muḥammad and traditions about his death. *Caxtigox para lax gentex* (*Junta* 8) contains a number of traditions on the birth of Muḥammad.

36. See below, Chapter 20.

37. *BNM* 5337.

38. *Códice de miscelánea* (*Junta* 3, pt. 3); *Códice de miscelánea* (*Junta* 4) also contains various items concerning 'Alī, the son-in-law of the Prophet, traditions about the caliph 'Umar, the emergence of the Turks, and several Islamic personalities.

39. Mainly history of prophets, who include such figures as Abraham, Job, Moses, Jacob, and Solomon (*BNM* 5305, 5253).

40. *Recontamiento de Rey Alixandre* (*BNM* 5254); Guillén Robles, *Leyenda de José y de Alejandro Magno*; Saavedra, *Discurso*, pp. 159ff. It should be indicated that fragments of unknown authorship were written in Arabic during the sixteenth century; among several stories in them is that of Alexander the Great (Escorial 1668). For an Arabic version of the story of Alexander, see Muḥ al-Shāṭibī, *Kitāb fīh qiṣṣat dhī al-Qarnaym* (*BNM* 5379).

The principal works on Alexander are Florencio Janer, *Libro de Alexandre* (Madrid, 1864); E. García Gómez, *Un texto árabe occidental de la leyenda de Alejandro* (Madrid, 1929); A. R. Nykl, "Aljamiado Literature," pp. 466ff. (transliterates the *aljamiado* legend).

For the Syriac and Ethiopic versions of the legend of Alexander, see E. A. Wallis Budge, *The History of Alexander the Great* (Cambridge, 1888) and *The Life and Exploits of Alexander the Great* (London, 1896); Paul Meyer, *Alexandre le Grand dans la littérature française du Moyen Âge* (Paris, 1888).

41. See Qu'rān 18:83f.

42. *BNM* 5292. The poem of Joseph (*BNM* 247) was edited by H. Morf (Leipzig, 1883). Cf. Menéndez Pidal, "Poema de Yuçuf." It is of interest here to mention that 'Umar Ibn Ibrāhīm Ibn 'Umar al-Awsī (d. 1350) of Murcia is supposed to have composed *Kitāb zahr al-kamām fī qiṣṣat Yūsuf 'alayh al-salām* (Escorial 1659).

43. Qu'rān 12.

44. *Leyendas*, vol. 1, pp. 117ff.; *BNM* 5305, 4 and 5.

45. This attitude is already conveyed in Qu'rān 19:22ff. See al-Shāṭibī, *Qiṣṣat Yaḥyā wa-Maryam wa-'Īsā* (*BNM* 5375).

46. *Leyendas*, vol., 1, pp. 181–224; cf. Saavedra, *Discurso*, pp. 164ff.; *Junta* 3, 2.

47. *Leyendas*, vol., 1, pp. 225–266; cf. *BNM* 5305, 6.
48. *Leyendas*, pp. 267–280.
49. *Ibid*., pp. 281–314; cf. *BNM* 5305, 9.
50. *Leyendas*, pp. 315–381; for another version of Moses' dialogue, see González Palencia, *Noticias*, no. 10, 7; *BNM* 5305, 1.
51. *Leyendas*, vol., 2, pp. 27–96.
52. *Ibid*., pp. 97–130.
53. *Ibid*., pp. 131–144.
54. *Ibid*., pp. 145–158; cf. *BNM* 5337, 1.
55. *Leyendas*, vol., 2, pp. 159–166.
56. *Ibid*., pp. 167–216; cf. *BNM* 5337, 6.
57. *Leyendas*, vol. 2, pp. 217–232.
58. *Ibid*., pp. 233–258.
59. *Ibid*., pp. 259–268.
60. *Ibid*., pp. 269–300; cf. *BNM* 5053 and *Junta* 9, 3.
61. *Leyendas*, vol. 2, pp. 301–324; cf. *BNM* 5337, 4.
62. *Leyendas*, vol. 2, pp. 325–358; cf. *BNM* 5337, 2.
63. *Leyendas*, vol. 2, pp. 359–88; González Palencia, *Noticias*, no. 10, 13; and *Junta* 9, 4.
64. *Leyendas*, vol. 3, pp. 65–82; cf. *BNM* 4953.
65. *Leyendas*, vol. 3, pp. 83–186; *BNM* 5337, 8.
66. *Leyendas*, vol. 3, p. 187.
67. *Ibid*., pp. 201–230; cf. González Palencia, *Noticias*, no. 10, 1.
68. *Leyendas*, vol. 3, pp. 231–246.
69. *Ibid*., pp. 247–277; *BNM* 5337, 3 and 7.
70. *Leyendas*, vol. 3, pp. 278–286.
71. *Ibid*., pp. 287–306.
72. *Ibid*., pp. 307–320; cf. *BNM* 5301.
73. *Leyendas*, vol. 3, pp. 321–350.
74. *Ibid*., pp. 351–388; cf. *Junta* 4, 2.
75. Saavedra, "El alhadiz del baño de Zarieb."
76. First transliterated by Saavedra in *Revista Histórica* (Barcelona), 3 (1876), 33ff.; see Galmés's critical edition comparing the various texts, *Historia de los amores*.
77. Asín Palacios, "El original árabe."
78. Galmés, *Historia de los amores*, pp. 21ff.
79. *BNM* 4944, 5302.
80. "Memoria de los cuatros del año" (*BNM* 4937); also *BNM* 5306, which deals with the months of the year.
81. "Libro y traslado de buenas doctrinas y castigos y buenas costumbres" (BNM 5267).
82. "Litanía para pedir agua" (*Junta* 23) and "Alquiteb de rogar por agua" (*Junta* 30).
83. "Libro de dichox marabilloxox" (*Junta* 22).
84. *BNM* 5300.
85. "El libro de moriscos" (*BNM* 5373).
86. "Alhaicales" (*BNM* 5380).
87. *BNM* 4908.
88. *BNM* 5452.
89. *BNM* 5073.
90. *BNM* 5238.
91. Saavedra, *Discurso*, pp. 169ff.
92. *Ibid*., pp. 155ff. El Mancebo de Arévalo wrote *Tafcira* (*Junta* 62; also *BNM* 245.

21. The Islamic Legacy

1. Andrés, *Dell' origine, progressi e stato attuale d'ogni letteratura*.
2. Sarton, *Introduction to the History of Science*.
3. Asín Palacios, *La escatología musulmana y la Divina Comedia*.

4. Ribera, *La música de las cántigas* and *Disertaciones y opúsculos* (Madrid, 1928).

5. González Palencia, *Moros y Cristianos en España medieval* and *Historia de la literatura arábigo-española*.

6. Farmer, *A History of Arabian Music to the Thirteenth Century* and "Clues for the Arabian Influence on European Musical Theory."

7. Nykl, *Hispano-Arabic Poetry* and *Troubadour Studies*.

8. Arnold and Guillaume, eds., *The Legacy of Islam*. One may add Hitti, *History of the Arabs*, pp. 567ff.; Lévi-Provençal, *La civilización arabe en España*; S. M. Imam al-Dīn, "The Influence of Spanish Muslim Civilization on Europe," *IL*, 11 (1959); De Lacy O'Leary, "Scientific Influence of Andalus," *IL*, 9 (1957), 331ff.; H. A. R. Gibb, "The Influence of Islamic Culture in Medieval Europe," *Bulletin of the John Rylands Library*, 38 (1955). Jean Lacam, *Les Sarrazins dans le haut Moyen Age français* (Paris, 1965).

For the general study of the Islamic influences on European sciences and art, see also Haskins, *Studies in the History of Medieval Science*; Dunlop, *Arabic Science in the West*; M. Steinschneider, "Die europäischen Übersetzungen aus dem Arabischen bis Mitte des XVII Fhdt.," *Sitzungsberichte der Akademie der Wissenschaften zu Wien*, 149 (1905) and 151 (1906); F. Gabrieli, "The Transmission of Learning and Literary Influences to Western Europe," in *The Cambridge History of Islam* (Cambridge, 1970), pp. 851–889. On astronomy, see Carmody, *Arabic Astronomical and Astrological Sciences*. On medicine, see Leclerc, *Histoire de la médecine arabe*; D. Campbell, *Arabian Medicine*; Khairallah, *Outline of Arabic Contributions to Medicine and the Allied Sciences*. On art, see E. Mâle, "Les influences arabes dans l'art roman," *Revue de Deux Mondes*, ser. 17, vol. 18 (1923); L. Bréhier, "Les influences musulmanes dans l'art roman du Puy," *Journal des Savants* (1936); G. Moreno, *Iglesias mozárabes, arte español de los siglos IX a XI* (Madrid, 1919); G. Gaillard, "La catalogue entre l'art de Cordoue et l'art roman," *SI*, 6 (1956). See also K. Mommsen, *Goethe und 1001 Nacht* (Berlin, 1960), *Goethe und die Moallakat* (Berlin, 1961), and *Goethe und der Islam* (Stuttgart, 1965); A. Mieli, *La science arabe et son rôle dans l'evolution scientifique mondiale* (Leiden, 1966).

9. Chejne, *The Arabic Language*.

10. Amari, *Storia dei musulmani di Sicilia*. Cf. R. Menéndez Pidal, "España como eslabón entre el cristianismo y el Islam," *RIEEI*, 1 (1953), 1–20.

11. Amari, *Storia*, as quoted by Hitti, *History of the Arabs*.

12. Translations from Arabic into Latin were not limited to one single place, but were carried on at Barcelona, Tarazona, Segovia, Leon, Pamplona, Toulouse, Narbonne, and Marseilles. See Haskins, *Studies in the History of Medieval Sciences*, p. 10; J. W. Thompson, "The Introduction of Arabic Sciences into Lorraine in the Tenth Century," *ISIS*, 38 (1929), 189ff.; M. C. Welborn, "Lotharingia as a Center of Arabic and Scientific Influence in the Eleventh Century," *ISIS*, 40 (1931), 188ff.; A. Clerval, *Les écoles de Chartres au Moyen Âge* (Paris, 1895); F. Wüstenfeld, *Die Ubersetzungen arabischer Werke in das Lateinnische Zeit dem XI Jahrhundert* (Göttingen, 1877).

For Toledo in particular, see the valuable work of J. M. Millás Vallicrosa, *Las traducciones orientales en los manuscritos de la Biblioteca Catedral de Toledo* (Madrid, 1942). This work contains inventories of books owned by clerics and deposited in the Cathedral of Toledo. Most of the works deal with philosophy, theology, astronomy, astrology, mathematics, medicine, alchemy, and agriculture. See also J. A. Jourdain, *Recherches critiques sur l â*ge et l'origine *des traductions latines d'Aristotes et sur les commentaires grecs ou aralies employés par les docteurs scholastiques* (Paris, 1843); G. Théry, *Tolède, grande ville de la renaissance médiévale* (Oran, 1944); J. M. Millás Vallicrosa, "La corriente de las traducciones científicas de origen oriental hasta fines del siglo XIII," *JWL*, 2 (1954–1955), 416ff.

13. A. González Palencia, *El Arzobispo Don Raimundo de Toledo* (Barcelona, 1942).

14. M. Alonso, "Traducciones del arcediano Domingo Gundisalvo," *al-Andalus*, 12 (1947), 295–338.

15. On Gerard of Cremona, see Sarton, *Introduction to the History of Science*, vol. 2, pp. 334–344.

16. M. Alonso, "Traducciones del arábe al latin por Juan Hispano (Ibn-Dāwūd)," *al-Andalus*, 17 (1952), 129–151.

17. On the role of Peter the Venerable, see Kritzeck, *Peter the Venerable*, pp. 51ff.

18. On the works of Alfonso X, see A. G. Solalinde, *Antología de Alfonso X el Sabio*; J. Soriano Viguera, *Contribución al conocimiento de los trabajos astronómicos desarrollados en la escuela de Alfonso X, el Sabio* (Madrid, 1916); O. J. Tallgren, *Los nombres árabes de las estrellas y la transcripción alfonsina* (Madrid, 1925).

19. Arnold and Guillaume, *Legacy of Islam*, pp. 272–273.

20. *Ibid*. On the Arabic influence on Lull, see M. Asín Palacios, "El lulismo exagerado," in *Cultura española* (1906); J. Ribera, "Orígines de la filosofía de Raimundo Lulio," in *Homenaje a Menéndez Pelayo*, pp. 191–216.

21. On this point, see above, Chapter 6.

22. The *Mi'rāj* is reproduced in Alfonso X's *Crónica general de España*, in Solalinde, *Antología*, pp. 92–95. Translations into French and Latin were also made at Alfonso's court. See the editions of *Mi'rāj* of Muñoz and Cerulli.

23. See Ribera, *Música de las cántigas*.

24. See Soriano Viguera, *Contribución al conocimiento de los trabajos astronómicos* and Tallgren, *Los nombres árabes*.

25. Daniel, *Islam and the West*, p. 84, n. 4. In *Summa contra gentiles, Summa Theologica*, and other works, St. Thomas makes ample references to Muslim authors, mainly Averröes.

26. See Hourani, *Averroës*.

27. For instance, *Convivio*, bk. 2, p. 9; *Epístola*, bks. 6, 7, p. 3; etc., as they appear in E. Moore et al., *Le opère di Dante Alighieri* (Oxford, 1963).

28. *Inferno*, bk. 28, pp. 22–63.

29. *Ibid*., p. 22, trans. A. Gilbert, *Dante and his Comedy* (New York, 1963), pp. 81–82.

30. *Inferno*, bk. 4, p. 129.

31. *Ibid*., p. 143.

32. *Ibid*., p. 144.

33. *Ibid*., pp. 64–151.

34. J. Muñoz Sendino, ed., *La escala de Mahoma* (Madrid, 1949).

35. E. Cerruli, ed., *Il "Libro della Scala" e la questione della fonti-arabo-espagnole della Divina Comedia* (Vatican, 1949); G. Levi Della Vida, "Nuova luce sulle fonti islamiche della *Divina Commedia*," *al-Andalus*, 14 (1949), and "Dante e l'Islam," *Accademia Nazionale dei Lincei*, 12 (1957).

36. For more recent studies, see T. Silverstein, "Dante and the Legacy of the Mi'rāj," *JNES*, 11 (1952), 89ff., 187ff.; V. Cantarino, "Dante and Islam: History and Analysis of a Controversy," in *A Dante Symposium* (Chapel Hill, 1965); M. Rodinson, "Dante et l'Islam d'après des travaux récents," *Revue de l'Histoire des Religions*, 124 (1951).

37. On Ibn al-'Arabī, see Afifī, *The Mystical Philosophy*.

38. On the influence of Arabic on European languages, see Dozy and Englemann, *Supplément aux dictionnaires arabes* and Dozy *Glossaire des mots espagnols et portugais dérivés de l'arabe*. See also L. Eguilaz, *Glosario etimológico de las palabras españolas de orígen oriental*; E. Lokotsch, *Etymologisches Worterbuch der europaischen Worter orientalischen Ursprungs* (Heidelberg, 1927); A. Steiger, *Origin and Spread of Oriental Words in European Languages* (New York, 1963) and *Contribución a la fonética del hispano-árabe y de los arabismos en el ibero-románico y el siciliano* (Madrid, 1932); L. Devic, *Dictionnaire etymologique des mots français d'origine orientale* (Paris, 1876); H. Lammens, *Remarques sur les mots français dérivés de l'arabe* (Beirut, 1890); E. Littmann, *Morgenländische Vörter in Deutschen* (Tübingen, 1924).

39. Nafis Ahmad, *Muslim Contribution to Geography* (Lahore, 1943).

40. See above, Chapter 13.

41. See above, Chapter 14.

42. T. Irving, "Arab Tales in Medieval Spanish," *IL*, 7 (1955), 509–514. See also

González Palencia, *Historia de la literatura arábigo-española*, Ch. 15, and *Moros y cristianos*, pp. 35ff.; M. Menéndez Pelayo, *Orígenes de la novela* (Madrid, 1962), esp. vol. 1.

For the epic, see Luṭfī 'Abd al-Badī', *La épica árabe y su influencia en la épica castellana* (Santiago, Chile, 1964); J. T. Monroe, "The Historical *Arjūza* of Ibn 'Abd Rabbihi, a Tenth-Century Hispano-Arabic Epic Poem," *JAOS*, 91 (1971), 67–95.

43. A recent critical edition of *Kalīlah wa-Dimnah* is by J. E. Keller and R. White Linker (Madrid, 1967); on its influence on the Spanish see Menéndez Pelayo, *Orígenes*, vol. 1, pp. 28ff.

44. Madrid, 1968. *El Conde Lucanor* reveals that its author, Juan Manuel, had great familiarity with Arabic and Arabic themes. In fact, it contains various stories about Arab personalities — al-Mu'tamid of Seville, the Caliph al-Ḥakam II, a Moorish lady — besides using of Arabic words and referring to Arabic musical instruments.

45. Ed. J. Keller (Madrid, 1958).

46. Ed. J. Keller (Madrid, 1961). The work consists of a compilation of 395 stories arranged alphabetically. It is joined by another collection of 58 stories entitled *Libro de los gatos*.

47. Ed. Juan Corominas (Madrid, 1967). *El libro de buen amor* resembles the Arabic genre called *adab*. It consists of fables, stories, maxims about love in its profane and spiritual aspects. It contains numerous Arabic words used with propriety besides Arabic themes pertaining to Moorish dancers.

48. Ed. A. González Palencia (Madrid, 1948). The work consists of proverbs, admonitions, and fables derived from Arabic sources.

49. Ed. A. González Palencia, *Versiones castellanas del Sendebar* (Madrid, 1946). On its influence on Spanish literature, see Menéndez Pelayo, *Orígenes*, vol. 1, pp. 42ff.

50. Ed. by F. Lauchert in *Romanische Forschung*, 7 (1893), 33–402. On its influence, see Menéndez Pelayo, *Orígenes*, vol. 1, pp. 47ff.

51. See Menéndez Pelayo, *Orígenes*, vol. 1, pp. 140ff.

52. J. Monroe, *Islam and the Arabs in Spanish Scholarship* (Leiden, 1970); M. Manzanares de Cirre, *Arabistas españoles del siglo XIX* (Madrid, 1972).

Bibliographies

Bibliography of Catalogues and Manuscripts

Catalogues

NOTE: For a guide to Arabic manuscripts throughout the world, see A. J. W. Huisman *Les manuscrits arabes dans le monde* (Leiden, 1967) and A. Chejne, *Hispano-Arabic Manuscripts in the Libraries of Morocco and Tunisia* (in preparation). Only catalogues consulted are listed below, along with the abbreviations used for them elsewhere.

BNM. F. Guillén Robles. *Catálogo de los manuscritos árabes existentes en la Biblioteca Nacional de Madrid*. Madrid, 1889.

BRAH. *Boletín de la Real Academia de Historia*. Madrid, 1860.

Casiri. M. Casiri. *Bibliotheca Arabico-Hispana Escurialensis*. 2 vols. Madrid, 1760–1770.

Escorial. H. Derenbourg et al. *Manuscrits arabes de l'Escurial*. 3 vols. Paris, 1884–1941.

IEIM, *Manuscritos en el Instituto de Estudios Islámicos en Madrid* (for the most part, on microfilm).

Junta. J. Ribera and M. Asín Palacios. *Manuscritos árabes y aljamiados de la Biblioteca de la Junta*. Madrid, 1912.

Marrākush. "Ibn Yūsuf Collection; catalogue en manuscript" by al-Ṣiddīq Ibn al-ʻArabī.

Qayrawīn. Qayrawīn Mosque Library, Fez.

Rabat. E. Lévi-Provençal. *Les manuscrits arabes de Rabat*. Paris, 1921.

Rabat-A. Awqāf Collection, General Library.

Rabat-AR. I. S. Allouche and A. Regragui. *Les manuscrits arabes de Rabat*. 2 vols. Paris, 1954–1958.

Rabat-IK. Ibrāhīm al-Kattānī. *al-Makhṭūṭāt al-ʻārabiyyah fī-l-khizānah al-ʻāmmah*. MS.

Rabat-K. The Kattānī Collection, General Library.

Rabat-R. The Royal Library.

Tetuan. General Library of Tetuan.

Zaytūnah. ʻAbd al-Ḥāfiẓ Manṣūr. *Fihris makhṭuṭāt al-maktabah al-aḥmadiyyah bi-Tūnis*. Beirut, 1969.

Zaytūnah-A. The Aḥmadiyyah Collection, Tunis.

Manuscripts

CLASSICAL TEXTS

al-ʻAbdarī, Abū Muḥammad. *al-Riḥlah al-maghribiyyah*. Escorial 1738. Published and edited by Muḥ. al-Fāsī. Rabat, 1968.
Abū ʻAbdallah al-Ilbīrī. *Sharḥ al-burdah*. Escorial 282.
Abū Ḥamīd al-Gharnāṭī. *al-Mughrib ʻan ʻajā'ib al-Maghrib*. *IEIM*-C-8. *BRAH* 23.
Abū Ḥayyān, Muḥ. Ibn Yūsuf. *al-Baḥr*. Rabat-K 2027.
———. *I'rāb al-Qur'ān*. Rabat-AR (D814) 676.
Abū-l-Ṣalt al-Dānī (d. 1134). *Ajwibat Abī-l-Ṣalt ʻan masā'il su'ila ʻanhā*. Escorial 646, no. 2, being a dialogue on astronomical problems.
———. *Taqwīm al-dhihn*. Escorial 646.
al-Aʻlam al-Shantarī (d.1083). *Taḥṣīl ʻayn al-dhahab fī maʻdan al-ʻArab jawhar al-adab*. Zaytūnah 3967.
al-Anṣārī al-Jayyānī, Burhān al-Dīn. *Dīwān al-shudhūr wa-taḥqīq al-umūr*. Rabat-AR (D1450) 2668; Rabat-R 1035, 1369.
al-Anṣārī al-Qurṭubī. *Manẕūmah fī-l-qirā'āt*. Rabat-AR (D503) 645.
al-Awsī, ʻUmar Ibn Ibrāhīm Ibn ʻUmar (d. 1350). *Kitāb zahr al-kamām fī qiṣṣat Yūsuf ʻalayh al-salām*. Escorial 1659; Rabat-AR (D614) 2212, (D1290) 2213.
al-Azdī, ʻAbdallah Ibn Abī Jamrah (d. 1296). *Bahjat al-nufūs wa-taḥlīluhā*. Rabat-AR (D621) 729.
al-Azdī, Ṣādiq al-Dīn (d. 1172). *al-Muqaddimah al-qurṭubiyyah*. Rabat-AR (D1164) 1354; Rabat-R 7198, 7222.
al-Azrafī, Muḥammad Ibn ʻAlī (d. 1491). *Badā'iʻ al-sulk fī ṭabā'iʻ al-mulk*. Zaytūnah 5068.
al-Bakrī, Abū ʻUbayd (d. 1094). *al-Masālik wa-l-mamālik*. *IEIM*-A-6; A-7; A-8.
———. *al-Mughrib fī dhikr bilād Ifrīqiyah wa-l-Maghrib*. *IEIM*-A-1.
al-Buqāʻī, Burhān al-Dīn (d. 1480). *al-Juz' al-thānī min aswāq al-ashwāq*. Escorial 468.
Dhikr bilād al-Andalus. Rabat 85.
Diccionario árabe español. Escorial 599; composed in the seventeenth century.
al-Ḥillī, Muḥammad Ibn ʻAlī (d. 1116). *Kitāb nuzhat al-mushtāq wa-rawḍat al-ʻushshāq*. Escorial 471.
Ibn ʻAbbād al-Rundī (d. 1390). *Fatḥ al-tuḥfah wa-idā'at al-sudfah*. Rabat-AR (D.984) 784.
———. *Ghayth al-mawāhib*. Rabat-AR (D890) 1115; Rabat-K 159; Rabat-R 4144.
———. *Kayfiyat al-duʻā' bi-asmā' Allah al-ḥusnā*. Rabat-AR (D1071) 1291; and (D1148) 1292; Rabat-R 8832.
Ibn al-Abbār, Muḥammad (d. 1260). *Ansāb al-ʻArab wa-l-ʻAjam*. Rabat-K 1437.
———. *Bahjat al-majālis wa-uns al-majālis*. *BRAH* 14, 16; Rabat-AR (D1692) 1901; Rabat-K 4007; Zaytūnah 4676.
———. *Durar fī-l-maghāzī wa-l-siyar*. Rabat-K 1447.
———. *Kitāb al-intiqā' fī akhbār al-thalāthah al-fuqahā'*. Escorial 1807.
———. *Kitāb fī tarājim al-rijāl*. Rabat-K 632.
Ibn ʻAbd al-Quddūs al-Qurṭubī (d. 1068). *Kitāb al-miftāḥ fī-ikhtilāf al-qirā'āt al-sabʻah*. *BNM* 5255.
Ibn ʻAbd al-Raḥmān al-Anṣārī (d. 1350). *Wathā'iq*. Rabat-AR (D1418); Rabat-R 3507; Marrākush 501.
Ibn Abī-l-Khiṣāl al-Ghāfiqī (d. 1147). *Kitāb al-manāqib al-ʻashrah*. Escorial 1745, no. 2.
———. *Zikr azwāj al-nabī*. Escorial 1745, no. 4.
———. *Ẓill al-ghanāmah wa-ṭawq al-ḥamāmah*. Escorial 1745, no. 3.
Ibn Abī Rabīʻ, ʻUbaydallah Ibn Aḥmad (d. 1289). *Barnāmaj*. Escorial 1785, no. 3.
Ibn Abī Ṭālib al-Qaysī (d. 1045). *Tafsīr al-Qur'ān*. *BNM* 4945.
Ibn Aflaḥ, Muḥammad. *Kitāb al-hay'ah*. Escorial 910.
Ibn ʻArabī, Muḥyy al-Dīn. *Durr al-durar*. Rabat-IK (D1986) 3537; Rabat-K 2681.
———. *al-Kibrīt al-aḥmar fī bayān al-kashf al-akbar*. Rabat-K 2585.
———. *Kitāb al-kashf wa-l-katm*. Rabat-K 518.

Ibn Arqām, Abū Yaḥyā (d. 1356). *al-sifr al-thānī min kitāb al-iḥtifāl fī istifā taḍayyuf mā li-l-khayl min al-aḥwāl*. Escorial 902.
Ibn 'Asākir, Muḥammad. *Tawāshī' al-tawshīḥ*: Escorial 438.
Ibn 'Āṣim, Muḥammad (d. 1427). *Ḥadā'iq al-azhār fī mustaḥsan al-ajwibah al-muḍḥikah*. Rabat-AR (D593) 1935; Rabat-R 1141, 3190.
Ibn Aslam al-Ghāfiqī, Muḥammad (12th c.). *Kitāb al-murshid fī ṭibb al-'ayn*. Escorial 835.
Ibn 'Aṭiyyah, Abū Bakr Muḥammad. *Fahrasah*. Escorial 1733, 1785.
———. *Tafsīr surat al-mā'idah*. *BNM* 4874.
Ibn al-Azdī, Muḥammad Ibn Aṣbagh (d. 1223). *al-jihādfī abwāb al-jihād*. Marrākush 216.
Ibn Badr, Muḥammad Ibn 'Umar. *Kitāb fī ikhtiṣār al-jabr wa-l-muqābalah*. Escorial 936; ed. and Spanish trans. Sánchez Pérez (Madrid, 1916).
Ibn Bājjah. *Jawāb 'alā risālat al-rāhib*. Escorial 538, no. 12.
Ibn Banna al-Tujībī, Abū-l-'Abbās. *al-Mabāḥith al-aṣliyyah min jumlat al-ṭarīqah al-ṣufiyyah*. Rabat-AR (D984) 1137; Rabat-IK (D1674) 3709; Rabat-R 7670.
———. *Sharḥ al-mabāḥith al-aṣliyyah*. Rabat-IK (D2284) 3590.
Ibn Gharsiyyah, Abū 'Āmir. *Risālah khāṭaba Abū 'Āmir Ibn Gharsiyyah Abā 'Abdallah Ibn al-Ḥaddād yu'ātibuh bihā wā yufaḍḍil al-'Ajam 'alā al-'Arab*. Escorial 538, no. 10; cf. 538, nos. 11 and 12.
Ibh Ḥabīb, 'Abd al-Malik. *al-Tārīkh al-kabīr*. *IEIM*-A-9.
Ibn Hānī. *Dīwān*. Marrākush 143; Zaytūnah 4566, 4567, 4568.
Ibn Ḥazm. *Ḥijjat al-wadā'*. *IEIM*-A-12.
———. *Marātib al-'ulūm*. Rabat-A 209.
Ibn Ḥijjah, Abū Bakr Ibn 'Alī (d. 1434). *Balāgh al-amal fī fann al-zajal*. Zaytūnah 4467.
Ibn Hishām, Muḥammad Ibn Aḥmad. *Kitāb al-radd 'alā al-Zubaydī fī laḥn al-'awāmm*. Escorial 46.
Ibn Hudhayl, 'Alī Ibn 'Abd al-Raḥmān. *Kitāb tuḥfat al-anfus wa-shi'ār sukkān al-Andalus*. *BNM* 5095; Escorial 1652; Rabat-AR (D904) 1397, and (D1108) 1398; Rabat-R 733.
Ibn Idrīs, Abū Bakr Ṣafwān. *Shi'r al-muwalladīn*. Escorial 355.
Ibn 'Iyāḍ, Abū Faḍl 'Iyād, *Qaṣīdah fī madḥ khayr al-bariyyah*. Rabat-AR (D774) 886.
———. *al-Shifā' bi-ta'rīf ḥuqūq al-muṣṭafā*. Rabat-AR (D1109) 785; Rabat-R 5; and Zaytūnah-A 1216. (Many other copies).
Ibn Jizzī al-Kalbī, Muḥammad (d. 1340). *Taqrīb al-wuṣūl ilā 'ilm al-uṣūl*. Rabat-IK (D1849) 3166.
Ibn Juljul. *Tafsīr min kitāb Diyāsqūrīdis*. *BNM* 4981.
Ibn Khalaf al-Qurṭubī (d. 1205). *Rawḍat al-azhār wa-bahjat al-nufūs wa-nuzhat al-abṣār*. Rabat-AR (D679) 1909; Rabat-R 2543.
Ibn Khalaf al-Ṭurṭūshī (d. 1127). *al-Majālis*. Rabat-AR (D1095) 707.
Ibn al-Khaṭīb. *'Amal man ṭabba li-man ḥabba*. *BNM* 4929.
———. *al-Ḥilal al-marqūmah*. *BNM* 4894, 4997; Casiri 1771.
———. *al-Iḥāṭah*. *BNM* 4891, 4892; Casiri 1668.
———. *al-Iḥāṭah fī adab al-wizārah*. Rabat-AR (D1092) 2410; Zaytūnah 5093.
———. *Kitāb nufāḍat al-jirāb fī 'ulālat al-ightirāb*. Escorial 1755.
———. *Kitāb al-rasā'il wa-l-mukātabāt*. Zaytūnah-A 462.
———. *Kitāb al-takmilah*. *BNM* 4889; Casiri 1669.
———. *al-Maqālah al-musammāh bi-muqāna'at al-sā'il 'an al-maraḍ al-hā'il*. *BNM* 5067; Casiri 1780.
———. *Mi'yār al-ikhtiyār*. Escorial 554. A portion was published by F. J. Simonet in his *Descripción del reino de Granada* (Madrid, 1861).
———. *Qaṣīdah fī madḥ khayr al-bariyyah*. Rabat-AR (D774) 887 and (D774) 888.
———. *Rasā'il ilā ba'ḍ al-mulūk wa-l-a'lām*. Rabat-AR (D784) 1932.
———. *Rawḍat al-ta'rīf bi-l-ḥubb al-sharīf*. Rabat-AR (D778) 1095; Rabat-K 3365.
———. *Rayḥān al-kuttāb wa-naj'at al-muntāb*. *BNM* 5183; Escorial 825; Rabat-AR (D988) 1927 and Rabat-R 437.
———. *Risālah fī aḥwāl khidmat al-dawlah*. Rabat-AR (D972) 2414.
———. *al-Siḥr wa-l-shi'r*. Escorial 455; Rabat-AR (D1295) 1833; (D121) 354.

———. *Ta'līf fī-l-adab*. Rabat-AR (D1373) 1930 and (D1233) 1931.
Ibn Khātimah, Aḥmad Ibn 'Alī (d. 1369). *Taḥṣīl al-gharaḍ al-qāṣid fī tafṣīl al-maraḍ al-wāfid*. Escorial 1785.
Ibn Layūn al-Tujībī, Sa'd (d. 1346). *Bughyat al-mu'ānis min bahjat al-majālis*. Rabat-AR (D1037) 1921; Rabat-R 2860, 4503, 6946; Zaytūnah 4677, 6176, and 6725.
———. *al-Iksīr fī-l-mubtaghā min ṣan'at al-taksīr*. Rabat-AR (D1588) 2427 and (D1590) 2428.
———. *al-Inānah al-'ilmiyyah min al-risālah al-'ilmiyyah fī ṭarīqat al-ṣufiyyah*. Rabat-AR (D1041) 1042; Rabat-IK 3579.
———. *Lamḥ al-siḥr min rūḥ al-shi'r*. Rabat-AR (D1033) 1924; Rabat-R 770; Zaytūnah-A 4721.
Ibn Lubb, Faraj (d. 1381). *al-Qaṣīdah al-laghziyyah*. Rabat-AR (D 1648) 1696.
Ibn Mālik (d. 1274). *Tashīl al-wā'id wa-takmīl al-maqāṣid*. Marrākush 54; Rabat-AR (D568) 1659; Rabat-R 912.
———. *Thulāthiyat al-af'āl*. Zaytūnah 3962.
———. *Tuḥfat al-mawdūd fī-l-maqṣūr wa-l-mamdūd*. Rabat-AR (D545) 1658; Rabat-R 1612, 6029.
———. *Urjūzah fī-l-ẓā' wa-l-ḍa'*. Rabat-AR (D1033) 1747; Tetuan 659m.
Ibn Nubātah, Muḥammad. *al-Mufākharah bayn al-qalam wa-l-sayf. BRAH* 29.
Ibn al-Qaṭṭā', Abū Qāsim Ibn Ja'far (d. 1221). *Kitāb al-af'āl*. Escorial 576.
Ibn al-Raqqām al-Awsī (d. 1315). *Ta'līf fī-l-ṭibb*. Rabat-AR (D1681) 2269.
Ibn Rushayd, Muḥammad Ibn 'Umar. *Kitāb ifādat al-naṣīḥ bi-l-ta'rīf bi-isnād al-jāmi' al-ṣaḥīḥ*. Escorial 1732, 1785.
———. *Riḥlah*. Escorial 1680, 1735, 1736.
Ibn Rushd. *Bidāyat al-mujtahid wa-nihayat al-muqtaṣid*. Marrākush 293, no. 1.
———. *Kitāb al-jawāmi'. BNM* 5000.
———. *Sharḥ urjūzat Ibn Sīnā fī-l-ṭibb*. Qayrawīn 342.
Ibn Rushd (al-jadd). *al-Bayān wa-l-taḥṣīl limā fī-l-mustadrijah min al-tawliyah wa-l-ta'līl*. Marrākush 17, nos. 1 and 2.
———. *al-Masā'il wa-l-nawāzil*. Marrākush 451.
Ibn Sab'īn. *Inshā' al-ḥikmah al-ilāhiyyah. IEIM*-B4 and B-5.
Ibn Sahl, Ibrāhīm. *Dīwān*. Rabat-AR (D979) 1824.
———. *al-Maslak al-sahl 'alā al-tawshīḥ al-badī'. IEIM*-C-14; from a Cambridge MS.
Ibn Sa'īd, Abū Muḥ. 'Abdallah. *Tafsīr gharīb al-Qur'ān BNM* 4911.
Ibn Sa'īd al-Būṣīrī (d. 1294). *al-Burdah*. Escorial 248.
Ibn Sa'īd al-Dānī, Abū 'Amr (d. 1052). *Kitāb al-taysīr fī-l-qirā'āt al-sab'ah*. Escorial 65 and 1387. Rabat-A (D541) 598; Rabat-R 6247.
———. *al-Ta'rīf fī-l-qirā'āt al-shawādh*. Rabat-AR (D1532) 587; Tetuan 125m.
Ibn Salmūn al-Kinānī, Salmūn (d. 1335). *al-'Iqd al-munaẓẓam li-l-ḥukkām*. Rabat-IK (D2108) 3313.
Ibn al-Sarrāj, Muḥammad (d. 929). *Uṣūl Ibn al-Sarrāj fī-l-naḥw*. Marrākush 399.
Ibn al-Sayyid al-Baṭalyūsī (d. 1030). *Risālah fī-l-ism wa-l-musammah wa-l-tasmiyah*. Marrākush 456; Zaytūnah-A 6816.
———. *al-Sifr al-awwal min kitāb al-iqtiḍāb fī sharḥ adab al-kuttāb*. Escorial 222, 503.
Ibn Ṭufayl. *Manẓūmah rajaziyyah fī 'ilm al-ṭibb*. Qayrawīn 3138.
al-Iflīlī, Ibrāhīm Ibn Muḥammad (d.1050). *Sharḥ 'alā shi'r al-Mutanabbī*. Rabat-AR (D1128) 1803; (D437) 324; Qayrawīn 600.
al-Ishbīlī, Bakr Ibn Ibrāhīm. *al-Taysīr fī ṣinā'at al-tafsīr*. Tetuan 82m.
Jean Leon of Granada (16th c.). *Diccionario árabe-español*. Escorial 598.
Jughrāfiyat al-Andalus. IEIM-B-15.
al-Khazrajī, Ḍiyā' al-Dīn. *al-Qaṣīdah al-khazrajiyyah*. Rabat-AR (D1299). 1754; (D1647) 1755.
al-Kulā'ī Sulaymān Ibn Mūsā (d. 1237). *al-Iktifā' fī maghāzī al-muṣṭafā wa-l-khulafā' al thalāthah*. Rabat-AR (D1276) 812; Rabat-R 2657; Marrākush 279; Tetuan 808m.

Mafākhir al-Barbar. Rabat 1275.
Majmū'ah. Escorial 1745, consisting of various biographies of Muḥammad by Andalusian writers.
al-Majrīṭī. *Risālah fī takwīn al-ḥayawān*. Escorial 900.
al-Mawwāq, Muḥammad Ibn Yūsuf (d.1492). *al-Tāj wa-l-iklīl li-mukhtaṣar Khalīl*. Rabat-AR (D842) 1374; Rabat-T 5687; Tetuan 721m.; Marrākush 36, nos. 1, 2.
al-Nawājī, Shams al-Dīn Muḥammad. *Kitāb 'uqūd al-la'āsī fi-l-muwashshaḥāt wa-l-azjāl*. Escorial 434; cf. 339, 424, 427.
Nuzhat al-'āshiq wa-uns al-muyattam al-wāmiq. *IEIM*-B-15.
al-Qundī, Ismā'īl Ibn Muḥammad (d. 1231). *Risālah fī tafḍīl al-Andalus 'alā barr al-'Awdah*. Zaytūnah 455.
Rasā'il murābiṭiyyah wa-muwaḥḥidiyyah. *IEIM*-P-24.
al-Rāzī, 'Umar Ibn Muḥammad. *Kitāb musāmarat al-nudmān wa-mu'ānasat al-ikhwān*. Escorial 501.
Risālat al-rāhib min Ifransah dammarahā Allah ilā al-Muqtadir bi-allāh Ṣāḥib Saraqusṭah. Escorial 538, no. 11.
al-Ru'aynī, Abū-l-Ḥasan 'Alī (d. 1268). *Fahrasah*. Escorial 1729.
al-Ru'aynī al-Shāṭibī, Qāsim (d. 1194). *al-Shāṭibiyyah*. Rabat-AR (D815) 602; Rabat-R 915, 3955.
al-Shaqūrī, Abū 'Abdallah Muḥammad. *al-Naṣīḥah*. Escorial 1785, no. 7; *BNM* 5069. A summary of his work entitled *Taḥqīq al-nabā' 'an amr al-wabā'*.
al-Sharīshī, Aḥmad Ibn Muḥammad (d. 1243). *Anwār al-sarā'ir wa-sarā'ir al-anwār*. Rabat-AR (D984) 1043; (D1204) 1044; Rabat-K 2482; Rabat-IK (D1611) 3561; Rabat-R 4658, 8900, 9322.
al-Shāṭibī, Ibrāhīm (d.1290). *al-I'tiṣām*. Marrākush 121.
al-Shāṭibī, Muḥammad Ibn 'Alī (d. 1465). *al-Anwār fī mushkilāt āyāt al-Qur'ān*. Tetuan 783m.
———. *Kitāb fīh qiṣṣat dhī al-Qarnayn*. *BNM* 5379.
———. *Kitāb al-jannān fī mukhtaṣar akhbār al-zamān*. *BNM* 5221; Rabat 371.
———. *Kitāb al-libāb fī mushkilāt al-kitāb*. Rabat-K 2065; Tetuan 2101m.
———. *Qiṣṣat Yaḥyā b. Zakariyyah wa-Maryam wa-'Īsā*. *BNM* 5375.
al-Tijānī al-Andalusī, 'Abdallah. *Kitāb tuḥfat al-'arūs*. Escorial 562.
al-Tujībī, al-Qāsim Ibn Yūsuf. *Barnāmaj*. Escorial 1756.
'Uddat al-kuttāb wa-'uddat dhawī al-albāb. *IEIM*-C-18.
Uns al-'āshiq. *IEIM*-C-15.
al-Wādī Āshī, 'Abdallah (d. 1345). *Barnāmaj*. Escorial 1726.
al-Zubaydī. *Mukhtaṣar kitāb al-'ayn*. *BNM* 5017; *Junta* 35 and 49; Escorial 517, 570, 569; Rabat-K 1662; Marrākush 468; Qayrawīn 363; Zaytūnah 4944.

ALJAMIADO TEXTS

Abdallah al-Kātib (?). (1) Disputa contra los judios; (2) Disputa contra cristianos. *BNM* 4944.
Albecri, Abulhasan Ahmad Ben Abdallah. *BNM* 4955.
Alhadits de los des amigos. *BNM* 5301.
Alhadits de Xarchil Ben Xarchon. *BNM* 4953.
Alhaicales y otros documentos Móriscos. *BNM* 5380.
Alhasan b. Abdallah b. Abbas b. Ja'far b. Moh. b. Ali. *Del fablimiento de Alcoran y del bien que se hace con el*. *BNM* 5081.
Alquiteb de preicax y exemplax y dotrinax para medicinar el alma y amar la otra bida y abarrecer exte mundo. *Junta* 53.
Alquiteb de suertes. *BNM* 5300.
El alquiteb del rogar por agua. *Junta* 30.
Azoras alcoranicas. *Junta* 18.
Batallas de los primeros tiempos del islamismo. *BNM* 5337.

Caxtigox para lax gentex. *Junta* 8.
Códice de miscelánea. *Junta* 3, 4, 9, 12, 13, 32.
Comentario del Alcorán (en aljamiado). *Junta* 47 and 51.
Devocionario morisco. *BNM* 5378.
Devocionario musulman. *BNM* 5223, 5346, 5377, 5384, 5385, 5389, 35c.; cf. *Junta* 55 and 56.
Discusion y opiniones mahometanas sobre N. S. Jesucristo. *BNM* 5302.
Documentos en árabe y aljamía. *BNM* 5238.
Documentos varios en castellano, árabe y aljamía referentes a los moriscos. *BNM* 5073.
Documentos varios en latin, árabe, castellano y lemosin. *BNM* 4934.
Documentos varios pertenecientes a moriscos. *BNM* 5452.
Documentos y fragmentos varios aljamiados, castellanos y árabes. *BNM* 4908.
Hakmum b. Abu Abdallah Moh. b. Salama. *BNM* 5354.
Ibn Shihāb, Abū-l-Qāsim ʻUbaydallah ibn al-Ḥusayn al-Baṣrī (d. 1007). *BNM* 4870.
Inventario de los bienes matrimoniales de doña mayor Alvarez. *BNM* 5052.
Kitāb Samarqandī. *BNM* 4871; *Junta* VI.
Letanía para pedir agua. *Junta* 23.
Leyendas aljamiadas. *BNM* 5305.
Libro de dichox marabilloxox. *Junta* 22.
Libro de moriscos. *BNM* 5373.
Libro y traslado de buenas dotrinas y castigos y buenas costumbres. *BNM* 5267.
Mancebo (el) de Arévalo. *BNM* 245, cf. *Junta* 73.
Memoria de los cuartos del año. *BNM* 4937.
Novelas árabes. *BNM* 5098.
Practicas religiosas musulmanas usadas entre los moriscos. *BNM* 5374.
Recontamiento de Yaḳub y de su hijo José. *BNM* 5292.
Recontamiento del Rey Alixandre. *BNM* 5254.
Recontamiento que recontó el annabi Moh. Cuando subió a las cielas y las maravillas que Allah le dió ver. *BNM* 5053.
Soler, Ali Ben Moh. Ben Moh. *Brevario*. *BNM* 5306; cf. *Junta* 1.
Tratado jurídico. (*BNM* 4987.
Tratado y declaración y guía para seguir y mantener el din del alislam. *BNM* 5252.

Bibliography of Western Works

al-'Abbādī, Aḥmad Mujtār 'Abd al-Fattāḥ. *Los eslavos en España, ojeada sobre su orígen, desarrollo y relación con el movimiento de la sh'ubiyya*. Madrid, 1953.

———. "Muḥammad V, al-Ghānī bi-llāh, Rey de Granada." *RIEI*, 11–12 (1963–1964), 209–308; 13 (1965–1966), 43–102; and 14 (1967–1968), 139–192.

Abel, A. "Spain: Internal Division," in *Unity and Variety in Muslim Civilization*, ed. G. E. von Grunebaum. Chicago, 1955.

Abbou, Isaac D. *Musulmans andalous et judeo-espagnols*. Casablanca, 1953.

Abd al-Badi, Luṭfi. *La épica árabe y su influencia en la épica castellana*. Santiago, Chile, 1964.

'Abd al-Jalil, J. M. *Histoire de la littérature arabe*. 2nd ed. Paris, 1960.

'Abd al-Wahhāb, H. H. "Le développement de la musique arabe en Orient, Espagne, et. Tunisie." *RT*, 25 (1918), 106–107.

———. "Coup d'oeil général sur les apports ethniques étrangers en Tunisie." *RT*, 24 (1917), 305–316 and 371–379.

Abun-Nasr, J. M. *A History of the Maghrib*. Cambridge, 1971.

Addison, J. T. *The Christian Approach to the Moslems.* New York, 1942.

Adler, G. J. *The Poetry of the Arabs of Spain*. New York, 1867.

Afīfī, A. E. *The Mystical Philosophy of Muḥyid dīn Ibnul 'Arabi*. Cambridge, 1939; Lahore reprint.

Afnan, A. M. *Avicenna, His Life and Works*. London, 1958.

Agrado Bleye, Pedro. *Manual de historia de España.* 6th ed. Madrid, 1947.

Ahlwardt, W. *The Divans of the Six Ancient Arabic Poets*. London, 1870.

Alarcón, Maximiliano. *Lámpara de los príncipes por Abubéquer de Tortosa*. 2 vols. Madrid, 1930–1931.

Alcalá, Pedro de. *Arte para ligeramente saber la lengua arábiga*. Granada, 1501. New York, 1928.

———. *Vocabulista arábigo en letra castellana*. Granada, 1505.

Alcalá Veceslada, Antonio. *Vocabulario andaluz*. Andujar, 1933.

Alcocer Martínez, Don R. *La corporación de los poetas en la España Musulmana*. Madrid, 1940.

Alemany, J. and A. G. Solalinde, eds. *Calila e Dimna*. Madrid, 1915, 1917.
———. "La Geografiá de la Península Ibérica en los escritores árabes." *RCEHG*, 9–11 (1919–1921).
Alfonso X (el Sabio). *Antologia de Alfonso X el Sabio*, ed. A. G. Solalinde. 4th ed. Madrid, 1960.
Ali, Ameer. *A Short History of the Saracens*. London, 1951.
Allouche, I. S. "La Poésie andalouse." *Hespéris*, 23 (1939).
Alonso, Amado. "Correspondencias arábigoespañolas." *RFE*, 8 (1946), 30–43, 57–60.
Alonso, Damaso. "Cancioncillas 'de Amigo' mozárabes (Primavera Temprana de la lírica europea)." *RFE*, 33 (1949), 297–349, and *al-Andalus*, 8 (1943), 129–253.
———. "Poesía arábigoandaluza y poesía gongorina," in *Estudios y ensayos gongorinos*. Madrid, 1955.
Alonso, Manuel. "Influencia de Algazel en el mundo latino." *al-Andalus*, 23 (1958), 2, 371–380.
———. *Pedro Hispano scientia libri de anima*. 2nd ed. Barcelona, 1961.
———. *Temas filosóficos medievales (Ibn Dawud y Gundisalvo)*, in *Miscelánea Comillas, serie filosófica*, vol. 10. Santander, 1959.
———. "Traducciones del arcediano Domingo Gundisalvo." *al-Andalus*, 11 (1947), 295–338.
Altamira y Crevea, R. *Historia de España y de la civilización española*. 3rd ed., 4 vols. Barcelona, 1913. English trans. M. Lee. London, 1949.
———. "Western Caliphate," in *Cambridge Medieval History*, vol. 3. Cambridge, 1922.
Alvaro, Bishop of Cordoba. *Alvari Cordubensio opera Indicus Luminosus*, ed. F. H. Florex. *Espana Sagrada*, 11 (1753), 273.
Amari, M. "Questions philosophiques adressées aux savants musulmans par l'Empereur Frederic II." *JA*, 5 ser., vol. 1 (1853).
———. *Storia dei Musulmani di Sicilia*. 3 vols. Catania, 1854–1858; rev. ed. titled *Biblioteca arabo-sicula*, ed. C. A. Nallino. Leipzig, 1933–1939.
Ambar, Mohamed Abd El Hamid. "Le probleme de l'influence arabe sur les premiers troubadours." Thesis, University of Paris, 1947.
Andrae, Tor. *Les origines de l'Islam et du christianisme*, French trans. J. Roche. Paris, 1955.
Andrés, Juan. *Dell' origine, progressi e stato attuale d'ogni letteratura.* 8 vols. Parma, 1782–1799. Spanish trans. *Orígen, progreso y estado actual de toda la literatura.* 7 vols. Madrid, 1784–1806.
Antuña, M. M. "La corte literaria de Alháquem II en Córdoba," in *Religion y Cultura*. San Lorenzo del Escorial, 1929.
———. *Sevilla y sus monumentos árabes*. San Lorenzo del Escorial, 1930.
Arberry, A. J. *Aspects of Islamic Civilization*. London, 1964.
———. *An Introduction to the History of Sufism*. The Sir Abdullah Suhrawardy Lectures for 1942. Oxford, 1942.
———. *Moorish Poetry*. Cambridge, 1953.
———, ed. *Poems of al-Mutanabbī*. Cambridge, 1953.
———. *Portraits of Seven Scholars.* London, 1960.
———. *The Seven Odes.* London, 1950.
———. *Sufism*. London, 1950.
Arie, Rachel, *Miniatures hispano-musulmanes*; *Recherches sur un manuscrit arabe illustré de l'Escurial*. Leiden, 1969.
Arnaldez, R. *Grammaire et théologie chez Ibn Hazm de Cordoue*. Paris, 1956.
Arnold, T. W. *The Caliphate*. Oxford, 1925.
———. *Painting in Islam*. Oxford, 1928.
———. *Preaching of Islam: A History of the Propagation of the Muslim Faith*. 2nd. ed. London, 1913.
——— and Alfred Guillaume, eds. *The Legacy of Islam*. Oxford, 1931.
Artega, Esteban. *Della influenza degli Arabi sull' origine della poesia moderna in Europa*. Rome, 1791.

Asensio, E. *Poética y realidad en el cancionero peninsular de la edad media.* Madrid, 1957.
Aschbach, Joseph. *Geschichte der Ommaÿaden in Spanien*. Frankfurt A.M. 1829. 2nd ed., 2 vols. Vienna, 1860.
———. *Geschichte Spaniens und Portugals zur Zeit der Herrschaft der Almoraviden und Almohaden*, Frankfurt A.M. 1833; Arabic trans. 'Inān. Cairo, 1958.
Asín Palacios, M. "El abecedario de Yusuf Benaxeij el malagueño." *BRAH*, 69 (1932), 195–228.
———. *Abenházam de Córdoba y su historia crítica de las ideas religiosas.* 5 vols. Madrid, 1927–1932.
———. "Abenmasarra y su escuela," in *Obras escogidas*. Madrid, 1946.
———. *Algazel*. Saragossa, 1901.
———. "Biografía de Ibn al-'Arīf (1088–1141)," in *Obras escogidas*. Madrid, 1946. Pp. 219–234.
———. "Un códice inexplorado del Cordobés Ibn Ḥazm." *al-Andalus*, 2 (1934), 1–56.
———. *Contribución a la Toponimia Árabe de España*. 2nd ed. Madrid & Granada, 1944.
———. *Crestomatia del árabe literal con glosario y elementos de gramática*. 3rd ed. Madrid, 1954.
———. "Una descripción nueva del Faro de Alejandria." *al-Andalus*, 1 (1933), 241–300.
———. *La escatología musulmana en la Divina Comedia.* Madrid, 1919, 1943, 1961; English trans. H. Sunderland, *Islam and the Divine Comedy*. London, 1926.
———. *La espiritualidad de Algazel y su sentido cristiano*. 4 vols. Madrid, 1934–1941.
———. *Glosario de voces romances registradas por un botánico anónimo hispano-musulmán (siglos XI–XII)*. Madrid & Granada, 1943.
———. *Huellas del Islam*. Madrid, 1941.
———. "El 'Intérprete Arábigo' de Fray Bernardino González." *BRAH*, 38 (1901), fasc. 1 15–28.
———. *El Islam cristianizado*. Madrid, 1931.
———. *El místico murciano Aben Arabi*. Madrid, 1925–1928.
———. "El origen del lenguaje y problemas conexos," in *Obras escogidas*. Madrid, 1948. Pp. 357–388. Also in *Historia y filología árabe*, vols. 2 and 3 (Madrid, 1948), pp. 377–378.
———. "Un precursor hispanomusulmán de San Juan de la Cruz," in *Obras escogidas*. Madrid, 1946, Pp. 243–336.
———. *La psicología según Mohidin Abenarabi*. Algiers, 1905.
———. "La tesis de la necesidad de la revelación en el Islam y en la escolástica." *al-Andalus*, 3 (1935), 345–389.
———. *Vidas de santones andaluces, la "Epístola de la santidad" de Ibn 'Arabī de Murcia*. Madrid, 1933.
Asso del Rio, Ignacio de. *Biblioteca arábigo-aragonensis*. Amsterdam, 1782.
Atiyeh, G. N. *al-Kindī: The Philosopher of the Arabs*. Rawalpindi, 1966.
Atkinson, William C. *A History of Spain and Portugal*. London, 1960.
d'Averny, M. T., and G. Vajda. "Mark de Tolède." *al-Andalus*, 16 (1951), 99–140, 259–308; 17 (1952), 1–56.
Avicenna. *Avicennae de congélatione et conglutinatione lapidum.* (Paris, 1927.
Ayala, F. "Fuente árabe de un cuento popular en el Lazarillo." *BRAE*, 45 (1965), 493–495.
Badawī, 'Abd ar-Raḥmān. *Aristoteles de Poetica*. Cairo, 1953.
Baer, Uotzjal. *A History of the Jews in Christian Spain*. Vol. 1. Philadelphia, 1961.
Ballesteros, Antonio. *Historia de España*. Barcelona, 1918–1934.
———. *Historia de España y su influencia en la historia universal*, vols. 2 and 3. Barcelona, 1920–1922.
———. *Sevilla en el siglo XIII*. Madrid, 1913.
Bammate Haidar, Georges Rivoire. *Visages de l'Islam*. Lausanne-Paris, 1946.
Barbier de Meynard. *Dictionnaire géographique, historique et littéraire de la Perse et des contrées adjacentes*; extracts trans. from Yaqūt, *Mu'jam al-buldān*. Paris, 1861.
Barbieri, Giammaria. *Dell' origine della poesia rimata*. Modena, 1790.

Bargebuhr, F. P. *The Alhambra*. Berlin, 1968.
Barthold, V. V. *Mussulman Culture*. Calcutta, 1934.
Basset, R. *La littérature populaire berbère et arabe dans le Maghreb et chez les Maures d'Espagne*, in *MAO*. Paris, 1915.
Bataillon, Marcel. "L'Arabe à Salamanque au temps de la Renaissance." *Hespéris*, 31 (1935).
———. "La poésie andalouse." *BH*, 41 (1939;, 187–191.
Baynes, N. H., and H. Moss. *Byzantium: An Introduction to East Roman Civilization*. Oxford, 1961.
Beazley, C. R. *The Dawn of Modern Geography*, Vols. 1–3. London, 1897–1901. 2nd ed., vol. 3. Oxford, 1906.
Bel, Alfred. *Les Banou Ghanya, derniers représentants de l'empire almoravide et leur lutte contre l'empire almohade*. Paris, 1903.
———. "Inscriptions arabes de Fes." *JA* (1917–1919; offprint, Paris, 1919).
———. "Quelques rites pour obtenir la pluie en temps de sécheresse chez les musulmans maghribins," in *Recueil de mémoires et de textes publiés en l'honneur du XIV Congres des Orientalistes*. Algiers, 1905. pp. 49–98.
———. *La religion musulmane en Berberie. Esquisse d'histoire et de sociologie religieuse*. Paris, 1938.
———. "Le sufisme en Occident musulman au XII et au XIII siècle de J.C." *AIEO*, 1 (1934), 145–161.
Bell, G. L. *The Origin of Islam in Its Christian Environment.* London, 1926.
———. *Palace and Mosque at Ukhaiḍir*. Oxford, 1914.
Bellver y Cacho. *Influencia que ejerció la dominación de los árabes en la agricultura, industria y comercio de la provincia de Castellón de la Plana.* Catellón, 1889.
Benhamouda, A. "Les noms arabes des étoiles (essai d'identification)." *AIEO*, 9 (1951), 76–210.
Berendes, J. *Die Pharmacie bei den alten Culturvolkern*. 2 vols. Halle, 1891.
Bergsträsser, G. *Hunain ibn Ishaq uber die syrischen und arabischen Galenubersetzungen.* Leipzig, 1925.
Bergua, José. *Psicología del pueblo español*. Madrid, 1934.
Berthelot, M. *La chimie au Moyen Âge*. Vol. 4. Paris, 1895.
Bertrand, Louis. *England and Arabic Learning: The History of Spain*. London, 1956.
Besthorn, R., et al. *Miscelánea de estudios y textos árabes*. Madrid, 1915.
Bevan, Bernard." The Mudejar Towers of Aragon." *Apollo* (May 1929).
Bewes, W. A. *The Romance of the Law Merchant*. London, 1923.
Blachère, R. *Histoire de la littérature arabe des origines à la fin du XVe siècle*. 3 vols. Paris, 1952–1966.
———. "Ibn Zumruk et son oeuvre." *AIEO*, 2 (1936), 291–312.
———. "L'Islam et l'Occident." *Cahiers du Sud* (Marseilles). August–September 1935.
———. "Un pionnier de la culture arabe orientale en Espagne au Xe siècle, Ṣā'id de Baghdad." *Hespéris*, 10 (1930), 15–36.
———. "Le Poète arabe al-Mutanabbī et l'Occident musulman." *REI* (1929), 127–135.
———. *Un poète arabe du IV siècle de l'Hegire (X siècle de J.C.): Abou ṭ-Ṭayyib al-Motanabbi (Essai d'histoire littéraire)*. Paris, 1935.
———. "Les principaux thèmes de la poésie érotique au siècle des Umayyades de Damas." *AIEO*, 5 (1939–1941).
———. "La vie et l'oeuvre d'Abou ṭ-Ṭayyib al-Mutanabbī," in *al-Mutanabbi Recueil publié a l'occasion de son Millenaire*. Beirut, 1936.
———. "La vie et l'oeuvre du poète-épistolier andalou Ibn Darrāg al-Qasṭallī." *Hespéris*, 16 (1933), 99–121.
———. "Vue d'ensemble sur la poètique classique des Arabes." *RES* (1938).
Blochet, E. *Les sources orientales de la Divine Comedie*. Paris, 1901.
Boissonnade, P. *Life and Work in Medieval Europe (Fifth to Fifteenth Centuries)*. London, 1937.

———. *Du nouveau sur la Chanson de Roland*. Paris, 1923.
Bolaguer. *Historia de los trovadores*. 6 vols. Madrid, 1878.
Borbon, Faustino de. *Cartas para ilustrar la historia de la España árabe*. Madrid, 1799.
Boronat y Barrchina, Pascual. *Los moriscos españoles y su expulsión*. Valencia, 1901.
Bosch Vilá, Jacinto. *Albarracīn musulmán*. Teruel, 1959.
———. *Los Almorávides*. Tetuan, 1956.
———. "Considerationes sobre 'al-tāgr en al-Andalus," in *Études d'Orientalisme*, vol. 1 (1952), 23–33.
———. "Los documentos árabes del archivo catedral de Huesca." *RIEI*, 5 (1957), 1–48.
———. "Escrituras oscenses en aljamía hebraico árabe," in *Homenaje a Millás Vallicrosa*. vol. 1. Barcelona, 1954. pp. 183–214.
———. *El Oriente árabe en el desarrollo de la cultura de la Marca Superior*. Madrid, 1954.
Bosworth, C. E. *The Islamic Dynasties*. Edinburgh, 1967.
Bourgoin, M. J. *Le trait des entrelacs*. Paris, 1879.
Bourke, Thomas. *A Concise History of the Moors in Spain from Their Invasion of That Kingdom to Their Final Expulsion from It*. London, 1811.
Bréhier, L. "Les influences musulmanes dans l'art roman du Puy." *Journal des Savants* (1936).
Breydy, Michel. *Michel Gharcieh al-Ghazīrī, orientaliste Libanais du XVIIIe siècle*. Beirut, 1950.
Briffault, R. *The Troubadours*. Bloomington, Ind., 1965.
Briggs, M. S. "Architecture" in T. Arnold and A. Guillaume eds. *The Legacy of Islam*. Oxford, 1931.
———. *Muhammadan Architecture in Egypt and Palestine*. Oxford, 1924.
Brockelmann, C. *Geschichte der arabischen Literatur*. 2 vols. and 3 sups. Weimar & Leiden, 1898–1942.
———. *History of the Islamic Peoples*, English trans. J. Carmichael and M. Perlmann. New York, 1960.
Browne, E. G. *Arabian Medicine*. Cambridge, 1921.
Brunches, Jean. *L'irrigation dans la Péninsule Ibérique et dans l'Afrique du Nord*. Paris, 1904.
Brunot, L. "La mer dans les traditions et les industries indigènes à Rabat et Salé." *PIHEM* (1921).
———. "Textes arabes de Rabat." *P.I.H.E.M.*, 20 (1931).
Brunschvig, R. "Deux récits de voyage inédits en Afrique du Nord au XV siècle: 'Abd al-Basiṭ b. Halil et Adorne." *AIEO*, 7 (1936).
——— and G. E. von Grunebaum. *Classicisme et declin culturel dans l'histoire de l'Islam*. Paris, 1957.
Buckler, Francis William. *Harūn al-Rashīd and Charles the Great*. Cambridge, Mass., 1931.
Burckhardt, Titus. *An Introduction to Sufi Doctrine*. Lahore, 1959.
Butler, A. J. *Islamic Pottery*. London, 1926.
Çabanelas Rodríguez, Darío. *Juan de Segovia y el problema islámico*. Madrid, 1952.
———. *El morisco granadino Alonso del Castillo*. Granada, 1965.
Cagigas, Isidoro de las. *Andalucía musulmana; aportaciones a la delimitación de la frontera del Andalus*. Madrid, 1950.
———. "Una carta aljamiada granadina." *Arabica*, 1 (1954), 271–275.
———. *Los mozárabes*. 2 vols. Madrid, 1947.
———. *Los mudéjares*. 2 vols. Madrid, 1948–1949.
———. *Sevilla almohade y útimos años de su vida musulmana*. Madrid, 1951.
———. *Tratados y convenios referentes a Marruecos*. Madrid, 1952.
———. *Los viajes de Ali Bey a través del Marruecos oriental*. Madrid, 1919.
Calvert, A. F. *The Alhambra*. London, 1907.
Campaner y Fuertes, A. *Bosquejo histórico de la dominación islamita en las Islas Baleares*. Palma, 1888.

Campbell, Donald. *Arabian Medicine and Its Influence on the Middle Ages*. 2 vols. London, 1926.

Camps y Cazorla. E. *Arquitectura caliphal y mozárabe*. Madrid, 1929.

Candolle, Alphonso de. *Origine des plantes cultivées*. Paris, 1883.

Cañes, Francisco. *Diccionario español-latino-arabico*. Madrid, 1776.

———. *Diccionario manual árabe y español*. Madrid, 1776.

———. *Gramática arábigo-española, vulgar, y literal con un diccionario arábigo-español*. Madrid, 1775.

Cantarino, Vincent. "Averroes on Poetry," in *Islam and Its Cultural Divergence*. Urbana, Ill., 1970. Pp. 10–26.

———. "Dante and Islam: History and Analysis of a Controversy," in *Dante Symposium*. Chapel Hill, N.C., 1965. Pp. 175–192.

———. "Ibn Arabi, Poet of Love: An Ode to Nizam." *Literature East and West*, 9 (1968), no. 2, 104–118.

———. "Ibn Gabirol's Metaphysic of Light." *SI*, 24 (1967), 49–71.

———. "Lyrical Traditions in Andalusian Muwashshahas." *Comparative Literature*, 21 (1969), no. 3, 213–231.

———. "Sobre los Espãnoles y sobre cómo llegaron a serlo." *Revista Hispánica Moderna*, no. 1–2 (1968), 212–226.

Canteras Burgos, F. "Los estudios orientales en la Espãna actual." *OM* (1955), 236–240.

———. "Versos españoles en las muwaššaḥas hispano-hebreas." *Safarad*, 9 (1949), 197–234.

Capellanus, Andreas. *The Art of Courtly Love*, English trans. J. J. Parry. New York, 1964.

Capmany, Antonio. *Memorias históricas sobre la marina comercio y artes de la antigua ciudad de Barcelona*. Vol. 3. Madrid, 1779.

Cardonne, Denis D. *Histoire de l'Afrique et de l'Espagne sous la domination des Arabes*. 3 vols. Paris, 1765.

Carmody, F. J. *Arabic Astronomical and Astrological Sciences in Latin Translation*. Berkeley, 1956.

Carande, Ramón. "Sevilla, Fortleza y Mercado." *AHDE*, 2 (1925).

Caro Baroja, Julio. *Los moriscos del reino de Granada.* Madrid, 1957.

———. *Una visión de marruecos a mediados del siglo XVI, la del primer historiador de los "xarifes," Diego de Terres*. Madrid, 1956.

Carra de Vaux, Baron. "Astronomy and Mathematics," in T. Arnold and A. Guillaume, eds., *The Legacy of Islam*. Oxford, 1931.

———. *Gazali*. Paris, 1902.

———. *Les penseurs de l'Islam*. 5 vols. Paris, 1921–1926.

Carrasco Urgoiti, María Soledad. *El moro de Granada en la literatura (del siglo XV al XX)*. Madrid, 1956.

Casiri, M. *Bibliotheca arábico-hispana escurialensis*. Madrid, 1760–1770.

Gaspar Remiro, M. *Historia de la Murcia musulmana*. Saragossa, 1905.

Castejón Calderón, Rafael. *Los juristas hispano-musulmanes*. Madrid, 1948.

Castellanos, Manuel P. *Apostolado seráfico en Marruecos; o sea, historia de las misiones franciscanas en aquel imperio desde el siglo XIII hasta nuestros días*. Madrid-Santiago, 1896.

———. *Historia de Marruecos*. 3rd ed. Tangiers, 1898.

Castries, Henry de. *Les sources inédits de l'histoire du Maroc*. 20 vols. Paris, 1918–1960.

Castro, Américo. *España en su historia: Cristianos, moros y judíos.* Burenos Aires, 1948. English trans. E. L. King, *The Structure of Spanish History*. Princeton, 1954.

———. *History of Religious Intolerance in Spain*, trans. F. Parker. London, 1953.

———. *La realidad histórica de España*. Mexico, 1954.

Cattan, Isaac. "L'orientaliste espagnol Francisco Codera y Zaidín." *RT*, 25 (1918), fasc. 126, 128–129.

Cerrada, Pio. "La riqueza agricola y pecuaria en España," in *Estatutos de la Real Academia de Ciencias morales y políticas*. Madrid, 1896.

Cerruli, E. "Dante e l'Islam." *Academia Nazionale dei Lineli*, 12 (1957).

———, ed. *Il "Libro della Scala" e la questione della fonti-arabo-espagnole della Divina Comedia*. Vatican, 1949.
Cesareo, G. *Le origini della poesia lirica e la poesia Siciliana sott gli Suevi*. 1924.
Chaplyn, M. A. *Le roman mauresque en France*. 1928.
Chateaubriand, F. R. de *Le génie du christianisme*, ed. Garnier. 12 vols. Paris, 1859–1861.
Chaytor, H. J. *The Troubadours and England*. Cambridge, 1923.
Chejne, Anwar. *The Arabic Language: Its Role in History*. Minneapolis, 1969.
———. "Hispano-Arabic Manuscripts in the Libraries of Morocco and Tunisia." In preparation.
———. *Plegaria bilingue árabe-aljamiada de un morisco*. Madrid, in press.
———. *Succession to the Rule in Islam*. Lahore, 1960.
Christie, A. H. "Islamic Minor Arts and Their Influence upon European Works," in T. Arnold and A. Guillaume, eds., *The Legacy of Islam*. Oxford, 1931. Pp. 108–151.
Cluzel, J. "Las jaryas et l'amour courtois." *Cultura Neolatina* (1960), 1–18.
Codera y Zaidín, Francisco. "Almacén de un librero morisco descubierto en Almonacid de la Sierra." *BRAH*, 5 (1884), 269–276.
———. *Decadencia y disaparición de los Almorávides en España*. Saragossa, 1899.
———. *Estudios críticos de la historia árabe española*. Saragossa & Madrid, 1903–1917.
———. "Mozárabes, su condición social y política." Doctoral thesis, Lérida, 1866.
———. *Numismática arábigo-española*. Madrid, 1879.
Cohen, Gustave. "Le problème des origines arabes de la poésie provençale médiévale." *Bullétin de l'Académie royale de Belgique (Classe des Littres)*, 32 (Bruxelles, 1946), 266–278.
Colbert, Edward P. *The Martyrs of Cordoba (850–859)*. Washington, D.C., 1962.
Colin, Georges S. "La Noria Marocaine et les machines hydrauliques dans le monde arabe." *Hespéris*, (1932).
———. "L'origine des norias de Fes." *Hespéris*, 15 (1933).
Colmeiro, Manuel, *Historia de la economía política en España*. Madrid, 1863.
Comparetti, D. and A. Bonilla y San Martin, *Researches Respecting the Book of Sindibad*. London, 1882; Madrid, 1904.
Conant, M. P. *The Oriental Tale in England*. New York, 1908.
Conde, J. A. *Historia de la dominación de los árabes en España*. 3 vols. Madrid, 1820–1821; Paris, 1840; Barcelona, 1844. English trans. Mrs. Jonathan Foster, *History of the Dominion of the Arabs in Spain*. London, 1854.
Coppée, Henry. *History of the Conquest of Spain by the Arab-Moors*. Boston, 1881.
Corbin, H. *Avicenna and the Visionary Recital*. London, 1961.
———. *Creative Imagination in the Sūfism of Ibn 'Arabī*, trans. Ralph Manheim. London, 1969.
———. *Histoire de la philosophie islamique*. Paris, 1964.
Coulson, N. J. *Islamic Law*. Edinburgh, 1964.
Cour, A. *La dynastie marocaine des Beni Waṭṭas*. Constantine, 1920.
———. "De l'opinion d'Ibn al-Ḥaṭīb sur les ouvrages d'Ibn Haqan considérés comme source historique." *Mélanges René Basset*, 2 (1925), 17–32.
———. *Un poète arabe d'Andalousie: Ibn Zaidoun*. Constantine, 1920.
Covarrubias Orozco, Sebastian de. *Tesoro de la lengua castellana*. Madrid, 1611.
Creasy, Edward. *The Fifteen Decisive Battles of the World*. New York, 1918.
Creswell, K. A. C. *A Bibliography of the Architecture, Arts and Crafts of Islam*. Cairo, 1961.
———. *Early Muslim Architecture*. 2 vols. Oxford, 1932–1940.
———. "The Lawfulness of Painting in Early Islam." *AI*, 11–12 (1946).
Cruz Hernández, M. *Historia de la filosofía española*. 2 vols. Madrid, 1957.
———. *La filosofía árabe*. Madrid, 1963.
Ḍaif, Aḥmad. *Eassai sur le lyrisme et la critique littéraire chez les arabes*. Paris, 1917.

Daniel, N. "The Church and Islam — The Development of the Christian Attitude to Islam," *Dublin Review* (1957).
———. "Holy War in Islam and Christendom." *Blackfriars* (1958).
———. *Islam and the West*. Edinburgh, 1960.
Dannenfeldt, K. "The Renaissance, Humanists and the Knowledge of Arabic." *Studies in the Renaissance*, 2 (1955), 96–117.
Dante, Alighieri. *La divina comedia*, Spanish trans. A. Aranda Sanjuan. Barcelona, 1958.
———. *Monarquia*, Spanish trans. A. Marino Pascual. Madrid, 1947.
———. *Vita nuova*, ed. Michele Barbi. Florence, 1932.
Dánvila y Collado, D. M. "Ajuar de una morisca de Teruel en 1583." *BRAH*, 6 (1885), 410–439.
———. *La expulsión de los moriscos españoles*. Madrid, 1889.
Darmstaedter, E. *Die Alchemie des Geber*. Berlin, 1922.
DeBoer, T. J. *The History of Philosophy in Islam*. London, 1903.
Delgado Hernández, A. *Memoria sobre el estado moral y político de los mudéjares de Castilla*. Madrid, 1864.
Delgado S. R. *Glosario Luso-asiático*. 2 vols. Coimbra, 1919, 1921.
Della Vida, G. Levi. "Nuova luce sulle fonti islamiche della *Divina Commedia*." *al-Andalus*, 14 (1949).
Denomy, Alexander J. "Concerning the Accessibility of Arabic Influence to the Earliest Provençal Troubadours." *Medieval Studies*, 15 (1953), 147–158.
———. "*Fin' Amors*: The Pure Love of the Troubadours, Its Amorality, and Possible Source." *Medieval Studies*, 7 (1945), 139–179.
———. *The Heresy of Courtly Love*. Gloucester, Mass., 1965.
———. "*Jovens*: The Notion of Youth among the Troubadours, Its Meaning and Source." *Medieval Studies*, 11 (1949), 1–22.
Dérenbourg, Hartwig. *Les manuscrits arabes de l'Escurial*. Paris, 1917.
Dermenghem, Emile. *Les plus beaux textes arabes*. Paris, 1951.
Devic, L. *Dictionnaire etymologique de mots français d'origine orientale*. Paris, 1876.
di Giacomo, Louis. "Une poètesse grenadine du temps des Almohades: Hafsa bint al-Hajj." *Hespéris* (Paris, 1949).
Díaz-Plaja, G. *Historia del español*. Buenos Aires, 1955.
Diccionario de autores. Barcelona, 1963.
Dickie, James. "Ibn Shuhayd: A Biographical and Critical Study." *al-Andalus*, 29 (1964), 243–310.
Diehl, C., and G. Marçais. *Le monde orientale de 395 à 1081 (histoire générale)*, vol. 3 of *Histoire du Moyen Âge*. Paris, 1936.
Dierx, G. *Die arabische Kultur in mittelalterischen Spanien*. Hamburg, 1887.
Diez, E. *Die Kunst der islamichen Volker*. Berlin, 1915.
Dimand, M. S. *A Handbook of Mohammedan Decorative Arts*. New York, 1958.
———. *A Handbook of Muhammadan Art*. New York, 1944.
Dioscorides, *see* Dubler, C. E.
Donaldson, D. M. *The Shī'ite Religion*. London, 1933.
Doutté, E. "Mahomet Cardinal." *Memóires de la Société d'Agriculture, Commerce, Sciènces, et Arts de la Marne*, 2 ser., 1:2 (1898–1899), 233–243.
———. *Merrakech*. Paris, 1905.
Dozy, R. *Catalogus codicum orientalium bibliothecae Academiae Lugduno-Batavae*. 6 vols. Leiden, 1851–1877.
———. *Le Cid d' après de nouveaux documents*. Leiden, 1860.
———. *Corrections sur les textes du Bayano 'l-Mogrib d'Ibn-Adhāri (de Maroc), des fragments de la chronique d'Arib (de Cordue) et du Hollato 's-siyara de 'Ibno-'l-Abbar*. Leiden, 1883.
———. *Dictionnaire détaillé des vêtements chez les arabes.* Amsterdam, 1845.
———. *Glossaire des mots espagnols et portugais dérivés de l'arabe*. Leiden, 1869.

———. *Histoire des musulmans d'Espagne jusqu'à la conquête de l'Andalousie par les almoravides (711–1110)*. 4 vols. Leiden, 1861; 2nd ed. E. Lévi-Provençal, 3 vols., Leiden, 1932. English trans. F. G. Stokes, *Spanish Islam*. New York, 1913.
———. *Recherches sur l'histoire et la littérature de l'Espagne pendant le Moyen Âge*. Leiden, 1847; 3rd ed. 2 vols., Paris, 1881.
———. *Scriptorum arabum loci de Abbadidis*. 3 vols. Leiden, 1848–1853.
——— and H. W. Englemann. *Supplément aux dictionnaires arabes*. Vols. 1 and 2. Leiden, 1881.
Dozy, R., et. al. *Analectes sur l'histoire et la littérature des arabes d'Espagne*. Leiden, 1855–1861.
Draper, John William. *A History of the Intellectual Development of Europe*. 2 vols. London, 1902.
Dressendorf, P. *Islam unter der Inquisition die Morisco-Prozesse in Toledo 1575–1610*. Wiesbaden, 1971.
Dubler, Céar E. "Über das Wirtschaftsleben auf der Iberischen Halbinsel." *JHRH*, 11–12 (Switzerland, 1943).
——— and Elias Teres Sadaba. *La "Materia Medica" de Dioscorides, transmission medieval y renacentista*, vol. 2, *La version arabe de la "Materia Medica" de Dioscorides (texto, variantes e indices)*. Tetuan-Barcelona, 1952–1957.
Dugat, G. *Histoire des orientalistes de l'Europe du XIIe au XIXe siècle*. 2 vols. Paris, 1868.
———. "Hodba, un poète arabe du I siècle de l'Hégire." *JA*, 5e ser., vol. 5 (1855).
———. *Introduction aux analectes d'al-Maqqari*. Leiden, 1855.
Duhem, H. *Le système de monde*. 5 vols. Paris, 1913–1917.
Dunlop D. M. "Arabic Medicine in England." *Journal of the History of Medicine and Allied Sciences*, 11 (1956), 166–182.
———. *Arabic Science in the West*. Karachi, 1958.
Dupin, H. *La courtoisie au Moyen Âge*. Paris, 1931.
Dureau de la Malle. *Climatologie comparée de l'Italie et de l'Andalousie anciennes et modernes*. Paris, 1849.
Dutton, Brian. "Delia Doura, Edoy Lelia Doura: An Arabic Refrain in a Thirteenth-Century Galician Poem?" *BHS*, 41 (Jan. 1964), 1–9.
East, W. G. *An Historical Geography of Europe*. London, 1950.
Ecker, L. *Arabischer, provenzalischer und deutscher Minnesang*. Berne & Leipzig, 1934.
Edrisi. *Geographie traduite de l'Arabe en français d'après des MSS, de la Bibliotèque du Roi et accompagnée de notes par Amedée Faubert*. Paris, 1836–1840.
Eguilaz y Yanguas, L. *Estudio sobre el valor de las letras arábigas en el alfabeto castellano*. Madrid, 1874.
———. *Glosario etimológico de las palabras españolas de orígen oriental*. Granada, 1886.
———. *El haditz de la princesa Zoraida, del Emir Abulhasan y del Caballero Aceja*. Granada, 1892.
———. *Poesía histórica, lírica y descriptiva de los árabes andaluces*. Madrid, 1846.
———. *Reseña histórica de la conquista del reino de Granada*. Granada, 1894.
———. *El talismán del diablo, novela fantástica-oriental*. Madrid, 1853.
Ehrenpreis, M. *Le pays entre Orient et Occident*. Paris, 1930.
Elisseeff, Nikita. *Themes et motifs des mille et une nuits. Essai de classification*. Beirut, 1949.
Entwistle, Wm. James. *The Spanish Language*. London, 1936; 2nd ed., 1962.
d'Erlanger, B. R. *La musique arabe*. 6 vols. Paris, 1930–1959.
Espalza, M. de "Recherches récentes sur les emigrations de 'Moriscos' en Tunisie." *CT*, 18 (1970), 139–149.
Ettinghausen, R. *Studies in Muslim Iconography*. Washington, D.C., 1950.
Fackenheim, E. L. "A Treatise on Love by Ibn Sīnā." *Mediaeval Studies*, 7 (1945). 208–228.
Fagnan, E. *Chronique des Almohades et des Macides atribué à Zarkechi*. French trans. Constantine, 1895.

———. *Extraits inédits relatifs au Magreb. Géographie et histoire*. Algiers, 1924.
Fahmy, 'Alī Muhammad. *Muslim Sea Power in the Eastern Mediterranean Sea*. London, 1950.
Farah, C. *The Dhayl in Medieval Arabic Historiography*. New Haven, 1967.
Faris, Bishr. *L'honneur chez les arabes avant l'Islam*. Paris, 1932.
Faris, N. A., ed. *The Arab Heritage*. Princeton, 1944.
Farmer, H. G. "Clues for the Arabian Influence on European Musical Theory." *JRAS*, Jan. 1929.
———. *Historical Facts for the Arabian Musical Influence*. London, 1930.
———. *A History of Arabian Music to the Thirteenth Century*. London, 1929.
———. "Ziryāb," in *EI* (1913–1914), vol. 4.
Fernández y González, F. *Estado social y político de los mudéjares de Castilla*. Madrid, 1866.
———. *La influencia de las lenguas y literaturas orientales en la nuestra*. Madrid, 1894.
Ferrand, G. *Relations de voyages et textes géographiques arabes, persans et turcs relatifs à l'Extreme-Orient des VIII au XVIII siècles*. 2 vols. Paris, 1913–1914.
Ferrandis Torres, J. *Marfiles y azabaches españoles (Colección Labor)*. Barcelona & Buenos Aires, 1928.
———. *La vida en el Islam español*. Leipzig, 1936.
Filgueira, Volverde J., ed. *Primera crónica general de España*. Madrid, 1949.
Fischel, W. J. *Jews in the Economic and Political Life of Medieval Islam*. London, 1937.
Fitzmaurice-Kelly, J. *A New History of Spanish Literature*. New York, 1926.
Flügel, G. *Die grammatischen Schulen der Araber*. Leipzig, 1862.
Fouillée, A. *Esquisse psychologique des peuples européens*. Paris, 1903.
Franz, J. *Die Baukunst des Islam*. Darmstadt, 1887.
Friedländer, N. *Maimonides: The Guide for the Perplexed*. London, 1951.
Fück, J. *'Arabiya*. Berlin, 1950. French trans. Cl. Denizeau. Paris, 1955.
———. *Die arabischen Studien in Europa bis in den Anfang des 20 Jahrhunderts*. Leipzig, 1955.
Funck-Brentano, F. *La Renaissance*. Paris, 1935.
Fyzee, Asaf A. A. *Outlines of Muhammadan Law*. London, 1955.
Gabrieli, Francesco. *Ibn Hamdis*. Mazara, 1948.
———. *Storia della letterature araba*. Milan, 1951.
———. *Storia e civilta musulmana*. Naples, 1947.
———. "The Transmission of Learning and Literary Influences to Western Europe," in *Cambridge History of Islam*. Cambridge, 1970. Pp. 851–889.
Gaillard, G. "La catalogue entre l'art de Cordoue et l'art roman." *SI*, 11 (1956).
Gallop, Rodney. *A Book of the Basques*. 1930.
Galmés de Fuentes, Alvaro. *Historia de los amores de Paris y Viana*. Madrid, 1970.
———. *Influencias sintácticas y estilísticas del árabe en la prosa medieval castellana*. Madrid, 1956.
———, ed. *El libro de las batallas*. Oviedo, 1967.
Galmette, J. *Le monde féodal*. Paris, 1934.
García Gómez, E. "A propósito del libro de K. Heger Sobre las jaryas." *al-Andalus*, 26 (1961), 453–465.
———. *Abū Isḥāq de Elvira: Un alfaquí español*. Madrid, 1944.
———. "Algunas precisiones sobre la ruina de la Córdoba Omeya." *al-Andalus*, 12 (1947), 267–294.
———. "Al-Ḥakam y los berberes según un texto inédito de Ibn Ḥayyān." *al-Andalus*, 13 (1948), 209–226.
———. "Bagdad y los reinos de Taifas." *RO*, 127 (1934), 1–22.
———. *Las banderas y los campeones: Traducción española del libro de Ibn Said al-Magribi titulado Rayat al-Mubarrizin*. Madrid, 1942.
———. *Cinco poetas musulmanes*. Madrid, 1944.
———. "Dos nuevas jaryas romances (XXV y XXVI) en muwaššahas árabes (MS. G. S. Colin), y adición al estudio de otra jarya romance." *al-Andalus*, 19 (1954), 390–391.

———. "Estudio del Dār al-ṭirāz." *al-Andalus*, 27 (1962), 21–104.
———. *Introducción a la traducción del Libro El Collar de la Paloma, tratado sobre el amor y los amantes, de Ibn Hazm de Cordoba*. Madrid, 1952.
———. *Las jarchas*. Madrid, 1963.
———. "La 'ley de Mussafia' se aplica a la poesía estrófica arábigoandaluza." *al-Andalus*, 27 (1962), 1–20.
———. "La lírica hispano árabe y la aparición de la lírica románica." *al-Andalus*, 21 (1956) 303–338.
———. "Más sobre las 'jaryas' romances en 'muwaššahas' hebreas." *al-Andalus*, 14 (1949), 409–417.
———. "La Muwaššaha de Ibn Baqi de Córdoba: *Ma laday ṣabrun m'inu* con jarya romance." *al-Andalus*, 19 (1954), 43–54.
———. *Poemas arábigo andaluces*. Madrid & Buenos Aires, 1940.
———. *Poesía arábigoandaluza. Breve síntesis histórica*. Madrid, 1952.
———. "La poésie politique sous le Califat de Cordoue." *REI*. Paris, 1949, pp. 5–11.
———. "Un 'pre-muwaššaha' atribuída a Abū Nuwās." *al-Andalus*, 21 (1956), 404–414.
———. *Qasīdas de Andalucía*. Madrid, 1940–1948.
———. "Siete zéjeles de Ben Quzmān." *RO*, 2 (1964), 129–145.
———. *Silla del moro y nuevas escenas andaluzas*. Madrid, 1948.
———. "Sobre un tercer tipo de poesía arábigoandaluza," in *Estudios dedicados a Menéndez Pidal*, 2 (1951) 397–408.
———. *Un texto árabe occidental de la leyenda de Alejandro*. Madrid, 1929.
———. *Todo Ben Quzmān*. 3 vols. Madrid, 1972.
———. "Usos y supersticiones communes a Persia y España." *al-Andalus*, 22 (1957), 459–462.
———. "Veinticuatro jaryas romances en muwaššahas árabes (MS. G. S. Colin)." *al-Andalus*, 17 (1952), 57–127.
———. *Una voz en la calle*. Madrid, 1933.
Gardet, L. *La cité musulmane; vie sociale et politique*. Paris, 1954.
———. *La pensée religieuse d'Avicenne*. Paris, 1951.
——— and M. Anawati. *Introduction à la théologie musulmane*. Paris, 1970.
———. *Mystique musulmane*. Paris, 1961.
Garrido Atienza, M. *Las capitulaciones para la entrega de Granada*. Granada, 1910.
Garrison, F. H. *An Introduction to the History of Medicine*. 4th ed. Philadelphia, 1929.
Gaspar Remiro, Mariano. *Historia de Murcia musulmana*. Saragossa, 1905.
Gaudefroy-Demombynes, M. "Une lettre de Saladin au calife almohade," in *Mélanges René Basset*, vol. 2. Paris, 1925.
———. *Muslim Institutions*. London, 1950.
———. "Observations sur le tome III du Bayan d'Ibn Idari," in *Mélanges René Basset*, vol. 2. Paris, 1925.
———. *Le pèlerinage à la Mekke. Étude d'histoire religieuse*. *AMG*, 33. Paris, 1923.
———. *La Syrie à l'époque des Mamlouks d'après les auteurs arabes*. Paris, 1923.
Gauthier, Léon. *Accord de la religion et de la philosophie: Traité d'Ibn Rochd*. Algiers, 1905.
———. *Ibn Rushd*. Paris, 1948.
———. *Ibn Tofail: Sa vie ses oeuvres*. Paris, 1909.
———. *Introduction à l'étude de la philosophie musulmane. L'esprit sémitique et l'esprit aryen. La philosophie grecque et la religion de l'Islam*. Paris, 1923.
Gautier, E. F. *L'islamisation de l'Afrique de Nord. Les siècles obscurs du Maghreb*. Paris, 1927. 2nd ed., *Le Passé de l'Afrique du Nord. Les siècles obscurs*. Paris, 1937.
Gayangos, P. de. "Escritores en prosa anteriores al siglo XV." *BAE*, 51 (Madrid, 1860).
———. "La gran conquista de Ultramar." *BAE*, 49 (Madrid, 1858).
———. *The History of the Mohammedan Dynasties in Spain*, partial trans. of al-Maqqarī's *Nafḥ al-ṭīb*. 2 vols. London, 1840–1843.
———. "Language and Literature of the Moriscos." *British and Foreign Review*, 8 (1839), 63–95.

———. "Libros de caballerías." *BAE*, 40 (Madrid, 1857).
———. "Memoria sobre la autenticidad de la crónica denominada del moro Rasis." *MRAH*, 8 (1852).
———. *Memorias del cautivo en la Goleta de Túnez*. Madrid, 1875.
———. "Tratado de legislación musulmana." *Memorial Histórico Español*, 5 (1853), 1–149.
——— and R. Menéndez Pidal, eds. *La crónica del moro Rasis*, in *El catálogo de crónicas de la Real Biblioteca*. Madrid, 1850.
Gayet, A. *L'art arabe*. Paris, 1893.
Ghali, Wacyf Boutros. *La tradition chevaleresque des Arabes*. Paris, 1919.
Gibb, H. A. R. *Arabic Literature, an Introduction*. Oxford, 1963.
———. " 'Arabiyya," in *EI* (1960).
———. "The Influence of Islamic Culture in Medieval Europe." *Bulletin of the John Rylands Library*, 38 (1955).
———. *Mohammedanism*. Mentor Book, 1955.
———. *Studies on the Civilization of Islam*. Boston, 1962.
Gibbon, Edward. *The Decline and Fall of the Roman Empire*, ed. J. B. Bury. London, 1911.
Gil, P., J. Ribera, and M. Sánchez. *Colección de textos aljamiados*. Saragossa, 1888.
Gilbert, Allan. *Dante and His Comedy*. New York, 1963.
Gilson, E. *Pourquoi Saint Thomas à critiqué Saint Augustin*, in *Archives d'histoire doctrinale et littéraire du Moyen Âge*. Paris, 1926.
Goichon, A. M. *La philosophie d'Avicenne et son influence en Europe médiévale*. Paris, 1944.
Goitein, S. D. *Jews and Arabs*. New York, 1955.
Goldziher, I. *Le livre d'Ibn Toumart*. Algiers, 1903.
———. *Muhammedanische Studien*. 2 vols. Halle, 1890.
———. "Die Šu'ūbiyya unter den Muhammedanern in Spanien." *ZDMG*, 53 (1899), 601–620.
———. *Die Ẓāhiriten*. Leipzig, 1884.
Gómez Moreno, M. *El arte árabe español hasta los almohades; arte mozárabe*, in *Ars Hispaniae*, 3 (Madrid, 1951).
———. *Iglesias mozárabes. Arte español de los siglos IX a XI*. 2 vols. Madrid, 1919.
Gómez Nogales, R. P. "Ibn 'Arabī eslabón cultural." *RIEI*, 13 (1965–1966), 25–42.
González, Joaquin de. *Fatḥo l-Andalusi, historia de la conquista de España*. Algiers, 1899.
González Palencia, A. "El amor platónico en la corte de los Califas." *Boletín de la Real Academia de Ciencias, Bellas Letras, y Noblas Artes de Cordova* (Cordova, 1929), 1–25.
———. *Arabes muricanos ilustres*. Murcia, 1957.
———. *El Arzobispo Don Raimundo de Toledo*. Barcelona, 1942.
———, trans. *El filósofo autodidácto* (Ibn Ṭufayl's *Ḥayy Ibn Yaqẓān*). 2nd ed. Madrid, 1948.
———. *Historia de la España musulmana*. 3rd ed. Barcelona, 1932. 4th ed., 1951.
———. *Historia de la literatura arábigo-española*. Barçelona, 1928.
———. *Historias y leyendas*. Madrid, 1942.
———. *Influencia de la civilisṭhación árabe*. Madrid, 1931.
———. *El Islam y Occidente*. Madrid, 1931.
———. *Moros y cristianos en España medieval*. Madrid, 1945.
———. *Los mozárabes de Toledo en los siglos XII y XIII*. 4 vols. Madrid, 1926–1930.
———. *Noticias y extractos de manuscritos árabes aljamiados*, in *Miscelánea de estudios y textos árabes*. Madrid, 1915.
———. "Posicion de Arteaga en la polémica sobre música y poesía arábigas." *al-Andalus*, 11 (1946), 241–245.
——— and Juan Hurtado y J. de la Serna. *Antología de la literatura española*. Madrid, 1926.
———. *Historia de la literatura española*. Madrid, 1922.
Gorze, Jean de. *Embajada del emperador de Alemania Oton I al califa de Cordoba Abderraham III*. Madrid, 1872.
Granja, Fernando de la. "Ibn García, cadí de los califas Ḥammūdies." *al-Andalus*, 30 (1965), 63–78.

———. "Origin árabe de un famoso cuento español." *al-Andalus*, 24 (1959), 319–332.

———. "Una opinión significativa sobre la poesía arábigo-andaluza." *al-Andalus*, 22 (1957), 215–220.

Grunebaum, G. E. von. "Avicenna's Risāla fî 'l-'išq and Courtly Love." *JNES*, 11 (1952), 233–238.

———. *Islam*. London, 1955.

———. *Medieval Islam: A Study in Cultural Orientation*. Chicago, 1946. 2nd ed., 1953.

———. *A Tenth-Century Document of Arabic Literary Theory and Criticism: The Sections on Poetry of al-Baqillānī's I'jāz al-Qur'ān*. Chicago, 1950.

Gruner, O. C. *A Treatise on the Canon of Medicine of Avicenna*. London, 1930.

Guillaume, A. *The Traditions of Islam*. Oxford, 1924.

Guillén Robles, F. *Leyenda de José y de Alejandro Magno*. Saragossa, 1888.

———. *Leyendas moriscas*. 3 vols. Madrid, 1885–1886.

———. *Málaga musulmana*. Málaga, 1880.

Gundisalvo, Domingo. *De scientiis, texto latino establecido por el P. Manuel Alonso Alonso, S.J.* Madrid & Granada, 1954.

Guttman, J. *Der Einfluss der maimonidischen Philosophie auf das christliche Abendland*. Leipzig, 1908.

Haines, C. R. *Christianity and Islam in Spain, A.D. 756–1031*. 1889. 2nd ed. New York, 1969.

Halphen, L. *Les barbares*. Paris, 1930.

———. *L'essor d'Europe*. Paris, 1932.

Hammer-Purgstalls, J. B. von. *Literaturgeschichte der Araber, von Ihrem Beginne bis zu Ende des zwölften Jahrhunderts der Hidschret*. 7 vols. Vienna, 1850–1856.

Hankin, E. H. *The Drawing of Geometric Patterns in Saracenic Art*. Calcutta, 1925.

Harris, C. R. S. *Duns Scotus*. Oxford, 1927.

Hartmann, M. *Das arabische Strophengedicht. I. Das Muwaššah*. Weimar, 1897.

Harvey, L. P. "Aljamía," in *EI*, vol. 1. London, 1960, Pp. 404–405.

———. "The Literary Culture of the Moriscos (1492–1609)." Ph.D. thesis, Oxford, 1958.

———. "Yuse Banegas, un moro noble de Granada bajo los Reyes Católicos." (MS. Extracto 3, *BNM* 245.) Also in *al-Andalus*, 21 (1956), 297–302.

Haskins, C. H. *The Renaissance of the Twelfth Century*. Cambridge, 1927.

———. *Studies in the History of Medieval Science*. 2nd ed. Cambridge, Mass., 1927.

Hassan, Zaky Mohamed. *Les Tulunids — Étude de l'Egypte Musulmane à la fin du IX siècle*. Paris, 1953.

Havell, E. B. *Indian Architecture*. 2nd ed. London, 1927.

Haywood, J. *Arabic Lexicography*. Leiden, 1960.

Hell, Joseph. "Al-'Abbās ibn al-Aḥnaf, der Minnesänger am Hofe Hārūn al-Rasīd's." *Islamica*, 2 (1926), 271–307.

———. *The Arab Civilization*. Cambridge, 1926.

Henriquez de Jorquena, Fr. *Anales de Granada*. Granada, 1934.

Hernández Jiménez, Féliz. *Arte musulman. La techumbre de la Gran Mezquita de Córdoba*, in *Archivo Español de Arte y Arqueología*, vol. 4. Madrid, 1928.

Herrera, Alonso de. *Agricultura general*. Madrid, 1945.

Hess, A. C. "The Moriscos: An Ottoman Fifth Column in Sixteenth-Century Spain." *American Historical Review*, 74 (1968), 1–25.

Heyd, A. *Histoire du commerce du Levant au Moyen Âge*. 3 vols. Leipzig, 1885–1886.

Hirschberg, J. *Geschichte der Augenheilkunde bei den Arabern*. Leipzig, 1905.

Hirschfeld, Haetwig. *Literary History of Jewish Grammarians and Lexicographers*. Oxford, 1926.

Hitti, P. K. *History of the Arabs*. 6th ed. London, 1958; New York, 1968.

———. *The Makers of Arab History*. New York, 1968.

Hodgson, M. *The Venture of Islam*. 3 vols. Chicago, 1970.

Hoernerbach, W. *Islamische Geschichte Spaniens*. Zurich, 1970.

———. *Spanisch-Islamische Urkunden aus der Zeit der Naṣriden und Moriscos*. Bonn, 1965.

———. "Teoría del 'zégel' según Safi al-Dīn Ḥillī." *al-Andalus*, 15 (1950), 297–334.
——— and H. Ritter. "Neue Materialien zum 'Zacal' I: Ibn Quzman." *Oriens*, 3 (1950), 266–315.
———. "Neue Materielien zum 'Zacal' II: Mugalis." *Oriens*, 5 (1952), 269–301.
Hole, Edwyn. *Andalus: Spain under the Muslims*. London, 1958.
Holmyard, E. J. *Book of Knowledge Concerning Cultivation of Gold by Abulqasim Muhammad ibn Ahmad*. Paris, 1923.
———. *Chemistry to the Time of Dalton*. Oxford, 1925.
Homenaje a D. Francisco Codera en su jubilación del pofesorado. Estudios de erudición oriental. Saragossa, 1904.
Hoogvliet, M. *Specimem e litteris orientalibus, exhibens diversorum scriptorum locos de regia Aphtasidarum familia et de Ibn Abduno poeta*. Leiden, 1839.
Hopkins, J. F. P. *Medieval Muslim Government in Barbary until the Sixth Century of the Hijra*. London, 1958.
Horovitz, J. *Koranische Untersuchungen*. Berlin & Leipzig, 1926.
Horten, M. *Die philosophischen Systeme de spekulativen Theologen im Islam.* Bonn, 1912.
Hourani, G. *Averroës on the Harmony of Religion and Philosophy*. London, 1961.
———. "The Early Growth of the Secular Sciences in Andalusia." *SI*, 32 (1970), 143–156.
Huart, C. *Histoire des Arabes*. Paris, 1913.
———. *Littérature arabe*. Paris, 1902.
Huici Miranda, A. "La cocina Hispano-Magribí durante la época almohade." *RIEI*, 5 (1957), 137–156.
———. *Colección de crónicas árabes de la Reconquista*, 4 vols.: Vol. 1, *Al-Ḥulāl Al-Mawšiyya, crónica árabe de las dinastías almorávide, almohade y benimerín*. Tetuan, 1952. Vols. 2 & 3, *al-Bayān al-Mugrib fi Ijtisār Ajbār Mulūk al-Andalus wa al-Magrib por Ibn 'Idhārī al-Marrakuši. Los almohades*, vols. 1, 2. Tetuan, 1953–1954. Vol. 4, *Kitāb al-Mu'yib fī Taljīs Ajbār al-Magrib por Abū Muḥammad 'Abd al-Wāḥid al-Marrakušī*. Tetuan, 1955.
———. *Colección diplomática de Jaime I, el Conquistador, años 1217 a 1253*, vol. 1. Valencia, 1916.
———. *Las crónicas latinas de la Reconquista, estudios prácticos de latín Medieval*. 2 vols. Valencia, 1913.
———. *Estudio sobre la compaña de Las Navas de Tolosa*. Valencia, 1916.
———. *Las grandes batallas de la Reconquista*. Madrid, 1956.
———. *Historia musulmana de Valencia*. 3 vols. Valencia, 1970.
———. *Historia política del imperio almohade*. Tetuan, 1956–1957.
———, ed. "Kitāb aṭ-Ṭabīj fī l-Magrib wa l-Andalus fī 'Aṣr al-Muwaḥḥidīn li-Mu'allif Maŷhūl." *RIEI*, 9–10 (1961–1962), 15–242.
Humbert, Jean. *Anthologie Arabe*. Paris, 1819.
Hurtado, Juan, and A. González Palencia. *Historia de la literatura española*. Madrid, 1932.
Husik, I. *A History of Medieval Jewish Philosophy*. New York, 1916.
Imamuddin, S. M. "Cordovan Muslim Rule in Iqritish [Crete]." *JPHS*, 8 (1960), 296–312.
———. "Gardens and Recreations in Muslim Spain." *IC* (1962), 159–166.
———. "Music in Muslim Spain." IC (1959).
———. *A Political History of Muslim Spain*. Dacca, 1961.
———. *Some Aspects of the Socio-Economic and Cultural History of Muslim Spain*. Leiden, 1965.
Irving, Thomas. "Arab Tales in Medieval Spanish." *IL*, 7 (1955), 509–514.
———. *Falcon of Spain: A Study of Eighth-Century Spain with Special Emphasis upon the Life of the Umayyad Ruler Abdurrahman I, 756–788*. Lahore, 1954.
Irving, Washington. *Chronicle of the Conquest of Granada*. Philadelphia, 1829.
———. *Tales of the Alhambra*. Philadelphia, 1832.
Issawi, Ch. *Ibn Khaldun's Philosophy of History*. London, 1950.

Jacob, G. *Studien in Arabischen Geographen*. 4 vols. Berlin, 1891–1892.
Jadaane, F. *L'influence du stoïcisme sur la pensée musulmane*. Beirut, 1968.
Janer, Florencio. *Condición social de los moricos de Granada*. Madrid, 1857.
Jean-Léon l'Africain. *Description de l'Afrique*. French trans. A. Epaulard. 2 vols. Paris, 1956.
Jeanory, A. *La poésie lyrique des troubadours*. 2 vols. Toulouse & Paris, 1934.
Jeffery, A. *The Foreign Vocabulary of the Qur'ān*. Baroda, 1928.
———. *Materials for the History of the Qur'ān*. Leiden, 1937.
———. *The Qur'ān as Scripture*. New York, 1952.
———. *A Reader on Islam*. The Hague, 1962.
Jiménez de Rada, Rodrigo. *Historia Arabum*. Madrid, 1793.
Julien, C. A. *Histoire de l'Afrique du Nord*. Paris, 1951; 2nd ed., 1964.
Kamal, Youssouf. *Monumenta cartografica africae et aegypti*. Leiden, 1935.
Kamen, H. *The Spanish Inquisition*. New York, 1965.
Kennedy, E. S. "A Survey of Islamic Astronomical Tables." *Transactions of the American Philosophical Society*, 46 (1956), 123–177.
Khadduri, M. *Law in the Middle East*. Washington, D.C., 1955.
Khairallah, A. *Outline of Arab Contributions to Medicine and the Allied Sciences*. Beirut, 1946.
Khoury, P. "Jean Damascene et l'Islam." *Proche Orient Chrétien*, 7 (1957), 8 (1958).
Khudā Bakhsh. *Islamic Civilization*. 2 vols. Berkeley, 1929–1930.
Kimble, G. H. T. *Geography in the Middle Ages*. London, 1938.
Kleinhans, Arduinis. *Historia Studii Linguae Arabicae et Colegii Missionum Ordinis Fratrum Minorum in Conventu ad S. Petrum in Monte Aureo Romae Erecti*, in *Biblioteca Bio-Bibliografica della Terra Santa e dell' Oriente Francescano*, vol. 13. Florence, 1930.
Knust, Hermann. *Mittheilungen aus dem Eskurial*. Tübingen, 1879.
Koechlin, Raimundo, and Gaston Migeon. *Arte musulman, cerámicas, tejidos, tapices*. Barcelona, 1930.
Krachkovskii, I. I. *Arabskaīa Kul'tura v Ispanii* (The Arab Culture in Spain). Moscoe & Leningrad, 1937.
———. *Istoria Arabiskoi geograficheskoi Literatury*. 2 vols. Moscow, 1957. Arabic trans. Salāḥ al-Dīn 'Uthmān Hāshim Cairo, 1963–1965.
Kramers, J. H. "Geography and Commerce," in T. Arnold and A. Guillaume, eds., *The Legacy of Islam*. Oxford, 1931.
Kritzeck, James. *Peter the Venerable and Islam*. Princeton, 1964.
Lacam, Jean. *Les sarrazins dans le haut Moyen Âge français*. Paris, 1965.
Lafuente Alcántara, M. *Historia de Granada*. Paris, 1913–1915.
———. *Historia general de España*. Barcelona, 1889.
———. *Inscripciones árabes de Granada*. Madrid, 1860.
———. *Relaciones de algunos sucesos de los últimos tiempos del reino de Granada*. Madrid, 1868.
Lambert, E. "L'art hispano-mauresque et l'art roman." *Hespéris*, 17 (1933), 29–43.
———. "Histoire de la Grande Mosquée de Cordoue au XIIe et IXe siècles." *AIEO*, 2 (1936), 165–179.
———. *Tolède*. Paris, 1925.
Lammens, H. *Remarques sur les mots français dérivés de l'arabe*. Beirut, 1890.
Landau, R. *The Philosophy of Ibn 'Arabī*. London, 1959.
Lane, E. W. *Arabic English Lexicon*. 4 vols. Edinburgh, 1867.
Lane-Poole, S. *The Mohammadan Dynasties*. London, 1893.
———. *The Story of the Moors in Spain*. New York, 1886, 1911.
Lapesa, R. *Historia de la lengua española*. 6th ed. New York, 1965.
Lapeyre, H. *Géographie de l'Espagne morisque*. Paris, 1959.
Laprade, A. *Croquis*. Paris, 1958.

Larra, Mariano José de. *Artículos de costumbres*. Madrid, 1959.
Lathan, J. D. ''Towards a Study of Andalusian Immigration and Its Place in Tunisian History.'' *CT*, 5 (1957), 203–252.
Latrie, Le Comte de Mas. *Relations et commerce de l'Afrique septentrionale au Magreb avec les nations chrétiennes au Moyen Âge*. Paris, 1886.
———. *Traités de paix et de commerce et documents divers concernant les rélations des chrétiens avec les arabes et l'Afrique septentrionale au Moyen Âge*. Paris, 1866.
Lea, Charles H. *A History of the Inquisition of Spain*. New York, 1906.
———. *The Moriscos of Spain*. London, 1901.
Le Bon, Gustave. *La civilisation des arabes*. Paris, 1884.
Leclerc, L. *Histoire de la médecine arabe*. 2 vols. Paris, 1876.
———. *Traité des simples par Ibn al Beithar*. 3 vols. Paris, 1877.
Le Gentil, P. *La poésie lyrique espagnole et portugaise à la fin du Moyen Âge*. Rennes, 1949–1953.
Lelewel, J. *Atlas*. Brussels, 1850.
———. *Géographie du Moyen Âge*. 2 vols. Brussels, 1852.
Lemay, Richard. ''À propos de l'origine arabe de l'art des troubadours.'' *Annales, Économies, Sociétés, Civilisations* (1966), 990–1011.
Lerchundi, J., and J. Simonet. *Cretomatia arábigo-española*. Granada 1881.
Lerner, R., and Mahdi. *Medieval Political Philosophy*. Glencoe, Ill., 1963.
Le Strange, G. *Baghdad during the Abbasid Caliphate*. Oxford, 1900.
Le Tourneau, Roger. *The Almohad Movement in North Africa in the Twelfth and Thirteenth Centuries*. Princeton, 1969.
Levasseur, E. *Histoire du commerce de la France*. Paris, 1911.
Lévi-Provençal, E. ''Le Cid de l'histoire.'' *Revue Historique*, 180 (Paris, 1937), 58–74.
———. *La civilisation arabe en Espagne, vue générale*. Cairo, 1938. 3rd ed., Paris, 1961. Spanish trans. de las Cagigas. Buenos Aires, 1953.
———. ''Deux nouveaux fragments des mémoires du roi Ziride 'Abd Allah de Grenade.'' *al-Andalus*, 6 (1941), 1–63.
———. *Documents arabes inédits première série: Trois traité hispaniques de Hisba*. Paris & Cairo, 1955.
———. *Documents inédits d'histoire almohade*. Paris, 1928.
———. *España musulmana*. Spanish trans. E. García Gómez. Madrid, 1950.
———. *Histoire de l'Espagne musulmane*. 3 vols. Paris, 1950–1953.
———. *Les historiens de chorfa*. Paris, 1922.
———. *Inscriptions arabes d'Espagne*. Leiden, 1931.
———. *Islam d'Occident*. Paris, 1948.
———. *Mafākhir al-Barbar, Fragments historiques sur les Berbères au Moyen Âge* in *Collection de textes publiée par l'Institut des Hautes Études Marocaines*, vol. 1 Rabat, 1934.
———. ''Un manuscrit de la bibliothèque de calife al-Ḥakam II.'' *Héspéris*, 18 (1934), 198–200.
———. ''Poésie arabe d'Espagne et poésie d'Europe médiévale.'' *IO* (Paris, 1948), 283–304.
———. ''Quelques considérations sur l'essor des études relative à l'Occident musulman.'' *RIEEI*, 2 (1954;, 73–76.
———. *Trente-sept lettres officielles almohades*. Rabat, 1941.
———. ''Les vers arabe de la chanson V de Guillaume IX d'Aquitaine.'' *Arabica*, (1955), 208–211.
Levy, R. *A Baghdad Chronicle*. Cambridge, 1929.
———. *The Social Structure of Islam*. Cambridge, 1957.
Lewis, Archibald R. *Naval Power and Trade in the Mediterranean, A.D. 500–1100*. Princeton, 1951.
Lewis, B. *The Arabs in History*. London, 1954.
Lida de Malkiel, María Rosa. *Two Spanish Masterpieces, The ''Book of Good Love'' and ''The Celestina''* in *Illinois Studies in Language and Literature*, 49 (1961).

Lippmann, O. von. *Entstebung und Ausbreitung der Alchemie*. Berlin, 1919.
Littman, E. *Morgenländische Vörter im Deutschen*. 2nd ed. Tübingen, 1924.
Llampillas, Javier. *Ensayo histórico-apologético de la literatura española contra las opiniones preoccupadas de algunos escritores modernos italianos*. Madrid, 1789.
Llorente, A. *Historia crítica de la inquisición de España*. Madrid, 1817.
Lokotsch, K. *Etymologisches Worterbuch der europaischen Worter orientalischen Ursprungs*. Heidelberg, 1927.
Longás, Pedro. *Vida religiosa de los moriscos*. Madrid, 1915.
———. "Un documento sobre los mudéjares de Nuez (Zaragoza), siglo XV." *al-Andalus*, 28 (1963), 431–444.
Lópes, D. *Textos en aljamía portuguesa*. Lisbon, 1897.
López de Ayala, J. *Contribuciones e impuestos en Leyon y Castilla durante la Edad Media*. Madrid, 1896.
López Ortíz, José. "El clero musulmán." *Religión y cultura*, 6 (1929), 198–206.
——— *Derecho musulmán*. Barcelona & Buenos Aires, 1932.
———. "Fatwas granadinas de los siglos XIV y XV." *al-Andalus*, 6 (1941), 73–127.
———. "Figuras de jurisconsultos hispano-musulmanes. *Yaḥya ben Yaḥya*." *Religion y Cultura*, 16 (1931), 94–104.
———. "La recepción de la escuela malequí en España." *AHDE*, 7 (Madrid, 1931), 1–169.
Lot, F. *Les invasions barbares*. Paris, 1937.
Luna, Miguel de. *The History of the Conquest of Spain by the Moors*. 2nd ed. London, 1963.
Lyall, Charles. *Ancient Arabian Poetry*. Edinburgh, 1885.
———. *A Commentary on the Ancient Arabic Poems*. Calcutta, 1894.
———. *Translations of Ancient Arabian Poetry*. New York, 1930.
Lynch, John. *Spain under the Hapsburgs*. Vol. 1, *Empire and Absolutism, 1516–1598*. New York, 1964.
MacCabe, Joseph. *Splendour of Moorish Spain*. London, 1935.
McCarthy, R. C. *The Theology of al-Ash'arī*. Beirut, 1953.
MacDonald, D. B. *Development of Muslim Theology, Jurisprudence and Constitutional Theory*. New York, 1903.
———. *The Religious Life and Attitude in Islam*. Chicago, 1909.
Madkour, I. *La place d'al-Fārābī dans l'école philosophique musulmane*. Paris, 1934.
Mahdi, Muhsin. *Ibn Khaldūn's Philosophy of History*. London, 1957.
Makkī, Maḥmūd 'Alī. *Ensayo sobre las aportaciones orientales en la España musulmana*. Madrid, 1968.
———. "El sī'ismo en al-Andalus." *RIEEI*, 2 (1954), 93–149.
Mâle, E. *Art et artistes du Moyen Âge*. Paris, 1927.
———. "Les influences arabes dans l'art roman." *Revue de Deux Mondes*, 18 (1923).
Manuel, Juan. *El Conde Lucanor*. 4th ed. Madrid, 1968.
Manzanares de Cirra, M. *Arabistas españoles del siglo XIX*. Madrid, 1972.
Manzano Martos, Rafael. "La Capilla Real de Cholula y su mudejarismo." *al-Andalus*, 26 (1961), 219–224.
Marçais, G. *Les Arabes en Berberie du XI au XIV siècles*. Constantine & Paris, 1913.
———. *L'architecture musulmane d'Occident*. Paris, 1954.
———. *La Berbérie musulmane et l'Orient au Moyen Âge*. Paris, 1946.
———. *Le costume musulman d'Alger (1839–1930). Collection du centenaire de l'Algérie: Archéologie et histoire*. Paris, 1930.
———. "Le dialecte arabe parlé à Tlemcen." *Publications de l'École des Lettres d'Alger*, vol. 26, Paris, 1902.
———. *Manuel d'art musulman. L'architecture. Tunisie, Algérie, Maroc, Espagne, Sicile*. 2 vols. Paris, 1926–1927.
———. *Les monuments arabes de Tlemcen*. Paris, 1903.
———. "Note sur les ribats en Berberis," in *Mélanges René Basset*, vol. 2 (Paris, 1925), 395–430.

———. *Sur un bas-relief musulman du Musée Stephane Gsell*. *AIEO*, 1 (Paris, 1935), 162–175.
———. *Textes arabes de Takrouna*. *BELOV*, vol. 8 Paris, 1925.
Marceira, A. G. *Apuntes y noticias sobre la agricultura de los árabes españoles*. Zamora, 1876.
———. *La cana de azucar*. Madrid, 1875.
Margoliouth, D. S. *Lectures on Arabic Historians*. Calcutta, 1930.
Mármol Carvajal, Luis del. *Descripción general de Africa*. Madrid, 1953.
———. *Historia de rebelión y castigo de los moriscos del Reino de Granada*, in *BAE*, vol. 21. Madrid, 1946.
Martinenche, E. *À propos d'Espagne*. Paris, 1905.
Martínez Montávez, Pedro. *Poesía árabe contemporanea*. Madrid, 1958.
Martino, Pierre. *L'Orient dans la littérature française au XVII et au XVIII siècles*. Paris, 1906.
Massad, P. "Casiri y uno de sus estudios inéditos." *BRAH*, 5 (1959), 15–47.
Maspero, Jean, and Gaston Wiet. *Matériaux pour servir à la géographie de l'Egypte*, in *Mémoires de l'Institut Français d'Archéologie Orientale*, vol. 36. Cairo, 1914–1919.
Massé, H. *Anthologie persane (XI–XIX siècles)*. Paris, 1950.
———. "Un chapître des analectes d'al-Maqqari sur la littérature descriptive chez les arabes," in *Mélanges René Basset*, vol. 1 (Paris, 1923), 235–258.
———. *Les épopées persanes, Firdousi et l'épopée nationale*. Paris, 1935.
———. "Ibn Zaidun." *Hespéris*, 1 (1921), 183–193.
Massignon, Louis. *La passion d'al-Ḥallāj*. Paris, 1922.
———. "Recherches sur Shushtarī, poète andalou enterré à Damiette," in *Mélanges William Marçais* (Paris, 1950), 251–276.
———. "Time in Islamic Thought." *Papers from the Eranos Yearbooks*, Bollingen Series, 30. New York, 1956.
Melber, J. *The Universality of Maimonides*. New York, 1968.
Mélida, José Ramón. "Memoria acerca de algunas inscripciones arábigas de España y Portugal." *Boletin de la Institución Libre de Enseñanza*, 7 (1883), 366–367.
Mendoza, Diego Hurtado de. *De la guerra de Granada*, in *BAE*, vol. 21. Madrid, 1946.
Mendoza y Bobadilla. *El tizon de la nobleza española y sambenitos de sus linajes*. Barcelona, 1880.
Menéndez Pidal, R. *Cantar de mío Cid*. Madrid, 1906–1911.
———. "Cantos románicos andalusíes (continuadores de una lírica latina vulgar)." *BRAE*, 31 (Madrid, 1951), 187–270.
———. *El Cid campeador*. Buenos Aires, 1950.
———. "España como eslabón entre el cristianismo y el Islam." *RIEEI*, 1 (1953), 1–20.
———. *La España del Cid*. 2 vols. Madrid, 1947. English trans. Harold Sunderland, *The Cid and His Spain*. London, 1934.
———. *Estudio linguístico de la Península Ibérica hasta el siglo XI*. Madrid, 1929.
———. *Historia de España*. Madrid, 1950–1957.
———. *Historia y epopeya*. Madrid, 1934.
———. *El idioma español in sus primeros tiempos*. 5th ed. Madrid, 1957.
———. *Orígenes del español*. Madrid, 1950.
———. "Poema de Yūçuf: materiales para su estudio." *RABM*, 8 (1902). Reprinted Granada, 1952.
———. *Poema del Cid*, English verse trans. W. S. Merwin. New York, 1960.
———. *Poesía árabe y poesía europea*. Madrid, 1941, 1963. *Revista Cubana* (Jan.–Mar. 1937).
———. *Poesía juglaresca*. Madrid, 1957.
———. *Poesía juglaresca y juglares*. Madrid, 1924.
———. *Primera crónica general de España*, in *NBAE*, vol. 5. Madrid, 1906.
———. "La primitiva lírica europea." *RFE*, 43 (1960).

——— and P. de Gayanogs, eds. *La crónica del moro Rasis*, in *El catálogo de crónicas de la Real Biblioteca*. Madrid, 1850.
Menéndez y Pelayo, M. *Antología de poetas líricos castellanos*, vol. 1. Madrid, 1914.
———. *Antología general*, ed. José Ma. Sánchez de Muniain. 2 vols. Madrid, 1956.
———. "De las influencias semíticas en la literatura española," in *Obras completas, Estudios de crítica literaria*, in *Colección de escritores castellanos*, vol. 106. 2nd ed. Madrid, 1912.
———. *Introducción y programa de literatura española*. Madrid, 1934.
Merril, J. E. "John of Damascus on Islam." *MW*; 41 (1951) 88–97.
Meyerhof, M. *Le monde islamique* Paris, 1926.
———. "Science and Medicine," in T. Arnold and A. Guillaume, eds., *The Legacy of Islam*. Oxford, 1931, Pp. 311–355.
———. ed. *The Ten Treatises on the Eye, by Hunain B. Ishaq*. Cairo, 1928.
Meynard, C. Barbier de. *Dictionnaire géographique, historique et littéraire de la Perse et des contrées adjacentes, extrait du Modjem al-Bouldan de Yaquot et complète à l'aide de documents arabes et persans*. Paris, 1861.
Mez, A. *Renaissance des Islams*. Heidelberg, 1922. English trans. Salahuddin Khuda Buksh and D. S. Margoliouth, *The Renaissance of Islam*. Patna, 1937; London, 1937. Spanish trans. Madrid, 1936.
Michel, André. *Histoire de l'art*. Paris, 1905.
Mieli, A. *La science arabe et son rôle dans l'évolution scientifique mondiale*. Leiden, 1966.
Migeon, Gaston. *Manuel d'art musulman. Arts plastique et industriels.* 2 vols. Paris, 1927.
Miles, G. C. *The Coinage of the Umayyads in Spain*. New York, 1950.
Millás Vallicrosa, J. M. "Albaranes mallorquines en aljamiado hebraico árabe." *Sefarad*, 4(1944), 275–286.
———. *Assais d'historia de les ideas fisiques i matematiques a la Catalunya medieval*. Barcelona, 1931.
———. "La ciencia geopónica entre los autores hispanoárabes; conferencia pronunciada el dia 5 de marzo de 1953 en el Club Edafos." Madrid, 1954.
———. *Estudios sobre Azarquiel*. Madrid & Granada, 1943–1950.
———. *Estudios sobre la historia de la ciencia española*. Barcelona, 1949.
———. *Influencia de la poesía popular hispano-musulmana en la poesía italiana. RABM* (1920–1921).
———. "El literalismo de los traductores de la corte de Alfonso el Sabio." *al-Andalus*, 1 (1933), 155–187.
———. *Nuevas aportaciones para el estudio de la transmisión de la ciencia a Europa a través de España*. Barcelona, 1943.
———. *Nuevos estudios sobre historia de la ciencia española*. Barcelona, 1960.
———. *La poesía sagrada hebraico-española*. Madrid, 1940, 1949.
———. "El quehacer astronómico de la España árabe." *RIEEI*, 5 (1957), 49–64.
———. "Solución del problema de la patria de Colón," in *Tesoro de los judíos sefardíes*, vol. 6. Jerusalem, 1953. Pp. vii–svi.
———. *Las traducciones orientales en los manuscritos de la Biblioteca Catedral de Toledo*. Madrid, 1942.
———. *Tres polígrafos judaicos en la corte de los Tuchibies de Zaragoza*. Barcelona, 1948.
Miller, K. *Mappae Arabicae*. 4 vols. Stuttgart, 1926–1929.
Millet, R. *Les Almohades, histoire d'une dynastie berbère*. Paris, 1923.
Milliot, L. *Introduction à l'étude du droit musulman*. Paris, 1953.
Mommsen, Katharina. *Goethe und 1001 Nacht*. Berlin, 160.
———. *Goethe und die Moallakat*. 2nd ed. Berlin, 1961.
———. *Goethe und der Islam*. Stuttgart, 1965.
Monneret de Villard, Ugo. *Lo Studio dell' Islam in Europa nel XII e nel XIII secolo. Studi e Testi*, vol. 110. Vatican, 1944.
Monroe, James T. "A Curious Morisco Appeal to the Ottoman Empire." *al-Andalus*, 31 (1966), 281–303.

———. *Hispano-Arabic Poetry: A Student Anthology*. Berkeley, 1970.
———. "The Historical *Arjūza* of Ibn 'Abd Rabbihi, a Tenth-Century Hispano-Arabic Epic Poem." *JAOS*, 91 (1971), 67–95.
———. *Islam and the Arabs in Spanish Scholarship*. Leiden, 1970.
———. "The Muwashshaḥāt," in *Collected Studies in Honor of Américo Castro's 80th Year*. Oxford, 1965. Pp. 335–371.
———. *The Shu'ūbiyya in al-Andalus: The Risāla of Ibn García and Five Refutations*. Berkeley & Los Angeles, 1970.
Montague, R. *Les Berbères et le Makhzen dans le Sud du Maroc*. Paris, 1930.
Moore, E., et al. *Le opère di Dante Alighieri*. 4th ed. Oxford, 1963.
Mora, José Joaquín de. *Cuadros de la historia de los árabes, desde Mahoma hasta la conquista de Granada*. London, 1926.
Moraleda, V. L. "Edición de un manuscrito morisco del Corán. M.A. thesis, University of Barcelona, 1965.
Moreno, G. *Iglesias mozárabes, arte español de los siglos IX a XI*. Madrid, 1919.
Moreno Nieto, J. *Estudio crítico sobre los historiadores arábigo-españoles*. Madrid, 1864.
Müller, M. J. *Beitrage zur Geschichte der Westlichen Araber*. Munich, 1866–1878.
———. *Die Letzten Zeiten von Granada* (Munich, 1863).
Mu'nis, Ḥusayn (Hussain Mones). "Abd al-Raḥmān III y su papel en la historia general de España." *RIEI*, 9–10 (1961–1962), 233–252.
———. "Los Almoravides." *RIEI*, 14 (1967–1968), 49–102.
———. "Classificación de las ciencias según Ibn Ḥazm." *RIEI*, 13 (1965–1966), 7–16.
———. "De nuevo sobre las fuentes árabes de la historia del Cid." *RIEI*, 2 (1954).
———. "La división político-administrativa de la España musulmana." *RIEI*, 5 (1957), 79–135.
———. *Essai sur la chute du califat Umayyade à Cordoue en 1009*. Cairo, 1948.
Munk, S. *Mélanges de philosophie juive et arabe*. Paris, 1857, 1927.
Muñoz Sendino, J., ed. *La escala de Mahoma*. Madrid, 1949.
Munro, D. C. "The Western Attitude toward Islam during the Period of the Crusades." *Speculum*, 6 (1931), 338ff.
Murray, H. J. R. *A History of Chess*. Oxford, 1913.
Muwaffak, Abu Mansu. *Liber fundamentorum pharmacologiae*, ed. R. Seligmann. Vindobonae, 1830–1833.
Nafīs, Aḥmad. *Muslim Contribution to Geography*. Lahore, 1943.
Naṣr, Ḥossein. *Three Muslim Sages, Avicenna-Suhrawardy-Ibn 'Arabī*. Cambridge, Mass., 1964.
Netanyahu, B. *The Marranos of Spain from the Late 14th to the Early 16th Century*. New York, 1966.
Neuburger, Max. *History of Medicine*. 2 vols. English trans. Oxford, 1910–1925.
Neuman, A. *The Jews in Spain: Their Social, Political and Cultural Life during the Middle Ages*. 2 vols. Philadelphia, 1948.
Nicholson, R. A. *The Idea of Personality in Sufism*. Lahore, 1964.
———. *A Literary History of the Arabs*. Cambridge, 1956.
———. *The Mystics of Islam*. London, 1914, 1966.
———. *Studies in Islamic Mysticism*. London, 1921.
Noeldeke, Th. *Beitrage zur Kenntniss der Poesie der alten Araber*. Hanover, 1864.
———. *Delectus veterum carminum arabicorum*. Berlin, 1890.
———. *Geschichte des Qorans*. 2nd ed. 3 vols. Leipzig, 1909–1938.
Nykl, A. R. *El cancionero del seih, nobilismo visir, maravilla del tiempo, Abu Bakr ibn 'Abd-al-Malik Abén Guzmán*. Madrid, 1933.
———. "A Compendium of Aljamiado Literature." *RH*, 77 (1929), 448–465.
———. *Hispano-Arabic Poetry and Its Relations with the Old Provençal Troubadours*. Baltimore, 1946.
———. "Ibn Ḥazm's 'Treatise on Ethics.' " *AJSLL*, 40 (1923), 30–36.

———. "L'influence arabe-andalouse sur les troubadours." *BH*, 41 (1939) 305–315.
———. "The Latest Troubadour Studies." *AR*, 19 (1935), 227–235.
———. "La poesía a ambos lados del Pirineo hacia el año 1110." *al-Andalus*, 1 (1933), 355–408.
———. *Selections from Hispano-Arabic Poetry*. Beirut, 1949.
———. *Troubadour Studies*. Cambridge, Mass., 1944.
Ocaña Jiménez, M. "La inscripción fundacional de la mezquita de Ibn Adabbas." *al-Andalus*, 12 (1947, 145–151.
———. "Notas sobre cronología hispano-musulmana." *al-Andalus*, 8 (1943), 333–381.
———. "Nuevas excavaciones en Madīnat al-Zahrā'." *al-Andalus*, 10 (1945), 147–159.
———. *Repertorio de inscripciones árabes de Almería*. Madrid & Granada, 1964.
———. *Tablas de conversión de datas islámicas a cristianas y viceversa, fundamentadas en nuevas fórmulas de coordinación y compulsa*. Madrid & Granada, 1946.
Oliver Asín, Jaime. "Maŷšar (Cortijo) — orígines y nomenclatura árabe del Cortijo Sevillano." *al-Andalus*, 10 (1945), 109–126.
———. "Un morisco de Túnez, admirador de Lope." *al-Andalus*, 1 (1933), 409–450.
———. "Origen árabe de rebato, arrobda y sus homónimos." *BRAE*, 15 (1928), 347–395, 496–542.
Ortega y Gasset, J. "Abenjaldún nos revela el secreto." *El Espectador*, 8 (Madrid, 1934).
Ovid. *The Art of Love*, English trans. R. Humphries. Bloomington, Ind., 1962.
Pano y Ruata, Mariano de. *Las coplas del peregrino de Puey Monçon, viaje a la Meca en el siglo XVI*. Saragossa, 1897.
Pareja, F. M. Alessandro Bausani, Ludwig von Hertling, and Elias Teres Sadaba, *Islamologia*. 2 vols. Madrid, 1952–1954.
Pareja Casañas, F. M. *Libro de ajedrez*. Madrid, 1935.
Pastor, Antonio. *The Idea of Robinson Crusoe*. Watford, 1930.
Pearson, J. D. *Index Islamicus: 1906–55*; Cambridge, 1958.
Pedregal y Fantini, J. *Estado social y cultura de los mozárabes y mudéjares españoles*. Seville, 1878.
Pellat, C. *Langue et littérature arabes*. Paris, 1952.
Penella Roma, J. "Los moriscos españoles emigrados al norte de Africa después de la expulsión." Ph.D. thesis, University of Barcelona, 1971.
Pérès, Henri. "Les éléments ethniques de l'Espagne musulmane et la langue arabe, au Ve/XIe siècle." *Études d'Orientalisme*, 2 (1962), 717–731.
———. "L'Espagne vue par les voyageurs musulmans de 1610 à 1930." *AIEO*, 6 (Paris, 1937).
———. "La langue arabe et les habitants de l'Andalousie au Moyen Âge." *Majma'*, 19 (1944), 393–408.
———. *La poésie andalouse en arabe classique au XIe siècle, ses aspects généraux et sa valeur documentaire*. Paris, 1953.
———. "La poésie arabe de l'Andalousie et ses relations possibles avec la poésie des troubadours." *IO* (Marseilles, 1947), 107–130.
Perron, D. *Femmes arabes avant et depuis l'islamisme*. Paris & Algiers, 1958.
Pigeonneau. *Histoire du commerce de la France*. Paris, 1885.
Piles Ibars, A. *Valencia árabe*. Valencia, 1901.
Pirenne, Henri. *Economic and Social History of Medieval Europe*. New York, n.d.
———. *Mahomet et Charlemagne*. Brussels & Paris, 1937.
Plessner, M. *Die Geschichte der Wissenschaften in Islam.* Tübingen, 1931.
Pons Boïgues, F. *Apuntes sobre las escrituras mozárabes toledanas existentes en el archivo histórico nacional*. Madrid, 1897.
———. *Ensayo bío-biliográfico sobre los historiadores y géografos arábigo-españoles*. Madrid, 1898.
Power, George. *The History of the Empire of Musulmans in Spain and Portugal*. London, 1815.
Prieto y Vives, Antonio. *Los reyes de Taifas*. Madrid, 1926.
Rabadan, M. *Mahometanism Fully Explained*, English trans. J. Morgan. London, 1723.

Ramírez de Arellano, Rafael. *Historia de Córdoba desde su fundación hasta la muerte de Isabel la Católica*. Real, 1915.
al-Rāzī, Aḥmad. *La crónica denominada del moro Rasis*, Spanish trans. Pascual de Gayangos in *MRAH*, 8 (Madrid, 1852).
Reinaud, A. *Introduction générale à géographie des orientaux.* Paris, 1848.
Renan, E. *Averroès et l'averroisme*. Paris, 1852; 3rd. ed., 1925.
Rescher, O. *Excerpte und Ubersetzungen aus den Schriften des Philologen und Dogmatikers Gahiz aus Bacra*. Stuttgart, 1931.
Riano, J. F. *Spanish Arts: The Industrial Arts in Spain.* London, 1879.
Ribera y Tarragó, Julián. *Bibliófilos y bibliotecas en la España musulmana*. Saragossa, 1896.
———. *El cancionero de Abéncuzmán*. Madrid, 1912.
———. *Disertaciones y opúsculos*. 2 vols. Madrid, 1928.
———. "La enseñanza entre los musulmanes españoles," in his *Disertaciones y opúsculos*. Madrid, 1928.
———. *Historia de la conquista de España*. Madrid, 1926.
———. *Historia de la música árabe medieval y su influencia en la española*. Madrid, 1927.
———. "Huellas, que aparecen en los primitivos historiadores musulmanes de la Península, de una poesía épica romanceada que debió florecer en Andalucía en los siglos IX y X," in *Discursos leídos ante la Real Academia de la Historia*. Madrid, 1915.
———. *La música andaluza medieval en las canciones de trovadores, troveros y minnesinger*. Madrid, 1922–1925.
———. *La música de las cántigas de Santa María*. Madrid, 1922. Trans. Eleanor Hague and Marion Leffingwell, *Music in Ancient Arabia and Spain.* London, 1929.
———. *Opúsculos dispersos*. Tetuan, 1952.
———. "El sistema de riegos en la huerta Valenciana no es obra de los árabes," in his *Desertaciones y opusculos*, vol. 2. Madrid, 1928.
———. and Miguel Asín. *Manuscritos árabes y aljamiados de la Biblioteca de la Junta; noticia y extractos por los alumnos de la seccion árabe bajo la dirección de Ribera y. M. Asín.* Madrid, 1912.
Rice, D. T. *Islamic Art*. New York, 1965.
Richmond, E. T. *Moslem Architecture, 623–1516; Some Causes and Consequences*. London, 1926.
al-Rikābī, J. *La poésie profane sous les Ayyubides et ses principaux représentants*. Paris, 1949.
Rivoira, G. T. *Moslem Architecture: Its Origin and Development*. Oxford, 1918.
Robson, J. *An Introduction to the Science of Tradition*. London, 1953.
——— and H. G. Farmer. *Ancient Arabian Musical Instruments as Described by al-Mufaddal Ibn Salama*. Glasgow, 1958.
Roca Traver, F. A. *Un siglo de vida mudéjar en la Valencia medieval*. Saragossa, 1952.
Rodinson, M. "Dante et l'Islam d'arprès des travaux récents." *Revue de l'Historie des Religions*, 140 (1951), 203–235.
Romano, D. "Un texto en aljamía hebraico árabe." *Sefarad*, 29 (1969), 313–318.
Ron de la Bastida, C. "Los MSS. árabes de Conde (1824)." *al-Andalus*, 21 (1956), 113–124.
Ronciere, Ch. de la. *Le découverte de l'Afrique au Moyen Âge*. 3 vols. Cairo, 1925–1927.
Rosenthal, E. I. J. "La filosófia política en la España musulmana." *RO*, 78 (1969), 259–280.
———. *Political Thought in Medieval Islam*. Cambridge, 1962.
Rosenthal, F. *Aḥmad b. aṭ-Ṭayyib as-Sarahsī*. New Haven, 1943.
———. *History of Muslim Historiography*. Leiden, 1952, 1968.
———. *Knowledge triumphant*. Leiden, 1970.
Rougemont, Denis de. *Love in the Western World*. New York, 1966.
Ruíz, Juan. *Libro de buen amor*, ed. J. Corominas. Madrid, 1967. English trans. Mario A. Di Cesare and Rigo Migani, *The Book of Good Love*. Albany, N.Y., 1970.
Runciman, Steven. *A History of the Crusades*. 2 vols. New York, 1964.
Ruska, Julius. *Arabische Alchemisten*. 2 vols. Heidelberg, 1924.
——— and P. Kraus. *Der Zusammenbruch der aeschabir-Legende*. Berlin, 1930.

———. *Tabula Smaragdina*. Heidelberg, 1926.
Russell, Peter. *Arabic Andalusian Casidas*, trans. Joan Penelope Cope. London, 1953.
Saab, Hasan. "Communication between Christianity and Islam," *MEJ*, 18 (1964), 41–62.
Saavedra, Eduardo. "El alhadit del baño de Zarieb," *Mundo Ilustrado*, 86 (1881).
———. "Escritos de los musulmanes sometidos al dominio cristiano, discurso de ingreso a la Real Academia Española," in *MRAE*, 6 (Madrid, 1889), 141–328.
———. *Estudio sobre la invasión de los árabes en España*. Madrid, 1882.
———. *La geografía de España del Edrisi*. Madrid, 1881.
———. "Note sur un astrolabe arabe," in *Atti del IV Congresso Internazionale digli Orientalisti, 1878*. Florence, 1880.
Sabbe, E. *Quelques types de marchands des IX*[e] *et X*[e] *siècles*. *RBPH*, 13 (Brussels, 1934).
Saladin, H. *Manuel d'art musulman. Vol. 1, Architecture*. Paris, 1907.
Salem, A. *Political Theory and Institutions of the Khawārij*. Baltimore, 1956.
Sánchez-Albornoz y Menduina, Claudio. *España: Un enigma histórico*. 2 vols. Buenos Aires, 1956.
———. *La España musulmana según los autores islamitas y cristianos medievales*. 2 vols. Buenos Aires, 1946.
———. *España y el Islam*. Buenos Aires, 1943.
———. *Estampas de la vida en León durante el siglo X*. Madrid, 1926.
———. *Estampas de la vida en León hace mil años*. Madrid, 1928.
Sánchez Pérez, J. A. "Un arabista español del siglo XVIII, Fray Patricio José de la Torre." *al-Andalus*, 18 (1953), 450–455.
———. *Biografías de matemáticos árabes que florecieron en España*. Madrid, 1921.
———. *La ciencia árabe en la edad media*. Madrid, 1954.
———. *Compendio de álgebra de Abenbéder*. Madrid, 1916.
———. *Cuentos árabes populares*. Madrid, 1952.
Sarnelli, C. D. *Mujāhid al-'Āmiri*. Cairo, 1961.
Sarre, F. *Jahrbuch des Kgl. Preussischen Kunst-sammlungen*. 1904.
Sarthou Carreras, C. *Castillos de España*. Madrid, 1952.
Sarton, G. *Introduction to the History of Science*. 3 vols. Baltimore, 1927–1948.
Saunders, John J., ed. *The Msulim World on the Eve of Europe's Expansion*. Englewood Cliffs, N.J., 1966.
Sauvaget, J. *Introduction à l'histoire de l'Orient musulman, éléments de bibliographie*. Paris, 1961.
Schacht, J. *Introduction to Islamic Law*. Oxford, 1964.
———. *The Origins of Muhammedan Jurisprudence*. Oxford, 1950.
Schack, A. F. von. *Poesie und Kunst der Araber in Spanien und Sizilien*. Berlin & Stuttgart, 1865–1877. Spanish trans. J. Valera, *Poesía y arte de los árabes en España y Sicilia*. Seville, 1881.
Schelenz, H. *Geschichte der Pharmazie*. Berlin, 1904.
Schiaparelli, G., ed. *Vocabulista in arabico*. Florence, 1871.
Schoy, C. "The Geography of the Moslims of the Middle Ages," in *The Geographical Review*. New York, 1924.
Scott, Samuel Parsons. *History of the Moorish Empire in Europe*. 3 vols. Philadelphia, 1904.
Seco de Lucena Vázquez, L. "Arabismo granadino. El Centro de Estudios Históricos de Granada y su reino y su revista (1911–1925)," in *Miscelánea de Estudios Árabes y Hebraicos*, (1958), 99–135.
Seco de Lucena y Paredes, Luis. *Los Abencerrajes, leyenda e historia*. Granada, 1960.
———. *Documentos arábigo-granadinos*. Arabic texts and Spanish trans. Madrid, 1961.
———. *Los Hammudies señores de Málaga y Algeciras*. Málaga, 1955.
Sentenach, Narciso. "Bosquejo histórico sobre la orfebrería española, IV, Orfebrería hispano-arábiga," in *RABM*. Madrid, 1909.
Setton, Kenneth M., ed. *A History of the Crusades*. 2 vols. 2nd ed. Madison, Wis., 1969.
Sharif, M. M., ed. *History of Muslim Philosophy*. 2 vols. Wiesbaden, 1963–1966.

Siddiqi, Z. A. *Philosophy of Ibn Tufayl*. Aligarh, 1965.

Silver, D. J. *Maimonidean Criticism and the Maimonidean Controversy, 1180–1240*. Leiden, 1965.

Silverstein, T. "Andreas, Plato and the Arabs: Remarks on Some Recent Accounts of Courtly Love." *Modern Philology*, 47 (1949), 119–121.

———. "Dante and the Legacy of the Mi'rāj." *JNES*, 11 (1952), 89ff., 187ff.

Simonet, F. J. *El cardenal Jiménez de Cisneros y los manuscritos arábigo-granadinos*. Granada, 1885.

———. *Descripción del reino de Granada bajo los Nazarites*. Madrid, 1860.

———. *Glosario de voces ibéricas y latinas usadas entre los mozárabes*. Madrid, 1888.

———. *Historia de los mozárabes de España*. Madrid, 1897–1903.

———. *L'influence de l'élément indigene dans la civilisation des maures de Grenade*. Brussels, 1895.

———. *Leyendas históricas árabes*. Madrid, 1858.

———. *Santoral hispano-mozárabe escrito en 961 por Rabi Ben Zaid, obispo de Ilíberis*. Madrid, 1871.

———. *El siglo de oro de la literatura arábigo-española*. Granada, 1867.

Singer, C. *From Magic to Science*. London, 1928.

Singer, D. W. *Catalogue of Latin and Vernacular Alchemical Manuscripts in Great Britain and Ireland*. 3 vols. Brussels, 1928–1929.

Singer, S. "Arabische und europäische Poesie im Mittelalter." *Abhandlung Preussischen Akademie der Wissenschaften*, vol. 13. Berlin, 1918.

Slane, W. McGuckin de. *Descriptions de l'Afrique Septentrionale*, trans. of al-Bakrī's work. Algiers, 1911, 1913.

———, ed. and trans. *Histoire de Berbères et des dynasties musulmanes de l'Afrique septentrionale*, trans. of Ibn Khaldūn, *'Ibar*. 4 vols. Algiers, 1852–1856; new edition, 3 vols. Paris, 1925–1934.

Smith, Dulcie Laurence. *The Poems of Mu'tamid King of Seville Rendered into English Verse*. London, 1915.

Smith, M. *al-Ghazālī, the Mystic*. London, 1944.

Sobhy, G. *The Book of al-Dhakhira*. Cairo, 1928.

Solalinde, A. G. *Alfonso X el Sabio: Antología*. Madrid, 1921.

———. *Antología de Alfonso el Sabio*. 4th ed. Madrid, 1960.

Sordo, E. *Moorish Spain*, trans. I. Michael. London, 1963.

Soriano Viguera, J. *Contribución al conocimiento de los trabajos astronómicos desarrollados en la escuela de Alfono X el Sabio*. Madrid, 1916.

Sourdel, D. *Le Vizirat*. Damascus, 1959–1960.

———. "Wazīr' et 'Hāgib' en Occident," in *Études d'Orientalisme*, vol. 2 (Paris, 1962), 747–755.

Sousa, de. *Vestigios de la lingua arabica en Portugal*. Lisbon, 1789.

Southern, R. W. *Western Views of Islam in the Middle Ages*. Cambridge, Mass., 1962.

Spaulding, R. K. *How Spanish Grew*. Berkeley & Los Angeles, 1967.

Spitzer, Leo. "La lírica mozárabe y las teorías de Theodor Frings," in *Lingüística e historia literaria*. Madrid, 1961.

Steiger, A. *Contribución a la fonética del hispano-árabe y de los arabismos en el ibero-románico y el siciliano*. Madrid, 1932.

———. *Origin and Spread of Oriental Words in European Languages*. New York, 1963.

Steinschneider, M. "Constantinus und seine arabischen Quellen." *Virchow's Archiv*, 37 (1866), 352–354.

———. "Études sur Zarakli, astronome arabe du XIe siècle, et ses ouvrages." *Bulletino di Bibliographia e di Storia delle Scienze, Matematiche, e Fisiche*, 14 (1881), 16 (1883), 17 (1884).

———. "Die Europaischen Übersetzungen aus dem Arabischen bis Mitte des 17 Jahrhunderts." *Sitzungsberichte der Akademie der Wissenschaften zu Wien*, 149 (1905), 151 (1906).

Stephenson, J. *Zoological Section of the Nuzhatu-l-Qulūb of al-Qazwini*. London, 1928.
Stern, S. M. "Four famous muwaššaḥs from Ibn Bušra's Anthology." *al-Andalus*, 23 (1958), 339–370.
———. In *Arabica*, 1 (1955), 150–192.
———. In *Hispanic Studies in Honor of I. González Llubera*. Oxford, 1959. Pp. 367–386.
———. *Les chansons mozárabes*. Oxford, 1964.
———. "Les vers finaux en español dans les muwaššaḥas hispano-hébraiques." *al-Andalus*, 13 (1948), 299–346.
———. "Muḥammad Ibn 'Ubada al-Qazzāz: un andaluz author de 'muwaššaḥs.'" *al-Andalus*, 15 (1950), 79–109.
———. "Studies on Ibn Quzman." *al-Andalus*, 16 (1951), 379–425.
Stevenson, Robert. *Spanish Music in the Age of Columbus*. The Hague, 1960.
Strzygowski, J. *Origin of Christian Church Art*. Oxford, 1923.
Suter, H. *Die Mathematiker und Astronomen der Araber und ihre Werke*. Leipzig, 1900.
Tallgren, O. J. *Los nombres árabes de las estrellas y la transcripción alfonsina*. Madrid, 1925.
Terés Sábada, Elías. "Abbās Ibn Firnas." *al-Andalus*, 25 (1960) and 29 (1964).
———. "Linajes árabes en al-Andalus (primera parte)." *al-Andalus*, 22 (1957), 55–112.
———. "Linajes árabes en al-Andalus, según la 'Ŷamhara' de Ibn Ḥazm (conclusión)." *al-Andalus*, 22 (1957), 337–376.
———. *Literatura arábigo-española*. Madrid, 1952–1954.
———. "Préstamos poéticos en al-Andalus." *al-Andalus*, 21 (1956), 415–419.
Terrasse, H. *L'art hispano-mauresque des origines au XIII*[e] *siècle*. Paris, 1932.
———. *Histoire du Maroc, des origines à l'établissement du protectorat français*. 2 vols. Casablanca, 1949–1950.
———. *Islam d'Espagne, une rencontre de l'Orient et de l'Occident*. Paris, 1958.
Théry, R. P. G. *Tolède, grande ville de la renaissance médiévale*. Oran, 1944.
Thompson, E. A. *The Goths of Spain*. Oxford, 1968.
Thorndike, Lynn. *History of Magic and Experimental Science*. 2 vols. 2nd ed. Cambridge, Mass., 1927.
Ticknor, George. *History of Spanish Literature*. 3rd ed. Boston, 1866.
Tiraboschi, Girolamo. *Storia della letteratura Italiana*. 10 vols. Rome, 1782–1798.
Torres Balbás, L. "Alcaicerias." *al-Andalus*, 14 (1949).
———. *La Alcazaba y la catedral de Málaga*. Madrid, 1960.
———. *La Alhambra y el Generalife de Granada*. Madrid, n.d.
———. *Arte almohade, arte nazarí, arte mudéjar*. vol. 4. Madrid, 1949.
———. *Arte hispanomusulmán hasta la caída del califato de Córdoba*, in R. Menéndez Pidal, ed., *Historia de España*, vol. 4. Madrid, 1957. Pp. 331–788.
———. *Artes almorávide y almohade*. Madrid, 1955.
———. "Ciudades — musulmanes de nueva fundación." *Études d'Orientalisme*, vol. 2, pp. 781–803.
———. "Los edificios hispano-musulmanes." *RIEI*, 1 (1953), 92–121.
———. *La Mezquita de Córdoba y las ruinas de Madīnat al-Zahrā'*. (Madrid, 1952, 1965.
———. "Las norias fluviales en España." *al-Andalus*, 5 (1940).
———. "Nuevos datos sobre la Mezquita de Córdoba cristianizada." *al-Andalus*, 14 (1949).
———. "Plazas, zocos y tiendas de las ciudades hispano-musulmanas." *al-Andalus*, 12 (1947).
———. "La primitiva Mezquita Mayor de Sevilla." *al-Andalus*, 11 (1946), 425–436.
———. "La vivienda popular en España," in *Folklore y costumbres de España*, vol. 3. Barcelona, 1953.
———, Cervera, Chueca, and Bidagor. *Resumen histórico del urbanismo en España*. Madrid, 1954.
Torrey, C. C. *The Jewish Foundation of Islam*. Oxford, 1924.
Trabulsi, Amjad. *La critique poétique des arabes jusqu'au V*[e] *siècle de l'Hégire*. Damascus, 1955.
Trend, J. B. in *Hispanic Studies in Honor of I. González Llubera*. Oxford, 1959. Pp. 415–428.

———. *The Language and History of Spain*. London, 1953.
———. "Spain and Portugal," T. Arnold and A. Guillaume, eds., *The Legacy of Islam*. Oxford, 1931.
Tritton, A. S. *The Caliphs and Their Non-Muslim Subjects*. London, 1930.
———. *Muslim Theology*. London, 1947.
Turben Ville, A. S. *The Spanish Inquisition*. London, 1932.
Tyan, E. *Histoire de l'organization judiciaire en pays d'Islam*. 2 vols. Paris, 1938.
Üllman, M. *Die Medizin im Islam*. Leiden, 1970.
Vadet, Jean-Calude. *L'espirt courtois en Orient dans les cinq premiers siècles de l'Hégire*. Paris, 1968.
Valbuena Prat, Ángel. *Historia de la literatura española*. 6th ed. Barcelona, 1960.
Valdeavellano, Luis G. de. *Historia de España I, de los orígenes a la baja edad media*. 3rd ed. Madrid, 1963.
Van Den Bergh, S. *Die Epitome der Metaphysik des Averroes*. Leiden, 1924.
Vasiliev, A. A. *History of the Byzantine Empire*. Madison, Wis., 1964.
Velázquez Bosco, R. *Excavaciones en Medina Azahara*. Madrid, 1923.
———. *Medina Azzahara y Amiriya*. Madrid, 1912.
Vernet Ginés, Juan. "Una bibliografía de la historia de las ciencias matemáticas y astronómicas entre los árabes (años 1942–1956)." *al-Andalus*, 21 (1956), 431–440; 23 (1958), 215–236.
———. "Dos instrumentos astrónomicos de Alcazarquivir." *al-Andalus*, 18 (1953), 445–449.
———. "España en la geografía de Ibn Saʿīd al-Magribī." *Tamuda*, 6 (1958), 307–326.
———. *Literatura árabe*. Barcelona, 1968.
———. *Los musulmanes españoles*. Barcelona, 1961.
———. "Traducciones moriscas del Corán," in *Der Orient der Forschung, Festscrift für Otto Spies*. Wiesbaden, 1967. Pp. 686–705.
———. "El valle del Ebro como nexo entre Oriente, occidente." *BRABL*, 32 (1950), 249–286.
Viardot, L. *Historia de los árabes y de los moros en España*. Barcelona, 1844; Paris, 1851.
Vicens Vives, J. *Aproximación a la historia de España*. 2nd ed. Barcelona, 1960.
Vives y Escudero, A. *Monedas de las dinastías arábigo-españolas*. Madrid, 1893.
Walzer, R. *Greek into Arabic*. Oxford, 1962.
———. *History of Philosophy, Eastern and Western*. London, 1953.
Watt, W. M. *Free Will and Predestination in Early Islam*. London, 1948.
———. *A History of Islamic Spain*, with additional sections on literature by Pierre Cachia. Edinburgh, 1965.
———. *Islamic Philosophy and Theology*. Edinburgh, 1962.
———. *Muslim Intellectual: The Struggle and Achievement of al-Ghazālī*. Edinburgh, 1963.
Webb, C. J. *A History of Philosophy*. London, 1915.
———. *Studies in the History of Natural Theology*. Oxford, 1915.
Wensinck, A. J. *The Muslim Creed*. Cambridge, 1932.
Whishaw, B., and E. M. *Arabic Spain*. London, 1912.
White, J. G. *The Spanish Treatise on Chess-Play Written by Order of King Alfonso the Sage in the Year 1283*. Leipzig, 1913.
Wiedemann, E. *Beitrage zur Geschichte der Naturwissenschaften*. Erlangen, 1904–1929.
———. "Al-Kimiya," in *EI*, vol. 2. Leiden & London, 1927.
Wiet, G. *Introduction à la littérature arabe*. Paris, 1966.
——— and L. Hautecoeur. *Les mosquées du Caire*. 2 vols. Paris, 1932.
Wittmann, M. *Die Stellung des bl, Thomas von Aquin zur Avencebrol*. Munster, 1900.
———. *Zur Stellung Avencebrol's im Entwicklungsgang des Zwölften Jahrhunderts in ihren Verbaltnis zur aristotelischen und judischarabischen Philosophie*. Munster, 1915.
Wüstenfeld, F. *Geschichte der arabischen Arzte und Naturforscher*. Göttingen, 1840.
Zambaur, E. *Manuel de généalogie et de chronologie pour l'histoire de l'Islam*. Hanover, 1927.
Ziegler, A. K. *Church and State in Visigothic Spain*. Washington, D.C., 1930.

Bibliography of Eastern Works

al-'Abbādi, Aḥmad Mujhṭār. *Los eslavos en España*, Arabic text with Spanish trans. by F. de la Granja Santamaría. Madrid, 1953.

———. "Siyāsat al-fāṭimmiyyin naḥw al-Maghrib wa-l-Andalus." *RIEI*, 5 (1957), 1923–226.

'Abbās, Iḥsān. "al-Adab fi-l-Andalus wa-l-Maghrib," in *al-Adab al-'arabī li-l-dārisīn*. Beirut, 1961. Pp. 254–290.

———. "Akhbār al-ghinā' wa-mughannīn bi-l-Andalus." *al-Abḥāth*, 16 (1963), pp. 3–19.

———. (ed.) *Akhbār wa-tarājim andalusiyyah*. Beirut, 1963.

———. *al-'Arab fī Ṣiqilliyah*. Beirut, 1959.

———. *al-Muwashshaḥāt al-andalusiyyah) Nash'atuhā wa-taṭawwuruhā*. Beirut, 1965.

———. "al-Naqd al-adabī fī-l-Andalus." *al-Abḥāth*, 12 (1959), 509–527.

———. *Tārīkh al-adab al-andalusī: 'aṣr al-Muwaḥḥidīn*. Beirut, 1960.

———. *Tārīkh al-adab al-andalusī: 'aṣr siyādat Qurṭubah*. Beirtu, 1960, 1969.

———. *Tārīkh al-adab al-andalusī: 'aṣr al-Ṭawā'if wa-l-Murābiṭīn*. Beirut, 1962.

'Abdallāh, *Mudhakkirāt Emir 'Abdallāh*. Ed. and trans. E. Lévi-Provençal, *Les "Mémoires" de 'Abd Allāh, dernier roi Ziride de Grenade*, Madrid, Granada, 1936; Cairo, 1955.

'Abd al-Badī', Aḥmad. *al-Islām fī Isbānīya*. Cairo, 1958.

'Abd al-Ḥakīm, Maḥmūd. *Falsafat Ibn Ṭufayl wa-risālatuh*. Cairo, n.d.

'Abd al-Ḥaqq al-Badīsī. *al-Maqṣad (Vie des saints du Rif)*, trans. G. S. Colin. *Archives marocaines*, vol. 26, Paris, 1926.

'Abd al-Jabbār al-Jūmard. *al-Aṣma'ī: ḥayātuh wa-āthāruh*. Beirut, 1955.

al-'Abdarī, Muḥammad. *Riḥlat al-'Abdarī*, ed. M. al-Fāsī. Rabat, 1968.

Abū-l-Faraj al-Iṣfahānī. *Kitāb al-aghānī*. 21 vols. Beirut, 1956–1957.

Abū-l-Fidā'. *al-Mukhtaṣar fī akhbār al-bashar*. 4 vols. Cairo, A.H. 1325.

———. *Taqwīm al-buldān*. Paris, 1840. French trans. Reinaud and St. Guyard, 2 pts. in 3 vols. Paris, 1848–1883.

Abū Ḥāmid al-Andalusī al-Gharnāṭī. *Tuḥfat al-albāb wa-nukhbat al-a'jāb*, ed. G. Ferrand. *JA* (1925), 1–304.

Abū Ḥayyān. *Dīwān*. Cairo, A.H. 1286; Beirut, A.D. 1951.

Abū Isḥāq al-Ilbīrī. *Dīwān*, ed. E. García Gómez. Madrid & Granada, 1944.

Abū-l-Khashab, I. *Tārīkh al-adab al-'arabī fī-l-Andalus*. Cairo, 1966.
Abū-l-Khayr al-Shajjār. *Kitāb al-filāḥah*. French trans. A. Charbonneau. Algiers, 1946.
Abū Nuwās. *Dīwān*. Ed. I. Aṣāf. Cairo, 1898. Ed. Maḥmūd Kāmil Farīd. Cairo, 1351/1932.
Abū-l-Qāsim al-Gharnāṭī. *Raf' al-ḥujūb al-mastūrah fī maḥāsin al-maqṣūrah*. 2 vols. Cairo, A.H. 1344.
Abū-l-Qāsim al-Ḥasan ibn Muḥammad ibn Ḥabīb al-Naysabūrī, *'Uqalā' al-majānīn*. Damascus, 1924.
Abū Rahab, Ḥassān. *al-Ghazal 'ind al-'Arab*. Cario, 1947.
Abū-l-Ṣalt of Denia. *Taqwīn al-dhihn*, ed. with Spanish trans. A. González Palencia. Madrid, 1915.
Abū Ṭālib, 'Abd al-Hādī. *Wazīr gharnāṭah: Lisān al-Dīn ibn al-Khaṭīb*. Cairo, 1950.
Abū Tammām, *Dīwān al-ḥamāsah*. Beirut, 1905.
Abū Zahrah, Muḥammad. *Ibn Ḥazm: ḥayātuh wa-'aṣruh*. Cairo, 1954.
al-'Adawī, Ibrāhīm Aḥmad. *al-Dawlah al-islāmiyyah wa-imbaraṭūriyat al-rūm*. Cairo, 1958.
Adham, 'Alī. *Manṣūr al-Andalus*. Cairo, n.d.
———. *Ṣaqr Quraysh: dirāsah bi-ḥayāt al-amīr 'Abd al-Raḥmān al-awwal, al-mulaqqab bi-l-Dākhil, mu'assis al-dawlat al-Umawīyah bi-l-Andalus*. Cairo, 1938.
al-Afghānī, Sa'īd. *Ibn Ḥazm al-andalusī*. Beirut, 1969.
'Afīfī, A. E. *al-Taṣawwuf*. Cairo, 1963.
al-Ahwanī, 'Abd al-'Azīz. "al-Azjāl al-andalusiyyah." Thesis, University of Cairo, 1951.
———. "Kitāb al-muqtaṭaf min azāhīr al-ṭuraf de Ibn Sa'īd." *al-Andalus*, 13 (1948), 28–31.
———. *al-Zajal fī-l-Andalus*. Cairo, 1957.
Akhbār al-'aṣr fī-inqiḍā' dawlat Banī Naṣr. Cairo, A.H. 1343.
Akhbār majmū'ah, ed. and Spanish trans. E. Lafuente y Alcántara. Madrid, 1867.
'Alī 'Allām, 'Abdallah. *al-Da'wah al-muwaḥḥidiyyah fī-l-Maghrib*. Cairo, 1964.
al-'Āmilī, Bahā' al-Dīn. *Asrār al-balāghah*. Cairo, A.H. 1317.
Amīn, Aḥmad. *Ḍuḥā al-islām*. 3 vols. Cairo, 1933–1936.
———. *al-Naqd al-adabī*. 3rd ed. Cairo, 1963.
———. *Ẓuhr al-Islām*. Cairo, 1955.
'Aqīqī, N. *al-Mustashriqūn*. 3 vols. Cairo, 1964–1965.
'Aqqād, 'A. *Athar al-'Arab fī-l-ḥaḍārah al-urubbiyyah*. Cairo, 1946.
al-A'rābī, Abū Misḥal. *Kitāb al-nawādir*. 2 vols. Damascus, 1961.
Arslān, Shakīb. *al-Ḥulal al-sundusiyyah fī-l-akhbār wa-l-āthār al-andalusiyyah*. 3 vols. Cairo, 1936–1939.
al-Ash'arī. *al-Ibānah*, English trans. R. C. McCarthy. New Haven, 1940.
———. *Maqālāt al-islāmiyyīn wa-ikhtilāf al-muṣallīn*, ed. H. Ritler. 2 vols. Istanbul, 1929–1930.
Ashtor, Eli. *Korot ha-Yehudim bi-Sefarad ha-muslemit*. Jerusalem, 1966.
al-'Askarī, Abū Hilāl. *Kitāb al-ṣinā'atayn*. Constantinople, A.H. 1320.
al-Aṣma'ī. *Kitāb al-khayl*, ed. A. Haffner. Vienna, 1895.
al-'Asqalānī, Shihāb al-Dīn A. ibn 'A. ibn Ḥajar. *Lisān al-mīzān*. 6 vols. Hyderabad, A.H. 1329–1331.
'Awḍ al-Karīm, Muṣṭafā. *Abū Bakr ibn 'Ammār*. Doctoral thesis, University of London, 1958.
———. *Fann al-tawshīḥ*. Beirut, 1959.
al-Awsī, Ḥāzim. *Minhāj al-bulaghā' wa-sirāj al-'udabā'*, ed. Muḥammad Ḥabīb ibn al-Khawjah. Tunis, 1966.
Ayātī, Muḥammad Ibrāhīm. *Andalus yā tārīkh-i ḥukūmat-i Muslimin dar Urūpā*. Teheran, A.H. 1340.
'Azzām, 'Abd al-Wahhāb. *al-Mu'tamid ibn 'Abbād*. Cairo, 1959.
Badī' al-Zamān. *Maqāmāt*, ed. Mu. 'Abduh. Beirut, 1889.
Badr, Aḥmad. *Dirāsāt fī tārīkh al-Andalus wa-ḥaḍarātuhā*. Damascus, 1969.
al-Baghdādī, 'Abd al-Qādir. *Khizānat al-adab*. 4 vols. Cairo, A.H. 1348–1351.
al-Baghdādi, 'Abd al-Qādir Ibn Ṭāhir. *Kitāb al-farq bayn al-firaq*. English trans. *Moslem Schisms and Sects*, pt. 1 by K. C. Seelye (New York, 1920); pt. 2 by A. S. Halkin (Tel Aviv, 1936).

———. *al-Mukhtaṣar*, ed. P. K. Hitti. Cairo, 1924.
Bāghī, 'Abd al-Raḥmān. *Ḥayāt al-Qayrawān wa-mawqaf ibn Rashīq minhā*. Beirut, 1961.
al-Bakrī, Abū 'Ubayd Allāh. *Faṣl al-mawāl fī sharḥ kitāb al-amthāl*, eds. Iḥsān 'Abbās and 'Abd al-Majīd 'Abdīn. Khartoum, 1958.
———. *al-Mughrib fī dhikr bilād Ifrīqiyah wa-l-Maghrib*, ed. W. McGuckin de Slane. Algiers, 1857. French trans. de Slane. Algiers, 1913.
———. *Mu'jam mā ista'jam*, ed. F. Wüstenfeld. 2 vols.; Göttingen & Paris, 1876. 4 vols.; Cairo, 1945.
———. *al-Tanbīh 'alā awhām Abī 'Alī fī āmālihi*. Cairo, 1954.
al-Balādhurī, Aḥmad ibn Yaḥya. *Futūḥ al-buldān*. Ed. M. J. de Goeje (Leiden, 1866). English trans. *The Origins of the Islamic State*, by P. K. Hitti and F. C. Murgotten (New York, 1916–1924).
al-Balawī, Yūsuf Ibn al-Shaykh. *Kitāb alif-bā'*. 2 vols. Cairo, A.H. 1287.
al-Barqūqī, 'Abd al-Raḥmān. *Ḥaḍārat al-'Arab fī-l-Andalus*. Cairo, 1923.
al-Batanūnī, Muḥammad Labīb. *Riḥlat al-Andalus*. Cairo, 1927.
al-Baṭliyūsī, *see* Ibn al-Sayyid.
al-Baṭṭānī. *Kitāb al-zīj*, ed. and Latin trans. C. A. Nallino. Rome, 1903.
al-Bayḍāwī. *Anwār al-tanzīl*. 2 vols. Cairo, A.H. 1315.
al-Baydhaq. *Akhbār al-Mahdī Ibn Tūmart wa-ibtida' dawlat al-muwaḥḥidīn*, ed. and French trans. E. Lévi-Provençal. Paris, 1928.
al-Bayhāqī. *Kitāb al-maḥāsin*. Giessen, 1902.
Ben Cheneb. *Classes des savants de l'Ifrīqiya*. Arabic text with French trans. by Abū Muḥ. b. Aḥmad b. Tamīn and Muḥ. b. al-Ḥārith b. Asad al-Khushānī. Algiers, 1920.
al-Bukhārī. *Saḥīḥ*. 4 vols. Paris, 1903–1914.
al-Bustānī, Buṭrus. *Ma'ārik al-'Arab fī-l-Andalus*. Beirut, 1950.
———. "al-Muwashshaḥāt al-andalusiyyah." *al-Mashriq*, 33 (1935), 368–380.
———. *Udabā' al-'Arab fī-l-Andalus wa-'aṣr al-inbi'āth*. Beirut, 1947.
al-Bustānī, Fu'ād. "Ta'āwun al-shi'r wa-l-mūsīqā fī nash'at al-muwashshaḥāt al-andalusiy yah." *al-Mashriq*, 36 (1938), 499–509.
Chenery, Thomas, *see* al-Ḥarīrī.
Una crónica anónima de 'Abd al-Rahmān III al-Nāṣir, ed. and Spanish trans. by E. Lévi-Provençal and E. García Gómez. Madrid & Granada, 1950.
al-Dabbāgh, 'Abd al-Raḥmān ibn Muḥammad. *Ma'ālim al-īmān fī ma'rifat ahl al-Qayrawān*. 4 vols. Tunis, 1901.
al-Ḍabbī, Aḥmad ibn Yaḥyā ibn Aḥmad ibn 'Amīrah. *Bughyat al-multamis fī tārīkh rijāl al-Andalus*, ed. F. Codera. Madrid, 1885. Cairo, 1955.
al-Darārī' al-sab' aw-al-muwashshahāt al-andalusiyyah. Beirut, 1876.
Darwīsh, A. *al-Ma'ājim al-'arabiyyah*. Cairo, 1956.
al-Darwīsh, Nadīm 'Alī. *al-Muwashshaḥāt al-andalusiyyah*. Aleppo, 1955.
al-Dāyah, Muḥammad Riḍwān. *Tārīkh al-naqd al-adabī fī-l-Andalus*. Beirut, 1968.
Ḍayf, A. *Balāghat al-'Arab fī-l-Andalus*. Cairo, A.H. 1342 / A.D. 1924.
Ḍayf, Shawqī. *al-Balāghah: taṭawwur wa-tārīkh*. Cairo, 1965.
———. *Ibn Zaydūn*. Cairo, 1953.
al-Dhahabī, Abū 'Abd Allāh. *Tadhkirat al-ḥuffāẓ*. 4 vols. Hyderabad, 1955–1958.
Faḍā'il al-Andalus wa-ahlihā, ed. S. al-Munajjid. Beirut, 1968. Includes the *Rasā'il's* of Ibn Ḥazm, al-Shaqundī, and Ibn Sa'īd.
Fakhrī, M. *Ibn Rushd: faylasūf Qurṭubah*. Beirut, 1960.
al-Fākhūrī, Ḥanna. *Tārīkh al-adab al-'arabī*. Beirut, 1951.
al-Fārābī, Abū al-Naṣr. *Iḥṣā' al-'ulūm*, ed. U. M. Amīn (Cairo, 1948). Also, ed. A. González Palencia (Madrid, 1933).
———. *Kitāb al-mūsīqā al-kabīr*, ed. Ghiṭās 'Abd al-Malik Khashabah. Cairo, n.d.
———. *al-Madīnah al-fāḍilah*, ed. F. Najjār. Beirut, 1964.
———. *al-Siyāsah al-madaniyyah*, ed. A. Nader. Beirut, 1959.
al-Farazdaq. *Dīwān*, ed. Boucher. 4 vols. Paris, 1870–1875. Beirut, 1960.
Farrūkh, 'Umar. *'Abqariyat al-'Arab fī-l-'ilm wa-l-falsafah*. Beirut, 1945.

———. *Abū Nuwās*. Beirut, 1946.
———. *Ibn Bājjah*. Beirut, 1946.
———. *Ibn Ṭufayl wa-qiṣṣat Ḥayy Ibn Yaqẓān*. 2nd ed. Beirut, 1959.
al-Fīrūzābādī. *al-Qāmūs al-muḥīṭ*. 4 vols. Cairo, A.H. 1330.
al-Ghazālī. *Iḥyā' 'ulūm al-dīn*. 4 vols. Cairo, 1933.
———. *al-Munqidh min al-ḍalāl*. Cairo, A.H. 1309.
——. *Tahāfut al-falāsifah*, ed. M. Bouyges. Beirut, 1927.
al-Ḥajjī, 'Abd al-Raḥmān 'Alī. *Andalusīyāt*. 2 vols. Beirut, 1969.
Ḥajjī, Khalīfah. *Kashf al-ẓunūn*, ed. G. Flügel. 7 vols.; Leipzig & London, 1835–1858. 2 vols.; Istanbul, 1941–1943.
al-Ḥakīm, 'Alī b. Yūsuf. *al-Dawḥah al-mushtabikah fī ḍawābiṭ dār al-sikkah*, ed. H. Mu'nis. Madrid, 1960.
Ḥammūdah, 'Alī Muḥammad. *Tārīkh al-Andalus al-siyāsī wa-l-'umrānī wa-l-ijtimā'ī*. Cairo, 1957.
———. *Tārīkh al-islām fī-l-Andalus*. Cairo, 1953.
al-Ḥarīrī. *Maqāmāt*. Beirut, 1886. Ed. with English trans. *The Assemblies of al-Hariri*, pt. I by Thomas Chenery (London, 1867) and pt. II by F. Steinglass (London, 1898).
Hārūn, 'Abd al-Salām. *Nawādir al-Makhṭūṭāt*. Cairo, 1953.
Ḥasan, Zāki, *al-Raḥḥālah al-muslimūn fī-l-'uṣūr al-wuṣṭā*. Cairo, 1945.
Haykal, Aḥmad. *al-Adab al-andalusī min al-fatḥ ilā suqūṭ al-khilāfah*. 4th ed. Cairo, 1968.
Ḥāzim al-Qarṭajannī. *Dīwān*. Beirut, 1964.
al-Ḥijārī, T. *Fī tārīkh al-naqd wa-l-madhāhib al-adabiyyah*. Alexandria, 1953.
———. *Kitāb al-mushib fī gharā'ib ahl al-Maghrib*. Source for Ibn Sa'īd.
al-Ḥillī, Ṣafī al-Dīn. *al-'Āṭil al ḥālī*, ed. W. Hoenerbach, Wiesbaden, 1955.
al-Ḥimyarī, Abū-l-Walīd. *al-Badī' fī waṣf al-rabī'*, ed. H. Pérès. Rabat, 1940.
al-Ḥimyarī, Ibn 'Abd al-Mun'im. *Kitāb al-rawḍ al-mi'ṭār (La péninsule Ibérique au Moyen Age)*, ed. E. Lévi-Provençal. Leiden, 1938. Cairo, 1948.
———. *Ṣifat jazīrat al-Andalus*, ed. E. Lévi-Provençal. Cairo, 1934.
al-Ḥulal al-mawshiyyah fī dhikr al-akhbār al-marrākushiyyah. Tunis, A.H. 1329. Ed. I. S. Allouche (Rabat, 1936). Spanish trans. A. Huici Miranda (Tetuan, 1952).
al-Ḥumaydī, Muḥammad ibn Fattūḥ. *Judhwat al-muqtabis*, ed. M. T. al-Ṭanjī. Cairo, A.H. 1372 / A.D. 1952.
Ḥusayn, Ṭāhā, ed. *Ta'rīf al-'ulamā' bi Abī-l-'Alā*. Cairo, 1944.
al-Huṣrī al-Qayrawānī, Abū Isḥāq. *Zahr al-ādāb*. 4 vols. Cairo, 1953–1954.
al-'Ibādī, 'Abd al-Ḥamīd. *Mujmal fī tārīkh al-Andalus*. Caior, 1958.
Ibn 'Abbād al-Rundī. *al-Rasā'il al-ṣughrā*, ed. Fr. Nwyia, S.J. Beirut, n.d.
———. *Sharḥ ibn 'Abbād al-Rundī li-ḥikam al-'aṭā'iyyah*. Cairo, A.H. 1324.
Ibn al-Abbār. *al-Ḥullah al-ṣiyarā'*, ed. H. Mu'nis. 2 vols. Cairo, 1963.
———. *I'tāb al-kuttāb*, ed. Ṣāliḥ al-Ashtar. Damascus, 1961.
———. *al-Mu'jam fī aṣḥāb al-qāḍī Abī 'Alī al-Ṣadafī*. Madrid, 1886.
———. *al-Muqtaḍab min tuḥfat al-qādim*, ed. I. al-Abyārī. Cairo, 1957. Also in *Majallat al-Sharq*, 31 (Cairo), 351–543.
———. *al-Takmilah li-kitāb al-ṣilah*. Ed. F. Codera in *BAH*, 5–6 (1887–1890). Ed. 'Izzat al'Iṭār al-Ḥusaynī (Cairo, 1955). Ed. A. González Palencia and Alarcón in *Miscelánea* (Madrid, 1915).
Ibn 'Abd al-Barr. *Jāmi' bayān al-'ilm wa-faḍlih*. Cairo, A.H. 1320.
———. *al-Intiqā' fī faḍa'il al-thalāthā al-fuqahā'*. Cairo, A.H. 1350.
Ibn 'Abd al-Ghafūr al-Kilā'ī of Seville. *Iḥkām ṣan'at al-kalām*. Beirut, 1966.
Ibn 'Abd al-Ḥakam. *Futūḥ Miṣr wa-l-Maghrib wa-l-Andalus*. Ed. Ch. Torrey (New Haven, 1922). Trans. T. Harris Jones (Göttingen, 1858).
Ibn 'Abd al-Malik al-Marrākushī, M. *al-dhayl wa-l-takmilah*, ed. I. 'Abbās. Vols. 4 and 5. Beirut, 1964–1965.
Ibn 'Abd Rabbihi. *Kitāb al-'Iqd al-farīd*, ed. Aḥmad Amīn et al. 7 vols. Cairo, 1948–1953.
Ibn 'Abdallāh, 'Abd al-'Azīz. *Ibn al-Khaṭīb: ḥayātuh wa-kutubuh*. 2 vols. Morocco, 1953–1954.

Ibn 'Abdūn. *al-Basāmah bi-aṭwāq al-ḥamāmah*, ed. Muḥiyy al-Dīn Ṣabrī al-Kurdī. Cairo, A.H. 1340.

———. *Risālat Ibn 'Abdūn fī-l-qaḍā' wa-l-ḥisbah*. Ed. E. Lévi-Provençal (1934). Also in *Thalāth rasā'il andalusiyyah* (Cairo, 1955). French trans. E. Lévi-Provençal, *Séville musulmane au début du XIIe siècle* (Paris, 1947). Spanish trans. E. García Gómez, *Sevilla musulmana a comienzos del siglo XII* (Madrid, 1948).

Ibn Abī Bakr al-Taṭwānī, Muḥ. *Ibn al-Khaṭīb min khilāl kutubih*. Tetuan, 1959.

Ibn Abī Dīnār. *al-Mu'nis fī tārīkh Ifriqiyā wa-Tūnis*. Tunis, 1869.

Ibn Abī-l-Ghāfiyah al-Maknāsī. *Jadhwat al-iqtibās fī man ḥalla al-a'lām madīnat Fās*. Fez, A.H. 1309.

Ibn Abī Rabī'ah, 'Umar. *Dīwān*, ed. Paul Schwarz. 2 vols. Leipzig, 1901.

Ibn Abī Uṣaybi'ah. *'Uyūn al-anbā' fī ṭabaqāt al-aṭibbā'*, ed. A. Müller 2 vols. Cairo, 1882–1884. Beirut, 1956.

Ibn Abī Zar'. *al-Anīs al-muṭrib bi-rawḍ al-qirṭās fī akhbār mulūk al-Maghrib*. Fez, n.d. Ed. with Latin trans. C. J. Tornberg (Upsala, 1843–1846). French trans. A. Beaumier (Paris, 1860).

Ibn al-Aḥmar, Ismā'īl b. Yūsuf. *Nathīr farā'id al-jumān fī naẓm fuḥūl al-zamān*, ed. Muḥammad Riḍwān al-Dāyah. Beirut, 1967.

Ibn 'Ammār. *Dīwān*, ed. Ṣalāḥ Khāliṣ. Baghdād, 1957.

Ibn 'Aqīl. *Sharḥ Ibn 'Aqīl 'alā Alfiyat Ibn Mālik*. 2 vols. Cairo, 1951.

Ibn 'Arabi, Muḥiyy al-Dīn. *Aḥkām al-Qur'ān*. 2 vols. Cairo, A.H. 1347.

———. *Dīwān Ibn 'Arabī*. Cairo, 1855.

———. *Fuṣuṣ al-ḥikam*. Cairo, A.H. 1252, 1309. French trans. T. Burckhardt, *Sagesse de prophètes* (Paris, 1955).

———. *al-Futuḥāt al-makiyyah*. 4 vols. Cairo, 1295 / 1946.

———. *Inshā' al-dawā'ir; 'Uqlat al-mustawfiz; al-Tadbīrāt al-ilāhiyyah*, in H. S. Nyberg, ed., *Kleiner Schriften des Ibn al-'Arabī*. Leiden, 1919.

———. *Muḥāḍarāt al-Abrār*. Cairo, 1924.

———. *Rasā'il Ibn 'Arabī*. Hyderabad, 1948.

———. *al-Rūḥ al-quds and al-Durrat al-fākhirah*, English trans. R. W. Austin. Berkeley, 1971.

———. *Tarjumān al-ashwāq*. Beirut, 1961. English trans. R. A. Nicholson (London, 1911).

Ibn al-'Arīf. *Maḥāsin al-majālis*. Cairo, A.H. 1315. Ed. M. Asín Palacios (Paris, 1933).

Ibn 'Askar, Muḥammad ibn 'Alī Maṣbāḥ. *Dawḥat al-nāshir li-maḥāsin man kāna bi-l-Maghrib min mashāyikh al-qarn al-'āshir*. Fez, A.H. 1309.

Ibn al-Athīr. *al-Kāmil fī-l-ta'rīkh*, ed. C. J. Tornberg. 14 vols. Leiden, 1851–1876. The section on Spain was translated into French by E. Fagnan, in *Annales du Maghreb et de l'Espagne*. Algiers, 1901.

Ibn al-'Awwām, Abū Zakarīyā Yaḥyā ibn Aḥmad. *Kitāb al-filāḥah: Libro de Agricultura*, ed. with Spanish trans. by José Antonio Banqueri. 2 vols. Madrid, 1802.

Ibn Badrūn. *Sharḥ qaṣīdat Ibn 'Abdūn*, ed. R. Dozy. Leiden, 1846.

Ibn Bājjah. *Tadbīr al-mutawaḥḥid*. Ed. with Spanish trans. by M. Asín Palacios, *El régimen del solitario* (Madrid, 1946). Partial English trans. D. M. Dunlop in *JRAS* (1945), 61–81; and by L. Berman in R. Lerner et al., *Medieval Political Philosophy* (Glencoe, Ill., 1963), 122–133.

Ibn Bashkuwāl, Abū-l-Qāsim Khalaf ibn 'Abd al-Malik. *al-Ṣilah*, ed. Fr. Codera. Madrid, 1882–1883. Ed. 'Izzat al-'Iṭār al-Ḥusaynī. 2 vols. Cairo, 1955.

Ibn al-Baṣṣāl Muḥammad ibn Ibrāhīm Abū 'Abd allāh of Toledo. *Kitāb al-qaṣd wa-l-bayān*. Ed. with Spanish trans. by J. Millás Vallicrosa and Mohammad Aziman, *Libro de agricultura* (Tetuan, 1955).

Ibn Bassām, Abū-l-Ḥasan 'Alī. *al-Dhakhīrah*, pts. 1 and 2 from vol. 1 and pt. 1 from vol. 4. Cairo, 1939–1942, 1951. Ed. Lévi-Provençal, 4 vols. (Cairo, 1945). Ed. Sobhy, *The Book of al-Dhakhira* (Cairo, 1928).

Ibn Buṭṭūtah. *Tuḥfat al-nuẓẓār fī 'ajā'ib al-amṣār*. Ed. and French trans. C. Defremery and B. R. Sanguinetti (Paris, 1953). English trans. H. A. R. Gibb, *Travels in Asia and Africa*

1325–1354 (London, 1958). Ed. Beirut, 1960. Abridged ed. S. Lee, *Travels of Ibn Batuta* (London, 1829). Also in *The Broadway Travellers*, ed. Sir E. Denison Ross and Eileen Power (London, 1929).

Ibn Bayṭār. *al-Jāmi' li-mufradāt al-adwiyah wa-l-aghziyah*. 4 vols. Cairo, A.H. 1291.

Ibn Darrāj al-Qasṭallī. *Dīwān*, ed. Maḥmūd 'Alī Makkī. Damascus, 1961.

Ibn Dawūd al-Iṣfahānī. *Kitāb al-Zahrah*, ed. A. R. Nykl and Ibrāhīm Ṭūqān. Chicago, 1932.

Ibn Durayd. *Jamharat al-lughah*. 4 vols. Hyderabad, 1925.

———. *Kitāb al-ishtiqāq*, ed. F. Wünstenfeld. Gotha, 1853–1855.

Ibn Faḍl Allāh al-'Umarī. *Waṣf Ifrīqiyah wa-l-Andalus*, ed. Ḥasan Ḥusnī. Tunis, n.d.

Ibn al-Faraḍī. *Kitāb ta'rīkh 'ulamā' al-Andalus*. Ed. F. Codera, *Historia de los varones doctos de Andalusia*, in *BAH*, 7, 8 (1891–1892). Ed. 'Izzat al-'Iṭār al-Ḥusaynī, 2 vols. (Cairo, 1954, 1966).

Ibn Farḥūn. *al-Dībāj al-mudhahhab*. Cairo, A.H. 1351.

Ibn Fāris. *al-Mujmal fī-l-lughah*. Cairo, A.H. 1361.

———. *al-Ṣāḥibī fī fiqh al-lughah*. Cairo, 1910.

Ibn Gabirol. *Yanbū' l-ḥayāt*. Abridged English trans. H. E. Wedeck (New York, 1962). Spanish trans. F. de Castro y Fernández (Madrid, n.d.).

Ibn Ghālib al-Andalusī. *Kitāb farḥat al-anfus*, ed. Luṭfī 'Abd al-Badī. Cairo, 1956. A part of this book was published in the *Periodical of the Arabic Manuscripts Institute* (Cairo, 1956).

Ibn Ḥamdīs. *Dīwān*. Ed. Iḥsān 'Abbās (Beirut, 1960). Ed. Schiaparelli (Rome, 1897).

Ibn Hānī. *Dīwān*. Cairo, A.H. 1274.

Ibn Ḥawqal, Abī-l-Qāsim. *Kitāb al-masālik wa-l-mamālik*. Ed. M. J. de Goeje, pt. 2 (Leiden, 1873). Ed. Kramers (Leiden, 1938).

———. *Ṣūrat al-arḍ*. Beirut, n.d.

Ibn Ḥayyān, Abū Marwān Ḥayyān ibn Khalaf. *Kitāb al-muqtabis fī-tārīkh rijāl al-Andalus*. Ed. M. Melchor Atuña, *Chronique du règne du calife umaiyade 'Abdallah à Cordoue* (Paris, 1937). The part dealing with the reign of al-Ḥakam II was edited by 'Abd al-Raḥmān 'Alī al-Ḥajjī (Beirut, 1965). Spanish trans. E. García Gómez (Madrid, 1967).

Ibn Ḥazm. *al-Fiṣal fī-l-milal wa-l-ahwā' wa-l-niḥal*. Cairo, A.H. 1347–1348. Spanish trans. M. Asín Palacios, *Abenházam de Córdoba y su historia crítica de las ideas religiosas*. 5 vols. Madrid, 1927–1932.

———. *Ḥijjat al-wadā'*, ed. Mamdūḥ al-Ḥaqqī. Beirut, 1966.

———. *Jamharat ansāb al-'Arab*. Ed. 'Abd al-Salām Muḥammad Hārūn (Cairo, 1962).

———. *Kitāb al-akhlāq wa-l-siyar fī mudāwāt al-nufūs*. Spanish trans. M. Asīn Palacios, *Los caracteres y la conducta* (Madrid, 1916). Ed. with French trans. by Nada Tomiche, *Epître morale* (Beirut, 1961).

———. *Kitāb al-iḥkām fī uṣūl al-aḥkām*. 8 vols. Cairo, A.H. 1345–1348.

———. *Marātib al-'ulūm* in *Rasā'il*, ed. I. 'Abbās. Cairo, 1952.

———. *al-Muḥallā*. 11 vols. Cairo, A.H. 1351.

———. *Naqṭ al-'Arūs*, ed. Sh. Ḍayf in *Majallat kulliyat al-adab*, vol. 13. Cairo, 1951.

———. *Rasā'il Ibn Ḥazm*, ed. Iḥsān 'Abbās. Cairo, 1952.

———. *Risālah fī faḍl al-Andalus*, in al-Maqqarī, *Nafḥ al-ṭīb*, vol. 4, 154–170.

———. *al-Taqrīb li-ḥidd al-manṭiq*, ed. I. 'Abbās. Beirut, 1959.

———. *Ṭawq al-ḥamāmah*. Ed. D. K. Petrof (Leiden, 1914; Cairo, 1950). English trans. A. R. Nykl, *The Dove's Ring* (Paris, 1931). Trans. A. J. Arberry (London, 1953). Spanish trans. E. García Gómez, *El collar de la paloma* (Madrid, 1952). French trans. by L. Bercher (Algiers, 1949). Russian trans. A. Salil (Moscow & Leningrad, 1933). German trans. Max Weisweiler (Leiden, 1941). Italian trans. F. Gabrieli (Bari, 1949).

Ibn 'Idhārī. *Kitāb al-bayān al-mughrib fī akhbār mulūk al-Andalus wa-l-Magrib*. Ed. G. S. Colin, E. Lévi-Provençal, and I. 'Abbās. 4 vols. (Paris, 1930). Vols. 1 and 2 ed. R. Dozy (Leiden, 1848–1851). Vol. 4 ed. I. 'Abbās (Beirut, 1967).

Ibn Idrīs, Muḥammad Ibn Ja'far al-Kattānī. *Salwat al-anfus wa-muḥādathat al-akyās fī man uqbira min al-'ulamā' wa-l-ṣāliḥīn bi-madīnat Fās*. Fez, A.H. 1312.

Ibn Idrīs, Ṣafwān Abū-l-Baḥr. *Zād al-musāfir*. Beirut, 1939.
Ibn Iḥyah al-Kalbī. *al-Muṭrib min ash'ār al-Maghrib*, ed. Muṣṭafa 'Awḍ al-Karīm. Khartoum, 1954.
Ibn al-'Imād, 'Abd al-Ḥayy. *Shadharāt al-dhahab fī akhbār man dhahab*. 8 vols. A.H. 1350–1351.
Ibn al-Jarsīfī, 'Umar. *Risālah fī-l-ḥisbah*, ed. E. Lévi-Provençal in *Thalāth rasā'il andalusiyyah*. Cairo, 1955.
Ibn Jubayr. *Riḥlat Ibn Jubayr*. Cairo, 1935.
Ibn Juljul. *Ṭabaqāt al-aṭibbā' wa-l-ḥukamā'*, ed. F. Sayyid. Cairo, 1955.
Ibn al-Kattānī. *Kitāb al-tashbīhāt*, ed. I. 'Abbās. Beirut, 1966.
Ibn Khafājah, Abū Isḥāq. *Dīwān*. Cairo, A.H. 1286. Beirut, n.d.
Ibn Khaldūn. *Kitāb al-'ibar wa-diwān al-mubtadā wa-l-khabar*. 7 vols. Cairo, A.H. 1284; Beirut, 1957–1967. Partial French trans. by W. McGuckin de Slane, *Histoire de berberes et des dynasties musulmanes de l'Afrique septentrionale*, 3 vols. (Paris, 1834–1838; Algiers, 1852–1856).
———. *al-Muqaddimah*, English trans. F. Rosenthal, 3 vols. New York, 1958.
———. *al-Ta'rīf bi-Ibn Khaldūn*, ed. M. al-Ṭanjī. Cairo, 1951.
Ibn Khallikān, Shams al-Dīn Aḥmad Ibn Muḥammad. *Wafāyāt al-a'yān (Biographical Dictionary)*. Ed. in 3 vols. (Cairo, A.H. 1299); French trans. W. McGuckin de Slane in 4 vols. (Paris, 1842–1871).
Ibn Khalūf al-Andalusī al-Tūnisī. *Dīwān*. Beirut, 1873. Damascus, 1874.
Ibn Khāqān, Abū Naṣr al-Fatḥ. *Maṭmaḥ al-anfus wa-masraḥ al-ta'annus*. Constantinople, A.H. 1302.
———. *Qalā'id*. Būlāq, A.H. 1277.
Ibn al-Khaṭīb, Lisān al-Dīn. *A'māl al-a'lām fī man buyi'a qabl al-iḥtilām min mulūk al-islām*. Ed. E. Lévi-Provençal (Rabat, 1934; Beirut, 1956). Ed. Aḥmad Muḥammad al-'Abbādī (Damascus, 1964). Partial ed. and French trans. E. Lévi-Provençal, *Histoire de l'Espagne musulmane* (Rabat, 1934). German trans. with suppl. text by W. Hoenerbach, *Islamische Geschichte Spaniens* (Zurich, 1970).
———. *al-Ḥulal al-mawshiyyah fī dhikr al-akhbār al-marrākushiyyah*. Tunis, n.d. (Attributed to Ibn al-Khaṭīb.)
———. *al-Iḥāṭah fī akhbār Gharnāṭah*. Cairo, A.H. 1319. Ed. Muḥammad 'Abd Allāh 'Inān. Cairo, 1955.
———. *Jaysh al-tawshīḥ*, ed. J. Nājī. Tunis, 1967.
———. *al-Katībah al-kāminah*, ed. I. 'Abbās. Beirut, 1963.
———. *al-Lamḥah al-badriyyah fī tārīkh al-dawlah al-naṣriyyah*. Cairo, A.H. 1347.
———. *Mushāhadāt Ibn al-Khaṭīb fī bilād al-Maghrib wa-l-Andalus*, ed. Aḥmad Mukhtār al-'Abbādī. Alexandria, 1958. Fez, A.H. 1325.
———. *Raqm al-ḥulal fī naẓm al-duwal*. Tunis, A.H. 1316.
———. *Rawdat al-ta'rīf bi-l-ḥubb al-sharīf*, ed. 'Abd al-Qādir 'Aṭā. Cairo, 1968.
Ibn Khayr, Abu Bakr Muḥammad. *Fahrasah*, ed. F. Codera and J. Ribera. Saragossa, 1893. Baghdād, 1963.
Ibn Khayyāṭ, Khalifah. *Tārīkh: hiwāyat Bāqiyy Ibn Makhlad*, ed. Suhayl Zakkār. Beirut, 1967–1968.
Ibn Kurdādhbih. *al-Masālik wa-l-mamālik*, ed. M. J. de Goeje. Leiden, 1889.
Ibn Maḍā' al-Qurṭubī. *Kitāb al-radd 'alā-l-nuḥāh*, ed. Sh. Ḍayf. Cairo, 1948.
Ibn Mājid, Aḥmad. *Instructions nautiques et routiers arabes et portugais des XVe et XVIe siècles*, ed. Gabriel Ferrand. Paris, 1921–1922.
Ibn Mālik. *Alfiyyah*, ed. and French trans. A. Goguyer. Beirut, 1888.
Ibn Manẓūr. *Lisān al-'arab*. 20 vols.; Cairo, A.H. 1300–1307. 15 vols.; Beirut, 1955–1956.
Ibn Muḥammad al-Andalusī. *al-Ḥulal al-sundusiyyah fī-l-akhbār al-tūnisiyyah*. Tunis, A.H. 1278.
Ibn al-Muqaffa' *al-Adab al-kabīr*. Beirut, 1898.
———. *al-Adab al-ṣaghīr*, ed. M. Amīn. Cairo, 1913.
Ibn al-Mu'tazz. *Dīwān*. Beirut, A.H. 1331.

———. *Fuṣūl al-tamāthīl fī-tabāshīr al-surūr*. Cairo, 1925.
———. *Kitāb al-badī'*, ed. I. Kratchkowsky. London, 1935.
Ibn Nabātah. *Sharḥ al-'uyūn fī sharḥ risālat Ibn Zaydūn*. Cairo, A.H. 1278.
Ibn al-Nadīm. *al-Fihrist*, ed. G. Flügel. Leipzig, 1871–1872. Cairo, A.H. 1348.
Ibn al-Nafīs. *al-Risālah al-kāmiliyyah fī-l-sīrah al-nabawiyyah*, ed. with English trans. by M. Meyerhof and J. Schacht, *The Theologus Autodidacticus of Ibn al-Nafīs*. London, 1968.
Ibn al-Qaṭṭān. *Juz' min kitāb naẓm al-jumān*, ed. Maḥmūd 'Alī Makkī. Tetuan, n.d.
Ibn Qudāmah. *Kitāb al-tawwābīn*, ed. G. Makdisi. Damascus, 1961.
Ibn Qutaybah. *Adab al-kātib*, ed. Max Grünnert. Leiden, 1900.
———. *Kitāb al-shi'r wa-l-shu'arā'*, ed. M. J. de Goeje. Leiden, 1904.
———. *Ta'wīl mushkil al-Qur'ān*, ed. al-Sayyid Aḥmad Ṣaqr. Cairo, A.H. 1373.
———. *'Uyūn al-akhbār*. 4 vols. Cairo, 1925–1930.
Ibn al-Qūṭiyah. *al-Af'āl al-thulāthiyyah wa-l-rubā'iyyah*, ed. I. Guidi. Leiden, 1894.
———. *Ta'rīkh iftitāḥ al-Andalus*. Ed. P. de Gayangos (Madrid, 1868). Ed. and Spanish trans. by Julián Ribera, *Historia de la conquistas de España* (Madrid, 1926). French trans. O. Houdas (Paris, 1889). Ed. 'Abdallāh Anīs al-Ṭabbā' (Beirut, 1957).
Ibn Quzamān, M. ibn 'I. ibn 'Abd al-Malik. *Dīwān Ibn Quzmān*. Ed. D. Gunzburg (Berlin, 1896). Transliterated into Latin characters and partially trans. into Spanish by A. R. Nykl, *El cancionero de Aben Guzman* (Madrid, 1933). Partial ed. by O. J. Tuulio (Helsinki, 1941). Also E. García Gómez, *Todo Ben Quzmān*, 3 vols. (Madrid, 1972).
Ibn Rashīq. *al-Nutaf min shi'r Ibn Rashīq wa-zamīlih Ibn Sharaf*, collected by 'Abd al-'Azīz. Silfiyah, A.H. 1343.
———. *Qirādat al-dhahab fī naqd ash'ār al-'arab*. Cairo, A.H. 1344.
———. *al-'Umdah fī ṣinā'at al-shi'r wa-naqdih*. 2 vols. Cairo, A.H. 1344.
Ibn al-Ra'ūf. *Fī ādāb al-ḥisbah wa-l-muḥtasib*, ed. E. Lévi-Provençal in *Thalāth rasā'il andalusiyyah*. Cairo, 1955.
Ibn Rushd. *Bidāyat al-mujtahid wa-nihāyat al-muqtaṣid*. 2 vols. Cairo, n.d.
———. *Faṣl al-maqāl*. Ed. G. Hourani (Leiden, 1959). Text, trans., and notes by Léon Gauthier in *Bibliothèque arabe-français*, vol. 1 (3rd ed.; Algiers, 1948). *On the Harmony of Religion and Philosophy*, trans. G. Hourani. London, 1961.
———. *Rasā'il*. Hyderabad, 1947.
———. *Tafsīr mā ba'd al-ṭabī'ah* (Commentary on Aristotle). Beirut, 1938.
———. *Tahāfut al-tahāfut*. Ed. Sulaymān Dunyā, 2 vols. (Cairo, 1964–1965). English trans. S. van den Bergh, 2 vols. (Oxford, 1954).
———. *Talkhīṣ kitāb al-maqūlāt*. Beirut, 1932.
Ibn Sab'īn, 'Abd al-Ḥaqq ibn Ibrāhīm. *Kitāb al-iḥāṭah*, ed. 'Abd al-Raḥmān Badawī. *RIEI*, 6 (1958), 11–34.
———. *Rasā'il Ibn Sab'īn*, ed. 'Abd al-Raḥmān Badawī. Cairo, 1965.
Ibn Ṣāḥib al-Ṣalāh. *al-Mann bi-l-imāmah*, ed. 'Abd al-Hādī al-Tāzī. Beirut, 1964.
Ibn Sahl al-Andalusī. *Dīwān*, collected by al-Shaykh Ḥasan al-'Itāiṭ. Cairo, A.H. 1289, 1297, 1302, 1328, 1344. Beirut, A.H. 1885.
———. *al-Maslak al-sahl fī sharḥ tawshīḥ Ibn Sahl li-l-Ifrānī al-Marrākushī*. Fez, A.H. 1324.
Ibn Sahl al-Isrā'īlī. *Dīwān*, compiled by A. Ḥusayn al-Qarnī. Cairo, 1926.
Ibn Sa'īd, Abū-l-Ḥasan 'Arīb. *Kitāb awqāt al-sanah*, ed. with Latin trans. by R. Dozy, *Le calendrier de Cordoue*. Leiden, 1873.
Ibn Sa'īd al-Maghribī. *al-Ghuṣūn al-yāni'ah fī maḥāsin shu'arā' al-mi'at al-sābi'ah*, ed. I. al-Abyārī. Cairo, 1954.
———. *Kitāb rāyāt al-mubarrizīn wa-l-ghāyāt al-mumayyizīn*. Ed. and trans. E.García Gómez, *Libro de las banderas y campeones* (Madrid, 1942). English trans. A. J. Arberry, *Anthology of Moorish Poetry* Cambridge, 1953).
———. *al-Mughrib fī akhbār ahl al-Maghrib*, ed. Sh. Ḍayf. 2 vols. Cairo, 1954.
———. *Risālah*, in al-Maqqarī, *Nafḥ al-ṭīb*, vol. 4, 171–177. Cairo, 1949.
———. *'Unwān al-murqiṣāt wa-l-muṭribāt*, ed. 'Abd al-Qādir. Agliers, A.D. 1949. Cairo, A.H. 1286.

Ibn Sanā' al-Mulk. *Dār al-ṭirāz fī 'amal al-muwashshaḥāt*, ed. J. al-Rikābī. Damascus, 1949.
———. *Dīwān*, ed. M. 'Abd al-Ḥaqq. Hyderabad, 1958.
Ibn Sayyid al-Baṭliyūsī, Abū Muḥammad 'Abdallāh. *al-Ḥadā'iq fī-l-maṭālib al-'āliyah al-falsafiyyah*, ed. Muḥammad Zāhid ibn al-Ḥasan al-Kawtharī. Cairo, A.H. 1365.
———. *al-Inṣāf fī-l-tanbīh*. Cairo, A.H. 1319.
———. *al-Intiṣār min man 'adala 'an al-istibṣār*, ed. Ḥamīd 'Abd al-Majīd. Cairo, 1955.
———. *al-Iqtḍāb fī sharḥ al-kuttāb*. Beirut, 1901.
———. *Sharḥ saqṭ al-zand*. 5 vols. Cairo, 1945–1948.
Ibn Sharf al-Qayrawānī. *I'lām al-kalām*, ed. Ḥasan Ḥusnī 'Abd al-Wahhāb. Damascus, 1912. Cairo, 1926.
Ibn Shuhayd. *Dīwān*. Beirut, 1963.
———. *Risālat al-tawābi' wa-l-zawābi'*. Ed. Buṭrus al-Bustānī (Beirut, 1951). English trans. J. Monroe (Berkeley, 1971).
Ibn Sīdah, 'Alī Ibn Ismā'īl. *al-Muḥkam wa-l-muḥīṭ al-a'ẓam*. 3 vols. Cairo, 1958.
———. *al-Mukhaṣṣaṣ*. 17 vols. Cairo, A.H. 1316–1321.
———. "Urjūzah li-Ibn Sīdah," ed. Ḥabīb al-Ziyyāt. *al-Mashriq*, 36 (1936), 181–192.
———. *al-Najāt*. Ed. M. S. al-Kurdī (Cairo, 1944). Partial English trans. F. Raḥmān, *Avicenna's Philosophy* (London, 1952).
Ibn Sulaymān, al-Shaykh Ḥasan Khūjah. *al-Dhayl li-kitāb bashā'ir al-a'yān* Tunis, A.H. 1324.
Ibn Ṭufayl. *Ḥayy Ibn Yaqẓān*. Beirut, 1962. Ed. Aḥmad Amīn (Cairo, 1952). Ed. Jamīl Ṣalībā and Kāmil 'Iyāḍ (Damascus, 1949). Trans. S. Ockley, *The Improvement of Human Reason* (London, 1708); rev. A. S. Fulton (London, 1929). German trans. G. Pritius (Frankfurt, 1726). English trans. Paul Bonnle, *The Awakening of the Soul* (London, 1904); Spanish trans. A. González Palencia, *El Filósofo autodidacto* (Madrid, 1934, 1948). French trans. Léon Gauthier (Beirut, 1936). Latin trans. with Arabic text ed. E. Pococke (Oxford, 1671, 1700).
Ibn Tūmart. *Kitāb a'azzu mā-yuṭlab*. Ed. J. D. Luciani, *Le livre de Mohammed Ibn Toumert*. Algiers, 1903.
———. *al-Muwaṭṭa'*. Algiers, 1905.
Ibn Ṭumlus. *Kitāb al-madkhal li-ṣinā'at al-manṭiq*, ed. with Spanish trans. by M. Asín Palacios. Madrid, 1916.
Ibn al-Wāfid, Abū-l-Muṭarrif 'Abd al-Raḥmān al-Lakhmī. *Tratado de Agricultura*, Spanish trans. J. M. Millás Vallicrosa. *al-Andalus*, 8 (1943), 280–332.
Ibn Ya'īsh. *Sharḥ al-mufaṣṣal*, ed. Jahn Leipzig, 1882–1886.
Ibn Yūsuf, 'Alī. *Ḍawābiṭ al-sikkah*, ed. H. Mu'nis. Cairo, 1958.
Ibn Ẓāfir. *Badā'i' al-badā'i'*. Cairo, A.H. 1278.
Ibn al-Zaqqāq al-Balansī. *Dīwān*, ed. 'Afīfah Maḥmūd Dīrānī. Beirut, 1964.
Ibn Zaydūn, 'Abd al-Raḥmān. *Ittiḥāf a'lām al-nās bi jamāl akhbār hāḍirat Miknās*. Rabat, n.d.
Ibn Zaydūn, Abū-l-Walīd. *Dīwān*. Ed. Sayyid Kīlānī (Cairo, 1932). Ed. Karam al-Bustānī Beirut, 1951).
———. *al-Risālah al-hazliyyah*, commented on and published by Ibn Nabātah, *Sharḥ al-'uyūn fī sharḥ risālat Ibn Zaydūn*. Cairo, A.H. 1278, 1321. Alexandria, A.H. 1290. Istānah, A.H. 1275.
———. *al-Risālah al-jiddiyyah*. Cairo, 1906, 1926.
———. *Tamām al-mutawwam fī sharḥ risālat Ibn Zaydūn*. Ed. Salāḥ al-Ṣafdī (Baghdād, A.H. 1327).
Ibn al-Zubayr. *Ṣilat al-ṣilah*, ed. E. Lévi-Provençal. Rabat, 1938.
al-Ibshīhī. *al-Musṭaṭaf fī kull fann mustaẓraf*. Cairo, A.H. 1330. French trans. G. Rat, 2 vols. (Paris, 1902).
al-Idrīsī, al-Sharīf. *Kitāb nuzhat al-mushtāq fī ikhtirāq al-āfāq*. Ed. and French trans. R. Dozy and M. J. de Goeje, *Description de l'Afrique et de l'Espagne* (Leiden, 1866). Partial French trans., *Description de la Grande Mosquée de Cordoue*, by Alfred Dessus Lamare (Algiers, 1949) and by P. A. Jaubert (Paris, 1836–1840).
Ikhwān al-Ṣafā'. *Rasā'il, risālat māhiyyat al-'ishq*. Bombay, A.H. 1305–1306. Ed. Khayr al-Dīn al-Ziriklī, 4 vols. (Cairo, A.H. 1347).

'Inān, Muḥammad 'Abdallah. *'Aṣr al-Murābiṭīn wa-l-Muwaḥḥidīn*. 2 vols. Cairo, 1964.
———. *al-Āthār al-andalusiyyah*. Cairo, 1956, 1961.
———. *al-Dawlat al-'āmiriyyah*. Cairo, 1958.
———. *Dawlat al-Islām fī-l-Andalus*. 2 vols. Cario, 1943–1958. 3rd ed.; Cairo, 1960.
———. *Duwal al-Ṭawā'if*. Cairo, 1960.
———. *Lisān al-Dīn Ibn al-Khaṭīb*. Cairo, 1968.
———. *Nihāyat al-Andalus wa-ta'rīkh al-'Arab al-mutanāṣṣirīn*. 2nd ed.; Cairo, 1958.
———. *Tarājim islāmiyyah sharqiyyah wa-andalusiyyah*. Cairo, 1947.
al-Iskandarī, Aḥmad. "Ibn Khafājah al-andalusī." *Majallat al-majma' al-'ilmī al-'arabī*, 11 (1931), 724–735 and 12 (1932), 26–39.
———. "Ibn Zaydūn. *al-Majma'*, 11 (1931), 513–527, 577–592, 656–669.
Iṣṭakhrī, Abū Isḥaq Ibrāhīm ibn Muḥammad al-Fārisī. *Kitāb masālik wa-l-mamālik*, ed. M. J. de Goeje. Leiden, 1870.
'Iyāḍ al-Qāḍī, *Tartīb al-madārik wa-taqrīb al-masālik li-ma'rifat a'lām madhhab Mālik*, ed. A. B. Mahmūd. 4 vols. Beirut, n.d.
Jabbūr, J. *Ibn 'Abd Rabbihi wa-'iqduh*. Beirut, 1933.
———. *'Umar Ibn Abī Rabī'ah*. 2 vols. Beirut, 1935–1939.
al-Jāḥiẓ. *al-Bayān wa-l-tabyīn*, ed. 'Abd al-Salām Hārūn. 4 vols. Cairo, 1961.
———. *al-Bukhalā'*, ed. van Vloten. Leiden, 1900.
———. *al-Ḥayawān*, ed. 'Abd al-Salām Muḥammad Hārūn. 7 vols. Cairo A.H. 1323–1325; A.D. 1945.
———. *Majmū'āt rasā'il*. Cairo, A.H. 1324.
Jahshiyārī. *Kitāb al-wuzarā'*. Cairo, 1938.
Jamāl al-Dīn, Muḥsin. *Udabā' baghdādiyyūn fī-l-Andalus*. Baghdād, 1962–1963.
al-Jamānah fī izālat al-ratānah, ed. Ḥasan Ḥusnī. Cairo, 1953.
Jāmātī, Ḥabīb. *Andalus al-'Arab*. Cairo, 1962.
al-Jarsīfī, 'Umar. *Risālah fī-l-ḥisbah*, ed. E. Lévi-Provençal. Cairo, 1955.
al-Jundī, Muḥammad Salīm. *al-Jāmi' fī akhbār Abī-l-'Alā' wa-āthāruh*. 2 vols. Damascus, 1962.
Kaḥḥālah, 'Umar R. *Mu'jam al-mu'allifīn*. Damascus, 1957.
Kanūn, Abdallah. *al-Nubāgh al-maghribī fī-l-adab al-'arabī*. Beirut, 1961.
———. *Madkhal ilā tārīkh al-Maghrib*. Tetuan, 1944.
Khafājah, Muḥammad. *Qiṣṣat al-adab al-'arabī fī-l-Andalus*. Beirut, 1962.
al-Khafājī, Shihāb al-Dīn. *Shifā' al-'alīl fīmā warada fī kalām al-'Arab min al-dakhīl*. Cairo, A.H. 1325.
Khāliṣ, Ṣalāḥ. *Ishbīliyyah fī-l-qarn al-khāmis al-hijrī*. Beirut, 1965.
———. *Muḥammad Ibn 'Ammār al-andalusī*. Baghdād, 1957.
———. *al-Mu'tamid Ibn 'Abbād al-Ishbīlī*. Baghdād, 1958.
al-Khaṭīb, Muḥibb al-Dīn. *Tārīkh madīnat al-zahrā'*. Cairo, A.H. 1343.
Khaṭṭāb Maḥmūd. *Qādat fatḥ al-Maghrib al-'arabī*. 2 vols. Beirut, 1966.
al-Khushanī, Muḥammad Ibn Ḥārith. *Ṭabaqāt 'ulamā' Ifrīqiyah*, ed. Ibn Abī Shanab. Algiers, 1914.
———. *Ta'rīkh quḍāt Qurṭubah*. Ed. and Spanish trans. J. Ribera, *Historia de los jueces de Córdoba* (Madrid, 1917). Ed. I. 'A. al-Ḥusaynī (Cairo, A.H. 1372).
al-Khuwārizmī. *Ḥisāb al-jabr wa-l-muqābalah*, ed. with English trans. by F. Rosen. London, 1831.
———. *Mafātīḥ al-'ulūm*, ed. G. van Vloten. Leiden, 1895.
Kīlānī, K. *Muqaddimat dīwān Ibn Zaydūn*. Cairo, 1932.
———. *Nāẓarāt fī ta'rīkh al-adab al-andalusī*. Cairo, 1342/1924.
al-Kindī. *Rasā'il al-Kindī al-falsafiyyah*, ed. M. A. Abū Riḍā. 2 vols. Cairo, 1950–1953.
al-Kulā'ī, Abū-l-Qāsim. *Iḥkām ṣan'at al-kalām*, ed. M. al-Dāyah. Beirut, 1967.
Kurd 'Alī, Muḥammad. *Ghābir al-Andalus wa-ḥāḍiruhā*. Cairo, 1923.
———. *Gharā'ib al-gharb*. Cairo, 1923.
———. *al-Islām wa-l-ḥaḍārah al-'arabiyyah*. 2 vols. Cairo, 1936.

———. *Rasā'il al-bulaghā'*. Cairo, A.H. 1331.
al-Kutubī, M. ibn Shākir. *Fawāt al-wafāyāt*, ed. M. al-Ḍīn 'Abd al-Ḥamīd. 2 vols. Cairo, 1956.
Labīb al-Batnūnī, Muḥ. *Riḥlat al-Andalus*. Cairo, n.d.
al-Ma'arrī, Abū-l-'Alā'. *al-Lūzumīyāt*, ed. Amīn 'Abd al-'Azīz al-Khānijī. 2 vols. Cairo, A.H. 1342.
———. *Risālat al-Ghufrān*. Ed. K. Kilānī (Cairo, 1923). Partial trans. by R. A. Nicholson, *JRAS* (1900), 673–720, (1902), 75–101, 337–362, and 813–847.
Mafākhir al-Barbar, ed. Lévi-Provençal. Rabat, 1937.
Maḥmūd, Ḥasan A. *Qiyām dawlat al-Murābiṭīn*. Cairo, 1957.
Maimonides. *Guide to the Perplexed*, English trans. M. Friedlander. New York, 1956.
Makkī, Maḥmūd 'Alī. *Madrīd al-'arabiyyah*. Cairo, n.d.
———. "al-Tashayyu' fi-l-Andalus." *RIEEI*, 2 (1954), 93–149.
Mālik Ibn Anas. *Muwaṭṭa' al-imām Mālik*. Cairo, A.H. 1349.
al-Mālikī, Abū Bakr. *Riyāḍ al-nufūs*, ed. Ḥusayn Mu'nis. Cairo, 1951.
al-Mālikī, Burhān al-Dīn. *al-Dībāj al-mudhahhab*. Cairo, A.H. 1351.
Manūnī, Muḥ. *al-'Ulūm wa-l-adab wa-l-funūn 'alā 'ahd al-Muwaḥḥidīn*. Tetuan, 1952.
Maqdisī, Shams al-Dīn Abī 'Abd Allāh. *Kitāb aḥsān al-taqāsīm fī ma'rifat al-aqālīm*, ed. M. J. de Goeje. Leiden, 1906.
al-Maqqarī, Shihāb al-Dīn A. ibn Muḥammad. *Azhār al-riyāḍ*, ed. Muṣṭafā al-Siqā, I. al-Abyārī, and A. H. Shalabī. Cairo, 1939–1942.
———. *Nafḥ al-ṭīb min ghuṣn al-Andalus al-raṭīb*. Ed. R. Dozy et al., *Analectes*, 2 vols. (Leiden, 1855–1860). Ed. M. Muḥyy al-Dīn 'Abd al Ḥamīd, 10 vols. (Cairo, 1949). Ed. I. 'Abbās, 8 vols. (Beirut, 1968). Partial English trans. by P. de Gayangos, *The Mohammedan Dynasties in Spain*, 2 vols. (London, 1840–1843).
al-Maqrīzī, Taqiyy al-Dīn. *al-Mawā'ith wa-l-i'tibār*. 2 vols. Cairo, 1853.
al-Marrākushī, 'Abd al-Wāḥid. *Kitāb al-mu'jib*, ed. R. Dozy, 2nd ed.; Leiden, 1885.
———. *al-Mu'jibfī talkhīṣ akhbār al-Maghrib*. Ed. R. Dozy (Leiden, 1848). Ed. Mu. Sa'id al-'Iryān (Cairo, 1963). French trans. E. Fagnan, *Histoire des Almohades* (Algiers, 1893).
al-Mashrifī, M. Muḥiyy al-Dīn. *Ifrīqiyah al-shamāliyyah*. Rabat, 1950.
al-Mas'ūdī. *Murūj al-dhahab*, ed. and French trans. by C. Barbier de Meynard and Pavet de Courtielle. 9 vols. Paris 1861–1877.
al-Mawā'inī. *Rayḥān al-albāb wa-ra' yān al-shabāb*. Excerpts in R. Dozy, *Scriptorum arabum loci de Abbadidis*, vol. 2. Leiden, 1946–1963. pp. 1–10.
al-Mawardī. *al-Aḥkām al-sulṭāniyya*, French trans. Léon Ostrorog. Paris, 1901.
Mawsawī, M. Bāqir. *Rawḍāt al-jannāt fī aḥwāl al-'ulamā' wa-l-sādāt*. 2nd ed. Tehran, A.H. 1347.
Mubārak, Zakī. *Madāmī' al-'ushshāq*. Cairo, A.H. 1353.
———. *al-Muwāzanah bayn al-shu'arā'*. Cairo, A.H. 1344.
al-Mubarrad, Abū-l-'Abbās. *Kitāb al-kāmil fi-l-lughah wa-l-adab*, ed. Abū-l-Faḍl Ibrāhīm. 4 vols. Cairo, 1956.
al-Muḥāsibī, Ḥarīth ibn As'ad. *Ri'āyah li-ḥuqūq allāh*, ed. M. Smith. London, 1940.
Mu'jam fiqh Ibn Ḥazm al-ẓāhirī. Compiled by Lajnat Mawsū'at al-fiqh al-Islamī. Damascus, 1966.
Mulīn, Muḥ. Rashīd. *'Aṣr al-Manṣūr al-muwaḥḥidī*. Rabat, 1946.
Mu'nis, Ḥusayn. *Fajr al-Andalus*. Cairo, 1959.
———. *Fatḥ al-'Arab li-l-Maghrib*. Cairo, 1947.
———. "Ghārāt al-nūrmaniyyīn 'alā-l-Andalus" *The Periodical of the Egyptian Historiacal Society*, 2, pt. 1 (1949).
———. *Tārīkh al-jughrāfiyah wa-l-jughrāfiyyīn fi-l-Andalus*. *RIEI*, 7 (1959), 199–359. Also published Madrid, 1967.
———. *Riḥlat al-Andalus*. Cairo, 1963.
al-Murābiṭ, Jawād. *'Ibar wa-'abarāt min Dimashq al-Andalus*. Beirut, 1969.
Murād, Ḥasan. *Tārīkh al-'Arab fi-l-Andalus*. Cairo, 1931.
al-Mu'tamid ibn 'Abbād. *Dīwān*, ed. Dr. Badawī and Ḥāmid 'Abd al-Majīd. Cairo, 1951.

al-Mutanabbī. *Dīwān, with the Commentary by Abī-l-Ḥasan ʻAlī ibn Aḥmad al-Wāḥidi an-Naisabūrī*, ed. F. Dieterici. Berlin, 1861.
Muṭlaq, Albīr Ḥabīb. *al-Ḥarakah al-lughawiyyah fī-l-Andalus mundh al-fatḥ al-ʻarabī ḥattā nihāyat ʻaṣr mulūk al-ṭawā'if*. Sidon & Beirut, 1967.
Nājī, Munīr. *Ibn Hānī' al-andalusī: dars wa-naqd*. Beirut, 1962.
al-Nāsirī al-Salāwī. *al-Istiqṣā' li-akhbār duwal al-Maghrib al-aqṣā*. 9 vols. Casablanca, 1954–1955. French trans. in *Archives marocains*, vols. 30–33 (Paris, 1923–1924).
Naṣṣār, H. *al-Muʻjam al-ʻarabī*. 2 vols. Cairo, 1956.
al-Nubāhī, Abū-l-Ḥasan ibn ʻAbd Allāh. *al-Marqabah al-ʻulyā, tārīkh quḍāt al-Andalus*, ed. E. Lévi-Provençal. Cairo, 1948.
al-Nuṣulī, Anīs Zakariya. *Al-dawlat al-umawiyya fī Qurṭubah*. Baghdād, 1926.
al-Nuwayrī. *Nihāyat al-arab*. 18 vols. Cairo, A.H. 1345. Chs. 5 and 6, bearing on Muslim Spain, were translated into Spanish by M. Gaspar Remiro in *RCEH*, 2 (1917–1919).
Nykl, A. R. *Mukhtārāt min al-shiʻr al-andalusī*. Beirut, 1949.
al-Qālī, Abū ʻAlī. *al-Amālī*. 2 vols. Cairo, 1953–1954.
———. *al-Kitāb al-bāriʻ fī-l-lughah*, ed. A. van Vlöten. London, 1933.
al-Qalqashandī, Abū-l-ʻAbbās. *Ṣubḥ al-aʻshā*. 14 vols. Cairo, 1913–1919.
al-Qazwīnī. *ʻAjā'ib al-makhlūqāt* (*Cosmographia*), ed. F. Wüstenfeld. Göttingen, 1849.
———. *Athār al-bilād*, ed. F. Wüstenfeld. Göttingen, 1848.
al-Qifṭī. *Inbā' al-ruwāh ʻalā anbā' al-nuḥāh*. 3 vols. Cairo, 1950–1955.
———. *Ta'rīkh al-ḥukamā'*. Ed. A. Müller and J. Lippert (Leipzig, 1903). Ed. A. Müller (Cairo, 1882–1884).
al-Qurashī, M. ibn Abī-l-Khaṭṭāb. *Jamharat ashʻār al-ʻArab*. Beirut, 1963.
al-Qurṭubī, A. ibn ʻAbd al-Raḥmān ibn Maḍā'. *al-Radd ʻalā-l-nuḥah*, ed. Sh. Ḍayf. Cairo, 1947.
al-Qurṭubī, Shams al-Dīn. *al-Jāmiʻ li-aḥkām al-Qur'ān*. 20 vols. Cairo, 1933–1950.
al-Qushayrī, Abū Qāsim. *Risālah*. Cairo, A.H.1287; A.D. 1948.
al-Rafīʻī, Muṣṭafā Ṣādiq. *Tārīkh ādāb al-ʻArab*. 3 vols. Cairo, 1953–1954.
al-Rāghib al-Iṣfahānī. *Mufradāt fī gharīb al-Qur'ān*. Cairo, A.H. 1324.
Rasā'il Ikhwān al-Safā'. Cairo, 1928.
al-Rāzī, Muḥammad ibn ʻAlī ibn ʻAbd al-Qādir. *La Crónica denominada del moro Rasis*, Spanish trans. P. de Gayangos and R. Menéndez Pidal. *MRAH*, 8 (1850).
———. *Mukhtaṣar al-ṣiḥaḥ*. Cairo, A.H. 1308.
al-Rikābī, Jawdat. *Fī-l-adab al-andalusī*. 2nd ed. Cairo, 1966.
———. *al-Ṭabīʻah fī-l-shiʻr al-andalusī*. Damascus, 1959.
al-Ruʻaynī, Abū-l-Ḥasan ʻAlī Ibn Muḥammad b. ʻAlī. *Barnāmaj shuyūkh al-Ruʻaynī*. Damascus, 1962.
al-Ruṣāfī al-Balansī. *Dīwān*. Beirut, 1960.
Saʻd Zaghlūl ʻAbd al-Ḥamīd. *Tārīkh al-Maghrib al-ʻarabī*. Cairo, n.d.
al-Ṣafadī, Ṣalāḥ al-Dīn. *Nakt al-himyān*. Cairo, 1911.
———. *Tawshīʻ al-tawshīḥ*, ed. A.H. Muṭlaq. Beirut, 1966.
———. *al-Wāfī bi-l-wafayāt*, ed. H. Ritter. Leipzig & Istanbul, 1931. (This book is also at the Library of Ahmad III, MS. 660.)
Ṣafwān Ibn Idrīs al-Mursī. *Zād al-Musāfir wa-ghurrat muḥayya al-adab al-sāfir*, ed. A. Mahad. Beirut, 1938.
Ṣāʻid. *Ṭabaqāt al-umam*. Cairo, n.d. Ed. L. Cheikho (Beirut, 1912). French trans. R. Blachère, *Le livre des "Categories des nations"* (Paris, 1935).
al-Sakkākī, Yūsuf. *Miftāḥ al-ʻulūm*. Cairo, A.H. 1317.
Salām, Mu. Zaghlūl. *Tārīkh al-naqd al-ʻarabī ilā-l-qarn al-rābiʻ al-hijrī*. Cairo, 1964.
Ṣāliḥ Aḥmad ʻAlī. *al-Tanẓīmāt al-ijtimāʻiyyah fī-l-Baṣrah fī-l-qarn al-awwal al-hijrī*. Baghdād, 1953.
Sālim, ʻAbd al-ʻAzīz. "Baʻḍ al-muṣṭalaḥāt al-ʻarabiyyah li-lʻamārah al-maghribiyyah al-andalusiyyah. *RIEI*, 5 (1957), 241–253.
———. "Baʻḍ al-ta'thīrāt al-andalusiyyah fī-l-ʻamārah al-miṣriyyah." *al-Majallah*, 12 (Dec. 1957).

———. "al-Mariyyah qā'idat al-usṭūl al-islāmi fī-l-Andalus." *al-Rābiṭa*, 8 and 9 (1958).
———. al-usṭūl al-islāmi fī-l-Andalus." *al-Rābiṭa*, 8 and 9 (1958).
———. "Masjid al-muslimīn bi-ṭulayṭilah." *Faculty of Arts Periodical* (University of Alexandria, 1958).
———. "al-Takhṭīṭ wa-maẓāhir al-'imrān fī-l-quṣūr al-islāmiyyah al-wusṭā." *al-Majallah*, 9 (Sept. 1957).
———. *Ta'rīkh al-muslimīn wa-āthāruhum fī-l-Andalus*. Beirut, 1962.
al-Sāmirra'ī, Ibrāhīm. *Rasā'il fī-l-lughah*. Baghdād, 1964.
Sarnelli, C. D. *Mujāhid al-'Āmirī*. Cairo, 1961.
al-Sarrāj, Abū Naṣr. *Luma'*, ed. R. A. Nicholson. London, 1914.
al-Shabībī, Muḥammad R. *Adab al-maghāribah wa-l-andalusiyyīn*. Cairo, 1961.
al-Shahrastānī. *al-Milal wa-l-niḥal*. Cairo, A.H. 1317.
al-Shaqundī. *Risālah*. Spanish trans. E. García Gómez, *Elógio del Islam español* (Madrid & Granada, 1934). Arabic text in al-Maqqarī, *Nafḥ al-ṭīb*, vol. 4, 177–208. Cairo, 1949.
al-Sharīshī. *Sharḥ maqāmāt al-Ḥarīrī*. 2 vols. Cairo, A.H. 1314.
al-Sharqāwī, M. 'Abd al-Mun'im, and Muḥammad Maḥmād al-Ṣayyād. *Mamālik al-Maghrib al-'arabī*. Alexandria, 1959.
al-Shāṭibī, Ibrāhīm Ibn Mūsā. *al-I'tiṣām*. 3 vols. Cairo, 1914.
al-Shāṭibī, Abū Muḥammad al-Qāsim. *Ibrāz al-ma'ānī min ḥarz al-amānī*. Cairo, A.H. 1349.
———. *al-Shāṭibiyyah*. Cairo, A.H. 1347.
Shaybūb, Ṣiddīq. "Jumhūriyyah andalusiyyah bi-l-iskandariyyah." *al-Kitāb* (Feb. 1949).
al-Shushtarī. *Dīwān*. Cairo, 1960.
Sibawayhi. *al-Kitāb*. 2 vols. Cairo, A.H. 1316–1317. Ed. H. Derenbourg, 2 vols. (Paris, 1881–1887).
al-Silafī, Aḥmad ibn Muḥammad. *Akhbār wa-tarājim andalusiyyah*, ed. I. Abbās, Beirut, 1963.
al-Ṣufī. Khālid. *Ta'rīkh al-'Arab fī Isbāniya: Jumhuriyyat Banī Jahwar*. Damascus, 1959.
———. *Ta'rīkh al-'Arab fī Isbāniyā; nihāyat al-khilāfah al-umawiyyah fī-l-Andalus*. Aleppo, 1963.
al-Suhaylī, Abū-l-Qāsim 'Abd al-Raḥmān. *al-Ta'rīf wa-l-i'lām bimā ubhima fī-l-Qur'ān min al-asmā' wa-l-a'lām*, ed. Maḥmūd Rabī'. Cairo, 1938.
al-Sulamī, Abū 'Abd al-Raḥmān. *Kitāb ṭabaqāt al-ṣufiyyah*, ed. J. Pederson. Leiden, 1960.
al-Ṣūlī. *Adab al-kuttāb*. Baghdād, A.H. 1341.
al-Suyūṭī, Jalāl al-Dīn. Bughyat al-wu'ah fī ṭabaqāt al-lughawiyyīn wa-l-nuḥāh. Cairo, A.H. 1326.
———. *Itqān*. 2 vols. Cairo, A.H. 1279.
———. *al-Ishtibāh wa-l-naẓā'ir fī-l-naḥw*. Hyderabad, A.H. 1316.
———. *al-Muzhir*. 2 vols. Cairo, 1958.
al-Ṭabarī. *Akhbār al-rusul wa-l-mulūk*. 3 vols. ed. M. J. de Goeje and others under *Annales*. Leiden, 1879–1901.
———. *Tafsīr al-Qur'ān*. 30 vols. Cairo, n.d.
al-Taftazānī, Abū-l-Wafā al-Ghunaymī. "Ibn 'Abbād al-Rundī: ḥayātuh wa-mu'allafātuh." *RIEI*, 6 (1958), 221–258.
al-Tamgrūtī. *al-Nafḥah al-miskiyyah fī-l-sifārat al-turkiyyah (Rélation d'une ambassade marocaine en Turquie 1589–1591)*, trans. and annotated by H. de Castries. Paris, 1929.
al-Tha'ālibī. *Yatīmat al-dahr*. 4 vols. Damascus, A.H. 1304. Cairo, 1956.
Tha'lab, Abū-l-'Abbās Aḥmad. *Majālis tha'lab*, ed. 'Abd al-Salām Muḥammad Hārūn. 2 vols. Cairo, 1965.
al-Tijānī, 'Abdallah. *Riḥlah*, ed. W. Marçais. Tunis, A.H. 1345.
———. *Tuḥfat al-'arūs*. Cairo, A.H. 1301.
al-Ṭūd, 'Abd al-Salām Aḥmad. *Banū 'Abbād bi-Ishbīliyyah*. Tetuan, 1947.
Tuhfat al-'aṣr fī inqiḍa' dawlat Banī Naṣr, ed. M. J. Müller, Munich, 1863.
Ṭurkhān, Ibrāhīm 'Alī. *Dawlat al-qūṭ al-gharbiyyīn*. Cairo, 1958.
al-Turṭūshī, Abū Bakr. *Sirāj al-mulūk*. Cairo, A.H. 1287. Trans. Maximiliano Alarcón, *Lámpara de los príncipes*, 2 vols. Madrid, 1930–1931.
al-Ṭuṭīlī. *Dīwān*, ed. Iḥsān 'Abbās. Beirut, 1963.

al-'Udhrī. *Nuṣūṣ 'an al-Andalus* (Being fragments of his larger work, *Kitāb tarṣī' al-akhbār wa-tanwī' al-āthār wa-l-bustān fi gharā'ib al-buldān wa-l-masālik ilā jamī' al-mamālik*), ed. 'Abd al-'Azīz-Ahwānī. Madrid, 1965.
Wathā'iq 'arabiyyah gharnāṭiyyah, ed. by L. Seco de Lucena. Madrid, 1961.
al-Wansharīshī, Abū al-'Abbās Aḥmad ibn Yaḥyā. *Asnā al-mutājir*, ed. Husayn Mu'nis. *RIEI*, 5 (1957), 129–191.
———. *Kitāb al-mi'yār*. 12 vols. Fez, A.H. 1315.
al-Yāfi'ī, Abū Muḥammad 'Abd Allāh ibn As'ad. *Mir'āt al-janān*, 4 vols. Hyderabad, A.H. 1337–1339.
Yaḥyā Ibn Yaḥyā al-Laythī. *Muwaṭṭa' al-imām Mālik*, ed. Aḥmad R. 'Armūsh Beirut, 1971.
Yāqūt. *Irshād*, ed. D. S. Margoliouth. 7 vols. Leiden & London, 1907–1927. 20 vols.; Cairo, 1938.
———. *Mu'jam al-buldān*. Ed. F. Wüstenfeld, 6 vols. (Leipzig, 1866–1873). 8 vols. Cairo, 1323/1906. Beirut, 1955.
Yūsuf III of Granada. *Dīwān*. Cairo, 1965.
al-Zabīdī, Murtaḍā. *Tāj al-'arūs*. 10 vols. Cairo, A.H. 1307.
al-Zajjājī, 'Abd al-Raḥmān. *al-Jumal fi-l-naḥw*, ed. Ibn Abī Shanab. Paris, 1957.
al-Zajjāli al-Qurṭubī, A. *Amthāl al-'awwām fi-l-Andalus*, ed. Muḥammad b. Sarīfah. Fez, 1971.
al-Zamakhsharī. *Asās al-balāghah*. 2 vols. Cairo, A.H. 1299.
———. *al-Kashshāf 'an ḥaqā'iq al-tanzīl*, ed. W. H. Lees. 4 vols. Calcutta, 1856.
al-Zarkashī. *Tārīkh al-dawlatayn bi-bilād al-Maghrib*. Tunis, A.H. 1289.
———. *Tārīkh al-dawlatayn al-muwaḥḥidiyyah wa-l-ḥafsiyyah*. Tunis, A.H. 1289. French trans. E. Fagnan (Constantine, 1895).
Zaydān, Jurjī. *Tārīkh ādāb al-lughah al-'arabiyyah*. 4 vols. Cairo, 1957.
———. *Tārīkh al-tamaddun al-islāmī*. 4 vols. Cairo, 1905.
al-Ziriklī, Khayr al-Dīn. *al-A'lām*. 10 vols. Cairo, 1954–1959.
al-Zubaydī, Abū Bakr Muḥammad. *Kitāb al-istidrāq 'alā Sībawayhi*, ed. I. Guidi. Rome, 1890.
———. *Laḥn al-'awām*, ed. R. 'Abd al-Tawwāb. Cairo, 1964.
———. *Ṭabaqāt al-naḥwiyyīn wa-l-lughawiyyīn*, ed. Muḥammad Abū-l-Faḍl Ibrāhīm. Cairo, 1954.

Index

Index

Note: Titles of books are usually abbreviated and followed by the author's name. Ibn, meaning son, is abbreviated b.; Muḥammad is abbreviated Muḥ. The article *al-*, which is prefixed to a noun in normal usage, is here inverted when it would begin an entry (thus, al-Manṣūr appears as Manṣūr, al-); within entries *al-* is disregarded in alphabetizing.